What's That Sound?

An Introduction to Rock and Its History

What's That Sound?

An Introduction to Rock and Its History

John Covach

UNIVERSITY OF ROCHESTER
AND THE EASTMAN SCHOOL OF MUSIC

W. W. Norton & Company
Independent and Employee-owned
New York · London

W. W. Norton & Company has been independent since its founding in 1923, when William Warder Norton and Mary D. Herter Norton first published lectures delivered at the People's Institute, the adult education division of New York City's Cooper Union. The Nortons soon expanded their program beyond the Institute, publishing books by celebrated academics from America and abroad. By mid-century, the two major pillars of Norton's publishing program—trade books and college texts—were firmly established. In the 1950s, the Norton family transferred control of the company to its employees, and today—with a staff of four hundred and a comparable number of trade, college, and professional titles published each year—W. W. Norton & Company stands as the largest and oldest publishing house owned wholly by its employees.

Copyright © 2006 by W. W. Norton & Company, Inc.

Printed in the United States of America
First Edition

Manufacturing: Courier
Book Design: Anna Palchik
Director of Manufacturing, College: Roy Tedoff
Electronic Pagination: Carole Desnoes
Editor: Pete Lesser
Manuscript Editor: Patterson Lamb
Project Editor: Lory A. Frenkel
Editorial Assistant: Birgit Larsson

Library of Congress Cataloging-in-Publication Data

Covach, John Rudolph.
  What's that sound? : an introduction to rock and its history / John Covach. — 1st ed.
    p. cm.
  Includes bibliographical references and index.
  ISBN-13: 978-0-393-97575-8 (pbk)
  ISBN-10: 0-393-97575-4 (pbk)
  1. Rock music—History and criticism. I. Title.
  ML3534.C7 2006
  781.6609—dc22

                                                      2006002220

W. W. Norton & Company Inc., 500 Fifth Avenue, New York, N.Y. 10110
www.wwnorton.com

W. W. Norton & Company Ltd., Castle House, 75/76 Wells Street, London W1T 3QT

  2 3 4 5 6 7 8 9 0

Contents

The 1950s   54

Chapter 2:
The Birth and First Flourishing of Rock and Roll (1955–1960)   58

The 1960s 148

Chapter 6:
Motown Pop and Southern Soul (1960–1970) 224

Chapter 7:
Psychedelia (1966–1969) 254

The 1970s

Chapter 8:
The Growing Rock Monster (1970–1975)

Chapter 10:
Mainstream Rock, Punk, and New Wave (1975–1980) 396

The 1980s 436

Chapter 11:
I Want My MTV (1980–1990) 440

Listening Guides

Acknowledgments

Like most textbooks, the one you are about to read developed over the course of many years—in this case, over ten years of teaching university-level courses in rock music. As a consequence of this prolonged period of gestation, I owe debts of gratitude to many more people than I can list here. My apologies in advance to those I overlook in what follows.

During my time at the University of North Texas College of Music, Thomas Sovik and David Joyner gave me the chance to offer my first courses in the history of rock music. When I moved to the University of North Carolina at Chapel Hill, John Nadas and Mark Evan Bonds were especially supportive in helping establish a series of rock-music courses there.

In many ways, I owe a significant debt to the many students (well over 3,000) who took my courses at Carolina; much of what is contained in this book was tried out on them first, and I benefited immensely from their feedback. Over the years my graduate students have helped educate me on a number of the finer points of rock history; this group of students includes Mark Spicer, David Carson Berry, Tim Hughes, Andy Flory, John Brackett, Paul Harris, Marc Medwin, Akitsugu Kawamoto, Sarah Nicholson, Jason Titus, Anna Stephan-Robinson, Martha Bausch, Christina Brandt, Joel Mauger, Joe Gennaro, and Richard Rischar. Thanks also to Tim Hughes for writing the featured boxes in each chapter.

During the years I was working on this book, many friends and colleagues gave me wise, helpful, and encouraging advice, including Kim Kowalke, Walter Everett, Albin Zak, James Grier, Jocelyn Neal, Mark Butler, Betsy Marvin, Tim Riley, Jonn Buzby, Paul Cole, Chris Chamis, and Stefan Zajic.

The excellent staff at Norton also deserve a big thanks, including Michael Ochs and Suzanne LaPlante, who convinced me to write this book, Roby Harrington, Steve Hoge, and Maribeth Payne who offered wisdom and guidance along the way, proofreader Ben Reynolds, project editor Lory Frenkel, and especially Peter Lesser, who worked tirelessly to shepherd the book through the editing and production process.

Most of all, I would like to thank my family, Julie, Jonathan, and Ricky, who suffered my many obsessed moments with grace and loving support.

John Covach
Rochester, New York
September 2005

What's That Sound?

An Introduction to Rock and Its History

Recorded in 1951 by Jackie Brenston and His Delta Cats, "Rocket '88'" is considered by some to be the first rock and roll record. Though it was first released as a 78-rpm single, this is a photograph of an original 1955 pressing—one of only a handful of "Rocket '88'" 45s in existence.

Studying Rock

Rock music has often been controversial, and its rebellious, ne'er-do-well image has always been part of its attraction for fans. In the mid 1950s, for instance, many adults used to the fatherly crooning of Bing Crosby and the suave, swinging delivery of Frank Sinatra were shocked by Elvis Presley with his emphatic blues-influenced singing and sexually suggestive dance moves. Teenagers, of course, loved him. Similarly, the Beatles' moptop haircuts upset a lot of parents in the mid 1960s, while setting a fashion trend among youngsters. Rock continued to push the envelope in later years: Jim Morrison, Alice Cooper, and David Bowie challenged cultural values in the late '60s and early '70s, while Madonna and Prince did the same in the 1980s. Rap and heavy metal compact discs (CDs) have even been the focus of federal government hearings. While there has certainly been a lot of rock music that is not the source of such controversy and cultural struggle, rock makes the most headlines—or at least the most sensational headlines—when it misbehaves.

Considering rock's frequent (and sometimes militant) opposition to the status quo, some people are surprised to learn that colleges and universities across the country have been offering courses in rock for many years. But as music historians look back on the twentieth century, it is obvious that popular music has played an enormous role in the development of the Western musical tradition. As historians note the importance of modern concert-music composers, such as Claude Debussy, Igor Stravinsky, Arnold Schoenberg, Olivier Messiaen, Aaron Copland, and Karlheinz Stockhausen, they must also figure the jazz of Duke Ellington and Miles Davis into the picture, as well as the Tin Pan Alley songs of Irving Berlin and Cole Porter, among the many styles of music that coexisted—sometimes more, sometimes less comfortably—in the previous century. During the second half of the twentieth century, rock music was dominant among popular styles, and even music historians whose work does not focus on rock during those decades must take into account its many and often far-flung effects on the world of music in general. Rock definitely plays a role in music history.

Despite the acknowledged importance of rock music, however, determining exactly what "rock" means is not so easy. Some scholars prefer the term "rock and roll," for instance, to designate the first wave of rock from 1954 to 1959 (covered in Chapter 2); for these scholars, music after 1964 is "rock," and using these two distinct terms preserves what they see as an important difference. This book will employ the term "rock" in a broad sense, however, and it will designate popular music that is produced specifically for a youth audience. But even this more encompassing usage is not without problems and seeming contradictions. Can 1960s soul be considered rock, for example? How about folk or rap? Is all pop also rock, and is all rock also pop? It often turns out that the problem with labels in any musical style is never at the center, but at the edges. Few will argue that a definition of rock has little value if it does not include Elvis Presley, the Beatles, the Rolling Stones, Jimi Hendrix, Led Zeppelin, the Police, and U2. But should we think of the Supremes and the Four Tops as rock? How about the Kingston Trio or even the Archies?

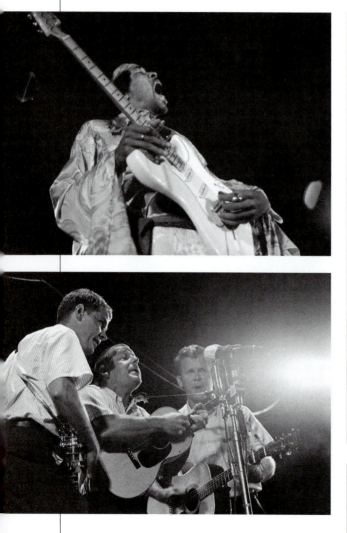

Almost any listener would agree that "rock" includes Jimi Hendrix (top left). But what about the Supremes (above) or the Kingston Trio (bottom left)?

This book will not completely resolve these kinds of stylistic questions, which will probably continue to be hashed out by critics, scholars, and fans for years to come. Rather, it will unfold a history of popular music that focuses on rock but includes many other kinds of styles along the way. The main purpose of the book is to organize this repertory—an enormous body of music that covers at least fifty years of popular-music history—to make it and its development easier to understand and appreciate. Anyone who has ever browsed a CD store, online or in person, knows that there is a lot of popular music for listeners to choose from. In fact, there is probably a better selection of music available today than at any other time in the history of recorded music, and almost all listeners have ready and convenient access to great pop music of the 1950s, '60s, '70s, '80s, or '90s (often remastered and repackaged with bonus tracks), in addition to all of rock's more recent music. In many ways, this half-century of music can be thought of as a vast territory, some of which you may have already begun to chart for yourself, but most of which probably remains relatively unknown. You may end up being surprised by how much rock you are unfamiliar with. In the chapters that follow, we will explore this musical territory in a comprehensive way, organizing the music into styles and eras that will not only make the rock repertory easier to understand and appreciate but will also provide a broad stylistic and historical perspective. Unexpected similarities between artists, groups, and styles will emerge as we work through the material, and your newly won perspective on rock and its history may even change the way you listen to and think about music in general.

Elements to Consider

Rock History in the Media. Thinking about rock's history is not new, and most fans of rock music will have had some exposure to the style's history. For those who have never studied rock as a scholarly or academic subject, this historical information will most likely have come from books, magazines, and newspapers, and perhaps also from radio and television programs as well as the Internet. Well-known magazines such as *Rolling Stone* or *Mojo* often provide readers with useful information about rock musicians, their music, and aspects of the entertainment industry. Books targeted at the general reader—often written by journalists and music critics—are plentiful and varied. Cable networks such as VH-1 and MTV regularly offer profiles of artists and styles, frequently taking larger historical patterns into account, at least to some degree. The development of the classic-rock radio format in the early 1990s has also encouraged a growing sense of rock's history, along with the time-tested oldies format that has been around for decades. All these sources of information about the history of rock music can be useful, and indeed many have been employed in the writing of this textbook—a list of some of the best general sources can be found at the end of this chapter, and references to more specifically focused material are provided at the ends of subsequent chapters. Realize, however, that a scholarly approach to the history of rock is bound to differ in a number of significant ways from these other accounts. Such differences arise because information about rock music that is found in the popular media is designed primarily for entertainment rather than for educational or research purposes. Some of this information may be quite accurate, well researched, and balanced, but some of it is also skewed, gossipy, or unreliable. Always remember that magazines and broadcast stations generate revenue primarily through the sale of advertising; the worst thing that can happen in such businesses is for people put the magazine down, change the radio station, or turn off the TV. It is therefore in the best interests of such media outlets to deliver what they believe people want most, and this can lead them to focus on the more sensational and titillating aspects of biography at the expense of serious consideration of the music. At best, such sources of information can viewed as "historically flavored" entertainment; as such, they are still first and foremost entertainment.

This textbook will provide as balanced and fair an account of the history of rock music as possible. Its job is to capture a sense of the time during which each artist, group, or style prospered. Often this means that many more artists and groups will enter the story than may typically appear in other kinds of accounts, or that some artists or groups may turn out to have been more important in their day than they have been since, or, conversely, are more important now than they were in their day. This richness is to let you experience the broadest possible range of artists, groups, and styles. There will be no attempts to convince you to like this or that style of music, to elevate one style over another, or to dismiss or otherwise discredit any artist or group. These chapters will equip you with enough reliable information and historical context for you to defend your own ideas in an articulate manner. There is no better debate than an informed debate, and I encourage you to discuss your ideas with fellow students whenever possible.

I Know What I Like: The Fan Mentality. This is a good time to raise the issue of what might be called the "fan mentality." All of us who enjoy music are fans to some degree—nobody is really excluded from this group. But what does it mean to be a fan? Being a fan of an artist, group, or style entails frequently listening to the music itself as well as gathering interesting facts about both the artists and the music. At the same time we do this, however, we also reject a lot of other music. As a fan, there is absolutely nothing wrong with ignoring other artists, groups, or styles that do not interest us. This is perfectly natural. But as students of rock music, we cannot be so quick to ignore music we do not like. We must strive to be as fair as we can as we study rock's history and development, and this often forces us to consider carefully music we probably wouldn't choose to listen to otherwise. Being fair also means that we don't use every fact we encounter in a perpetual quest to prove that our favorite band really is the best band in the history of music. If you were studying American history, it wouldn't be acceptable to consider only presidents who shared your political persuasion. A balanced history of the last few decades would consider both John F. Kennedy and Richard M. Nixon, Ronald Reagan and Jimmy Carter, and Bill Clinton and George W. Bush. When it comes to music, however, we are all most interested in the bands or artists we like most. You don't have to suspend your sense of judgment to study rock's history, but you do have to work to keep the fan mentality at bay.

The Ups and Downs of Chart Positions.   To guard against presenting biased accounts of rock history in the chapters that follow, this book will make frequent citation of chart positions. While these are only one factor in determining what to include or leave out, they can be very helpful.

Almost everyone is familiar with charts of hit songs and albums, showing their ranking by popularity for a given week, and the most widely cited of these are the charts that appear in *Billboard Magazine.* Among scholars, charts in *Billboard* and elsewhere are viewed with some suspicion because much about the ways they have been put together over the years is unknown, making these weekly rankings susceptible to manipulation. Clearly, charts are not a precision instrument for measuring a song or album's success or popularity; it is not very useful to attempt to distinguish between a number one and a number five single. It is, however, much more viable to give credibility to the distinction between a number one hit and a number twenty-five hit. Charts are thus good at helping us make general kinds of distinctions about the popularity of a song or album during the time when it was released. They can also be useful when we compare how certain songs did on pop charts with the way they fared on rhythm and blues or country charts, or even on the British charts. But the best thing about chart numbers for this book is that they help us avoid the fan mentality—in a sense, they keep us honest. It is true that they do not accurately reflect the popularity or influence of some songs or albums; a record can occasionally chart well and have little influence, or chart moderately well (or even poorly) and have a lot of influence. But in a broad sense, charts are still the best instrument we have available, even if their measurements are flawed in some respects. It would be great if we could have extensive data on radio playlists of various eras, or on the actual number of records sold of any song or album. But thus far scholars have not comprehensively retrieved and collated playlists, and actual record sales are even more prone to manipulation than chart numbers (this has been a frequent complaint of artists and bands since the beginning of recording). The Record Industry Association of America (RIAA) awards gold records for sales of 500,000 units and platinum records for sales of one million units, and these distinctions can also be helpful as we measure the success of an album or single. You may find the RIAA website (www.riaa.com) interesting, since you can look up any record and track its award history. It may surprise you to realize that some records hit gold or platinum status several years—sometimes even decades—after their initial release!

The Four Themes.   The following chapters each take a three- to ten-year stretch of rock's history and organize the music along stylistic lines. Some chapters cover the same years from different angles, as in the chapters devoted to the British invasion and American response in the mid 1960s, for instance, years also covered in the chapter devoted to black pop in the '60s. Each chapter will also raise a set of interpretive issues that may help you glimpse how scholars and critics have debated the music and its historical circumstances or aesthetic impact or value. In the discussion of psychedelia in Chapter 7, for instance, the differences between mainstream popular culture of the mid 1960s and the hippie subcultures in both London and San Francisco are highlighted, and the questions that arise in this discussion are representative of the kinds of issues that can surface generally whenever a strong subculture can be identified. While these interpretive angles mostly change from chapter to chapter, some important themes are pursued throughout the book and return time and again in the discussions:

- social, political, and cultural issues
- issues of race, class, and gender
- the development of the music business
- the development of technology

All these themes play an important role in the way rock music develops and changes as a general musical style and as a force in popular culture. Changes in the music business, for example, play a crucial role in the how and why of the rock story, as the style goes from a ragamuffin challenger of the status quo in the 1950s to the dominant style of popular music in the decades that follow. In the realm of technology, the rise of radio in the 1920s and the emergence of television in the years following World War II are central to an understanding of how rock exploded into mainstream American culture in the mid 1950s, as is the development of cable television that facilitated the introduction of MTV in the early 1980s. As the chapters unfold, you will be urged to examine the ways these themes work into the story of rock's development. No style of music ever exists in a vacuum, and consideration of these broader perspectives will help us come to a deeper understanding of the forces that have shaped the repertory, as well as those that have shaped the ways this repertory has been interpreted, both by scholars in academia and by writers in the popular media.

Tracking the Popularity Arc. As we study rock's history and progress from the 1950s through the 1990s, you may notice a pattern that often arises regarding particular styles within rock music. In many cases, a specific style will seem to appear first within a relatively restricted geographic region and remain virtually undetected by most fans of popular music. For instance, few rock fans were aware of the punk scene in New York during the mid 1970s, and bands such as Television, the Ramones, and Blondie played to small local audiences, often containing only the members of the other bands playing on the bill that night. The American punk style, which would morph into new wave by the end of the decade, developed within this small subculture for a few years before breaking into the national spotlight in 1978. By the early 1980s, however, new wave had begun to change; some bands and artists merged into the rock mainstream, while the more die-hard, aggressive punk groups retreated back into a punk underground, mostly off the mainstream radar. The rise of punk out of a small, regionally based underground scene and into mainstream pop culture, and its subsequent retreat back into an often nationally dispersed underground scene, follows a pattern we will see often enough that we can give it a name: the popularity arc. Over and over, the story of specific styles in rock music follows the template of this popularity arc. Typically, histories of rock music account for the time each style spends in the pop limelight—the peak of the popularity arc—

creating a chronology of how such styles come and go without accounting much for their pre-mainstream roots or their existence after the commercial boom years. In a certain sense, it is difficult to avoid such a historical account, and similar problems arise in histories of other musical styles (such as jazz and classical music) as well. To keep the popularity arc in mind for any given style, you may ask yourself the following questions:

- How did this style arise?
- When did it peak in popularity?
- Does this style continue to exist in a subculture somewhere?

The chapters will give you the information you need to answer the first two questions. To answer the third, you will need to search the Internet. In fact, you may be surprised to discover how many older rock styles are still alive and celebrated, often long after they have fallen out of the mainstream spotlight. Old rockers, it turns out, never die—they just go online.

Elements of Music: An Introduction

Throughout the book, Listening Guides will direct your attention to individual songs that illustrate specific musical features of the styles discussed. As interesting as the circumstances surrounding a style, band, or song may be, the way the music itself sounds is probably the element that attracts most listeners in the first place. The analysis of rock music can get extremely complicated and even require a high level of specific music-analytical training. Many books and doctoral dissertations by music theorists and musicologists in the past several years have demonstrated how interesting rock music can be in terms of the many dimensions of its musical structure, and this area of scholarly research continues to expand every year. The Listening Guides in this book will help you listen for the structural features in rock music, and the focus of these guides will be musical form. In the broadest sense, musical form refers to the way the different sections in a song or piece are structured and organized. Rock uses a limited number of common formal types; once you are familiar with these types, you will begin to notice that most songs fit relatively neatly into one or another of them (though often with certain exceptions). Understanding these songs in terms of their formal structure will not only help you hear new things in the music

Jackie Brenston, who is credited with writing "Rocket '88'"—perhaps the first rock and roll record.

itself, but will also help you to perceive similarities between musical styles that may otherwise seem very different.

Form, Rhythm, and Meter: "Rocket '88'." The basic formal types will be introduced as they arise in Chapters 1 and 2, and Interlude 1 will further refine and organize this information. But to give you a start on listening for some of these musical features, here is a brief analysis of a classic track from rock's past: Jackie Brenston and His Delta Cats' 1951 single, "Rocket '88'." Recorded in Memphis and produced by Sam Phillips (who would later become central in the emergence of Elvis Presley), "Rocket '88'" is often claimed to be the first rock and roll song. While it is legally credited to Brenston, the singer may have written only the lyrics and lifted the music from an earlier song called "Cadillac Boogie" (such "borrowings" are relatively common in early rock and roll). To show how the song is laid out, I provide a formal diagram that breaks the song into sections and lists them according to CD timings. These timings may differ slightly from CD to CD, so don't let that throw you; they simply give you an idea about where in the song a specific section begins and ends. Each section is also marked by a snippet of lyrics or some other description to help you locate it as the song goes by. The formal diagram for "Rocket '88'" is in the Listening Guide below.

In the first section, labeled "Instrumental Verse" in the diagram, note that the description "12 mm." is given. This indicates that the section is twelve *measures* in length ("mm." is commonly used to abbreviate measures in musical writing). Let's figure out how to count measures in music. You have probably heard musicians begin a song by counting out "one, two, three, four!" The Beatles' "I Saw Her Standing There" might be the most famous rock example of this. Musicians commonly count the beats in music in groups of four (though groups of two or three beats can also be found). This simply means that you count "one, two, three, four" and then continue by counting "one, two three, four" again rather than "five, six, seven, eight." Each group of four beats is called a "measure" or "bar" of music—these terms are synonymous and are commonly used interchangeably. Note that each verse and instrumental verse (except one) in "Rocket '88'" is twelve measures (bars) in length. You might count it like this:

mm.:	1	2	3	4	5	6	7	8	9	10	11	12
beats:	1234	1234	1234	1234	1234	1234	1234	1234	1234	1234	1234	1234

Verse 2 is the exception and is only eight measures in length; it seems to break off early by comparison with the twelve-measure pattern shown above. It is likely that this is actually a mistake, because you can hear the musicians scrambling a bit musically to come back together as a band. Verse 2 can be seen like this:

mm.:	1	2	3	4	5	6	7	8	9??
beats:	1234	1234	1234	1234	1234	1234	1234	1234	???

Despite the irregularity of verse 2, if you count the measures and watch the CD timings, you should be able to follow the diagram as the song goes by. If you are having trouble keeping up, try pausing the music at the section boundaries given by the timings; this may help you hear the sections more clearly.

Simple Verse Form.   "Rocket '88'" repeats a single section of music eight times, and each is labeled either "Verse" or "Instrumental Verse." The only exception is verse 2, which, as we mentioned, seems to be a botched version of the structure found in all the other sections. Because this song simply repeats the same verse structure over and over, it will be classified as a *simple verse form*. Simple verse form is common in rock music and we will see many instances of it in the chapters that follow. Notice that the song does not have a chorus or distinctive contrasting section of any kind; other common forms will incorporate these elements, as we shall see in the next two chapters. For this song, focus on being sure that you can follow the form and count the measures. After you have followed the form with the diagram, see if you can follow it without the diagram. Once you begin hearing form in music, you may find that it can be difficult *not* to hear form in music!

Instrumental Listening.   In addition to form and rhythm in this song, it is also useful to listen for the instrumentation. This particular track uses drums, bass, electric guitar, acoustic piano, two saxes, and lead vocals. See if you can listen to the song all the way through following only one of these instruments; don't let your attention be drawn away by what's happening in another part. Then, play the song again and see if you can follow a different instrument all the way

---

🎧 **LISTENING GUIDE**   GET MUSIC ▶▶ wwnorton.com/rockhistory

Jackie Brenston and His Delta Cats, "Rocket '88'"

Words and music by Jackie Brenston, produced by Sam Phillips. "Rocket '88'" hit #1 on the Billboard Rhythm and Blues charts in 1951.

CD timings	Section	Description
0:00–0:19	Instrumental Verse	12 mm., piano featured.
0:19–0:38	Verse 1	12 mm., "You women have heard of jalopies . . ."
0:38–0:57	Instrumental Verse	12 mm., saxes featured.
0:57–1:10	Verse 2 (partial)	8 mm., "V–8 motor . . .", breaks off early.
1:10–1:28	Instrumental Verse	12 mm., sax solo.
1:28–1:47	Instrumental Verse	12 mm., sax solo continues.
1:47–2:05	Instrumental Verse	12 mm., sax solo continues.
2:05–2:23	Verse 3	12 mm., "Step in my rocket . . ."
2:23–2:46	Instrumental Verse	12 mm., sax and guitar featured.

A Note on Rhythm and Meter

Generally, "rhythm" refers to the ways musical sounds are organized in time; "beat" refers to a regular rhythmic pulse. Most of the music in this book will employ four-beat measures. Measures may also contain two or three beats, and these are counted "one two, one two" and "one two three, one two three" respectively. It is even possible for a measure to contain five, six, seven, or more beats per measure. These ways of organizing rhythm and beats in music are called "meter." A fuller consideration of a song's meter takes into account not only how many beats are in each measure, but also how each beat may be subdivided. A single beat can be divided into either two or three equal parts; in the first case you would evenly count, "one &, two &, three &, four &," and in the second, "one & uh, two & uh, three & uh, four & uh." When each beat is evenly divided into two parts, we call this "simple," and when each beat is divided evenly into three parts, we call this "compound." Meters are grouped by combining the number of beats per measure with the way each beat is divided, as shown in the following chart:

	Simple (2 parts)	*Compound (3 parts)*
Duple (2 beats)	duple simple (2/4)	duple compound (6/8)
Triple (3 beats)	triple simple (3/4)	triple compound (9/8)
Quadruple (4 beats)	quadruple simple (4/4)	quadruple compound (12/8)

When the meter employs two beats per measure, and each beat is evenly divided into two parts, we classify the meter as "duple simple," and this can be seen in the chart. Notice that a time signature is given in parentheses next to each meter classification. In each case, the time signature given represents the most common one used to indicate this meter classification in written music. You may have noticed that sheet music almost always has a time signature provided at the beginning of the song or piece; this tells the performer what the meter classification of the rhythm will be in that song. The meter classification plays a crucial role in establishing the rhythmic "feel" of a song, though it is not the only element that influences this. In the rock music we will study in this book, most songs will be in quadruple time, with both simple and compound divisions in play. "Rocket '88'," for instance, is in quadruple compound time, which many musicians simply think of as a "shuffle" in four.

through. Typically, our attention darts from part to part in a song, usually when something new comes in to grab our interest. While listening to "Rocket '88'," for instance, we may focus on the piano in the first instrumental verse, then on the vocals in verse 1, and then on the saxes in the next section, and so on. You may be surprised at how difficult it can be to remain focused on one part as you listen, but if you can train yourself to do this, you will hear things going on in the music that you've never noticed before. The topic of instrumentation is covered in Interlude 2, so feel free to look ahead to that section if you'd like to learn more about this topic. If you have never learned an instrument or played in a rock band, you may find it difficult to pick out the differences or characteristic features of certain instruments. If that is the case, try going out to hear live music and concentrating on each player in the band. Sometimes it is easier to pick out an instrument's sound when you can see it performed. And by all means, ask the band members questions between sets—most musicians are flattered by the attention!

Now that we have discussed the organization of the book and listened carefully to some music, it is time to dive in and explore rock music's history and repertory. Before we consider the emergence of rock and roll in the mid 1950s, however, we will need to get a clear picture of how the music business was configured in the first half of the twentieth century. Chapter 1 will help us understand what the popular music world was like before the advent of rock and roll.

General Sources for the History of Rock Music

Simon Frith, *Sound Effects: Youth, Leisure, and the Politics of Rock 'n' Roll* (Pantheon Books, 1991).

Theodore Gracyk, *Rhythm and Noise: An Aesthetics of Rock* (Duke University Press, 1996).

Greil Marcus, *Mystery Train: Images of America in Rock 'n' Roll Music*, 3rd rev. ed. (Plume, 1992).

James Miller, *Flowers in the Dustbin: The Rise of Rock and Roll, 1947–1977* (Fireside, 1999).

Robert Palmer, *Rock & Roll: An Unruly History* (Harmony Books, 1995).

Dafydd Rees and Luke Crampton, *Rock Stars Encyclopedia*, new rev. ed. (Dorling Kindersley, 1999).

The Rolling Stone Illustrated History of Rock Music, ed. Anthony DeCurtis and James Henke (Random House, 1992).

The Rolling Stone Encyclopedia of Rock & Roll, 3rd ed., ed. Holly George-Warren and Patricia Romanowski (Fireside, 2001).

Martin C. Strong, *The Great Rock Discography* (Times Books, 1998).

Ed Ward, Geoffrey Stokes, and Ken Tucker, *Rock of Ages, The Rolling Stone History of Rock & Roll* (Rolling Stone Press, 1986).

1920s–'40s

The decades of the 1920s, '30s, and '40s in America were to a great extent shaped by three crucial events: the end of World War I ("The Great War"), the stock market crash of 1929, and World War II. But both before and after these crushing events, Americans conquered flight, fought for the right to vote, battled for and against prohibition, danced new dances, and made new music.

When World War I ended, 10 million soldiers were dead. Though American casualties accounted for only 1 percent of the total, the Great War had taken a costly toll on American culture generally. The war was bloody, fought with gas as well as bullets and old-world strategies that could not accommodate modern weaponry. The modern world was torn apart and people everywhere were horrified.

With the war finally over, Americans felt relief and fear at the same time, and the result was a sense of desperate recklessness. Upheaval in world politics was reflected in the arts, with the emergence of riotous new forms of literature, dance, and music. Songs remained the dominant form of popular music in the 1920s, but the radical sounds of Louis Armstrong, Glenn Miller, Duke Ellington, and others helped define the decade musically. F. Scott Fitzgerald (author of *The Great Gatsby*) dubbed the 1920s "the jazz age," and jazz's strong rhythms, jagged melodies, and big sound made people get up and dance, with young, single, female "flappers" dancing (and smoking and drinking) right alongside their male counterparts.

But the excitement and freedom of the "roaring" twenties were quickly snuffed out in one day, with the stock market crash of October 29, 1929, forever known as "Black Tuesday." The crash sent the American economy into turmoil: 26,000 businesses failed in 1930. By 1932, 11 million Americans—25 percent of the labor force—were out of work. People were forced to move from their homes into shantytowns and many stood in line for bread every day.

In 1932, with the nation out of work and looking to its government for help, Franklin Delano Roosevelt was elected president. Roosevelt promised Americans a "New Deal" and he used the power of the federal government to get people back to work, using workers in government-paid jobs to improve the nation's roads, bridges, tunnels, and forests and national parks. Roosevelt also established the Works Progress Administration (WPA) whose most famous contributions came in the arts. With the creation of federal agencies like the WPA

This cover of Life magazine from February 18, 1926, shows a "flapper" teaching an older man the charleston, a popular dance of the time. Many women smoked, danced, and drank in public for the first time in the 1920s.

During the Great Depression, nearly 25 percent of the American labor force was out of work. Here, hundreds of homeless and unemployed people wait in line seeking shelter in New York in 1930.

along with the establishment of the Social Security system, Roosevelt defined a new role for the federal government that some argue broke the United States out of its psychological, if not wholly its economic, depression.

No sooner had Americans started to leave the Great Depression behind than a new enemy emerged: Adolf Hitler. Like Roosevelt, Hitler was dealing with a severe economic crisis in his nation. Hitler, however, began to solve Germany's economic problems in a different way. He chose expansion, eventually leading his military forces into Austria, Czechoslovakia, and Poland and pitting the German "master race" against "undesirables," most notably Jews— 6 million of whom were killed in Nazi death camps by 1945. Joining forces with Italy and Japan, Germany led the Axis powers in what soon became World War II. At first the United

States did not join in the fighting against the Axis powers, but when Japan attacked Pearl Harbor on December 6, 1941, America entered the fray in the Pacific, and after Germany declared war on the United States, in Europe as well. The war on the European front ended with Germany's surrender in May 1945. The Japanese fought on until September, when they surrendered after the United States dropped atomic bombs on both Hiroshima and Nagasaki. The war was over but the world had entered the atomic age.

While war had ravaged Europe and rocked the world, American soldiers returned home

as conquering heroes. Optimism reigned at home, signaled by the G.I. Bill, which allowed more Americans to attend college than ever before, and a dramatically increased birth rate—a "baby boom" that would have long-range consequences for American culture, and especially for popular music and its audience. Being such a large (and prosperous) generation had its benefits. There were lots of baby boomers and soon they would have their own money to spend. Many would spend it on music, a music that was also all their own: rock and roll.

Irving Berlin's "White Christmas" is one of the most successful songs in the history of popular music. Originally featured in the 1942 movie Holiday Inn starring Bing Crosby and Fred Astaire, the song has been recorded by a wide range of performers, including Crosby, Frank Sinatra, Perry Como, Rosemary Clooney, and Pat Boone. In the mid 1950s Clyde McPhatter and the Drifters recorded a doo-wop version, which Elvis Presley imitated almost note-for-note on his famous Christmas album a couple of years later. Among the many versions of this song that have been recorded are one by Otis Redding (1968), a Phil Spector–produced version featuring Darlene Love from the early 1960s, and an up-tempo dance treatment by Al Green from the early '80s. Crosby's version is often reported to be the biggest selling record in history, and it returned to the upper regions of the pop charts during the Christmas season almost every year until 1962, hitting number one in 1942, 1945, and 1946. While the song has come to conjure up nostalgic and warm images of snowy winter nights in front of a crackling fire, in Holiday Inn Crosby's character is stuck in sunny southern California during the Christmas season, lamenting the balmy climate.

The World before Rock and Roll

In 1956 a young, slim Elvis Presley appeared on the *Ed Sullivan Show*, a weekly television variety program that aired Sunday evenings on CBS. Presley's appearance on the show was the source of considerable controversy; in an earlier performance of "Hound Dog" on Milton Berle's show, Elvis had launched into an improvised ending to the tune, grinding his hips suggestively as he sang. Such on-stage antics earned the singer the nickname "Elvis the Pelvis," and caused such a public uproar that when Presley appeared on Sullivan's show, the cameras were not permitted to show his body below the chest. Despite the heated protests of parents—or maybe because of them—Elvis became the central figure in a new kind of popular music intended especially for teenagers: rock and roll.

We'll discuss Elvis and his music in further detail in the next chapter. For now, recognizing the importance of Elvis's early television performances can help us approach the ways rock and roll developed in the mid 1950s. Consider, for instance, that Presley appeared before a national audience, making his performance one that the entire country reacted to. As rock and roll erupted in 1955 and 1956, a new and interesting feature of its success was that it was a national style of music almost from the beginning—it didn't spread gradually from town to town and region to region around the country but rather broke onto the national cultural scene relatively suddenly. How was it possible, then, for this first wave of rock and roll to saturate American culture so quickly and thoroughly? What kinds of cultural conditions and commercial means of production and distribution had to be in place for a new musical style to "catch fire" as rock and roll did? And what were the musical and stylistic sources of this new style?

This chapter will examine these issues as well as outline the world of popular music before rock and roll made its rowdy entrance onto the national scene. Few musical styles emerge fully formed and in isolation from other styles of their time, and rock and roll is no exception. Rock and roll developed out of three principal sources that preceded it: mainstream popular music, rhythm and blues, and country and western. Each of these styles has its own history and development in the decades before rock and roll. This chapter will examine how these styles developed in the 1930s, '40s, and early '50s, providing a historical backdrop and music-stylistic context that will help us understand how and why rock and roll emerged as it did and when it did. It will also explore how the development of new technologies like radio and television played a crucial role in preparing the ground for this critical shift in the pop-music landscape.

Part 1. The World of Mainstream Pop in the Years Leading Up to 1955

Building a National Audience for Music and Entertainment

National versus Regional. One of the important changes that took place in popular music in the first half of the twentieth century was the emergence of a national audience. In today's world, in which satellite TV and the Internet provide us convenient and instant access to even remote parts of the globe, it is difficult to imagine an America in which most culture was regional. But at the end of the nineteenth century, the majority of Americans lived in a world very much conditioned by their local and regional surroundings. People tended not to travel nearly as much as we do now, and in many parts of the country there was no quick access to news of national and world events. In terms of popular-musical styles, this meant that styles often could be identified with particular regions of the country. Early gramophone cylinders and disks made recorded performances available to many Americans, but the music that people knew still tended to be mostly the music they could either play or hear performed in person. If someone played the piano and read music—and many Americans did—he or she could purchase the sheet music to a favorite song, often at the local Woolworth's five-and-dime store where pianists were on hand to personally play the music for customers trying to decide among competing titles. Music was also available through oral tradition, and one could learn to play tunes by ear, without having to read music. The technological and marketing developments in radio and motion pictures played a central role in making the same kinds of popular entertainment available in all parts of the country during the first few decades of the century, in many ways breaking down regional differences. The 1930s and '40s are often thought of as a golden age in the history of motion pictures, as Hollywood churned out a long series and wide variety of films that played movie houses in towns across America. Later we will consider the role films played in the music business during those years, but the central role of radio in building a national audience is probably just as crucial.

Radio technology was developed at the end of the nineteenth century and used initially for military purposes and to communicate with ships at sea; the first radio broadcasts of consequence for our story date back to 1920, when KDKA in Pittsburgh and WWJ in Detroit went on the air with a blend of news, local information, and live music. It would be hard to exaggerate the marked effect early radio had on American culture, and especially on the history of popular music. For the first time, listeners within range of a regional radio station could enjoy music that might otherwise be unavailable to them: listeners way out in farm country could hear performances from far-off big city nightclubs, for instance. When NBC went coast-to-coast with its national radio network in 1928, regional boundaries in popular culture began to blur. Now it no longer mattered as much where one lived: the same news, music, drama, and comedy were simultaneously available to significant portions of the country. Listeners within the transmitting range of stations in Philadelphia, Buffalo, Detroit, Chicago, and Los Angeles, for instance, could all hear the same programming at the same time. Network radio audiences suddenly became national audiences.

Especially important to the history of popular music is the way some pop styles became national while other kept their regional identities. To a great extent this can be attributed to the programming of the networks: the mainstream pop music of performers such as Bing Crosby, the Andrews Sisters, the big bands, and later Frank Sinatra were heard frequently on network radio; country and western, and rhythm and blues were not. Because mainstream pop developed a national audience, regional distinctions are not particularly useful when we chart the development of that particular style in the 1930s, '40s, and '50s; instead, experts tend to stress how similar pop was in most markets across the country. Also, the mainstream pop played on network radio during the 1930s and '40s was directed at a white, middle-class listening audience. Music that music-business people thought might appeal only to low-income white or black listeners (rural or urban) was mostly excluded, or at best, given a marginal role in radio programming. Since country and western and rhythm and blues were considered music for such low-income listeners, these styles were not often programmed on network radio; as a consequence, they retained their regional distinctions. We will want to keep track of such regional differences within and among country and western and rhythm and blues styles, and this will be discussed in more detail later in this chapter and in Chapter 2.

The Rise of the Radio Networks in the 1920s (How Did They Work?)

The early years of radio were an exciting time, and as broadcasters worked to get radio into every home in America, they discovered there were two reliable ways of reaching ever-larger audiences. The first was to broadcast the radio signal via a high-power transmitter. Under the most favorable atmospheric conditions, such "superstations" could reach listeners within a radius of several hundred miles of the transmitter. The federal government even licensed a few stations not only for high power but also for exclusive use of a particular frequency. With no local stations to mask the signal,

Many of the first radio stations developed from very modest beginnings. This photo shows the original facilities used to broadcast results of the 1920 presidential election. This small set-up, originally housed in a garage, would soon become Pittsburgh's KDKA.

such "clear channel" stations could regularly reach entire multistate regions of the country. Other enterprising broadcasters placed their transmitters in Mexico, just south of the border where the U.S. government had no licensing authority. These "X-stations" (named after their first call letter) could sometimes be picked up as far north as Chicago.

A more effective way of reaching a large audience was to link a number of local and regional stations together to form a network. NBC used ATT telephone lines to link up sixty-nine stations across the country for its first coast-to-coast broadcast in 1928. Soon NBC was running two networks and other networks were getting into the business as well. The network system had a number of distinct advantages: programming could be run from one central location (most often a studio in New York), and it was also possible to run live programming from member stations (called "affiliates"). This gave the networks a tremendous range of programming from which to choose. When networks could get one of the clear-channel stations on board, this offered the best of both worlds. This network system survives today relatively intact in the television industry, where most of the prime-time programming originates from the main studios in Los Angeles or New York, while other shows and newscasts originate locally. Current talk radio also employs this model, as shows originate from many parts of the country but play to a national audience. All of this was originally developed for radio in the 1920s.

Perhaps the biggest difference between today's radio and radio before 1945 was that back then it was considered unethical to play records on the air. It was thought that by playing a record you were trying to fool people into believing a performance was live when it really was not, so most music was performed live on the air. Modern radio listeners expect that the music they hear is recorded, but from the first broadcast moments of radio, listeners assumed and expected that what they heard over the airwaves was occurring live and in real time. This was, of course, a happy situation for most musicians, who eagerly took advantage of the opportunities for ample work. Even though affiliates were fed network programming for large segments of the broadcast schedule, most larger stations also employed a studio band for local programming. In addition, stations had to work to fill the remaining on-air time when no network programs were broadcast, and this created plenty of opportunity for entrepreneurial local bandleaders, who were often eager for a chance to promote their groups. In this context, it is not surprising that the musician's union (American Federation of Musicians) took strong political steps in the 1940s to keep records ("canned

Many today might consider Amos 'n' Andy to be politically incorrect, but during the heyday of radio, the show was enormously popular nationwide. Amos and Andy are shown here—uncharacteristically—in costume while filming a movie.

music") off the airwaves—keeping music live meant keeping musicians (and union members) working.

Network radio programming offered listeners a wide range of entertainment: soap operas, adventure, and comedy shows were popular, along with variety shows and feeds from dance clubs across the network. *The Guiding Light* appeared in 1937, while *The Lone Ranger* and *Superman* entertained listeners throughout most of the 1930s and '40s. One of the great successes of the era was the comedy *Amos 'n' Andy*, which premiered in 1929. Though its use of racial stereotypes would be unacceptable by today's standards, during its heyday the adventures and mishaps of Amos and Andy had the undivided attention of the country (not unlike success later enjoyed by television shows such as *All in the Family*, *M*A*S*H*, *Cheers*, *Seinfeld*, and *Friends*). Network radio created an audience that reached from the east to the west coast, and in so doing created a national popular culture in which music played a central role. Once radio came on the scene, a song could become popular almost overnight; no more waiting for word to spread from town to town and from region to region: with radio, a song could be heard far and wide in a single performance.

The Migration of Big Corporate Money Away from Radio to Television.
Network radio helped create a national audience, but by the late 1940s that audience was beginning to move away from radio and toward the newest technological marvel: television. The Radio Corporation of America (RCA), under the direction of David Sarnoff, had been a key player in the development of radio since the beginning. Sarnoff had been the young man decoding radio transmissions from the *Titanic* as she went down in 1912, and as a rising executive in the radio industry, he led RCA in building the NBC networks in the 1920s and '30s. In the 1940s Sarnoff's attention turned to television, and soon RCA would increasingly redirect its resources from radio to television in the period after World War II, betting that sound with pictures would be even more popular—and profitable—than sound alone. As more Americans could afford to acquire television sets in the late 1940s and 1950s, the national audience migrated away from radio and toward television. This changeover occurred slowly but steadily and could be seen in programming as well; some of the most popular radio shows— *The Guiding Light*, *Amos 'n' Andy*, *The Lone Ranger*, and *Superman*—all made the leap and

Among many of the radio shows that survived the move to television, The Lone Ranger *became one of the most popular small-screen staples of the 1950s. The* Lone Ranger *(Clayton Moore, left) is shown here with his faithful sidekick, Tonto (Jay Silverheels).*

Bing Crosby and the *Kraft Music Hall*

During the golden age of radio, network programs helped turn the airwaves into a communal space shared by the entire nation. One particularly important example was a Thursday night variety show hosted by Bing Crosby, called the *Kraft Music Hall*. Variety shows had their roots in vaudeville, where a range of different acts were scheduled on a single show. These included music, dancing, comedy routines and sketches, magic tricks, or other types of performances. By presenting many different forms of entertainment, a variety show usually had something for everyone. This format proved equally successful on radio, where a number of variety shows rose to national prominence. The *Kraft Music Hall* was as successful as any of them and had a large impact on American popular culture.

Kraft began sponsoring the *Kraft Music Review* in 1933 to promote Miracle Whip. The original host was Al Jolson, but Bing Crosby took over as host in 1936 after the show was renamed *Kraft Music Hall*. It is difficult to appreciate today how enormously popular Bing Crosby was at the time. As a singer, Crosby had thirty-eight number one hits in his career, nearly as many as the Beatles (24) and Elvis Presley (18) combined. He charted an astounding total of 396 records and recorded "White Christmas," the most popular record in history. As a movie star, Crosby was the top box-office attraction in America for five consecutive years (1944–48). In many ways, he was the first true popular music superstar and his multidimensional career was a model for many singers

The popularity of the Kraft Music Hall *was enormous, with nearly 50 million listeners each week. At the time, host Bing Crosby was a major force in American music and Kraft Foods made the most of his appeal by closely connecting him to their products. Pictured here is a lid to a canister of Kraft cheese, prominently featuring Crosby and the popular show.*

became popular TV shows. Along with motion pictures, radio had created a national audience, and television now inherited radio's share of that audience.

Our discussion has thus led us back to television in the 1950s and provided us with a greater context for interpreting Elvis's 1956 appearance on the *Ed Sullivan Show*. It was crucial to the rapid and broad success of rock and roll that this new style appear before a national audience. Only fifteen years earlier this audience could have been reached via network radio, but by the mid 1950s they were gathered around the television set. Thus, the national audience that television enjoyed had been brought together for the first time by radio. Rock and roll was able to spread as fast as it did because this audience could be reached with a single Sunday evening television broadcast. As television grew in national prominence, however, radio was left out in the cold in many ways. With its national audience dwindling, radio returned to its local and regional audiences.

turned movie stars, like Frank Sinatra, Elvis Presley, and Will Smith.

Crosby was one of the first "crooners," a vocal style based on nuance and intimacy. He used the power of the microphone to sing very gently, as if he were right in the ear of each listener. His stage and screen persona was that of the likeable everyman. The combination of these two traits—a gentle, baritone voice and an affable, charismatic image—were ideal for a variety show host who had to provide the glue that kept the show together, from act to act and from week to week. Crosby kept the banter to a minimum and didn't allow applause from the audience. His commercial announcements were as unobtrusive as possible and he rarely performed them himself. The acts on his show were a mixture of highbrow classical music, lowerbrow popular music, comedy routines and skits, and jazz that was both sophisticated and popular. By freely intermingling classical, jazz, and pop music on *Kraft Music Hall*, Crosby reinforced the traits of his own musical style, which combined pop and jazz with a clean, classicist aesthetic. As both a singer and variety show host, he helped create a style of American song that was popular and sophisticated, yet still had swing. Through both his music and his eclectic variety show, Crosby also became a subtle force for integration, uniting races and cultures *within* the music as well as through it.

The popularity and influence of the *Kraft Music Hall* was enormous. At the peak of its success, nearly 50 million listeners tuned in each week. As a point of comparison, the Beatles' first appearance on *The Ed Sullivan Show*—one of the most widely seen musical broadcasts in history— was watched by 73 million people. The variety show format outlasted the golden age of radio and was a direct precursor to television variety shows like Ed Sullivan's, live sketch-comedy shows like *Saturday Night Live*, and talk shows like *The Tonight Show* or *The Late Show with David Letterman*. Both directly and through its many imitators, Bing Crosby's *Kraft Music Hall* was a powerful unifying force in American popular culture.

The migration of the networks (and their audiences) toward television, though it might be seen as a major blow to the radio industry, actually opened up new kinds of opportunities for entrepreneurial station owners and managers. The transformation of local and regional radio stations in response to the early age of television played a critical role in the development of country and western and rhythm and blues, and, in turn, figured prominently in the emergence of early rock and roll.

Tin Pan Alley

Sheet Music Publishers and Professional Songwriters. The development of radio and television technologies and was one influence on the mainstream popular-music business in the decades before rock and roll. A second important dimen-

Is It Live or Is It Memorex? A Note on Recording Technology

As a result of the popularity of the books-on-tape format in recent years, recordings of some old radio broadcasts have been released and are readily available in bookstores. Many assume that these shows are tapes of original broadcasts; it is important to note, however, that recording tape was not widely used in radio until the late 1940s. Most of us are familiar with magnetic tape, which is used in cassette and reel-to-reel formats. This technology was employed by the Germans during World War II for military purposes and was intended to protect Adolf Hitler from attack by Allied forces. The Germans were concerned that the Allies might detect the exact source of specific radio transmissions, and so could possibly attack the station from which Hitler was delivering one of his many radio speeches to the German people. They refined magnetic tape recording in order to produce the most realistic recorded version of Hitler's voice, and then the tape was broadcast at a later time, while Hitler was far away from the radio studio. When the Allies conquered Germany, they found that the radio stations all had sophisticated tape machines, and this new technology quickly made its way into the radio business.

For those radio programs that date from before 1945, most of the broadcasts are lost forever. But of those that are preserved, many are "transcription disc" recordings, made on sixteen-inch discs that resemble LP records and were made for circulation only among stations and not for general sale. It says a good deal about the importance of radio in the lives of Americans in the 1940s that the U.S. government made certain that transcription discs of popular radio shows were shipped to armed forces stations overseas and played for the troops. In addition to letters and packages from home, familiar radio shows helped ease the strain for servicemen of being a long way from home and often in hostile conditions.

sion in the pop-music business from the same years is music publishing. In the first half of the twentieth century, sheet music was the principal way to sell music. This all changed with the emergence of rock and roll, as recordings came to dominate the business. The sheet music industry was concentrated in an area often referred to as Tin Pan Alley. Strictly speaking, Tin Pan Alley is an area of New York City where, about a hundred years ago, the high concentration of songwriters plunking out their song ideas on rows of pianos sounded like people banging on tin pans; it was the place where songwriters and song publishers were clustered to form the geographical heart of the sheet music business. Tin Pan Alley has since come to denote more than just a few blocks in Manhattan; the term is now shorthand not only for a body of music but also for a way of doing business in popular music. The body of music consists of the thousands of popular songs written and made popular mostly in the first half of the twentieth century by such professional songwriters as Irving Berlin, Cole Porter, George and Ira Gershwin, and Jerome Kern. The way of doing business has to do with how these songs were sold.

Musically speaking, Tin Pan Alley songs follow a standard, though very flexible, formal pattern. Many of these songs make use of a *sectional verse-chorus* format, in which the *sectional chorus* is the song listeners are likely to recognize, while the *sectional verse* is a kind of introduction that sets the scene for the song.

Most listeners, for instance, know only the sectional chorus of the perennial favorite "White Christmas" (sung by many but made famous by Bing Crosby); the song actually has a sectional verse that explains how Christmas doesn't seem the same in California with all the bright sunshine, though most listeners who have not seen the 1942 movie *Holiday Inn* do not know this. Sectional choruses are often cast in a 32-measure structural pattern called *AABA form*. Judy Garland's performance of "Over the Rainbow"—a song featured in the classic 1939 film *The Wizard of Oz*—provides a representative example of how the 32-bar AABA form is structured. While there are some standard variations on this common structural pattern in the Tin Pan Alley repertory—ABAC, for instance—the basic 32-bar sectional chorus length remains intact in most instances. Thus what holds this repertory together musically is a fairly uniform approach to musical form, practiced by a majority of the professional songwriters of Tin Pan Alley, along with a consistent approach to the many other musical elements that are used to help delineate the form. The sectional verse-chorus format is rare in rock music, but the AABA form common to so many Tin Pan Alley sectional verses plays a central role in rock.

This repertory is unified not only in the way it is structured but also in the way it was marketed. In rock music, the basic unit of trade is a specific recorded performance, available on a record, tape, CD, MP3, or some other form. But in the Tin Pan Alley era, the basic unit of trade was the song itself, not a specific recording of the song. A successful song was recorded by a series of artists, each trying to tailor the tune to suit his or her personal style, and the more versions, the more money that could be made by the songwriter and his or her publisher. In this practice, professional songwriters composed the songs and publishers then worked to get each tune heard by the public. The songwriters

Judy Garland, playing the role of Dorothy Gale in The Wizard of Oz, sings "Over the Rainbow" as her faithful dog Toto looks on. This song, written by E. Y. Harbaugh (lyrics) and Harold Arlen (music), is representative of Tin Pan Alley songwriting. Its AABA form is one of the most common of the mainstream pop formal designs during the 1900–1950 period.

themselves were rarely performers, so publishers needed ways of "pitching" songs to performers who might consider working them into their perform-ances. In the first few decades of the twentieth century, some were pitched in all kinds of ways—some more ethical than others. The usual way to get a song known was to convince a professional to perform the tune as part of a show. Another more aggressive method was to plant a "song plugger" in the audience who would stand up during the show and offer a rendition of a new song—an action that could land him either in the street, or worse, in jail.

With the rise of musical theater, Broadway musicals became a prime vehi-cle for getting songs heard, and some early Broadway shows had only the skimpiest of plots, provided merely to give some sense of sequence to the songs themselves (later musicals were far more integrated). The first movies had no sound, though music was in many instances furnished by local musicians—sometimes even an orchestra—and occasionally musical scores were provided by the film studio for specific movies. When sound films became popular in the 1930s, musicals were often released in film versions, and new musicals were

LISTENING GUIDE

GET MUSIC ▶▶ wwnorton.com/rockhistory

Judy Garland with Victor Young and His Orchestra, "Over the Rainbow"

Words by E. Y. Harbaugh, music by Harold Arlen. Reached #5 on the Billboard Pop charts in fall 1939.

FORM: This example uses AABA form. This form is closely associated with Tin Pan Alley songwriting and is one of the most common of the mainstream pop formal designs during the 1900–1950 period. Typically an AABA form presents two verses, followed by a contrasting bridge, and a return to the verse. To fill out a particular per-formance arrangement of an AABA song, verses and the bridge may be repeated. Here two verses are repeated, as well as part of the bridge, after the complete verse-verse-bridge-verse structure has been presented. Interlude 1 provides a fuller discus-sion of form in pop music. Note that the verses within the AABA form are not the same as the sectional verse employed in the sectional verse-chorus format.

TIME SIGNATURE: 4/4. Note the frequent speeding up and slowing down of the tempo. These tempo variations help shape the vocal phrases and make them more expressive. Such changes of tempo are not common in dance music or in any style that uses a drummer. In this case, a conductor directs the changes of tempo and dynamics.

INSTRUMENTATION: Vocalist with orchestra.

composed expressly for the movies. Thus musical theater and movies provided convenient vehicles for promoting Tin Pan Alley songs. Records could also help promote songs, though when we think of recordings during the pre-rock era we have to remember that the central element in a record was the song, not the particular performance of it. By far the best way to get a song out during the 1930s and '40s was to get it on the radio, and radio was dominated during the 1935–45 period by big bands, and then in 1945–55 by star singers. By getting a song performed on national radio, a publisher could expect the best chance of success. In some instances sales of a recorded version of a song could outsell the sheet music, but the usual mode of success for Tin Pan Alley came in the form of sheet music sales. During the years before rock and roll, songs were seen as entities separable from particular performances of them. For a Tin Pan Alley music publisher, the best thing that could happen to a song was for it to be recorded by a wide variety of artists (this is still true for music publishers today). But until the advent of rock and roll, the heart of the business was squarely in sheet music sales.

0:00–0:11	**Introduction**, 4 mm.	String melody with pulsating winds accompaniment set the dreamy mood for the song
0:11–0:34	**A-Verse**, 8 mm.	Vocal enters, "Somewhere . . . way up high . . ." Listen for the large leap in the melody, which then works its way back to Earth, paralleling the words.
0:34–0:55	**A-Verse**, 8 mm.	As before, "Somewhere . . . skies are blue . . ."
0:55–1:18	**B-Bridge**, 8 mm.	"Some day I'll wish . . ." Notice how the first half of each vocal phrase seems to rush forward, then slow down toward the end.
1:18–1:40	**A-Verse**, 8 mm.	As before, "Somewhere . . . bluebirds fly . . ." Note the nice melodic support in the orchestra.
1:40–2:01	**A-Verse**, 8 mm.	Vocal gets a rest and the melody is played by clarinet and answered by orchestra.
2:01–2:25	**A-Verse**, 8 mm.	Vocal returns with variations that make the melody seem fresh, "Somewhere . . . bluebirds fly"
2:25–2:46	**B-Partial Bridge**, 4 mm.	Beginning of bridge serves as the basis for the ending, "Some day . . ."

The Singers and the Big Bands. One important objective for all Tin Pan Alley publishers was to get their songs on the radio, and this is where our discussions of radio and Tin Pan Alley come together. Because most radio performances until the late 1940s were live, promoting a song meant much more than just getting a record out: bandleaders and singers had to be convinced to perform a song, and in the process persuaded that using that song in their live shows would also serve their own career interests—and for most musicians during that era (much as today), "career interests" meant "future bookings for more money." Publishers thus had to bargain with bandleaders and singers, as well as radio producers, to get their songs included in those live radio broadcasts that the bands and singers were using to prompt future bookings. The radio networks, performers, and song publishers thus needed one another to succeed, and much of the behind-the-scenes action in the music business during those years had to do with which artists would perform on which shows, and which songs they would play or sing.

Often referred to as the King of Swing, Benny Goodman was a top bandleader during the big band era. The virtuoso jazz clarinetist is shown here performing a beach-side concert with his band and singer Martha Tilton. In most big bands, the instrumental playing was featured, with the singer providing variety—a practice that would reverse itself as the big band era ended.

The era from about 1935 to 1945 is considered the big band era. During this time, dance bands employed a rhythm section of bass, drums, piano, and guitar with horn sections of trumpets, trombones, and saxophones to create arrangements of Tin Pan Alley songs designed to provide music appropriate for dancing while also featuring the instrumental prowess of the musicians and the virtuosity of the arranger. Big bands were led by instrumentalists such as Benny Goodman, Tommy Dorsey, Jimmy Dorsey, and Glenn Miller, and singers were merely featured soloists. Thus, the celebrity in the band was its leader; the musicians and singers could (and did) change frequently. Arrangements during the big band era gave more emphasis to the band, often allotting only one time through the sectional chorus of a song for the singer; sections of the band, and perhaps instrumental soloists, might also be featured both before and after the singer. Many arrangements, such as the Glenn Miller Band's 1942 number one hit "A String of Pearls" employed no vocals at all. Such an emphasis on the band may seem strange to many rock listeners. The rock music practice that developed later is exactly the opposite of the big band practice: in rock music the vocalist is usually the focus of the song and an instrumental solo takes a verse of the song to provide variety. In big band music, the vocalist provides the variety! Perhaps because of the emphasis on instrumental playing in the big bands, there is a close relationship between big band music and jazz, which developed both within and alongside big band music.

Despite the general focus during the big band era on the bands themselves, a number of performing artists developed careers independent from any particular band. The most important pop singer in the 1930s and 1940s was Bing Crosby, whose relaxed, easygoing crooning made him a favorite in both the United States and abroad. Crosby enjoyed a long string of hit recordings, including "I've Got a Pocketful of Dreams" (1938), "Only Forever" (1940), and "Swinging on a Star" (1944), along with "White Christmas," which topped the pop charts in 1942 and again in 1945. In addition to being perhaps the most successful solo performer of his era, Crosby acted in films (often with comedian Bob Hope) and hosted his own radio variety show (sponsored by Kraft Foods). In contrast to some of the pop singers who would come to fame in the years after World War II, Bing Crosby projected a wholesome, friendly, and paternal image; in many ways, he was America's dad (or favorite uncle). The Andrews Sisters and the Mills Brothers were also important figures in the 1935–45 period, each ringing up a long series of hit records. Both groups made harmony singing their trademark and in some ways the vocal arrangements of each group owe something to big band horn arrangements. This can be heard especially in the Andrews Sisters' "In the Mood," which is a vocal rendition of a song made popular by the Glenn Miller Band. The Andrews Sisters enjoyed their greatest commercial success with "Bei Mir bist du Schoen" (1938), "Shoo-Shoo Baby" (1943), and "Rum and Coca Cola" (1945), while the Mills Brothers scored biggest with "Tiger Rag" (1931), "Paper Doll" (1943), and "You Always Hurt the One You Love" (1944). The Andrews Sisters' and Mills Brothers' approach to harmony singing served as a precursor to the doo-wop and girl groups that played an important role in rock and roll in the 1950s and 1960s.

Frank Sinatra. To somebody inside the entertainment business in the period before 1945, it would probably have seemed crazy to think that a big band singer could strike out on his own and have a viable career; Bing Crosby had enjoyed considerable success as a solo act, but he was considered more the exception than the rule. Frank Sinatra, however, established a new model for the

Starting out as a featured singer with the Harry James and Tommy Dorsey bands, Frank Sinatra set out on a solo career in 1943. The singer—an early example of the many "teen idols" in pop music—was especially popular with young ladies, who often swooned while Sinatra crooned.

pop-music singer; building in part on Crosby's accomplishments, Sinatra made the singer, not the band, the star of the show, and thus paved the way for later rock and roll singers like Elvis Presley and Pat Boone. Sinatra came up through the big band ranks as a singer with the Harry James and Tommy Dorsey bands, singing the occasional solo but mostly sitting on the sidelines. He went solo in 1943, and perhaps owing to his good looks and slightly rebellious sensuality, Sinatra became a teen idol almost immediately. In a preview of the rock and roll hysteria to come a decade later, teenage girls mobbed Sinatra performances, fainting or grabbing at him. Sinatra enjoyed the fanatical attention and advantages of success that came with it, though he continued to think of himself as a musician, frequently acknowledging that he owed much of his vocal phrasing and technique to his study of the musicians with whom he had worked during the big band era. Of Sinatra's many important records from the late 1940s, perhaps his rendition of "I've Got a Crush on You" (1948) is the best example of his distinctive singing style, employed in a song that reinforced his teen idol image. Sinatra went on to become one of the most successful singers of the post–World War II era, selling millions of records and playing to packed houses well into the 1980s.

In the wake of his first successes, Sinatra drew many imitators, as singers now replaced the big bands as the focus of music-business attention and many of the now-former big band vocalists took center stage in the wake of Sinatra's success. At the same time, financial pressures forced many of the big bands to break up; after about 1945 it simply became too expensive to employ so many musicians, and smaller combos became a more cost-effective way making a suitable living playing dancehall gigs. By the end of the 1940s, the big band era was over and increasingly new singers emerged who had no significant previous association with any particular big band. For many involved with the big bands, this was

Les Paul and Mary Ford were among the most popular acts during the first half of the 1950s. The couple is shown here recording at home, using a roomful of Paul's custom modified equipment.

Les Paul, Electric Guitars, and Multitrack Recording

A new role for the electric guitar in pop was pioneered by guitarist and inventor Les Paul, whose innovations in electronics and recording during the 1950s had a lasting impact on popular music. Here are the ways in which Les Paul changed pop:

As Guitarist and Arranger for Les Paul and Mary Ford Les Paul was one of the country's leading guitarists during the big band era. While his own musical preference was for up-tempo jazz, he was a master of many styles. In fact, in the early years of his career he posed as the country singer Rhubarb Red, singing traditional "hillbilly" music on a local radio show in his home state of Wisconsin. Paul met country singer Mary Ford in 1945; in 1949 the two married and formed a musical duo that also featured spirited husband-and-wife banter and gags on stage. Paul arranged all of the duo's music, playing guitar and employing his latest electronic inventions to create a distinctive pop style that made Les Paul and Mary Ford records unmistakable and enormously successful.

As Inventor of the Solid-body Electric Guitar Les Paul was one of the first to experiment with building a solid-body electric guitar. Before Paul's experiments, electric guitars were traditional hollow-body jazz guitars with an electric pickup attached. Paul was convinced that to produce the purest electric sound the pickup needed to be free from vibrations caused by the guitar body on which it was mounted. In 1941 this led Paul to design a guitar with a solid body that would vibrate far less. By mounting a pickup on this guitar—Paul actually constructed it out of a railroad tie and called it "the log"—Paul invented one of the first solid-body electric guitars. He later negotiated with the Gibson Guitar Company in 1951 to produce the Gibson Les Paul guitar. This guitar has gone on to be one of the most frequently used models in the history of rock music. As it turns out, Leo Fender was also experimenting with the same idea in southern California in the late 1940s, resulting in his Broadcaster/Telecaster guitars; Fender's slightly later Stratocaster design rivals that of the Les Paul in popularity among rock guitarists.

As Inventor of Sound-on-sound Recording ("Overdubbing") Les Paul was one of the first musicians to experiment with sound-on-sound recording—the process by which a musician records one part and then records another part so that the two parts sound together when played back. By extending this process, one musician can record several parts to an arrangement that would take many musicians to play in real time. Using discs in his first recordings, Paul figured out how to lay one take over the previous one, painstakingly building up the parts according to a method that allowed for no error—any mistake could only be corrected by starting the process all over again. In the early 1950s, Paul developed the first multitrack tape machine by designing a way that several tape machines could be synchronized to produce a more flexible method of "overdubbing." In his hit records with Mary Ford, such as "How High the Moon" (1951) and "I'm Sittin' on Top of the World" (1953), Paul overdubs choruses of guitars and vocals to create complex arrangements that reveal his big band roots. Paul also developed a technique of recording guitar parts at half speed so that when the machine runs at full speed the parts are not only higher, but much faster as well (the same technique was originally used to record the voices of the cartoon Chipmunks—Alvin, Simon, and Theodore). Multitrack recording came to prominence in rock music with the Beatles' *Sgt. Pepper's Lonely Hearts Club Band*, released in 1967—almost twenty years after Paul's first sound-on-sound recordings!

an unfortunate turn of events. As far as Tin Pan Alley was concerned, however, it was a good thing. The new singers continued to depend on Tin Pan Alley for songs, and the focus on singing created a stronger vehicle for song sales. Rock and roll would upset this applecart in 1955, but until then it was business as usual for the New York publishers: the big bands were out and singers were in.

The Sound of Pop in the Early 1950s. Pop music in the first half of the 1950s is sometimes dismissed as being hopelessly corny and stiff, especially in comparison to the rhythm and blues of the same time. Patti Page's "How Much Is That

---

LISTENING GUIDE

GET MUSIC ▶▶ wwnorton.com/rockhistory

Les Paul and Mary Ford, "I'm Sittin' on Top of the World"

Words and music by Sam Lewis, Joe Young, and Ray Henderson, produced by Les Paul. The song reached #10 on the pop charts in 1953 and was featured in the 1946 film *The Jolson Story*.

FORM: AABA, with three presentations of the complete verse-verse-bridge-verse structure. The first and third presentations are sung, while the second one features a guitar solo. The verses in the second presentation are adapted from the sung verses, and so do not match these earlier and later verses exactly. During the first two verses in the third presentation, the time signature changes from 2/4 time to 4/4 time, and while the tempo does not change, this creates the impression that the music slows down. The 2/4 time signature returns at the bridge and continues to the end. The change of key that occurs in the last verse helps drive the music toward a big ending.

TIME SIGNATURE: 2/4, with verse in 4/4 as indicated.

INSTRUMENTATION: Layered electric guitars and lead vocals. The highest and fastest guitar lines were recorded at half speed to create the "chipmunk" sound.

0:00–0:09	**Introduction**, 8 mm.	Layered guitar melody; note the echo effect on the guitar—this is the trademark Les Paul sound.
0:09–0:17	**A-Verse**, 8 mm.	Multitrack harmony vocals, all recorded by Mary Ford, with "chipmunk" guitar lines filling in the gaps, "I'm sittin' . . ."
0:17–0:25	**A-Verse**, 8 mm.	As before, "I'm quittin' . . ."
0:25–0:34	**B-Bridge**, 8 mm.	Harmony vocals continue, layered guitars create a nice descending cascade effect, "Hallelujah . . ."

Doggie in the Window?" might be thought of as representative of the generally wholesome and inoffensive approach found in much early to mid 1950s pop, but there was more to pop in the first half of the decade than hopelessly happy tunes with canine obbligato. Singers such as Eddie Fisher and Tony Bennett scored hit records in the new, more youth-oriented mold cast by Sinatra; Fisher's sentimental "Oh! My Pa-Pa" (1954) and Bennett's swinging "Rags to Riches" (1953) each placed the musical focus squarely on the singer with the orchestra in a supporting role. Johnnie Ray took the male vocalist role from suave and controlled to overtly emotional and romantically melodramatic with his ballad, "Cry," creating

0:34–0:43	**A-Verse**, 8 mm.	As before, "I'm sittin' . . ."
0:43–0:51	**A-Instrumental Verse**, 8 mm.	Guitar solo, music adapted from earlier verses. Les Paul's skill as a jazz soloist comes to the fore throughout this sectional verse.
0:51–0:59	**A-Instrumental Verse**, 8 mm.	Guitar solo continues.
0:59–1:08	**B-Instrumental Bridge**, 8 mm.	Guitar solo continues, high and fast "chipmunk" guitar lines created as described above.
1:08–1:16	**A-Instrumental Verse**, 8 mm.	Guitar solo continues.
1:16–1:33	**A-Verse**, 8 mm.	As before but now in 4/4 time, creating a sense that the music slows down. Note the addition of new backing vocals, "I'm sitting . . ."
1:33–1:50	**A-Verse**, 8 mm.	Continues in 4/4, "I'm quitting . . ."
1:50–1:58	**B-Bridge**, 8 mm.	Music goes back to 2/4, creating a sense that the music is speeding up, "Hallelujah . . ."
1:58–2:06	**A-Verse**, 8 mm.	This last verse changes key and this helps drive the song effectively to its ending, "I'm sittin' . . ."
2:06–2:15	**Coda**, 8 mm.	A showy ending adapted from last verse, "I'm sittin' . . ."

an international hit in 1951. In addition to the success enjoyed by Page—whose "The Tennessee Waltz" topped the charts for thirteen weeks in 1950—female vocalists were well represented in the pre–rock and roll hit parade; Jo Stafford's "You Belong to Me" (1952) and Kay Starr's "Wheel of Fortune" (1952) both follow the singer-up-front format with the band relegated to an accompanimental role.

The most important aspect of mainstream pop in the years preceding rock and roll is that much of this music was produced for a family audience—teenagers were expected to enjoy this music as readily as their parents and grandparents might. As family entertainment, pop music mostly avoided any topics that might be considered unsuited for general audiences. "I'm Sittin' on Top of the World," a hit in 1953 for guitarist Les Paul and and vocalist Mary Ford, is a representative example of the happy, wholesome sound of early 1950s mainstream pop.

As discussed in the next chapter, early rock and roll was a style directed primarily at young people, serving as a marker of generational difference. In the first half of the 1950s, however, mainstream pop was designed to appeal to a broad, mostly white middle-class audience. Aspects of this music that might seem corny and naïve in retrospect resulted from trying to produce music that would be acceptable to a wide range of listeners. But even within this relatively constrained context it is possible to detect features that point to the emergence of the rowdier, youth-oriented rock and roll: the sensual appeal of Sinatra and the emotional directness of Johnnie Ray. By the mid 1950s many of the elements were in place for rock and roll. Singers were dominating pop music, with some placing more emphasis on emotional performances and sensuality, and a national audience for popular music was well established.

As some aspects of popular music were preparing the way for rock and roll, the Tin Pan Alley part of the music business was caught entirely off guard by the new style, and part of this had to do with the rise of two other styles that the big music publishing houses had previously ignored: rhythm and blues and country and western. Big publishers, along with major record companies like Columbia, Decca, and RCA-Victor, had tended to stay out of the rhythm and blues and country and western markets, partly because they considered their profitability to be limited, and partly because they had tried to work in these markets and found that they were not very good at it. Both rhythm and blues and country and western developed in their own way during the 1930s, '40s, and '50s. To understand clearly how rock and roll was forged from combining these two styles with mainstream pop, we will now need to trace these separate but in many ways parallel developmental paths. We turn first to country and western music.

Part 2. The Growth of Country and Western Music

Regional Styles

"Country" Music in the Southeast in the 1920s and '30s. Country and western music generally remained regional until after 1945: unlike the mainstream pop heard on the radio networks, the regional musical styles that would ultimately come together under the umbrella of "country and western" after World War II mostly kept their distinctive regional accents until Nashville was established as the central location for this type of music in the late 1940s. These regional styles can be divided up into folk styles that could be found in the southeast and Appalachia, called "country" music, and styles that were prevalent in the west and southwest, called "western" music. Country music in the southeast can be traced to the folk traditions of the region, which are themselves derived in part from the folk music of the British Isles. Some of the first recordings of country music were made by Ralph Peer, a producer who traveled the south in search of what record companies would soon call "hillbilly music." These early recordings are probably as close as historians will ever get to capturing an authentic, regional folk music unaffected by other nonindigenous styles, and Peer recorded many of the earliest country performers, including "Fiddlin'" John Carson and Gid Tanner and His Skillet Lickers. Peer went from small town to small town, setting up his gear as he went; these country musicians then lined up and recorded a few numbers each on his recording apparatus. The Carter Family is a representative example of this down-home country style. Accompanied by an acoustic guitar and an autoharp (played by Maybelle and Sara Carter, respectively), the three voices of Maybelle, Sara, and A. P. Carter sing together in a style very much influenced by white gospel music. "Can the Circle Be Unbroken" (1935) captures both the musical style and the confessional spirit of much of this music, as does "Great Speckled Bird" (1936) of Roy Acuff and his Crazy Tennesseans. The Acuff group also adds the Hawaiian slide guitar to the mix (a more developed version of the slide guitar, the pedal steel guitar, would later play a central role in country and western instrumentation).

"Western" Music in the Southwest and California in the 1920s and '30s. If country music is most often associated with the Appalachian Mountains, western music is most closely linked with the wide open prairie of the cowboys—or at least Hollywood's portrayal of it. Gene Autry was the first of the singing cowboys to appear in a long string of movies set in the wild west. His "Back in the Saddle Again"—complete with a "whoopie ti yi yea"—is representative of the kind of song that he and Roy Rogers sang throughout their careers on the silver screen. Patsy Montana made her mark as the singing cowgirl with "I Want to Be a Cowboy's Sweetheart" (1935) and featured a yodeling style very much under the influence of Jimmie Rodgers (discussed below). Historians may dispute how authentically western some of this music was, but for the national movie-going public, these artists defined "cowboy music."

Perhaps more interesting than the music of the Hollywood cowboys was western swing, a style of music that gave the big band idea a cowboy twist. Made popular by Bob Wills and his Texas Playboys and Milton Brown and His Musical Brownies, western swing eventually featured not only the rhythm section and horns one would expect to find in a radio dance band, but also fiddles, a steel guitar, and even at times Mariachi-style trumpet parts, imported from south of the border. Wills's "New San Antonio Rose" (1940) is an example of this eclectic stylistic blend of the urbane dance band of the northeast with the rough-and-tumble western hoedown stompers of the southwest. When this

Often considered the first star of country music, Jimmie Rodgers appears here in his "Singing Brakeman" attire. Though Rodgers's career was short, his musical influence was felt for decades.

song was redone by Bing Crosby in 1941 and became a national hit, it helped gain western swing far more attention than it might have received otherwise, and Wills's band especially benefited from this. By the 1940s Wills and the Playboys were appearing in Hollywood films and expanding Americans' sense of western music beyond cowboy songs.

Jimmie Rodgers, the First Star of Country Music.

As we think about country and western music, it is important to consider not only how it developed but when and how it began to come to the attention of the mainstream pop audience. The movies helped promote western music, and Gene Autry and Roy Rogers were its biggest stars. The most important figure in the early history of country music is Jimmie Rodgers. Rodgers's music and performances made him a national star, though only for a brief time; he died at the age of thirty-six from tuberculosis. His performances were almost always solo, with Rodgers accompanying his singing on the acoustic guitar. His "Blue Yodel" (1927)—often called "T for Texas" and later covered by Lynyrd Skynyrd—is a representative example of Rodgers's style, complete with his trademark yodel. Rodgers's singing style was much imitated by later country and western singers, including Gene Autry, Ernest Tubb, and Eddy Arnold. During his brief career, Rodgers was known as both "The Blue Yodeler" and "The Singing Brakeman." The Blue Yodeler image cast Rodgers as a kind of rustic backporch guitar picker and singer, while the Singing Brakeman image had Rodgers as something of a roving hobo, wandering the country in the back of a freight car and stopping only long enough to sing a song about his lonely nomadic existence. Neither of these images was an accurate portrait of Rodgers, who, according to many reports, frequently performed in stylish clothes of his day. These rustic images played on stereotypes of the time and seem to have been contrived simply to sell sheet music and records. This manipulation of Rodgers's image marks an early awareness in country music of the importance of marketing. Constructing homespun images would increasingly become the specialty of the country barn-dance radio shows, the most successful of which was the *Grand Ole Opry*. Thus Rodgers's legacy to country music is not only his music, but the way in which he and those who represented him crafted its reception.

The Development Toward a National Sound for Country and Western Music

Superstation Radio Broadcasts in Prime Time. Mainstream pop in the 1930s and '40s played to a national audience, but country and western was limited to mostly regional radio exposure during those years. In 1922 Atlanta's WSB went on the air featuring local country music (including "Fiddlin'" John Carson and Gid Tanner), while WBAP in Ft. Worth began a barn-dance program, featuring hoedown fiddle music. Within a few years, local and regional radio stations across the south were programming country music, especially WSM in Nashville (the *Grand Ole Opry*) and WLS in Chicago (the *National Barndance*). At first broadcasting to the middle Tennessee region, in 1932 WSM became a clear-channel station whose signal reached most of the southeast and could even be picked up in Texas. This made *Opry* broadcasts available to a significant portion of the country, and when NBC picked up a half-hour version in 1939, the *Opry* could be heard coast-to-coast. As the listening audience for the show increased, so did the clamor from musicians to appear on these broadcasts; performers were happy to make the trip to Nashville to sing and play on the show, since the large radio audience could provide enormous exposure for ambitious performers.

While the *Grand Ole Opry* blanketed southern evenings with country music, the *National Barndance* did the same for the midwest. And although the *Opry* eventually became the more prominent and influential radio venue in country and western music, the *Barndance* enjoyed a national audience much sooner when a one-hour segment of it was programmed on the NBC network in 1933. In addition to hearing country and western music on NBC, listeners in the northeast could tune to the *Wheeling Jamboree* beginning in 1933 from WWVA in Wheeling, West Virginia. Combined with numerous other barndance shows that emanated from local and regional stations across the United States, at least some country and western music was readily available to many radio listeners, even if the style remained something of a novelty on network radio, receiving far less exposure than mainstream pop of the day. This prime-time national exposure—however limited—does help explain one way in which country and western music became known across the nation.

Country Music during World War II (War Buddies). Other important factors that led to the dissemination of country music among

*With her trademark "Howdy!", Minnie Pearl would launch into one of her stand-up comedy routines on the **Grand Ole Opry**. Like many Opry regulars, Pearl played up the idea that country folk are simple and honest, but somewhat backward and naïve.*

In the period after 1945, Nashville emerged as the center of country and western music, and Hank Williams became one of its most important and distinctive performers. Williams started out as a songwriter, and many of his songs are considered staples of the country repertory.

northerners (and those outside the south generally) developed as a result of World War II. Military personnel hailing from all regions of the country found themselves living together overseas during the war, and as people got to know one another they naturally shared their favorite music. Many northerners got their first sustained exposure to country and western music from the southerners with whom they served. Country singers became so popular among the U.S. Armed Forces during the war that Roy Acuff was voted best singer by the troops in Munich (over Frank Sinatra); and hoping to insult American soldiers, Japanese attackers on Okinawa raised the battle cry, "To hell with Roosevelt! To hell with Babe Ruth! To hell with Roy Acuff!" When the troops headed home after the war, many took their newfound affection for country and western music with them and sought it out in their hometowns. But soldiers were not the only ones who found themselves among new company because of the war. Stateside, many southerners migrated north to fill the great number of factory jobs created by the war effort. Detroit had long been a popular destination for southerners before the war because of its automobile manufacturing, but during the early 1940s a number of cities—including Baltimore, Washington, D.C., Cincinnati, Chicago, and Los Angeles—became home to southerners from the surrounding regions as they followed wartime production jobs. These relocated country and western fans brought their music with them, and jukebox records in these cities show that in some places country and western music was the most popular style in local bars and clubs.

Nashville Becomes Country and Western Headquarters. In the years after World War II, Nashville became the center of much professional activity in country and western music. The West Coast also saw growth in this type of music, but Nashville increasingly assumed the role of the capital of country and western. Nashville had been home to the *Grand Ole Opry* since its first broadcast in 1925, and by the late 1940s the *Opry* had become the most highly regarded radio show in country music. But in the postwar years Nashville also became a center for country music recording and publishing; and to meet the demand created by the nation's new interest in the style, the business of country and western music became more sophisticated. As these musicians increasingly made their way to Nashville to record (especially in the studios of Castle Recording Company), promoters, booking agents, and record company representatives soon moved their offices there as well—it was just more convenient to have everything in one place. The catalyst for this new kind of music industry growth in Nashville was a publishing firm established in 1942 by singer Roy Acuff and songwriter Fred Rose. Acuff-Rose did not rely on sheet music sales the way Tin Pan Alley publishers might; instead, they primarily worked to have the firm's songs recorded and performed by country artists. When Patti Page's version of "The Tennessee Waltz"—an Acuff-Rose song—became a hit pop record in 1950, the resultant financial success allowed the company to expand its operation and extend its influence. And while in some ways country and western publishing in the postwar years differed from mainstream pop publishing, it was the same in needing talented songwriters. In 1946 Fred Rose signed the then-unknown Hank Williams to Acuff-Rose—not as a singer, but as a songwriter.

Hank Williams, Country Music Singer–Songwriter in the Big Business of Country and Western

A Short Career that Cast a Long Shadow. In the minds of many Americans in the early 1950s, Hank Williams stood for country and western music. Though Jimmie Rodgers, Gene Autry, and Roy Acuff had enjoyed considerable commercial success, none matched the popular appeal of this singer-songwriter from rural Alabama. It is therefore surprising that the first of his songs to be recorded was sung by Molly O'Day, a singer Fred Rose was promoting in 1946. But by 1948 Williams was enjoying his first taste of success as a performer in his own right, appearing as a regular on the new *Louisiana Hayride* radio show out of KWKH in Shreveport (a young Elvis Presley would get his start on the same show only a few years later). Williams's first important hit was not one of his own songs, but rather a Tin Pan Alley number entitled "Lovesick Blues." On the strength of its popularity, Williams became a regular on the *Grand Ole Opry* in the summer of 1949 and enjoyed tremendous success until his death on New Year's Day, 1953, at the age of thirty-three. While Williams himself enjoyed fewer than five years of success, his music would be recorded by generations of country singers to follow. The story of the hard-living singer-songwriter who died too young would become a romantic image for future rock singers as well.

Williams's singing style shows the influence of both Roy Acuff and Ernest Tubb, and his many vocal inflections create an impression of sincere emotional expression. He pours out his personal romantic anguish in "Your Cheatin' Heart," "Cold, Cold Heart," and "I'm So Lonesome I Could Cry"; he radiates confident excitement in "Hey, Good Lookin'"; and he offers prayerful testimony in "I Saw the Light." His

Starting out as members of Bill Monroe's band, Lester Flatt (right) and Earl Scruggs (left) left Monroe to establish their own act. Scruggs's virtuosic banjo playing was a model for many bluegrass musicians who followed.

lyrics are direct and simple, and his performances seem to come straight from the heart. Whether Williams's songs really are autobiographical (some are) is less important than the fact that most listeners took them to be so. To most listeners in the early 1950s, Hank Williams was "pure country"—a country boy right down to the bone. His music and performance style thus became an important influence on subsequent country performers and writers.

Bluegrass, the New, Old-Time Country Music

Bill Monroe and His Blue Grass Boys. Fans of 1960s television can call to mind the banjo-dominated theme from the popular television show *The Beverly Hillbillies* ("The Ballad of Jed Clampett"). And fans of classic movies

---

LISTENING GUIDE   GET MUSIC ▶▶ wwnorton.com/rockhistory

Hank Williams, "Hey Good Lookin'"

Words and music by Hank Williams, produced by Fred Rose. Hit #1 on the Billboard Country and Western charts and #29 on the pop charts in 1951.

FORM: AABA, with three presentations of the complete verse-verse-bridge-verse structure. This song is similar to "I'm Sittin' on Top of the World" in terms of its arrangement. But where the Les Paul and Mary Ford track devotes the middle presentation of the AABA to a guitar solo, Williams's track splits the solo between the steel guitar and violin, with the steel taking the verses and the fiddle taking the bridge. Note also that Williams composes new lyrics for the last presentation of the verses and bridge, completing the story.

TIME SIGNATURE: 4/4.

INSTRUMENTATION: Acoustic guitars, bass, steel guitar, violin, and lead vocal. Note that there are no drums, which were forbidden in the early years of the *Grand Ole Opry*. The piano and steel guitar take turns playing fills behind the vocals, seeming to comment on each vocal line, often echoing some part of it at the ends of phrases.

0:00–0:07	**Introduction,** 4 mm.	The steel guitar is featured, its notes sliding gracefully into one another.
0:07–0:21	**A-Verse,** 8 mm.	Vocal enters, "Hey good lookin' . . ." Note how the rhythm of the accompaniment is driven by the acoustic guitars and piano. The piano echoes the vocal at the ends of phrases.
0:21–0:34	**A-Verse,** 8 mm.	As before, "Hey sweet baby . . ."

may even remember "Foggy Mountain Breakdown" from *Bonnie and Clyde* or "Dueling Banjos" from *Deliverance*. These songs are all in a style of country music called "bluegrass." To most ears, this music sounds as old as the hills, but bluegrass music actually developed during the same post–World War II period that saw the growth of country music in Nashville. The origin of the style can be traced to Bill Monroe and His Blue Grass Boys, whose first performance at the *Grand Ole Opry* occurred in 1939 but who gained far greater popularity in the late 1940s. The group's lineup after 1945 featured Monroe playing mandolin and singing high harmony, Robert "Chubby" Wise on fiddle, Lester Flatt on guitar and lead vocals, and Earl Scruggs on banjo, and this version of the Blue Grass Boys cast the musical mold that most other bluegrass groups would imitate.

0:34–0:47	**B-Bridge,** 8 mm.	"I got a hot-rod Ford . . ." The chords now change more quickly beneath the melody, creating a sense of excitement and anticipation. The steel guitar steps forward.
0:47–1:01	**A-Verse,** 8 mm.	As before, "Hey good lookin' . . ." Piano commentary returns.
1:01–1:15	**A-Verse,** 8 mm.	Steel guitar solo, plays an arrangement of vocal melody.
1:15–1:28	**A-Verse,** 8 mm.	Steel guitar solo continues. This simple solo is considered a classic by fans of the steel guitar.
1:28–1:41	**B-Bridge,** 8 mm.	Fiddle picks up the melody to provide contrast.
1:41–1:55	**A-Verse,** 8 mm.	Steel guitar returns to round off this AABA presentation.
1:55–2:08	**A-Verse,** 8 mm.	Vocal returns, "I'm free and ready . . ." Now steel echoes vocal, instead of piano.
2:08–2:22	**A-Verse,** 8 mm.	Note that the story develops this last time through the AABA form, "No more lookin' . . ."
2:22–2:35	**B-Bridge,** 8 mm.	"I'm gonna throw my datebook . . ." Piano adds new part in its high register.
2:35–2:51	**A-Verse,** 8 mm.	As before, "Hey good lookin' . . ." Steel "commentary" returns as song drives to ending.

While bluegrass numbers often feature singing, they also showcase virtuosic instrumental soloing, causing some to compare bluegrass with jazz. Monroe's late-1940s band had three dynamic and technically accomplished soloists—Wise, Scruggs, and Monroe himself—and the solos were frequently more the focus of the group's music than the singing. Banjoist Earl Scruggs's playing is especially noteworthy in this context: Scruggs developed a technique called the "three-finger roll," which allowed him to play passages of greater complexity than banjo players had done previously. Along with developing other technical innovations, Scruggs raised the level of banjo playing to new heights. In 1948, Flatt and Scruggs left the Blue Grass Boys to form their own group, as many other musicians, inspired by the playing of Monroe's classic lineup, were attracted to bluegrass in subsequent years.

By the early 1950s, country and western music had gone from a mostly regional musical style to one known at least to some extent by most Americans. Building on the exposure of the national audience to cowboy and western swing music in the movies, as well as to a broad range of country and western via the barn-dance shows that played as novelty programs on the network radio stations, and powered by stars such as Gene Autry, Jimmie Rodgers, Roy Acuff, and Hank Williams, country and western began to make its mark as a national style at just about the time that rock and roll was poised to explode. Despite its growth throughout the 1930s, '40s, and '50s, country and western music remained separate from mainstream pop, which still could boast a national market share that dwarfed country and western in terms of sales and profitability. Early rock and roll would challenge the lines that separated pop and country and western, but for the time being that boundary was clear and secure. Rhythm and blues was also seen as a style set apart from both mainstream pop and country and western. While country and western was assumed to be the music of low-income whites, rhythm and blues was assumed to be the music made for and by black Americans. In many ways, the growth of rhythm and blues in the decades before rock and roll parallels the rise of country and western, and so it is to this third stylistic ingredient in the recipe for early rock and roll that we now direct our attention.

Part 3. Rhythm and Blues in the 1940s and 1950s

Rural (Delta) and Urban Blues

Migration Patterns from the Rural South to the Urban North. The music that came to be called "rhythm and blues" in the years immediately after World War II was popular music played by black musicians intended for black listening audiences. In a manner that might be thought of as "separate but not very equal," it developed as an entire music business that remained almost completely outside the world of mainstream pop. While country and western had at least a marginal presence in mainstream American pop in the years leading up to the emergence of rock and roll, rhythm and blues played almost no role: most white listeners had no familiarity with either its artists or their music. This situation was a result of

Bessie Smith, the Empress of the Blues, was one of the most famous blues singers of the 1920s. Her 1923 recording of Alberta Hunter's "Down Hearted Blues" sold over a million copies. Her style influenced many singers, including Billie Holiday in jazz and Janis Joplin in rock.

racial segregation in American culture generally; most white, middle-class Americans were simply unaware of any aspect of black culture. But the same forces that drove white southerners to migrate to large cities in the north were also a factor in the migration of black southerners. Many left their field jobs in the south in hopes of finding better work in the north; and when they arrived in Memphis, Chicago, and Detroit, they brought their music with them.

In the years immediately after World War I, blues had enjoyed several years of popularity with mainstream white pop listeners, partly through the popular sheet music of W. C. Handy, whose "Memphis Blues" and "St. Louis Blues" sold well nationally, and partly through records by female black singers. The historical roots of the blues may be unclear but the roots of selling blues records can be traced to the 1923 million-selling hit "Down Hearted Blues," sung by Bessie Smith. Originally from Tennessee, Smith enjoyed enormous success in the years following this hit record. Her style is considered more authentically blues-based than some of the other female blues singers of her day, and this is probably because she toured the south as a youngster performing in tent and minstrel shows where she was undoubtedly exposed to early blues music. Her recordings were made in New York, however, where she was able to use the best jazz musicians of the day, including Louis Armstrong. But by the end of the decade, Smith's career began to fade and the blues fell off the mainstream radar.

As rural blacks began to migrate to urban centers in the 1930s and '40s, many were drawn to Memphis. As a result, the city developed a strong black music scene as musicians adapted their rural blues approach to fit an urban, club environment. Many of the rural blues recordings of the 1920s and '30s are the result of record companies heading into the south in an attempt to find new blues artists who might repeat Bessie Smith's success. Among the many blues artists representative of the rural approach is Robert Johnson, whose recordings of the 1936–37 period became enormously influential on rock guitarists in the 1960s, in large part owing to Eric Clapton's enthusiastic endorsement (discussed in Chapter 5). Like many rural blues singers, Johnson performed solo and, similar to Jimmie Rodgers during a slightly earlier period, he sang to the accompaniment of his own acoustic guitar playing. The rural blues style allowed for tremen-

Legend has it that Robert Johnson made a deal with the devil to acquire his forceful skill as a blues guitarist. Johnson's 1930s recordings were embraced by the 1960s British blues revival, making him a guitar hero decades after his death.

dous flexibility, and artists could easily add extra beats or measures as the spirit moved them; this can be heard clearly in Johnson's "Cross Roads Blues" (1936), as he alters the regular blues structural patterns whenever it suits his sense of musical expression. But as blues musicians moved into city bars and clubs, they often formed combos, using electric guitars, bass, piano, drums, and harmonica (in addition to microphones to amplify the singer's voice); this arrangement forced them to stick more closely to a prearranged structure. This style of electric blues quickly made its way to other cities, and by the early 1950s Chicago had become the most important blues center in the country. The scenes in Memphis and Chicago remained relatively isolated from one another, as well as from similar music in other cities across the country. Musicians might move from city to city, but records from one area often remained in that area, creating regional distinctions much like those in country and western music of the time.

While much of the development of rhythm and blues during the 1940s remained regional and outside the pop mainstream, the jump blues of Louis Jordan and his Tympani Five became popular with pop listeners through a series of hit singles, including "G.I. Jive" (1944), "Caldonia Boogie" (1945), and "Choo Choo Ch'boogie" (1946). Jordan adopted the fast tempos of swing dance music but pared down the instrumentation to only a rhythm section and his saxophone, a move that worked both musically and financially, considering the expenses of traveling with a larger band. Jordan's vocal delivery was upbeat and often comical, though his humorous lyrics could lightly touch on pressing social issues such as racism and poverty. Jordan's influence can be seen in the comical hits of the Coasters, as well as in the spirited delivery and clever wordplay of Chuck Berry.

Regional Radio and the Black Experience in 1950s America. A new approach to radio played an important role in the dissemination of rhythm and blues outside of regional black communities, and to understand how radio changed in the years following the introduction of television, it is important to know what makes a radio station work financially. Commercial radio makes its profits by selling advertising time; to reach a particular kind of listener, radio stations program music they hope will attract that specific group. These stations can then offer that audience to sponsors, who often will also have developed an idea of the kind of person who might be most interested in their products. We know from our earlier discussions that by the early 1950s the national audience for popular music had largely shifted from radio to television. This meant that radio needed to adapt considerably to survive, and many stations opted for a local or regional approach. As black populations began to grow in urban areas, it soon became clear that they constituted a distinctive community with needs for particular goods and services. In 1948, WDIA in Memphis began programming and advertising especially to the local black population, playing rhythm and blues records supported by a roster of sponsors who welcomed a black clientele. Soon black stations—or programs directed to a black audience on otherwise white stations—began to pop up around the country. These programs and stations not only provided black listeners with music they could enjoy; they also informed them of which advertisers would welcome their business. In those days of racial segregation, when black patrons were required to sit only in the back of a bus, often ate in sections of restaurants designated for "colored" customers, and could in many cases not even use the same drinking fountains or bathrooms as whites, this was useful information.

Independent Labels Target Regional Audiences.   As radio stations devoted to rhythm and blues arose across the country, so also did record labels specializing in black popular music. Sun Records in Memphis, Chess Records in Chicago, King Records in Cincinnati, and Atlantic Records in New York were just a few of the more successful of these new rhythm and blues labels. Most of the new record companies were independents—that is, they were not one of the few major labels that dominated the music industry at the time: Decca, Mercury, RCA-Victor, Columbia, Capitol, and MGM. Major labels had enormous financial resources, manufacturing plants, and sophisticated distribution networks that allowed them to get their newest records out quickly to most areas of the country; independent labels were sometimes just the owner and perhaps a secretary, driving from store to store, distributing records out of the trunk of a car. This meant that independents had to focus on local or regional markets. But independent labels could prosper precisely because the major labels were so big; and since the rhythm and blues market was not nearly as profitable as the mainstream pop one, the majors tended to devote their resources to pop, leaving room for the independents to survive—and in many cases, to thrive. (Independent labels also played a role in country and western music at the same time, and these labels likewise took advantage of opportunities created by the majors' focus on pop and neglect of almost everything else.)

In both radio and records, then, rhythm and blues in the 1945–55 period was a style of popular music intended specifically for black urban listeners. Nobody expected that white listeners would hear this music; if they did and bought some records, so much the better, but no one within the rhythm and blues industry was counting on that. White teenagers could pick up the black stations on their radios just as well as anybody, however, and when they developed a taste for rhythm and blues, the stage was set for rock and roll to emerge. It is important to understand that rhythm and blues in the decade before rock and roll was not a single musical style; rather, it was a collection of popular-music styles tied together as much by its audience as by its specific musical characteristics. Within the music business, if a record was expected to have a black listening audience, it was rhythm and blues, and this has led to a number of distinctive black pop styles being grouped together under that single label.

Rhythm and Blues as a Marketing Category That Includes a Broad Range of Musical Styles

The Influence of Gospel Music (Rural Southern Church Traditions).   One trait shared by most rhythm and blues styles during this era was a debt to gospel music. Much like the southern whites who sang country music, many of the southern blacks who would eventually sing in secular pop styles learned to sing in church. The often sophisticated harmony singing that characterized doo-wop also had roots in the mainstream pop vocalizing of the Mills Brothers, the Ink Spots, and the Andrews Sisters, but it was clearly influenced by gospel harmony singing in the black church. The vocal emphases and embellishments that rhythm and blues singers frequently employed, as well as the call and response between the soloist and the chorus, were drawn from typical gospel practices. Sometimes—as in the case of Ray Charles's "I Got a Woman"—the religious lyrics to gospel songs were changed to make them pop songs. This borrowing from religious music by pop music was a source of controversy within the black community, as some viewed such stylistic secularization as a sacrilege. Sometimes performers who moved from gospel music into pop had feelings of guilt that they might have "sold out," and this ambivalence over popular music would continue to affect both white and black singers after the emergence of rock and roll.

Chicago Electric Blues. As a talent scout for Sam Phillips's Sun Records in Memphis, Ike Turner would typically search in two types of places for new performers: churches and bars. Gospel was clearly grounded in the sacred, and blues was strongly secular. By the early 1950s Chicago's electric blues scene had developed into the most important one in the country, a growth due in part to an independent label founded in 1947 by two white fans of black music, Phil and Leonard Chess. Along with its subsidiary label Checker, Chess collected an impressive roster of blues artists: Howlin' Wolf, Muddy Waters, John Lee Hooker, Little Walter, and Bo Diddley, among others. The Chess style emphasized a sometimes rough-edged emotional directness, with vocals that were more expressive than beautiful or technically accomplished, and instrumental playing that blended technical prowess with raunchy bravura. Early Chess recordings were made with the simplest of equipment, producing a raw, technically unsophisticated recorded sound, in marked contrast to the kinds of records the major labels were releasing. This lack of studio polish, combined with the directness of many of the performances, would give Chess records an aura of honesty for many of the white rock and rollers who came along later. But at the time, the Chess brothers were simply doing the best they could with the resources they had. Howlin' Wolf's "Evil" (1954), Muddy Waters's "I Just Wanna Make Love to You" (1954), and Bo Diddley's "I'm a Man" (1955) are representative examples of Chicago electric blues, with adult-oriented lyrics delivered with more gusto than

Leonard Chess (left) is shown here in the Chess recording studio with three of the most influential artists in electric blues: (from left) Muddy Waters, Little Walter, and Bo Diddley. Chess blues recordings defined the sound of Chicago electric blues. Their style was often rough-edged and direct, with expressive, if unpolished, vocals. Early Chess recordings used simple equipment, which produced a raw, unsophisticated sound—contrasting with the kinds of records the major labels were releasing.

polish and accompanied by accomplished instrumental playing. Chess also recorded other artists who had the potential to appeal to a white audience, but their electric blues records made few concessions to white, middle-class sensibilities, and it is these records that had the most impact on rock and roll.

Atlantic and Black Pop. One independent label that did at times make some attempt to reach a broader audience was Atlantic Records in New York. Founded in 1948 by Ahmet Ertegun and Herb Abramson, Atlantic worked for a more polished pop sound, influenced by the production practices of mainstream pop and featuring accomplished singers such as Ruth Brown, Big Joe Turner, Clyde McPhatter, and Ray Charles. While Atlantic also offered its share of blues records, in general its most characteristic releases followed the mainstream pop practice of focusing on the singer and the song. Ruth Brown's "Mama, He Treats Your Daughter Mean" (1952) is a good example of this tendency and has clear ties not only to blues and gospel, but also to big band pop. Atlantic singles tended not to focus on instrumental playing; backup arrangements were structured and controlled, with solos occurring only rarely. In comparison with the electric blues records released by Chess, Atlantic singles are cleaner, more vocally oriented, and generally more pop oriented. Taken together, the music of these two labels begins to suggest the wide stylistic range found within 1950s rhythm and blues—and these are just two of many regional labels that produced R&B records during this era, though they are the most prominent.

Doo-wop (Urban Vocal Music). In the years immediately following World War II, singing groups began to form within the neighborhoods of American urban areas. The singers in these groups often could not afford the instruments they needed to accompany themselves, so their vocal arrangements were designed to be completely self-contained and without need of accompaniment ("a cappella"). A common practice was for groups from one block in an urban neighborhood to challenge groups from nearby blocks, leading to group-singing contests in the street. As independent labels sought out local talent to record, many invited these singing groups into the recording studio. Professional studio musicians would then learn the group's arrangements in order to accompany them on piano, bass, drums, and sometimes guitar. The result of these sessions was a style of music called "doo-wop," named after the nonsense syllables singers would often use in their arrangements. Doo-wop groups would typically feature a solo singer against the vocal accompaniment of the other singers, with one section of the song, usually toward the end, reserved for a sophisticated harmony-vocal rendition of one of the song's verses. The songs were often in the AABA form derived from Tin Pan Alley and cast in a rolling rhythm—called "compound time"—in which the beat is divided into three equal parts and in many instances pounded out as chords on the piano (imagine this as one-anduh, two-and-uh, three-and-uh, four-and-uh). The Chords' "Sh'Boom" (1954) is a representative example of doo-wop, with the syllables "sh'boom" used in the vocal accompaniment as a solo singer delivers the initial verses. A contrasting section features different singers from the group, and a last verse features the entire group singing together in harmony. "Sh'Boom" is a bouncy up-tempo number, but doo-wop songs were frequently ballads appropriate for slow dancing; the Five Satins' "In the Still of the Night" (1956) is a good example of this kind of song. Doo-wop is easily distinguished stylistically from Chicago blues or Atlantic pop (though Chicago Blues labels and Atlantic also recorded doo-wop groups), but in the eyes (and ears) of the market, it was all rhythm and blues.

Rhythm and Blues as a "Dangerous Influence" on American (White) Youth

Stagger Lee and the Black Male Swagger. As white teenagers were increasingly drawn to rhythm and blues in the early 1950s, their parents worried about the effects this music might have on their children. Much of this concern—which at times ran to fear—resulted from racial stereotypes circulating within the white community that are well known and have been thoroughly discussed by social historians. Of these, the image that seemed the most threatening is one scholars call the Stagger Lee myth: the idea that black men are especially driven sexually, and that their greatest conquests are white women. These often super-virile and swaggering black men are thought to be constantly on the lookout for virginal white women, and teenage girls are thought to be especially vulnerable targets. This is not the place to explore the origins of such ugly stereotypes; it is enough to realize that when many white listeners heard Muddy Waters singing "I Just Wanna Make Love to You," it confirmed the stereotype for them. Such stereotypes are almost always based on fundamental sociocultural misunderstanding. A song that is understood one way within the black community can be interpreted in an entirely different way by white listeners unfamiliar with that culture. This misunderstanding had the unfortunate consequence of convincing many white parents that rhythm and blues was a dangerous influence on their teenagers, and many worked to have this music, and the later rock and roll that developed out of it, abolished.

Hokem Blues and Fun with Double Meanings. Popular songs with lyrics containing sexual double-entendres can be traced back centuries; songs by Elizabethan composer John Dowland (1563–1626), for instance, are full of subtle wordplay designed for adult amusement. Within American popular music, Jimmie Rodgers's "Pistol Packin' Papa" features one line after another about the singer's need to shoot his "gun," and so on. Within black culture at mid-century, there was a well-established musical tradition of similar kinds of songs called "hokem blues" that poked fun at various aspects of adult relationships, mostly centered on sexual relations and the many situations that can arise in this context. Earlier hokem blues numbers like "Let Me Play with Your Poodle" took this kind of fun about as far as one can and still have a double meaning, but others were far more gentle in their references. "Hound Dog," recorded by blues singer Big Mama Thornton and written by white songwriters Jerry Leiber and Mike Stoller, features these lines: "You ain't nothin' but a hound dog, snoopin' 'round my door. You can wag your tail, but I ain't gonna feed you no more." In the context of such a tradition, the words "snoopin' 'round my door," "wag your tail," and "feed you" suggest a more sexual interpretation than they might in isolation.

Big Joe Turner's "Shake, Rattle, and Roll," released on Atlantic Records in 1954, provides a representative example of the hokem blues (the lyrics are provided below). This song was also recorded by Bill Haley and His Comets (a band made up entirely of white musicians). Haley adapts the song to make the lyrics acceptable to white audiences, since Turner's original lyrics would have never been allowed on the mainstream pop airwaves. In Turner's rendition, for instance, a man tells his lover to get out of bed and make him some breakfast. He then casts the reasons for his attraction to this woman in increasingly colorful terms: she looks great in a light cotton dress and nylon hose, though he complains about the way she spends his money. The "one-eyed cat" is definitely a metaphor for something more suggestive, as is the "seafood store." When Turner gets to gritting his teeth in the last verse, any doubt about what "Shake, Rattle, and Roll" of the chorus refers to is dispelled. As innocuous as this song may be by today's standards, it would have been considered obscene

LISTENING GUIDE

GET MUSIC ▶▶| wwnorton.com/rockhistory

Big Joe Turner, "Shake, Rattle, and Roll"

Words and music by Jesse Stone (Charles Calhoun), produced by Ahmet Ertegun and Jerry Wexler. Reached #1 on the Billboard Rhythm and Blues charts in late 1954.

FORM: This song contains both verse and chorus sections, though the music underpinning these sections is exactly the same. We used the term "sectional chorus" to describe an entire AABA form in our discussion of "Over the Rainbow"; this should not be confused with the use of "chorus" here to indicate a section that repeats the same lyrics. When the verse and chorus sections like those found in "Shake, Rattle, and Roll" are closely based on the same music, the formal type is called **simple verse-chorus.**

TIME SIGNATURE: 12/8 (shuffle in 4).

INSTRUMENTATION: Piano, saxes, guitar, bass, drums, and lead vocals.

0:00–0:07	**Introduction**, 4 mm.	Piano featured. Note the easy, rolling rhythmic feel.
0:07–0:25	**Verse 1**, 12 mm.	Vocal enters and musical focus remains almost entirely on the singing, with the saxes answering the ends of vocal lines "Get out of that bed . . ."

in white middle-class culture in the mid 1950s. Accordingly, Haley changes the lyrics enough to make the song seem harmless: the references to bed and sensuality are gone, replaced with more wholesome images. Note that while Haley retains the line about the one-eyed cat, it no longer seems sexual in this new context.

Another aspect of the song that gets changed in Haley's version is the rhythmic feel. While Turner's version projects a laid-back rhythmic feel that comes from not "pushing" the beat, Haley's version is somewhat frantic by contrast, pushing the beat as if the musicians can't wait to get to the next measure. This gives the Haley version a peppier, happier feel and helps in creating the impression that the song is really only about good, clean fun. In many ways, Haley's adaptation is a prototype of the pop adaptation of rhythm and blues that came to define rock and roll in its early years.

The ways white musicians adapted rhythm and blues for the pop market is discussed in more detail in the next chapter. For now, remember that rhythm and blues in the first half of the 1950s was in many ways very different from

0:25–0:43	**Verse 2**, 12 mm.	The story begins to unfold, "You're wearin' those dresses . . ."
0:44–1:02	**Verse 3**, 12 mm.	"I believe you know . . ." New horn lines added.
1:02–1:21	**Chorus**, 12 mm.	This sing-along type chorus uses the same background music as the verses; at this point, it still is not clear how these lyrics relate to the verses, "Shake, rattle, and roll . . ."
1:21–1:40	**Instrumental Verse**, 12 mm.	Sax solo.
1:40–1:58	**Verse 4**, 12 mm.	Sexual double meanings increase, "I'm like a one-eyed cat . . ." Simpler sax commentary returns.
1:58–2:17	**Chorus**, 12 mm.	The connection is getting clearer, "Shake, rattle, and roll . . ."
2:17–2:36	**Verse 5**, 12 mm.	This verse almost stops having a double meaning, horn parts from earlier return, "I said, over the hill . . ."
2:36–3:00	**Chorus** with ending, 12 mm.	Now the connection is clear, "Shake, rattle, and roll . . ."

the mainstream pop of the same period. Like the market for country and western, the market for rhythm and blues was assumed to be quite distinct: industry insiders believed that nobody but black listeners would be interested in this music. But as things turned out, white middle-class teenagers were interested in both rhythm and blues and country and western by the middle of the decade, and because both styles of music were available over the radio, they could hear music from neighborhoods and communities their parents would prefer they avoided. Still, until 1955, the music business remained highly segregated into pop, rhythm and blues, and country and western markets, with most of the media exposure and industry dollars devoted to pop. Pop was deeply invested in Tin Pan Alley music publishing, but this was not the case with rhythm and blues or country and western. Pop was focused on the song; the other two styles were focused on the record. When rock and roll broke out in 1955, it not only challenged the boundaries of style but it also threatened the way the popular music business was run—as well as some white Americans' sense of moral decency. Elvis the Pelvis seemed to assault middle-class sensibilities and Tin Pan Alley appeared to be under siege by styles and practices

Two versions of "Shake, Rattle, and Roll"

Turner's version:

Get out of that bed, wash your face and hands
git in that kitchen, make some noise with those
pots and pans

You're wearin' those dresses, the sun comes
shinin' through
I can't believe my eyes, all of this belongs to you

I believe you know you're the devil in nylon hose
as fast as I work, the faster my money goes

(I said) Shake, Rattle, and Roll
you won't do right to save your doggone soul

I'm like a one-eyed cat, peepin' in a seafood store
well I could look at you till you ain't no child no
more

(I said) Shake, Rattle, and Roll
you won't do right to save your doggone soul

(I said) Over the hill and way down underneath
you make me roll my eyes, baby make me grit my
teeth

(I said) Shake, Rattle, and Roll
you won't do right to save your doggone soul

Haley's version:

Get out in that kitchen and rattle those pots and
pans
(well) Roll my breakfast 'cause I'm a hungry man

(I said) Shake, Rattle, and Roll
(well) You'll never do nothin' to save your doggone
soul

Wearin' those dresses, your hair done up so nice
You look so warm but your heart is cold as ice

(I said) Shake, Rattle, and Roll
(well) You'll never do nothin' to save your doggone
soul

I'm like a one-eyed cat, peepin' in a seafood store
I can look at you till you don't love me no more

I believe you're doin' me wrong and now I know
The more I work, the faster my money goes

(I said) Shake, Rattle, and Roll
(well) You'll never do nothin' to save your doggone
soul

that originated in the other two, smaller areas of the music business. The next chapter focuses on the first tumultuous years of this musical and cultural onslaught: rock and roll.

Questions for Discussion and Review

1. What are some of the important similarities in the rise of country and western and rhythm and blues, especially during the 1945–55 period? What are some significant differences?
2. What was the relationship between mainstream pop, country and western, and rhythm and blues in the 1940s and '50s? How did the music business separate out these styles? Why?
3. Radio plays a central role in the discussions in this chapter. How does it affect each of the three styles under consideration? What role does television play?
4. What's the difference between focusing on the sale of songs and focusing on the sale of records? How does this relate to the three styles under consideration?
5. If many Americans had prejudices against country and western and rhythm and blues music, was this because of their perceptions of the intended audiences for each style? Did country and western and rhythm and blues have features that may be seen to reinforce negative stereotypes?

Further Reading

Glenn C. Altschuler, *All Shook Up: How Rock 'n' Roll Changed America* (Oxford University Press, 2003).

Philip K. Eberly, *Music in the Air: America's Changing Tastes in Popular Music, 1920–1980* (Hastings House, 1982).

Phillip H. Ennis, *The Seventh Stream: The Emergence of Rocknroll in American Popular Culture* (Wesleyan University Press, 1992).

Gary Giddings, *Bing Crosby, a Pocketful of Dreams: The Early Years, 1903–1940* (Little, Brown, 2001).

Charlie Gillett, *The Sound of the City: The Rise of Rock and Roll*, rev. and expanded ed. (Pantheon, 1983).

Charles Hamm, *Yesterdays: Popular Song in America* (Norton, 1979).

Tom Lewis, *Empire of the Air: The Men Who Made Radio* (HarperCollins, 1991).

Bill C. Malone, *Country Music U.S.A.* (University of Texas Press, 1985).

Russell Sanjak, updated by David Sanjek, *Pennies from Heaven: The American Popular Music Business in the Twentieth Century* (Da Capo, 1996).

Mary Alice Shaughnessy, *Les Paul: An American Original* (William Morrow, 1993).

Nick Tosches, *Unsung Heroes of Rock 'n' Roll: The Birth of Rock in the Wild Years before Elvis* (Harmony Books, 1991).

Jerry Wexler and David Ritz, *Rhythm and the Blues: A Life in American Music* (Knopf, 1993).

The Nineteen Fifties

1950s

After the roaring 1920s, the depressed '30s, and the war-ravaged '40s, the 1950s seemed to some a kinder, simpler, more innocent decade. But while popular TV shows like *Father Knows Best* and *Leave It to Beaver* and grandfatherly President Dwight Eisenhower reflected much of the 1950s' conservative (and, some would say, puritanical) values, the decade also saw the birth of the modern civil rights movement, *Playboy* magazine, and rock and roll.

While visible wars erupted in Korea (ending in 1953) and began to boil in Vietnam, Americans were much more aware of a bloodless battle they were fighting at home and abroad: the Cold War. During World War II, the Americans and Soviets had been allies in the struggle against the Axis powers. But this partnership arose almost entirely out of necessity, and both parties remained acutely suspicious of one another. Many Americans were convinced that the communists were trying to infiltrate their culture and overthrow the U.S. government. In 1948 (due in large part to the efforts of young congressman Richard Nixon from California), Alger Hiss was

indicted for smuggling secrets to the Soviets (he was convicted in 1950), and Julius and Ethel Rosenberg were famously tried and convicted on espionage charges in 1951 (they were executed in 1953). Riding what many viewed as a wave of communist paranoia (often called the "red scare"), Senator Joseph McCarthy used a Senate subcommittee he chaired to lead an anti-communism campaign (some would call it a witch hunt) during the first half of the decade. McCarthy's subcommittee undertook a series of well-publicized hearings and private investigations dedicated to exposing the communists lurking among U.S. citizens, in politics, film, and labor unions.

The Soviets did have secrets: while the United States had stunned the Soviets with the development and use of the atomic bomb in 1945, the Soviets surprised American scientists by launching the first satellite into space in 1957. Called *Sputnik*, this satellite reinforced American fears of Soviet ambitions and fueled an intense race for superiority in technology between the two countries—a battle that was won when America landed the first men on the moon over a decade later.

Out of this strange brew of technology, spaceflight, and communist paranoia came a distinctly American passion for science-fiction stories and movies. Evil aliens seemed to be dropping out of the skies every night, and films such as *Invasion of the Body Snatchers* (1956) captured the sense that these intruders might well be moving quietly among us, waiting for just the right moment to execute their diabolical plan for domination of the Earth.

Along with communist paranoia, economic prosperity increased after World War II. The American economy boomed, spurred by strong demand for new houses and goods like televisions, home appliances, and cars. Most new homes were constructed in the suburbs, and new highways and automobiles made commuting to and from these towns easy.

Levittown, New York, 1954. In the 1950s, the explosion of new car sales and the construction of interstate highways made suburbs like Levittown more accessible than ever. For many, the American dream—your own home and car, plenty of space, and peace and quiet—was to be found in suburbia.

Racial segregation was one of the most divisive issues of the 1950s. This picture's original caption says it best: "9/4/1957—Little Rock, AR: Arkansas National Guardsmen turn away Elizabeth Eckford, a Negro Girl, as she attempts to enter Central High School here, Sept. 4th. The troops stopped eight Negro students from entering the school. The soldiers, called out to prevent the desegregation of the school because it might set off rioting between Negroes and whites, stopped the students in defiance of a Federal Judge's order that the school was to be integrated." President Eisenhower eventually sent troops in to enforce the judge's order and integrate the school.

Americans spent more time in cars than ever before, and many automobiles were equipped with AM radios. These car radios would play a significant role in the development of rock and roll as teens tuned in to rock and roll and rhythm and blues, well out of earshot of their parents.

Though rock and roll rebelliousness was finding its way into teenagers' cars, traditional middle-American values were strongly reinforced on 1950s television (evidenced by *Leave It to Beaver*'s popularity), and sexuality was almost totally absent from the small screen. In fact, most married couples on TV

slept in twin beds, and if a couple were seated on the bed together, network censors required that each had to have at least one foot touching the floor. In the midst of this obsession with sexually prudent normality, Hugh Hefner introduced *Playboy*, a magazine devoted to such modern and sophisticated topics as fine wines, clever writing, and naked women. Hefner caused a considerable stir when he launched the magazine with a calendar featuring pictures of a nude Marilyn Monroe in 1953, thus beginning a debate over sexuality that would continue for decades. And it was not only adults who were subject to this cultural shift in sexuality: in 1959 Mattel Toys introduced the shapely Barbie doll—a toy that for better or worse defined an ideal of female beauty for an entire generation of girls and boys.

While some in 1950s America were worrying over the communist threat, which new car or television to buy, and changing notions of sexuality, others were struggling against racism and America's legacy of discrimination against African Americans. In 1954, the Supreme Court ruled on a landmark case concerning a black child named Linda Brown, who had been denied the opportunity to attend an all-white public school in Topeka, Kansas. In *Brown v. Board of Education*, attorney Thurgood Marshall argued that no one should be kept out of a school on the basis of race; the justices concurred and the practice of racial segregation in schools was ruled unconstitutional. In 1955 in Montgomery, Alabama, a black woman named Rosa Parks refused to give up her seat to a white passenger, as was required by law. When Parks was arrested, Martin Luther King Jr. organized a peaceful citywide bus boycott that held until Parks's case made it to the Supreme Court in 1956. When the court ruled that Montgomery's bus segregation law was unconstitutional, the city's blacks returned to the buses and sat wherever they wanted.

The effects of these antisegregation decisions by the Court extended well beyond Topeka and Montgomery. They strengthened the growing civil rights movement across America, though some (especially, but not exclusively, in the south) staunchly resisted these new social changes. In fact, racial tensions reached such a fever pitch that Eisenhower had to send American troops to a high school in Little Rock, Arkansas, in 1957 to defend nine black students who had won the right in federal court to attend the all-white school. In the early 1960s folk music aligned itself with the civil rights movement that had developed throughout the 1950s, and by the end of the '60s, civil rights would be widely accepted as an important cause by the country's burgeoning rock-music counterculture. In the context of such mid 1950s racial struggles, it is easier to understand how so many could view rhythm and blues as a threat to white culture, and how a new style of youth music called rock and roll could become so controversial.

The 1950s were a time of great contradictions. Joseph McCarthy and Martin Luther King Jr., *Leave It to Beaver* and *Playboy*, consumerism and the civil rights movement all existed in the same time and space. And out of these tensions arose a new music that would bring together black and white, urban and rural, and north and south. That music was rock and roll.

A fan of both country and western music and rhythm and blues, Chuck Berry came to Chicago to record with Chess Records on the advice of Muddy Waters. Berry's 1955 hit "Maybelline" was followed by a string of crossover hits, including "Johnny B. Goode." Beginning with one of Berry's trademark guitar riffs, the song tells the story of a young country boy who is destined to be a big star, because he can "play the guitar like ringing a bell." Notably, the song steers clear of any suggestive language, eliminating an obstacle that kept many rhythm and blues hits off mainstream pop radio until white artists re-recorded them in cleaned-up cover versions. Berry was happy to write about typical topics in teenager life (school, dancing, parents), though he is perhaps most admired for the clever wordplay found in many of his lyrics. "Johnny B. Goode" became a classic and was covered by guitar-oriented acts from the Beatles to Johnny Winter.

The Birth and First Flourishing of Rock and Roll

Historians love dates they can use to define the end of one historical period and the beginning of another. In American history, for instance, we think of 1776 as the year when the United States broke with England to become a country in its own right. Of course, a more careful study of the American Revolution reveals that many events before 1776 were vital to what happened that year, and many important events in the next few years were also central to how the United States came to be organized as a sovereign nation. Important years or specific dates are ways historians have of organizing history, but they should be understood as only representative markers in the flow of a broad range of historical events. Music historians are no exception in their use of important dates to account for the development of musical styles; so when many scholars distinguish 1955 as the first year of rock and roll, remember that there is not really a clean dividing line between rock and roll and rhythm and blues in the first few years of the new style. As a way of organizing the history of rock music, 1955 is nonetheless a useful marker and it will help us draw a kind of imaginary line between the world before rock and roll and everything that follows.

In the last chapter we saw that country and western and rhythm and blues were clearly established styles by the early 1950s, with each directed at specific though different audiences; we also briefly explored how regional radio stations made this music available to middle-class white youth. These middle-class white kids are central to the emergence of rock into the popular-music mainstream in 1955. In the period before 1955, rhythm and blues and country and western were still mostly out of the mainstream of American popular music, which was dominated by the major record labels and the Tin Pan Alley publishers. But as a youth culture developed in America in the decade or so after the end of World War II, rhythm and blues increasingly became the music of these young people. The music business eventually realized that rhythm and blues records were popular among white youth, and when the songs were "cleaned up" a bit to make them suitable for radio stations directed to a white audience, record companies could sell more of these records than they had ever imagined possible. When rhythm and blues broke into the mainstream of American popular music in 1955, rock and roll was born.

This chapter will consider the "first wave" of rock and roll, encompassing the years 1955 to 1960. During this time, artists such as Fats Domino, Little Richard, Chuck Berry, Bill Haley, Elvis Presley, Jerry Lee Lewis, and Buddy Holly established rock and roll as a style distinct from the Tin Pan Alley pop, rhythm and blues, and country and western from which it emerged. During these early years of rock and roll, white teenagers thought of rock and roll as their music—something distinct from the culture of their parents and grandparents. For its part, white adult culture mostly viewed rock and roll as dangerous, thinking it led to juvenile delinquency and/or unacceptable adoption of attitudes and cultural practices associated with black culture. Eventually the pressure of adult culture would become more than this first wave could bear, and most of these original artists, as well as many of the independent labels they worked for, were out of the music business by 1960. But these first years proved to be crucial in establishing rock as a musical style and as a central element in youth culture; and despite repeated attempts by the major record labels to domesticate rock, future musicians would frequently look back to these first few years as a kind of Golden Age of Rock and Roll. Popular music had crossed a line, and in many fundamental ways, the music business would never be the same again.

Many elements fit together to create a picture of how rock and roll erupted in the second half of the 1950s. The rise of a youth culture is central, but so are the roles of independent radio and record labels. Rock and roll played a crucial role in challenging Tin Pan Alley's dominance in the music business and in breaking down borders between the three markets that had remained separate up until that time: mainstream pop, country and western, and rhythm and blues. In 1955 and the years that followed, songs and records moved among these three markets in a way that astounded industry pros working for the major labels. Since these markets had been divided along racial and socioeconomic lines, the integration of musical styles was bound to have reverberations throughout American culture, and indeed it did. But none of this could have happened if middle-class teenagers in large numbers hadn't been listening to the music, creating a lucrative market for record companies, radio stations, and others involved in the pop-music business. How these mostly white teens discovered the music of mostly black artists is where this part of our story begins.

The Rise of Youth Culture in the 1950s

The First Wave of War Babies Reaches Adolescence (This Is Not Your Father's Pop Music).　　The end of World War II saw the rise of a new and extremely significant phenomenon in American society: a pop culture devoted exclusively to teenagers and their almost-teenage siblings. While earlier generations of teenagers had been expected to assimilate into adult culture as soon as they left high school, white middle-class teens in the 1950s were allowed to remain teenagers and avoid adult responsibility longer than any similar group in history. They had fashions, music, dancing, movies, and even a bevy of slang terms that belonged exclusively to them. In part, this phenomenon arose as a result of the country's relative political stability and affluence in the post–World War II years: teens had money to spend on leisure activities and luxury items. There was also a general attempt within the middle class to return to "normalcy" following the war. Middle-class parents, in many cases recovering from the domestic disruption of the war, now focused increasingly on family life, devoting considerable attention and resources to the health, education, and overall happiness of their children. Children born in the years just before the American involvement in the war (December 1941) were the first beneficiaries of this new attention; by 1955 many of these children were in high school. In a pattern that has since become familiar with teenagers (but was new at the time), these adolescents wanted music that did not sound like their parents' music or the music of their older, college-age siblings. To these kids, rhythm and blues—easily accessible via local black radio—seemed exotic, dangerous, and sexual in ways that excited them; they knew their parents would find this music unsettling or worse. Imagine the reaction of conservative *Leave It to Beaver* TV-parents Ward and June Cleaver to Big Joe Turner's "Shake, Rattle, and Roll" lyrics.

Listening to rhythm and blues was not simply a forbidden pleasure to white teens, it could also be an act of social rebellion—a way of resisting assimilation into the adult world of responsibilities and commitments. Among adults during the 1950s there was much worrying about juvenile delinquency, a concern reflected in several movies that appeared mid-decade. Marlon Brando plays the rebellious young leader of a motorcycle gang in *The Wild One* (1953). The anger of Brando's "Johnny" is not particularly focused in the film; Johnny seems bent on disruption of normal life for its own sake. When asked at one point what he's against, he replies simply, "Whaddya got?" *Rebel Without a Cause* (1955) features James Dean in what is considered a classic portrayal of a tragically misunderstood teenager. In the same year the film was released, Dean was killed in a car crash. His untimely death at the age of twenty-four made him an icon not only for misunderstood youth but also for moping teenage tragedy. While both of these films directly addressed teen angst and rebellion, neither used rhythm and blues music in the soundtrack. By contrast, *Blackboard Jungle* (1955)—a film about the perils of juvenile delinquency in an urban high school setting—featured Bill Haley's "(We're Gonna) Rock Around the Clock" over the opening credits. The success of the movie, which actually caused youth riots in some theaters in both the United States and the United Kingdom, catapulted the Haley song to the top of the pop charts. The success of the song and its association with the movie marked an important moment in the emergence of rock and roll in 1955. Not only was "Rock Around the Clock" one of the top pop records of that year—thus, not simply a top rhythm and blues hit—but its placement in a film dealing with juvenile delinquency forever cemented in American culture the association of rock music with teenage rebellion and rowdiness. As far as many parents were concerned, listening to rhythm and blues—now being called rock and roll—led to far worse things, and it was just this reaction that made the music all the more appealing to teens. As we shall see, Haley was not

In the mid 1950s, several films helped establish the image of restless and rebellious youth that soon would become associated with rock and roll. Directed by László Benedek, The Wild One (1953, top) starred Marlon Brando as the charismatic and troubled leader of a motorcycle gang. James Dean also played a troubled youngster in Rebel Without a Cause (1955, middle), later that year becoming a legend after his untimely death in an automobile accident. In 1955, Blackboard Jungle (bottom, starring, from left, Vic Morrow, Sidney Poitier, and Glenn Ford) gave rise to adult concerns when teenage viewers got rowdy as the song "Rock Around the Clock" was played in the film.

the only one to have a pop hit with a rhythm and blues record; and once it became clear that such records would sell, the market was flooded with them.

Radio and Records

The Rise of the Disc Jockey in Regional Radio.   Many white teenagers got their first taste of rhythm and blues by hearing it on the radio. By the end of the 1950s the development of the transistor made small portable radios affordable to almost anyone. Earlier in the decade, however, small and inexpensive tube-driven tabletop models were common among the middle class, and the majority of black urban households had at least one radio of some kind as well. By mid-decade, no one needed an expensive cabinet-style unit to hear music; radios were more plentiful and portable than ever. In 1951, Alan Freed was working as an announcer at a radio station in Cleveland, hosting an evening classical-music show sponsored by one of Cleveland's largest record stores—the Record Rendezvous, owned by Leo Mintz. Mintz had noticed that teenagers were buying significant numbers of rhythm and blues records in his store. He proposed that Freed host a late-night show devoted to this music and sponsored by Mintz's company. Freed was reluctant at first, but on July 11, 1951, *The Moondog Show* premiered on WJW, a clear-channel station with a signal that reached far beyond the Ohio state line. The most often-told version of this story holds that the teenagers who bought rhythm and blues records in the Record Rendezvous were white, but it is almost certain that they were black; white kids were exposed to rhythm and blues only after hearing the music on radio shows directed primarily at black listeners. These white teens could tune in the rhythm and blues shows either on a small portable radio—well out of their parents' hearing—or on the radios that were now becoming more common in automobiles. Either way, radio programming that had been targeted at a black audience was now being enjoyed by white teens, and at first, even disc jockeys (DJs) like Freed didn't know these teenagers were listening.

As it turns out, Freed was not the first disc jockey to play rhythm and blues on the radio, though he is easily the best remembered and was perhaps the most influential in rock and roll's breakthrough into the popular-music mainstream. In 1949, Dewey Phillips began his *Red, Hot, and Blue* show on WHBQ in Memphis, and at about the same time, Gene Nobles, John R. Richbourg, and Hoss Allen were playing rhythm and blues at WLAC in Nashville, as were Zenas "Daddy" Sears in Atlanta (WGST) and Hunter Hancock in Los Angeles (KFVD). Freed was reportedly a WLAC listener and modeled his early shows on those in Nashville, even calling occasionally to find out what records were hot there. All of these early DJs were white, though most listeners assumed they were black on the basis of their on-air voices. According to one survey, of the three thousand or so disc jockeys on the air in the United States in 1947 (playing all styles of music), only sixteen were black. But during the late 1940s and throughout the '50s black DJs increasingly made their mark on the radio: Vernon Winslow ("Doctor Daddy-O") in New Orleans, Lavada Durst ("Doctor Hepcat") in Austin, William Perryman ("Piano Red" and "Doctor Feelgood") in

Atlanta, Al Benson in Chicago, Jocko Henderson in Philadelphia, and Tommy Smalls ("Doctor Jive") in New York were among many black DJs on the airwaves. WDIA in Memphis featured an all-black on-air staff, including Rufus Thomas, B. B. King, and Martha Jean ("The Queen") Steinberg. When he debuted his rhythm and blues radio show in 1951, Freed was simply doing something in Cleveland that was already going on in other parts of the country.

Freed was enormously successful in Cleveland, and reports of his popularity there drew the attention of WINS in New York. In September of 1954 he debuted in the Big Apple, where he repeated his midwestern success on a much larger media stage. Just a few months after his show began airing in New York, however, Freed was forced to stop using the Moondog moniker, since there was already an eccentric vagabond street musician in town by that name. Freed's show became *The Rock and Roll Party* and was soon syndicated nationally and even eventually in Europe. Thus, in the waning months of 1954 and into 1955, Freed created a considerable buzz over rhythm and blues among white teenagers in one of the country's major markets, and this gives more support to the idea that 1955 was an important year for rock and roll. But Freed, ever the entrepreneur, did not stop at being one of New York's major radio personalities. He had promoted rhythm and blues concerts during his stint in Ohio and now continued doing so in New York, capitalizing on the tremendous success his radio show enjoyed. He took his 1958 concert show, *The Big Beat* (which included Jerry Lee Lewis and Buddy Holly), on the road across the United States. Freed brought out several movies at about this time, though *Rock Around the Clock* (1956), *Rock Rock Rock* (1956), and *Don't Knock the Rock* (1957) were all hastily produced affairs with flimsy plots as excuses for appearances by a number of early rhythm and blues and rock and roll acts, such as Bill Haley, Chuck Berry, Frankie Lymon, and the Moonglows. Freed also hosted a dance show on TV from 1958 to 1960. To many teenagers, Alan Freed was the father of rock and roll, so it came as no surprise when the almost continual backlashes against the music were often directed at him and especially his concert shows, which the press often portrayed as teen riots. As Freed enjoyed celebrity on the national level, his popularity was paralleled in every major city by local DJs who were stars in their own communities. These DJs also aggressively promoted the new youth music whose name was now being changed—thanks to Freed's high profile—from rhythm and blues to rock and roll.

Starting out playing rhythm and blues records on a Cleveland-area radio station late at night, Alan Freed was to become one of the most important disc jockeys in the early years of rock music. After moving his show to New York in 1954, he dubbed it The Rock and Roll Party *and took credit for giving the new style its name. While in Cleveland, Freed began to promote rhythm and blues shows for what he thought was his African American listening audience, but soon white teens who had also tuned in his show began to attend these events.*

Aggressive Marketing by Independent Labels. Most of the rhythm and blues that teens heard on the radio was recorded by and released on independent labels. In the discussion of "indies" in the last chapter, we noted that these labels tended to be much smaller operations than those run by the major labels, and while the majors were national, the indies were mostly regional. The majors—Decca, Mercury, RCA-Victor, Columbia, Capitol, and MGM—each had their own manufacturing plants and national distribution networks; the indies had to farm out the manufacturing of their records and set up whatever distribution system they could, at first cooperating with indie labels in other parts of the country to establish reciprocal arrangements ("You distribute my records, I'll distribute yours") until independent distributors were established. This competitive disadvantage was significant and meant that a successful indie label needed to be aggressive about marketing: selling records meant first getting them played on the radio and then making sure they were in stores and jukeboxes. To get a record played, it helped to develop relationships with DJs, who could often be influenced through gifts ranging from cash and merchandise to nights on the town and even vacation trips. Record stores might receive extra copies of records to sell at full profit in order to push a record. Jukeboxes were a fixture in many bars and restaurants; if a label could get a regional distributor to pick up a record for use in such jukeboxes, this not only constituted significant sales but also stimulated new sales. Here again, developing relationships was the key, and gifts could always facilitate a business friendship.

While much of this kind of practice was later called "payola"—a scandal in the music business discussed below—and was not restricted to indie labels, these methods were part of a strategy to overcome the great advantage held by major labels in the marketplace. Those who worked for a major label were often working with the company's money, but the owner of an indie label had his own money on the line with a record. In addition, indie labels also competed with one another. This led not only to more aggressive marketing but also to a willingness to be innovative in the styles of music recorded and the kinds of artists who performed it. In the early 1950s, the conventional wisdom held that an indie could not beat a major label in the pop market, so rhythm and blues—and secondarily country and western—was the area in which independents could make money. In many ways, the emergence of rock and roll in the 1950s can be attributed to the entrepreneurship of both indie labels and DJs, each working on the outskirts of their respective business worlds: indie labels were fighting for a place on the margin of the recording industry while independent radio stations were battling in regional markets with the local affiliates of the national networks. Rhythm and blues had been largely ignored by the major corporate powers in the post–World War II music business, mostly because these companies found that the profit generated by such music did not justify the effort to develop, record, and market it. This opened up the opportunity for entrepreneurship, and independent labels and radio stations across the country took advantage of the opening. All of this occurred, for the most part, outside the powerful corporations and institutions that had shaped popular music in the United States for decades. When rhythm and blues records started showing up on the pop charts in the early 1950s, however, the music industry was headed for a significant shake-up.

Crossovers and Covers

Hit Records and the Charts.   By the middle of the twentieth century, the music business was extremely lucrative and highly organized. In order to be successful in the music business, people who sell music for a living ultimately have to view it as a business; it's great if a record company executive, radio station manager, record store owner, or jukebox distributor likes some of the music he or she sells, but this is by no means a necessity. Businesspeople think in terms of markets, product, distribution, and promotion—especially given the fickle character of many listeners when it comes to popular music—and it is tremendously beneficial to be able to identify trends. If you can spot a trend, your chances are greatly increased for having the right amount of product where it needs to be, timed precisely to meet the peak consumer demand. If your timing is right, your profits soar; if you time it wrong, they plummet. This kind of "inside" information is usually not very interesting to most listeners, who just want to hear the music, so magazines devoted to the more dollars-and-cents aspect of the business, directed primarily at music-industry people, developed over the first half of the century to help these professionals keep close and detailed track of the music business. The most important of these periodicals for the history of rock and roll are *Cashbox* and *Billboard*. Both of these industry news magazines regularly contained charts that attempted to predict trends in record and jukebox sales. Based on the most recent issue of *Billboard*, a record store owner might decide to order additional copies of a record that is climbing the charts, while making sure to get rid of extra copies of a record that is falling; such a businessperson wants to have the hot records on hand and not be stuck with piles of records that nobody wants anymore. Likewise, a jukebox owner wants the most popular songs in her machine; the more they play, the more they pay. Jukebox distributors will use the most recent *Cashbox* charts to make decisions to add new records and remove old ones on their regular visits to service their regional clients.

The charts in these industry periodicals were divided up according to the ways the professionals believed consumers could most effectively be separated out, and so the divisions were driven by purchasing patterns. Thus, pop charts listed records that would likely be marketed to white, middle-class listeners. Rhythm and blues (originally called "race" and then "sepia") charts followed music that was directed to black urban audiences, and country and western (originally called "hillbilly") charts kept track of music directed at rural or urban low-income whites. This system of three parallel charts was based on assumptions about markets and audience tastes, and not primarily on musical style. This arrangement suggests that listeners enjoying rhythm and blues would not also enjoy country and western or pop, but all it really tries to predict is who is most likely to buy these records or play them on the jukebox. According to this system, if you owned a record store on Main Street that had few black customers and almost none from the country, you would likely not have paid much attention to the rhythm and blues and country and western charts, as most of your customers (though not all) would have been interested in pop records.

Contrary to beliefs about such segregated listening, anecdotal evidence suggests that many black listeners enjoyed pop and country and western, and that many country and western listeners enjoyed pop and rhythm and blues. Young middle-class white listeners already knew some country and western from the network broadcasts, though most white adults seem not to have been interested in rhythm and blues. It was the middle-class white teens who discovered rhythm and blues, and this led to the softening of the boundaries between chart classifications.

When a record or song appears first on one chart, then appears on one of the other two, this is called a "crossover." A crossover can occur in two ways: the record itself may cross over, or the song, recorded by a different artist, may cross over. A new version of a song is called a "cover," so a simple way to think of the possibilities is that either the record or a cover version of it can cross over. Until 1955, the chart boundaries between the three categories of American popular music were relatively reliable; for the most part, records and songs popular on one chart stayed on that chart and crossovers were more the exception than the rule. In the 1950–53 period, for instance, about 10 percent of the hits appearing on the rhythm and blues charts crossed over. Beginning in 1954, a clear trend can be seen, as rhythm and blues records increasingly began to cross over onto the other charts; in that year 25 percent of the rhythm and blues hits crossed over, and by 1958 the figure increased to 94 percent. Sometimes two versions of the same song would appear on the pop charts—the original rhythm and blues performance, most often performed by a black artist, and a cover version, most often performed by a white artist. With only a few notable exceptions, the versions by white artists performed better on the pop charts than the rhythm and blues originals. When the original version appeared on a small independent label, a larger independent label (or a major label) could cover the song and get its records out faster and to more outlets; to some extent, this explains the success of these cover versions. But race played a significant role in pop listeners' tastes, and this was the source of much resentment among the black artists whose records were copied.

The First Rock and Rollers Cross Over

Fats Domino.   Among the first of the early rockers to enjoy consistent crossover success was Antoine "Fats" Domino. Based in New Orleans and

Reading the Chart Numbers

Throughout this book, Billboard chart positions will be noted and sometimes these numbers will be cited in an abbreviated form. Rhythm and blues positions will be abbreviated with an "r": "r1, 1955" indicates a record that hit the number one slot on the R&B charts in 1955. Pop records will be abbreviated with a "p," and later in the book, British chart positions will be abbreviated with the letters "uk." Using these abbreviations, a record's chart success might be cited as "r1 p3, 1956," meaning it rose as high as number one on the R&B charts and number three on the pop charts in 1956. Bear in mind that chart numbers are not a precision instrument and are subject to manipulation in some cases; they provide only a general indication of a record's success. We are using them here mostly for comparison purposes and to keep the "fan mentality" in check, as discussed in the Introduction.

recording on the west coast independence label Imperial, Domino scored a series of rhythm and blues hits in the early 1950s, including "The Fat Man" (r6, 1950), "Goin' Home" (r1, 1952), and "Something's Wrong" (r6, 1953). His "Ain't It a Shame" was a number one hit on the rhythm and blues charts in 1955 and crossed over to the pop charts, rising as high as number ten in the summer of that year. In the 1955–63 period, Domino released thirty-seven Top 40 singles, the most successful of which were "I'm in Love Again" (r1 p3, 1956), "Blueberry Hill" (r1 p2, 1956), and "I'm Walkin'" (r1 p4, 1957). Domino delivered his songs from the piano, gently pounding out repeated triplet chords and singing his often lyrical melodies in a relaxed manner. Domino projected a warm, friendly image that could hardly trigger the kind of racial anxiety in white listeners that a Big Joe Turner might. Domino's biggest pop hit, "Blueberry Hill," had even been a hit for Glenn Miller in 1940, and it provides a representative example of Domino's easygoing crossover style.

Based in New Orleans, Fats Domino had a series of rhythm and blues hits before crossing over onto the pop charts. His easygoing style is characterized by rolling triplets in the piano and a smooth vocal delivery.

Chuck Berry: Blending Rhythm and Blues and Country and Western while Targeting a White Youth Audience.

According to Fats Domino's producer, Dave Bartholomew, close musical associates thought of Domino as a country and western singer. But another black artist who was even more influenced by country would become the next important early rock and roller to cross over. Charles Edward Anderson (Chuck) Berry grew up in St. Louis and was introduced to Leonard Chess of Chess Records by blues great Muddy Waters. Chuck Berry's first hit for Chess was "Maybelline," his version of a traditional country fiddle tune called "Ida Red," which had been recorded by both Roy Acuff and Bob Wills. Though there are several stories of how the words got changed—Chess reported that he got the idea from a makeup case that was handy, though Berry claims this was the name of a cow in a book he read as a child—"Maybelline" was a number one hit on the rhythm and blues charts and crossed over to reach number five on the pop charts in the fall of 1955. Berry followed with several more hit singles in the next few years, including "School Day" (r1 p3, 1957), "Rock and Roll Music" (r6 p8, 1957), "Sweet Little Sixteen" (r1 p2, 1958), and "Johnny B. Goode" (r2 p8, 1958). Berry's vocal delivery in these early rock hits seems influenced by his love for country music; in fact, reports from early personal appearances chronicle a sense of surprise among many white audience members who had assumed from his records that Berry was white. Berry had a more flamboyant performance style than Fats Domino; especially striking was Berry's trademark "duck walk," which he would do during his guitar solos. But overall, there was not much about Berry's music or performing that would strike white audiences as threatening or menacing.

Knowing the negative reaction of adult white listeners to many cover versions of songs, Chuck Berry may have sized up his situation in 1955 like this: if rhythm and blues numbers are too adult for white, middle-class teenage listeners, why not write songs directly for them? In fact, Berry has stated that his main intention was not to reach adult black listeners but to write songs specifically geared to the average teenager. "Roll Over Beethoven" gently celebrates the idea that the thought of teens listening to rhythm and blues music—which is

 LISTENING GUIDE   GET MUSIC ▶▶ wwnorton.com/rockhistory

Fats Domino, "Blueberry Hill"

Words and music by Al Lewis, Larry Stock, and Vincent Rose, produced by Dave Bartholomew. Reached #1 on the Billboard Rhythm and Blues charts and #2 on the pop charts in 1956.

FORM: AABA form, with only the bridge and last verse repeated.

TIME SIGNATURE: 12/8, with the characteristic easy, loping New Orleans feel. Each measure contains four beats, with each beat divided into three parts (compound). Note how the piano chords play these three parts of each beat, creating a rolling 1 & uh, 2 & uh, 3 & uh, 4 & uh rhythmic undercurrent.

INSTRUMENTATION: Piano, electric guitar, acoustic bass, drums, horns, and lead vocal.

0:00–0:12	**Introduction**, 4 mm.	Piano featured as the New Orleans feel locks in.
0:12–0:33	**A-Verse**, 8 mm.	Vocal enters. Note the repeated chords high on the piano, and the rolling line in the bass and guitar below. Sustained horns support the vocal, "I found my thrill . . ."
0:33–0:53	**A-Verse**, 8 mm.	As before, "The moon stood still . . ."
0:53–1:14	**B-Bridge**, 8 mm.	New horn line enters to emphasize contrast, "The wind in the willow . . ."
1:14–1:35	**A-Verse**, 8 mm.	As before, "Though we're apart . . ."
1:35–1:56	**B-Bridge**, 8 mm.	Supporting horn line returns, "The wind in the willow . . ."
1:56–2:18	**A-Verse**, 8 mm.	As before, "Though we're apart . . ."

playfully cast as a contagious virus—would probably be enough to make Beethoven turn over in his grave. Of course, the real target here is not classical music, but what classical music stands for: conservative and serious adult culture. Rhythm and blues emerges as a way of marking resistance to adult culture. Early in his professional career Berry developed an affection for what he called "story songs," and "School Day" (originally titled "A Teenager's Day") is one such song, chronicling the daily life of the average teen—off to school in the morning, classes, lunch, and the final bell, after which everyone goes down to the local meeting place to play rock and roll on the jukebox. In this case, the conservative and oppressive institution is not the stuffy world of classical music and culture, but rather school life, and again rhythm and blues (here referred to as "rock and roll") is the music of resistance. The ending chorus of the tune, "Hail, hail, rock and roll," has become an anthem for school-hating rock fans ever since.

Such lyrics might have been delivered with an earnestness that could prove tedious or directly rebellious. But Berry's clever allusions and good humor make the songs harmless in terms of advocating or affecting social change; they are more of a friendly ribbing of adult culture than a full frontal assault. Later rock

musicians, such as John Lennon and Bob Dylan, among many others, admired Berry's lyrics and imitated his careful and creative wordplay. Berry's songs do not all deal with teen life, and some can be interpreted on at least two levels. "Memphis" is perhaps the best example of a more adult story song that expertly plays on the expectations of the listener. Throughout the song the listener is led to believe that Berry is trying to reach his estranged wife by telephone, revealing details of his personal life to the operator; in the last line we find out that this is not the case—listen to the song to find out how it turns out. It may perhaps come as no surprise that early in their collective career the Beatles covered this song very closely, with Lennon singing the lead. Even "Maybelline," which seems to alternate between unrelated stories of the singer racing Maybelline's Cadillac in his Ford with a chorus complaining of Maybelline's unfaithfulness, can be read at a second level. The problem with Maybelline is that she is a "fast woman," represented in this case by a fast car (the Cadillac). Trying to keep up with her is thus like a car race, as the allusions follow one after another. The singer begins by "motorvatin' over the hill" but soon they are "bumper to bumper, rolling side to side"; later Berry describes "rainwater flowin' all under my hood, knew that was doin' my motor good," and at the end of the song the Ford catches the Cadillac "at the top of the hill." Yet another interpretation might take this song as a thickly veiled song about sexuality, ultimately not much different from "Sixty Minute Man" or "Shake, Rattle, and Roll."

Berry's Musical Influence. Most of Berry's songs are in simple verse or simple verse-chorus form, often employing a chord structure influenced by the 12-bar blues (see Interlude 1 for a detailed discussion of the 12-bar blues). His songs are relatively easy to learn, and with their catchy lyrics, they have been favorites with rock bands ever since the late 1950s. Most of the musicians who created the rock music of the '60s and '70s could have played half a dozen Berry tunes without even thinking about it, and many often did so in live shows. Berry's guitar style became one of the most imitated in rock. His chordal accompaniments often featured a characteristic two-string boogie-woogie pattern on the low strings, and his solos used frequent double stops (playing two notes at the same time) on adjacent high strings. These can be heard clearly on a number of songs, but "Johnny B. Goode" is perhaps the best example.

Little Richard. The most flamboyant performer in the early years of rock and roll was probably Little Richard, born Richard Wayne Penniman. Recording on the Hollywood-based Specialty independent label, Richard's high-energy "Tutti Frutti" climbed the rhythm and blues charts in late 1955, hitting number two and crossing over onto the pop charts where it peaked at number seventeen. In the next few years, Richard placed nine hits on the pop Top 40, including "Long

A consummate showman, Chuck Berry decided early on that he would write and perform songs that didn't need to have the words changed to be appropriate for white radio. Berry's attention to lyrics provided a model for many songwriters who followed, as did his lead-guitar bursts.

Tall Sally" (r1 p6, 1956), "Keep a Knockin'" (r2 p8, 1957), and "Good Golly, Miss Molly" (r4 p10, 1958). With his sometimes-manic singing (and even screaming), aggressive piano pounding (he frequently played with one leg propped up over the keyboard of the piano), and strong driving beat in the rhythm section, Richard provided a remarkable contrast to the gentler Fats Domino. Berry may have named a song after makeup, but Richard was the first rocker to *wear* makeup. There is little doubt that he cultivated the image of being the first "wild man" of rock and roll; while this made him attractive to white teens, it

---

LISTENING GUIDE   GET MUSIC ▶▶| wwnorton.com/rockhistory

Chuck Berry, "Johnny B. Goode"

Words and music by Chuck Berry, produced by Leonard and Phil Chess. Reached #8 on the Billboard Pop charts and #5 on the Rhythm and Blues charts in 1958.

FORM: Simple verse-chorus.

TIME SIGNATURE: 4/4, with a tendency to blend in a shuffle, but not completely.

INSTRUMENTATION: Electric guitars, piano, acoustic bass, drums, and lead vocal. Note how the drums tend to shuffle, while the guitar stays stubbornly in simple time.

0:00–0:17	**Introduction**, 12 mm.	Famous guitar intro using double stops, with stop time in first 4 mm. and band entering in m. 5.
0:17–0:34	**Verse 1**, 12 mm.	Vocal enters; note the constantly changing piano fills in the background throughout the song, "Deep down in Louisiana . . ."
0:34–0:51	**Chorus**, 12 mm.	Vocal punctuated by characteristic Chuck Berry guitar bursts, "Go, Go Johnny . . ."
0:51–1:08	**Verse 2**, 12 mm.	As before, note Berry's vocal sound—does it sound country-influenced? "He used to carry . . ."
1:08–1:26	**Chorus**, 12 mm.	As before.
1:26–1:43	**Instrumental Verse**, 12 mm.	(Like Intro), guitar solo, more double stops, full of rhythmic drive but technically simple.
1:43–2:00	**Instrumental Verse**, 12 mm.	(Like Intro), guitar solo continues.
2:00–2:18	**Verse 3**, 12 mm.	As before, "His mother told him . . ."
2:18–2:38	**Chorus**, 12 mm.	As before, driving to ending.

Richard Penniman was the most flamboyant figure in rock's first years, as can be seen from the position of his legs in this picture. Little Richard had a string of crossover hits before quitting rock music for a time to enter the ministry.

also made it more difficult for him to advance his career in the mainstream pop market. Perhaps the country and western influence made it easier for Fats Domino and Chuck Berry to be accepted by white audiences, but there was little that was country and western about Richard. Lyrics such as "Good golly, Miss Molly, you sure like to ball" and "I got a girl named Sue, she knows just what to do" did not make things any simpler. Richard was a prime target for cover versions; if a white artist covered the song and took much of the sexual innuendo out of the lyrics, his record could often outperform Richard's on the charts and in sales, even if it was less vital and exciting than the original.

Bill Haley, Pat Boone, and the "Whitening" of Rhythm and Blues. As we saw in the previous chapter, Bill Haley's version of "Shake, Rattle, and Roll" removes a good deal of the sexual playfulness from the song as performed by Big Joe Turner. These changes were clearly done to make the song more successful with white listeners. Indeed, the resulting record, like much of Haley's music that followed it, exudes a kind of innocent excitement by replacing references to sexuality with references to dancing. Though not many listeners think of the song in this way now, when viewed from a rhythm and blues context of the time, "(We're Gonna) Rock Around the Clock" can be seen as one of a series of songs that deal with sexual stamina. Prompted by the success of the Dominoes' "Sixty Minute Man"—a number one rhythm and blues hit in 1951 that actually crossed over to the pop charts briefly—a series of songs followed, including Ruth Brown's "5-10-15 Hours" (r1, 1952), the Ravens' "Rock Me All Night Long" (r4, 1952), and both "Work with Me, Annie" (r1, 1954) and "Annie Had a Baby" (r1, 1954) by the Midnighters with Hank Ballard. In early 1955 Georgia Gibbs had a number two pop hit with "Dance with Me Henry," a reworked version of the Midnighters' tune that makes the substitution of dance for sex even clearer. Adjustments to both the lyrics and the music of rhythm and blues began to establish a model for rock and roll in the early years, and Haley was an important figure in what might be called the "whitening" of rhythm and blues.

In the early 1950s William John Clinton Haley Jr. was a disc jockey also playing in a Philadelphia-area country swing band, Bill Haley and His Saddlemen. At the suggestion of a local record-label owner, Haley recorded a cover of Jackie Brenston's number one rhythm and blues hit, "Rocket '88'" (the original record was produced by Sam Phillips, soon to found Sun Records, and released on Chess). Haley's version was a commercial flop, though he enjoyed some success in 1953 with "Crazy Man Crazy." In 1954 Bill Haley and His Comets signed with the major label Decca and released "Shake, Rattle, and Roll" and "(We're Gonna) Rock Around the Clock." Neither crossed over to the pop charts, though the group did place three other hits in the pop Top 40 in late 1954/early 1955; none of these made the Top 10. With the release of *Blackboard Jungle*, "(We're Gonna) Rock Around the Clock" topped the pop charts for eight weeks in mid 1955 (r3), making it one of the top pop records of the year. In the next few years Haley and the group placed nine more hits in the pop Top 40, including "Burn That Candle" (r9 p9, 1955) and "See You Later, Alligator" (r7 p6, 1956).

Many listeners who associate rock and roll with the raucousness of Chuck Berry and Little Richard might be surprised to learn that Charles Eugene "Pat" Boone (a direct descendant of Daniel Boone) was one of the most successful artists of the early years of rock and roll. Recording for the independent, Nashville-based Dot Records, Boone scored thirty-two Top 40 hits—sixteen of these in the Top 10—during the 1954–59 period. Boone's cover of Fats Domino's "Ain't It a Shame"—which he renamed "Ain't That a Shame"—outperformed the original on the pop charts, hitting number one for two weeks in the fall of 1955, and his covers of Little Richard's "Tutti Frutti" (p12, 1956) and "Long Tall Sally"

Fueled by the success of "Rock Around the Clock," Bill Haley and His Comets became one of the first successful white acts in rock and roll. The band's roots in country swing are noticeable in this picture by the presence of the accordion and steel guitar—hardly rock and roll instruments in the 1950s!

(p8, 1956) equaled or surpassed the originals in the pop market. Rock historians and critics tend to consider Boone's contribution to rock and roll only in terms of these cover versions, which are often judged inferior to the originals; but Pat Boone had many other hit records during the same period, including "Don't Forbid Me" (p1, 1956), "Love Letters in the Sand" (p1, 1957), and "April Love" (p1, 1957). "Don't Forbid Me" was offered to Elvis Presley, who may have regretted not recording the song first after Boone's success with it. In contrast to Elvis and at least a year before Presley was known to a national audience, Pat Boone cultivated a polite, clean-cut personal image; his musical approach in many ways continued in the mainstream pop style of Frank Sinatra while extending it to include country and western, rhythm and blues, and gospel. If Little Richard presented a musical and personal image that many white parents found threatening, Boone's music and manner were much more readily assimilated into middle-class white culture. Most important for the history of early rock music, Boone's popularity both depended on the rise of rock and roll and fueled that rise. More than just a

Doo-wop and Crossover

Vocal group music played an important role in rhythm and blues in the years leading up to 1955. Originating in urban areas and basing their ensemble singing on the music of the Mills Brothers, the Ink Spots, and big band horn arrangements, these groups frequently sang without instrumental accompaniment; this was later added in the recording studio to fill out the sound. One of the first doo-wop records to cross directly over to the pop charts was "Cryin' in the Chapel" by the Baltimore-based Orioles (on the Jubilee independent label). The Chords' "Sh'boom" was also a crossover hit on Atlantic in 1954, though it was quickly covered for the white market by the Crew Cuts. The success of these records sent independent labels into their local streets searching for whatever vocal groups they could find. Some groups used their own arrangements, lending many of the classic doo-wop recordings an amateurish quality that fans of the style find especially endearing. In such cases, the label brought the group into the studio, added a rhythm section—often consisting of drums, bass, piano, and guitar, and recorded the tunes the group had worked up, releasing the best of them. Consequently, most doo-wop groups had one hit, maybe two; a follow-up hit was difficult because the first hit was often the best arrangement a group had and it had developed over months of rehearsing. In some cases a label would work with a group to help them develop material and arrangements, as Atlantic did with Clyde McPhatter and the Drifters, who had a series of rhythm and blues hits, including "Money Honey" (r1, 1953) and "Whatcha Gonna Do?" (r2, 1955). Recording for Mercury, the Platters were among the most successful of the 1950s vocal groups, charting eighteen pop Top 40 hits during the 1955–60 period, including "Only You (and You Alone)" (r1 p5, 1955), "The Great Pretender" (r1 p1, 1955), "My Prayer" (r1 p1, 1956), "Twilight Time" (r1 p1, 1958), and "Smoke Gets in Your Eyes" (r3 p1, 1958).

If Elvis Presley seemed dangerous to middle-class parents, Pat Boone was the answer. Boone's cover versions of songs by Fats Domino and Little Richard outperformed the originals on the pop charts, and together with his other hit records made him one of the top-grossing pop artists of the second half of the decade.

singer who covered rhythm and blues records for a white audience, Boone played a crucial role in establishing rock and roll within mainstream pop music in the 1955–59 period.

The Controversy over Cover Versions.   The early rock and roll cover versions remain a controversial and hotly debated topic among scholars and critics of rock music, but as with most issues that are the source of debate over long periods of time, there are at least two ways to interpret the facts and events of those years. It is easy to see how many black rhythm and blues artists would have resented white cover versions. In some cases, the arrangements were copied in great detail; the only substantial differences were that the new record was on a different label and the artist or group was white. These white cover versions thus seemed intent on replacing the original versions on the charts, in jukeboxes, on the radio, and in stores. With the success of Bill Haley, Fats Domino, Little Richard, Pat Boone, and Chuck Berry, it became common practice in the record business to watch the rhythm and blues charts for hits and then to cover these hits for the pop market. This procedure significantly reduced the crossover potential not only for the original records but also for the original artists, who were almost always black. The way many see it, black artists were "ripped off." Rhythm and blues artists were often paid a flat fee for recording a number; in many cases they signed away any rights to future royalties they might be entitled to as songwriters. For musicians in the habit of going from town to town and from gig to gig, it was far more prudent to get their money up front than to sign any agreement for future royalties with a small and financially fragile record company. Under this practice, however, the only beneficiaries of cover versions were record company people—who were almost always white—and white performers.

Others have argued that the situation was not so clear-cut. To begin with, the unit of trade within American popular music since the late nineteenth century had been the song, not a particular recording of it. This was still true in the early 1950s, when the top thirty records of 1955 featured three different performances of the same song, "The Ballad of Davy Crockett." It was a well-established practice among record companies to get a version of the latest popular song out on their label to capitalize on its success while it lasted. In fact, our current understanding of the term "cover version" is based on the idea that a particular recording is the primary source of reference. But as we will see in a later chapter, this idea of the cover version did not develop until the 1960s, as rock musicians and producers explored the possibilities of the recording studio and recordings become primary. It seems silly, for instance, to imagine a band covering the Beatles' *Sgt. Pepper's Lonely Hearts Club Band* in the weeks after its release in June 1967. But in 1955, copying someone else's record was the norm, a practice that went back decades. There is an important difference in the early white covers of rhythm and blues hits, however, that must be considered. Record labels in the pre-rock music business invested in particular singers, whose distinctive approach, it was hoped, set them apart and fostered "brand loyalty." If you liked a song, for instance, you might especially want to hear the Frank Sinatra or Tony Bennett version. The formula was thus largely a matter of matching songs with "song stylists." None of these stylists would dream of closely copying another's version of a song, since that would diminish his or her own mark of musical distinction. With the white rhythm and blues covers, however, most are not distinctive versions but almost note-for-note replications of the originals. Rather than being versions by artists who might be interested in advancing their own approach to the music, they are very close copies designed in some degree to directly replace the original.

If this seems to further complicate the issue, consider as well that most of the Pat Boone and Bill Haley records discussed here are distinct versions that would not be confused with the originals by most listeners. In fact, the extent to which these covers can be distinguished from their rhythm and blues models begins to map out the important features that will ultimately distinguish rock and roll from rhythm and blues. Pat Boone has remarked that the records he covered would never have been played on white radio anyway; to Boone, the changes were necessary to bring this music to a white pop audience. Haley might have said the same thing. Little Richard strongly disagrees. Our discussion here does not settle the issue, but using the context established by this discussion, consider the issue for yourself: Were black artists ripped off, or were these cover versions understandable within the context of music-business practices of the day?

The Rise of Elvis Presley: In Steps Corporate America

Elvis at Sun.   If the music of Bill Haley, Fats Domino, Little Richard, Pat Boone, and Chuck Berry began to break down the boundaries separating the three markets—pop, country and western, and rhythm and blues—then Elvis Presley would take this process one giant leap forward. Presley was not only the first rock and roller to repeatedly have hits on all three charts simultaneously, he was also the first rock and roll artist to draw intense interest from the major labels. When Elvis moved from Sun Records to RCA in November 1955, RCA set music-business mechanisms in motion to support their new rising star that would not only lead to Elvis's success but would also firmly establish rock and roll in the pop mainstream. In many ways, the story of Presley's early music is also the story of Sun Records, the Memphis-based independent label that first signed him.

Born in Tupelo, Mississippi, Elvis and his parents moved to Memphis when he was only thirteen. Raised in a poor family and in a city with a rich and thriving black music scene, Elvis became well versed not only in the country music that one might expect a youngster growing up in the post-1945 south to hear, but also in the rhythm and blues music of the black community. As a teenager Elvis performed in his neighborhood and at school, gaining a reputation as a flashy dresser who seemed to buy much of his wardrobe at Memphis's leading clothing store for blacks, Lansky Brothers. In 1950, radio announcer and technician Sam Phillips opened his Memphis Recording Service, making a specialty of recording black blues singers (including Joe Hill Louis, B. B. King, Howlin' Wolf, and Roscoe Gordon) but also taking whatever other recording jobs might come his way. Phillips started out licensing his recordings to other labels such as the Los Angeles–based Modern and Chicago-based Chess. Phillips recorded Jackie Brenston's 1951 rhythm and blues hit, "Rocket '88'," which he then licensed to Chess. In 1952 Phillips decided to start his own label and Sun Records was born. He continued to focus his efforts on black blues, releasing records by Rufus Thomas, Little Junior Parker, Little Milton, and the Prisonaires, a group of singing inmates from the Tennessee State Penitentiary. Not long after that, a teenage Elvis Presley started showing up at Phillips's studio, first to make a private demo in 1953 and then perhaps just hanging around (Elvis was reportedly at a Prisonaires session at which he offered advice before Phillips decided it was not a good place for a teenager to be). Eventually Phillips decided to try Elvis on a song he needed to record, and while Elvis didn't ultimately seem right for the two songs recorded that day in 1954—"It Wouldn't Be the Same without You" and "I'll Never Stand in Your Way"—he did ask guitarist Scotty Moore and bassist Bill Black to work up some other tunes with Elvis to see what he might be able to do.

Phillips had a flair for spotting talent; as a producer, he also had the patience to let the performers loosen up and explore in the recording studio. Part of his routine was to roll tape and let the musicians just keep working until they hit on something interesting. The story of the July 1954 Elvis Presley sessions can be understood in this context. After trying several numbers without much success and perhaps a bit tired and slap-happy, Elvis grabbed his guitar and started to bang out an Arthur "Big Boy" Crudup number called "That's All Right (Mama)." Bassist Black joined right in and Moore began fiddling with a guitar part. Phillips, who was busy doing something else in the studio at the time, asked the group to start again as he hit the record button. Before long they had recorded the single that would both launch Presley's career and establish Sun Records as an independent label of national stature. The band recorded a rocked-up version of Bill Monroe's classic bluegrass number "Blue Moon of Kentucky" as the B-side. Phillips rushed a copy of the recording to DJ Dewey Phillips, who played it repeatedly on his popular *Red, Hot, and Blue* radio show, making Elvis a local celebrity. Elvis and the group began touring, landing a spot on the *Grand Ole Opry* (which did not go well) and then a regular spot on the competing *Louisiana Hayride* out of Shreveport. Despite the strong influence of rhythm and blues on his music, Elvis was marketed as a country and western artist, earning the title "The Hillbilly Cat" early on.

The Big RCA Deal. As Elvis's success increased and word spread of his dynamic performances, he began to draw the attention of professionals within the music business. One of these was Colonel Tom Parker, who had managed country singer Hank Snow and who now began working with Elvis, first as a promoter and later as his personal manager. Sam Phillips also began hearing about Elvis from colleagues inside the business, receiving at least two serious queries about buying out the young singer's contract. Phillips turned these down, but as 1955 wore on he found himself in need of funds to keep Sun afloat. Parker believed that Elvis could never make the important career step to the national level as long as he was with Sun; he felt Phillips did not have the necessary capital to promote Presley. Parker brokered a deal with RCA that paid Phillips the unheard of sum of $35,000 for Presley's contract while Elvis received an additional $5,000 in back royalties. Phillips had quoted a sum to RCA that he thought they would never be willing to pay; to his surprise, they were. Phillips invested the money in his label as well as in a radio station he had purchased, going on to produce artists at Sun such as Carl Perkins, Johnny Cash, Jerry Lee Lewis, and Roy Orbison. Presley went to RCA and recorded "Heartbreak Hotel," which hit number one on both the pop and country and western charts in early 1956 and rose as high as number five on the rhythm and blues chart. Television appearances followed in 1956, including the one on Ed Sullivan's *Talk of the Town* variety show (discussed at the beginning of Chapter 1), as Parker also began to work on movie deals for his young star. By the end of the year and into 1957, Presley had begun to ring up the kinds of sales and chart numbers that would establish him as one of the most successful entertainers of all time. Tom Parker and RCA had indeed elevated Presley from a regional sensation to an international star.

The importance of Presley's deal with RCA is hard to exaggerate. Before he jumped to RCA, most major labels were not interested in rock and roll, seeing it as a mere fad they did not want to be involved in; they would let the independents have it (Columbia Records' Mitch Miller even saw his label's lack of involvement in rock and roll as a point of personal pride!). But when industry leader RCA paid an enormous sum (by the standards of the day) for a rock and roll singer, it was clear that the game was changing. True, it was the country division of RCA that made the deal; however, the other major labels soon began to add rock and roll artists to their rosters. And when Presley scored one tremendous success after another, the race was really on. The effect of all this was to push rock and roll even more toward the center of the pop mainstream, and compared to its place at the very margins of the business just a couple of years before, things had changed considerably. Maybe rock and roll was not going to be just a passing fad after all.

Covers in Elvis's Early Career.   Unlike Chuck Berry, Elvis was not a songwriter; thus his particular contribution to the history of rock music is not a creative one in the traditional sense. Presley is best thought of as a master song-stylist. What he was able to do well was pick songs to record and discover engaging ways to interpret them. Right from the beginning of his recording career, Elvis had almost total control over this aspect of his music making; if there was a song or version of a song he didn't like, neither Sun nor RCA would release it (since Presley's death in 1977 many of these recordings have been issued). Elvis Presley recording sessions were often a series of tries at a wide variety of

"Ladies and Gentlemen: Elvis Presley!"

At the beginning of 1956, Presley was still a regional star only recently signed to a major label. For his first nationally televised performances, Elvis appeared on six episodes of *The Stage Show*, a poorly rated Saturday night variety show hosted by Tommy and Jimmy Dorsey. The first episode, on January 28, attracted little attention outside of Memphis. The promoter literally couldn't give away all the tickets. Although he performed well, Presley was tentative and played two Big Joe Turner songs, "Shake, Rattle, and Roll" and "Flip, Flop, and Fly," instead of the newly recorded "Heartbreak Hotel." The next week he played Little Richard's "Tutti Frutti" and "Baby, Let's Play House." Elvis finally used his own material on his third appearance, although "Heartbreak Hotel" worked poorly with Jimmy Dorsey's orchestra and "Blue Suede Shoes" was still known as Carl Perkins's song. By his sixth appearance on *The Stage Show* in late March, Presley was finally a comfortable television performer. But because these early shows were not widely seen, it is unclear whether they had any impact on Presley's record sales—although he did earn a much-publicized Hollywood screen test.

Presley's next television appearance was on the much more popular *Milton Berle Show* on April 3. His performances of "Heartbreak Hotel" and "Blue Suede Shoes" went particularly well and Berle even appeared with Elvis in a skit as his twin brother Melvin Presley—complete with clown-sized blue suede shoes. But it was a return engagement on June 5 that sparked a national controversy. Presley played his new single "Hound Dog" and appeared without his guitar for the first time. Perhaps as compensation for the guitar or perhaps because of his growing confidence, Presley's stage moves were notably sexual, particularly during the grinding, half-tempo ending of the song. Because of Berle's popularity and Elvis's rising stardom, this was the first time that older Americans and the mainstream media had really noticed him; the media, at least, were shocked. The *New York Daily News* declared that music "had reached its lowest depths in the 'grunt and groin' antics of one Elvis Presley." Presley was attacked in the *New York Times*, the *San Francisco Chronicle*, and the catholic publication *America.* Ed Sullivan loudly declared that he would never book Elvis on his show. Elvis Presley had now become not just a phenomenon, but a threat.

Despite the controversy—or because of it—network executives knew that a Presley performance guaranteed strong ratings. He appeared on Steve Allen's Sunday night show in July, although Allen made him wear a tuxedo and even reassured the audience that this would be "a show the whole family can watch and enjoy." By the time Presley appeared on the season premiere of the *Ed Sullivan Show* on September 9, he was the biggest star in America, was already shooting his first film (*Love Me Tender*), and needed Ed Sullivan less than Sullivan needed him—enough to earn him $50,000 for three appearances. Of course, Sullivan's cameras still pulled away from Presley's legs in order to maintain propriety.

During the span of nine months from his first televised performance to the triumphant appearance on the *Ed Sullivan Show*, Elvis Presley had matured greatly as an on-camera performer and had progressed from a rising talent to a true superstar. Presley had become the first rock and roll musician to gain the full attention of a nationwide adult audience, permanently opening the door for many stars to follow. Television and America would never be the same again.

Referred to early in his career as "The Hillbilly Cat," Elvis Presley became one of the biggest stars in show business when RCA bought his contract from Sun Records. The young Elvis was handsome, sexy, and dangerous, and this was enough to scandalize some parents and cause Ed Sullivan to order cameras to show Presley only from the chest up when the singer appeared on his television variety show in 1956.

songs—some Elvis knew from recordings; others were supplied to him on acetates (inexpensive demonstration records not designed for commercial release) by professional songwriters. "Don't Forbid Me" was offered to Elvis, for instance, but Pat Boone recorded it first and had a number one hit, as mentioned above. In this way, Elvis joins Boone as a singer in the pop tradition of Bing Crosby, Frank Sinatra, and Tony Bennett. And like Boone but in a more extreme manner, Elvis extended this tradition by drawing broadly from folk, country and western, rhythm and blues, and gospel sources for his tunes. His first sessions for Sun featured not only Crudup's "That's All Right (Mama)" and Monroe's "Blue Moon of Kentucky," but also "I Love You Because," which had been made famous by Eddie Fisher, and "I Don't Care If the Sun Don't Shine," which had been recorded by Patti Page.

The Sun recordings are often viewed as some of Elvis's best, and they established a style that came to be called "rockabilly." These songs are mostly recorded without drums, featuring Presley singing to the accompaniment of Black's acoustic bass, Elvis's acoustic guitar, and Moore's Chet Atkins–influenced electric guitar. The warm reverberation and short echo (called "slapback echo") are sonic features that Sam Phillips pioneered, and this general ambience has come to be much imitated by rockabilly artists ever since Elvis's first release. Though these recordings often featured light percussion, the absence of drums is a clear marker of their country and western roots: drums were important to pop dance music and rhythm and blues generally, but country musicians tended not to use them, and the *Grand Ole Opry* even had a long-standing policy against the use of the drum set in performances. From the very first recordings, Elvis's distinctive vocal style is as much a stylistic hybrid as his repertory; much of the swooping in his voice can be traced to many early '50s pop singers, especially Dean Martin, while other vocal mannerisms derive from rhythm and blues sources. A quick comparison of two recordings makes this easy to hear. Clyde McPhatter and the Drifters recorded "White Christmas" for Atlantic in 1954. Elvis copied that recording fairly closely in a version that appeared on *Elvis' Christmas Album* in 1957 (recorded for RCA but still good for comparison purposes). While the Drifters are a vocal group and pass the melody around from singer to singer, Elvis takes all the parts in his version. His recording sounds fairly typical of his trademark style, but comparison with the Drifters' version shows that elements usually associated with Elvis are often adapted from other styles.

Elvis's Move to RCA for Broader Appeal. Ironically, while Elvis's move to RCA is important because it signals the greater involvement of the major recording studio in rock and roll, the plan almost from the beginning of Presley's tenure with RCA was to broaden his appeal beyond a teenage audience. The movies he began to make were part of that strategy, but the mainstreaming process can be seen most clearly in the period after 1960. Elvis's career was interrupted by a stint in the U.S. Army, which ran from 1958 to 1960. While much happened in popular music while Presley was stationed in Germany, his return was celebrated by a television performance hosted by Frank Sinatra and featuring some of Sinatra's Rat Pack buddies, including Sammy Davis Jr. The career plan seems to have been to turn necessity into a virtue, and Elvis was transformed from the hip-swiveling menace to society into a patriotic G.I., doing his part to protect the American way of life. Musically, his three number one hits from 1960 show this new broadening. "Stuck on You" is a clear continuation of Elvis's earlier RCA rock and roll hits such as "Hound Dog," "Too Much," and "Teddy Bear." But "It's Now or Never" is reminiscent of Italian crooner Mario Lanza, while "Are You Lonesome Tonight," recorded because it was a favorite song of Tom Parker's wife, features a narration in the middle that leaves the last shred of Elvis the Pelvis far behind. Separating Elvis from the rock and roll he played such a crucial role in establishing was a prudent business move at the time. Rock and roll had always been viewed by many in the music business as a fad that would pass with time. By the late 1950s (as we'll see below), the first wave of rock and roll was almost played out. Since so much had been invested in Elvis, it was important that he not fade as the public grew tired of rock and roll. By mid 1960, Elvis was a pop song-stylist who had established himself in rock and roll but moved on; and despite an excellent 1968 television special that was meant to reestablish his rock roots, it would be Elvis's music from before 1960 that would influence future rock musicians.

When Elvis (center in background, choosing his uniform from clothing bins) was drafted into the U.S. Army, many predicted his career would be over. Elvis's manager, Tom Parker (second from right, talking to two RCA executives), calculated that military service would help show that Presley was a good, upstanding American boy and position the singer closer to the center of the entertainment-business mainstream. Presley recorded several records before he shipped out to boot camp, and these singles were released while he was away, keeping his career alive until his return.

Rockabilly in the Wake of Elvis

Carl Perkins, Johnny Cash, and Jerry Lee Lewis at Sun. After Presley left Sun, Phillips began concentrating on other artists who would help develop rockabilly. Only weeks after signing over Elvis's contract to RCA, Phillips was recording Tennessee guitarist-vocalist Carl Perkins. In one December session in 1955, Perkins laid down four tracks, including "Honey, Don't" and his biggest hit, "Blue Suede Shoes." In the first half of 1956, "Blue Suede Shoes" rose as high as number two on the pop charts; but even more importantly, the record was a hit on all three charts. While some records crossed over from the rhythm and blues charts and others crossed over from the country and western charts, it was rare for the same record to climb all three. Elvis's records would do this routinely beginning with "Heartbreak Hotel," which raced up all three charts neck-and-neck with the Perkins single. "Blue Suede Shoes" was the first million-selling single for Sun and likely served to reassure Phillips that he had acted wisely in selling Presley's contract to RCA. Perkins's career ascent was dealt a severe blow when he and members of his band were involved in a serious auto accident en route to the taping of a national television show, leaving him unable to capitalize on the success of the single through live performances. He was unable to repeat with a second hit single, though several of his songs were later covered by the Beatles (George Harrison admired Perkins so much that at one point before the Beatles became famous he adopted the stage name Carl Harrison!).

Johnny Cash played a key role in the development of country and western music in the 1960s and after. But in 1956 he was another of Sam Phillips's young hopefuls at Sun. Early that year he had become a regular on the *Louisiana Hayride* broadcasts out of Shreveport, barely overlapping with Presley, who was at that point on his way to bigger things. Cash's "Folsom Prison Blues" was climbing the country and western charts at the same time as "Heartbreak Hotel" and "Blue Suede Shoes," but unlike those other two, did not cross over. By late 1956, however, his "I Walk the Line" had indeed crossed over, reaching number seventeen on the pop charts and becoming the first of four Top 40 pop singles Cash would release on Sun. By the end of 1957, Cash and then Perkins had followed Elvis's lead and signed new recording deals with the same major label, Columbia. Perkins was perhaps prompted to follow Cash in leaving Sun by the arrival from Ferriday, Louisiana, of a dynamic young musician to whom Perkins believed Phillips had shifted the label's attention: Jerry Lee Lewis.

In late July of 1957—about a year after Elvis's first provocative national television appearances—viewers of the *Steve Allen Show* tuned in to see and hear

---

LISTENING GUIDE   GET MUSIC ▶▶| wwnorton.com/rockhistory

Elvis Presley, "That's All Right (Mama)"

Words and music by Arthur Crudup, produced by Sam Phillips. Recorded and released on Sun Records in July 1954.

FORM: Simple verse, with measures added in guitar verse, and both added and subtracted in last verse.

TIME SIGNATURE: 2/4, employing a country two-step feel with alternating bass notes.

INSTRUMENTATION: Electric guitar, acoustic guitar, acoustic bass, and lead vocals. Note that the slapping sound that might be mistaken for a snare drum is actually Bill Black slapping on his bass.

0:00–0:06	**Introduction**, 5 mm.	Note strummed guitar and country feel, and entrance of the slap bass after the guitar begins alone.

Jerry Lee Lewis tearing his way through "Whole Lotta Shakin' Goin' On." Lewis pounded the piano as he belted out the lyrics, at one point tossing the piano bench across the stage only to have Allen toss it back. This performance fueled the record's ascent on all three charts; it hit number one on the rhythm and blues and country and western charts and peaked at number two on the pop charts. Lewis's manic style was by this point nothing new—Little Richard had beat him to that punch by two years. Nevertheless, in the next twelve months Lewis would have three additional records become hits on all three charts: "Great Balls of Fire" (1957), "Breathless" (1958), and "High School Confidential" (1958). Lewis might have continued to turn out more hit records for Sun had he not been involved in a scandal that threw him into public disgrace. On a concert tour of Britain, Lewis let it slip that his new bride, Myra Gale Brown, was fourteen years old (she was actually thirteen and also his cousin) and the British press picked up on this, revealing further that Lewis had already been married twice before. These discoveries played into the stereotypical notions of American southerners as well as negative images of rock and roll musicians, and Lewis was almost drummed out of the entertainment business in both the United States and England for several years.

Gene Vincent and Eddie Cochran. Sam Phillips continued to develop new talent at Sun in the wake of Elvis's move to RCA as other rockabilly artists emerged on other labels and bore a striking stylistic resemblance to The Hillbilly Cat. Virginian Gene Vincent scored three Top 40 hits for Capitol, the most noteworthy of which is his "Be Bop a Lula," which rose as high as number

0:06–0:26	**Verse 1**, 18 mm.	Vocal enters, note electric guitar fills, "That's all right, Mama . . ."
0:26–0:47	**Verse 2**, 18 mm.	Listen to how Presley swoops and shades the vocal line, sometimes moving from a low chest voice to a higher and thinner head voice. "Mama, she done told me . . ."
0:47–1:10	**Instrumental Verse**, 20 mm.	Chet Atkins–influenced guitar solo, 18 mm. verse extended by 2 mm.
1:10–1:30	**Verse 3**, 18 mm.	As before, "I'm leavin' town . . ."
1:30–1:53	**Verse 4**, 20 mm.	Presley improvises a bit using "di" during the first part of the vocal, the previous 18 mm. verse is shortened to 16 mm. then extended by 4 mm. to create ending.

seven in 1956. Guitarist-vocalist Eddie Cochran hailed from Oklahoma City and also enjoyed three Top 40 hits; his "Summertime Blues" hit number eight in the second half of 1958. Both Vincent and Cochran appeared in the 1956 film, *The Girl Can't Help It*, and Cochran's performance of "Twenty Flight Rock" in that movie strongly impressed the teenage Paul McCartney. Both Vincent and Cochran were very popular in England and it was during a UK concert tour they undertook together in 1960 that Cochran was killed and Vincent injured in an auto accident.

Buddy Holly. As rockabilly moved into the pop mainstream, new artists emerged who put greater stylistic stress on pop at the expense of the country and western and rhythm and blues influences. The Everly Brothers and Ricky Nelson both warrant discussion in this regard, but their music will be considered in the next chapter since both acts continued to have hits after 1960. Because of this, they act as transitional figures from the era under consideration here to the 1960–64 period. The next important figure, Buddy Holly, had a career that was cut brutally short by a tragic plane crash in early 1959, so his important contributions to the history of rock music are complete by the beginning of the new decade.

Charles Hardin (Buddy) Holly was one of the first major figures in rock music to have been significantly influenced not only by rhythm and blues and country and western, but also by the rock and rollers who emerged in 1955 and 1956. Growing up in Lubbock, Texas, Buddy Holly was first exposed to the

Why Would Sam Phillips Sell Elvis's Contract?

To understand why Sam Phillips would have benefited by selling Presley's contract to RCA, it is necessary to know a bit about the way independent labels were forced to operate in the mid 1950s. When an independent put out a record, the owner needed to pay up front everyone who was concerned with manufacturing the actual records—so the businesses making the labels, sleeves, records, and so on were all paid before any income from the record was realized. Independent distributors, however, paid for the records that were shipped to them *after* these records were sold. This meant that there was a lag of weeks or months from the time the producers paid for the records to be made and when he was paid for record sales. Once records were being released on a regular schedule, profits and expenses could begin to balance one another after the initial expenses were absorbed. Ironically, a big hit record could throw everything into disarray, since unusually large sums would need to be paid out to manufacture large numbers of records, potentially placing the label in great financial jeopardy until the profits were realized. Elvis's fame was rising at about the same time his contract was close to expiring. Phillips judged that the smart thing to do was to sell Elvis's contract while it was still worth something and use the money to put his label in a better financial position overall.

music of Elvis Presley, Little Richard, and Chuck Berry as their records were played on the radio. Like many other teenagers, Holly was glued to the screen when Elvis appeared on Ed Sullivan's *Talk of the Town*, though he had seen Presley perform in Lubbock in January of 1955. Holly spent time with Presley on his subsequent trips through Lubbock, as he did with Little Richard, who even had dinner in Buddy's home during one visit (an event that was greeted with great uneasiness by Holly's conservative parents).

In early 1956 the Columbia and Decca offices in Nashville were searching for young rockabilly artists to compete with Presley on RCA and Decca signed Holly. The recording sessions for Decca did not go well as far as Holly was concerned, and when the records from them went nowhere, Holly was dropped by the label. Holly and his band, the Crickets, had already begun recording for Norman Petty in his independent studio in Clovis, New Mexico. When some of these recordings were shopped around to labels, it turned out that Coral, ironically a Decca subsidiary, was interested. Within the company it was decided that another subsidiary,

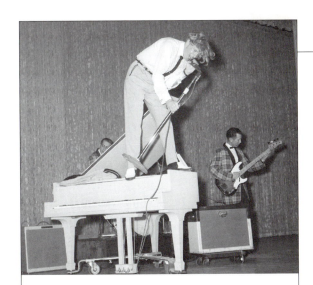

After Elvis left RCA, Sam Phillips invested in a number of other artists, including the blonde-haired, piano-banging Jerry Lee Lewis. Lewis enjoyed a string of hits until being chased briefly from the business when reporters learned that his wife was only fourteen.

Brunswick, was a better home for the Crickets, and then later that it would be a good marketing ploy to release Buddy Holly records on Coral. This explains why some Holly hits are credited to him while others are credited to the Crickets, despite the fact that there is little difference in personnel on the actual recordings. Holly's first hit, "That'll Be the Day," reached number one on the pop charts in the second half of 1957, roughly about the same time Jerry Lee Lewis was emerging with "Whole Lotta Shakin' Goin' On." During the period between his emergence onto the national scene in August of 1957 and his death in early February of 1959, Holly had seven Top 40 hits, including "Peggy Sue" (p3, 1957), "Oh, Boy!" (p10, 1957), and "Maybe Baby" (p17, 1958). He also recorded a number of other tracks that have since become classics covered by later groups, such as "Not Fade Away" (the Rolling Stones), "It's So Easy" (Linda Ronstadt), and "Words of Love" (the Beatles). As with so many tragic deaths, Holly's has prompted much speculation about what his music would have sounded like had he lived longer. One indication is provided by two of his last recordings, "It Doesn't Matter Anymore" and "True Love Ways." Both employ orchestral accompaniment and suggest that Holly might have joined Presley in moving to a more mainstream pop style.

In many ways, Buddy Holly and Chuck Berry offer an interesting comparison: both were guitarists who wrote most of their own songs and performed them in a distinctive manner. And both wrote music directly for a pop audience with strong elements from country and western and rhythm and blues mixed in. The influence of country can be heard in Berry's vocals, his penchant for telling stories with his lyrics, the occasional upbeat country tempos (as heard in "Maybelline," for instance). Berry's guitar playing is for the most part derived strongly from the electric blues tradition, however, relying often on muted, low-register chords for rhythm playing and distorted string bends and double stops for leads. Holly, by contrast, tends to strum full chords energetically with an open, clean guitar tone on his electric guitar, much the way traditional country guitarists do on an acoustic guitar. Combined with a clear country twang in his voice and the vocal hiccups that came to be his trademark, Holly's west-Texas musical roots in country and western are perhaps one of the most obvious features of his style. But Holly was also fascinated with Elvis's assimilation of rhythm and blues singing into his rockabilly vocals, as well with the records of Clyde McPhatter and others who influenced Elvis. It is thus interesting to see how, using the same styles that had influenced so many other early rockers, Holly comes up with his own distinctive blending of features.

Much of the distinctiveness of Holly's stylistic approach can be heard in his recording of "Oh, Boy!" (one of the few Holly hits not from his own pen). A very open, countrified guitar sound accompanies Holly's eager and excited delivery of the lyrics. A closer listen reveals that the song is in AABA form with the verses built up from the 12-bar blues structure (see Interlude 1 for a discussion of the 12-bar blues), revealing the influence of both country and western and rhythm and blues on the track. While the guitar part on another Holly tune, "Peggy Sue," is initially quite muted, Holly eventually breaks into a guitar solo that is nothing more than aggressively strummed open chords. The 12-bar blues structure is also present in the verses of this Holly-composed song. "Peggy Sue" is perhaps also the best example of Holly's vocal technique. During the course of the tune, Holly never delivers any of the verses in exactly the same way; to vary the verses, he not only changes the notes and rhythms around a bit, but he

Hailing from Lubbock, Texas, Buddy Holly blended country twang with R&B rhythm to become an important songwriter and performer during rock's first wave. Shown here with the Crickets, Holly died in a plane crash in February 1959—an event singer-songwriter Don McLean would later describe as "the day the music died."

also changes the timbre of his voice by producing the sound either back in his throat and chest or very forward and through his nose. His manipulation of these timbral changes reveals in Holly's singing an extension of Presley's approach (though Holly's direct tribute to Elvis can be heard on his "Rock Around with Ollie Vee"). It is also noteworthy that the drums are used in an interesting way on "Peggy Sue": Crickets drummer Jerry Allison employs only tom-toms in the drum set—no cymbals or snare drum are heard.

Holly the Songwriter.   As engaging as his recorded performances may be, Buddy Holly was most influential among later rockers as a songwriter. Unlike Berry's lyrics, Holly's are not clever or filled with veiled references. They are mostly happy and positive, but not exceptional in the way that Berry's are. But as with Berry, the fact that Holly wrote those songs himself served as a model for many of the rock musicians who would emerge in the 1960s and '70s. If Berry's songs were more accomplished in terms of lyrics, Holly's were much more adventurous in terms of formal design. Holly employed 12-bar blues, AABA, simple verse-chorus, and contrasting verse-chorus forms in his song-writing, thereby avoiding the impression that a song was simply poured into a preexistent mold. In addition, his stylistic range was broader than that of most rock and roll songwriters of the time. Compare the excitement of "That'll Be the Day" (a listening guide is provided in Interlude 1) or "Maybe Baby" with the gentle pop lyricism of "Words of Love" or "True Love Ways," for instance. While Leiber and Stoller (whose music is discussed in the next chapter) may have been the premiere songwriters of the early years of rock and roll, and Elvis may have been the most engaging and versatile song stylist, Buddy Holly and Chuck Berry were the models of how to be a successful songwriter and performer—a model that would come to define much rock music after the Beatles used it to shake up the music industry in early 1964.

The Day the Music Died

The Misfortunes of Many in Rock and Roll's First Wave.   The 1950s ended with rock and roll suffering two kinds of setbacks that threatened to eliminate the style. The first of these involved the removal of some of the first wave's principal figures from the music business. During a tour of Australia and at the height of his success in 1957, Little Richard believed he received a calling to go into the ministry. He promptly quit music and began a course of study that led to his being ordained as a minister in the Seventh Day Adventist Church. In December of 1957, Elvis received his draft notice, and after a deferment and boot camp at Fort Hood, he was on his way to Germany by late September 1958. In May of 1958, the British press broke the story of Jerry Lee Lewis's marriage to his thirteen-year-old cousin—a scandal that sent his career on a steep decline from which it would take years to recover. Buddy Holly's plane went down on February 3, 1959, a date singer-songwriter Don McLean dubbed "the day the music died." In 1959 Chuck Berry was charged with violating the Mann Act (transporting a minor across state lines for immoral purposes). He was convicted but the verdict was overturned on appeal; he was then tried again and convicted in February of 1961, receiving a three-year sentence (of which he served less than two years). By the end of 1959, many of rock and roll's most important figures were out of the pop-music picture, and rock and roll seemed to be a played-out fad, fading away just as many of its biggest critics had predicted it would.

The Payola Investigations.   As bad as the exit of these key figures was for rock and roll's future, that unfortunate situation was matched by a series of legal and political machinations called the payola scandal that officially began in late 1959. As mentioned above, record labels and distributors often paid disc jockeys to play records on the radio—sometimes the payment was cash; other times it was in goods or services. This practice of paying to get your song heard goes back to the nineteenth century in the American popular music business. In the first decades of the twentieth century, singers received payola to include particular songs in their acts; during the big band era, bandleaders received it to play and record certain numbers; and during the 1950s, disc jockeys were paid off play records on the radio. The reason this occurs is very simple: in each of these eras, certain professionals were "gatekeepers"—they had the power to expose a song to a broad audience and hopefully increase record or sheet music sales by doing so. In the first half of the century, there were periodic squabbles over this, either because the publishers resented having to pay the fees or because they paid the fees and did not get the song played as much as they wanted. So from inside the music business, there was nothing new about the articles and news items regarding payola that began appearing again in the trade magazines in the early 1950s.

By the end of the 1950s, a major shake-up had taken place in the music business over the course of the decade—and this was new. Early in the decade, most hit pop records were recorded and released by major labels. By 1958, because of rock and roll's breakthrough into the pop mainstream, a significant portion of the hit pop records were now on independent labels. From the perspective of the old-school major-label executives, these new indies presented a substantial competitive threat that had to be eliminated. And not only record money was at stake in this shake-up; there was also a struggle between the two organizations that collect royalties for songwriters. ASCAP (the American Society of Composers, Artists, and Publishers) represented the traditional pop song composers; they were very selective about who could be a member, and those who composed rhythm and blues or country and western songs were not welcome to join their ranks. BMI (Broadcast Music Incorporated) was a newer organization and welcomed the very kinds of songwriters that ASCAP was proud to reject. The majors and ASCAP therefore represented music's powerful and well-entrenched old guard (Tin Pan Alley and Hollywood songwriters, mainstream pop performers and their record companies) and the indies and BMI represented rock and roll. Clearly the musical establishment had much to gain by attacking both the indie labels and the songwriters who provided them their material. The payola scandal was the means by which the old guard attempted to win back its market share.

It is important to understand just how little respect rock and roll had in the minds of most seasoned musical professionals in the late 1950s. Most music executives had come up in the business during the 1930s and '40s and had achieved their greatest success promoting the music of the big bands and then the song-stylists. They considered rock and roll—and the rhythm and blues and country and western from which it was developed—to be a crude and unrefined kind of music. Of course, most listeners over the age of thirty felt the same way, so many of this generation had a tough time understanding how rock and roll could have gotten so big so fast. Why weren't they playing good music on the radio anymore, many wondered. There was an explanation that made some sense to such cranky opponents of rock and roll: these ragamuffin indie labels were buying their time on the air—paying the disc jockeys to play that primitive musical garbage—and *that's* why people were buying it. The argument was presented in just such terms to the listening public as the industry began ratcheting up the payola rhetoric. As it happened, a congressional committee was just winding up its investigation into television quiz shows (some of which were rigged, they discovered) and now decided to turn its attention to payola in the music business. In November 1959 the House Special Subcommittee on Legislative Oversight, chaired by Oren Harris (an Arkansas Democrat), began taking testimony.

From the start, the focus of the committee's investigation was radio stations that played rock and roll. The testimony offered no significant acknowledgment that payola had been a part of the music business for decades and that both majors and indies, marketing rock and roll as well as other styles, were involved. It unfortunately played too easily into deeply ingrained American stereotypes that people involved in rhythm and blues were likely to be dishonest, and thus the cultural struggle over the segregation of black and white culture played itself out on a new field of conflict. The Federal Trade Commission and Federal Communications Commission eventually got involved, causing most stations to take some kind of action, if only for show; disc jockeys were fired and formats were changed. Strangely enough, there was nothing illegal about taking money or gifts in exchange for playing a record on the radio. There were two catches, however; by FCC rules the gift had to be acknowledged on the air, and any money received had to be claimed on the recipient's income tax form. The problem for many of the disc jockeys under scrutiny was thus not that they took gifts, but rather that they never declared them. For most of the radio stations

The U.S. government hearings into payola in the radio business became the undoing of many in radio, including Alan Freed. Dick Clark, however, emerged from the investigation relatively unscathed and went on to become one of the most powerful figures in pop-music broadcasting.

involved in the investigation, it was a matter of public perception and working to guard against losing their broadcast license with the FCC. Disc jockeys and the rock and roll format were disposable in this context.

The two highest profile subjects in the payola investigations were Alan Freed and Dick Clark. Clark was extremely cooperative and emerged from the proceedings being praised as a hard-working young businessman. He was forced to divest himself of a significant number of financial interests that might have created a conflict of interest with his broadcast activities. Freed, on the other hand, resisted the entire idea that there was anything wrong with his activities. He argued that he would never take money to play a record he didn't like; but if he'd played a record and a company wanted to show its appreciation, he was happy to accept the gift. Such honest but rebellious declarations made him a liability to his broadcast employers, and he in turn lost his radio job at WABC and his television show on WNEW-TV. There is little doubt that Freed took a wide variety of payments; he was even credited as one of three authors of Chuck Berry's "Maybelline," even though he had no role in its composition. The practice of sharing publishing rights was common within the business; Norman Petty's name, for instance, appears on a number of Buddy Holly songs that Holly composed alone. But as a "gatekeeper," Freed was in the position to push a song that he had a financial interest in, and to the congressmen doing the investigating, this was at least a questionable practice. In December 1962 Freed eventually pleaded guilty to a charge of taking bribes. While he received only a six-month suspended sentence and a $300 fine, the damage had been done. The payola scandal had driven Alan Freed out of the music business. With the severe shake-up in both the personnel and the business of rock and roll, by 1960 it seemed to many that the Golden Age of rock and roll was over.

Having considered the first wave of rock and roll in some detail, we can now step back to see the broader picture and gain a greater sense of historical perspective. Clearly many of the circumstances that led to the emergence of rock and roll were developing before 1955. But a number of significant events occurred in fairly close succession in 1955: "Rock Around the Clock" was a pop hit associated with a movie about juvenile delinquency; Alan Freed's radio show rose to prominence in New York; and Fats Domino, Chuck Berry, and Little Richard enjoyed their first crossover hits, all on independent labels. By the end of the year, Elvis was signed to RCA and on his way to becoming the most commercially successful entertainer in rock and roll, launching a major-label search for rock and roll singers during the next two years that brought recording deals to figures such as Gene Vincent and Buddy Holly. As exciting as rock and roll was, it also represented a serious threat to established music-business interests; because of this, these interests pulled political strings to shut down the upstart music-business entrepreneurs, and by 1960 the first wave of rock and roll was all but over.

The big record companies and music publishers were not about to let this new market in youth music fade away, however; youth music was now a lucrative aspect of the business. In the years that followed, by the big companies once again took control of American popular music, for the most part producing music for middle-class teens that would not offend their parents. In the next chapter we will explore how popular music returned to its Tin Pan Alley ways, with a wide variety of artists and styles hoping to duplicate the kind of success Elvis Presley and rock and roll had enjoyed.

Questions for Discussion and Review

1. How many important elements can you cite from 1955 that support its designation as the year rock and roll was born? What is the problem with assigning such a specific date to the beginning of rock music?
2. Why was youth culture important to rock and roll? What were some of the elements of youth culture in the 1950s?
3. What role was played by radio and record labels in the birth of rock and roll?
4. What is the difference between a cover and a crossover? What roles did they play in early rock and roll? What important debates surround this?
5. Discuss important covers and crossovers. Which songs and/or artists are important and why?
6. Why are Pat Boone and Bill Haley particularly representative of the whitening of rhythm and blues?
7. What are some important features of Chuck Berry's music? Compare and contrast Berry with Buddy Holly.
8. What role did Elvis Presley play in the first wave of rock and roll?
9. What was the payola scandal and why was it important?

Further Reading

Howard A. DeWitt, *Chuck Berry: Rock 'n' Roll Music* (Pierian Press, 1985).

Colin Escott with Martin Hawkins, *Good Rockin' Tonight: Sun Records and the Birth of Rock 'n' Roll* (St. Martin's Press, 1991).

Ben Fong-Torres, *The Hits Just Keep On Coming: The History of Top 40 Radio* (Miller Freeman Books, 1998).

Charlie Gillett, *Making Tracks: Atlantic Records and the Growth of a Multi-Billion-Dollar Industry* (E. P. Dutton, 1974).

John A. Jackson, *Big Beat Heat: Alan Freed and the Early Years of Rock & Roll* (Schirmer, 1991).

Ernst Jorgensen, *Elvis Presley: A Life in Music* (St. Martin's, 1998).

Myra Lewis with Murray Silver, *Great Balls of Fire: The Uncensored Story of Jerry Lee Lewis* (St. Martin's Press, 1982).

Craig Morrison, *Go Cat Go! Rockabilly Music and Its Makers* (University of Illinois Press, 1996).

Philip Norman, *Rave On: The Biography of Buddy Holly* (Simon & Schuster, 1996).

Kerry Segrave, *Payola in the Music Industry: A History, 1880–1991* (McFarland, 1994).

Wes Smith, *The Pied Pipers of Rock 'n' Roll: Radio Deejays of the 50s and 60s* (Longstreet Press, 1989).

The Bigger Picture: Typical Formal Types in American Popular Music

As you have seen from the Listening Guides presented thus far, the analysis of musical form is a study of the way sections are structured in a piece of music, and the way these sections combine to produce larger structures. If all the individual pieces of music that scholars studied had distinctively different formal designs, the study of musical form might involve endless lists of the many ways particular works unfold. But one important thing that form teaches us is that most musical styles work within the constraints of a relatively small number of formal types, so that formal analysis of any single work usually consists in noting its similarities and differences against the backdrop of some formal design common to a large number of works in the style. Because of this, particular formal types and particular musical styles are often linked to one another. For our purposes, it will be useful to pause in our study of rock's historical development to look at the common formal types that occur in rock music. This interlude will guide us in listening to the rest of the music discussed in this book, reveal some of the unexpected kinship among contemporary musical styles, and show the influence of earlier styles of rock on later ones.

The 12-Bar Blues

Perhaps the best place to begin the study of form in rock is with the 12-bar blues. This is a common structural pattern in much rhythm and blues and a pattern that can be found in much rock music as well. A *12-bar* blues is a structural pattern that consists of twelve groups of four-beat measures. The twelve-measure structure is not what makes the 12-bar blues distinctive, however; instead it is the way these twelve measures fall into three groups of four. The first four measures, which are called a "phrase," can often feature a lyric that is repeated in the next four measures. The last four measures provide a lyric that completes the thought. Think of this pattern as "question, question again, answer" (though the lyrics don't literally have to ask a question); the first phrase poses a question, the second poses the same question in a slightly different way, and the third phrase answers the question. A good example of a 12-bar blues in rhythm and blues is Big Joe Turner's "Shake, Rattle, and Roll," discussed earlier. The first line in each verse is repeated in the second phrase, with the third phrase completing the thought with a new line. This is shown below.

bars	1	2	3	4	5	6	7	8	9	10	11	12
chords	I	(IV)	I	I	IV	IV	I	I	V	(IV)	I	(V)
	1st phrase (question)--------				2nd phrase (question)--------				3rd phrase (answer)--------			
	get out of that bed . . .				get out of that bed . . .				git in that kitchen . . .			

Notice that Roman numerals occur under each measure number in the preceding figure. This shows the chords that typically are played in those measures. Chords are combinations of notes played together—think of somebody strumming chords on the guitar or banging them out on the piano, for instance. Chords in any key can be organized by the scale for that key, and the Roman numerals show which note of the scale the chord is based on. If we are in C, for instance, the scale goes C – D – E – F – G – A – B – C. The I chord is a C chord, the IV is an F chord, and the V is a G chord, since the notes C, F, and G are the first, fourth, and fifth notes of the scale. You might well wonder why musicians would bother with arcane Roman numerals when they could just write C, F, and G. The reason is more pragmatic than you might think: there are twelve distinct keys in which this pattern can occur; the specific labels C, F, and G cover only one of those, while the Roman numerals generalize across all twelve. If a musician knows the Roman numerals, she can play the pattern in any key as easily as in C.

On the basis of our discussion, we can see that the 12-bar blues is a pattern that is defined by its measure length, phrasing, lyrics, and chord structure. Once this twelve-measure pattern is in place, an entire song will often repeat this structure several times, with new lyrics and instrumental solos added to make these repetitions fresh. Listen to Big Joe Turner's "Shake, Rattle, and Roll" while following the listening guide provided in Chapter 1. After you have listened to the song in this way two or three times, you will begin to hear the 12-bar blues structure clearly. Notice how the song employs a chorus, which is that ear-catching lyric and melody that returns without change—in this case "Shake, Rattle, and Roll." Despite the use of a chorus, the 12-bar blues structure remains unchanged between verse and chorus sections. You may recall that we identified the form of this song as simple verse-chorus. We will delve a bit deeper into verse-chorus forms a little later in this interlude.

Of the tracks we have already encountered in Listening Guides, both Jackie Brenston's "Rocket '88'" and Chuck Berry's "Johnny B. Goode" employ the 12-bar blues pattern throughout. "Johnny B. Goode" alternates verses and choruses in a manner similar to "Shake, Rattle, and Roll," while "Rocket '88'" uses the pattern for each of its verses (except the shortened one, as discussed). One way that Berry's tune breaks with standard blues practice is in the organization of the lyrics. Berry does not repeat the lyrics of the first phrase in the second; instead he opts for a more continuous narrative. Listen to "Johnny B. Goode" and "Rocket '88'" again and try to detect the 12-bar blues. Another example of a simple verse-chorus form is Little Richard's "Tutti Frutti." This song uses the

12-bar blues, but slightly alters the progression during the last four bars of each verse. Listen to this Little Richard track and see if you can follow the form and detect the slight change Richard makes in the verse sections.

Verse and Verse-Chorus Forms

Simple Verse-Chorus.   As common as it is to early rock and roll, 12-bar blues is not a formal type; it is, rather, a distinctive pattern that can be used to build a larger form. As mentioned, "Rocket '88'," "Shake, Rattle, and Roll," "Johnny B.

LISTENING GUIDE   GET MUSIC ▶▶▏   wwnorton.com/rockhistory

Little Richard, "Tutti Frutti"

Words and music by Richard Penniman, Robert Blackwell, and Dorothy LaBostrie, produced by Bumps Blackwell. Reached #21 on Billboard Pop and #2 on the rhythm and blues charts.

FORM: Simple verse-chorus, beginning with chorus.

TIME SIGNATURE: 4/4.

INSTRUMENTATION: Piano, acoustic bass, drums, saxes, and lead vocal.

0:00–0:18	**Chorus**, 12 mm. + 2 mm.	Vocal intro, "Wop bop . . ."
0:18–0:34	**Verse 1**, 12 mm. (with slight change from chorus),	"I got a girl . . . Sue . . ."
0:34–0:49	**Chorus**, 12 mm.	"Tutti frutti . . ."
0:49–1:04	**Verse 2**, 12 mm.	"I got a girl . . . Daisy . . ."
1:04–1:20	**Chorus**, 12 mm.	"Tutti frutti . . ."
1:20–1:35	**Instrumental Verse**, 12 mm.	Sax solo.
1:35–1:50	**Chorus**, 12 mm.	"Tutti frutti . . ."
1:50–2:06	**Verse 3**, 12 mm.	(Same lyrics as Verse 2).
2:06–2:22	**Chorus**, 12 mm.	"Tutti frutti . . ." ends on vocal intro "Wop bop . . ."

Goode," and "Tutti Frutti" all use the 12-bar blues throughout; but the last three of these are in simple verse-chorus form, while the first is in simple verse form. To determine the form of these songs, we need to examine the relationship of the verses to the choruses. Remember that whenever a single pattern is used as the basis for both verses and choruses in a song, the resulting form is called simple verse-chorus; when no chorus is present, the form is simple verse. Identifying the 12-bar blues in these songs helps us to understand how the verses (and choruses, when present) are structured; but while these tunes use the 12-bar blues in their respective verses and choruses, a simple verse or verse-chorus form can also be composed of a repeating pattern that is not a 12-bar

 LISTENING GUIDE   GET MUSIC ▶▶ wwnorton.com/rockhistory

The Carter Family, "Can the Circle Be Unbroken"

Words and music by A. P. Carter, recorded in 1935.

FORM: Simple verse-chorus.

TIME SIGNATURE: 2/4, with dropped beats.

INSTRUMENTATION: Acoustic guitar, two female and one male voice, with one female voice taking the lead during voices and choruses sung in three-part harmony.

0:00–0:06	**Introduction**, 3 mm.	Guitar accompaniment.
0:06–0:26	**Verse 1**, 16 mm. (only 1 beat in m. 12)	Solo vocal, "I was standin' . . ."
0:26–0:44	**Chorus**, 16 mm. (only 1 beat in mm. 4 and 12)	Choral vocal, "Can the circle . . ."
0:44–1:04	**Instrumental Verse**, 16 mm. (no dropped beats)	Guitar solo.
1:04–1:23	**Verse 2**, 16 mm.	As before, "I told the undertaker . . ."
1:23–1:41	**Chorus**, 16 mm.	As before, "Can the circle . . ."
1:41–2:00	**Verse 3**, 16 mm.	As before, "I followed close behind her . . ."
2:00–2:18	**Chorus**, 16 mm.	As before, "Can the circle . . ."
2:18–2:28	**Instrumental Verse** (partial), 8 mm.	Guitar solo.
2:28–2:47	**Verse 4**, 16 mm.	"Went back home, Lord . . ."
2:47–3:04	**Chorus**, 16 mm.	"Can the circle . . ."

blues. Consider "Can the Circle Be Unbroken" as recorded by the Carter Family. The verses and choruses in this tune are built on a 16-bar progression that cannot be considered a variation of the 12-bar blues pattern. While the verse and chorus may seem different on first hearing, repeated hearings reveal that the verse and chorus use the same melody and harmony, with only slight changes made between them. Listen to this track and see if you can hear the similarity.

In order to count the measures in "Can the Circle Be Unbroken," you will need to keep two things in mind. First, rather than the four-beats-per-measure rhythmic pattern we encountered in the 12-bar blues, this song uses a two-beats-per-measure pattern. You thus need to count one-two, one-two, and so on. The other aspect of this song is subtle and can cause confusion when you try to count it out: during the verses, the 12th bar contains only one beat, while in the choruses the 4th and 12th measures contain only one beat. Musicians often refer to this situation as "dropping a beat," meaning in this case that the second beat in each instance is dropped. The only instance of this 16-bar pattern not to drop these beats is the first instrumental verse on the guitar; in this verse Maybelle Carter "corrects" the dropped beats from the sung verses and choruses by playing sixteen full measures of two beats. This passage is a fine example of Maybelle Carter's distinctive guitar style as well.

Simple Verse Form.   Verse can also be built on other structures than the 12-bar blues in simple verse form. Like "Rocket '88'," "That's All Right (Mama)" uses simple verse form. A quick look back to the Listening Guide in Chapter 2 reveals that Elvis's cover of the Big Boy Crudup tune has no chorus and is made up of repeated verses, each of which is eighteen bars in length. While the structure of the verses in "That's All Right (Mama)" are derived from the blues, they do not conform to the standard 12-bar structure. Elvis's recording of "Heartbreak Hotel" provides another clear example of simple verse form: each 8-bar verse is based on the same chord progression, which is actually an abbreviated version of the 12-bar blues (though it is not a 12-bar blues). As you listen, notice how the song consists only of repetitions of the same music.

Contrasting Verse-Chorus.   The verses and choruses of "Tutti Frutti" are slight variations of one another, but there are also songs in which verse and chorus sections contrast much more strongly. When the verses and choruses of a song employ distinctively different music, we call this contrasting verse-chorus form. Chuck Berry's "Rock and Roll Music" offers a clear instance of this. The 14-measure choruses alternate with the 8-measure verses, and the different measure count for each of these sections already indicates the musical contrast between them. As you listen, notice how central the choruses seem and how subordinate the verses are. The most memorable part of the song is its chorus, and this tends to be true of most verse-chorus forms, simple or contrasting.

Another rock and roll example of contrasting verse-chorus form is Buddy Holly's "That'll Be the Day." As you listen to this track, note the clear difference between the 8-bar verse and chorus sections. Note especially the instrumental bridge; while neither of these 8-bar sections is blues-based, notice that this bridge uses the 12-bar blues pattern.

Elvis Presley, "Heartbreak Hotel"

Words and music by Mae Boren, Tommy Durden, and Elvis Presley, produced by Steve Sholes. Reached # 1 on the Billboard Pop and Country and Western charts, and #5 on the rhythm and blues charts in 1956.

FORM: Simple verse.

TIME SIGNATURE: 12/8 (shuffle in four).

INSTRUMENTATION: Electric guitar, piano, acoustic bass, drums, and lead vocals.

0:00–0:22	**Verse 1**, 8 mm.	"Well, since my baby left me . . ."
0:22–0:42	**Verse 2**, 8 mm.	"Oh, though it's always crowded . . ."
0:42–1:01	**Verse 3**, 8 mm.	"Now, the bellhop's tears . . ."
1:01–1:22	**Verse 4**, 8 mm.	"Well, if your baby leaves you . . ."
1:21–1:42	**Instrumental Verse**, 8 mm.	Guitar solo for first 4 mm., then piano solo.
1:42–2:05	**Verse 5**, 8 mm.	"Oh, though it's always crowded . . ."

Chuck Berry, "Rock and Roll Music"

Words and music by Chuck Berry, produced by Phil and Leonard Chess. Reached #8 on the Billboard Pop charts and #6 on the rhythm and blues charts in 1957.

FORM: Contrasting verse-chorus, beginning with the chorus rather than the verse.

TIME SIGNATURE: 4/4, with a tendency toward shuffle.

INSTRUMENTATION: Electric guitar, acoustic bass, piano, drums, and lead guitar.

0:00–0:22	**Chorus**, 14 mm. + 2 mm. introduction	"Just let me hear . . ."
0:22–0:34	**Verse 1**, 8 mm.	"I have no kick . . ."
0:34–0:54	**Chorus**, 14 mm.	"That's why I go for that . . ."
0:55–1:06	**Verse 2**, 8 mm.	"I took my lover over . . ."
1:06–1:26	**Chorus**, 14 mm.	"That's why I go for that . . ."

continued

1:26–1:38	**Verse 3**, 8 mm.	"Way down south . . ."
1:38–1:58	**Chorus**, 14 mm.	"And started playin' that . . ."
1:58–2:10	**Verse 4**, 8 mm.	"Don't care to hear 'em . . ."
2:10–2:30	**Chorus**, 14 mm.	"So I can that . . ."

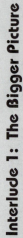

LISTENING GUIDE   GET MUSIC ▶▶ wwnorton.com/rockhistory

The Crickets, "That'll Be the Day"

Words and music by Buddy Holly, Jerry Allison, and Norman Petty, produced by Norman Petty. Reached # 1 on the Billboard Pop charts and #2 on the rhythm and blues charts in 1957.

FORM: Contrasting verse-chorus with instrumental bridge.

TIME SIGNATURE: 12/8 (shuffle in 4).

INSTRUMENTATION: Electric guitar, acoustic bass, drums, lead and backup vocals.

0:00–0:04	**Introduction**, 2 mm.	Solo guitar featured.
0:04–0:19	**Chorus**, 8 mm.	"Well, that'll be the day . . ."
0:19–0:34	**Verse**, 8 mm.	"Well, you give me . . ."
0:34–0:49	**Chorus**, 8 mm.	"Well, that'll be the day . . ."
0:49–1:12	**Instrumental Bridge**, 12 mm. (guitar solo over 12–bar blues).	
1:12–1:27	**Chorus**, 8 mm.	"Well, that'll be the day . . ."
1:27–1:42	**Verse**, 8 mm.	"Well, when Cupid shot . . ."
1:42–1:58	**Chorus**, 8 mm.	"Well, that'll be the day . . ."
1:58–2:14	**Ending**, 8 mm.	Based closely on chorus, "That'll be the day . . ."

AABA Form

Perhaps the song form most associated with mainstream pop in the decades preceding the birth of rock and roll is the AABA form. In Tin Pan Alley songs, this formal pattern is one of the most common and usually occurs in a 32-bar scheme that combines four 8-bar phrases. We use the designation AABA to show that the first two 8-bar phrases are very similar, the third 8-bar phrase is contrasting, and the last 8-bar phrase is similar to the first two.

A	A	B	A
8 mm.	8 mm.	8 mm.	8 mm.

Of the songs we have already seen in Listening Guides, "Over the Rainbow," "I'm Sittin' on Top of the World," "Hey Good Lookin'," and "Blueberry Hill" have all employed the standard 32-bar AABA form. As it turns out, most AABA songs would be too short if the song consisted of only one time through the 32-bar pattern, so usually all or some part of the pattern is repeated. In "I'm Sittin' on Top of the World" and "Hey Good Lookin'," the entire AABA form returns. But in "Over the Rainbow" and "Blueberry Hill," only part of the AABA structure is repeated. When the entire AABA form is repeated, this is called a "full reprise": when only part of the AABA form returns, the term "partial reprise" is used.

While the 32-bar AABA is common, this form can also be modified to include sections that exceed eight measures. Jerry Lee Lewis's recording of

LISTENING GUIDE

GET MUSIC ▶▶ wwnorton.com/rockhistory

Jerry Lee Lewis, "Great Balls of Fire"

Words and music by Otis Blackwell and Jack Hammer, produced by Sam Phillips. Reached #2 on the Billboard Pop charts, #1 on the country and western charts, and #3 on the rhythm and blues charts in 1957.

FORM: AABA, with full reprise.

TIME SIGNATURE: 4/4.

INSTRUMENTATION: Piano, drums, acoustic bass, and lead vocals.

0:00–0:13	**A-Verse**, 8 mm.	Vocals delivered in stop time, "You shake my nerves . . ."
0:13–0:25	**A-Verse**, 8 mm.	Full band in, "I led your love . . ."
0:25–0:43	**B-Bridge**, 12 mm.	"Kiss me baby . . ."
0:43–0:55	**A-Verse**, 8 mm.	"I chew my nails down . . ."
0:55–1:06	**A-Instrumental Verse**, 8 mm.	Raucous piano solo.
1:06–1:18	**A-Instrumental Verse**, 8 mm.	
1:18–1:37	**B-Bridge**, 12 mm.	"Kiss me baby . . ."
1:37–1:49	**A-Verse**, 8 mm.	"I chew my nails . . ."

"Great Balls of Fire" provides a good rock and roll example of this. The A sections are of the typical 8-measure length found in the AABA forms we've encountered thus far, but the bridge consists of twelve measures of music. This extended bridge structure produces a complete AABA pattern of thirty-six measures, not the usual thirty-two. Note that "Great Balls of Fire" employs a full reprise of this 36-bar pattern to form the second half of the song.

There may be many differences between the manic music of Jerry Lee Lewis and the more lyrical soft rockabilly of the Everly Brothers, but one difference is not in their respective uses of form. "All I Have to Do Is Dream" offers a nice instance of the use in rock and roll of the 32-bar AABA pattern with partial reprise. The only deviation occurs when two measures are added to ease the transition to the bridge at 1:31. This song is also exceptional in the way that it

---

LISTENING GUIDE

GET MUSIC ▶▶▶ wwnorton.com/rockhistory

The Everly Brothers, "All I Have to Do Is Dream"

Words and music by Boudleaux Bryant, produced by Archie Bleyer. Reached #1 on Billboard Pop, Country and Western, and Rhythm and Blues charts in 1958.

FORM: AABA, with partial reprise. The "Dream" refrain from the introduction returns just before the repeat of the bridge and then again at the end as the song fades.

TIME SIGNATURE: 4/4, with a slightly latin feel.

INSTRUMENTATION: Electric guitars, acoustic guitar, acoustic bass, drums, and two-part harmony vocal throughout.

0:00–0:12	**Introduction,** 4 mm.	Guitar chord, and then vocals enter, "Dream . . ."
0:12–0:30	**A-Verse,** 8 mm.	"When I want you . . ."
0:30–0:49	**A-Verse,** 8 mm.	"When I feel blue . . ."
0:49–1:07	**B-Bridge,** 8 mm.	"I can make you mine . . ."
1:07–1:31	**A-Verse,** 10 mm. (8 mm. + 2 mm. drawn from intro)	"I need you so . . ."
1:31–1:49	**B-Bridge,** 8 mm.	"I can make you mine . . ."
1:49–2:18	**A-Verse,** 8 mm. and fade on intro	"I need you so . . ."

works the "dream" refrain into the introduction, the transition to the bridge, and the ending.

The diagram below summarizes the four common formal types found in rock music that we have discussed. While we will encounter a couple of more complicated formal designs later in the book, these four will apply to a large majority of the songs we study from here forward.

Four Common Formal Types

Simple verse	All verses based on same music, no chorus
Simple verse-chorus	Verses and choruses based on same music
Contrasting verse-chorus	Verses and choruses based on different music
AABA	Verses and bridge based on different music; can employ full or partial reprise

12-bar blues may occur as the basis for any of the sections in any of the above forms

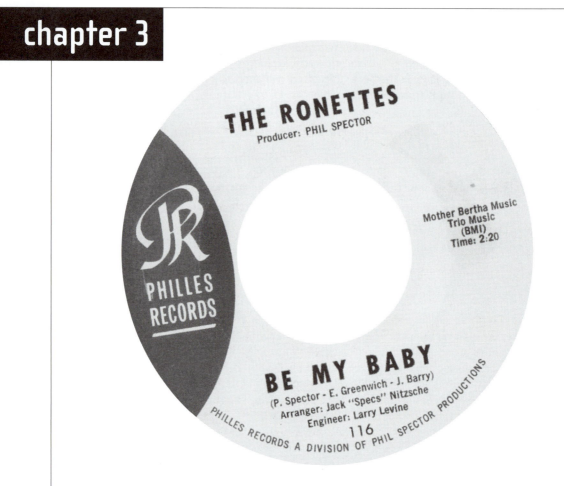

chapter 3

THE RONETTES
Producer: PHIL SPECTOR

PHILLES RECORDS

Mother Bertha Music
Trio Music
(BMI)
Time: 2:20

BE MY BABY
(P. Spector - E. Greenwich - J. Barry)
Arranger: Jack "Specs" Nitzsche
Engineer: Larry Levine
116
PHILLES RECORDS A DIVISION OF PHIL SPECTOR PRODUCTIONS

An original pressing of the Ronettes' "Be My Baby," produced by Phil Spector in 1963. Though early '60s rock and roll is seen by some as a mere pause between Elvis and the Beatles, others cite the period's many musical innovations. Spector was one of the early 1960s' most important producers—drawing influence from Leiber and Stoller before him and influencing the Beatles and Brian Wilson after. Spector demanded total control over the music and was famous for his "Wall of Sound": a unique recording technique in which he would use many instruments—sometimes multiple guitars, other strings, sleigh bells, and others—in a very small space. This created a complex, richly textured sound that was complimented by strong vocals from female singers like Darlene Love and Veronica Bennett (Ronnie Spector). "Be My Baby," featuring Ronnie Spector, is representative of Phil Spector's Wall of Sound.

The Demise of Rock and the Promise of Soul

By the end of the 1950s, many of the important figures in rock and roll's first wave were out of the music business. The radio stations that had played rock and roll and the independent labels that had supplied the records were shaken by the payola scandal. In addition to posing a cultural challenge to the values of many Americans, rock and roll also posed a threat to the music-business old guard. The basic problem, as some older hands in the business saw it, was that the wrong people had been in control of rock and roll: musicians, disc jockeys, and independent label owners seemed to be running things. According to these old pros, all this hustling led to a market for youth music that was destined to run into trouble sooner or later, because none of these small-time operators could be depended on to act responsibly and consistently: too much free choice had resulted in too many variables that could not have been predicted, and thus the entire enterprise fell apart. Despite these seeming failures, rock and roll *had* accomplished something important in the eyes of the music-business establishment: it had demonstrated convincingly that youth culture provided a significant and profitable market. What was needed now was for seasoned professionals to step in, pick up the pieces, and bring some order to the chaos Elvis and Little Richard has created—a lot of money could be made if the processes of creating and selling music to a youth market could be more tightly organized and controlled. As we saw in the last chapter, however, rock and roll did not collapse entirely on its own; the music-business establishment played a significant role in hastening the fall of the first wave.

The era after the demise of the first wave and before the arrival of the Beatles is the source of controversy among rock historians. For some, the perspective outlined above explains why rock music was so mediocre during these years; big corporate types attempted to domesticate rock music, turning it into a slickly and cynically produced commercial product that quickly became a mere shadow of its former self. Teen idols, girl groups, and music composed and produced by music-publishing professionals are often seen to represent the severe decline in rock that was reversed only with the "British invasion" in 1964. There are other, more positive evaluations of these years, however, and some writers and historians argue that this era was filled with important music and musical accomplishments. They cite the music of Leiber and Stoller, Phil Spector, and the rise of sweet soul, for instance, as marking an important maturation in rock and roll that, as some of the most partisan forms of this argument run, were unfortunately cut short by the British invasion. As we will see in this chapter, the 1959–63 period was indeed filled with a wide variety of music. Rock and roll had brought an audience (and a market) together, but many had always considered it only a fad, and now it seemed to be over. Nearly everyone in the music business was on the lookout for the "next big thing" that would focus the attention of youth culture as Elvis and company had done in the immediately preceding years. As it turned out, that next big thing was the Beatles, but the Fab Four did not hit in the United States until early 1964. A number of styles thus ended up vying for center stage—a spot that none would ultimately win. This chapter surveys the variety of pop styles that made up the youth market in the early 1960s. The way you view this time—as years of decline or years of promise—will likely depend on how much you like the music of this era. From the historical point of view, however, it is probably best to focus on how rock and roll during these years grew out of the popular music that preceded it while also preparing the way for the rock music that followed later in the 1960s.

Splitting up the Market: Teenyboppers and Their Older Siblings

In many ways, the period from 1959 to 1963 was a time of transition in the history of rock. Music-business people took advantage of the opportunities provided by the youth market during this time by noticing that, by 1960, the youth market was no longer one market. Many of the kids who had been excited by Little Richard, Chuck Berry, and Elvis in the mid 1950s had graduated from high school by the end of the decade and were now eager—in time-honored fashion—to be treated as adults. This meant that there were now at least two distinct markets: one focused on the new generation of teenagers (the younger brothers and sisters of the first-wave rock and roll fans) and another directed at the now college-age former rock and rollers. Teen idols and dance music, concerned with nonsexual romance and dancing, would be the styles most clearly directed at the younger set; for the older set, folk, a style that grappled with issues of social, cultural, political, and economic issues, would have appeal.

The Adults in the Room: Brill Building and Aldon Publishing. The return of pre–rock and roll practices to teen pop music can clearly be seen in the music that came out of the Brill Building in the early 1960s. The Brill Building is in fact an actual place, but "Brill Building" is also used as a stylistic label, much like "Tin Pan Alley" refers both to a place as well as a type of popular music and a set of business practices. Located in midtown Manhattan, the Brill Building housed the offices of many of the music business's most important music publishing companies of the time. Aldon Music, run by Al Nevins and Don Kirschner, became one of the most important of these in popular music of the late 1950s and early 1960s, and provides a representative example of how Brill Building pop worked. The Aldon offices contained a number of small rooms, each equipped with a piano; songwriters or songwriting teams would work all day writing new pop songs. Carole King and Gerry Goffin, Cynthia Weil and Barry Mann, Neil Sedaka and Howard Greenfield, Jeff Barry and Ellie Greenwich, and Doc Pomus and Mort Shuman were all professional songwriters turning out a new song every day or so and competing with one another to have their song the next one recorded. Once a song was selected by Aldon, it was then matched to the appropriate performing group, who were almost never the songwriters themselves. A professional producer, in charge of organizing the session, and a cast of professional studio musicians would then record the tune, which might end up released on any of a number of record labels. This was a very organized way of producing pop music, with duties assigned to specialists and songs cranked out with machine-like efficiency and precision. In such a situation, the actual recording artist was obviously not at the center of the process. The Brill Building approach—which can be extended to other publishers not based in the actual Brill Building—was one way that professionals in the music business took control of things in the time after rock and roll's first wave. In the Brill Building practice, there were no more unpredictable or rebellious singers; in fact, a specific singer in most cases could be easily replaced with another. No more temperamental songwriters to deal with or songs with lyrics that might offend middle-class sensibilities. Songs were written to order by pros who could custom fit the music and lyrics to the targeted teen audience. In a number of important ways, the Brill Building approach was a return to the way business had been done in the years before rock and roll, since it returned power to the publishers and record labels, and made the performing artists themselves much less central to the music's production. In the perception of the public, however, these performers still seemed to be the center of attention, and teen idols, along with girl groups (discussed later in the chapter), were the principal means of delivering Brill Building tunes to the pop audience.

Teen Idols for Idle Teens. The rise of Pat Boone and Elvis during the first wave had created two distinct images for rock and roll song stylists. Boone was meant to suggest the "good boy"—the kind of clean-cut and respectable young man middle-class parents would feel comfortable with if he took their teenage daughter on a date. Elvis started out as the "bad boy"—the kind of tough, sex-obsessed hoodlum that parents tried hard to keep their girls away from (these roles of good and bad boys would be reworked in the 1960s, with the Rolling Stones as troublemakers and the Beatles as the charming, good boys). During his stint in the army, Elvis's image was reformed, suggesting that the strict discipline of the army had made a respectable man out of him. By 1957 it was clear that preteen and younger teenage girls would buy—or have their parents buy—a lot of records by young handsome men singing songs about love. These "good boy" teen idols were cast as ideal boyfriends: well groomed and attractive, sensitive, and absolutely not interested in anything more than holding hands and an occasional kiss. It was again a measure of the low regard in which rock and roll was held within the music business that record companies figured anybody could be a rock singer; as long as the songs were written by pros and the backing music was played by experienced studio musicians, all that was needed was somebody who could carry a tune, or be coached to do so. The crucial thing was that these teen idols look and act the part effectively.

Teen idols recorded for both independent and major labels with almost equal success during the 1957–63 period (though the indies involved were often not those that had been releasing rock and roll previously). Philadelphia-based teen idols enjoyed a string of successful hits, including Frankie Avalon's "Dede Dinah" (p7, 1958) and "Venus" (p1, 1959), Bobby Rydell's "Wild One" (p2, 1960), and Freddy Cannon's "Palisades Park" (p3, 1962). Other teen idol hits were scored by Bobby Vee ("Take Care of My Baby"; p1, 1961), Bobby Vinton ("Roses Are Red"; p1, 1962), and three singers who also wrote many of their own hits: Paul Anka ("Diana"; p1, 1957), Bobby Darin ("Dream Lover"; p2, 1959), and Neil Sedaka ("Breaking Up Is Hard to Do"; p1, 1962). As popular as some of these records were, Fabian Forte's "Turn Me Loose" (p9, 1959), a product of Bob Marcucci's Philadelphia-based Chancellor label, is a good example of the kinds of musical problems that the teen-idol adaptation of rock and roll could produce for fans well versed in the first-wave music. The song was written by Brill Building songwriters Doc Pomus and Mort Shuman and the backup playing is proficient but nondescript—another day at the office for these musicians. Fabian's vocals are tenuous, creating the impression that he can just barely sing the tune. For many listeners old enough to have experienced the excitement of the first few recordings of Elvis and Little Richard, this was discouragingly tame stuff. Despite the cynical system in which this strategically accommodating music was produced, there were also some genuine highlights. Paul Anka, Neil Sedaka, and Bobby Darin all got their starts as teen idols, and

Teen idols Frankie Avalon (left) and Fabian. After the chaos that surrounded Elvis, Jerry Lee Lewis, and the payola scandal, many of the larger record companies exerted control over the music business and promoted clean-cut teen idols like Avalon and Fabian. These singers projected the image of the "perfect boyfriend"—well-groomed, attractive, and sensitive—and produced a smooth, tame vocal style.

each later translated that success into careers in songwriting and performing for a broader audience. Darin was even nominated for an Oscar in 1963 for his role in the film *Capt. Newman, M.D.* The emergence of the teen idols in the late 1950s inaugurated a segment of the market that has since been termed "bubblegum music." Though the ways in which they were packaged would transform to follow changing fashions through the decades to follow, ideal boyfriends would continue to be marketed to young girls. In the early 1960s, teen idols were marketed both on the radio and on special television shows devoted to teen pop, the most important of which was *American Bandstand*.

The Dance Craze,* American Bandstand, *"The Twist." By the early 1960s many American teenagers were in the habit of heading straight home from school most days to watch a new television show developed especially for them. The idea of *American Bandstand* was simple: get a bunch of teenage kids together in the studio, play the current hit records as the kids dance, and have a few musical guests "performing" their most recent hits. *Bandstand* was yet another instance of the migration of entertainment from radio to TV; the show was essentially a familiar rock and roll radio program format adapted to television. Though he made the show famous, Dick Clark was not the first host of the program; Bob Horn was the host when the show debuted locally on Philadelphia's WFIL in 1952. And *Bandstand* was not the only television rock and roll show; Alan Freed and others had done rock and roll TV programs as well. But *Bandstand* was the one that survived and succeeded. Debuting nationally on the ABC network in 1957, the show was broadcast every weekday afternoon as well as on Saturday nights. In his first years of network broadcast, Dick Clark had almost every important rock and roll performer on his show at one time or another. Most of these performances were not exactly live. Unlike Jerry Lee Lewis's appearance on *The Steve Allen Show* or Elvis's on Ed Sullivan's *Talk of the Town, Bandstand* appearances were almost always lip-synched—another symptom of the perceived need to control the music. No flying piano benches or provocative hip swiveling here—just good clean fun and dancing. Of course, the lip-synching practice worked out well for the teen idols who were often the featured performers on Clark's show. The last thing anybody needed was for some of those acts to actually have to sing.

Most of the focus of *American Bandstand* was not on the controlled "performances," however; it was on dancing. The high profile of Clark's show created new interest in dancing to pop music. Dancing had never been absent from rock and roll, especially since references to dancing had been the crucial substitute for references to sex in the original rhythm and blues that so much rock and roll appropriated. But with all that was sometimes going on onstage during the first wave, dancing was often secondary, as the performance itself was the focus of the experience. In 1960 Clark introduced a cover version of Hank Ballard's "The Twist" done by a young singer named Ernest Evans, who went by the stage name Chubby Checker. The record quickly rose to number one in the pop charts and initiated a craze for named dances: the fly, the fish, the mashed potato were among those that would be demonstrated by the teens on Clark's show. The fad over the twist reached far beyond youth culture, as even affluent Manhattan

American Bandstand

One reason *American Bandstand* was so important is that it was a powerful force for musical and cultural diversity at precisely the time that the major labels and media conglomerates were working hard to regain control of popular music. The show's flexibility was largely due to its independence: *American Bandstand* was made as an independent, local television show but had the influence of a hit series on a major network.

In the 1950s there were very few outlets on network television for the new music of the rising youth culture. CBS and NBC continued to fill the airwaves with the older, established, mainstream styles of music favored by their major advertisers, who preferred middle-class, adult audiences. One of the ways that independent television stations and, to a lesser extent, ABC competed was to seek out other audiences, including younger viewers. As a result, newer or non-mainstream styles, particularly rhythm and blues, rock and roll, and country and western, received their television exposure on these outlets. This division was reinforced by the similar split between major and independent record labels; the major labels developed close relationships with the networks, while the independent labels did the same with independent stations.

"Video DJ" programs were an early, inexpensive way for independent stations to grab market share. It was a simple concept: take a popular local DJ and convert his radio show to television. The DJ would introduce short films (similar to modern-day music videos) and in-studio, lip-synched performances, interspersed with variety segments like comedy sketches and dance parties. By the mid 1950s, video DJ shows were on the air in dozens of large markets across the country.

In 1952, Philadelphia DJ Bob Horn was asked to convert his weekday afternoon show on WFIL-AM, *Bob Horn's Bandstand*, to television. At first, *Bandstand* was a conventional video DJ show. But after some experimentation, Horn emphasized the dance-party aspect and *Bandstand* became wildly popular. Horn was fired in 1956 after a drunk-driving arrest and replaced by Dick Clark, who had been hosting the radio version. The show grew in popularity and was picked up by ABC and broadcast nationally as *American Bandstand*.

For *American Bandstand* to be produced independently in Philadelphia while being broadcast on a major network was most unusual. Because of this unique status, and because the show was a big hit, Clark had remarkable freedom in choosing his material. Within four weeks of premiering on ABC, *American Bandstand* was the top-rated daytime show on television, drawing as many as 20 million viewers. ABC also added the show to its Saturday night lineup. Dick Clark used this unusual combination of freedom and popularity very well. He continued to broadcast music and in-studio performances by both black and

Dick Clark, host of American Bandstand, *1959. Unlike Elvis's performance on Ed Sullivan's show or Jerry Lee Lewis's performance on Steve Allen's,* Bandstand *was just good clean fun: lip-synched performances by current pop stars with teenagers dancing. Clark's show featured both black and white artists and was seen as a force for racial integration.*

white artists. As a result, *Bandstand* became a daily, national force for racial integration—not just for music but also for social interaction in general.

American Bandstand continued to be popular and important until the arrival of MTV in the mid 1980s. Throughout its long history, it continually adapted to changing musical tastes: the first song Clark played on ABC was Jerry Lee Lewis's "Whole Lotta Shakin' Goin' On," and the last was Laura Branigan's "Shattered Glass." The artists on the show ranged from Twist-king Chubby Checker to the infamous former Sex Pistol Johnny Rotten (as John Lydon, leader of Public Image Limited). Despite the changes, however, *American Bandstand* always maintained its identity as a dance-music showcase because Dick Clark let music fans and dancers—not network executives and sponsors—dictate its programming content.

socialites began frequenting the Peppermint Lounge in New York City to do the twist—a situation that prompted a spin-off song, Joey Dee's "The Peppermint Twist" (p1, 1962). Hoping to re-create the previous year's success, Checker released "Let's Twist Again" in 1961, which rose as high as number eight. "The Twist" then returned to the number one slot for a second time in 1962, a feat that had been accomplished before only by Bing Crosby's "White Christmas."

While *American Bandstand* was responsible for igniting the early 1960s dance craze, its greater importance is the role it came to play in youth culture during the era we are considering in this chapter. Having a network television show exclusively for young people reinforced the idea that there was a national youth culture, creating a sense that while there might be regional differences in the way people spoke and acted, when it came to music most teens were united by a common bond. Movies also played a role in building this sense of community and shared concern. Elvis—at this point as much a teen idol as anything else—was making family-oriented films, and Frankie Avalon (among many other teen idols) made the jump to movies, appearing in a series of music- and dance-filled, teen-targeted beach movies with Annette Funicello (who had been a Mouseketeer on the original Mickey Mouse Club television show). As commercially successful as this movie and television exposure was for pop music and pop performers in the early 1960s, it also prepared the way for the Beatles—a group as charming as they were musically talented who would prove to be the darlings of the television and movie audiences that were now assembling. *American Bandstand* also helped to make rock and roll more acceptable to adults. Although the show had been designed to appeal to teens, Clark soon discovered that adults were tuning in too. He has remarked that he considers "The Twist" to be one of the most important songs in the history of rock and roll because its reception constituted the first time that most adults could freely admit that they liked rock and roll. Hardliners might reply that this is precisely the problem: rock and roll should be about resistance to adult culture, not assimilation into it. But like "(We're Gonna) Rock Around the Clock" appearing in *Blackboard Jungle* and Elvis signing with RCA and appearing on Ed Sullivan's show, the popularity of "The Twist," *American Bandstand*, and teen movies clearly indicated that rock and roll was becoming firmly established within American culture.

Chubby Checker, inventor of the dance (and performer of the song) "The Twist" in performance in London, England. Dick Clark, host of American Bandstand, *said that "The Twist" was one of rock and roll's most important songs: it swept the nation and reached into Europe, and young, old, black, and white all did the dance with ease.*

Folk Music and the Putting Away of Childish Things.   No matter how much teens and their parents might have been enjoying *American Bandstand*, some college-age listeners were looking for something else in music more consistent with their new standing as adults. While they may have consigned rock and roll to their high school past, many were not quite ready to enter the cultural world of their parents. Some remained devoted to rock of the first wave, while others were assimilated into adult culture; but many—college students especially—looked around for music that seemed more "real" than what the mainstream commercial music business was offering. In some cases these listeners were attracted to jazz or blues and sometimes even to classical music, but the most popular style of alternative music among these former rock and rollers became folk music.

Folk had enjoyed a certain amount of popular appeal throughout the 1940s, with traditional performers such as Pete Seeger and Woody Guthrie reaching larger and larger audiences, both as soloists and together in the Almanac Singers. During the first half of the 1950s, the Weavers (with Pete Seeger) had a series of pop hits, including "Good Night Irene" (p1, 1950), "So Long (It's Been Good to Know Ya)" (p4, 1951), and "On Top of Old Smokie" (p2, 1951). Folk had a long history of addressing the problems faced by the less-fortunate in American society, and folk singers often advocated social change from a markedly left-wing political position. As a consequence, many ran into problems during the McCarthy era of the early 1950s, as the U.S. government attempted vigorously to identify communists within its borders. The Weavers' career, for instance, was cut short when they were blacklisted for reportedly being in sympathy with the Communist Party. By the mid 1950s, politically engaged folk music was forced out of mainstream pop. By the late 1950s, fueled largely by its appeal to college audiences and downplaying any overt political

One of the most important groups in American folk, the Weavers: (from left) Pete Seeger, Lee Hayes, Fred Halterman, and Ronnie Gilbert. Folk was characterized by its focus on social issues, musical and instrumental simplicity, and appeal to a college (and decidedly non-teen) audience. After many hits, the Weavers' career was cut short when they were blacklisted for reportedly being in sympathy with the Communist Party.

connections, folk music experienced a revival that pushed it back into the pop mainstream. By the early 1960s, some folk artists were once again openly political, as many aligned themselves with the civil rights movement, and, later in the decade, with the opposition to the Vietnam War.

One of the key components of folk that attracted many listeners was its marked populist character. Folk seemed to be music devoted to a greater sense of community than commercial pop: to its adherents, it was music for regular people, performed by regular people. Performers in this populist context were not perceived to be above their audience; they were thought to be in some sense representative of it. Virtuosic or theatrical performance practices were rejected in favor of a sense of unpretentious and direct musical expression. Folk lyrics frequently told stories that illustrated various kinds of societal problems, and the meaning of the lyrics was much more important to folk listeners than the musical prowess of the folksinger, or his or her good looks. No matter how accurate such a description might be of folk-music culture during the original folk song movement (1935–48), it is clear that much of the untutored quality of folksingers and their audiences during the later folk revival period (1958–65) was studied and self-conscious. To the college-age people who were drawn to it, a big part of folk culture's appeal was its break with the norms of middle-class life. The music itself was in many cases not so new to these young people; they had been humming and strumming folk tunes on camping trips and in public school music classes almost all their lives. Its democratic ethos, combined with seriousness of purpose and its cultural distinctions from adult culture, made folk music very popular on college campuses by the turn of

The Kingston Trio—(from left) Bob Shane, Dave Guard, and Nick Reynolds—at a recording session. The group was the most popular one in the "folk revival" of the late '50s and early '60s. Their first album, The Kingston Trio (1958), stayed on the pop album charts for 195 weeks.

the decade. One index of the popularity of folk is the steep increase in the number of acoustic guitars that were sold in the United States about this time—it must have seemed as if collegiate folkniks were popping up all across the country. And the great thing about folk music was that, equipped with a passable singing voice and the ability to strum a few easy guitar chords, almost anyone could play it, and this reinforced the idea that folk was "for the people and by the people."

The rise of folk in pop was preceded by a brief fascination with calypso music. Harry Belafonte's "Jamaica Farewell" (p14, 1957) and "Banana Boat (Day-O)" (p5, 1957) are the best examples of this easygoing, soft pop style with Caribbean folk inflections that seemed exotic at the time. Inspired by a Pete Seeger performance they heard while auditioning in a San Francisco club, Dave Guard, Bob Shane, and Nick Reynolds began performing folk to collegiate audiences while adopting a name inspired by Belafonte's Jamaican-drenched hits. The Kingston Trio's version of the traditional "Tom Dula"—which they called "Tom Dooley"—began to climb the pop charts in late 1958, hitting number one in early 1959 and initiating the folk revival in the mainstream pop market. This track serves as a representative example of the group's easygoing and polished approach, with a carefully scripted verbal introduction to the tune followed by an elegant arrangement. The Kingston's Trio's pop-sensitive approach to folk proved to be a winner; during 1958–65 the group placed ten singles in the pop Top 40, all of which were recorded for the Los Angeles–based Capitol label, including "Where Have All the Flowers Gone" (p21, 1962) and "Reverend Mr. Black" (p8, 1963). While pop singles give us some picture of an artists' success in the youth market, a better measure of pop success for folk artists among adults and college students is album sales. Long-playing 33-rpm records were only a secondary concern for teen-oriented pop acts, but they were the primary format for two other more "serious" styles of music at the time: jazz and classical. It suited the cultural aspirations of folk listeners to be part of the more sophisticated, album-buying—as opposed to singles-buying—public. The Kingston Trio had a series of nineteen Top 40 albums through 1964, with thirteen of these reaching the Top 10 (five of these hit number one). The group's first album, *The Kingston Trio* (1958), stayed on the pop album charts for 195 weeks. In the first few years of the 1960s, the Kingston Trio were among the most consistently successful acts in popular music and in many ways defined what folk music was in the perception of most general listeners.

In the years that followed the first hit records of the Kingston Trio, two sides of the folk revival developed. Listeners interested in folk's roots and tradition began exploring the rich literature of folk that had already begun to be documented by musicologists and folklorists such as Charles Seeger and Alan Lomax in the preceding decades. Singers such as Joan Baez and Bob Dylan emerged from that side of the folk revival and were popular and respected among the folkniks; neither had a hit single during this period, though each charted Top 40 albums. To the discriminating fan of folk, singers like Baez and Dylan were the real thing. The Kingston Trio, and other groups that followed in their wake such as the Highwaymen ("Michael Row the Boat Ashore"; p1, 1961), the Rooftop

Singers ("Walk Right In"; p1, 1963), and the New Christy Minstrels ("Green Green"; p14, 1963), were seen as pop-music imitators who paled by comparison. Even groups that had successful albums but no hit singles, such as the Chad Mitchell Trio or the Limelighters, were not exempt from such criticism. However much the most uncompromising folk fans may have disparaged the Kingston Trio and other commercially successful folk groups, by music-business standards these acts were enormously successful and many within the business did all they could to stoke the fire that was now burning under folk music.

Formed in New York's Greenwich Village in 1961, the group known as Peter, Paul, and Mary eventually eclipsed the Kingston Trio as the most successful folk-pop group of the 1960s. After the success of "Lemon Tree" (p35, 1962), they followed up with "If I Had a Hammer" (p10, 1962), "Puff the Magic Dragon" (p2, 1962), and a cover of Bob Dylan's "Blowin' in the Wind" (p2, 1963). The group released ten Top 40 albums during the decade; two hit number one, while the first album, *Peter, Paul, and Mary* (1962), stayed on the album charts for 185 weeks. The members of the group all had different backgrounds in music: Peter Yarrow had been a solo folk artist, Paul Stookey had previously played in a rock and roll band, and Mary Travers had sung in the chorus of an

---

LISTENING GUIDE

GET MUSIC ▶▶ wwnorton.com/rockhistory

The Kingston Trio, "Tom Dooley"

Words and music by Frank Warner, John Lomax, and Alan Lomax, produced by Voile Gillmore. Reached #1 on the pop charts in 1959.

FORM: Simple verse-chorus, beginning with the chorus. The entire song repeats the same 8-bar music for verses and choruses. The verses are presented the same way each time, with the lead vocal supported by two-part backups. The chorus is presented first in unison (all three voices sing the same notes), then in three-part harmony, and then in a more complicated arrangement for three voices that introduces a new melody over the chorus melody. To end, the last 2 bars of the chorus are repeated three times, a technique often used to close out a tune and called a "tag."

TIME SIGNATURE: 12/8, a gently rolling four-beat feel.

INSTRUMENTATION: Acoustic guitar, banjo, acoustic bass, lead vocal, and two backup vocals.

0:00–0:28	**Introduction**, 16 mm.	Spoken introduction, banjo plays melody.
0:28–0:46	**Chorus**, 8 mm.	Choral unison vocal, strummed rhythm kicks in, "Hang down your head . . ."

unsuccessful Broadway musical. While he was a full-fledged folkie, at the time the group formed Yarrow was working as a stand-up comic and Travers was just getting back into singing. Manager Albert Grossman was responsible for bringing the three together, and the idea from the start was to capitalize on the folk revival ignited by the Kingston Trio. This was not a group formed to tour small coffeehouses and perform for the sheer joy of sharing the message of the music: Peter, Paul, and Mary were assembled in a manner that did not differ much from the way other pop acts of those years were assembled. One might suspect that an act born of such music-business calculating would be rejected within the folk community, which often made a show of denouncing commercialism. But even though part of their fame rested on slick pop-flavored cover versions of Bob Dylan originals, Peter, Paul, and Mary were mostly well received by die-hard folkniks, perhaps owing to their strong commitment to the civil rights protest movement.

A comparison of Peter, Paul, and Mary's version of "Blowin' in the Wind" with Dylan's shows clearly that Dylan makes no concessions to pop sensibilities. While the Peter, Paul, and Mary version is professionally sung, played, and arranged (by Milton Okun)—all this increasing its likelihood of appealing

0:46–1:01	**Verse 1**, 8 mm.	Solo vocal w/ backup vocals, "I met her on the mountain . . ."
1:01–1:16	**Chorus**, 8 mm.	Three-part harmony vocal introduced, "Hang down your head . . "
1:16–1:32	**Verse 2**, 8 mm.	Solo vocal w/ backups as before, "This time tomorrow . . . Tennessee."
1:32–1:47	**Chorus**, 8 mm.	Energetic new solo melody against two-part harmony, music gets much louder, "Hang down your head . . ."
1:47–2:02	**Chorus**, 8 mm.	New texture continues, "Hang down your head . . ."
2:02–2:17	**Verse 3**, 8 mm.	Music gets quiet again, solo vocal w/ backups as before, "This time tomorrow . . . tree."
2:17–2:32	**Chorus**, 8 mm.	Three-part harmony vocal as in first chorus presentation, "Hang down your head . . ."
2:32–3:00	**Chorus**, 14 mm.	Music gets louder, energetic 8-bar chorus is extended by tag.

to a pop audience—Dylan's version, in stark contrast, was never going to be heard on pop radio. To pop sensibilities of the time, Dylan's performance would have seemed too rough and amateurish (the very qualities the folkies embraced). Of course, such perceptions of Dylan's marketability would change dramatically later in the decade when American folk rock emerged as a response to the music of the Beatles and other British bands, but that will be considered in more detail in Chapter 5. For now, it is enough to point out that folk's image of sincerity and authenticity—as it was perceived by pop audiences in the early 1960s mostly through the tremendous success of the Kingston Trio and Peter, Paul, and Mary—was largely a construction of the music industry. Like the old adage—"sincerity: if you can fake that you've got it made"—folk performers worked carefully at projecting a homespun image. This parallels the "construction of authenticity" discussed in Chapter 1 regarding the development of the *Grand Ole Opry* and the country music business. To a significant degree, such constructions of authenticity bear out the notion that no matter what a performer does in the music business, he or she is always still part of the entertainment business. Even if a performer actually is sincere and homespun in his or her everyday personal manner, it will never be enough to simply show up and be oneself; these qualities must be projected from the stage, and most performers have to learn how to do this. The issue of authenticity will return in later chapters, since later rock musicians (the singer-songwriters especially) used the perceived authenticity of the folk revival as a model of artistic integrity.

Peter, Paul, and Mary—(from left) Mary Travers, Paul Stookey, and Peter Yarrow—were constructed not for the small coffeehouses that had been the traditional home of folk, but for the larger concert halls of rock. Though their music was decidedly more polished than many folk artists', even die-hard folkniks embraced Peter, Paul, and Mary—mostly because of their passionate involvement in the civil rights movement.

It is surprising to see the striking similarities between folk music and Brill Building pop; these styles were indeed two faces of the same music business in the early 1960s, each carefully crafted to appeal to a distinct age group within the youth culture. The images of the two styles contrasted strongly—pop was superficial and cute, folk was serious minded and intellectually engaged—but the business mechanisms that marketed the music were often the same. Both Brill Building pop and folk were strikingly polite in comparison with much of the music of the first wave of rock and roll, and much of this family orientation can be attributed to the control being exercised within the music business during those years. The music-business pros had gained control of the business again, and the music clearly reflected that. Later in the decade artists would begin to exert far more muscle; but for now, pop and folk remained relatively safe and pleasant.

Ambitious Pop: The Rise of the Producer

Many who defend the music of the early 1960s often cite the rise of producers such as Leiber and Stoller and Phil Spector, and the music they produced, as evidence for the accomplishment of those years. To understand this aspect of early 1960s music, we need to take a closer look at just what a "producer" is. During the first years of rock and roll, many of the first wave of performers brought fully worked-up songs and arrangements into the recording studio. Sometimes, as in the case of Presley and Boone, a number of songs were tried out before the best ones were chosen, and less often, as with Chuck Berry and Buddy Holly, the songs were written by the artist. Often these artists had a strong voice in the recording process, deciding what would be recorded and how the arrangement would go. In mainstream pop, by contrast, artists had for years used songs written by professional songwriters and arrangements done by professional arrangers. The record company employed A&R (artists and repertoire) men whose job was to organize and coordinate the various professionals involved in making the record, including hiring the musicians who played on the tracks; this was an early version of the record producer. The mainstream pop approach put more of the crucial decision-making authority in the hands of the A&R man, leaving the artists relatively powerless in some cases. Buddy Holly's unsuccessful sessions for Decca, for instance, were the casualty of an A&R man who had no feel for Holly's strengths and weaknesses. As the business took greater control of rock and roll, the model employed in mainstream pop increasingly became the norm for making rock and roll records. But as this aspect of the business was changing, the role of the A&R man/producer was also shifting, and the role of record producer began to develop. Replacing the mostly organizational role of the label's A&R man, the producer became a specialist in charge of shaping the sound of the record, from details of arranging to fine points in the recording process. In some cases, the record became the result of the producer's vision rather than that of the artist or songwriter; in most cases, it was the producer, not the performing artists, who was responsible to the record company for how a record turned out.

The first important production team was Jerry Leiber and Mike Stoller, and their success with a variety of artists was imitated by others such as Carole King and Gerry Goffin, Shadow Morton, and, perhaps most important, Phil Spector. As the role of the producer in pop developed, there was also parallel growth in the ambition with which song ideas were executed; producers increasingly experimented with ways to make their records more sophisticated musically, some establishing a trademark "sound" that distinguished a particular producer's record. Drawing from classical music and musical theater, as well as from the sounds available only in the recording studio, productions of early 1960s teen pop records initiated an important shift away from the idea that a record is a live performance that has been recorded (as it had been until then) to the idea that a record is a kind of performance in its own right. This increased focus on the recording studio and the sounds it could produce would continue to resonate in almost all the rock music that followed, establishing an approach to recording that the Beach Boys and the Beatles would adopt and extend later in the decade.

Leiber and Stoller with the Coasters and Ben E. King with the Drifters. Jerry Leiber and Mike Stoller initially made their mark as the most important songwriting team in rock and roll music during the period before 1956–64. In 1956, Elvis Presley's version of their song "Hound Dog" went to number one, prompting the team to write more music for Presley to record, including "Jailhouse Rock" (p1, 1957) and "Don't" (p1, 1958). Leiber and Stoller, however, had roots in the west coast rhythm and blues scene and had enjoyed hits on the R&B charts such as Charles Brown's "Hard Times" (r7, 1952), Big Mama Thornton's original version of "Hound Dog" (r1, 1953), and the Robins's "Smokin' Joe's Cafe" (r10, 1955) before crossing over with Presley's record. Almost from the beginning, Leiber and Stoller wanted more control over the recording process than songwriters were typically allowed. In 1953, they formed their own label based in Los Angeles, Spark Records, and began "producing" their songs in what would soon become the standard sense of the term. The pair has often said, "We don't write songs, we write records," and with this approach the recording artists' task became more a matter of realizing the concept for the song that Leiber and Stoller had devised than of finding their own personal expressive interpretation of the tune. In many ways, Leiber and Stoller already had a clear idea of how the record should sound before the performers entered the studio.

Leiber and Stoller had already produced three rhythm and blues hits with the Robins on Spark when they got an offer to produce records for Atlantic. The songwriting duo had found the business end of running an independent label unrewarding, so they welcomed the chance to move to a bigger label and leave the bookkeeping chores behind. The business arrangement they made with Atlantic was exceptional for its time: rather than become A&R men working exclusively for the label, as was the industry norm, Leiber and Stoller retained the right to work with other artists and labels if they chose to, making them among the first independent producers in pop music. They had had great success working with the Robins and wanted to take the group with them to Atlantic. Dissension within the group over the move caused only two members to go with Leiber and Stoller. Two new members were added and the new group was called the Coasters; this group became the focus of Leiber and Stoller's most creative work over the next several years.

Mike Stoller (left) and Jerry Leiber (right) helped to define the important role producers would play in the music of the early 1960s. Their songs were characterized by strong rhythm and blues influences and complex arrangements, often recounting mini-dramas (called "playlets") for example, as in "Smokin' Joe's Cafe" and "Down in Mexico."

The Coasters recorded "playlets": short, songs that told an often-humorous story. In writing for the Coasters, Leiber and Stoller were inspired by Broadway and radio play traditions. As Jerry Leiber has remarked, the very first song they wrote for the Coasters, "Riot in Cell Block #9," was inspired by a radio show called *Gangbusters*. The group would frequently act these tunes out in performance, sometimes using costumes, and in this context the similarity to the Broadway stage is evident. A few of these records deal with teen life, not unlike the songs of Chuck Berry or the Everly Brothers or Ricky Nelson, discussed later in this chapter. Of these, "Yakety Yak" (p1, 1958)—about household chores and teenage disputes with parents—and "Charlie Brown" (p2, 1959)—about a kid who always gets in trouble at school—were the most popular. Mostly, however, the Coasters' playlets dealt with topics in black culture and were directed at a black audience (even if they also became popular with white audiences). Original Coasters member Carl Gardner has marveled at how these two white songwriters so expertly captured aspects of black culture. Leiber and Stoller responded, "We thought we were black—we were wrong, but that's what we thought."

The Coasters were important collaborators with Leiber and Stoller. This team produced a number of hits, including the playlets "Smokin' Joe's Cafe" (when the Coasters were still the Robins) and "Down in Mexico."

"Smokin' Joe's Cafe" and "Down in Mexico" are good early examples of playlets by the Coasters. "Smokin' Joe's Cafe" was recorded when the Coasters were still the Robins, and was initially released on Spark in 1955. After Leiber and Stoller signed with Atlantic, the song was released on the subsidiary Atco and rose to number ten on the rhythm and blues charts (but only as far as number seventy-nine on the pop charts). The lyrics proceed in an AABA formal pattern: two verses develop the story, a bridge brings the action to a climax, and a return of the verse forms a kind of epilogue. In this case, the singer is sitting in Smokin' Joe's Cafe when a sexy woman sits next to him and starts to flirt very suggestively. Other patrons warn him about the woman's jealous boyfriend just as the boyfriend emerges from the kitchen, wielding a knife and telling the singer to finish his meal and get out. In the last verse the singer explains how he'll never go into that cafe again. "Down in Mexico" reached number eight on the rhythm and blues charts in 1956 but missed the pop charts entirely. This song takes the barroom action south of the border; in the first two verses, we hear about a "honky tonk, down in Mexico." At this Mexican bar, there's a guy named Joe who works there and "wears a red bandana" and "plays a blues piana." The bridge narrates how a sexily clad dancer enters the bar to the accompaniment of Joe's piano playing; she grabs the singer and dances with him, doing "a dance I never saw before." The last verse advises the listener to visit the bar if ever in the neighborhood. Both of these

The Coasters, "Down in Mexico"

Words and music by Jerry Leiber and Mike Stoller, produced by Leiber and Stoller. Reached #8 on the rhythm and blues charts in 1956.

FORM: AABA form. Each 16-bar verse is divided into an 8-bar section with lyrics that change from verse to verse, and a section beginning with the lyrics "He wears a red bandana" that are repeated in each verse. Such a section with repeated lyrics occurring at the end of a verse is called a "refrain," and refrains may be found in AABA, simple verse, or verse-chorus forms, though most refrains are not as lengthy as this one. The bridge repeats a 2-bar section eight times, building to the song's comic punch line. Note the dramatic introduction and the spoken fade-out, both of which heighten the comedy of this classic playlet.

TIME SIGNATURE: 4/4. There are three distinct latin-tinged feels on this track, one with the first half of the verse, another with the second half of the verse (refrain), and a third with the bridge. These changes of feel are unusual in pop music of the time, and reinforce the influence of Broadway stage numbers, in which such changes are common.

INSTRUMENTATION: Piano, bass, electric guitar, nylon-string guitar, percussion, lead and backup vocals. Mike Stoller plays piano on this (and most) Coasters tracks. Famous jazz guitarist Barney Kessel plays guitar on this track.

0:00–0:21	**Introduction**, 6 mm., 2 mm.	Rubato (sax and guitar), and then 4 mm. in time to begin sultry latin feel.
0:21–0:57	**A-Verse 1 w/refrain**, 16 mm., 8 mm. verse + 8 mm. refrain	The verse uses the sultry latin feel, while the refrain uses a brighter latin feel employing nylon-string guitar and castanets, "Down in . . ."
0:57–1:32	**A-Verse 2 w/refrain**,	As before, "The first time . . ."
1:32–2:06	**B-Bridge**, 16 mm., eight 2 mm. phrases	Employing a more violent latin feel to suggest sensual dance show, building to the song's dynamic high point, "All of a sudden . . ."
2:06–3:13	**A-Verse 3 w/refrain**, 16 mm.	As before, then fade on intro material, "If you're . . ."

songs are clear extensions of the hokem blues discussed in Chapter 1 in connection with Big Joe Turner's "Shake, Rattle, and Roll," and seduction and seductive strippers were hardly the kind of thing that would sell to white listeners in the mid 1950s. "Down in Mexico" is interesting because Leiber and Stoller's production makes the south-of-the-border theme more vivid through the use of Mexican sounding nylon-string guitars and percussion. The bridge is sung to music the dancer might have performed to, a kind of latin striptease music with emphasis on the conga drums.

As unsuited as these two early playlets might have been for white radio, it is interesting to compare them to "Little Egypt (Ying Yang)," a number sixteen rhythm and blues hit that reached number twenty-three on the pop charts. Here the Mexican scene is shifted to a carnival, and the seductress is a belly dancer. The first two verses describe this dancer, Little Egypt, who wears "nothing but a button and a bow" and does "the hootchie-kootchie real slow." The bridge pulls back from being too suggestive, describing instead an acrobatic performance during which she reveals a picture of a cowboy tattooed on her back. The last verse says that Little Egypt no longer dances because now she and the singer are married and she is busy taking care of their seven children. The final verse also features the singing of high, speeded up voices (similar to those of Alvin and the Chipmunks from the same period), meant to be those of the children, and creating an almost irresistible comic effect. Despite its clear connections to songs with a more adult theme, this playlet represents both literally and figuratively a domestication of the topic and thus serves as another instance of the changes needed for crossover to be possible for rhythm and blues. Like the Chuck Berry lyrics discussed in Chapter 2, Leiber and Stoller's lyrics can also be read on more than one level. "What About Us" from 1959 (r17, p47) is a thinly veiled comment on racial inequality. "Run Red Run" hit number thirty-six on the pop charts in early 1960 (r29) and tells the story of a monkey whose owner, Red, teaches him how to play poker. When the monkey learns to play, he also learns that Red has been cheating him. The monkey grabs a gun and chases Red until he catches him, takes his keys, watch, hat, and suit, and heads back into town. While the lyrics seem to focus the listener's attention on the comedy of a man being chased around town by a gun-toting monkey, the deeper message addresses the exploitation of blacks in American culture. Leiber and Stoller claim to have many more socially motivated songs that were never recorded, partly because the Coasters were not interested in becoming controversial.

The Important Collaboration between Songwriter/Producers and Performers.
Leiber and Stoller had considerable control over their records with the Coasters, though group members were free to change things or reject entire numbers they didn't like. Many aspects of the arrangements were composed in advance. Stoller, who was trained as a classical composer, even wrote out many of the saxophone lines played by King Curtis that became so closely associated with the pop hits "Yakety Yak," "Charlie Brown," and "Along Came Jones" (p9, 1959). As important as the unprecedented degree of control that Leiber and Stoller exercised in producing these records was the close and long-lasting relationship the

duo formed with the Coasters; both were essential elements in the success of those records.

In composing playlets such as "Smokin' Joe's Cafe," "Down in Mexico," "Shoppin' for Clothes," and "Little Egypt," Leiber and Stoller drew from a broad range of music styles, often blending these within a single track. In 1959 they recorded "There Goes My Baby" with the Drifters (featuring Ben E. King at the time) and the song's arrangement employed the orchestra in a manner reminiscent of classical music. This blending of easygoing rhythm and blues with orchestral backing would soon be dubbed "sweet soul" and will be discussed in more detail later in this chapter. Such a stylistic blending was unusual for its time, prompting Atlantic's Jerry Wexler to remark that "There Goes My Baby" sounded like a radio stuck between two stations.

Taking on Social Issues.   Leiber and Stoller had shown that rock and roll could aspire to greater sophistication: their playlets were carefully crafted to tell a story, and their arrangements employed elements drawn from a wide range of styles. This would seem to make girl-group music a poor prospect for ambitious production, focused as it is in most cases on teen love. But as it turns out, some of the most ambitious pop music during this time came from girl-group records. One of the first records to approach a subject that might have been considered provocative was the Shirelles' "Will You Still Love Me Tomorrow?" (p1, 1960). Produced by Aldon's Carole King and Gerry Goffin (two young songwriter/producers very influenced by Leiber and Stoller), this song dealt with a topic many teenage girls were likely to face during the course of their dating: whether or not engage in sexual intimacy. While such a topic seems mild by today's standards, in 1960—just as payola and the struggle against the negative influences of rock and roll were beginning to subside—lyrics dealing with teenage sex posed a commercial risk. But King was especially dedicated to this song, at one point taking the mallets and playing the tympani part herself when the professional percussionist could not get it just the way she heard it. Becoming a number one hit that further fueled the public's enthusiasm for girl-group music, the song addressed the topic with enough thoughtful sensitivity to quell any parental fears. With its serious-minded lyrics and orchestral accompaniment, the song extended the ambition of Leiber and Stoller's productions.

Producers in the Brill Building: The Rise of the Girl Groups.   By the late 1950s Leiber and Stoller's approach to record production had spread throughout the music business. At Aldon Music, the songwriting teams of Neil Sedaka and Howie Greenfield and Carole King and Gerry Goffin began making demonstration records of their songs (demos), and these records were sometimes so nicely done that they were released without even being re-recorded. Like Leiber and Stoller were doing, other Brill Building songwriting teams such as Cynthia Weil and Barry Mann and Jeff Berry and Ellie Greenwich were increasingly in the studio directing the recording process. By the early 1960s, many of the groups they were directing were female vocal groups, often referred to as "girl groups." The Chantels, Shirelles, Crystals, Chiffons, Cookies, Dixie Cups, and Ronettes were among the many girl groups that came and went during the first half of the 1960s. These groups were mostly made up of black teenagers with little professional experience (there were some exceptions; Claudine Clark was a singer who had an undergraduate degree in music composition and wrote much of her own music). A few groups used one male (the Exciters) or were made up of white teens (the Angels). Girl groups provided a performance and an image to go with the song, but in most cases the crucial musical decisions were made by the producer at the session; as a result, the performing talent, as with the teen idols discussed above, was almost completely interchangeable. Girls were regularly changed out between recordings and tours and sometimes, as in the case of the Crystals, the entire group could be replaced.

Female singers had not been completely absent from teen pop before the girl groups; Connie Francis enjoyed a string of thirty-nine hit records during the 1958–64 period (including Neil Sedaka and Howie Greenfield's "Stupid Cupid," which hit number fourteen in 1958), while Connie Stevens ("Kookie, Kookie [Lend Me Your Comb]"; p4, 1959) and Annette Funicello ("Tall Paul"; p7, 1959) had Top 10 hits as well. These singers were more or less the female counterparts to the male teen idols. After 1960, many female solo singers such as Little Eva ("The Loco-Motion"; p1, 1962), Mary Wells ("My Guy"; p1, 1964), and Leslie Gore ("It's My Party"; p1, 1963) fit well into the girl-group stylistic category, since most of their records featured backup vocals and thus differed from girl-group records only in terms of image. This easy crossing of the stylistic border between teen-idol and girl-group music underscores the principal similarity between the styles: the Brill Building approach.

More that any other style of music discussed in this chapter, girl-group music was dominated by the music industry's drive to control the music; there was no way a performer could rock the boat, since so little depended on her in most cases. The creative control had shifted from the performer (who, to the

The Brill Building approach to music-making involved strong, long-lasting song-writing teams including Carole King (left) and Gerry Goffin (right), pictured here with another young singer/songwriter, Paul Simon (center). Strongly influenced by Leiber and Stoller, King and Goffin exerted a lot of control over the production of their songs.

public at least, still seemed to be important) to the producers and songwriters (who worked behind the scenes with multiple groups, often having more than one record on the charts at the same time). However much rock and roll purists might distain this system, it was tremendously successful. During 1960–65, girl groups were responsible for dozens of hit records, including the Shirelles' "Will You Still Love Me Tomorrow?" (p1, 1960) and "Soldier Boy" (p1, 1962), the Crystals' "He's a Rebel" (p1, 1962), the Chiffons' "He's So Fine" (p1, 1963) and "One Fine Day" (p5, 1963), the Angels' "My Boyfriend's Back" (p1, 1963), and the Dixie Cups' "Chapel of Love" (p1, 1964).

Phil Spector and the Wall of Sound. The most ambitious producer of the early 1960s, and the most important producer of girl-group pop, was Phil Spector. While still a teenager, he had a number one hit as both a performer and songwriter with the Teddy Bears in 1958. The idea for the song, "To Know Him Is to Love Him," is reported to have come from the inscription on Spector's father's gravestone. Having had a taste of national success but unable to repeat it with subsequent releases, Spector came to New York to work under Leiber and Stoller, helping at sessions and undoubtedly learning a lot about how to produce records. More than any other aspiring producer during the early 1960s, Spector demanded total control of the recording process; and while it took him a while to achieve such control, when he did, he developed an approach to production that he called "the Wall of Sound." Spector wanted his records to have a signature sound. Most groups, of course, have a distinct sonic identity, often resulting from the singing voices involved. But for Spector, the group was not the star of the record; the production was the star. Spector's trademark sound came from recording an enormous number of instruments in a relatively small space. Often several guitars, pianos, basses, and drum sets would be crammed

Phil Spector defined the role of the dominant producer. He ferociously controlled his music—the songwriting and production. Spector was also an innovator in recording techniques. His "Wall of Sound" was built by packing many instruments into a small room and recording them as they all played together. Notice the four guitarists at this recording session.

into one room at Gold Star Studios in Los Angeles; the sound from one instrument would spill into the microphone of the next, and all of this would be mixed together into a monophonic backing track. Like the ingredients in a fine sauce, the idea was for a single sonic "taste" to emerge that could not easily be broken down into its component parts. Vocals were layered over this mono backing track, with strings added to finish it off (see Interlude 3 for a fuller technical discussion of the Wall of Sound).

The most important Wall of Sound hits are the Crystals' "Da Doo Ron Ron" (p3, 1963) and "Then He Kissed Me" (p6, 1963), featuring the lead vocals of Darlene Love, and the Ronettes' "Be My Baby" (p2, 1963), featuring Veronica Bennett (later to become Ronnie Spector). In addition to their great popularity, these Wall of Sound records also made an enormous impression on others in the music business. As a producer, Spector was characterized as an eccentric genius who followed nothing but his own artistic impulses in creating innovative and ambitious records. The comparisons to great classical composers and conductors abounded; Spector referred to these singles as "teenage symphonies" while others characterized him as a Wagner-like figure (a reference to the German opera composer, Richard Wagner). The fact that Spector had blended the instruments into a single timbral entity made the records almost impossible to cover and added to the mystery of Spector's technique. In the face of the British invasion in early 1964, Spector continued to have hits, though by the end of the year the girl-group sound in which he played such a crucial role began to fade. In late 1964, however, Spector had yet another production innovation up his sleeve; the Righteous Brothers' "You've Lost That Lovin' Feelin'," written by Jeff Barry, Ellie Greenwich, and Spector, was the result. Topping the pop charts in early 1965, the record was longer and more musically ambitious than anything Spector had tried up to that point. After two statements of the verse and chorus sections, the music moves into a bridge section with a contrasting rhythmic feel. In pop music of the time, to change the feel of a tune like this was considered unwise; it delays the return of the chorus and could prevent listeners from remembering. Barry, Greenwich, and Spector may have had similar middle sections from Coasters records in mind when they wrote this tune, and in any event the gamble paid off as the record became enormously successful.

Girl-group pop in the early 1960s might be thought of as a study in opposites: it was blatantly commercial as the songs were written to recipe by pros who tried almost cynically to project a kind of "wholesome" teen lifestyle, much as can be found in teen-idol records. In the hands of producers such as Carole King and Phil Spector, however, girl-group records became perhaps the most artistically ambitious music that rock and roll had yet produced. As innocent and frivolous as some of these records seemed at the time, many would have a lasting impact on the music that followed: the ambitious experimentation that became so characteristic of psychedelic rock of the later 1960s can be traced directly back to groups like the Shirelles and the Ronettes, and we will follow this story in the chapters that follow. The innovations of Leiber and Stoller had many consequences, however, and a parallel one to ambitious girl-group records was the development of a gentler style of black pop called sweet soul.

Sweet Soul on the Rise

Leiber and Stoller at Atlantic. The blending of rhythm and blues with strings that occurs on "There Goes My Baby" served as the prototype for a new and softer approach to black pop that turned out to have tremendous crossover potential. Working with the Drifters as well as with Ben E. King, Leiber and Stoller produced a long series of hits through 1964 in a style that came to be called "sweet soul." In addition to the rhythm and blues and rock and roll artists we have discussed thus far, other black singers had already appeared regularly on the pop charts since the mid 1950s. Nat King Cole scored a number of soft-pop hits, including "Send for Me" (p6, 1957) and "Looking Back" (p5, 1958). Johnny Mathis was also a familiar artist on the pop Top 40, with such releases as "It's Not for Me to Say" (p5, 1957), "Chances Are" (p1, 1957), and "Misty" (p12, 1959). Neither of these singers were rock and rollers, since they tended to record easy-listening pop ballads in much the same way as other mainstream-pop song stylists of the era such as Al Martino, Eddie Fisher, and Dean Martin. It would also be difficult to find much rhythm and blues influence in their music. Singing in a light pop style that *did* have marked elements of black music was Sam Cooke, who placed twenty-nine singles in the pop Top 40 during 1957–65, including "You Send Me" (p1, 1957), "Wonderful World" (p12, 1960), "Chain Gang" (p2, 1960), "Twistin' the Night Away" (another twist record; p9, 1962), and "Another Saturday Night" (p10, 1963).

Cooke came to the pop side of the business from gospel, where he had sung with the Soul Stirrers. Ray Charles had a number two rhythm and blues hit in 1955 by setting a gospel tune to secular lyrics with "I Got a Woman"; he went on to have a number of important hits, surprising many in the music business with pop and country and western influenced records such as "Georgia on My Mind" (p1, 1960), "Hit the Road Jack" (p1, 1961), and "I Can't Stop Loving You" (p1, 1962). With the success of "I Got a Woman," record companies began looking to promising and even successful gospel artists as potential rhythm and blues hit-makers. These gospel artists were deeply conflicted about turning to pop, since gospel was "the Lord's music," while many considered pop the Devil's music. Many rhythm and blues singers had backgrounds singing in the church, but these singers already had careers in gospel that would likely be ruined by making a pop record. Because of this, Cooke's first record was released under the name Dale Cooke, to test his marketability without adversely affecting his gospel reputation. What Cooke brought to pop from gospel was a clear tenor voice and a penchant for frequent melodic embellishment that often sounded improvisatory.

Sam Cooke at a recording session. Like many artists, including Ray Charles, Cooke was strongly influenced by gospel. Cooke combined this sensibility with a sweet soul style to make a sound all his own. After a string of hits, including "You Send Me," Cooke's career came to a tragic end when he was shot at a motel in 1964.

The influence of Cooke's signing can be found throughout Ben E. King's performance on "There Goes My Baby," especially in the melodic passages in the higher range of his baritone voice.

During the mid 1950s, the Drifters were one of the most successful vocal groups on the Atlantic roster. At first featuring Clyde McPhatter, the group scored a series of rhythm and blues hits. By 1958, however, the Drifters were floundering and Atlantic Records was reluctant to let the group dissolve since the name had become so strongly associated with a string of hits. Manager George Treadwell found another vocal group, the Crowns, to take over as the Drifters. In fact, the Drifters and the Crowns appeared together on the same bill at the Apollo in Harlem one evening in 1958, after which the Crowns became the Drifters. To rebuild the group's career, Atlantic brought in Leiber and Stoller to produce; "There Goes My Baby" was the first fruit of this new combination, followed by a string of hits, including "Save the Last Dance for Me" (p1, 1960) with King singing lead, "Up on the Roof" (p5, 1962) and "On Broadway" (p9, 1963) with Rudy Lewis singing lead ("On Broadway" features an uncredited electric guitar solo by Phil Spector). Atlantic staff producer Bert Berns took over from Leiber and Stoller in 1963; his "Under the Boardwalk" reached number four in 1964 with Johnny Moore on lead vocals.

Ben E. King was fired from the Drifters in May 1960, reportedly because he complained to Treadwell that the members of the group were not being paid enough to live on, despite their chart success. Leiber and Stoller quickly stepped in and offered to produce King as a solo act for Atlantic. At the first session King recorded four tracks, "Spanish Harlem," "First Taste of Love," Young Boy Blues," and at the last minute, a song King wrote himself called "Stand by Me." Out of this first session, both "Spanish Harlem" (p10, 1961) and "Stand by Me" (p4, 1961) reached the pop Top 10, initiating a series of five Top 40 hits in 1961–63 period. (In yet another instance of the interconnectedness of figures and styles in the early 1960s, "Spanish Harlem" was written by Jerry Leiber and Phil Spector because Mike Stoller was out of town one weekend.) Taken together, the music of the Drifters and Ben E. King established sweet soul as a style characterized by a fluid lead vocal melody often supported by doo-wop backup vocals, counter melodies in the strings, and a rhythm section laying down a medium-tempo beat, sometimes influenced by latin music (remember that Harry Belafonte had just had a couple of hits employing a calypso sound).

After the first few successful records from the Drifters, others had hits with similarly styled releases. Jerry Butler scored with "He Will Break Your Heart" (p7, 1960) and "Find Another Girl" (p27, 1961), while Chuck Jackson hit with "I Don't Want to Cry" (p36, 1961) and "Any Day Now (My Wild Beautiful Bird)" (p23, 1962). While the string of hits from the Drifters and Ben E. King was mostly over by the end of 1964, other artists took some of the elements of sweet soul into the British invasion years and beyond. Pop song-stylist Dionne Warwick was first noticed by composer Burt Bacharach while singing backup at a Drifters session; she became the most important performer of Burt Bacharach-Hal David songs, hitting the charts in 1964 with "Anyone Who Had a Heart" (p8) and "Walk On By" (p6)—two of many hits that would follow. Motown artists were also influenced by sweet soul, while rhythm and blues

singers with a more strongly pronounced gospel element—such as Solomon Burke, Otis Redding, and Wilson Pickett—emerged early in the 1960s and paved the way for soul music later in the decade. The story of Motown and southern soul is covered in Chapter 6.

Rockabilly Popsters

While Brill Building pop in one form or another tended to dominate pop music in the early 1960s, other styles vied for the public's attention as well. We have already seen how folk defined itself in opposition to the commercialism of Brill Building offerings, even if in many ways folk paralleled teen pop in its careful construction and marketing of its anti-commercial image. Rockabilly is not usually associated closely with Brill Building pop, perhaps because the style is seen to have its roots in the south, far away from big cities like New York and Philadelphia. But the development of rockabilly after the fall of the first wave is very much influenced by Brill Building practices, as the wilder music of early Elvis, Carl Perkins, and Jerry Lee Lewis became the sweeter country-inflected pop of the Everly Brothers, Roy Orbison, and Ricky Nelson. The development of rockabilly does not divide up into neat chronological divisions. In the last chapter we discussed Elvis Presley, Carl Perkins, Jerry Lee Lewis, and Buddy Holly, and the music of the Everly Brothers, Roy Orbison, and Ricky Nelson overlaps significantly with that of these other artists during the 1957–59 period. But by 1959, Presley, Perkins, Lewis, and Holly were no longer playing a role in rockabilly, while the Everlys and Nelson continued to develop without losing a step on the pop charts, and Roy Orbison began to make his mark only in 1960. There is thus a kind of dovetailing between these two groups of musicians, as well as a general stylistic tendency of the second group of artists to soften the rockabilly sound by incorporating a more marked pop component, under the general influence of the Brill Building approach. Especially after 1958 and perhaps in reaction to the controversy that began to swirl around the principal figures and the payola scandal, this second group of rockabilly popsters seemed eager to please a teen audience without offending parents or other authorities in any way.

The Everly Brothers perform for children at the Hudson Guild Neighborhood House in New York City, 1957. The Everly Brothers used lush harmonies, combining them with elements of country to create a sweet, seemingly simple vocal sound. Their hits include the up-tempo "Bye Bye Love" and the smoother ballad "All I Have to Do Is Dream."

The Everly Brothers. Coming from a strong background in traditional country music of the southeast—their father Ike was a professional musician who had the brothers performing together from an early age—the Everly Brothers' easygoing rockabilly sound emerged in 1957 when their first single for the New York-based independent Cadence label, "Bye Bye Love," raced up all three charts. Like Carl Perkins's "Blue Suede Shoes" and Elvis Presley's "Heartbreak Hotel," "Bye Bye Love" reached the Top 10 on each chart, hitting number one on the country and western chart, number two on the pop charts, and number five on the rhythm and blues charts. The duo had signed with Columbia in 1955 but they were dropped after only one release; they were then rejected by a number of labels, until their manager Wesley Rose (an important song publisher in Nashville whose father had managed Hank Williams) convinced Archie Bleyer at Cadence to sign the brothers in 1957, even though Bleyer had declined the chance to do so the previous year. After their hit with "Bye Bye Love," the Everlys went on to score fifteen additional Top 40 hit singles on Cadence through 1960, and seven more after switching to Warner Brothers through 1964.

Don and Phil Everly each wrote songs, some of which were hits; Don wrote "('Til) I Kissed You" (p4, 1959), "Cathy's Clown" (p1, 1960), and "So Sad (to Watch Good Love Go Bad)" (p7, 1960), while Phil wrote "When Will I Be Loved" (p8, 1960), which was later covered by Linda Ronstadt (p2, 1975). But in the first few years of their success, the Everlys depended on the well-crafted songs of Boudleaux and Felice Bryant and the backup of top Nashville studio musicians under the production of Bleyer. The Everly Brothers released a consistent stream of hits under this system, two of which went to number one on all three charts ("Wake Up, Little Susie" and "All I Have to Do Is Dream" in 1957), while "Bird Dog" hit number two on the rhythm and blues chart in 1958 and reached the top slot in the two others. The country influence can be readily heard in the earlier hits, where the energetic strumming on jumbo acoustic guitars by both brothers provides the rhythmic drive. Both "Bye Bye Love" and "Wake Up, Little Susie" reveal the influence of rhythm and blues in their respective guitar introductions, played here—as in much Everly Brothers music—not on the electric guitars that can be heard on Chuck Berry or Buddy Holly's recordings, but rather on the steel-string acoustic guitar. The lyrics address teenage love life, the best example of which is "Wake Up, Little Susie," which deals with a young couple who go to a drive-in and fall asleep during the movie; waking up after the movie is concluded, they worry that their reputations will be shot, since their parents will likely suspect them of having been involved in sexual activity.

The most distinctive feature of the Everly Brothers' music is the duet singing of Don and Phil. The songs are often sung by the two of them in harmony throughout, their voices tending toward the high end of the male vocal range and using a relatively straight tone, free of vibrato. Arguably their best duet singing occurs on "All I Have to Do Is Dream," a soft ballad that the brothers treat with a gentle touch, blending their voices in close-knit harmony in a very controlled manner. This high, light vocal quality not only gives their music its distinctive sound, but was also very influential on later artists, especially the Beatles, Simon and Garfunkel, and the Hollies. A number of Everly Brothers tunes seem to resonate through the early singing of John Lennon and Paul McCartney, especially "Cathy's Clown" and "So Sad (to Watch Good Love Go Bad)." The Everlys' tendency toward a generally softer style brought a more pronounced mainstream-pop influence to rockabilly. Unlike the recordings that Jerry Lee Lewis was making for Sun at about the time of the Everlys' first chart success and much more like the teen-idol music discussed above, one never gets the sense that there is anything dangerous or slightly out of control about the music.

Roy Orbison.   Hailing from Wink, Texas, Roy Orbison toured the west Texas region with the Wink Westerners before ending up at the University of North Texas (called North Texas State at the time) as a fellow student of Pat Boone. Orbison's first release, "Ooby Dooby," was written by two of his North Texas school buddies and was chosen because it was a crowd favorite with Orbison's band. The song was initially recorded in Fort Worth by Columbia (which rejected it) and then again by Norman Petty in Clovis (this second version was released on Je-Wel). On the advice of Johnny Cash, Orbison sent the record to Sam Phillips at Sun, who subsequently re-recorded and released it in 1956. None of Orbison's Sun releases were significant hits ("Ooby Dooby" reached number 59), nor were the ones he did in the late 1950s for RCA with Chet Atkins producing. Orbison then signed with a new independent label, Monument, and released "Only the Lonely (Know How I Feel)," which rose as high as number two in 1960. Orbison followed with a string of nineteen hit records for Monument through 1965, including "Running Scared" (p1, 1961), "Crying" (p2, 1961), "Dream Baby (How Long Must I Dream)" (p4, 1962), "In Dreams" (p7, 1963), and his biggest hit, "Oh, Pretty Woman," which occupied the number one slot for three weeks in the fall of 1964 during the middle of the Beatles-led British invasion.

Roy Orbison in concert. While usually associated with rockabilly, Orbison's music spans a range of influences and styles: country and western ("Ooby Dooby" and "Rockhouse"), doo-wop (in Orbison's trademark use of falsetto), pure pop ballads ("Runnin' Scared" and "Crying") and rhythm and blues ("Candy Man" and "Mean Woman Blues").

Like Buddy Holly, Orbison wrote most of his own material and the style of this music ranges broadly. Orbison's "Ooby Dooby" and "Rockhouse" singles for Sun are squarely in the up-tempo, country-influenced rockabilly style of Presley and Perkins. With his Monument releases, however, Orbison's west Texas roots in country and western are less perceptible, replaced with a haunting ballad singing style that features both Elvis-like low chest singing and frequent and almost operatic passages in which Orbison flips into his falsetto voice. The verses of "Oh, Pretty Woman"—beginning "Pretty woman, walkin' down the street"—offer a nice example of the lower, Presley-esque delivery; the "mercy" and growl that follow are reminiscent of Presley's mannerisms in "Don't Be Cruel." The stop-time sections of "Only the Lonely (Know How I Feel)" provide a good example of Orbison's characteristic and singular use of his higher, falsetto voice; in the second verse, after delivering a pair of lines in his chest voice and beginning with the lyrics "Maybe tomorrow," Orbison builds to the song's expressive climax on the words "but that's the chance you gotta take." Orbison's trademark use of falsetto voice is an adaptation of doo-wop practice, and the backup vocals—da da da dum diddly do wah—are clearly derived from doo-wop and help make the stylistic derivation clear. Orbison's next two hits, "Blue Angel" (p9, 1960) and "I'm Hurtin'" (p27, 1960), follow the same general pattern, using the standard pop practice of succeeding a hit with another record that is very similar. The follow-ups to these, "Runnin' Scared" and "Crying," are by contrast pure pop ballads without a hint of doo-wop backups; Orbison's delivery, however, is very similar, building to a dramatic climax in each case. "Candy Man" (p25, 1961) is straight rhythm and blues, as is "Mean Woman Blues" (p5, 1963). Roy Orbison's vocal style influenced several later rockers, among them Bruce Springsteen; his songs have been covered in well-known versions by artists as diverse as Linda Ronstadt ("Blue Bayou"; p3, 1977) and Van Halen ("Oh, Pretty Woman"; p12, 1982).

LISTENING GUIDE   GET MUSIC ▶▶   wwnorton.com/rockhistory

Roy Orbison, "Only the Lonely (Know How I Feel)"

Words and music by Roy Orbison and Joe Melson, produced by Fred Foster. Reached #2 on the pop charts in 1960.

FORM: Derived from AABA form, this song is a special formal instance. The first 11-bar verse takes the place of the first two A-section verses usually found in AABA forms, and is followed by an 8-bar B-section bridge, before a return to the A-section verse, here 6 bars in length. The first 11-bar verse is tricky to count, since Orbison flips the regular accent on beat one over to beat three to create bars of 2/4 time. If you keep counting in four, however, everything will work out, though you may feel you are off for a couple of measures. A 10-bar interlude connects up the two presentations of this special AABA-derived form, and this music is taken directly from the Introduction. The second time through the structure is similar to the first time through, except that the end of the bridge is much more dramatic, and the return to the verse is shorter and more connected to the bridge melodically and lyrically than it was before.

TIME SIGNATURE: This song in 4/4 throughout, though there are measures of 2/4 created in the verse sections. You may challenge yourself to see if you can place the measures of 2/4 and create a metric scheme that makes the entire verse section count out cleanly.

INSTRUMENTATION: Piano, bass, electric guitar, acoustic guitar, orchestral strings, vibraphone, lead and backup vocals.

Ricky Nelson. In many ways, Ricky Nelson's music during 1957–64 draws together a number of issues that have been discussed thus far. Eric Hilliard Nelson was the son of bandleader Ozzie Nelson and singer Harriet Hilliard. He played himself in the Ozzie and Harriet radio show from 1949 on, moving with the show to television in 1952. Inspired by his girlfriend's enthusiasm for Elvis, a seventeen-year-old Nelson boasted that he was also making a record. Father Ozzie was quickly convinced of the commercial possibilities of Ricky singing rock. Nelson's first single was a cover version of Fats Domino's "I'm Walkin'," which went to number four in 1957, followed by the other side of the record, "A Teenager's Romance" which climbed even higher to the number two slot. Suspecting that there would be problems collecting royalties from the Verve label on which these hits appeared, Ozzie signed Ricky to the Los Angeles–based Imperial (ironically, Fats Domino's label). Starting with "BeBop Baby" (p3, 1957), Nelson scored a series of twenty-six Top 40 singles for Imperial through 1962, and a few more after switching to Decca. Growing up in a family of professional musicians, Nelson had a knack for singing from the very start of his career. That singing career was launched through exposure on

0:00–0:21	**Introduction**, 10 mm.	Doo-wop style backup vocals, "Dum dum dum . . ."
0:21–0:43	**Verse 1**, 11 mm.	Lead vocal enters, backups continue, "Only the lonely . . ."
0:43–0:59	**Bridge**, 8 mm.	Dramatic solo vocal with stop-time string orchestra and vibraphone chords to add musical emphasis, "There goes my baby . . ."
0:59–1:11	**Verse**, 6 mm.	Added string melody in dialogue with lead vocal, "But only the lonely . . ."
1:11–1:30	**Interlude**, 10 mm.	Repeat of introduction, "Dum dum dum . . ."
1:30–1:52	**Verse 2**, 11 mm.	As before, "Only the lonely . . ."
1:52–2:14	**Bridge**, 8 mm.	Solo vocal with stop-time chords as before, but now driving to the song's dramatic high point on highest vocal notes, "Maybe tomorrow . . ."
2:14–2:24	**Verse**, 4 mm.	Tempo resumes to end, "if your lonely heart breaks . . ."

the popular television show, where he sang regularly after enjoying his first chart success. And his good looks and clean-cut image made him one of the first teen idols.

Musically, Nelson's records are well crafted. He did not write his own music and thus depended on songwriters for material, especially Baker Knight, Johnny Burnette, and Dorsey Burnette. He often used some of the same musicians on his records that Elvis did during his RCA period, with guitarist James Burton featured on lead guitar in most cases (Burton would later play in Presley's band). The Presley influence is clear on Nelson's "Stood Up" (p2, 1957), "Believe What You Say" (Johnny and Dorsey Burnette; p4, 1958), and "Just a Little Too Much" (Johnny Burnette; p9, 1959); they sound quite a bit like Elvis's up-tempo rockers on RCA like "Too Much," "All Shook Up," and "Teddy Bear," all of which antedate Nelson's first hit for Imperial. Nelson's "Lonesome Town" (Baker Knight; p7, 1958) seems to draw on "Heartbreak Hotel" (which is "down at the end of lonely street") for its lyrics and "Love Me Tender" for its gentle acoustic ballad style. Gene Vincent's "BeBop a Lula" may have been the initial inspiration for "BeBop Baby," though Nelson's record is bouncier and has none of Vincent's swagger. The lyrics and vocal delivery of Nelson's "Waitin' in School" (Johnny and Dorsey Burnette; p18, 1958), dealing with going through the school day in anticipation of dancing later, seem inspired by Chuck Berry's "School Day"; the lyrics and vocal delivery on the chorus ("one-two, buckle my shoe, three-four, get out on the floor") are reminiscent of Bill Haley's "Rock Around the Clock." The lyrics to "It's Late" (Dorsey Burnette; p9, 1959) deal with the singer's getting in trouble for bringing his girlfriend home too late and parallels the Everly Brothers' "Wake Up, Little Susie," which deals with the same topic. Far from being overly derivative, however, Ricky Nelson's music emerges as a rich product of its times. Stylistically, Nelson combines the pop rockabilly approach of the Everly Brothers with the good-boy image of Pat Boone to imitate the music of Elvis Presley.

In the development of rockabilly music in the early 1960s, we can clearly see the influence of Brill Building practice, perhaps resembling the teen idols more than the girl groups. But we can also see a distinct and mostly unbroken connection with the first wave of rock and roll. The Everly Brothers and Ricky Nelson were as much continuations of Elvis and Carl Perkins as they were parallels to Frankie Avalon and Fabian. Unlike the teen idols, rockabilly artists sometimes wrote their own music, though they depended on professional songwriters for hits at times as well. Maybe the best way to view these later rockabillies is as a more controlled and polite extension of the first wave of southern rockers, filtering the original rockabilly sound through a Brill Building sensibility.

Surfin' USA: It's Just Good, Clean, White-Suburban Fun

The Beach Boys, Jan and Dean, and Vocal Surf Music. Aside from a handful of labels that were based in Los Angeles (majors MGM and Capitol and indies Modern, Imperial, and Specialty), most of the music business that was creating rock music in the first half of the 1960s was east of the Mississippi (and most of that in New York and Philadelphia). Elvis and a few other teen idols were in Hollywood making movies, and Ricky Nelson was in southern California as well, but with *American Bandstand* broadcasting from Philadelphia and many of the songwriters and producers headquartered in the Brill Building in Manhattan, California was in many ways a long way from the pop-music action. This may explain why the influences that came together in the Beach Boys' music seem so eclectic. Growing up in suburban Los Angeles in the late 1950s, this quintet of three brothers, a cousin, and a high school friend were influenced by both black doo-wop groups and mainstream white vocal groups like the Four Freshmen, and as much by Chuck Berry's driving rock and roll as by Phil Spector's Wall of Sound. Along with their fellow Los Angelinos Jan and Dean, the Beach Boys created a style of music that seemed devoted to the ideal teenage world of summer fun: surf music.

The Beach Boys first enjoyed success in late 1961 with a regional hit single, "Surfin'," written by group leader Brian Wilson and released on the small Candix label. The group then signed with Capitol in 1962 and soon began releasing a series of Top 40 hits—twenty-six by the end of the decade—including "Surfin' Safari" (p14, 1962), "Surfin' U.S.A." (p3, 1963), "Surfer Girl" (p7, 1963), "Be True to Your School" (p6, 1963), and "Fun, Fun, Fun" (p5, 1964). While the British invasion was taking American pop by storm in the first half of 1964, the Beach Boys enjoyed their first number one hit, "I Get Around," the B-side of which, "Don't Worry Baby," also rose as high as number twenty-four. The tremendous popularity of the Beatles only made Wilson and the Beach Boys work that much harder, and while we will take up that aspect of the group's music in Chapter 5, note that in the years between the Beatles' arrival in the United States and the release of their *Sgt. Pepper's Lonely Hearts Club Band* in the summer of 1967, the Beach Boys had fourteen Top 40 singles, ten of which were in the Top 10 and two of which hit number one.

In 1961–64, the Beach Boys' music held fairly close to the same surf-music formula that was followed as well by Jan and Dean. Song lyrics are usually about three topics: cars, girls, or surfing; at times lighthearted (as in Jan and Dean's 1964 number-three hit, "Little Old Lady from Pasadena," which tells the story of a hot-rod granny), the lyrics hardly ever deal with adult sexuality. The vocals seem to draw in equal parts from doo-wop, girl group, and glee-club traditions, with some vocal jazz elements perceptible from time to time. The instrumental

The Beach Boys—(from left) Al Jardine, Carl Wilson, Dennis Wilson, Brian Wilson, and Mike Love—performing on television. While the Beach Boys' music seems like simple, catchy pop, their harmonies and arrangements were very complex. Influenced by Phil Spector, Brian Wilson wrote and produced many of the Beach Boys' songs, and like Spector, Wilson was an innovator of recording techniques.

accompaniments lean heavily on Chuck Berry's music. In fact, "Surfin' U.S.A." is an obvious reworking of Berry's "Sweet Little Sixteen," and consequently Berry sued the group for copyright infringement (most copies of this song currently list the songwriters as Berry/Wilson). Nevertheless, the song is a good example of the band's early surf style. Wilson's new lyrics list all the hot surf spots in southern California, while the back-up vocals alternate between "ooo" and "inside, outside, U.S.A.," all sung in multivoice harmony. Wilson's ringing falsetto on "Everybody's gone surfin'" provides the song's hook, while the

---

🎧 **LISTENING GUIDE**　　　　　　　GET MUSIC ▶▶ | wwnorton.com/rockhistory

The Beach Boys, "Surfin' U.S.A."

Words and music by Brian Wilson and Chuck Berry, produced by Nik Venet. Reached #3 on the pop charts in 1963. Based on Chuck Berry's "Sweet Little Sixteen."

FORM: Simple verse form. Each verse ends with the refrain "surfin' U.S.A.," though verses 2 and 4 feature the high falsetto "everybody's gone surfin'," making these verses seem to function like choruses, even though they are not actually choruses. The song ends with an instrumental verse shared by organ and guitar; the refrain here is sung as in verse 2 and 4, with a tag made up of four repetitions of the refrain.

TIME SIGNATURE: 4/4, with stops during verses 1 and 3. Note the constant bass drum during stops.

INSTRUMENTATION: Electric guitars, bass, drums, organ, lead and backup vocals.

0:00–0:03	**Introduction**, 4 mm.	Chuck Berry–style guitar intro, note the heavy reverb.
0:03–0:27	**Verse 1 w/refrain**, 16 mm.	Lead vocal with "oo" backups; note the stop time with bass drum beats that continue, "If everybody had an ocean . . ."
0:27–0:50	**Verse 2 w/refrain**, 16 mm.	Backup vocals sing lyrics as lead vocal continues, band plays in regular time to add rhythmic drive, "You can catch 'em at Del Mar . . ."
0:50–1:15	**Verse 3 w/refrain**, 16 mm.	As verse 1, in stop time, "We'll all be plannin' out a route . . ."
1:15–1:39	**Verse 4 w/refrain**, 16 mm.	As verse 2, regular time, "At Haggarty's and Swami's . . ."
1:39–2:04	**Instrumental Verse w/ refrain**, 16 mm.	Organ solo, guitar solo, and then sung refrain.
2:04–2:24	**Tag (refrain)**, 16 mm.	Repeat of refrain and fade.

instrumental solos provide a slice of early 1960s beach music, featuring a very "electronic" organ followed by a clean, Berry-esque electric guitar solo soaked in electronic reverb.

As formulaic as these early singles can often be, the Beach Boys were also capable of great musical subtlety and sophistication; the slow ballads "Surfer Girl" and "In My Room" are elegant Wilson compositions that, despite their teen themes, are compositionally innovative and reveal the group's prowess as a vocal ensemble. Jan and Dean also had a series of surf-music hits; in addition to "Little Old Lady from Pasadena," the duo hit with "Surf City" (co-written by Brian Wilson; p1, 1963), "Honolulu Lulu" (p11, 1963), "Drag City" (p10, 1963), and "Ride the Wild Surf" (p16, 1964). An important element in the Beach Boys' success was the writing and production of Brian Wilson. While initially the band were assigned a producer by the label in what was then typical music-business fashion, Brian soon demanded that he produce the records. Under the strong influence of Phil Spector's most ambitious records, Brian worked to create the biggest recorded sound for the band that he could muster, increasingly emphasizing innovation. Wilson's records with the Beach Boys are a clear continuation of the ambitious producer story this chapter has been tracing, though his most creative and ambitious work would not be done until 1965 and 1966.

Dick Dale, King of the Surf Guitar. While the Beach Boys and Jan and Dean were placing one single after another on the Top 40 charts, there was also another side to southern California surf music. Dick Dale and the Del-Tones pioneered a style of guitar-based surf music that produced a handful of hits for as many groups. While only one of the Beach Boys (Dennis Wilson) ever spent any time surfing, Dale's music grew straight out of the surf culture; Dale has described routinely coming in from the beach, drying off, and then stepping directly onstage to play. Dick Dale and the Del-tones' "Misirlou" (1962) features his trademark rapid tremolo picking on the guitar, set to a tune that had been a Greek pop standard in the 1940s and a quick tempo emphasizing a rock rhythmic feel. His "Let's Go Tripping" hit number sixty in 1961 (two months before the Beach Boys' first single) and was very popular on the west coast. Dale's tendency to slide his hand down the guitar strings (from high to low) while picking rapidly created a sound he thought was similar to the sound of a wave as it crashes around a surfer. That trademark sound can be heard in introduction to the Chantay's instrumental hit, "Pipeline" (p4, 1963). Other instrumental surf hits were the Duals' "Stick Shift" (p25, 1961) and the Surfaris' "Wipe Out" (p2, 1963).

Duane Eddy, the Ventures. While Dale and the surfers developed the guitar-band instrumental, in many ways they were building on the success of guitarist Duane Eddy, whose "Rebel Rouser" hit number six in 1958 and was followed by a series of instrumental hits through 1962. Eddy's distinctively twangy guitar records inspired the Seattle-based Ventures, who hit number two with their "Walk, Don't Run" in 1960. Driven by two guitars, bass, and drums, the group placed five hits in the Top 40 by 1964. It is some measure of how much the music business had changed in the fifteen years since the end of World War II that instrumental records by Dale, Eddy, and the Ventures in the early 1960s could be considered a novelty. During the Big Band era, many records were instrumental, and often when singing did occur, it was secondary to the playing of the band. The rise of the singers, led by Sinatra, had changed all that, and most rock and roll focused on vocal performances. In the period after 1964, however, increased attention would be given to instrumental playing, as young guitarists, inspired by electric blues and jazz, would make accomplished instrumental playing as much a feature of rock music as the vocals.

Baby, Baby, Baby: A Case Study in Record Production

"There Goes My Baby."   One of the central ideas this chapter has presented is that, during the 1959–64 period, the role of the record producer became increasingly important to rock music. To further illustrate this, we will consider three songs that provide a chronological sense of how production developed over this period. Leiber and Stoller were the most important producers in the early stages of this development; since we have already considered their work with the Coasters in some detail, we turn now to their important 1959 hit for the Drifters, "There Goes My Baby." While the song was written by Ben E. King (aka Benjamin Nelson), it is credited to Benjamin Nelson, Lover Patterson, George Treadwell, Jerry Leiber, and Mike Stoller. With the deals that were typically made on publishing rights, it is possible that none of the others were involved in the song's composition but were credited as part of the compensation for their services. At any rate, it is certain that the lead singer is Ben E. King and the record hit number one on the rhythm and blues charts (number two on the pop charts) in the summer of 1959. As mentioned earlier, fellow producer Jerry Wexler was so confused by the sound of the record at first that he thought it sounded like a radio stuck between two different stations. This comes from the fact that orchestral strings had not been used on rhythm and blues records much before this song was released, and the classically oriented strings combined with a relatively square-cut doo-wop introduction would have seemed incongruous to many listeners.

The track begins with a male vocal-harmony passage led by the bass, who sings a pattern outlining a chord progression common to much doo-wop (I–vi–IV–V). But set against this are tympani, followed by an ascending flourish from the strings (actually four violins and a cello, according to Mike Stoller). Finally King enters with the chorus, as his melody is accompanied not only by the rest of the Drifters but also by a counter melody played by the violins. When King gets to the verse lyrics, "I want to know, did she love me," the strings introduce a melodic figure with resonances of nineteenth-century orchestral music (perhaps Russian composers Borodin or Rimsky-Korsakov) in a call-and-answer exchange that sounds like it could have come from the gospel tradition. This track encapsulates well the eclectic musical influences that fed Leiber and Stoller's songwriting and producing. As a classically trained musician, Stoller was now drawing from that element; and since both partners were eager to try new things within the context of rhythm and blues music, this likely seemed no more risky to them than doing a playlet about a stripper. It is questionable whether many other producers could have gotten away with releasing such a record at the time; by 1959, however, Leiber and Stoller had an established record of success to back them up, giving them the influence needed to get the track issued. As discussed below, this record not only influenced the history of record production, but it also became the prototype for a new style of black pop: sweet soul.

"Be My Baby."   By the time Phil Spector began work in Los Angeles' Gold Star Studios in the summer of 1963, the Leiber and Stoller approach to record production had found its way into most early 1960 musical styles. Having apprenticed under the duo, Spector had already gone on to develop his Wall of Sound approach, with the Crystals' "Da Doo Ron Ron" and "Then He Kissed Me" enjoying great success. Written along with Jeff Barry and Ellie Greenwich, "Be My Baby" would feature a new group of singers—the Ronettes—led by the distinctive voice of Ronnie Bennett. As with almost all his Gold Star sessions, Spector utilized a cast of Los Angeles' top studio musicians, nicknamed the Wrecking Crew and often including drummer Hal Blaine, pianist Leon Russell, bassists Larry Knechtel and Carole Kaye, and guitarists Glen Campbell and Barney Kessel. The recording was done on a three-track machine that allowed each track to be recorded separately; the usual procedure was to record the guitars, basses, pianos, and percussion on the first track, record all vocals on the second track, and add the strings last on the third track. This three-track version was then mixed down to the mono version that would appear on the record. By the time "Be My Baby" was recorded, Spector had developed a reputation as a perfectionist, asking for multiple playbacks and re-recording until the sound was just as he imagined it in his head. This method made for some tremendously successful records that were also, however, very expensive to make.

From the opening moments, the contrasts with "There Goes My Baby" are clear. In the place of tympani, we instead get a heavy drumbeat from Blaine, delivered with plenty of reverberation that establishes a bigness of aural space. Bennett delivers the first two lines of the verse to the accompaniment of the rhythm section; at the lyrics "So won't you say you love me," the background vocals enter along with the low saxophone, and build to the chorus ("Be my baby"), in which the sound opens up as Bennett's lead vocal is set in call and response to the backup vocals and the drum beat changes to create a sense of greater forward drive. After a return to the verse, the second chorus adds another brick to the Wall of Sound by bringing in the strings, which then take the melody for the abbreviated third verse. After this, the entire ensemble plays out two statements of the chorus, interrupted only by Blaine's drumbeat from the introduction, before beginning the fade-out. The form is simple (see Interlude 1) and the song is short (less than three minutes). But somehow the track created an aural impression of grandness of scale that made it stand out from the rest of what was on the radio at the time.

The Drifters, "There Goes My Baby"

Words and music by Benjamin Nelson, Lover Patterson, and George Treadwell, produced by Jerry Leiber and Mike Stoller. Reached #1 on the rhythm and blues charts and #2 on the pop charts in 1959.

FORM: Simple verse-chorus. The same 8-bar pattern is used for the entire song, underpinning the introduction, verses, and chorus. The song begins typically enough, with a doo-wop inflected vocal intro, two verses, and a chorus. Verse 4 introduces what sounds like an improvised verse over a melodic figure in the cellos that might have been borrowed from a classical composer (Stoller has suggested the line resembles Rimsky-Korsakov). The rest of the song continues to create this impression of improvising over the repeated 8-bar progression, with the background vocals from the introduction returning, as well as the chorus, before the song fades out.

TIME SIGNATURE: 12/8.

INSTRUMENTATION: Acoustic guitar, electric guitar, bass, tympani, orchestral strings, lead and backup vocals.

0:00–0:15	**Introduction**, 8 mm.	Doo-wop vocals led by bass voice.
0:15–0:30	**Verse 1**, 8 mm.	Lead vocal enters, along with backing string melody, "There goes my baby . . ."
0:30–0:45	**Verse 2**, 8 mm.	String melody continues, backup vocals enter, "I broke her heart . . ."
0:45–0:59	**Chorus**, 8 mm.	Main melody sung in backup vocals, with lead vocal improvising over top, "There goes my baby . . ."
0:59–1:14	**Verse 4**, 8 mm.	Classical-style cellos enter, improvised lead vocal melody, tympani can be heard clearly in this section, "I want to know . . ."
1:14–1:29	**Verse 5**, 8 mm.	Cellos continue, backup vocals added, "I wonder why . . ."
1:29–1:44	**Verse 6**, 8 mm.	String melody replaces cellos, no backup vocals, "I was going to tell her . . ."
1:44–1:59	**Verse/Intro**, 8 mm.	String melody continues, backup vocals reenter, "Where am I . . ."
1:59–2:08	**Chorus**, 8 mm.	Backup vocals take melody as before, lead vocal improvises over top, "There goes my baby . . ."

The Ronettes, "Be My Baby"

Words and music by Phil Spector, Ellie Greenwich, and Jeff Barry, produced by Phil Spector. Reached #1 on the pop charts in 1963.

FORM: Contrasting verse-chorus; verses and choruses employ different music. Note how verse 1 builds, starting with only the lead vocal for the first 8 bars, then adding backup vocals and saxes for the second 8 bars, and finally bringing all the instruments and vocals in for the chorus, which is clearly the "hook"—that part of the song that sticks in the listener's memory. Verse 2 pulls back again, but not all the way back to the level of verse 1, before building to the chorus. The orchestral strings take the melody in the instrumental verse, though only the first 8 bars are used before breaking into the chorus again. Just when it seems like there's not much more the tune can do, Spector brings back the catchy drum intro, and launches once more into the chorus and the track then fades out.

TIME SIGNATURE: 4/4. Note the way hand claps and percussion are used to build excitement and drive toward the chorus.

INSTRUMENTATION: Piano, bass, electric guitar, drums, horns, orchestral strings, percussion, hand claps, lead and backup vocals.

0:00–0:08	**Introduction**, 4 mm.	2 mm. drum intro and then 2 mm. in time. Note the heavy reverb on the drums.
0:08–0:37	**Verse 1**, 16 mm.	Solo vocal in first 8 mm., then backup vocals; saxes added in second 8 mm., "The night we met . . ."
0:37–0:52	**Chorus**, 8 mm.	Lead and backup vocals, this is the song's hook, "Be my baby"
0:52–1:22	**Verse 2**, 16 mm.	Mostly as before, though first 8 mm. are fuller than before, "I'll make you happy . . ."
1:22–1:37	**Chorus**, 8 mm.	As before, "Be my baby . . ."
1:37–1:52	**Instrumental Verse** (partial), 8 mm.	Violins play first half of melody with vocal backups.
1:52–2:07	**Chorus**, 8 mm.	As before, "Be my baby . . ."
2:07–2:10	**Reprise of intro**, 2 mm.	Drum intro returns to re-launch the chorus.
2:10–2:25	**Chorus**, 8 mm.	As before, with lead vocals improvising over top.
2:25–2:36	**Chorus**, 8 mm.	As before, with fade-out.

"Don't Worry Baby."   Describing the first time he heard "Be My Baby" on the radio, Brian Wilson recalls that while he was fascinated by the first verse, he was so captivated by the chorus that he had to pull his car over to avoid an accident. Wilson's enthusiasm for the Ronettes/Spector record was so great that, together with Los Angeles disc jockey Roger Christian (who is mostly responsible for the lyrics), he wrote a song especially for the Ronettes to record. When Spector rejected Wilson's "Don't Worry Baby," Wilson and the Beach Boys recorded it; it hit number twenty-four in the summer of 1964. Wilson's song is modeled closely on "Be My Baby," featuring a similar form and series of chord progressions. The similarity can be heard right from the start, as the tune begins with a drumbeat strongly reminiscent of the one that begins the Spector tune. This beat is played by Hal Blaine who with other members of the Wrecking Crew provided the instrumental accompaniment on this record. After Wilson sings the first two lines of the verse, the backup vocals enter on the third line at the lyrics "but she looks in my eyes," building the texture to drive toward the chorus, where Wilson's voice and the backup vocals take up a call and response—all of this in direct imitation of "Be My Baby."

There are some differences between the songs; "Don't Worry Baby" does not use strings and is not a girl-group number. Rather than dealing with romantic longing as in "Be My Baby," Christian's lyrics describe the singer's reluctant involvement in a drag race. As Wilson tells the story, he was concerned he would never be able to equal Spector's achievement and his wife reassured him with the phrase, "Don't worry, baby." Perhaps the drag race described in "Don't Worry Baby" is a metaphor for Wilson's sense of competition with Spector. In any case, "Don't Worry Baby" is closely related to "Be My Baby," and through it, to Leiber and Stoller's "There Goes My Baby." The bass vocal part in the chorus of "Don't Worry Baby" further enforces the Leiber and Stoller connection, as it clearly refers to doo-wop stylistically and resembles the part at the beginning of "There Goes My Baby."

Narrative Lyrics Run Amok: The Splatter Platter

Teenage Romanticization of Death.   The 1959–64 period saw the release of a number of songs dramatically portraying teenage death. Most of these records are maudlin at best and downright tasteless at worst. Mark Dinning's "Teen Angel" (p1, 1960), for instance, tells the story of a young couple whose car stalls on the railroad tracks just as a train is approaching. They escape the car, but the girl goes back to the car to retrieve the boy's class ring and is killed. The song is cast as a prayer by the boy to the girl, who is now a "teen angel." Similarly gruesome and hyper-melodramatic stories were taken up by Ray Peterson's "Tell Laura I Love Her" (p7, 1960), the Everly Brothers' "Ebony Eyes" (p8, 1961), and J. Frank Wilson and the Cavaliers' "Last Kiss" (p2, 1964). Perhaps the most infamous of these records—sometimes called "death disks" or "splatter platters"—is the Shangri-Las' "Leader of the Pack." One might expect that such records only warrant a brief mention in a study of the era, but splatter platters are far more emblematic of teen pop during the early 1960s than they first appear. To understand how these strange records, especially "Leader of the Pack," pull together a number of threads we have been following in this chapter, it is important to know a bit about the history of the song and the people involved in making and releasing the record.

In perhaps the first move that spelled the end of the the Brill Building domination of teen pop, the publishing firm Aldon Music was sold to Columbia Pictures-Screen Gems in the summer of 1963 (at about the same time that the Beatles were enjoying their first overwhelming success in England). Founder Don Kirshner joined the corporation, running its Colpix label, while Al Nevins was hired as a consultant (we will hear from Kirschner and some of his Brill Building associates again in Chapter 5). At about the same time, Leiber, Stoller, and George Goldner founded Red Bird Records (one reason that Leiber and Stoller turned production of the Drifters over to Berns was to concentrate more energy on developing the new label). Jeff Barry and Ellie Greenwich had begun writing and producing for Red Bird, having a number one hit in 1964 with the Dixie Cups' "Chapel of Love," a song they had written with Spector and which he had recorded with both the Crystals and the Ronettes but never released. An old acquaintance of Greenwich's, George "Shadow" Morton, worked with Barry and Greenwich on a new single by the Shangri-Las, "I Remember (Walking in the Sand)," which was released on Red Bird and rose to number thirteen in August of 1964. The three then began writing the follow-up, "Leader of the Pack," produced by Barry and Morton.

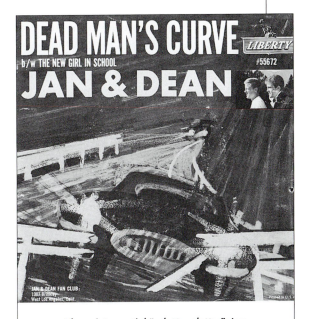

True to the death-disk genre, "Leader of the Pack" chronicles the untimely demise of a teenager, in this case a motorcycle hoodlum named Johnny (paralleling Marlon Brando's character in *The Wild One*). Johnny's violent motorbike death is represented by taped crash sounds and screams, a feature that caused some consternation among parents. This girl-group splatter platter is perhaps best viewed as a death-disk playlet. The involvement of Leiber and Stoller further underscores this; the verses set up the middle section, which provides the climax (the bike crash), and a final verse offers an epilogue. Also, the sound-effect technique was employed earlier, in their first Coasters single, "Riot in Cell Block #9" (released as the Robins on Spark), featured taped guns and police siren noises to represent the jailbreak. In a strange way, "Leader of the Pack" brings the Leiber and Stoller story back to where it began, incorporating a number of events that happened in their careers. "Leader of the Pack" would be among the last records to come out of the Brill Building

The quintessential "splatter platter": Jan and Dean's "Dead Man's Curve." "Splatter platters" or "death disks" told the stories of teenagers meeting gruesome deaths, usually at the hands of a car or motorcycle crash. These records reveal the strong storytelling style of Leiber and Stoller productions.

establishment, since by 1964 the British invasion had arrived on American shores, causing yet another shake-up of the American popular-music business.

A far more tragic epilogue to the splatter-platter genre is the true story of Jan and Dean. In 1964 Jan and Dan also had a teenage tragedy hit, "Dead Man's Curve," which rose to number eight. The song chronicles a car crash on a stretch of road so treacherous that it has earned the nickname "dead man's curve." On April 19, 1966, Jan Berry was involved in an auto accident in which three passengers were killed and he was critically injured, effectively ending his career.

As mentioned at the beginning of this chapter, the period between the first wave of rock and roll and the arrival of the Beatles is viewed by some as a period of decline—a kind of "dark ages" in rock history—while others see it as an important era filled with a lot of great music. For those who champion early 1960s pop, the British invasion was an unfortunate turn of events that snuffed out a number of pop styles prematurely and before they were allowed to blossom fully. For those who view the early 1960s as dark days, Brill Building pop was rock and roll with all its vitality removed, cynically neutered for crass commercial purposes. Whatever position one takes, it is clear that these years saw the music business gain control of a youth market that was cultivated during the first wave. Almost no aspect of pop during the early 1960s was completely immune from the influence of Brill Building practices, which were in themselves merely a return to the practices that had dominated mainstream pop before rock emerged in the mid 1950s. If teens generally thought the new, more controlled pop constituted a demise, they certainly did not abandon pop music as a result. With business booming, it must therefore have seemed enormously frustrating to the music-business establishment to experience once again a serious challenge to their control of youth music: just when they thought they had it all figured out, a band arrived from England in February 1964 and radically changed the business.

Questions for Discussion and Review

1. How does the Brill Building approach to teen pop differ from the approach found in rock and roll of the 1955–59 period?
2. How many different styles came out of the Brill Building songwriters and producers? Which styles discussed in this chapter seem at first to have little connection to Brill Building practices?
3. What does a record producer do, and how did producers get increasingly ambitious during the early 1960s? Who are the most important producers?
4. Why did folk music appeal to college-age listeners?
5. How did rockabilly develop in the early 1960s? In what ways does it reflect its roots in the first wave of rock and roll, while also evincing the influence of Brill Building practices?
6. What are some important influences on surf music?

Alan Betrock, *Girl Groups: The Story of a Sound* (Delilah Books, 1982).

Hal Blaine with David Goggin, *Hal Blaine and the Wrecking Crew: The Story of the World's Most Recorded Musician* (MixBooks, 1993).

Robert Cantwell, *When We Were Good: The Folk Revival* (Harvard University Press, 1996).

John A. Jackson, *American Bandstand: Dick Clark and the Making of a Rock 'n' Roll Empire* (Oxford University Press, 1997).

Mark Ribowsky, *He's a Rebel: The Truth about Phil Spector—Rock and Roll's Legendary Madman* (E. P. Dutton, 1989).

Ronnie Spector with Vince Waldron, *Be My Baby* (HarperCollins, 1990).

Timothy White, *The Nearest Faraway Place: Brian Wilson, The Beach Boys, and the Southern California Experience* (Henry Holt, 1994).

Brian Wilson with Todd Gold, *Wouldn't It Be Nice? My Own Story* (HarperCollins, 1991).

THE DEMISE OF ROCK AND THE PROMISE OF SOUL

The Nineteen Sixties

1960s

Although the 1960s in America began with great hope, it was a decade that saw tremendous turbulence and war. The true spirit of the time was reflected in the rise and fall of President John F. Kennedy. Some historians say the '60s ethos began with Kennedy's election—that his youthfulness and passion for grand ideas epitomized the growing influence of youth culture. Others say the sixties truly began with Kennedy's assassination in 1963, the resulting despair and conspiracy theories foreshadowing the many social movements that were deeply critical of government and traditional economic, social, and religious institutions. Wherever one places the beginning of the '60s, it is clear that both themes are present in these chaotic years: youth culture presented itself more forcefully than ever, and social movements became more vigorous, critical, and violent. The music of this time—revealing and heightening these trends—provided the appropriate soundtrack. The world was exploding, and rock musicians were listening more closely than ever.

Among the issues that divided Americans, none loomed larger than the Vietnam War and civil rights movement. Although the struggle for the rights of African Americans began when the first blacks were brought to America (1619) and continued through the landmark desegregation case, *Brown v. Board of Education of Topeka, Kansas*, the intensity and organization of the movement increased greatly in the 1960s. To protest racial segregation that lingered after *Brown*, four young African Americans students "sat in" at a segregated lunch counter in 1960 at Woolworth's in Greensboro, North Carolina. Their protest set off many more across the country and caused Woolworth's to integrate its lunch counters. The movement for African American civil rights continued in many locales, with major protests in Birmingham and Montgomery, Alabama.

A watershed moment in the movement came on August 28, 1963, when 250,000 Americans—black and white—took part in the "March on Washington." At this historic event, Martin Luther King Jr. delivered his "I Have a Dream" speech, which vocalized the movement's goals and spirit to

ll Americans. Following the
March, Congress passed the
Civil Rights Act (1964), making
discrimination based on race
illegal. Despite this, racial tensions remained high in some
big cities. Race riots erupted in
the Watts neighborhood of Los
Angeles in 1965, in Newark and
Detroit in 1967, and in many
cities following the assassination of King in 1968. As the
decade rolled on, the movement
became more militant, and earlier calls for integration and non-
violence gave way to "Black
Power"—promoted by the Black
Panthers, among others.

The antiwar movement paral-
eled the civil rights movement.
By mid-decade, America had

combat troops in Vietnam and
the number of American casualties began to increase. Many
young Americans questioned
the wisdom of the war, and dis-
sent became increasingly vocal
and organized, especially on college campuses. Students—
white and black, rich and
poor—"sat in" and burned their
draft cards; some even escaped
to Canada to avoid the war. Like
the civil rights protests, antiwar
demonstrations could also turn
violent, as did one at the 1968
Democratic National
Convention in Chicago. In 1970,
four students were killed at Kent
State University in Ohio, and
two more at Jackson State
College in Mississippi.

*Martin Luther King Jr.
delivering his "I Have a
Dream" speech during the
March on Washington,
August 28, 1963. King
preached a message of
racial unity and was the
most visible spokesperson
for African American civil
rights.*

Anti-Vietnam war protesters taunt military police during a demonstration at the Pentagon, in Washington, D.C., October 21, 1967. Throughout the 1960s antiwar sentiment increased, especially among students, as more and more young American soldiers died in battle.

In addition to the civil rights and antiwar movements, many other movements familiar to us today first appeared on the radar of national awareness in the 1960s. The feminist movement was nurtured significantly by Betty Friedan's 1963 best-selling book *The Feminine Mystique*, which argued that women were constrained by the traditional role of homemaker. In 1966, the National Organization of Women (NOW) was founded with Friedan as its first president. Environmentalism grew when Rachel Carson's *Silent Spring* (1962) drew the country's attention to the dangers resulting from the indiscriminate and persistent use of pesticides such as DDT. Similarly, the consumer protection movement got its spark from Ralph Nader's 1965 book *Unsafe at Any Speed*, which accused automobile companies of placing profits and style ahead of safety in the design of their vehicles. Nader went on to challenge the practices of many industries as these affected consumer safety, leading to changes in attitudes and laws. All of these causes raised serious doubts about previously accepted beliefs concerning American life and culture, taking on the status quo with militant passion.

The entertainment business was also going through important, and in same cases turbulent, changes. By the beginning of the decade, network programming had almost entirely migrated from radio to television. Driven by advertising demographics, AM radio continued to be mostly a regional or local affair, devoted to hit records and old favorites; FM radio, however, at first a kind of undeveloped wilderness of college lectures, religious programming, and classical music, began developing into the musical home of the hippie counterculture after 1967.

In television, ideas of 1950s "normalcy" reinforced by shows such as *Leave It to Beaver* continued in the 1960s, typified by inoffensive shows like *My Three Sons*. The first show to challenge this sense of domestic normalcy was *The Beverly Hillbillies* (1962), which placed a Tennessee backwoods family in the center of Beverly Hills. At first, the hillbillies seemed to be the target of the show's humor, but then it became clear that a better strategy was to use the hillbillies to make the "normal" folks look foolish. This soft critique of 1950s normalcy contin-

ued in *My Favorite Martian*, *Bewitched*, and *I Dream of Jeannie*—all shows based on the idea that unique, supernatural powers needed to be concealed from public view, lest the one who had them be considered "abnormal." The youth counterculture of the second half of the 1960s would be far less playful in its critiques of 1950s values.

Movies in the '60s reflected the pressures of the Cold War as well as the emergence of the elegant "jet set." Beginning with *Dr. No* in 1962, James Bond (Agent 007) fought communist secret agents in a continuing series of feature films, jetting around the globe, ordering his martinis "shaken, not stirred," and employing technically advanced gadgets. While James Bond might represent the West's confidence in foiling its Cold War enemies, some filmmakers were much more skeptical. Stanley Kubrick offered a stinging critique of the Cold War

arms race in his *Dr. Strangelove, or: How I Learned to Stop Worrying and Love the Bomb* (1964). And though some saw Kubrick's *2001: A Space Odyssey* (1968) as a celebration of space travel, others saw it as posing a fundamental question regarding man's reliance on technology.

The 1960s drew to a close the same way they began: with a mixture of hope and fear. On July 20, 1969, the United States was unified in celebration: astronauts Neil Armstrong and Buzz Aldrin had realized President Kennedy's challenge to put a man on the moon by the end of the decade. However, this brief moment of unity did nothing to heal the country's wounds over Vietnam and civil rights. Wars and riots raged on, and rock was raging with them.

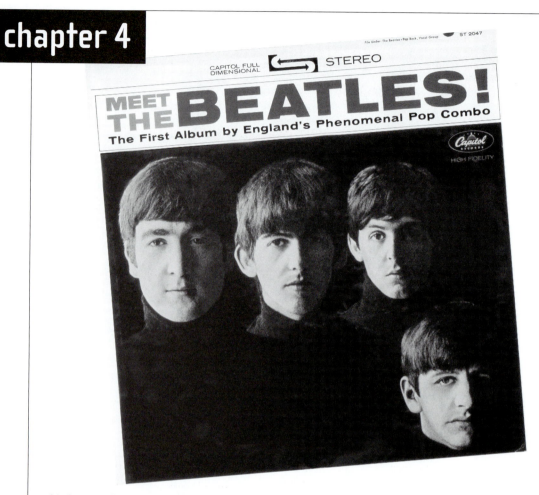

This famous album cover was almost never seen in the United States. Capitol Records, the American subsidiary of the British label EMI, was confident that a British act could never sell enough records in the United States to be profitable. After declining to release the British hit singles "Love Me Do," "Please Please Me," and "She Loves You" in the States, however, Capitol finally decided to release "I Want to Hold Your Hand" in the last week of 1963. By early 1964, the single had gone to number one on U.S. charts. The other three singles were climbing the charts as well, but on independent labels Swan and Vee Jay, which had picked them up when Capitol rejected them. Scrambling to recover from this costly mistake, Capitol quickly put together an album for American release, combining tracks from the first two British albums with both sides of the "I Want to Hold Your Hand" single. The resulting album, Meet the Beatles!, *was the first Beatles album most American fans owned, though it differs somewhat from the similar British release called* With the Beatles. *Capitol continued carving up Beatles albums through the first few years of the band's career in the United States, creating several albums that have no direct British counterpart, such as* The Beatles' Second Album *(1964),* Beatles VI *(1965), and* Yesterday and Today *(1966).*

The Beatles and the British Invasion

The early 1960s offered a wide variety of musical styles to American youth, from the simple teenybopper love songs of the teen idols to the more complicated traditionalism and social conscientiousness of folk. Somewhere in the music-stylistic space between these two opposing poles were girl-group music, rockabilly, surf music, and sweet soul. All these styles seemed to be competing to be the "next big thing" in rock and roll; following the overwhelming popularity of rock's first wave with teen listeners, musicians and business people were hoping to duplicate the enormous success of Elvis Presley. In early 1964, the American music business was taken entirely by surprise when the "new Elvis" turned out to be four young men from Liverpool, England. On February 9, 1964, the Beatles appeared on Ed Sullivan's Sunday evening variety show, just as Elvis had done almost eight years earlier. A record-breaking 73 million viewers are estimated to have tuned in to that broadcast in 1964, making the Beatles a household name across America practically overnight. The press even reported later that the crime rate in the United States went down during the time the show was on the air; perhaps even criminals stopped to watch.

The overwhelming success of the Beatles created a national fad for British groups; during most of 1964 it seemed that any group of young men with British accents, long hair, and matching suits could make a fortune in America. This "British invasion" of American pop in general and the enormous success of the Beatles in particular altered the music business in several significant and important ways. This chapter will focus on these English groups, their music, and the effect the British invasion had on American popular music in terms of both musical style and music-business practice. We will also focus on the British popular-music scene during the late 1950s and early '60s, since the impact of the Beatles was felt first in the UK, and the British pop market was transformed by the same music and musicians that would invade the colonies only slightly later. The story of the British invasion is therefore not a single one, but rather two interdependent stories: the first is a chronicle of British pop in the decade before 1964, and the second an account of how that music strongly affected American pop after the arrival of the Beatles.

British Pop in the Late 1950s and Early 1960s

The Music Business in the UK. As hard is it might be to imagine today, in the period before 1964 Britain was viewed as a secondary force in popular music; the UK was mostly a consumer of American-made music, importing far more popular music than it exported. A comparison of the pop hits in Britain during the late 1950s and early '60s with those in the United States reveals that most of the same records, performed in almost all cases by American artists, were popular in both countries. British artists were far more likely to achieve success at home than in the states, though occasionally a British artist would have success in the United States. Orchestra leader Mantovani, for instance, had twenty-six albums in the American Top 40 during 1955–63, as well as two singles in the U.S. pop Top 40—the movie themes from *Around the World in Eighty Days* (p12, 1957) and *Exodus* (p31, 1961)—but this was a level of American success unmatched by other British artists. To a significant extent this American dominance in popular music was a product of the differences in British and American society. In the years following the end of World War II in 1945, there was tremendous enthusiasm in Britain for American popular culture. American armed forces took their culture overseas with them during the war, and many Britons developed a taste for American pop during this time. Many areas in Britain, and London especially, were devastated by German bombing and the years after the war were marked by struggle and rebuilding in the UK. Many Britons looked to America as a country full of hope and confidence, affluent and unburdened by the scars of war or the weight of history and tradition. All this seemed to come through in the music. When rock and roll began to emerge in the United States, teens in Britain became enthusiastic listeners to the new style as well. The entire idea of the "teenager" was seen as an American innovation; to many young people in Britain, teens in the United States led lives of rock and roll, dancing, cars, and drive-in movies. In the sometimes dreary rebuilding years of the 1950s, British teens found such images enormously attractive and for them, as for their American cousins, rock and roll was the music of teenage rebellion.

Big companies influenced the music business in Britain much more than in the United States, and this affected the way rock and roll was understood by listeners in the UK. Britain had four major record labels—EMI, Decca, Pye, and Philips—and two radio stations—the BBC and Radio Luxembourg. These major labels licensed music from American majors and indies for release in the UK, with Decca and EMI being the most active. The BBC was government-owned, and featured three channels, only one of which ever played rock and roll—beginning in 1958, the BBC's two-hour radio show *Saturday Club* (hosted by Brian Matthew) became an important weekly source of rock and roll music and information. Radio Luxembourg was a commercial station broadcast from the European continent. Rock and roll was mostly played on shows financed by the major labels, which used these broadcasts as a way of promoting their own records. Unlike the United States, England had no independent radio stations before 1964, and as a consequence, very few independent labels as well.

Running an indie in the UK was a tough business: since radio access was controlled by the government or wealthy major labels, an independent stood little chance of ever getting a record played. While rock and roll records that appeared on the American pop charts were mostly available in stores, rhythm and blues was much more difficult to find, as was some country and western music. Information about such music was even scarcer, though magazines such as *Melody Maker*, *New Musical Express*, and later, *Record Mirror* increasingly devoted attention to rock and roll. Movies became an important resource for young people interested in rock and roll during this period; films made to capitalize on the first wave that featured a series of performances (the Freed movies and *The Girl Can't Help It*) and Elvis films were very popular. British tours by performers such as Bill Haley, Buddy Holly, and the Everly Brothers were important events for young rock and roll fans as well, giving them a chance to see some of their favorite artists perform in person.

These British rock and roll enthusiasts were not the first to seek out American pop music; in addition to loving American pop, the English have a long-standing (and perhaps surprising) infatuation with American folk and jazz that dates back to before World War II. In the years after 1945, both these lesser-known styles experienced a resurgence of interest in the UK and in many ways, the British infatuation with rock and roll was a continuation of that cultural tendency. Traditional jazz ("trad"), which stuck very close to the early twentieth-century New Orleans style, was championed by bandleader Ken Colyer and was later broadened stylistically to include other jazz styles by Chris Barber, Kenny Ball, and Acker Bilk. Barber's band featured banjo player Tony Donegan, who recorded a version of the traditional folk song "Rock Island Line" in a new style called "skiffle" that blended folk music with an up-tempo big band rhythmic feel. Credited to Lonnie Donegan and his Skiffle Group (Donegan on vocals and guitar, Barber on bass, and Beryl Bryden on washboard), the single rose to the number eight slot on the UK charts in 1956, igniting an English pop craze for skiffle music. In a parallel to the folk boom that took hold in the United States slightly later, this tuneful yet easy-to-play music encouraged the participation of many English teenagers, John Lennon and Jimmy Page among them. Donegan's "Rock Island Line" crossed the Atlantic to hit number eight on the U.S. pop charts in 1956, and Donegan followed his success in England by placing thirty-one hits on the UK charts by 1962, including a cover version of "Tom Dooley," which rose to number

Regarded as the most important figure in the late-1950s skiffle movement in Britain, Lonnie Donegan and his band blended American folk music with a traditional jazz beat. This photo shows Donegan (left) and a second guitarist strumming folk guitars while the other two band members play a stand-up bass and drum set, as might be found in a jazz dance band.

three in the UK in 1958. By the late 1950s, however, the skiffle fad was replaced by a preference for trad on the British charts, with the bands of Ball, Barber, and Bilk each scoring a series of hits. Some of these hits even crossed the Atlantic, such as Barber's "Petite Fleur" (uk3 p5, 1959), Ball's "Midnight in Moscow" (uk2, 1961; p2, 1962), and Bilk's "Stranger on the Shore" (uk2, 1961; p1, 1962).

The most pressing challenge facing the British music business in the late 1950s and early 1960s was not how to place more English records on the American charts, however; it was how to place more English records on the British charts which, despite the success of home-grown artists like Donegan, Barber, Ball, and Bilk, were still dominated by Americans. Similar to the American music business, English companies had already begun to produce teen-idol singers modeled on Elvis Presley. The first was Decca's Tommy Steele, who hit in 1956 with "Rock with the Caveman" (uk13) and followed later the same year with the number-one British hit, "Singin' the Blues," as well as sixteen more hits through 1961. The most successful British rocker was EMI's Cliff Richard; in the 1958–63 period alone, Richard scored twenty-seven UK hit singles. His backup band, the Shadows, was the English equivalent of the Ventures and placed a consistent series of instrumental hits on the UK charts, beginning with "Apache" (uk1, 1960). For all the UK success that Richard and the Shadows enjoyed, however, only one record ever crossed the Atlantic before 1964: "Living Doll," which rose only to number thirty on U.S. charts in 1959. In a parallel to Bob Marcucci's star-making machinery in Philadelphia, London's Larry Parnes managed a stable of teen idols; building on his success managing Tommy Steele, Parnes developed Marty Wilde, Billy Fury, Georgie Fame, and Joe Brown, each of whom had a series of hits in the UK. Despite the increased success of English artists, in 1962 the UK charts were still full of Americans; four Elvis Presley records hit number one, along with one each by Ray Charles and B. Bumble and the Stingers ("Nut Rocker," later covered by 1970s progressive rockers Emerson, Lake & Palmer). The turnaround for British performers would occur in 1963 with the emergence of what Britons call the "beat boom"— a style led by a group from Liverpool who had been turned away by almost every label and subsidiary in the UK.

The Beatles as Students of American Pop, 1960–1963

Formation and First Gigs. Studying the British music scene in the late 1950s and early 1960s helps us to understand better how young British musicians absorbed American rock and subsequently brought their version of it back to the United States. The Beatles formed in Liverpool in 1957, calling themselves the Quarrymen and playing skiffle in imitation of Lonnie Donegan, then moving on to rock and roll as the popularity of skiffle waned. John Lennon was born in 1940 and Paul McCartney in 1942, meaning that they were fifteen and thirteen years old, respectively, when rock and roll broke out on both sides of the Atlantic. They were among the first generation of rock musicians for whom rock was the music of their youth; Elvis Presley, by contrast, was fifteen in 1950 and twenty-one when he hit nationally in 1956. Coming along a few years after the first wave, young British musicians learned to play by imitating these older American rock and rollers, and this meant that the music of the first wave would leave an indelible imprint on British rock in the 1960s. The Beatles are among the best examples of this influence; the first recording of the group from 1958 (as the Quarrymen and now including a fifteen-year-old George Harrison on lead guitar) features Buddy Holly's "That'll Be the Day," clearly performed in close imitation of Holly's record. Also in imitation of Holly's musical style, the group recorded an original song, written by Harrison and McCartney, called "In Spite of All the Danger."

Like many other young British bands, the Beatles knocked around their hometown looking for paying gigs and learning any American record they could get their hands on. After performing in 1959 locally and with some success in a talent contest under the name Johnny and the Moondogs, Lennon, McCartney, and Harrison auditioned in 1960 for Larry Parnes, who decided not to sign them as a feature act, but to use them (now the Silver Beetles, after Holly's Crickets) to back one of his singers (not Fury or Wilde, but Johnny Gentle) on a brief tour of Scotland. Earlier that year Lennon's art-college buddy Stuart Sutcliffe had joined the band on bass, and by the summer Pete Best joined on drums. It was this lineup, with Lennon, McCartney, and Harrison all playing guitar and singing, that set out to play a four-month stint in two clubs in the red-light district of Hamburg, Germany. The group made three extended stays in Hamburg, playing 106, 92, and 48 nights in the period between August 1960 and May 1962 and returning for two shorter stays (14 and 13 appearances) in late 1962.

Hamburg and Liverpool (1960–1962).   The Beatles' first stay in Hamburg was at the small Indra Club and then the larger Kaiserkeller. The group had been booked through a Liverpool agent, Allan Williams, who had already sent another Liverpool band, Derry and the Seniors, to Hamburg. Among the other bands in Hamburg at the time were the Jets, from London, led by singer Tony Sheridan, and Rory Storm and the Hurricanes, from Liverpool, featuring drummer Ringo Starr. The Beatles played six-hour evenings in which they were constantly being prompted to "make a show." In order to fill the on-stage time, the Beatles learned every song they could find, especially the high-energy rock and roll numbers that excited the German patrons. The second stint, at the Top Ten Club, had the band playing from 7 P.M. until 2 A.M. with a fifteen-minute break each hour. Conditions were better on the third visit, during which the group played the Star Club, where at one point they even shared the bill with Little Richard. In an intense professional situation like this, musicians will either rise to the challenge or quickly be swept aside. These long nights in tough German bars worked to refine the Beatles' performing skills, making professionals out of these aspiring rock and rollers. The Beatles also became regulars at Liverpool's Cavern Club, with their first appearance in February 1961, two months after they returned from their first stay in Hamburg and only a few weeks after a tremendously successful dance gig at the Litherland Town Hall in Liverpool (perhaps the first hint of things to come in the UK). Arranged by Cavern Club DJ Bob Wooler, the Beatles played almost 300 times at the Cavern through early 1962. Many of the Cavern shows were lunchtime affairs, with the crowd and the band eating their lunches during the performance. Between shows at the Cavern and stints in Hamburg, the Beatles were performing frequently and continually developing their skills while building an enthusiastic following.

In November 1961, Brian Epstein saw the Beatles perform for the first time at the Cavern. Epstein had been running a record store owned by his family and heard of the group's success partly through requests from store customers for a rocked-up version of "My Bonnie Lies over the Ocean" performed by Tony Sheridan backed by the Beatles, a record that had been a hit in Germany. Epstein soon became the Beatles' manager, immediately setting to work on cleaning up the band's stage appearance. In addition to the "Beatle haircuts" the band now donned matching tailored suits. After helping the group to get better jobs for more money, Epstein set his sights on securing a recording contract; using his contacts inside the English record industry, he was able to get the band a recording audition for Decca in the company's London studios. Based on this fifteen-song session (January 1, 1962) and after months of consideration, Decca's Dick Rowe chose to sign Brian Poole and the Tremeloes over the Beatles, earning himself the informal title of "the man who passed up the Beatles" (he reportedly told Epstein that guitar bands were on the way out). The Beatles were allowed to keep the Decca demo tape, however, and in early May 1962, while the group was in Hamburg for the second time, Epstein made the rounds of record company offices in London. After being turned down by several labels, Epstein was introduced to George Martin, then serving as A&R man for a small EMI label called Parlophone. Martin heard promise in the Decca tape and set up an EMI recording audition for the group on their return from Germany in June 1962. By September Martin was producing the group's first release for Parlophone, Lennon and McCartney's "Love Me Do." The Hurricanes' Ringo Starr had joined the band in August (replacing Best), but Martin, wary of Starr's amateurish playing at the audition, had hired a professional session drummer for the recoding date. Martin also had the group record "How Do You Do It?" written by Mitch Murray, though the band successfully lobbied to release an original song as its first single. "Love Me Do" rose to number seventeen on the UK

Before they became worldwide stars, the Beatles regularly played the Cavern Club in their hometown of Liverpool. As Paul belts out a vocal, George and Ringo accompany on guitar and drums, while John is probably standing just out of the picture on the right.

charts by late 1962, and "How Do You Do It?" went to number one in 1963 when it was released by another Epstein-managed Liverpool group, Gerry and the Pacemakers.

By the end of 1962, the Beatles had done what no Liverpool band had done before: gone to London, signed a recording contract, and placed a single on the UK charts. There were advantages and disadvantages to being a Liverpool group. An important advantage was that Liverpool was a seaport—a stop for seamen who traveled the Atlantic regularly and brought back American records. This gave the young Beatles greater exposure to American pop than they might have had even in London. A similar situation in Hamburg added to the band's knowledge of American pop, rhythm and blues, and country and western music. The major disadvantage in coming out of Liverpool was that the entire British music business was centered in London, making it very difficult for groups outside of London, especially bands from the more working-class north, to find a way in. The Beatles were the first northern band to break through, and with their growing success more and more bands from Liverpool, Manchester, and Birmingham made their way south to the welcome of record company people eager to capitalize on the success of what was soon called "the Mersey Beat" (pop music originating in the mid 1960s around Liverpool and northwest England).

Beatle Influences

Since Lennon and McCartney later emerged as important songwriters, it is interesting to survey the kinds of songs the Beatles played during the Hamburg and Liverpool period. Young songwriters often learn their craft by modeling new songs on ones they know; some of the songs the Beatles played during these years likely served as models for their later hits. Recordings of the Beatles performing at the Star Club in 1962 have been available since the 1970s, and though they are of poor quality, these tapes provide documentation of the kinds of music the band played during those years. Perhaps the richest source for this repertory are tapes the band made especially for a variety of BBC radio broadcasts, including Brian Matthew's *Saturday Club*, in the first years of their British success (1963–65); these recordings largely duplicate songs played on the Star Club tapes but are of much higher audio quality. Known as *The Beatles Live at the BBC*, these tapes reveal the extent of the band's fascination with American rock and roll. The tapes feature four Elvis Presley covers, including McCartney performing a close copy of "That's All Right (Mama)"; and nine Chuck Berry covers, including Lennon singing the lyrically sophisticated "Memphis." Among the other first-wave rockers, Little Richard and Carl Perkins are also represented multiple times. The band also shows an appreciation for Leiber and Stoller's Coasters records, as well as Phil Spector's "To Know Him Is to Love Him." The first of the *Anthology* CD sets, released in 1995, further fills in the picture, providing five selections from the band's audition tape for Decca (including two Coasters tunes) and an excerpt from Ray Charles's "Hallelujah I Love Her So" recorded in the Cavern Club. Finally, their first two British albums, *Please Please Me* and *With the Beatles* (both 1963), contain several cover versions, among them girl-group numbers ("Chains" and "Baby It's You"), Motown tracks ("You Really Got a Hold on Me," "Please Mr. Postman," and "Money"), and a movie theme ("A Taste of Honey"). It is clear that Lennon and McCartney were already experienced students of American pop by the time they entered the EMI Abbey Road studios with Martin to make their first hit record in the fall of 1962.

Beatlemania, 1963–1966

Success in England.   The success of "Love Me Do" in late 1962 was a sign of things to come for the Beatles, though nobody expected the level of success they enjoyed in the UK in 1963 and in the United States and the world in 1964. They began the year by touring and recording their first album, *Please Please Me*. By August 1963, they had three more hit singles—"Please Please Me" (uk2), "From Me to You" (uk1), and "She Loves You" (uk1)—as well as a chart-topping album. That summer, the British press began to use the term "Beatlemania" to describe the tremendous excitement created among fans at the band's live performances. The group's national breakthrough in England occurred when they performed on *Sunday Night at the London Palladium*, a national television broadcast similar to the *Ed Sullivan Show* in the United States and watched by millions of British viewers. This was followed in early November by another high-profile television performance on the *Royal Variety Performance* in the presence of the Queen Mother, Princess Margaret, and Lord Snowdon. By late November the group's second album, *With the Beatles*, had entered the UK charts on its way to number one. In December "I Want to Hold Your Hand" hit the number one slot on the UK charts, where it replaced "She Loves You" and became the fourth consecutive hit for the band in 1963. Late in December *The Times'* music critic William Mann named Lennon and McCartney the outstanding English composers of the year.

The Beatles' tremendous success opened the English popular-music business up to dozens of other groups (many of which are discussed below). Most of the number one hits on the UK charts in 1963 were by British artists, a number of whom made their debuts in that year. If the first goal of the British music business had been to place more English acts on the UK charts, 1963 had been an important year. Despite Beatlemania and all that followed in its wake, however, none of this British success and excitement made any impact in the United States in 1963. Capitol Records, EMI's American subsidiary, declined the right to issue the first Beatles hits in the United States. George Martin was forced to license these singles to American indies—"Please Please Me" and "From Me to You" appeared on Vee Jay, while "She Loves You" was released by Swan. None of the three records had much chart impact. As strange as it seems today, Capitol was reluctant because they were sure that the Beatles would fail in the United States. This was logic based on experience: most British artists, even Cliff Richard, had been unable to establish themselves as consistent hit-makers in America. The Beatles were so afraid of failing in America that they told Brian Epstein they did not want to go to the United States until they had a number one hit there. Despite their reluctance, Epstein had been busy since the summer of 1963 trying to get the band booked in the United States. In November 1963 he visited New York and worked out a deal for two appearances on the *Ed Sullivan Show* in February 1964. Since Sullivan had agreed that the Beatles would get top billing on the show, Epstein and Martin were finally able to get Capitol to release "I Want to Hold Your Hand" in late December 1963. By the beginning of February 1964 the single had hit number one in the the United States, just in time for the first Sullivan performance on February 9.

The American Experience.   With the breakthrough success of the first Sullivan appearance (see p. 162), the Beatles became the hottest act in the American entertainment business almost overnight. Of course, success did not come to the group as easily as it seemed to Americans in 1964; few fans during those years knew of the long, grueling hours in Hamburg or the many shows at the Cavern and across England that had filled the previous four years. The Beatles followed the success of "I Want to Hold Your Hand" with thirty additional Top 40 U.S. hits through 1966 (including the two records that had been rejected by Capitol and released by Vee Jay and Swan), and twelve going to number one, including "Can't Buy Me Love" (1964), "A Hard Day's Night" (1964), "Ticket to Ride" (1965), "Help!" (1965), and "Paperback Writer" (1966). In the week following the first Sullivan show, *Meet the Beatles!* hit the top of the American album charts, staying in the top spot for almost three months and being replaced by *The Beatles' Second Album*; all the group's studio albums would go to number one in both the UK and the United States, although the American albums often differ from the English releases in titles and in the songs included. In July 1964 the band was featured in their first full-length movie, *A Hard Day's Night*, followed in August 1965 by *Help!* Both were tremendous box-office successes, taking advantage of a lucrative market for teen movies that had been established by Alan Freed, Elvis, and many others. Everyone involved with the Beatles initially expected that their success might dry up just as quickly as it had appeared; as with the first wave of rock and roll, the Beatles and the British invasion were thought by many in the music business to be a fad that would soon be replaced. The Beatles thus labored under the idea that they had to make the most of their brief moment of opportunity and worked at a furious pace, touring and recording almost without a break. The result was one of the most impressive runs of hit records ever posted in popular music. In this sense, the Beatles had become the new Elvis.

Things eventually turned sour for the band when a controversy erupted in the United States over some remarks that John Lennon had made in an English interview. When asked about the role religion played in the lives of British youth, Lennon remarked that it was a sign of the poor health of religion in England that a Beatles concert could outdraw a church service. These remarks were made in the context of a larger debate that had been taking place in

The Beatles on the *Ed Sullivan Show*

When the Beatles were preparing to come to New York in early 1964, they were concerned about their ability to succeed in the United States. As John Lennon said, "We didn't think we stood a chance. We didn't imagine it at all. Cliff [Richard] went to America and died. He was fourteenth on the bill with Frankie Avalon." Ringo Starr added, "We were doing countries: we'd conquered Sweden, we'd conquered France, we conquered Spain and Italy; but we were worried about America. . . . But the deal went down with Capitol [Records]. Then Ed Sullivan was getting off a plane at Heathrow at the same time that we were getting off one from Sweden, saw all the fans at the airport, and booked us on the spot."

After the Beatles were booked on the *Ed Sullivan Show*, Capitol and Sullivan both put their public relations muscle behind the band. It was a well-made marriage. For Sullivan, booking an unproven British band with no established American following for three consecutive weeks on a top-rated show was a big gamble, but he recognized that they could help expand his audience and make his show an event. Likewise, the Beatles knew that Sullivan could immedi-

ately offer them broad, national exposure that would otherwise take years to build. As a result of all the promotion, "I Want to Hold Your Hand" was number one on the pop charts at the time of the Beatles' appearance.

When the band arrived in New York they were greeted by thousands of fans. On February 9, they gave two performances before the studio audience for the *Ed Sullivan Show*. The first performance was taped to be broadcast two weeks later, but the second was broadcast live. Sullivan opened the show with his customary remarks, and then the Beatles played "All My Loving," "'Til There Was You," and "She Loves You." The audience reaction was nothing short of hysterical. A wide variety of family-friendly acts followed the Beatles, showing just how foreign the band must have seemed to Sullivan's regular viewers: first came magician Fred Kaps, followed by the cast of the Broadway musical *Oliver!* (including future Monkee Davy Jones), comedian Frank Gorshin, Olympian Terry McDermott, Broadway singer Tessie O'Shea, and comedians McCall & Brill. The Beatles then returned to play "I Saw Her Standing There" and finished with their big hit, "I

Want to Hold Your Hand." On February 16, the Beatles' segments were broadcast live from Miami. They played "She Loves You," "This Boy," and "All My Loving" in the first set and "I Saw Her Standing There," "From Me to You," and "I Want to Hold Your Hand" in the second, this time followed by a team of comedy unicyclists. On the third show (their taped performances of "Twist and Shout," "Please Please Me," and, again, "I Want to Hold Your Hand"), they at least shared the bill with jazz legend Cab Calloway.

If you examine these shows today, the much-discussed "generation gap" between the baby boom generation and their parents is obvious. To youngsters who had grown up with rock and roll, the arrival of the Beatles on a show full of Broadway medleys, acrobats, unicyclists, and card tricks must have been electric. To many of their parents, it was shocking in a different way. Rock singer Alice Cooper describes the reaction in his household: "I just sat there in my living room in Phoenix with a huge smile on my face. . . . My parents looked [stunned] like they were in the audience of 'Springtime for Hitler' from *The Producers*."

The Beatles' first appearance on the *Ed Sullivan Show* drew a record audience of 73 million viewers and propelled them to unprecedented heights of popularity: by April, they held the top five positions on the pop singles charts, a feat that has never been duplicated. What is more important, however, is that the show became an important musical and cultural landmark. The Beatles on the *Ed Sullivan Show* became an iconic moment that signified large-scale social change. Like the Kennedy assassination and the Apollo 11 moon landing, this was a vivid experience shared by almost every person in America old enough to comprehend it. When combined with an understanding of the great social and cultural changes that these shows heralded, the communal memory of the Beatles' performances became a powerful unifying force in the history of our culture.

The Beatles' first performance on the Ed Sullivan Show, *February 9, 1964, is among the most storied in rock. A record television audience tuned in to watch the British invasion storm the home shores.*

England about youth and the Church—a debate prompted in part by the changes brought by the Roman Catholic Church through the Vatican II reforms. Lennon's remarks were taken out of this context by American reporters and he was cast as having claimed that the Beatles were bigger than

LISTENING GUIDE

GET MUSIC ▶▶ wwnorton.com/rockhistory

The Beatles, "I Want to Hold Your Hand"

Words and music by John Lennon and Paul McCartney, produced by George Martin. Reached #1 in UK charts in late 1963 and #1 on the Billboard Pop charts in early 1964.

FORM: AABA, with partial reprise, since the bridge and verse sections are repeated after the complete verse-verse-bridge-verse structure has been presented. Each verse ends in a 4-bar refrain, employing the song's title in the lyrics and featuring two-part vocal harmony; the previous bars in the verse are always sung in two-part unison. Note that the first bridge is sung in unison (except at the very end), while the repeated bridge is sung in two-part harmony. The introduction is built from the last 4 bars of the bridge, while the song's ending is created by tagging the last bars of the refrain in a clever manner.

TIME SIGNATURE: 4/4. This lighthearted, driving pop feel with accents on beats 2 and 4, was called the "Mersey beat" in the UK.

INSTRUMENTATION: Electric guitars, bass, drums, hand claps, two-part lead vocal, with sections in unison and in harmony.

0:00–0:08	**Introduction**, 4 mm.	Instrumental with lots of driving rhythm guitar, derived from bridge.
0:08–0:29	**A-Verse w/refrain**, 12 mm.	Mostly unison vocals, hand claps enter, "Oh yeah I'll tell you . . ."
0:29–0:51	**A-Verse w/refrain**, 12 mm.	As before, "Oh please, say to me . . ."
0:51–1:11	**B-Bridge**, 11 mm.	Unison until end, quieter to provide contrast, but building at end, "And when I touch you . . ."
1:11–1:33	**A-Verse w/refrain**, 12 mm.	As before, hand claps return, "Oh you got that somethin' . . ."
1:34–1:54	**B-Bridge**, 11 mm.	New two-part harmony vocals, quiet until the end as before, "And when I touch . . ."
1:54–2:22	**A-Verse** with tag, 15 mm.	As before, three bars added at ending, "Yeah you got that . . ."

Jesus. An uproar in the American south resulted, with Beatles records and other merchandise burned in large bonfires in major cities. The Ku Klux Klan threatened violence at Beatles concerts and the group began to fear for their lives. As a result of this controversy, as well as the toll taken by constant work, the Beatles played their last public concert in San Francisco's Candlestick Park on August 29, 1966. The next stage of the band's career will be taken up in our discussion of psychedelia in Chapter 7.

The Beatles' Music Develops: From Craftsmen to Artists. A clear development can be seen in the Beatles' music during the 1964–66 period. Early on the band seemed content to imitate American models, combining often diverse but nonetheless identifiable elements from 1955–63 in sometimes surprising ways. From the remarks about the impact of the Beatles in 1964 made by musicians and others inside the music business, one might well expect that the music was a significant departure from American pop. But in many ways the Beatles took American pop of the late 1950s and early '60s, blended some of its hallmark stylistic elements, and sold it back to Americans as British pop. The sources employed by the group tell us how much of the Beatles' music extends the American tradition; the surprising juxtapositions begin to mark the distinctive ways in which the band reinterpreted American rock and roll. The Beatles' first American hit, "I Want to Hold Your Hand," is a good example. The driving guitars, playing Chuck Berry–like chords in the low register as the Ventures and the Beach Boys were doing at the time, recall "Johnny B. Goode" or "Roll over Beethoven," while the hand claps could have come from a number of girl-group tunes of the early 1960s (such as "My Boyfriend's Back"). The duet singing in the song's bridge is reminiscent of the Everly Brothers, while the trademark "ooo's" are lifted directly from Little Richard. The form of the song is AABA with abbreviated reprise—a structural design common in American pop (see Interlude 1).

Much of the Beatles music recorded in 1963–64 relies heavily on a reworking of a limited number of musical elements, most of which can be traced back to the music the band was playing in 1960–62. The group can hardly be faulted for this, since they considered their success to be fleeting and accordingly wrote and recorded quickly. In this context, it is impressive how much variety they achieved in the beginning. This approach to producing songs according to a "formula" can be considered an aspect of the craft of songwriting. Brill Building songwriters worked in precisely the same manner, as had the Tin Pan Alley songsmiths before them. Another approach to writing music is usually associated with classical-music composers from the nineteenth and twentieth centuries; for composers such as Beethoven, Brahms, or Schoenberg, one never solves the same musical problem in precisely the same way. Rather than finding a formula, the composer always strives for novel solutions posed by each piece of music. We can thus, at least for the purposes of this discussion, place craft and art in opposition to one another and in so doing reveal something crucial about the Beatles' music and its effect on popular music. Across the 1964–66 period, the Beatles increasingly moved away from the craftsperson approach to songwriting and toward the artistic one. Though this transition began in very small ways, by the time the band entered the studio in early 1966 for the sessions that produced *Revolver*, they had already begun experimenting with studio effects, stylistic juxtapositions, and novel timbral and structural elements.

"Tomorrow Never Knows" is a good example of how far the Beatles had

---

LISTENING GUIDE　　　　GET MUSIC ▶▶　wwnorton.com/rockhistory

The Beatles, "Tomorrow Never Knows"

Words and music by John Lennon and Paul McCartney, produced by George Martin. Included on the album *Revolver*, which rose to #1 on the U.S. and UK album charts in 1966.

FORM: Simple verse, with each verse built on the same 8-bar structure that is repeated over and over. The droning of the bass makes the harmonic dimension of the music sound static, suggesting the influence of Indian music, while the tape loops, backward guitar, and processed lead vocals create an otherworldly atmosphere.

TIME SIGNATURE: 4/4. Notice the constant repeated notes in the bass, which interact with the repeated drum pattern in an interesting way, creating a rhythmic feel that seems unrelenting.

INSTRUMENTATION: Bass, sitar, drums, organ, backward guitar, tape loops, piano (at end), and electronically processed lead vocal.

0:00–0:12	**Introduction**, 4 mm.	Opens with sitar, then other instruments and tape loops enter. Note persistent but catchy drumbeat and drone bass.
0:12–0:26	**Verse 1**, 8 mm.	Vocals enter, tape loops slip in and out, "Turn off your mind . . ."
0:26–0:42	**Verse 2**, 8 mm.	As before, "Lay down all thoughts . . ."
0:42–0:56	**Verse 3**, 8 mm.	As before, "That you may see . . . "
0:56–1:12	**Instrumental Verse**, 8 mm.	Tape loops and then backward guitar prominently featured.
1:12–1:27	**Instrumental Verse**, 8 mm.	Continues loops and "backward" guitar.
1:27–1:42	**Verse 4**, 8 mm.	Vocals return, as before, "That love is all . . ."
1:42–1:57	**Verse 5**, 8 mm.	As before, "That ignorance and hate . . ."
1:57–2:13	**Verse 6**, 8 mm.	As before, "But listen to the color . . ."
2:13–2:55	**Verse 7 w/ tag and fade**, 20 mm.+	Fades out with piano, "Or play the game . . ."

come from "I Want to Hold Your Hand" in terms of these characteristics and in just over two years. The song is in simple verse form, built on a single 8-measure structure played nine times with no chorus. Lennon draws his lyrics from the Tibetan Book of the Dead, an ancient spiritual text that offers to those who will soon die advice that may help them in the next life (Lennon found the verses adapted in Timothy Leary's *The Psychedelic Experience*). The music creates a kind of static meditative drone, using a repetitive drumbeat and a limited number of harmonies. The strange sounds that occur throughout the work and especially during the instrumental verse include tape loops that have been manipulated to suggest an otherworldly sonic landscape. In an experimental manner, these loops were mixed into the final recording in real time; because of the randomness of this procedure, the same result cannot have been easily duplicated either in the studio or in live performance. "Tomorrow Never Knows" is a one-time solution to the challenges presented by the ideas behind this particular track: the band did not repeat this exact approach again in subsequent tracks (though other tape techniques were often employed). In this way, "Tomorrow Never Knows" is more art than craft.

The Growing Importance of Lyrics. One way to see the band's tendencies toward a more artistic approach is in the song lyrics. The words for "She Loves You," "I Want to Hold Your Hand," and "A Hard Day's Night" typify early lyrics in their dedication to teenage love and are no more suggestive than words contemporary teen idols were singing. The lyrics for songs like "Help!" and "Norwegian Wood," however, begin to move into more unconventional territory. In "Help!" Lennon confesses that he has lost his confidence and needs to be reassured, looking back on his youth when his own naïveté provided a self-confidence that maturity has stripped away. The story of "Norwegian Wood" concerns a one-night stand that leaves the singer sexually frustrated. In a surprising turn not unlike the one found in Chuck Berry's "Memphis," the singer then burns the apartment down, sarcastically admiring the quality of the wood as it goes up in flames. Much of the more ambitious lyric writing came from Lennon, though McCartney's "Eleanor Rigby" paints a dark picture of alienation, perhaps influenced by the German students the band befriended in Hamburg, whom McCartney has since described as existentialists. McCartney would follow this song with "She's Leaving Home" on *Sgt. Pepper's Lonely Hearts Club Band* (1967), rendering as overly facile and misleading any characterization of Lennon as the "lyric man" and McCartney as the "music man." The Beatles' fascination with increasingly complex lyrics led them to print the complete lyrics on the album sleeve of *Sgt. Pepper*, a move that until then was uncommon among pop acts but has since been much imitated. The band's focus on lyrics was clearly influenced by the importance of lyrics in folk music, and especially in the music of Bob Dylan. Dylan, whom the band met in the fall of 1964, was the first to challenge Lennon and McCartney to move past teenage love tunes. The folksinger is also perhaps responsible for introducing the Beatles to marijuana (though this claim has been disputed)—an event that would have tremendous influence on pop culture by 1967.

Developing Greater Stylistic Range.　The Beatles' early songs stay within a rather narrow stylistic range, but ranged increasingly wider during 1964–66. The first important album to begin incorporating new stylistic approaches is *Help!* (1965); Lennon's "You've Got to Hide Your Love Away" is clearly influenced by Dylan and an oboe is employed in the ending, while McCartney's "Yesterday" features chamber-string accompaniment. With *Rubber Soul* the folk influence becomes even more pronounced, with Harrison introducing the sitar into the band's sound on "Norwegian Wood." *Revolver* ranges even more widely, from McCartney's "Eleanor Rigby" to Lennon's "Tomorrow Never Knows" and from the children's song "Yellow Submarine" to the show-band horns of "Got to Get You into My Life." The much-noted stylistic eclecticism of *Sgt. Pepper* was thus reached over the course of several albums. The Beatles were not the only band to experiment by adding new elements to rock music; the Beach Boys' Brian Wilson, working under the inspiration of earlier Leiber and Stoller and Phil Spector records, was also bringing new elements to rock. But few other bands could have gotten away with as much experimentation as the Beatles were allowed. Being the most successful band in the world brought with it a certain freedom not usually extended to young pop musicians. In taking advantage of this opportunity, the Beatles established a model for the rock musician as recording artist. The Beatles' development from craft to art in the 1964–66 period marks a shift to a new level of seriousness and self-consciousness among rock musicians and their listeners, paving the way for something that would have seemed like an oxymoron earlier in the decade: rock culture.

The British Invade

Haircuts, Accents, and Guitars.　In the wake of the Beatles' overwhelming American success in early 1964, a number of British bands flooded the U.S. charts. The most significant band after the Beatles was the Rolling Stones, a group who positioned themselves image-wise as the bad boys of the British invasion. If the Beatles were charming, cute, and friendly, then the Stones were sensual, dangerous, and often rude—in short, they were the anti-Beatles. In reality, the Stones and the Beatles were good friends and as people were much more similar than different. But to image-makers this hardly mattered, and many American teenage communities split between Stones and Beatles fans. The other British bands can be roughly divided into Beatles-type and Stones-type groups. Beatles-type bands such as Gerry and the Pacemakers and the Dave Clark Five were more pop and vocally oriented, while Stones-type groups—like the Animals and the Yardbirds—were more blues oriented. A few bands, such as the Who and the Kinks, do not fit well into either category.

It is important to realize that the term "British invasion" means primarily that all of these groups were British, played guitars, and, at least at first, wore long hair. Stylistically, there is a broad range of music within the British invasion, so while the term is useful very generally as a stylistic marker (these bands did have a number of things in common musically), it is most useful in terms of marketing and image. As discussed later in this chapter, the British invasion was clearly a fad at first; in many ways, it hardly seemed to matter whether the music was influenced by the slick production of Motown or the direct expressiveness of Chess. Initially, the Beatles and the British-invasion bands that followed in their wake were simply another version of the teen idols from the early 1960s, even if they did arrive quite unexpectedly from foreign shores.

Gerry and the Pacemakers, the Dave Clark Five, and Other Beatles-type Bands.
In retrospect we can see that the Beatles' success overshadows that of almost every other British band in the 1960s, but this was not as obvious in the months before and after their American arrival in February 1964. At home in the UK, Gerry and the Pacemakers, another Brian Epstein–managed Liverpool band, were giving the Beatles a run for their money on the British charts. This band copied the Beatles' arrangement of "How Do You Do It" with George Martin and saw it become a number one single in 1964. The Pacemakers followed with two more chart-topping British singles that year: "I Like It" and "You'll Never Walk Alone." While Gerry and the Pacemakers eventually scored seven Top 40 hits in the United States through 1966, with "Don't Let the Sun Catch You Crying" rising as high as number four in the summer of 1964, none ever reached the top spot. London's Dave Clark Five had a series of UK hits, though only "Glad All Over" (late 1963) went to number one. The band fared much better in the United States; the group had nine Top 40 American hits in 1964 alone, doing far better than Gerry and the Pacemakers, and leading some in the business to predict that they would topple the Beatles. By the end of the same year, however, the Beatles had nineteen Top 40 hits. Another Liverpool band, Billy J. Kramer and the Dakotas, also did well in the United States, placing four singles in the Top 40 in 1964, as did the Searchers, fellow Liverpudlians, who hit the Top 40 with five singles that year. The fact that many in the music business were on the lookout for the next big band at just the time the Beatles were enjoying their first success reveals how widely rock music, or at least particular rock acts, were still viewed as passing fads. A number of music business professionals at the time saw the Beatles, the Dave Clark Five, Gerry and the Pacemakers, Billy J. Kramer and the Dakotas, and the Searchers as all pretty much the same act. In many ways, these professionals were right; but while the Beatles' success survived the demise of the British invasion in 1966, the careers of these other groups ended.

Herman's Hermits, Freddy and the Dreamers, and the Hollies.
A second wave of Beatle-esque Manchester bands began to hit U.S. shores in 1965, led by Herman's Hermits, whose "I'm Into Something Good" went to number thirteen late in 1964. The group followed up with seventeen more Top 40 hits through 1968, including "Mrs. Brown You've Got a Lovely Daughter" (p1, 1965), "I'm Henry the VIII" (p1, 1965), "Listen People" (p3, 1966), and "There's a Kind of Hush" (p4, 1967). The boyish good looks of singer Peter Noone made him an immediate teen heartthrob at just the time the Beatles were beginning to move away from their mop-top, pop image. Another Manchester group, Freddy and the Dreamers, topped the U.S. charts early in 1965 with "I'm Telling You Now," following with three more Top 40 hits that year. Singer Freddy Garrity took a

Calculating that the Beatles owned the "good boy" image, the Stones cultivated a "bad boy" status. Note here the clean look of the Beatles' matching suits compared to the less-organized and scruffier attire of the Stones.

cue from the Beatles' flair for comedy by performing a silly dance while singing "Do the Freddy" (p18, 1965). The Hollies rounded out the "Manchester sound," placing six hits in the U.S. Top 40 in 1966–67, the best known of which is "Bus Stop" (p5, 1966). The Hollies' music emphasizes and expands the precise harmony singing that can be heard on many Beatles records, a feature that their lead vocalist, Graham Nash, would further develop with the group Crosby, Stills, and Nash.

The Rolling Stones and the British Blues Revival

Bad Boys, Blues, and Rhythm and Blues. The Beatles cultivated a wholesome image and, until the furor in the United States over Lennon's remarks concerning Christianity, the group's music and popularity met with only mild resistance from parents. The British invasion bands mentioned above followed the Beatles in this regard, keeping their clothes clean and their hair combed, and posing no significant threat to middle-class values and lifestyles. But a second

During the first year of the Beatles' success, fellow Liverpudlians Gerry and the Pacemakers rivaled the Fab Four's chart success in the UK. Lead singer Gerry Marsden is shown here playing a twelve-string electric like the one George Harrison played in A Hard Day's Night.

collection of British bands, mostly following the lead of the Rolling Stones, projected a more brash, nonconformist, and rebellious image. The music of these groups depended less on the vocal- and song-oriented pop styles of the late '50s and early '60s and drew more on the blues tradition, especially that of 1950s Chicago electric blues, featuring slide guitar, harmonica, and styles of vocal delivery more indebted to Muddy Waters, Elmore James, and Little Walter than to the Everly Brothers, Buddy Holly, or the girl groups. These blues-oriented bands emerged from a blues revival scene in the UK that flourished during the early 1960s but gained popularity in the United States well after the Beatles broke into the American market. Despite at times significant differences in musical style between these Beatles- and Stones-type bands, all were packaged in the matching suits and haircuts ushered in by Beatlemania—even if some of the Stones-type groups did tend to loosen their ties a bit more or lose parts of their outfits from time to time.

Blues Enthusiasts. The UK blues revival was mostly centered in London and was fueled by the same kind of British enthusiasm for American folk styles that had launched trad and skiffle. The catalysts for this scene were guitarist Alexis Korner and harmonica player Cyril Davies, who began by playing blues during breaks at performances of Chris Barber's trad band. Soon Korner and Davies regularly gathered blues enthusiasts together in London's Marquee Club (which Barber owned) and later in the Ealing Club. These sessions brought together aspiring blues musicians who generally played versions of American electric blues numbers, trying to get the music as close to the sounds on the records as possible; recordings of the Korner-Davies group Blues Incorporated from 1962 demonstrate how faithful these cover versions were. American blues records were not easy to come by in the UK, however, and many English blues musicians and fans bought them by mail order directly from the indie labels in the United States, with Chess as a favorite. The relative scarcity of American blues records led to trading and borrowing among members of the London-based blues culture—a practice that further reinforced the subculture aspects of the UK blues revival. A number of musicians who would later become important in the history of rock music came through the London blues scene, including John Mayall, Stevie Winwood, Eric Clapton, Jack Bruce, and John McLaughlin. Sitting in on Davies and Korner jam sessions some evenings were a pair of teenagers from London's Dartford suburb, guitarist Keith Richards and singer Mick Jagger.

The Rolling Stones.   While our current image of the Rolling Stones tends to focus on Jagger and Richards, through much of its first years the group was led by guitarist Brian Jones. Jones was a talented and close student of American blues; during a time when he was especially enthralled by the slide-guitar playing of Elmore James, he even changed his first name to "Elmo." The Rolling Stones were formed by Jones as a blues band after the model of Blues Incorporated to cover American blues records in the clubs that made up the London underground blues scene. Jagger and Richards were also enthusiastic fans of Chuck Berry's music, though this music was at first viewed with some suspicion by dedicated blues aficionados like Jones. The group got its start in July 1962 filling in for Blues Incorporated at the Marquee and later played regularly at the Ealing Club. By January 1963 bassist Bill Wyman and drummer Charlie Watts had joined forces with Jones, Jagger, Richards, and pianist Ian Stewart, and excitement for the band's live performances started to build when they established a regular weekly gig at the Richmond Crawdaddy Club in February. Giorgio Gomelsky, an entrepreneurial filmmaker who was also involved in the London music scene, managed the group during its early days and helped the Stones build a strong following at the Crawdaddy, which Gomelsky also managed. In May 1963 management of the band was taken over by Andrew Loog Oldham and Eric Easton. Easton was an experienced hand in the recording industry and Oldham had worked as a publicist for Larry Parnes and Brian Epstein (he had helped promote Gerry and the Pacemakers and Billy J. Kramer). When the Stones gave up their regular spot at the Crawdaddy, they were succeeded by the Yardbirds, whom Gomelsky also began to manage.

The Stones made their turn toward a more mainstream, pop-oriented style in the wake of the Beatles' first UK success in mid 1963. The two groups knew one another and were friendly, though the Beatles were by far the more successful and experienced group at first. At a Beatles show in London, members of the

Stones (who were not playing) even helped the Beatles load their equipment in and out of the van. The Stones recorded for Decca and were signed by Dick Rowe, "the man who turned down the Beatles." At one point Rowe was judging a talent contest in Liverpool on a panel that included George Harrison. After apologizing to Harrison about not signing the Beatles, he asked him if he knew any up-and-coming groups. Harrison enthusiastically endorsed the Stones and Rowe immediately sought them out at the Crawdaddy. Oldham and Easton negotiated an unprecedented deal with Decca specifying that while the label would have exclusive rights to distribute the band's recordings, the Stones would retain ownership of the recordings. Oldham had gotten the idea of retaining the rights to the recordings from a conversation he had had months before with Phil Spector when the American producer was in the UK. Even though he had no experience in the recording studio, Oldham immediately assumed the additional role of producer in the band.

The Stones did not initially write their own music; their first single was a cover version of Chuck Berry's "Come On" (uk21, 1963) and their third was a cover of Buddy Holly's "Not Fade Away" (uk3, 1964). The band's second single was a song Lennon and McCartney wrote for them, "I Wanna Be Your Man" (uk12, 1963), which both groups recorded. A comparison of the two versions provides an interesting contrast between these two bands in their early years. The Stones version shows much more of a blues influence, with an arrangement that sounds loose and prominently features the slide guitar. Like so much of their early music, the Beatles' version is tightly arranged and focuses on the vocals. Quickly understanding the financial advantages that writing music could provide, Oldham decided that Jagger and Richards should try their hand at songwriting, reportedly locking them in a room until they wrote a song. "The Last Time" was the band's first of many Jagger-Richards hits to come, reaching number one in the UK in 1965, though the budding songwriting team had an international hit in the second half of 1964 with Marianne Faithful's recording of "As Tears Go By" (uk9, p22). While the Stones would increasingly record more Jagger-Richards songs, their first six albums contain more cover versions than originals, and these cover versions reveal the band's dedication to American rhythm and blues artists such as Muddy Waters, Jimmy Reed, and Bo Diddley, among others. Two early hit singles show the band's range of influences: "It's All Over Now" (uk1, 1964) was originally recorded by Bobby Womack, and the Stones give it a country and western rhythmic feel, while Willie Dixon's "Little Red Rooster" (uk1, 1964) is a slow blues tune.

The Stones enjoyed great success in late 1963 and all through 1964 in the UK but this success did not extend in equal measure to the United States, where the Beatles, Gerry and the Pacemakers, and the Dave Clark Five were all much more warmly received. Late in 1964 things began to improve as "Time Is on My Side" hit number six in the United States and "The Last Time" reached number nine in the spring of 1965. Part of the reason for the Stones' slow start in the United States was that Andrew Oldham had encouraged the group's image as rock music's bad boys after it became clear that he would never be able to get them to project the same nice guy image that Brian Epstein had so effectively crafted for the Beatles. Oldham had bought the Stones matching outfits when he took over, but the band soon lost or hopelessly soiled parts of these stage clothes—and not entirely by accident. The Stones rode to fame in the UK as the antithesis of the Beatles, sporting scruffier clothing, longer hair, and rebellious attitudes that shocked adults. This, of course, was the key to the Stones' appeal to many young people in England; that appeal would soon spread to the United States also, starting with an American tour in late 1964 that—while not especially successful financially—generated several stories about the band that cast them as rock and roll troublemakers.

The band solidified its image as rock's bad boys with the single "(I Can't Get No) Satisfaction," which, driven by Richards' fuzz-guitar introduction, hit the top spot in the United States and the UK in the summer of 1965. Though the song's lyrics clearly express a general dissatisfaction with the superficiality of daily life, a rumor soon circulated that the topic of the song was masturbation, perhaps owing to the last verse, which refers to menstruation and a resultant sexual frustration. Jagger and Richards did little to calm the storm over the record, since the rumor fit well into the anti-Beatles image the band was now cultivating. What could have been better, after all, than a thin, swaggering Mick Jagger singing a song about something many American kids and their parents regarded—publicly at least—as a forbidden pleasure? The Stones followed with "Get Off of My Cloud" (p1 uk1, 1965), "As Tears Go By" (p6, 1966), "19th Nervous Breakdown" (p2 uk2, 1966), and "Paint It, Black" (p1 uk1, 1966). As the group's popularity rose in the United States, they appeared on American television and toured with increasing success, though their shows tended to be marked by fan riots and police interventions. After experiencing what was becoming the standard fan mania during the band's first appearance on his

The pandemonium of rock shows could sometimes turn violent. Here a Zurich crowd gets out of hand in April 1967 at a Rolling Stones concert. Considering the manic quality of many of these events, it seems remarkable that such chaos did not break out more often.

show in 1965, Ed Sullivan vowed the Stones would never return. By early 1967, however, Sullivan had changed his mind, and in a situation reminiscent of Elvis Presley's famous appearances on Sullivan's show several years earlier, the group was asked to change the chorus of "Let's Spend the Night Together" to "let's spend some time together." Jagger did not change the lyric, but rather mumbled it.

The Stones and the Blues Tradition.   Considering the importance blues music had for the Stones, it is somewhat surprising that there is hardly a twelve-bar blues number anywhere in their mid 1960s repertory that is not a cover version of a track recorded first by black artists ("19th Nervous Breakdown," which does employ the twelve-bar pattern, is one important exception). The Jagger-Richards originals tend to be influenced more by Chuck Berry and Motown than by Muddy Waters or Howlin' Wolf. This may reflect Jagger's opinion, expressed during the band's first years of success, that the idea of a blues song being written by a white Brit was preposterous. Whatever the reason, "Get Off of My Cloud" shows an approach used often by Jagger and Richards. While the Beatles employed mostly AABA forms as found in Brill Building pop, Jagger and Richards hardly ever used that form, preferring the contrasting verse-chorus form found in much of Chuck Berry and Buddy Holly's music. "Get Off of My Cloud" is the same contrasting verse-chorus as Holly's "That'll Be the Day" or Berry's "Rock and Roll Music."

The Animals, the Yardbirds, and the Spencer Davis Group.   When the Stones gave up their regular date at Giorgio Gomelsky's Crawdaddy Club in Richmond and took a step up in the music business under the management of Oldham and Easton in the spring of 1963, the Yardbirds took over their place in Gomelsky's club as well as under his managerial auspices. The group initially consisted of Keith Relf on vocals and harmonica, Paul Samwell-Smith on bass, Jim McCarty on drums, and Chris Deja and Tony Topham on guitar, but Topham was soon replaced by lead guitarist Eric Clapton. Clapton earned his nickname "Slowhand" during these early years because he often broke guitar strings and had to change them on-stage, as audience members joked with him about it by providing slow applause. The group was initially even more devoted to the blues tradition than the Stones had been, and Clapton was especially uncompromising in his resistance to pop music at the time. The Yardbirds developed long, improvisatory passages at the end of songs that they called "rave-ups"; these rave-ups emphasized the instrumental prowess of band members (Clapton especially) and were the forerunners of the much longer instrumental jam sessions that would characterize much rock music later in the decade. A good instance of this can be heard at the end of the band's version of Howlin' Wolf's "Smokestack Lightning," recorded at the Marquee in the spring of 1964 and released in the UK on the album *Five Live Yardbirds* in December.

Gomelsky had hopes that the Yardbirds could also follow the Stones' model as hit-makers, but the band's first two UK singles performed disappointingly: "I Wish You Would" failed to chart and "Good Morning Little

Schoolgirl" rose only as high as number forty-four in the UK. At this point Gomelsky, who was not only managing but also producing the band (with Samwell-Smith acting as musical director), decided that the group needed a sure-fire pop hit and was able to get songwriter Graham Gouldman's "For Your Love" for the Yardbirds. The verses of the tune primarily use studio musicians,

LISTENING GUIDE   GET MUSIC ▶▶   wwnorton.com/rockhistory

The Rolling Stones, "Get Off of My Cloud"

Words and music by Mick Jagger and Keith Richards, produced by Andrew Loog Oldham. Reached #1 on the U.S. and UK charts in 1965.

FORM: Contrasting verse-chorus, with an alternation of the 16-bar verse and the 8-bar chorus. Verses 2 and 3 are preceded by a 2-bar interlude to prepare the return of the vocal.

TIME SIGNATURE: 4/4.

INSTRUMENTATION: Electric guitars, bass, drums, hand claps, lead and backup vocals.

0:00–0:11	**Introduction**, 6 mm.	Drums intro, then entire band enters
0:11–0:42	**Verse 1**, 16 mm.	Vocals enter, note repeated melodic figure in the lead guitar, note that the vocals are more blues-oriented than the Beatles' vocals, "I live on . . ."
0:42–0:57	**Chorus**, 8 mm.	Lead vocals echoed by backup vocals, which are loose and simple, hand claps added. The chorus is more driving than the verse, giving it a sense of focus as well as offering contrast to the verse, "Hey you . . ."
0:57–1:32	**Verse 2**, 18 mm.	2-bar interlude and then the verse is performed as before, "The telephone is ringin'. . ."
1:32–1:47	**Chorus** , 8 mm.	Contrasting as before, "Hey you . . ."
1:47–2:23	**Verse 3**, 18 mm.	As verse 2 with interlude, "I'm sick and tired . . ."
2:23–2:38	**Chorus**, 8 mm.	Contrasting as before, "Hey you . . ."
2:38–2:54	**Chorus and fade**, 8 mm.+	Chorus repeats and fades out.

with the band as a whole playing only during the middle bridge section. While session musicians often played on pop records, this concession to pop music was more than Clapton could bear; after "For Your Love" was finished the guitarist left the group to join John Mayall and the Bluesbreakers while the Yardbirds single rose to number six in the United States and number three in the UK in the first half of 1965. Jeff Beck replaced Clapton on lead guitar and his more experimental nature can already be heard on the group's follow-up single, "Heart Full of Soul." As Keith Richards would do on "Satisfaction," Beck uses a fuzztone to create the tune's distinctive guitar lick. (As it turns out, "Heart Full of Soul" was recorded on April 20, 1965, while "Satisfaction" was recorded three weeks later on May 12, 1965). "Heart Full of Soul," also written by Gouldman (who would later go on to play in 10cc, a successful '70s rock band), reached number nine in the United States and number two in the UK in the summer of 1965.

While Clapton felt the band had not remained true to its blues roots, the Yardbirds themselves might not have agreed. The band was especially excited to record their first original single, "Shapes of Things" (p3 uk11, 1966), in the Chess studios in Chicago, where they also recorded a cover of Bo Diddley's "I'm a Man." The group recorded a version of "Train Kept a Rollin'," a Memphis rockabilly track most often associated with the Johnny Burnette Rock and Roll Trio version of 1956, in Sam Phillips's new recording studio (the successor to Sun Studios) in Memphis. In the spring of 1966, Simon Napier-Bell and Paul Samwell-Smith took over production duties from Gomelsky, and the result was the band's last hit single, "Over, Under, Sideways, Down" (p13 uk10). In June, Samwell-Smith left the band to devote himself full-time to producing, and session guitarist Jimmy Page was brought in. Page initially replaced Samwell-Smith on bass, but soon Dreja switched to bass and Beck and Page shared the lead-guitar spot for a couple of months in the fall of 1966. In October, Beck left the Yardbirds, going on to form the Jeff Beck Group, while Page, Dreja, Relf, and McCarty kept the band alive until the summer of 1968, when the Yardbirds disbanded. Page's new group played the remaining dates the Yardbirds had booked and then adopted a new name: Led Zeppelin.

A dedicated student of American blues, Eric Clapton was the original guitarist of the Yardbirds. When the group's music took a more commercial turn, Clapton quit and re-emerged with John Mayall and the Bluesbreakers.

While the Yardbirds in many ways followed in the footsteps of the Rolling Stones, another blues-based band enjoyed success in the UK and

United States before the Yardbirds or even the Stones did. Hailing from Newcastle in the north of England, the Animals made their reputation through their wild stage act. Fronted by the powerful blues singing of Eric Burdon, the group initially played clubs in the north of England and even did

By the summer of 1967, the original Animals lineup had dissolved and lead singer Eric Burdon forged ahead with a new band. Included in the concert advertised on this poster with Burdon are 1950s legend Chuck Berry—showing the continuing connection between classic rock and roll and the British invasion—and the Steve Miller Band, who would enjoy considerable success in the 1970s.

a two-month stint at Hamburg's Star Club before moving to London in early 1964. The Animals got a crucial break when they were chosen to play on a UK tour featuring Chuck Berry as headliner. Figuring that they needed a closing number that would make a strong musical impression on this important tour, the band turned to a slow traditional American folk-blues number, "House of the Rising Sun," calculating that it would be unwise to try to outrock Chuck Berry. Produced by Mickey Most (who would also produce Herman's Hermits while working with the Animals), the single hit number six in the UK and number seven in the United States during the summer of 1964. The group followed with a string of international Most-produced hits, including a cover of Nina Simone's "Don't Let Me Be Misunderstood" (p15 uk3, 1965), a version of a Barry Mann–Cynthia Weil song originally written for Paul Revere and the Raiders, "We've Gotta Get Out of This Place" (p13 uk2, 1965), and "It's My Life" (p23 uk7, 1965). After switching to producer Tom Wilson, the band continued to enjoy hit singles, including the traditional prison blues song "Inside Looking Out" (p34 uk12, 1966) and the Gerry Goffin–Carole King song "Don't Bring Me Down" (p12 uk6, 1966). By September the original Animals lineup had dissolved, though Burdon continued with new musicians as Eric Burdon and the Animals, while bassist Chas Chandler went on to manage Jimi Hendrix.

Not all the blues-based bands playing the London clubs achieved chart success in the United States, or even in the UK. Perhaps the busiest band on the London scene was Georgie Fame and the Blue Flames—a band that featured guitarist John McLaughlin and future Jimi Hendrix drummer Mitch Mitchell at various times. Fame, who was born Clive Powell but renamed by Larry Parnes while working for him in the early 1960s, scored several UK hits, including a couple of number ones with "Yeh Yeh" in 1965 (p21) and "Get Away" in 1966. Fame's playing on the Hammond B3 organ became his trademark, though other bands on the scene also featured the Hammond, including the Graham Bond Organization, which included Jack Bruce, future Cream drummer Ginger Baker, and McLaughlin, and Zoot Money's Big Roll Band, which included future Police guitarist Andy Summers. The Spencer Davis Group

---

🎧 **LISTENING GUIDE**   GET MUSIC ▶▶   wwnorton.com/rockhistory

The Yardbirds, "Heart Full of Soul"

Words and music by Graham Gouldman, produced by Giorgio Gomelsky. Reached #9 in the United States and #2 in the UK in 1965.

FORM: Contrasting verse chorus, with 16-bar verses and 7-bar choruses. The introduction employs a 2-bar, sitar-like guitar figure. This figure returns after each statement of the chorus as a way of preparing the return of the verse. This figure is used after the final chorus to create an ending.

TIME SIGNATURE: 4/4.

INSTRUMENTATION: Electric guitar, acoustic guitar, bass, drums, bongos, lead and backup vocals. Note how the rhythm of song is driven by the acoustic guitar (supported by the drums and bass), with the electric guitar present only in passages in which it takes the melody.

0:00–0:14	**Introduction**, 8 mm.	Based on four presentations of a 2-mm. sitar-like melodic figure in the guitar.
0:14–0:41	**Verse 1**, 16 mm.	Vocals enter, distant backup vocals answer each phrase, "Sick of heart and lonely . . ."
0:41–1:00	**Chorus**, 11 mm.	A 7-bar chorus, with a more intense rhythmic feel, then four bars drawn from intro, "And I know . . ."
1:00–1:13	**Instrumental Verse** (partial), 8 mm.	Lead guitar plays melody as it was sung previously.
1:13–1:32	**Chorus**, 11 mm.	Vocals return, 7-bar chorus + 4 bars from intro, as before, "And I know . . ."
1:32–1:59	**Verse 2**, as in verse 1	"She's been gone . . ."
1:59–2:26	**Chorus**, 14 mm.	7-bar chorus, then three presentations of 2-bar guitar and a final chord.

featured the Hammond playing of a young Stevie Winwood, who was also arguably the "blackest-sounding" lead vocalist in British rhythm and blues during the mid 1960s. Though Long John Baldry, Mick Jagger, and Eric Burdon might have wanted to compete for this distinction, the seasoned blues voice that came out of a young Englishman not yet out of his teens was uncanny. The Spencer Davis Group scored two chart-topping UK hits, "Keep On Runnin'" (1965) and "Somebody Help Me" (1966) before hitting internationally with "Gimme Some Lovin'" (uk2 p7, 1966) and "I'm a Man" (uk9 p10, 1967).

The Kinks and the Who: Raw Power and Ambitious Lyrics.   Two important British groups from the mid 1960s do not fit neatly into the categories of Beatles- or Stones-type bands. The Kinks emerged from the same rhythm and blues roots as the Stones-type groups but performed mostly as part of the package tours that featured the more pop-oriented acts, while the Who claimed no real roots in the blues but played the London rhythm and blues clubs regularly. Like the Beatles, both bands depended on strong songwriting from within the band for their best material (Ray Davies for the Kinks and Pete Townshend for the Who); and like the Stones, both groups emphasized the raw power and rhythmic drive of the best American rhythm and blues.

Formed in 1963, the Kinks featured brothers Ray and Dave Davies each on guitar and vocals, with Peter Quaife on bass and Mick Avory on drums. Both Ray and Dave had played in various blues-oriented groups around London,

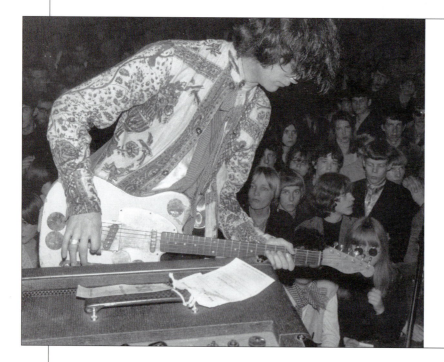

Jimmy Page was among London's most in-demand studio guitarists during the 1960s. He joined the Yardbirds initially to play bass but soon ended up on guitar, sharing the guitar duties with Jeff Beck until Beck quit to begin a solo career.

The Who were embraced by the British Mod movement in the mid 1960s, and the attention to snappy fashion so typical of mods is evident in this live shot from 1967. Not long after this, lead singer Roger Daltrey would trade in his fashionable suit for tight jeans and a fringe vest and guitarist Pete Townshend would opt for a one-piece cotton worksuit.

while Avory had been one of the first drummers for the Rolling Stones. The Kinks benefited early on from an aggressive management team and the production talents of Australian Shel Talmy. The band's first two singles, released in the first half of 1964, did not chart. The third single, "You Really Got Me" (which was reportedly written by Ray Davies in imitation of "Louie Louie" and became a hit again when covered by Van Halen in 1978), went to number one in the UK and number seven in the United States in the fall of 1964. The Kinks' aggressive pop approach in the early hits can be heard in the opening guitar chords, as well as in the wild guitar solo in the middle of the track. A series of Davies-written songs followed, including "All Day and All of the Night" (uk2 p7, 1964), "Tired of Waiting for You" (uk1, p6, 1965), and "Till the End of the Day" (uk6 p50, 1965). As the Beatles grew more serious and ambitious with their lyrics in 1965, so did Davies: his "A Well-Respected Man" (p13, 1965) and "Dedicated Follower of Fashion" (uk4 p36, 1966) offered clever and biting critiques of '60s culture and values.

Initially formed in 1962 as the Detours, the Who combined the guitar playing and songwriting of Pete Townshend with the singing of Roger Daltrey, the assertive bass playing of John Entwistle, and the manic drumming of Keith Moon. Though they eventually became one of the most important bands in the history of rock music, the Who were not an influential band until the late in 1960s. Their series of UK hit singles during the mid 1960s never made the U.S. Top 40, and the band's success was restricted to England until the release of "I Can See for Miles," which went to number nine in the United States in the fall of 1967. Like those of the Kinks, the first several Who singles were produced by Shel Talmy. Their first single, "I Am the Face," was released under the name the High Numbers in the summer of 1964 and failed to chart. As the Who, and now recording Townshend's songs, the band scored a series of top UK hits, including "I Can't Explain"(uk8, 1965), "Anyway, Anyhow, Anywhere" (uk10, 1965), "My Generation" (uk2, 1965), "Substitute" (uk5, 1966), "I'm a Boy" (uk2, 1966), and "Happy Jack" (uk3, 1966; p24, 1967). Appearing every Tuesday for six months at the Marquee Club during 1964–65, the group billed its music as "maximum R&B" and quickly became a favorite band among the Mod subculture in London.

Like the music of the Who during this time, the Mod movement never made it across the Atlantic to the United States, though "the mods" were a significant faction within the London youth culture of the mid 1960s. Mods listened to American R&B (Motown especially), dressed in very carefully controlled ways, worked but disdained advancement, sometimes rode Vespa motorscooters with many extra reflectors and mirrors installed, and danced late into the night—often under the influence of amphetamines—at select London clubs such as the Scene, where the Who often played. The mods were the opposite of "the rockers," who rode motorcycles and wore leather jackets in the style of Marlon Brando in *The Wild One*. The animosity between these two factions was serious enough for riots to break out, as they did in the quiet seaside resort town of Brighton in the summer of 1964, as the mods and rockers fought one another openly in the streets. The mod scene and lifestyle is captured in the Who's 1973 album *Quadrophenia*, a concept album in which the Brighton Beach rumble plays a crucial role, and in the 1979 movie of the same name. By the late 1960s, Townshend's songwriting had become increasingly ambitious, but the road from the mid 1960s mods through *Tommy* to *Quadrophenia* will be taken up in a later chapter.

The Mop Tops Threaten the Big Wigs

The rise of the Beatles transformed popular music in at least two important ways. First, it opened doors for British acts within the UK, allowing British artists to begin to reclaim their own popular-music charts and reap the benefits of such domestic success. This revitalized British popular music in a fundamental way. Second, the success of the Beatles in America—and indeed, the world—opened new opportunities for British acts outside the UK. Considering the broad stylistic range of the British bands that succeeded in the United States in the wake of the Beatles' success, it is clear that for many young Americans the British invasion was as much concerned with haircuts, clothing, and accents as it was with music. Strictly in terms of musical style, a Beatles concert and a Yardbirds concert were quite different from one another. But in the eyes of the Americans who came out to the shows, as well as those who saw the bands on television, heard them on the radio, or read about them in magazines, the groups were part of the same trend. The British invasion was thus—initially at least—a fad in which music was only one factor. Distinguishing between the more pop-oriented groups and the more blues-oriented ones helps to organize the music of the British invasion along music-stylistic lines that can be further understood within a broader historical perspective of music before 1964 and after 1966.

Writers on the history of rock often greatly emphasize the impact of the Beatles on the American scene in early 1964 and the subsequent flood of English bands. While it is clear that the British bands pushed many American groups off the charts, a look at the Billboard pop charts during 1964 also

---

LISTENING GUIDE   GET MUSIC ▶▶   wwnorton.com/rockhistory

The Kinks, "You Really Got Me"

Words and music by Ray Davies, produced by Shel Talmy. Reached #1 in the UK and #7 in the United States in 1964.

FORM: Simple verse form, with repeated 20-bar verses built on a two-chord pattern that is repeated progresssively higher on the guitar providing a sense of growing tonal intensification as the verse proceeds. This two-chord pattern is not transposed during the guitar solo, and a comparison of that partial verse with the other complete ones highlights this tonal difference.

TIME SIGNATURE: 4/4. Note the use of repeated piano chords and tambourine to underscore the beat and its division in two parts (simple time).

INSTRUMENTATION: Electric guitars, piano, bass, drums, tambourine, lead and backup vocals. While this track is professionally produced, the backup vocals give it a wild and almost amateurish quality, an impression reinforced by the manic but relatively primitive guitar solo.

0:00–0:07	**Introduction**, 4 mm.	Starts with 1-bar guitar figure played twice, then band enters. Note the distorted tone in the guitar.
0:07–0:42	**Verse 1 w/refrain**, 20 mm.	Vocals enter. Note how verse builds, first with solo vocal, then with added piano, then with added backup vocals, also getting increasingly louder to drive to refrain, "Girl, you really got me . . ."
0:42–1:17	**Verse 2 w/refrain**, 20 mm.	As before, "See, don't ever set . . ."
1:17–1:34	**Instrumental verse** (partial), 10 mm.	Guitar solo as the music breaks into a controlled frenzy.
1:34–2:12	**Verse 2 w/refrain**, 20 mm.	Repeats lyrics of second verse, last 2-bars changed to create ending.

reveals that much American music from the early 1960s continued to enjoy success after the British arrived: Phil Spector, the Beach Boys, and a host of Motown artists continued to score hit records. While the dividing line of February 1964 is convenient for articulating changes within popular music at the time, it is only a rough boundary. The most important aspect of the British invasion is that it established a more equal footing for American and British artists within popular music in the United States. The musical cross-fertilization between the States and the UK has been a feature of popular music in both countries ever since.

The British invasion certainly disrupted the American music business, and just at a time when the U.S. companies were thinking they had things back under control after the wild years of 1955–59. As in any business, a loss of market share is of great concern, and this is precisely what alarmed the major U.S. labels about the British invasion. Even though British bands did not completely take over the charts, they did make very significant inroads. This meant that a portion of the records Columbia or RCA might have sold to young listeners were now being sold by competitors offering a product that could not be quickly duplicated. As far as the major labels were concerned, something had to be done to win back this lost ground. In the next chapter we will see how American musicians reacted to the Brits and how the American music business worked to gain back its lost market share.

Questions for Review and Discussion

1. Before 1963, what was the general state of the British popular music industry? What accounts for the dominance of American pop during those years?
2. How did the success of the Beatles in the UK affect the British music business?
3. Outline the development of the Beatles' music from 1963 to 1966. What general tendencies can be found in the music and lyrics?
4. What other British bands seriously challenged the Beatles' popularity during 1964?
5. What are the important influences on the early music of the Rolling Stones? What American traditions played a role in the band's early days and how?
6. How did the Stones' music and the Beatles' music differ? How did the images of the two bands differ?
7. What other British bands of the mid 1960s were strongly grounded in the American blues tradition?
8. Compare and contrast the Kinks and the Who with the Beatles- and Stones-type bands.
9. How did the success of the British bands in the United States shake up the American music business?

Further Reading

Tony Bacon, *London Live* (Miller-Freeman Books, 1999).
Walter Everett, *The Beatles as Musicians: The Quarry Men through* Rubber Soul (Oxford University Press, 2001).

Walter Everett, *The Beatles as Musicians:* Revolver *through the* Anthology (Oxford University Press, 1998).

Dave McAleer, *The Fab British Rock 'n' Roll Invasion of 1964* (St. Martin's Press, 1994).

Philip Norman, *The Stones* (Penguin, 1993).

Philip Norman, *Shout! The Beatles in Their Generation* (MJF Books, 1981).

Harry Shapiro, *Alexis Korner: The Biography* (Bloomsbury, 1996).

Bill Wyman with Ray Coleman, *Stone Alone: The Story of a Rock 'n' Roll Band* (Da Capo, 1997).

The Byrds' distinctive version of Bob Dylan's "Mr. Tambourine Man," frequently cited as the first folk-rock hit, was part of an American response to the British invasion of the American pop charts. While the Byrds were steeped in the music of the American folk revival, they were also influenced by the Beatles' early music. After seeing A Hard Day's Night, the group added an electric twelve-string guitar to their already refined vocal harmonies, blending the Beatles, Dylan, the Kingston Trio, and a touch of surf music to create a trans-Atlantic number one hit in the summer of 1965. The Dylan version of "Mr. Tambourine Man" was released after the Byrds' version and is longer, containing two extra verses. Though the Byrds played as a band on subsequent releases, the only member of the group to play an instrument on this first single is Roger McGuinn, who plays the electric twelve-string. With the Byrds providing the vocals and McGuinn adding his trademark jingle-jangle guitar sound, the rest of the music is played by Los Angeles studio musicians—a bunch of top professionals who went by the nickname "The Wrecking Crew."

American Responses

The reaction of American teenagers to the music of the Beatles in early 1964 is easy to document; though the term "Beatlemania" had been coined in the UK in 1963 to describe the fans' reaction to the band's music there, it is an even more apt description of the reaction stateside—and not only among teenagers. Chapter 4 described the enormous commercial success enjoyed by the Beatles, the Rolling Stones, and a host of other British groups during 1964–66. Thought of in this audience-oriented context, the "American response" to the British invasion was as warm a welcome as any musician could hope for. This chapter will focus on the response of American musicians and the American popular music business to the competition offered by the Brits, showing that this reaction was not nearly as immediate as the one found among fans. The British bands did not erase all American pop acts from the charts; many groups who had hit records during 1963 continued to have success, seemingly undiminished by the enormous popularity of the Beatles and other British groups. Phil Spector, the Beach Boys, the Four Seasons, and most artists on the Motown label, for instance, vied neck-and-neck with the foreign invaders for top chart positions and radio airtime, sometimes winning.

By the summer of 1965, however, new musical styles in American pop were emerging as a result of the cross-fertilization of American styles with the Mersey beat. Folk rock is perhaps the most obvious response. Led by the Byrds and Bob Dylan but with dozens of acts soon jumping on the bandwagon, folk rock took the easy strumming-and-singing texture of folk and added Beatles-like electric guitars, bass, drums, and sometimes keyboards to create an American music-stylistic reaction to the British invasion. In many ways it is easy to see how and why this happened. American young people had already been hummin'-and-strummin' their way through the folk revival. During their early years on the charts the Beatles were essentially a guitar-oriented vocal group. Many performers who had been singing and harmonizing about social injustice to the accompaniment of the acoustic guitar or banjo made an easy transition to singing and harmonizing about social injustice to the accompaniment of the electric guitar and bass. Also in imitation of the Beatles' and Stones' guitar-dominated sound, a slew of garage bands formed across the country, most with only minimal playing and singing skills that tended not to impede their aggressive and energetic rock enthusiasm.

Pop music in the United States had been centered around New York early in the 1960s, but much of the new music after 1964 emerged from Los Angeles (though often still on New York–based record labels). Many of the folk rockers had made their way from New York's Greenwich Village to Los Angeles, and by 1965 the Hollywood-based television industry was getting into the picture. This industry produced several pop-music variety shows aimed at America's teens—one hosted by Paul Revere and the Raiders, emphasizing the American response by donning Revolutionary War costumes—and by 1966 put forward the most direct answer to the Beatles: the Monkees. The music business may have been surprised and stunned in 1964 by the overwhelming success of the Brits, but by mid 1965 American bands on American labels were once again scoring significant chart successes, partly by imitating the English and partly by adapting tried-and-true music-business practices. Perhaps the best instance of this blend of imitation and adaptation is folk rock.

Folk Rock

Dylan Plugs In. In December 1960, a young folksinger arrived in New York from his native state of Minnesota, where he had already been playing gigs in folk clubs and coffee houses. Within a few months, Bob Dylan was performing in Greenwich Village and becoming increasingly active in New York's burgeoning folk scene. By the beginning of 1964, Dylan was among the most respected young folksingers in the United States. Dylan was not particularly well known outside the folk community at this time, since "folk" to a general pop audience meant the music of the Kingston Trio or Peter, Paul, and Mary. Some pop listeners might have known that Dylan wrote "Blowin' in the Wind" and "Don't Think Twice It's Alright" (both hits in 1963 for Peter, Paul, and Mary), but most would not have enjoyed Dylan's own versions, which appear on his second album, *The Freewheelin' Bob Dylan* (p22 uk16, 1963). Like many folk artists, Dylan enjoyed success on the album charts in the absence of hit singles, with sales fueled by appearances in folk clubs and on college campuses. His first album did not chart, but the third, *The Times They Are A-Changin'* (p20 uk20, 1964), and fourth, *Another Side of Bob Dylan* (p43 uk8, 1964), did well enough in both the American and English markets to make Dylan one of the most respected and emulated folksingers of this period.

Dylan was a skilled performer but an even more accomplished songwriter. It was common for folksingers to write their own music, often basing new songs on tunes drawn or adapted from traditional folk melodies. Dylan's idol Woody Guthrie frequently reworked familiar music with new lyrics that chronicled social injustice. Dylan initially followed this model; "Blowin' in the Wind," for instance, addressed civil rights while "Masters of War" challenged the Vietnam conflict. Dylan's songs soon became increasingly focused on his own feelings and attempts to understand the world, however, prompting some in the folk world to observe that he had a tendency to replace the "we" in folk with "me." Early songs such as "Girl from the North Country" and "Don't Think Twice It's Alright" already display Dylan's exceptional gifts as a songwriter; the personal lyrics are crafted with the painstaking aesthetic attitude more common among poets than folksingers.

After an enormously successful tour of the UK in 1965 (documented in the D.A. Pennebaker film *Don't Look Back*), Dylan began a break with the folk tradition that would have tremendous consequences for popular music. He had long been interested in using electric instruments in his music. A few sessions for his second album were recorded with a band, with Dylan even trying out a version of "That's All Right (Mama)." He was not satisfied with the results and only one of those tracks was used on the album ("Corrina, Corrina"); another, "Mixed Up Confusion," became his first single, but it did not chart when released in 1962. In January 1965 and under the pronounced influence of the Beatles, the Byrds recorded their version of Dylan's "Mr. Tambourine Man." Even though the single was not released until months later, Dylan heard the Byrds' version in late 1964 or early 1965 and decided to renew his attempts to electrify his music. Half the songs on Dylan's fifth album, *Bringin' It All Back Home* (p6 uk1, 1965) used electric instruments, including his first hit single, "Subterranean Homesick Blues" (p39 uk9, 1965). Perhaps because half the album was acoustic, the folk community did not express an overwhelmingly negative reaction to Dylan's new electrified music. It was not until he played the Newport Folk Festival in July 1965 that the con-

Bob Dylan first made his name as a folksinger, strongly influenced by the music and image of Woody Guthrie. Dylan appears here with his acoustic guitar and trademark harmonica holder; while he radiates folk earnestness in this shot, his performances were typically also filled with wit and humor.

troversy began. Dylan's electric numbers met with resistance among the more traditionally minded folkies in attendance, and while accounts of the events vary, it seems clear that many senior members of the folk establishment who had strongly supported Dylan up to this point (including Pete Seeger of the Weavers, who was a key player in the folk revival—see Chapter 3) felt betrayed by his turn to electric instruments. Many felt that Dylan had sold out to pop; as a result, he became the target of very strong criticism within folk circles.

Dylan's next single, "Like a Rolling Stone," again used electric backing and rose to number two in the United States (uk4) in the summer and fall of 1965. He followed with the album *Highway 61 Revisited* (p3 uk4, 1965) and the angry hit single, "Positively 4th Street" (p7 uk8, 1965). The folk music establishment continued to react negatively to Dylan's use of electric instruments, and Dylan

in turn felt betrayed by their response. As a traditional folksinger, Dylan had excelled in aggressively attacking those who exploited others to gain unfair social or economic advantage. Dylan referred to such tunes as "finger pointing" songs, and after the response to his 1965 Newport performance with electric instruments he decided to use "Positively 4th Street" to point his finger at the folk establishment he felt had unfairly criticized him. The fervor of Dylan's obsession on this issue can be seen in the song's structure, which is a simple verse form employing twelve verses. After a short four-measure introduction, Dylan plows away at verse after verse, all based on the same eight-measure harmonic pattern. The song concludes with part of a thirteenth time through the chord progression, with vocals absent and the focus on Al Kooper's organ part, until the song fades out. Anyone who does not get the clear feeling that Dylan is angry by the end of the tune is just not listening.

Dylan followed up with the single "Rainy Day Women Nos. 12 and 35" (p2 uk7, 1966), and using most of the Hawks (who would later be called the Band), recorded *Blonde on Blonde* (p9 uk3, 1966). In July 1966 Dylan was almost killed in a motorcycle accident in upstate New York. Although his injuries kept him out of the spotlight for months afterward, his records continued to influence other musicians, and his lyrics were especially important. Dylan's songs had shown that pop music could address issues other than teenage romance and leisure concerns, and this seriousness of purpose became a model for many other songwriters in the 1960s and later. And while the folk traditionalists may have believed Dylan's music had become too commercial, it was not nearly as commercial as much of the folk rock that followed in its wake.

The Byrds and the Jingle-Jangle of the Electric Twelve-String Guitar.

As a measure of Dylan's importance in the rise of American folk rock, the first international number one folk-rock single was a Dylan song. In the summer of 1965, the Byrds' recording of "Mr. Tambourine Man" hit the top of both the U.S. and UK charts. The Byrds formed in Los Angeles in 1964, and the band's leading members had been active in the folk music scene in the early 1960s. Roger McGuinn had studied folk music as a teenager at Chicago's Old Town School of Folk Music, before working with the Limelighters and the Chad Mitchell Trio on the folk circuit. McGuinn was active in the early 1960s folk scene in New York's Greenwich Village as well, playing its folk clubs by night while working as a Brill Building songwriter for Bobby Darin during the day. In 1964, McGuinn headed to Los Angeles to do a stint at the Troubadour Club where, under the influence of the British invasion, he played sets mixing folk

Dylan shocked the folk-music establishment when he turned to the electric guitar in 1965. In this posed publicity photo, Dylan not only holds an electric guitar with the amplifier in close proximity, but his acoustic guitar is on the floor and his harmonica holder is empty, seeming to underscore his shift away from traditional folk music.

numbers with Beatles songs. McGuinn met songwriter and singer Gene Clark while playing the Troubadour, and he and Clark, who had been a member of the New Christie Minstrels, began writing songs together. Soon singer-guitarist

LISTENING GUIDE

GET MUSIC ▶▶ wwnorton.com/rockhistory

Bob Dylan, "Positively 4th Street"

Words and music by Bob Dylan, produced by Bob Johnston. Rose to #7 on the Billboard Pop charts (uk8) in fall 1965.

FORM: Simple verse. Like many Dylan songs, this song has a lot of lyrics. In this case, Dylan delivers 12 verses over the same 8-bar structure, without much change in the accompaniment. In contrast to the technique of building an arrangement by adding instruments or vocal parts as the song progresses, this track remains static, leaving the listener to focus on the development of the lyrics.

TIME SIGNATURE: 4/4. Note the finger cymbals on beat four of each measure.

INSTRUMENTATION: Piano, organ, electric guitars, drums, finger cymbals, lead vocal. Pay particular attention to Al Kooper's organ playing, which came to be much imitated despite Kooper's insistence that he was not really an organist.

0:00–0:09	**Introduction**, 4 mm.	Organ melody featured.
0:09–0:26	**Verse 1**, 8 mm.	Vocals enter, organ adds melodic interest, while the other instruments keep a low profile, supporting the vocal, "You got a lot of nerve . . ."
0:26–0:44	**Verse 2**, 8 mm.	As before, "You got a lot of nerve . . ."
0:44–1:01	**Verse 3**, 8 mm.	As before, "You say I let you down . . ."
1:01–1:19	**Verse 4**, 8 mm.	As before, "You say you lost your faith . . ."
1:19–1:36	**Verse 5**, 8 mm.	As before, "I know the reason . . ."
1:36–1:53	**Verse 6**, 8 mm.	As before, "Do you take me . . ."
1:54–2:11	**Verse 7**, 8 mm.	As before, "You seen me on the street . . ."
2:11–2:28	**Verse 8**, 8 mm.	As before, "When you know . . ."
2:29–2:46	**Verse 9**, 8 mm.	As before, "Now I don't feel . . ."
2:46–3:03	**Verse 10**, 8 mm.	As before, guitar and piano get a little busier, but not much, "And now I know . . ."
3:04–3:21	**Verse 11**, 8 mm.	As before, "I wish that for just one . . ."
3:21–3:38	**Verse 12**, 8 mm.	As before, "I wish that for just one . . ."
3:39–3:51	**Instrumental Verse** (partial), 4 mm.+	Organ featured again, as track fades out.

David Crosby joined the group and bluegrass mandolin player Chris Hillman was recruited to play bass, while Michael Clarke joined on drums. The band rehearsed under the direction of manager Jim Dickson, who taped the rehearsals and then forced the group to listen to themselves. Surviving tapes from that period, released on *In the Beginning* (Rhino, 1988), document the band's progress from a folk vocal-harmony act to a rock band. The group's distinct jingle-jangle guitar sound plays a key role in that development; it resulted when members of the band saw *A Hard Day's Night* and noticed that George Harrison was playing an electric twelve-string guitar. The electric twelve-string was not widely used in pop at that time and Harrison was playing only the second one ever made by the Rickenbacker guitar company. McGuinn traded in his acoustic twelve-string for a Rickenbacker electric twelve, and it is the distinctive jingle-jangle sound of that guitar that is heard on the introduction to "Mr. Tambourine Man."

The Byrds initially made their mark with rock versions of folk songs; the group's first album, *Mr. Tambourine Man* (p6 uk7, 1965), included three additional Dylan covers, including "All I Really Want to Do," which hit number four in the UK but was stalled at number forty in the States when another version by Cher passed it on the way to number fifteen. The Byrds' second number one U.S. hit, "Turn, Turn, Turn" (uk26, 1966) was a version of a Pete Seeger number McGuinn remembered from a Judy Collins album he had played on years before. The second album, *Turn, Turn, Turn* (p17 uk11, 1966), again included Dylan covers, though like the first it also had originals, mostly written by Gene Clark. As Dylan's success performing rock versions of his own songs continued, the Byrds were forced to rely increasingly on their own songwriting, and Clark, McGuinn, and Crosby wrote the band's next hit, "Eight Miles High" (p14 uk24, 1966). The guitar introduction invokes jazz, employing a melodic figure borrowed from John Coltrane's "India," and the lyrics refer both to the cruising altitude of a trans-Atlantic jet (actually six miles high) and to drugs. When an American radio tip sheet listed the song as a "drug song" in the summer of 1966, stations immediately stopped playing it. By the release of their fourth album, *Younger Than Yesterday* (p24 uk37, 1967), the Byrds' music had broadened to include country, jazz, and avant-garde influences as they became one of the most influential bands within American psychedelia (discussed in Chapter 7).

The Byrds, Dylan, the Beach Boys, and the Music Business. The Byrds' recording of Dylan's "Mr. Tambourine Man" represents a point of convergence for several elements of the music business that are usually thought of as exclusive of one another. Over the years since this record was released, many writers and fans have thought of the Byrds' music as a kind of antithesis to the overtly manufactured Brill Building music or the sunny but frivolous sound of surf music. On this first hit single, however, separating the authenticity of folk music (Dylan especially) from the calculated aspects of teen pop is more difficult than one might expect. To begin with, all the members of the Byrds do not actually play on this record: McGuinn plays the electric twelve-string guitar and he and David Crosby sing, but the rest of the music is provided by the Wrecking

Crew—that cast of top-flight studio musicians (mentioned in Chapter 3) who played on many Phil Spector hits (the Byrds played on their own records after this, however). Wrecking Crew musicians had previously provided the musical backing for the Beach Boys' "Don't Worry Baby." They used the same rhythmic feel to back the Byrds' "Mr. Tambourine Man" at the suggestion of producer Terry Melcher. As you may recall from the discussion of "Be My Baby" and "Don't Worry Baby" in Chapter 3, Brian Wilson wrote "Don't Worry Baby" hoping that Spector would record it with one of his girl groups. Thus, "Mr. Tambourine Man" brings together the folk revival (Dylan's song), girl groups, surf music, and with the use of the electric twelve-string inspired by *A Hard Day's Night*, the British invasion as well. In addition, McGuinn has remarked that the signature guitar lick that begins "Mr. Tambourine Man" was inspired by a version of the J. S. Bach chorale, "Jesu, Joy of Man's Desiring," which McGuinn had been playing on the twelve-string around that time.

The Byrds adapted Dylan's tune from an acoustic folk version that Dylan had decided not to release. As the Listening Guide shows, the song is in a contrasting verse-chorus form. The Byrds use only one of Dylan's three verses, a decision made to keep the song at about the two-minute length typical for pop singles in 1965. The odd number of measures in the verse and chorus are unusual and arise because these sections are expanded (and in the case of the second chorus, contracted) from what would typically be sixteen-measure sections. As you listen, see if you can detect where the extra measures are added or dropped (this is especially obvious in the verse section).

Simon and Garfunkel Go Electric.   Perhaps no song better illustrates the transformation of folk into folk rock better than Simon and Garfunkel's "The Sounds of Silence" (p1, 1965). Paul Simon and Art Garfunkel began their professional

The Byrds are joined onstage by a harmonica-playing Bob Dylan. Note that Roger McGuinn (right) is playing his signature Rickenbacker electric twelve-string guitar, while David Crosby (left) plays a Gretsch Tennessean like the one George Harrison used on Beatles for Sale (1964).

careers as high school students in the late 1950s under the name Tom and Jerry. Modeling their act on the Everly Brothers, Tom and Jerry had a minor hit in late 1957/early 1958 with "Hey Schoolgirl"; the duo even appeared on *American Bandstand*. Simon and Garfunkel then turned to folk in the early 1960s, recording the album *Wednesday Morning, 3 A.M.* (1964). When the album sold poorly, Simon went to London to perform solo and Garfunkel went to graduate school. After "Mr. Tambourine Man" and "Like a Rolling Stone" became hits, somebody at Columbia Records remembered the Simon and Garfunkel album. Tom Wilson, who had produced Dylan's albums and *Wednesday Morning, 3 A.M.*, was brought in and, without the knowledge or participation of either Simon or Garfunkel, he augmented the acoustic version of "The Sounds of Silence" that

LISTENING GUIDE   GET MUSIC ▶▶   wwnorton.com/rockhistory

The Byrds, "Mr. Tambourine Man"

Words and music by Bob Dylan, produced by Terry Melcher. Rose to #6 on the Billboard Pop charts (uk7) in summer 1965.

FORM: Contrasting verse-chorus, beginning with the chorus. Dylan's original alternates the chorus with multiple verses, but the Byrds use only one of the original verses. The resulting form looks a little strange, but the band had to get the arrangement to fit the 2-minute format of AM radio at the time.

TIME SIGNATURE: 4/4, with a feel borrowed from "Don't Worry Baby."

INSTRUMENTATION: Electric 12-string guitar, electric 6-string guitar, bass, drums, solo and duet vocals.

0:00–0:08	**Introduction**, 4 mm.	Electric 12-string begins with lick inspired by J. S. Bach, then sliding bass enters, followed by the entire band.
0:09–0:41	**Chorus**, 17 mm.	Duet vocals, then 2-bar link to verse; note the jingle-jangle picking on the electric 12-string guitar, "Hey Mr. Tambourine Man . . ."
0:42–1:30	**Verse**, 25 mm.	Solo vocal; note the short, sharp chords played high on a second electric guitar, "Take me for a trip . . ."
1:30–2:00	**Chorus**, 15 mm.	Duet vocals as before; "Hey Mr. Tambourine Man . . ."
2:00–2:15	**Coda**, 6 mm. and fade	Music is the same as in the introduction.

appears on the album—the same master tape was used—with jangly guitar, electric bass, and drums in the style of the Byrds. The resultant folk-rock single topped the charts in the United States in late 1965, as Simon rushed home from the UK and the duo brought out an album, *The Sounds of Silence* (p21 uk13, 1966), to capitalize on their newfound and unexpected success as rock stars. Two follow-up singles, "Homeward Bound" (p5 uk9, 1966) and "I Am a Rock" (p3 uk17, 1966), continued in the folk-rock style, but by late 1966, the album *Parsley, Sage, Rosemary and Thyme* (p4), which contains the delicate "Scarborough Fair / Canticle" (p11, 1968), began the duo's move away from rock and back toward a more acoustic sound, though the single "A Hazy Shade of Winter" (p13, 1966) features a rock arrangement. Later in the 1960s, Simon and Garfunkel would enjoy their greatest commercial and aesthetic success with *Bookends* (p1 uk1, 1968) and *Bridge Over Troubled Water* (p1 uk1, 1970).

Modeling themselves on the Everly Brothers, Simon and Garfunkel enjoyed modest success in the late 1950s as Tom and Jerry. When folk rock became popular in mid 1965, electric guitar, bass, and drums were added to an earlier recording to create the duo's first hit single, "The Sounds of Silence."

California Dreamin': Barry McGuire, the Turtles, the Mamas and Papas. While many of the first folk-rock records simply set preexisting folk songs to a rock beat and instrumentation, soon songs were written specifically as folk-rock numbers. Perhaps the first of these—beside those songs Dylan wrote and recorded after he turned electric—was P. F. Sloan's "Eve of Destruction." Recorded by Barry McGuire, another former New Christy Minstrel who had made his way to Los Angeles from Greenwich Village, this song ascended to number one on the U.S. charts (uk3) in the fall of 1965. Producer Lou Adler had given Sloan the task of writing a batch of Dylan-like songs, and the songwriter did his best to mimic the earnest sense of social protest found in much folk. Groups continued to cover Dylan songs in hopes of scoring folk-rock hits as the Byrds had done, and the Los Angeles–based Turtles (who initially considered spelling their name "The Tyrtles") worked this trick successfully with "It Ain't Me Babe" (p8, 1965) and "Let Me Be" (p29, 1965) before moving on to a more mainstream pop style and a series of non-Dylan hits including "Happy Together" (p1 uk12, 1967), "She'd Rather Be with Me" (p3 uk4, 1967), "Eleanore" (p6 uk7, 1968), and "You Showed Me" (p6, 1969). The Turtles' arrangements often showcased the polished dual lead vocals of Howard Kaylan and Mark Volman, who later worked with Frank Zappa and the Mothers of Invention and then as the duo Phlorescent Leech (Flo) and Eddie.

Formed in New York in 1965, the Mamas and the Papas followed the folk migration westward and moved from Greenwich Village to Los Angeles, where

Updating the polished folk approach of Peter, Paul, and Mary with a folk-rock beat, the Mamas and the Papas focused on sophisticated vocal arrangements by John Phillips (second from left). Cass Elliot (right) would go on to enjoy success as a solo artist.

they first enjoyed commercial success in the wake of Dylan, the Byrds, and Simon and Garfunkel. Each member had worked previously in vocally oriented pop or folk acts. Led by singer/songwriter/arranger John Phillips and including Michelle Phillips, Denny Doherty, and Cass Elliot, the group showcased John Phillips's sophisticated four-part vocal arrangements, influenced by the close harmony singing found in much late 1950s/early 1960s folk (especially Peter, Paul, and Mary) and doo-wop (they had a hit with a cover of the Shirelles' "Dedicated to the One I Love") and often accompanied by a rock rhythm section of drums, electric bass, guitars, and keyboards. The Mamas and the Papas had nine hit singles, most written by Phillips and including "California Dreamin'" (p4 uk23, 1966), "Monday Monday" (p1 uk3, 1966), "I Saw Her Again"(p5 uk11, 1966), and the autobiographical "Creeque Alley" (p5, 1967), the lyrics of which mention both Roger McGuinn and Barry McGuire at one point. This run made the quartet one of the most successful of their era. The band's music is more folk than rock, and they adapted the polished, poppy, vocally oriented folk sounds of the Kingston Trio and Peter, Paul, and Mary to the new folk-rock beat, making for a pop/folk succession that reaches back to the late '50s and forward to the psychedelic era.

American Pop on Both Coasts

L.A.: Spector and His Legacy.   While the British invasion had a tremendous impact on American pop, this impact was not yet felt to its full extent in early 1964 when the Beatles arrived in New York. Phil Spector, who flew with the Beatles from London to New York on February 7, was yet to experience some of his greatest successes when the Beatles stormed the U.S. charts; the Crystals'

"Da Doo Ron Ron" (p3 uk5, 1964) and "Then He Kissed Me" (p6 uk2, 1964), as well as the Ronettes' "Be My Baby" (p2 uk4,1964), were all Spector-produced hits in the months *after* the Fab Four landed. The Righteous Brothers' "You've Lost That Lovin' Feeling" (discussed in Chapter 3), went to number one in both the United States and UK in early 1965, and to number three on the U.S. rhythm and blues charts. The Spector/Righteous Brothers team followed with "Unchained Melody" (p4 uk14, 1965) and "Ebb Tide" (p5 uk48, 1966) before Spector began to lose his hit-making touch. During this time, Spector could have produced the Young Rascals or the Lovin' Spoonful, but he declined offers from both bands. Instead, he pinned everything on what he hoped would be his greatest record yet; written by Spector with Jeff Barry and Ellie Greenwich and sung by Tina Turner, "River Deep, Mountain High" failed in the United States, rising only as high as number eighty-six in mid 1966. Even though the record went to number three in the UK (mostly through airplay on pirate stations), Spector was crushed by the failure and retired from the business. He would return to producing a few years later, enjoying the success of several Beatles-related projects in the early 1970s, including number one albums for the Beatles (*Let It Be*, 1970), George Harrison (*All Things Must Pass*, 1970), and John Lennon (*Imagine*, 1971).

The Beach Boys: Brian Stays Home.   Like Spector, the Beach Boys continued to have hits after the arrival of the Beatles in the United States, and while they eventually moved away from surf music, this had not occurred yet in 1964—a year in which they charted "Fun, Fun, Fun" at number five in the States in the midst of Beatlemania. That summer, they had their first number one U.S. hit (uk7), "I Get Around," while the world was also celebrating *A Hard Day's Night*. Contending with the Beatles' success was tougher for the Beach Boys than most other American pop acts, however, because both groups were with Capitol Records. This meant that the Beach Boys had to fight not only for the attention of pop listeners, but also for the attention of their record company. Around that time, the band's music began to change, and the change resulted less from the challenge offered by the Mop Tops than from Brian Wilson's decision in December 1964 to stop touring with the band; instead Wilson stayed at home, writing new music and recording backing tracks that only required the other members to add the vocal tracks that Wilson had carefully worked out for them. Glen Campbell and then Bruce Johnston replaced Brian on the road, and Wilson could now do as his idol Spector had done: focus entirely on making records.

The next two albums, *The Beach Boys Today!* (p4, 1965) and *Summer Days (and Summer Nights!!)* (p2, 1965) reflected Wilson's increasingly sophisticated approach to songwriting, arranging, and production. "Help Me Rhonda" (p1 uk27, 1965) and especially "California Girls" (p3 uk26, 1965) began to explore more complicated musical structures and employed a broader palette of instrumentation, including orchestral instruments. After the quickly recorded *Beach Boys' Party!* (p6 uk3, 1966), meant to be an informal taping of the band jamming and singing with friends that perhaps surprisingly produced the hit single "Barbara Ann" (p2 uk3, 1966), Wilson set to work on a much more musically

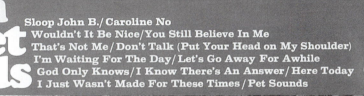

N-16156 A Capitol Re-Issue
MONOPHONIC

The Beach Boys Pet Sounds

Sloop John B./Caroline No
Wouldn't It Be Nice/You Still Believe In Me
That's Not Me/Don't Talk (Put Your Head on My Shoulder)
I'm Waiting For The Day/Let's Go Away For Awhile
God Only Knows/I Know There's An Answer/Here Today
I Just Wasn't Made For These Times/Pet Sounds

In late 1964, Brian Wilson decided not to tour with the Beach Boys, opting to stay at home working on new material while the band hit the road. By the time of Pet Sounds, *Brian was working long hours in the recording studio experimenting with new sounds, some of which he considered his "pet" sounds.*

The Beach Boys, "California Girls"

Words and music by Brian Wilson, produced by Brian Wilson. Rose to #3 on the Billboard Pop charts in fall 1965 (uk26).

FORM: Contrasting verse-chorus, with a 10-bar intro that leads into a 2-bar vamp that prepares the arrival of the first-verse vocals. The verse and chorus are both 8 bars in length, though their structure differs. Wilson builds his arrangement by employing solo lead vocals in the first two verses, then introducing a call-and-response scheme in the harmony vocals of the chorus, and then using doo-wop inspired backup vocals in the third and fourth verses. As Phil Spector does in "Be My Baby," Wilson uses a short musical interlude late in the song to allow a fresh return of the song's chorus; here it's a brief 2-bar organ and glockenspiel passage based on the "Happy Trails" bass line that prepares the way for the song's hook, "I wish they all could be . . . ."

TIME SIGNATURE: 12/8 (shuffle in four). Note that the repeated figure in the bass seems borrowed from the old cowboy song, "Happy Trails," giving the track a bouncy, easygoing rhythmic feel.

INSTRUMENTATION: Electric 12-string guitar, organ, bass, drums, glockenspiel, horns, percussion, lead and backup vocals.

0:00–0:26	**Introduction,** 12 mm.	10 mm. intro using harp and 12-string guitar, then bass and cymbals, and then horns, followed by a 2-mm. lead-in to verse 1 using the "Happy Trails" bass line.
0:26–0:43	**Verse 1,** 8 mm.	Solo lead vocal enters, "Well, east coast girls . . ."
0:43–0:59	**Verse 2,** 8 mm.	As before, "The midwest farmers' daughters . . ."
0:59–1:16	**Chorus,** 8 mm.	Arrangement gets fuller and louder, with call-and-answer harmony vocals, "I wish they all could be . . ."
1:16–1:32	**Verse 3,** 16 mm.	Doo-wop vocals, lightly doubled by horns, now backup solo lead vocal, "The west coast . . ."
1:32–1:49	**Verse 4,** 8 mm.	Texture continues as in verse 3, "I've been all 'round . . ."
1:49–2:06	**Chorus,** 8 mm.	Louder, fuller, with call-and-answer vocals, as before.
2:06–2:27	**Coda,** 10 mm. and fade	2 mm. interlude drawn from intro, and then 4 mm. drawn from chorus repeated as track fades.

ambitious project. Named after some of Brian's favorite studio sounds, *Pet Sounds* (p10 uk2, 1966) set a new standard for record production and musical sophistication within rock music. On the single released in advance of the album, "Sloop John B." (p3 uk2, 1966), you can hear the clear combination of Spector's Wall of Sound with Wilson's lush vocal-harmony arrangements. The echo-drenched harp introduction of the first track of the album, "Wouldn't It Be Nice," announces that what follows moves beyond the surf music that had made the band so successful. "God Only Knows," which Paul McCartney once called the perfect rock song and which features a lengthy (for its time) instrumental break that defies traditional tonal analysis, is the best illustration of how far Wilson's music had come during this period. Though it was not as commercially successful as the band's previous albums, *Pet Sounds* would soon become one of the most influential records of the 1960s, prodding the Beatles to even greater experimentation in the recording of their own *Sgt. Pepper's Lonely Hearts Club Band*. We will return to the friendly competition that developed between the Beach Boys and the Beatles in late 1966 and 1967 in Chapter 7, as we consider the single that followed *Pet Sounds*, "Good Vibrations," and the unfinished *SMiLE* album.

Ride the Ambitious Surf: Brian Wilson as Producer.

When Brian Wilson retired from touring, he began devoting his energies to increasingly complex and ambitious arrangements for the band; the introduction to "California Girls" is an early example of Wilson's blending of a symphonic sensibility with surf music. While the harmonies Wilson employs in this song are interesting and innovative, the formal design is the kind of straightforward contrasting verse-chorus design that is almost identical to Spector's "Be My Baby" (especially with the instrumental break after the second chorus and before the chorus fade). The introduction is the exceptional element in this song, and this short section builds from a brief two-measure figure played quietly at first and then repeated as new instruments enter. Finally, a growing series of chords in the horns drive this eight-measure introduction to the rhythmic two measures that lead into the first verse. There are other subtle touches throughout the rest of the song that signal Wilson's increased interest in expanding rock's musical vocabulary. Notice, for instance, how the drums during the chorus break from a steady four-beat pattern to provide an almost symphonic background, or the lushness of the backup vocals during the second verse. These relatively minor features in "California Girls" point the way to the more intensely experimental quality of the later *Pet Sounds* and "Good Vibrations."

Sonny and Cher: Dylan Meets the Wall of Sound.

Sonny Bono had been working in some capacity in the music scene around Los Angeles since the mid 1950s. A sometime songwriter, Sonny also worked at Specialty Records for a time and was the person at Specialty designated to deal with Little Richard when the singer decided to give up rock and roll for the ministry. Sonny eventually began handling promotion for Spector's Philles label and became one of the producer's most trusted aides. Sonny was present at many of the important Los Angeles recording sessions at Gold Star Studios, often singing backup or playing percussion on tracks, and thus had ample opportunity to soak up Spector's methods in the studio. He often brought his girlfriend, Cher (Cherilyn La Piere), to sessions to sing backup, where Sonny and Cher might find themselves singing along with members of the Ronettes or the Crystals. A failed Spector project that attempted to cash in on Beatlemania had Cher singing a song called "Ringo I Love You" under the name Bonnie Jo Mason. Sonny and Cher began performing together in 1963 under the name Caesar and Cleo and released three singles that did not chart. In late 1964, Sonny produced and wrote "Baby Don't Go" and "Just You" for the duo, and both singles enjoyed regional success in southern California in the first half of 1965. When the Byrds' "Mr. Tambourine Man" began to take off, Sonny produced a Cher cover of Dylan's "All I Really Want to Do"—which eclipsed the Byrds' version—and wrote and produced the duo's signature song, "I Got You, Babe." In the fall of 1965 "I Got You, Babe" hit number one in both the U.S. and UK charts. Soon the two previous regional hits "Baby Don't Go" (p8 uk11) and "Just You" (p20) took off, and Sonny and Cher, having gotten their start by capitalizing on the folk rock boom, moved increasingly away from folk rock into a more traditional brand of pop, enjoying a series of hits, including the Sonny Bono songs "But You're Mine" (p15 uk17, 1965), "Little Man" (p21 uk4, 1966), and "The Beat Goes On" (p6 uk29, 1967).

While Sonny extended the Spector legacy as Sonny and Cher followed in the husband-and-wife tradition of Les Paul and Mary Ford, one of the duo's most important roles was played in the area of hippie fashion. Sonny and Cher wore deliberately outlandish clothes, both on-stage and off, and this aspect of the act drew perhaps as much comment as their music. Even though Sonny and Cher were viewed as family entertainment only a few years later when they hosted their own very successful network television variety show, during the 1965–67 period they were considered somewhat subversive by establishment culture. Sonny's "Laugh at Me" is the singer-songwriter's response to an incident in which he was ridiculed over his clothing and haircut in one of the couple's favorite restaurants, and the duo were frequently refused at hotels both in the United States and abroad because of their appearance. While this became a common experience for hippies only a few years later, Sonny and Cher were among the first to insist that they had the right to dress any way they chose.

Gary Lewis and the Playboys, Johnny Rivers.   Another group that enjoyed tremendous chart success emerging out of Los Angeles was Gary Lewis and the Playboys, led by the son of comedian Jerry Lewis. In a situation reminiscent of Ricky Nelson's some years earlier, Gary had appeared in his dad's 1957 film *Rock-a-Bye Baby*. By 1964 he had formed a band that was booked as regular entertainment at Disneyland and earned a cameo appearance in the Raquel Welch film *A Swingin' Summer*. The group's first hit, "This Diamond Ring" (p1, 1965)—which Lewis performs with his father in the film *The Family Jewels*—was produced by veteran producer Snuff Garrett and featured arrangements by Wrecking Crew pianist Leon Russell (the song was actually co-written by Al

Kooper, who played organ on Dylan's "Like a Rolling Stone" and "Positively 4th Street"). Gary Lewis and the Playboys followed with eleven more U.S. hits in the next few years, including "Count Me In" (p2, 1965), "Save Your Heart for Me" (p2, 1965), "She's Just My Style" (p3, 1965)—clearly influenced by the Beach Boys' records of the same period—and "Green Grass" (p8, 1966). In another situation reminiscent of the late 1950s, Lewis and the band broke up when he was drafted into the U.S. Army.

Like Sonny Bono, Johnny Rivers had been in the music business for several years before having a hit record. Born John Ramistella, he took the stage name Rivers on the advice of Alan Freed in 1958. That same year, Ricky Nelson recorded Rivers's "I'll Make Believe," though it was not a hit. After playing in Louie Prima's band in Las Vegas and Lake Tahoe, Rivers made his way to Los Angeles. After a couple of failed singles, he established himself as a live act, eventually becoming a regular at the Whiskey-a-Go-Go, where he played mostly rock oldies and drew a star-studded crowd. On the strength of his popularity at the Whiskey, he was signed to Imperial Records by Lou Adler, who made the strange but inspired decision to make Rivers's first record a live album, *Johnny Rivers at the Whiskey-a-Go-Go*, which went to number twelve on the U.S. album charts. Rivers had his first two hit singles with covers of Chuck Berry tunes, "Memphis" (p2, 1964) and "Maybelline" (p12, 1964). He placed eleven more singles in the U.S. Top 40 during the 1960s and released eight Top 40 albums. In February 1965, before the Byrds or Dylan had hit with folk rock, Rivers enjoyed a number twenty hit with an up-tempo cover of the Weavers's "Midnight Special" (which became the theme song of the early 1970s music-variety show of the same name), and during the salad days of folk rock in late 1965, Rivers's cover of the Kingston Trio's "Where Have All the Flowers Gone?" went to number twenty six. In late 1966, the "Poor Side of Town," written by Rivers and Adler, hit number one in the United States, although Rivers is perhaps best known for his "Secret Agent Man" (p3) from earlier that year, which was written in part by P. F. Sloan ("Eve of Destruction") and

In addition to enjoying a string of hit records, Sonny and Cher were also trend-setters in the newly emerging sense of hippie fashion in the mid 1960s.

became the theme song of a popular television spy program. In 1966 Rivers started his own label, Soul City, signing songwriter Jimmie Webb and singing group the Fifth Dimension; he produced that group's version of Webb's "Up, Up, and Away," which went to number seven on the U.S. charts and earned Rivers a Grammy Award in 1967.

Meanwhile Back in New York: The Lovin' Spoonful, the Rascals. Judging by the steady migration of folk musicians from Greenwich Village to Southern California during 1964–65, one might wonder why this happened and if anybody was still in New York by 1966. Most of the folkies who headed west did so because they had grown weary of the neglect they suffered from the record labels in New York. This is ironic in that many of the Los Angeles–based folk-rock acts who received recording contracts in the summer of 1965 (when the folk-rock style emerged) were signed by New York–based labels; the Byrds, for instance, were on Columbia, and Sonny and Cher were on Atlantic. One Greenwich Village folkie who stayed in New York was John Sebastian, who had played on several folk albums (including an early version of Dylan's "Subterranean Homesick Blues") and performed with the Even Dozen Jug Band. Sebastian met Zalman Yanovsky at a Mugwumps recording sessions (the Mugwumps included future Mama Cass Elliot and papa Denny Doherty at the time) and, inspired by the Beatles, they formed the Lovin' Spoonful with bassist Steve Boone and drummer Joe Butler rounding out the quartet. Even though the new band became a popular attraction at the Night Owl Coffee House in Greenwich Village, it was not signed by a major New York label. Instead, the newly formed Kama Sutra Records released the band's John Sebastian–penned and Erik Jacobsen–produced "Do You Believe in Magic" in the summer of 1965 and the single rose to number nine on the U.S. charts. This easygoing melodic hit was followed by a string of catchy, playful, and mostly upbeat hit singles written by Sebastian and produced by Jacobsen, including "Daydream" (p2 uk2, 1966), "Did You Ever Have to Make Up Your Mind" (p2, 1966), "Summer in the City" (p1 uk8, 1966), and "Nashville Cats" (p8 uk26, 1967).

Formed in New York in early 1964 but emerging out of the area's rhythm and blues clubs rather than from the Greenwich Village folk scene, the Young Rascals (later simply the "Rascals") are probably better seen as the American precursors to the Spencer Davis Group rather than an answer to the Beatles. Nevertheless, the band caught the attention of New York promoter Sid Bernstein, who began managing the group, booking them as the opening act for the Beatles' 1965 performance at Shea Stadium. Led by the funky Hammond organ of Felix Cavaliere and the soulful vocals of Eddie Brigati, and backed by the Gene Cornish's guitar and Dino Danelli's drums, the band scored its first hit with a hard-rocking cover of the Olympics' 1965 rhythm and blues hit, "Good Lovin'," which rose to the top U.S. spot in the spring of 1966. Allowed to produce themselves with oversight from Atlantic's experienced house producers, the band followed with a series of rhythm and blues–inspired hits written by Cavaliere and Brigati, including "I've Been Lonely Too Long" (p16, 1967), "Groovin'" (p1 uk8, 1967), "How Can I Be Sure" (p4, 1967), "A Beautiful Morning" (p3, 1968), and "People Got to Be Free" (p1, 1968).

The Old Guard Hangs On: New York. By mid 1963 Aldon's Don Kirschner had left New York's Brill Building for the Los Angeles–based Colpix label—Kirschner would soon figure into the L.A. scene, as detailed below—and Leiber and Stoller had formed their Red Bird label. Leiber and Stoller continued to place hit records on the pop charts through 1965. The Ad Libs' "The Boy from New York City," for instance, hit number eight in the first half of 1965, while Red Bird releases such as the Dixie Cups' "Chapel of Love" and the Shangri-Las' "Leader of the Pack" (both discussed in Chapter 3) enjoyed chart success. When Leiber and Stoller formed Red Bird, they turned production of the Drifters over to Bert Berns. In 1965 Berns formed Bang! Records in partnership with his bosses at Atlantic, Ahmet and Neshui Ertegun and Jerry Wexler. In the fall of 1965, Berns produced an Indiana-based band, the McCoys (featuring guitarist Rick Derringer), doing a version of "Hang On Sloopy" that hit the top of the U.S. charts (uk5); it was a catchy reworking of "Louie Louie" with a fail-safe sing-along chorus. The McCoys followed with two more Top 40 hits for Bang!: "Fever" (p7 uk44, 1965) and "Come On Let's Go" (p22, 1966). But Berns had the most success with singer-songwriter Neil Diamond, who began his hit-making career on Bang!, scoring first with "Cherry, Cherry" (p6, 1966), and then with eight more hits before leaving the label. Diamond's "I'm a Believer" was to be a hit for the Monkees.

The Four Seasons, featuring lead vocalist Frankie Valli, were probably the New York–based act least affected by the British invasion. The group first had success in 1962 with successive number one Bob Crewe–produced singles, "Sherry" and "Big Girls Don't Cry," and then followed with twenty-five more U.S. Top 40 hits in the 1960s, including "Walk Like a Man" (p1, 1963), "Let's Hang On" (p4, 1965), and "Workin' My Way Back to You" (p9 uk50, 1966), the last one recorded under the name the Wonder Who? In early February, "Dawn (Go Away)" hit number three in the United States, kept out of the two top slots by the Beatles' "She Loves You" and "I Want to Hold Your Hand," and for two weeks in July 1964 "Rag Doll" occupied the top slot on the U.S. charts. Since the Four Seasons recorded for Vee Jay and that label had also released the Beatles' first album (in the months before Beatlemania when Capitol refused to release it), Vee Jay could not resist putting out a double album late in 1964 called *The Beatles vs. the Four Seasons*, which was a re-release of *Introducing the Beatles* combined with a Four Seasons greatest hits compilation. The Four

Emerging in the mid 1960s, the Young Rascals developed a reputation for a hard-driving, rhythm and blues–inspired approach to rock. In this shot from 1968, Eddie Brigati plays the piccolo during a show in Hollywood.

Seasons' doo-wop vocal style was very different from the music of the Beatles and other British invasion groups, however. Perhaps their closest musical parallel is the Beach Boys, who also depended on tight vocal harmonies and the high falsetto lead vocals of Brian Wilson. Frankie Valli's distinctive falsetto was much raspier and more aggressive than Wilson's, and while similar in many ways, one group would hardly be mistaken for the other. But despite the success of the Four Seasons and a handful of other New York–based groups, the

Top 40 Radio

Radio programming in the first half of the twentieth century was very different from what it later became. Each broadcast day was built around blocks of content, much of it set aside for nationally broadcast dramas, soap operas, mysteries, comedies, news, music, or variety shows—in much the same way that television is programmed today. With the advent of television in the late 1940s, listeners began to abandon radio programs for the televised equivalent. Radio ratings—and advertising revenue—started to drop. In the mid 1950s, the development of the transistor made cheap, portable radios widely available for the first time. Transistor radios were embraced by the baby boom generation, opening a younger, more active audience to radio. Most of these new listeners were very interested in music. Radio adapted to the challenge of television and the emerging market for young music fans with a new format: Top 40 radio.

No one knows exactly who invented the Top 40 format. It is clear, however, that Todd Storz, the owner and operator of KOWH in Omaha, Nebraska, developed a new type of format when he stopped broadcasting network programs and expanded music programming to fill the entire day. He did this because it was cheaper and because surveys showed that listeners enjoyed music more than any other kind of program. The all-music format was immediately successful and quickly spread around the nation.

This type of programming was called "formula radio." It was very simple: a disc jockey, or DJ, would play songs from a prescribed list provided by the station's programmer. Between songs, the DJ provided news, advertising, and personality. Formula radio became Top 40 radio when the majority of the songs on the playlist came from the Billboard Singles charts. The remaining songs on the broadcast would be elected either by the program director or the DJ.

Top 40 stations didn't simply play songs that were already popular, however.

They could also turn songs into hits. DJs made educated guesses about which new songs were likely to be popular and then would mix those songs with already established hits. If the audience responded to a song, the DJ would play it more often. The resulting exposure could generate record sales, jukebox selections, and requests at other stations—which would lead to a higher chart position and cause Top 40 stations to play the song even more. This feedback loop between Top 40 stations and the charts explains why hit songs—particularly novelty tunes or songs in distinctive, new styles—sometimes exploded in popularity.

Top 40 radio was also an important force in integrating music. Top 40 stations made their money by playing songs that were popular rather than those from a particular style. Variety was needed to keep a broad range of listeners tuned in for long periods of time: not everyone loved every hit, but if you played a variety of hits you could attract a variety of listeners. So if the audience

As Top 40 radio became increasingly popular, its disc jockeys became increasingly influential. As a high-profile disc jockey in New York, "Murray the K" Kaufman (pictured here) played an important role in whipping up enthusiasm for the Beatles and their music in early 1964.

responded strongly to a song by a musician from a different racial or ethnic group, it was in the financial interest of the station to play that song—even if there were strong political or social deterrents to it.

Once Top 40 radio became a widespread format with competing stations in each market, the personalities of the DJs became the main way that listeners differentiated between stations. Some DJs, like Wolfman Jack, Cousin Brucie, or Murray the K, became national stars. A star DJ with a strong broadcast signal or a major market could sometimes turn a song into a hit by playing it one time. Many of these DJs made a point of educating listeners about new styles or crossing color lines with their selections. In this way, Top 40 radio increased diversity and speeded change in popular music.

British invasion and the music-stylistic changes in American rock that it caused spelled the end of New York's domination of pop.

Garage Bands: No Professional Experience Necessary

From the Northwest: Garage Bands, the Kingsmen, and "Louie, Louie." Almost immediately after the Beatles landed in the United States, bands filled with teenage guys more equipped with enthusiasm than training or experience sprang up all across the country. As these bands began to play at local dances and clubs and gained some popularity, local record labels attempted to cash in by releasing records for the local or regional market. Many of these "local hero" bands rehearsed in basements or garages on inexpensive equipment, and their records were frequently recorded on very simple equipment as well. Like the doo-wop groups of the preceding years, garage bands often had only one hit, and most of these were only regional hits at that. When a garage band had more than one hit, the group's music almost always became more refined as the band migrated away from the charming but amateurish sound of their first success. There are literally dozens of garage-band singles from the 1960s and these records have spawned an entire culture of collectors who sometimes seem to prize records less for how they sound than for how rare or unknown they might be. Much of this interest grew out of a collection assembled in the early 1970s by writer and guitarist Lenny Kaye. Called *Nuggets,* this collection brought together many records that had never been widely heard, or if they had been heard, were already forgotten. Many of the bands in the early punk movement took their inspiration from the rough-and-tumble, amateurish character of the 1960s garage bands.

The first important national garage-band hit was "Louie, Louie"; this song, a live staple of a number of early garage bands in the Pacific Northwest, was the version recorded by the Kingsmen that rose to number two in late 1963/early 1964, at the same time that Beatlemania was breaking out. The song was written by Richard Berry and recorded in 1956 as a calypso-flavored rhythm and blues tune. The Kingsmen's version was recorded for $50 in a small studio in Portland, Oregon. This rendition is notably amateurish: at one point vocalist Jack Ely comes in at the wrong place and abruptly corrects himself. This moment, and the generally difficult-to-discern lyrics throughout, led to a rumor that the song contained foul language. At one point in early 1964, the governor of Indiana declared the song pornographic and the FCC was called in to investigate. As it turns out, the lyrics did not contain any profanity or overt sexual references, and the FCC ultimately concluded that they couldn't tell what the lyrics were anyway. Even though another Portland group, the Raiders, recorded their version of "Louie, Louie" soon after and in the same studio, it was the Kingsmen's version that took off, and the controversy did little more than stoke the curiosity of young listeners across the country. The versions by Paul Revere and the Raiders and the Kingsmen were initially released by local labels. When a record became a regional hit, a national label would sometimes license that particular record rather than sign the group. Columbia bought the Raiders record and Wand bought the Kingsmen one. When a DJ in Boston started playing the Kingsmen version, the response triggered a national hit for the band. The Kingsmen followed up with "Money" (p16, 1964) and "The Jolly Green Giant" (p4, 1965) before disappearing into the oldies circuit.

Despite the success of the Kingsmen in 1964, record companies did not turn to the practice of licensing records from unknown American bands until the folk-rock American response broke out in the summer of 1965. After that, a series of mostly one-time garage-band Top 40 hits regularly appeared on the U.S. pop charts. Among these groups and their hits were Cannibal and the Headhunters, "Land of 1000 Dances" (p30, 1965); the Count Five, "Psychotic Reaction" (p5, 1966); ? & the Mysterians, "96 Tears" (p1, 1966); the Seeds, "Pushin' Too Hard" (p36, 1966); Shadows of Knight, "Gloria" (p10, 1966); the Standells, "Dirty Water" (p11, 1966); and the Syndicate of Sound, "Little Girl" (p8, 1967). Some groups had more than one hit. Tommy James and the Shondells initially recorded their version of the Barry-Greenwich song "Hanky Panky" in 1963 at a studio in their hometown of Niles, Michigan. But when a Pittsburgh DJ began playing it a few years later, the song took off and eventually was released on Roulette and rose to number one in the second half of 1966. James then formed a new bunch of Shondells and followed with thirteen Top 40 hits over the next few years, including "Mony Mony" (p3, 1968), "Crimson and Clover" (p1, 1968), and "Crystal Blue Persuasion" (p2, 1969). Dallas-based Sam the Sham & the Pharaohs hit nationally with "Wooly Bully" (p2, 1965) and followed with five more hits through 1967, including "Little Red Riding Hood" (p2, 1966). But while these two groups may have moved toward a more commercial sound to sustain their success, the most successful garage band of the decade was Paul Revere and the Raiders—the other band that recorded "Louie, Louie."

Hailing from Portland, Oregon, the Kingsmen rose to national attention in 1963 with "Louie, Louie." Though famously rumored to contain obscene language, an FCC investigation pronounced the passage in question unintelligible.

TV Rock: The Industry Tries to Take Control Once More

One If by Land, Two If by Sea: Paul Revere and the Raiders. Part of the northwest garage-band scene in the early 1960s, Paul Revere and the Raiders had initially formed in Indiana and later made their commercial mark mid-decade after relocating to Los Angeles. After their single "Like, Long Hair" hit number thirty-nine on the national charts in 1961, the group moved to Portland,

Oregon; but when their version of "Louie, Louie" failed to break out of the regional market, lead singer Mark Lindsay and organist Paul Revere parted ways. Revere and Lindsay joined forces again in Los Angeles and, with the help of *American Bandstand* impresario Dick Clark, Paul Revere and the Raiders debuted in 1962 as musical hosts of Dick Clark's new rock variety show on CBS, *Where the Action Is*. (Clark's show was launched in response to ABC's *Shindig*, which had debuted earlier that year under the production of Englishman Jack Good, who had been responsible for producing similar shows in the UK. NBC joined the TV-rock race with its *Hullabaloo*, and together, the three shows targeted at America's teenagers provided wide exposure for British invasion and American acts.) The regular television exposure that *Where the Action Is* provided, combined with a Columbia Records recording contract and the production talents of Terry Melcher (who was also producing the Byrds), helped Paul Revere and Raiders score a series of hit singles on the American charts, making them the most successful of all garage bands. Beginning with "Just Like Me" (p11, early 1966), the band followed with "Kicks" (p4, 1966), "Hungry" (p6, 1966), and "Good Thing" (p4, early 1967). "The Great Airplane Strike" (p20, 1966) marked the first Paul Revere and the Raiders single to be written by members of the group (Lindsay and Melcher). The band continued to enjoy chart success through the rest of the decade, scoring their first number one hit with "Indian Reservation" in 1971. Singer Mark Lindsay also had a solo hit with "Arizona" in 1970.

A Collision of the Old and New: The Monkees' Tale. No group benefited as much from television exposure as America's most commercially successful answer to the Beatles: the Monkees. Initially, the Monkees was not formed as a band to make records that would be supported by a weekly television series; instead, a cast of players was formed to do a television series that would be supported by records. The brainchild of television producer Bert Rafelson and media executive Bob Schneider, *The Monkees* was a clear response to the Beatles' *A Hard Day's Night* and *Help!*; its intent was to reproduce the spirit of fun and wit that Richard Lester had captured with these two Beatles films. In forming the band that would be the focus of this project, Rafelson and Schneider sought four unknowns who could be trained primarily to become an on-camera acting team that could also play music. In August 1965, auditions for the series were advertised in an industry magazine and eventually four young men who had never worked together were selected. Guitarist and songwriter Michael Nesmith had played professionally in Texas and then in the Los Angeles folk clubs, while Peter Tork had

Dressed as American soldiers in Revolutionary War garb, Paul Revere and the Raiders battled the British invasion as hosts of a network television show, Where the Action Is.

been part of the Greenwich Village folk scene, where he and friend Stephen Stills were often mistaken for one another (when Stills was turned down for a spot in the band, he recommended Tork). Both Davy Jones and Mickey Dolenz had professional backgrounds in acting, Dolenz as star of the TV series *Circus Boy*, and Jones as a star of the musical *Oliver!* in London and New York (Jones performed in a selection from the show on the same Ed Sullivan broadcast that featured the Beatles' debut).

Since Rafelson and Schneider were primarily concerned with the success of the television show and not with the records that might be released by the band, they focused the new group's efforts on building their rapport and skills as actors. As a result, the musical aspect of the group's training was neglected and when the show was ready to begin production, Rafelson and Schneider needed songs. They turned to the songwriting-production team of Tommy Boyce and Bobby Hart (who had been strong candidates to become band members themselves), as well as to former Brill Building publisher Don Kirschner, now relocated to Los Angeles. The Monkees' Beatles-like music was created according to a distinctively old-school music-business procedure: songs were written by professionals (Boyce and Hart, Goffin and King, Neil Diamond), backing tracks were performed by studio musicians, and the records were produced by Boyce and Hart. Initially, the Monkees did little more than sing on their records, and when word of this leaked out, many in the rock community used it to discredit the group. None of this affected the band's popularity, however, and while Rafelson and Schneider may have hoped their series would be a hit (which it was), they could not have imagined the success the music would have. In the fall of 1966, after the show debuted Monday nights on NBC, the Monkees' "Last Train to Clarksville" went to number one on the U.S. charts. Soon the success spread to the UK, as "I'm a Believer" went to number one in the States and the UK at the end of 1966; the single's B-side, "I'm Not Your Stepping Stone" rose to number twenty on the U.S. charts in early 1967. The Monkees duplicated this double-sided chart topping with "A Little Bit Me, a Little Bit You" (p2 uk3, 1967)/"The Girl I Knew Somewhere" (p39, 1967); "Pleasant Valley Sunday" (p3 uk11, 1967)/ "Words" (p11, 1967), and "Valleri" (p3 uk12, 1968)/ "Tapioca Tundra" (p34, 1968). The band's first four albums went to number one in the United States and placed in the UK top 5; the first two Monkees albums together occupied the U.S. top slot for thirty-one consecutive weeks from late 1966 through the summer of 1967.

The Monkees themselves soon came to resent the entertainment-business machine they found themselves in—especially Nesmith, who felt that the band should be able to write its own music and play on the records. The struggle that resulted provides a clear illustration of how the new approach to popular music initiated by the Beatles came into conflict with the older approach best represented by the Brill Building. Taking their cue from the Beatles, the Monkees wanted to exercise control over the music they recorded; they wanted to write it, play it, and arrange it. The music-business people, led by Kirschner, insisted that they should control the singles, much as they had controlled the teen idols and girl groups only a few years earlier. Eventually the band did gain control, though its popularity quickly slipped away. Viewed in comparison with other

American bands of the mid 1960s, the fact that the Monkees did not initially play on their own records does not set Monkees records apart from most Beach Boys records or the Byrds' "Mr. Tambourine Man." Rather, the Monkees' eagerness to play and write is an indication of how much the idea that band members should exert greater control had begun to seep into rock record production. In a sense, the Monkees started out wanting to be the band that the Beatles had been in 1964, only to realize that they really wanted to be the kind of band the Beatles had become by 1967.

Monkee Complexitee. While the Monkees as a band were clearly modeled on the Beatles, their music was produced according to the established Brill Building pattern, and this association has led many to dismiss the Monkees' hits as uninteresting. With the exception of guitarist Michael Nesmith, the Monkees did not play on their early records; Mickey Dolenz or Davy Jones mostly sang songs written by professional songwriters to the accompaniment of studio musicians. "Last Train to Clarksville," however, gives some indication of the kinds of musical complexities that often resided behind the band's bubblegum image. This song is generally in simple verse form, presenting a series of five verses (the fifth repeats the lyrics of the first) with no real chorus. These verses are built on a sixteen-measure pattern, though the first and third verses come to only fourteen measures, owing to the truncation of what would have been the final two measures. Musical contrast is provided by two interludes, the first featuring a wordless vocal melody sung on the syllable "dooo." The second interlude is based on the first, but now guitar arpeggios and high background vocals rework the musical material and expand it to encompass sixteen measures. These interludes are the most unique feature of the song, and along with

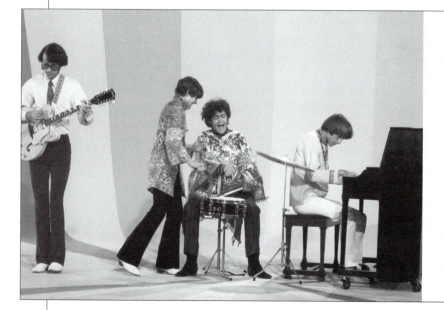

Modeled on the witty and fun-loving Beatles of A Hard Day's Night *and* Help!, *the Monkees were originally formed as an acting troupe, with the music intended to help promote their weekly television show. Written by professional songwriters and using a studio band, the music proved much more popular than the producers imagined it would, and the band enjoyed a string of hit singles and albums.*

The Monkees, "Last Train to Clarksville"

Words and music by Tommy Boyce and Bobby Hart, produced by Tommy Boyce and Bobby Hart. Rose to #1 on the Billboard Pop charts in fall 1966 (uk23, early 1967).

FORM: Modified simple verse, with verses of different lengths and two interludes not derived from the verses. While the first verse is 14 bars in length, the second is 2 measures longer, owing to a closing line that extends the verse, "and I don't know . . . ." The third verse is like the first, except that it is preceded by the 2-bar guitar figure from the introduction, while the fourth verse is like the second, with the extra concluding bars. The last verse repeats the lyrics of the first, while using the ending of the second. In the middle of all this, two instrumental interludes are inserted. These interludes are actually based on similar material, but sound different enough from each other to be heard as new when they appear in the arrangement.

TIME SIGNATURE: 2/4, with a hint of a country two-step feel, which is a lively one-two, one-two rhythm.

INSTRUMENTATION: Electric guitars, acoustic guitar, bass, drums, tambourine, lead and backup vocals. Note that the guitar lick employed here seems influenced by similar figures in the Beatles' "Ticket to Ride," "Day Tripper," and "I Feel Fine." Note as well that the background vocals imitate a train whistle in various ways throughout the track, picking up on the song's title.

0:00–0:10	**Introduction**, 8 mm., 2 mm.	Beatle-esque guitar lick played (w/ bass and tambourine) 4 times.
0:10–0:27	**Verse 1**, 14 mm. (last 2 mm. truncated)	Lead vocal enters, "Take the last . . ."
0:27–0:47	**Verse 2**, 16 mm.	As verse 1 (with 2 mm. ending added), train-whistle background vocals added, "'Cause I'm leaving . . ."
0:47–1:08	**Verse 3**, 18 mm.	4 mm. of guitar from intro, then 14 mm. verse, lead vocal with train-whistle backup vocals, "Take the last . . ."
1:09–1:18	**Interlude 1**, 8 mm.	Vocal melody without words, quieter, pulsating bass guitar.
1:18–1:38	**Verse 4**, 16 mm.	As in verse 2, new train-whistle backup vocals, "Take the last . . ."

continued

1:38–1:57	**Interlude 2**, 16 mm.	No vocal melody, based on the harmonies from interlude 1 but louder and brighter, verse 4 backup vocals enter toward end of this section.
1:57–2:17	**Verse 1**, 16 mm.	Same lyrics as verse 1, same ending as verse 2, "Take the last . . . ."
2:17–2:42	**Coda**, 20 mm.	Repetition of same four-measure phrase, with Beatle-esque guitar lick another variation of the train-whistle backup vocals.

the truncated verses, make the formal structure of this track more complex and subtle than it might otherwise have been.

In the mid 1960s, a clear division in the rock market had begun to open up again (much as it had in the early '60s) between the young teens who listened to the pop-oriented music of the Monkees and the older teens who were drawn to the increasingly more serious-minded and self-conscious rock of the Beatles. Music aimed at the younger listeners was called "bubblegum" or "teenybopper" music and it continued to be played on AM radio stations nationwide. After the Monkees, Don Kirschner went on to promote a group made up of cartoon characters that also had a TV show, the Archies. After hitting number twenty-two in the United States with "Bang Shang a Lang" in 1968, the fictitious Archies (whose music was written by Jeff Barry and played by studio pros) had a chart-topping hit in this country and the UK in 1969 with "Sugar Sugar." Other make-believe bands directed at young teens populated television in the late 1960s, including the Banana Splits (characters in fuzzy costumes) and Lancelot Link and the Evolution Revolution (a band of chimpanzees). Even episodes of the Hanna-Barbera cartoon *Scooby-Doo Where Are You?* featured an obligatory chase scene to the accompaniment of a pop tune. By the early 1970s, the Partridge Family would become America's foremost make-believe television band, with David Cassidy (Keith Partridge) sharing space in teen magazines with Bobby Sherman and members of the Brady Bunch.

As the younger teens listened to bubblegum pop, their older brothers and sisters were turning to psychedelia—a style of music that eschewed singles in favor of albums and was increasingly likely to be heard on FM instead of AM. We will turn to psychedelia in Chapter 7, but in Chapter 6 we will explore the rise of soul music in the 1960s as well as the story of one American label that seemed unaffected by the British invasion: Motown.

Questions for Review and Discussion

1. How did folk rock develop out of folk? How was folk rock influenced by both the British invasion and earlier American pop styles?

2. How did Bob Dylan's approach to songwriting begin to move away from the traditional folk practice? How were Dylan's stylistic changes received within the folk community?

3. What were the important acts emerging from southern California in the mid 1960s? What acts emerged from New York during the same period?

4. Which American bands or artists most successfully withstood the success of the British bands during 1964–65?

5. If you were asked to formulate a "garage-band aesthetic," what would it be?

6. What role did television play in the American response to the British invasion? Which bands benefited most from television exposure?

7. Make a case for the idea that the real action in the American pop-music business migrated from New York to Los Angeles in the mid 1960s. Offer as many examples as you can to support your argument.

Further Reading

Glenn A. Baker, with Tom Czarnota and Peter Hogan, *Monkee-Mania: The True Story of the Monkees* (St. Martin's Press, 1986).

Sonny Bono, *And the Beat Goes On* (Pocket Books, 1991).

Clinton Heylin, *Bob Dylan: The Recording Sessions, 1960–1994* (St. Martin's, 1995).

Patrick Humphries, *Paul Simon: Still Crazy after All These Years* (Doubleday, 1989).

Dave Laing, Karl Dallas, Robin Denselow, and Robert Shelton, *The Electric Music: The Story of Folk into Rock* (Methuen, 1975).

Michelle Phillips, *California Dreamin': The True Story of the Mamas and the Papas* (Warner Books, 1986).

Johnny Rogan, *Timeless Flight: The Definitive Biography of the Byrds* (Square One, 1990).

Robert Shelton, *No Direction Home: The Life and Music of Bob Dylan* (William Morrow, 1986).

Richie Unterberger, *Turn! Turn! Turn! The '60s Folk-Rock Revolution* (BackBeat Books, 2002).

Interlude 2

Who's Playing What? Instrumentation in Rock

The musical instruments used in rock music, and especially the ways these instruments are combined, are central to relationships between the myriad of styles discussed in this book. While any rock fan can tell the difference between an electric guitar and a keyboard, or a drum set and a saxophone, far fewer listeners understand exactly how these instruments typically work together in songs. This interlude will take a closer look at how rock musicians employ various methods of instrumentation to create the musical textures that are found in rock styles. Let's begin by reviewing the instruments themselves and how they tend to function in a rock context.

The Rhythm Section

Beat It: Drums and Percussion.   Instruments in rock frequently have specific roles within the music. The task of the rhythm section is to establish a solid foundation of rhythm and harmony that will provide a background for singers or instrumental soloists. At the heart of the rhythm section is the drummer, whose role is to establish not only the tempo and meter, but also the "feel" of each song. Most rock drummers employ a set consisting of a snare drum (which sits on a stand between the drummer's legs), a bass drum (played by the right foot), and a high-hat (two cymbals that can be clamped together using a special stand controlled by a foot pedal). The number of tom-toms used will vary from drummer to drummer; tom-toms that are mounted on the bass drum are called ride toms; those that stand on the floor are called floor toms. A drummer may also use several cymbals, though almost always there will be a ride cymbal and a crash cymbal included. The rhythmic patterns drummers play work something like the gears of a clock, with some gears moving quickly and others moving more slowly. The high-hat or ride cymbal is often used for the fastest notes, played in a regular stream. The bass and snare drums are slower and often seem to be in dialogue with one another. A typical drumbeat is shown below; the numbers across the top show the way the rhythm would be counted, while the x's show which drums (or high-hat) are used on which beats:

Count:	1	&	2	&	3	&	4	&			1	&	2	&	3	&	4	&		
High-hat	x	x	x	x	x	x	x	x			x	x	x	x	x	x	x	x	
Snare			x				x						x				x		
Bass	x				x	x					x				x	x			

A beat like the one shown above can be elaborated by the addition of other percussion instruments, such as tambourine, cowbell, conga drums, or even hand claps. Most drummers will use one pattern for verses and another for bridges or choruses, and also break the pattern to play drum fills that will help lead the music from section to section.

The Low Down: Electric Bass.   The bass player's job is to "lock in" with the drummer rhythmically, as well as to provide the important bass notes to the harmony played by the guitar and/or keyboards; the bassist is thus a kind of bridge between the rhythmic and harmonic dimensions of the music. Often the bass player will center his part around the rhythmic pattern played in the bass drum, making sure to stress those notes rhythmically while filling in other

Adolfo "Fito" de la Parra, drummer for Canned Heat, performing at the Woodstock Music and Art Fair (see Chapter 7). Here, de la Parra performs on a fairly standard rock drum set: bass drum (bottom left), snare drum (center), two mounted toms (attached to a second bass drum here), a floor tom (right), a ride and crash cymbal (right) and a high-hat cymbal (left).

notes in order to create an interesting bass line. Sometimes bass players will employ a walking bass line, in which the bass notes follow one after another in an even rhythm and mostly in a scale-wise manner. In this case, the bassist has to craft the line so that she sounds the root note of each chord on the first beat of each measure (the root note always shares the name of the chord, so that the root of a C-major chord is a C and the root of an A-minor chord is an A, etc.). Much early rock music used the upright bass, which, though acoustic, could be amplified; but by the early 1960s, the more easily amplified electric bass guitar was established as the preferred bass instrument for most popular music except jazz and country. The bass guitar has four strings, tuned an octave below the bottom four strings of the guitar and matching the tuning of the upright bass (making for easier switching from one to the other).

Harmony in Motion: Rhythm Guitar and Keyboards. While the bass usually provides the foundation for a song's harmony, the rhythm guitar really fleshes out the harmonic dimension by playing the full chords. The rhythm guitarist also has to be careful to fit his part in with the bass and drums, and sometimes if the bass locks in with the bass drum, the rhythm guitar will lock in with the snare, emphasizing the snare part while filling in the remaining space between beats. Rhythm guitar can be played on either acoustic or electric guitar. The electric guitar makes little sound on its own, but when connected to an amplifier it can reach high volume levels. In 1950s rockabilly, the acoustic rhythm guitar often replaces the drum set and provides the rhythmic propulsion that drives the song forward. More often, though, the rhythm guitar part complements the bass and drum parts, and together these three instruments work together to establish the harmonic and rhythmic basis for the song. Sometimes piano, organ, or synthesizer can be used along with, or even in place of, the rhythm guitar. If keyboards are used with rhythm guitar, the keyboards may play the same rhythmic figure as the guitar, though often if an organ is used, the organ will simply sustain chords while the guitar plays its more rhythmic part. However the parts are organized, the rhythm guitar and keyboard players have to be careful not to get in one another's way musically.

Parliament Funkadelic's Bootsy Collins playing the electric bass in concert. The electric bass plays a prominent part in much of rock and is central to the funk music of Collins and many others.

Singers and Solos

In the Spotlight: Lead Singers and Backup Vocals. With the rhythmic and harmonic dimensions of the piece firmly secured by the rhythm section, the singer can focus on the melodic dimension of the music. Singers are sometimes very free with the rhythmic placement of their melody notes, and this freedom translates not into rhythmic confusion (as it might if the rhythm guitarist were to take the same liberties) but rather into a lively dialectical tension between the tightly structured rhythmic grid of the rhythm section and the relative freedom of the vocal line. The singer's job is not only to create melodic interest but also to deliver the song's lyrics in a convincing manner—one that does not seem contrived or unnatural in comparison with normal speech. Many listeners attend as closely to the lyrics as to the melody that projects them, and so a vocal performer has to be sure that the words come across effectively. Sometimes a singer will have no backup vocals (Elvis Presley's "That's All Right (Mama)"), while other times the singer's melody will be accompanied by harmony vocals that either sing along with the melody (The Beach Boys' "Surfer Girl") or support and echo some part of it (The Beatles' "Twist and Shout"). Like the rhythm section parts described above, the vocals are usually coordinated with one another (as well as with the rhythm section) to avoid conflict between parts.

Paul Katner of Jefferson Starship playing a battery of keyboards at a secret, illegal concert in Golden Gate Park in San Francisco, May 1973.

Steppin' Up: Instrumental Solos. In order to create contrast in arrangements, an instrumental solo is often brought in somewhere past the midpoint in a song. This might be a saxophone solo (as in the Coasters' "Yakety Yak"), a guitar solo (Jimi Hendrix's "Purple Haze"), or a piano solo (Jerry Lee Lewis's "Great Balls of Fire"). Sometimes an arrangement can feature several solos, as in Yes's "Roundabout," for instance. In all of these cases, the instrumental soloist is the central focus of the music for the duration of the solo, taking the place in the spotlight usually reserved for the singer. The job of the rhythm section remains the same as it was during the other sections of the song: support the soloist. A good rhythm section will stay out of the soloist's way and follow the solo's lead, perhaps getting louder to build excitement if needed. The instrumental solo serves to make the return of the vocals sound fresh, since usually during the solo there has been no singing, and so in that regard the solo is itself subordinate to the sung sections of the track (though with some bands—like Santana, for instance—this relationship can be reversed).

Horns and Strings: Sweetening the Sound.   Some arrangements use horns or strings as a way of adding the finishing touches to a track. Horn sections consisting of some combination of trumpets, trombones, and saxophones are used frequently to give a tune a little more "punch," and much Memphis and Muscle Shoals soul is well known for this approach. Some producers are especially fond of adding strings, either real or synthesized—in some cases this is done after the band has left the recording studio. The most famous instance of this is the Beatles' "The Long and Winding Road," to which producer Phil Spector added strings without the knowledge of Paul McCartney. But most often the use of strings is far less controversial and has the effect of making an arrangement sound bigger and more elegant. Often strings are saved until late in the arrangement and employed to give the end of the track a convincing lift. In any case, an arranger has to be careful that the horns or strings added to sweeten a track stay out of the way of the rhythm section and singers, creating a backdrop that enhances without drawing too much attention to itself.

How It All Fits Together

"Smoke on the Water."   Now that we have briefly considered the instruments involved in rock music and sketched their respective roles, we will now explore two contrasting examples in order to observe in greater detail how instrumentation works. Deep Purple's "Smoke on the Water" provides a good example of how rock music from the mid 1960s forward is organized in terms of instrumentation. The track follows the contrasting verse-chorus formal pattern: after the introduction, four verse-chorus pairs occur (the third of which is instrumental), with a coda rounding the tune off. It is easy to hear each instrument during the introduction, since the band brings them in almost one at a time. The song begins with the electric guitar alone, playing a four-measure blues-inflected riff that is then repeated. Notice the guitar's distorted tone, which is a result of overdriving the amplifier; this tone is used extensively in rock. With the third time through the guitar riff the drums enter, first with the high-hat only, and then on the fourth time through, with the snare drum as well. Notice that the guitar is also doubled by the organ here, though the effect is subtle because the organ is also distorted and thus sounds a bit like a second guitar. With the fifth occurrence of the guitar riff, the bass guitar is added, and with the sixth time through the bass is doubled by the bass drum. As the vocals enter for the first verse, notice that the drummer is primarily playing the high-hat, bass drum, and snare, using crashes on the cymbal and bass drum to mark off the beginning and end of vocal phrases. The guitar and bass are playing almost the same part, while the organ takes the "rhythm guitar" role, playing the chords in a manner that plays off the drums and bass. As the chorus begins, note that the organ becomes somewhat more sustained, as do the guitar and bass, while more crashes and fills in the drums and a second vocal harmony are added. The verses and choruses that follow are mostly the same as the first pair, though the verse and chorus during the guitar solo are different.

Notice how the bass during the solo moves in faster notes, while the drum part emphasizes the snare drum on the faster notes rather than the high-hat. The arrival of the chorus during the solo is particularly dynamic, as is

LISTENING GUIDE

GET MUSIC ▶▶ wwnorton.com/rockhistory

Deep Purple, "Smoke on the Water"

Words and music by Ritchie Blackmore, Ian Gillan, Roger Glover, Jon Lord, and Ian Paice, produced by Deep Purple. Contained on the album *Machine Head*, which reached #1 in the UK and #7 on the Billboard Album charts in mid 1972. Reached #4 on the Billboard Pop charts when released as a single in mid 1973.

FORM: Contrasting verse-chorus, with guitar solo featured after second verse-chorus pair, employing music from the verses and an altered version of the chorus.

TIME SIGNATURE: 4/4.

INSTRUMENTATION: Drums, electric bass, electric guitar, and organ, with solo lead vocal on verses and one backup vocal on choruses.

0:00–0:51	**Introduction**, 24 mm.	4 + 4 + 4 + 4 + 4 + 4 using 4mm. guitar riff; instruments enter in turn.
0:51–1:25	**Verse 1**, 16 mm.	Vocals enter, as band supports, "We all came out . . ."
1:25–1:55	**Chorus**, 14 mm.	6 mm. chorus, second vocal enters, then 8 mm. link to verse 2 using guitar riff from intro.
1:55–2:28	**Verse 2**, 16 mm.	As before, "They burned down . . ."
2:28–2:58	**Chorus**, 14 mm.	As before, "Smoke . . ."
2:58–3:31	**Instr. Verse**, 16 mm.	Guitar solo, faster rhythm in bass, drums emphasize snare.
3:31–3:56	**"Chorus"** 12 mm.	Guitar solo continues, based on chorus but with some changes, then 8 mm. link using guitar riff from intro.
3:56–4:29	**Verse 3**, 16 mm.	As before, "We ended up . . ."
4:29–4:42	**Chorus**, 6 mm.	As before and then to coda.
4:42–5:35	**Coda**, 16+ mm.	4 + 4 + 4 + 4 using 4 mm. guitar riff, then fade on vamp.

the return to the guitar riff in the linking passage before the beginning of the last verse.

"Bye Bye Love." Deep Purple's "Smoke on the Water" employs an instrumentation that emphasizes all the musical power and drama that rock can frequently display. The Everly Brothers' "Bye Bye Love" takes a very different tack. The contrast can be heard already in the introduction to the Everly Brothers track: where Deep Purple began with the sound of a distorted electric guitar, "Bye Bye Love" starts with a bright acoustic guitar. In fact, the dual acoustic guitars of the Everlys play a central role in the rhythmic dimension of this track. The drums here are much lighter, played mostly with wire brushes (not sticks) on the snare drum, with no high-hat, cymbals, bass drum, or tom-toms, leaving it to the strummed acoustic guitars to drive the music forward. With the first chorus we hear the trademark duet vocals of the brothers, sung high and with little vibrato (which is a slight but regular variation of pitch often employed by singers and instrumentalists). The accompaniment during these sections con-

LISTENING GUIDE GET MUSIC ▶▶ wwnorton.com/rockhistory

The Everly Brothers, "Bye Bye Love"

Words and music by Boudleaux and Felice Bryant, produced by Archie Bleyer. Reached #2 on the Billboard Pop charts in mid 1957 (uk6); also reached #1 on the Billboard Country and Western charts and #5 on the rhythm and blues charts.

FORM: Contrasting verse-chorus, with choruses preceding each verse, rather than following.

TIME SIGNATURE: 12/8 (shuffle in four).

INSTRUMENTATION: Snare drum played with brushes, upright bass, and two acoustic guitars, with duet lead vocals on the choruses and solo vocals on the verses.

0:00–0:06	**Introduction**, 4mm.	Acoustic guitar featured.
0:06–0:32	**Chorus**, 19 mm.	Trademark Everly Bros. vocal duet, "Bye bye love . . ."
0:32–0:55	**Verse 1**, 16 mm.	Solo vocal used for contrast, "There goes my baby . . ."
0:55–1:21	**Chorus**, 19 mm.	As before.
1:21–1:44	**Verse 2**, 16 mm.	As before, "I'm 'a through with . . ."
1:44–2:18	**Chorus**, 19 mm.+	As before with fade.

sists of two acoustic guitars, snare drum, and acoustic bass. There is also an electric guitar present, and it can be heard much more clearly during the verses, where it plays a lick that follows the chord changes, though differently from verse to verse. Notice also that the verses are sung solo and this makes the return to the duet vocals in each subsequent chorus fresh by comparison.

Despite the contrasting character of these two tracks, they share a common approach to instrumentation. In both cases the singing is placed front and center with the rhythm section instruments working together to create a coordinated accompaniment. As can be seen from the chart below, the musicians combine their accompanimental parts in different ways: Deep Purple drives the rhythm and harmony with aggressive drumming, forceful bass playing, and distorted sounds in the organ and guitar, while the Everly Brothers propel the rhythm and harmony more through their far-less-forceful acoustic guitars. Both tracks employ solo vocals in the verses and duets during the chorus. There is no instrumental solo in "Bye Bye Love." The following chart helps highlight the different approaches to instrumentation between these two tracks.

Listening analytically to these two examples helps us focus our attention on the separate elements that make up these songs. Most listeners never really attend to the ways the musical parts in a track work together; they may only notice individual parts when one stands out in some particular way, and then only for a moment. As we continue our study of rock music in the following chapters, try to listen more carefully to the instrumentation, determining where you can detect how and in what ways the musicians are working together to make the music sound the way it does. As mentioned in the Introduction, it sometimes helps to follow a single part all the way through a tune, listening to the bass only, then playing the song again and focusing only on the drums, for instance. While rock music sometimes creates an impression of musical simplicity, there are often layers of complexity just below the surface waiting to be discovered. The tapestry of musical texture often does not draw attention to itself; in fact, good backing tracks help the listener to focus on the vocals or solos, making the background instrumentation relatively transparent aurally.

"Smoke on the Water"		
Rhythm section	**Singing**	**Solos**
Distorted guitar	Solo on verse	Guitar solo
Distorted organ	Duet on chorus	
Full drum set		
Electric bass		

"Bye Bye Love"		
Rhythm section	**Singing**	**Solos**
Snare drum w/ brushes	Solo on verse	None
Two acoustic guitars	Duet on chorus	
Upright (acoustic) bass		

But now you know the kind of thinking that goes into making the tracks, so you can attend to this dimension of the songs we study. In Interlude 3, we will explore how the recording process adds yet another dimension to the way we hear instrumentation, either by blending parts together or helping them to remain distinct. For now, it's enough to work at noting that the various instrumental parts have coordinated roles to play, and to appreciate modes of musical skill and artistry in rock that might otherwise go undetected.

chapter 6

DANCING IN THE STREET
MARTHA & THE VANDELLAS

While Motown was best known in the 1960s for its politely restrained pop music, Martha and the Vandellas represented the more soulful side of the Detroit-based label. Lead singer Martha Reeves (center) was a secretary at Motown before being tapped at the last minute to replace Mary Wells for a recording session. "Dancing in the Street" is probably the group's best-known record, and this Holland-Dozier-Holland–produced single rose as high as number two on both the pop and rhythm and blues charts in the summer of 1964. Martha and the Vandellas' style displays more gospel influence than that of their Motown rivals the Supremes, though the looser quality of their music did not translate into considerations of image. As exemplified in this "picture record," the dress and image projected by Motown and its artists was as polished and controlled as the music was often accused of being. Here, Reeves and company wear long, classy evening dresses, presenting an image of sophistication and elegance. One could imagine them performing for the president or the Queen of England as easily as in front of 10,000 screaming teenagers.

Motown Pop and Southern Soul

Judging only from the description of popular music in America provided by Chapters 4 and 5, we might conclude that the arrival of the Beatles and the other British invasion bands in the first months of 1964 swept most other forms of pop off the U.S. hit singles charts. True, the end of the Brill Building era was hastened by the British invasion, but we saw in Chapter 5 that Phil Spector, Leiber and Stoller, and others did not stop enjoying hit records in 1964: Leiber and Stoller's Red Bird label hit number one with the Shangri-Las' "Leader of the Pack" in late 1964, for instance, while Spector's production of the Righteous Brothers' "You've Lost That Lovin' Feeling" went to the top spot in the United States in early 1965. Black artists from the early '60s sometimes remark that the British invasion had a disastrous effect on the girl groups and sweet soul; to a certain extent this is true. Even if the Drifters went to number four with "Under the Boardwalk" during the summer of 1964 around the time *A Hard Day's Night* was released, and the Ronettes' "Walking in the Rain" climbed to number twenty-three in late 1964, it was clear that by 1965 the situation in the youth-music market had shifted for black artists hoping to score on the pop charts. With so many white Brits playing a brand of pop inspired by black American rhythm and blues, it is tempting to see a parallel in the mid '60s to the situation in the second half of the 1950s when white musicians appropriated musical styles developed by black musicians, leaving the black musicians behind and largely unrewarded for their work.

In the years between 1964 and 1970, however, there was a good deal of important music by black musicians on the pop charts. The difference was that this music now came from new artists and from other parts of the country than it had before—from Detroit, Memphis, Muscle Shoals (Alabama), and Atlanta. Some black pop was pushed off the charts by the British invasion, but new black pop flourished during this same period. This chapter covers the music that came out of Motown Records—an independent label whose most important era of success parallels that of the Beatles, almost to the day—as well as the emergence of southern soul from Memphis, which occurred about the same time the Byrds were introducing folk rock. The music of James Brown, who had his first success as early as 1956 and whose music stretches into the 1970s and beyond, will also be explored. The general question that arises in this chapter is not so much whether black popular music was shoved aside by the British invasion and the American response to it. It is, instead, a question that involves race in a new way: Can one form of this new black popular music be considered "blacker" than another? Motown is often cast as black pop music that made too many concessions to white sensibilities—that sold out its blackness to make money in the white market. Southern soul is often cast as music that makes no excuses for its blackness and stays closer to its origins in black culture. In this chapter we thus encounter a new dimension to issues of race that played an important role in previous chapters, because here we will consider not only questions of black and white, but also the question of black and blacker. Can such distinctions within black music be valid? In our study of black pop in the wake of the Beatles, we turn first to the music of Motown—a label that enjoyed enormous commercial success in the 1960s.

Berry Gordy Jr. and Black Music for White Audiences

Go Where the Money Is: White Kids and Disposable Income. By the end of the 1960s, Berry Gordy Jr. was head of one of the most important black-owned businesses in America. Gordy began Motown Records in 1959, after trying several other types of work. In the years between World War II and the founding of Motown, Gordy had been a professional boxer in the Detroit area, worked for his father's plastering company, owned a record store, and worked on the Ford assembly line. He spent a lot of time in Detroit's jazz clubs, though his experience with the record store taught him that—financially, at least—jazz was not the key to success in the music business. Gordy began writing songs when he learned that Detroiter and former boxer turned singer Jackie Wilson was looking for material to record. Working with Billy Davis (a.k.a. Tyran Carlo), Gordy wrote several songs that became hits for Wilson, including "Reet Petite" (1957), "Lonely Teardrops" (p7 r1, 1958), and "That's Why (I Love You So)" (p13 r2, 1959). During this time Gordy also wrote and produced songs using other local Detroit singers and musicians, leasing these recordings to other labels in New York or Chicago. His first hit record for Motown in early 1960, Barrett Strong's "Money (That's What I Want)" (p23 r2), was actually a re-release of a song he had leased to his sister's record company, Anna, only a year previously.

During his first few years in business, Gordy often modeled his releases on already successful records. The Marvelettes' "Please Mr. Postman" (p1 r1, 1961) resembles the kind of girl-group hits that were coming out of the Brill Building at about the same time, while the grittier "Do You Love Me" (p3 r1, 1962) by the Contours is similar to the Isley Brothers' style of the early '60s. From the founding of Motown, however, Gordy knew that there was enormous commercial potential in producing records that could cross over from the rhythm and blues charts onto the pop charts. Adopting the practice that Chuck Berry had initiated only a few years earlier, Gordy decided to make Motown singles acceptable to white listeners in the original Motown versions; and in the early to mid 1960s, this meant making records that would appeal especially to white teenagers. This willingness to accommodate white tastes is one of the keys to Motown's tremendous crossover success, but in the early years Motown's most regular success was in the rhythm and blues market. In fact, throughout the 1960s Motown releases frequently charted higher on the rhythm and blues charts than they did on the pop charts. And while the first target audience of crossover appeal may have been white teens, Gordy soon set his sights on the more middle-class audiences that frequented upscale supper clubs.

Adapting the Brill Building Production Model. Gordy was very good at borrowing ideas from other successful people in the music business. From the Brill Building, he took the idea of giving songwriting and production duties to a collection of specialized individuals and teams, using a model that had been established by Leiber and Stoller a few years before. From 1960 to 1964, Gordy, William "Mickey" Stevenson, and William "Smokey" Robinson handled many of the songwriter/producer duties. Gordy and Robinson wrote and Gordy produced the first Miracles hit, "Shop Around" (p2 r1, 1960), while Robinson wrote and produced the Miracles' "You've Really Got a Hold on Me" (p8 r1, 1962). Robinson probably had the most success of Motown producers in the early years; in addition to his work with other Motown artists, he took over songwriting and production for singer Mary Wells, enjoying a string of hits that included "The One Who Really Loves You" (p8 r2, 1962), "You Beat Me to the Punch" (p9 r1, 1962), "Two Lovers" (p7 r1, 1962), and "My Guy" (p1, 1964). The 1964–67 years at Motown were dominated by the tremendous success of the Brian Holland, Lamont Dozier, and Eddie Holland team; "H-D-H" were responsible for a string of hits by the Supremes, the Four Tops, and Martha and the Vandellas, among others. H-D-H left Motown late in 1967 over a royalty dispute, and Norman Whitfield then emerged as the label's most successful producer; his series of singles with the Temptations through the early 1970s especially made him a dominant figure in American pop. Later in the 1970s Frank Wilson, and the team of Valerie Ashford and Nick Simpson, had tremendous success at Motown.

The Studio, the Band, Quality Control. Throughout most of the 1960s, Motown productions were recorded in the studio contained within the two adjoining Detroit houses—called "Hitsville, USA"—that made up the business headquarters for the label. The studio was always open and often busy around the clock, as different artists and producers moved in and out working on various releases. Like Phil Spector in Los Angeles, Motown producers also had a gifted and experienced group of studio musicians to help them craft their arrangements. Drawn from Detroit's lively jazz scene, these players were adept at creating their parts on the spot, without the benefit of scored-out parts or even a completed formal design. Especially in the case of H-D-H sessions, the musicians would often be given only a general idea of the chords and rhythms the producers had in mind. Many musicians were used on Motown sessions over the decade, but the key players were pianist Earl Van Dyke, drummer Bennie Benjamin, and electric bassist James Jamerson. One key to what would by mid-decade be referred to as the "Motown Sound" was that most of the

Motown's founder Berry Gordy, seated left, had strong influence and control over the artists on his record label. Here he sits with the Supremes—Mary Wilson and Diana Ross to his left and Florence Ballard seated behind—discussing an upcoming performance. Gordy employed a large staff to help manage and perfect the Motown sound and image.

records featured the playing of this studio band, the Funk Brothers. Once a week, Gordy gathered Motown personnel together for "quality control" meetings, which served as the final test for each song, its arrangement, and its recorded sound. A number of freshly recorded potential releases would be presented and the members of the Motown staff would vote on the songs, with Gordy sometimes asking, "If you only had a dollar, would you buy this record or buy a sandwich?" Records that lost out to the sandwich would either be rejected or sent back for reworking.

Artist Development and Professional Choreography.   Since Gordy was drawing most of his talent from the lower-income areas of Detroit, he knew that most of his artists would need a certain amount of instruction in how to behave and carry themselves in a wide variety of social situations, especially since crossover was one clear objective for all Motown artists. He wanted the dance movements that accompanied singing in live performance be refined and graceful, not vulgar or amateurish. Motown artists had to project an image of class and sophistication. For the dancing and movement portion, he hired former Broadway choreographer Cholly Atkins. Atkins worked with each group for hours, carefully honing every on-stage movement and dance step. For what Motown performers playfully called "the charm school," Gordy hired Maxine Powell, who had run a finishing school within Detroit's black community since the early 1950s. Powell was charged with teaching both the women and men how to move and speak with grace. Gordy's goal was to prepare his acts for the highest echelons of success in the music business. Hit records were only one part of Motown's success formula; all Motown acts performed frequently and Gordy's plan was to book his best acts into elegant supper clubs such as the Copacabana in New York or the big hotel stages of Las Vegas. In light of Gordy's ambitious goals for his

artists, Powell told her charges that she was preparing them to perform and
socialize in two places especially: the White House and Buckingham Palace.

The Motown Artists

The Temptations.   Known for their athletic choreographed dance moves, the
Temptations were among the top Motown acts during 1964–72. The group
formed in 1961 in Detroit when Otis Williams, Melvin Franklin, and Al Bryant
of the Distants joined forces with Eddie Kendricks and Paul Williams (no relation to Otis) of the Primes. After a few unsuccessful releases for Motown,
Bryant left the group in 1963 and David Ruffin joined, completing the classic
Temptations lineup that would remain intact until Ruffin's departure in 1968.
After a few unsuccessful releases produced by Gordy and then Robinson, the
group hit the pop charts in early 1964 (at about the same time the Beatles were
making their first splash), with "The Way You Do the Things You Do" (p11), a
tune written and produced by Robinson and showcasing Kendricks's high tenor
lead vocal. This catchy track not only provides a representative example of the
early Temptations style, but it also showcases Robinson's clever approach to
writing lyrics. While lines such as "You got a smile so bright, you know you
could've been a candle" may ring a bit corny in isolation, when combined with
Robinson's sunny music, they come to life in a
distinctive and broadly appealing way. On the
basis of this song's success, the next several
Temptations releases were produced by
Robinson, including "My Girl" (p1 r1, 1965) featuring Ruffin on lead vocals, and "Get Ready"
(p29 r1, 1965). Perhaps disappointed that
Robinson could not duplicate the enormous success of "My Girl," Gordy decided to give Norman
Whitfield a chance to produce the group.
Beginning with "Ain't Too Proud to Beg" (p13 r1,
1966), Whitfield delivered a string of hits for the
group, including "I Know I'm Losing You" (p8
r1, 1966) and "You're My Everything" (p6 r3,
1967). With 1968's "Cloud Nine" (p6 r2),
Whitfield and the Temptations show the influence of Sly and the Family Stone's then most-
recent music; this recording also introduces
Ruffin's replacement, Dennis Edwards. The
group's more funk-oriented music will be considered in Chapter 9.

*The Temptations were one of Motown's
most consistently successful groups. They
were known for their smooth singing
style—drawing strongly on the doo-wop
tradition—and, as seen here, their
tightly choreographed dance steps.*

The Supremes.   If one group had to be chosen to
represent the Motown sound from the mid to
late 1960s, the Supremes would be the choice.
The Supremes extended the girl-group format to

The Temptations, "The Way You Do the Things You Do"

Words and music by William "Smokey" Robinson and Robert Rogers, produced by Smokey Robinson. Reached #11 on the Billboard Pop charts in 1964.

FORM: Simple verse. After an introduction based on a 1-bar, two-chord vamp, the first two verses follow the same lengthy structure. These verses employ a 16-bar section that leads into a 4-bar refrain and then a 3-bar ending subsection, based on the two-chord vamp from the intro. This extended structure is then truncated in the rest of the song, first in the 8-bar instrumental verse, then in the third verse, which pares the structure down to 12 mm. before launching into a coda based on the opening vamp. Robinson builds the arrangement by adding horns in verse 2, changing key for the sax solo, and scoring the horns in a higher register in verse 3 to create more excitement.

TIME SIGNATURE: 12/8 (shuffle in four).

INSTRUMENTATION: Electric guitar, piano, bass, drums, horns, lead and backup vocals.

0:00–0:08	**Introduction**, 4 mm.	Two-chord vamp featuring guitar with trebly tone.
0:08–0:53	**Verse 1 w/refrain**, 23 mm.	Harmony vocals take first part of each phrase, which is answered by Kendriks's high tenor, "You got a smile so bright . . ."
0:53–1:37	**Verse 2 w/refrain**, 23 mm.	Vocals continue call and response, though now the harmony parts adds some supporting "ooo's" derived from doo-wop. Horns are added. "As pretty as you are . . ."
1:37–1:52	**Instrumental Verse** (partial), 8 mm.	Verse is shortened, change of key, sax solo.
1:52–2:16	**Verse 3 w/refrain** (partial), 12 mm.	Horns are higher than before, and this gives the song an increased intensity, "You made my life so rich . . ."
2:16–2:38	**Coda**, 12 mm.	Vamp on chords from introduction, lead vocal improvises over the repeated backup vocals.

the highest reaches of commercial success. In Detroit in 1959, Diana Ross, Mary Wilson, Florence Ballard, and Betty McGlown formed a quartet initially called the Primettes—a sister group to the Primes (later to become the Temptations). McGlown soon left the group, and the remaining trio hung around the Motown headquarters during the early 1960s hoping to sing backup and to convince Gordy to sign them (he once told them to go home and finish school). Eventually the group did sign, though their first several singles, produced in turn by Gordy and Robinson, were so unsuccessful that the other Motown artists jokingly called them the "no-hit Supremes." Holland-Dozier-Holland took over production duties, and on their third try hit in the summer of 1964 with "Where Did Our Love Go?" (p1). Although Ballard was thought to be the most accomplished singer of the three, H-D-H experimented during the sessions for this single with both Wilson's and Ross's voices, deciding that Ross's was the more evocative. Once they found the formula, the H-D-H team chalked up an impressive string of five consecutive number one pop hits, following up "Where Did Our Love Go?" with "Baby Love" (1964), "Come See about Me" (r3, 1964), "Stop! In the Name of Love" (r2, 1965), and "Back in My Arms Again" (r1, 1965). A combination of professional frustration and personal problems led Ballard to leave the group in the summer of 1967 to be replaced by Cindy Birdsong. The group continued its chart-topping with "Reflections" (p2 r4, 1967), and after the departure of H-D-H, with "Love Child" (p1 r2, 1968). Diana Ross left the group in late 1969 to focus on her solo career. "Someday We'll Be Together" (p1 r1, 1969), an ironic title in retrospect, was her last hit single with the group. Ross became a very successful solo act, and Jean Terrell replaced her in the Supremes as the group went on to score more pop hits in the 1970s, including "Stoned Love" (p7, 1970).

The Supremes and Holland-Dozier-Holland.   During 1964–67, the teaming of the Supremes with the Holland-Dozier-Holland team produced a series of hit singles that made H-D-H one of the most successful writing and production teams in popular music and placed the Supremes among the top recording artists of the decade. A number one hit in the fall of 1964, "Baby Love" provides a good example of the H-D-H/Supremes approach during the mid 1960s.

The track begins with an introduction that features a series of pulsating piano chords accompanied by drums. Notice as well that the rhythm of the piano and drums is supported by what sound like hand claps or marching; this sound was actually produced by slapping together wooden 2 × 4's in the studio and makes the song's beat unmistakable. Also present in this introduction is the sound of the vibraphone (or "vibes"), a percussion instrument similar to the xylophone but featuring a sustained sound with vibrato. As Diana Ross enters with her sultry "ooo," followed by "baby love, my baby love," the song is off and running. Notice from the Listening Guide that the song is a simple verse form, with verses repeated mostly without much change in the accompaniment, which also includes electric guitar and bass after the introduction. The other Supremes provide backup vocals as Ross works her way through seven verses. There are a few nice twists to the arrangement: in the third verse, for instance, a saxophone takes over for the lead vocal for the last eight measures,

The Supremes, "Baby Love"

Words and music by Brian Holland, Lamont Dozier, and Edward Holland Jr., produced by Brian Holland and Lamont Dozier. Reached #1 on the Billboard Pop charts in the fall of 1964.

FORM: Simple verse, with a 12-bar verse structure repeated relatively unchanged throughout. The only significant alterations are in verse 3, where the saxes take over the melody after four bars, and in verse 5, which introduces a change of key via a 2-bar transition. The arrangement builds by adding instruments: the guitar enters in verse 2, as do call-and-response phrases between the lead and backup vocals; and saxes are added in verse 3. The change of key gives the song a lift after verse 4. The song structure is nevertheless very simple and its numerous repetitions would threaten to render this track boring if it weren't for the captivating vocal performance of Diana Ross.

TIME SIGNATURE: 12/8 (shuffle in four). Note how stomping boards pound out the beat throughout the song.

INSTRUMENTATION: Piano, vibes, electric guitar, bass, drums, saxes, stomping boards, lead and backing vocals.

0:00–0:09	**Introduction**, 5 mm.	Stomping boards, vibes, piano, and drums prepare the way for the vocals.
0:09–0:30	**Verse 1**, 12 mm.	Vocals enter, and Ross mostly sings solo with only a little backup. "Ooo, baby love . . ."
0:30–0:51	**Verse 2**, 12 mm.	Add guitar, as backup vocals add call and response to second half of verse. "'Cause baby love . . ."
0:51–1:13	**Verse 3**, 12 mm.	4 mm. of vocals with sax backup, and then saxes take melody, "Need ya . . ."
1:13–1:34	**Verse 4,**12 mm.	As verse 3, without the saxes, "Baby love . . ."
1:34–1:58	**Verse 5,**14 mm.	2 mm. key change peps up arrangement and then the regular 12 mm. verse follows, as the saxes return. "Need to hold you . . ."
1:58–2:20	**Verse 6**, 12 mm.	As verse 5, ". . . of me my love . . ."
2:20–2:40	**Verse 7**, 12 mm.	Fade out on second half of verse, "'Til it's hurtin' me . . ."

making the vocal return for verse 4 fresher than it might otherwise have been; and verse 5 introduces a change of key (up a half-step from D-flat to D) that also keeps the verses fresh. The pronounced rhythmic stomping in this tune is a continuation from the previous single, "Where Did Our Love Go?", as is the repetition of the word "baby"—showing that H-D-H were trying to repeat a winning formula with this second single. Both songs, as well as the next single, "Come See about Me," employ a simple verse form, though the next two hit singles, "Stop! In the Name of Love" and "Back in My Arms Again" employ contrasting verse-chorus form.

The Four Tops. In 1954, Levi Stubbs, Obie Benson, Lawrence Payton, and Duke Fakir formed the Four Tops and remained together for more than four decades. The group was originally signed to Chicago's Chess Records but moved to Motown in 1964. After initially recording a jazz album for Gordy's Workshop Jazz label, they were teamed with the Holland-Dozier-Holland team that had also begun working with the Supremes a few months earlier. Led by the lead vocals of Stubbs, the Four Tops were in many ways the male counterparts of the Supremes during 1964–67, enjoying a string of H-D-H–produced hits, including "Baby I Need Your Loving" (p11, 1964), "I Can't Help Myself (Sugar Pie, Honey Bunch)" (p1 r1, 1965), "It's the Same Old Song" (p5 r2, 1965), "Reach Out I'll Be There" (p1 r1, 1966), and "Standing in the Shadows of Love" (p6 r2, 1966).

Like those of the Supremes under H-D-H, most of the Four Tops' songs have a pronounced pop orientation, with frequent use of orchestral strings and other elements drawn from classical music. "Reach Out I'll Be There" offers a representative blend of rhythm and blues and classical music, with its classical sounding orchestral intro and harmonic progressions, combined with a strong beat and soulful vocals. After H-D-H left Motown, the group floundered somewhat but came back under Frank Wilson's writing and production (as did the post-Ross Supremes) to hit with "Still Water (Love)" (p11 r4, 1970), among others.

Martha and the Vandellas. Formed in Detroit in 1962 by former members of the Del-Phis, who had earlier recorded for Chess Records, Martha and the Vandellas had their first hit during the winter of 1963, when the Holland-Dozier-Holland–produced "Come and Get These Memories" hit number twenty-nine on the pop charts (r6). Martha Reeves had been performing in a Detroit club when she was spotted by Mickey Stevenson, who hired her not as a singer but as his secretary. When the backup singers hired for a Marvin Gaye recording session failed to show up, Reeves and her friends provided backup vocals on "Stubborn Kind of Fellow" (p46 r8, 1962), impressing Gordy enough that he had them record "I'll Have to Let Him Go" (which did not chart) as Martha and the Vandellas. By early 1963, the group consisted of Reeves on lead vocals, backed by Rosalyn Ashford and Annette Beard (Betty Kelly replaced Beard in 1964). After their first hit with H-D-H, the group followed up with "Heat Wave" (p4 r1, 1963) and "Quicksand" (p8, 1963) before Mickey Stevenson took over production duties for what would become the group's most successful and widely known single, "Dancing in the Street" (p2, 1964). By the time that single was on the charts, however, Holland-Dozier-Holland had already scored their first successes with both the Supremes and the Four Tops. This may have caused Motown to begin exercising a certain amount of caution about releasing Holland-Dozier-Holland–produced singles for Martha and the Vandellas, fearing that such records might dilute the tremendous success the Supremes were beginning to enjoy. In any case, Martha and the Vandellas continued to enjoy hit singles produced by H-D-H through 1967, including "Nowhere to Run" (p8 r5, 1965) and "Jimmy Mack" (p10 r1, 1967).

Roots in gospel and rhythm and blues are more apparent in the recordings of Martha and the Vandellas than in the records of the Supremes, who sound somewhat controlled by comparison. This contrast is due in large part to Martha Reeves's full-throated, soulful vocal style, which drives the group's music forward in a way that parallels southern soul and sets the stage for Aretha Franklin later in the decade.

Marvin Gaye, Stevie Wonder. With the notable exception of Smokey Robinson, most Motown artists were not allowed to produce their own records. The Supremes, the Temptations, and other Motown artists made suggestions and contributions in rehearsing and recording their music, but it was always clear that the producers at each session had the final say, and took the final responsibility. By the early 1970s, however, both Marvin Gaye and Stevie Wonder would gain considerable artistic control over their music, acting as artist/producers in a way that broke with earlier Motown practices. Gaye had a hit single as early as 1962 with "Stubborn Kind of Fellow," and during the remainder of the decade he placed sixteen more singles in the pop Top 40, as well as another ten in duets with Mary Wells, Tammi Terrell, or Kim Weston. He worked with most of the Motown producers, recording upbeat soul hits like "Pride and Joy" (p10 r2, 1963) for Mickey Stevenson, poppier hits like "How Sweet It Is to Be Loved by You" (p6 r4, 1965) for Holland-Dozier-Holland, and "Ain't That Peculiar" (p8 r1, 1965) for Smokey Robinson, as well as classic male-female duets like "Ain't Nothing like the Real Thing" (p8 r1, 1968), sung with Tammi Terrell and produced by Ashford and Simpson.

By the end of the decade, Gaye was also writing and producing for other artists. The Originals,

Marvin Gaye performing at the Miami Pop Festival in 1968. Gaye was a staple of Motown, scoring many solo hits, singing duets with Tammi Terrell and Mary Wells, and eventually writing songs for other Motown artists. As the 1960s came to a close, Gaye and other Motown artists (like Stevie Wonder) began to demand more control over their music. With this control, Gaye produced the highly influential album What's Going On *(1971), discussed in Chapter 9.*

a male vocal quartet that had been involved with Motown in one way or another for most of the 1960s, became Gaye's charges in the studio. The combination produced hits with "Baby I'm for Real" (p14 r1, 1969) and "The Bells" (p12 r4, 1970). His development as a producer at Motown is similar to that of Smokey Robinson, who also produced and performed, and Gaye's production experience prepared him for his most important solo project, the 1971 concept album *What's Going On.*

Stevie Wonder followed a path similar to Gaye's. At the age of thirteen, he scored a surprise number one hit on both the pop and rhythm and blues charts with "Fingertips, pt. 2" (1963). The record captures an impromptu moment during a live Motown Revue concert when Wonder launches into the tune without warning (bass player Larry Moses can be heard asking "What key? What key?"). The spontaneous and exuberant quality of that moment transferred well to vinyl, and Motown ended up with one of its most successful releases up to that time. After this initial success, Wonder floundered a bit—his voice changed and Motown seemed unsure how to advance his career. By early 1966, however, his "Uptight (Everything's Alright)" hit number three on the pop charts (r1), and began a string of hits, including "I Was Made to Love Her" (p2 r1, 1967), "For Once in My Life" (p2 r2, 1968), and "My Cherie Amour" (p4 r4, 1969), with Wonder earning partial songwriting credit for each. In 1970, he produced "Signed, Sealed, Delivered, I'm Yours" (p3 r1) and, like Gaye at about the same time, he felt ready to write and produce his own music. His first self-produced album, *Where I'm Coming From* (1971), was a disappointment as a whole, though the two singles, "If You Really Loved Me" (p8 r4, 1971) and a cover of the Beatles' "We Can Work It Out" (p13 r3, 1971), did well. His next few self-produced albums, however, made important contributions to 1970s popular music, and like the music of Marvin Gaye helped Motown to make the transition out of the 1960s. The music of Gaye and Wonder, and their role as producer/artists, will be considered further in Chapter 9.

> ### The Funk Brothers: Behind the Scenes
>
> The 2003 documentary film *Standing in the Shadows of Motown* chronicles well the contributions of the studio musicians behind the Motown sound. Most listeners focus their attention on the singers, and perhaps also on the songwriters. Few are aware that the backup musicians on a given record play a crucial role in how the record sounds, and by extension, in why a record is successful. Candid and intelligent interviews with the surviving Motown studio musicians make clear the important role these often unsung heroes played in the long succession of hits discussed in this chapter, bringing these players at last out of the shadows and into the spotlight.

Assimilation, Motown, and the Civil Rights Movement. The enormous crossover appeal of Motown records and artists in the mid 1960s, combined with Gordy's desire to appeal not only to white teens but also to a predominantly white, middle-class supper-club audience, has frequently prompted criticisms that Motown sold out to white America. In defense of Motown, even if this is so, black Americans never really tuned Motown out. In fact, if the pop charts are not taken into account at all, Motown remains one of the most important rhythm and blues labels of the 1960s. Black Americans listened to a lot of Motown records. Considerations of musical style aside, perhaps the carefully choreographed movements and the charm-school training are the most important signals of an assimilationist attitude on Gordy's part—the idea that blacks can or should assimilate into the larger American population (while retaining a strong sense of heritage). For many who oppose this idea, the black music that began coming out of the south—and Memphis especially—in the mid '60s is seen as the best counter-example. This southern soul music, some would argue, was actually much more in touch with its own roots in black culture. Whatever position you take, Berry Gordy remains a pivotal figure in the development of black pop music, and his success at Motown in the 1960s would inspire and serve as a model for 1970s artists like George Clinton (who was based in Detroit, see Chapter 9) and producer/songwriters like Gamble and Huff (who built their empire in Philadelphia).

Atlantic, Stax, and Southern Soul

Atlantic in the Early 1960s.   Although its records enjoyed enormous commercial success, Motown was not the only label crossing rhythm and blues hits onto the pop charts in the 1960s. As discussed at the end of Chapter 3, New York–based Atlantic Records enjoyed considerable success in the first years of the 1960s with hits from the Drifters, the Coasters, and Ben E. King. But while the highly produced and often relaxed style of sweet soul was the most public face of the label's activity, it was beginning to develop a new stylistic direction—a harder-edged brand of black pop that would soon be called southern soul.

Along with the label's co-founder Ahmet Ertegun, Jerry Wexler had been responsible for much of Atlantic's success in the second half of the 1950s. But with the emergence of other producers at the label, most notably Leiber and Stoller, Wexler found himself spending much of his time directing the label's business affairs. His interest in record producing was rekindled when Atlantic was able to sign gospel-influenced singer Solomon Burke in 1961. Working with Bert Berns, Wexler produced a series of successful singles for Burke, including "Just Out of Reach (Of My Two Open Arms)" (p24 r7, 1961), "If You Need Me" (p37 r2, 1963), "Goodbye, Baby (Baby Goodbye)" (p33, 1964), "Got to Get You off My Mind" (p22 r1, 1965), and "Tonight's the Night" (p28 r2, 1965).

There was an important stylistic difference between sweet and southern sou: sweet soul tended to be elegant and restrained (think of the Drifters' "Under the Boardwalk" or Ben E. King's "Stand by Me"); southern soul was a more openly enthusiastic emotional expression of the kind often found in black churches. This pronounced gospel influence made the music seem truer to its heritage than softer, more pop-oriented styles of black music. Wexler was quick to hear this quality, and he would play a crucial role in developing southern soul throughout the decade, either by signing artists directly to Atlantic or by licensing their recordings from other, smaller labels.

Soulsville, USA: The Memphis Connection. Larger labels often licensed a recording from a smaller label, either pressing new copies under their own label or simply pressing and distributing the record under its original label for the smaller company. This was a mutually beneficial relationship: it relieved the smaller company of the significant financial commitment that pressing large numbers of records required while giving them access to markets that would otherwise be closed to them; the larger companies benefited from sharing in the profits of records that were already in many cases proven regional hits and were often more innovative stylistically than records produced within the larger company. It was through such a licensing agreement that Atlantic and the Memphis-based Stax formed a very successful partnership. Founded in 1960 by Jim Stewart and his older sister Estelle Axton, Stax Records (called Satellite at first) came to the attention of Atlantic's Jerry Wexler later that year with a Stax single called "Cause I Love You." Written by Memphis DJ Rufus Thomas and sung as a duet with his daughter Carla, it become a regional hit in the south. Atlantic leased the national rights to the record, and a few months later the rights to a second single written and sung by Carla and produced by Stewart called "Gee Whiz"; this went to number ten on the pop charts and number five on the rhythm and blues charts in early 1961. Atlantic handled several Stax singles that scored success on the national pop and R&B charts, including the instrumentals "Last Night" (p3 r2, 1961) by the Mar-Keys and "Green Onions" (p3 r1, 1962) by Booker T. and the MG's, as well as Rufus Thomas's dance hit "Walkin' the Dog" (p10 r5, 1963). The leasing of rights thus worked out well for both Atlantic and for the much smaller Stax, and this success led to a closer relationship between the two labels.

In the first half of the 1960s, Stax was a much smaller operation than Motown. Like Motown, however, Stax often depended on its studio band, Booker T. and the MG's, to pull together the backing tracks on the spot, often without music or prepared arrangements. The band's membership shifted some in the early 1960s, but by the time of the classic recordings by Otis Redding, Wilson Pickett, and Sam and Dave of the mid 1960s, the members were Booker T. Jones on organ, Steve Cropper on guitar, Donald "Duck" Dunn on bass, and Al Jackson Jr. on drums. Different from Motown, where roles were mostly kept distinct, at Stax production duties and credits were shared among these musicians, Stewart, and other Stax regulars present at the sessions. The closest thing Stax had to songwriting/production specialists like Smokey Robinson, Holland-Dozier-Holland, or Norman Whitfield at Motown were songwriters David Porter and Isaac Hayes, though Cropper worked especially closely with Otis Redding, co-writing songs and playing the role of producer at many sessions. A Stax session was thus less regimented than a Motown session might have been, with the studio musicians taking up whatever role was needed in a given situation. Despite the differences between Stax and Motown, however, the Hitsville and Soulsville approaches were more similar to one another than either was to the standard music-business approach to making records at the time. One thing Wexler found liberating about recording at Stax—and later in Muscle Shoals—was the way the music often emerged so spontaneously from these sessions, though not without great musical experimentation and searching in some cases. This was not the way things had been done at Atlantic in New York.

Otis Redding and Stax. One of the most important artists recording for Stax during the 1960s was Otis Redding. He had scored a number twenty R&B hit in 1963 with "These Arms of Mine," but Redding and Stax both took a big step forward with Redding's series of crossover hits during 1965: "Mr. Pitiful" (p41 r10), "I've Been Loving You Too Long" (p21 r2), and "Respect" (p35 r4) brought the "Stax sound" to a larger national audience than the previous Stax hits had done. Redding's gospel-influenced vocals, combined with the driving accompaniment of Booker T. and the MG's, produced a style of southern soul that seemed less polished but more heartfelt and urgent than the slicker records coming out of Motown. Redding followed up his 1965 chart success with "Try a Little Tenderness" (p25 r4, 1966) and in early 1968 hit the top spot on both the pop and rhythm and blues charts with "Sittin' on the Dock of the Bay." Redding made significant inroads with the hippie rockers when he appeared, backed by Booker T. and the MG's, at the Monterey Pop Festival in the spring of 1967. Though most listeners today would not think this particularly strange, at the time the band was extremely apprehensive. As it turned out, the assembled flower children warmly embraced Redding and his music. Tragically, Redding never lived to see the full effect of this appearance or the crossover success of "Sittin' on the Dock of the Bay"; he died in a plane crash on December 10, 1967.

Isaac Hayes (left) and David Porter working at Stax Records. Hayes and Porter did at Stax what Holland-Dozier-Holland and Norman Whitfield did at Motown: they wrote songs for many artists, working consistently with a "house band"—in this case Booker T. and the MG's. Stax recordings were generally less regimented and more relaxed than Motown sessions, and the classic Stax sound is often "rougher" than Motown's.

Wilson Pickett and the Muscle Shoals Sound.
After singing with a Detroit-based vocal group called the Falcons, Wilson Pickett came to the attention of Jerry Wexler in 1963 under unlikely circumstances. Pickett had sung on the original demo recording from which Wexler, Bert Berns, and Solomon Burke had worked while recording "If You Need Me." By a strange error of omission, Atlantic had bought the rights to the song but not to the original demo, and Pickett's demo ended up being released on the Double L label, competing directly on the rhythm and blues charts with the Burke version on Atlantic. When Pickett showed up in the Atlantic offices in 1964 looking for a record deal, Wexler was happy to sign him as a solo act. After a few unsuccessful releases produced by Berns and recorded in New York, Wexler himself decided to take Pickett south to the Stax studios, where he hoped he might capture something of the

more unbuttoned quality that he heard in Redding's music. During the recording sessions for Pickett's "In the Midnight Hour," Wexler described to the musicians a dance he had seen in New York that featured a movement on beats two and four that seemed to delay those beats until the last possible moment. In trying to imitate this movement in music, the band discovered the "delayed backbeat" feel that became a regular element in the southern soul sound. Recorded in May of 1965, "In the Midnight Hour" hit number one on the rhythm and blues charts and number twenty three on the pop charts during the summer of '65—about the same time that Dylan and the Byrds were introducing listeners to folk rock. As it turned out, however, Pickett's days recording in the Stax studio were already numbered.

For reasons that remain unclear even today, Jim Stewart of Stax began denying Wexler recording time in the Stax studio, and Wexler's response was to take Pickett to Fame Studios in Muscle Shoals, Alabama. Atlantic's connection to Fame was through Joe Tex's hit "Hold What You've Got," which was recorded at Fame and hit number five on the pop charts (r2) in early 1965. Atlantic distributed the record for Nashville-based Dial Records. Wexler had also recently licensed Percy Sledge's "When a Man Loves a Woman," which went to number one on both the pop and rhythm and blues charts in the spring of 1966. The song had actually been recorded in the Quinvy studios in the Muscle Shoals area, but Wexler's contact in negotiations had been Rick Hall, who owned and operated Fame Studios as well as a music publishing company. Impressed by Sledge's record even before it became such a hit, Wexler brought Pickett to Hall's studio to record, and it was at Fame that Pickett recorded some of his best-known tracks, including "Land of 1000 Dances" (p6 r1, 1966), "Mustang Sally" (p26 r6, 1966), and "Funky Broadway" (p8 r1, 1967).

Like Stax, Muscle Shoals had a core of fine studio musicians, the most important of which were guitarist Jimmy Johnson, keyboardist Spooner Oldham, and drummer Roger Hawkins, who worked at Fame as well as other area studios. The success of "When a Man Loves a Woman" and Pickett's hits was attributed by many in the music business to "the Muscle Shoals sound," and this made Muscle Shoals a popular place to record in the years that followed, especially for later artists eager to harness the earthy sound of southern soul for their records.

Sam and Dave, Porter and Hayes.   A second part of Wexler's response to being shut out of the Stax studio was to offer Sam and Dave to Stax "on loan"—the group would remain under contract to Atlantic but Stewart could make records with them as if they were Stax artists. Stewart teamed Sam and Dave with Stax songwriters David Porter and Isaac Hayes, an arrangement that produced a series of successful singles, starting with the number seven R&B hit "You Don't Know Like I Know" in early 1966, and crossing over to the pop charts in mid 1966 with "Hold On, I'm Comin'" (p21 r1). The classic Sam and Dave number is "Soul Man," which was made even more famous in a 1979 close cover version by the Blues Brothers led by *Saturday Night Live* comedians John Belushi and Dan Aykroyd. "Soul Man" hit number two on the pop charts and number one on the rhythm and blues charts in the fall of 1967. The teaming of the songwriting/production team of Porter and Hayes with Sam and Dave to produce a string of hit singles is the closest parallel at Stax to the Motown practice of teaming specific producers with specific artists (Holland-Dozier-Holland with the Supremes or Norman Whitfield with the Temptations, for instance). This success at Stax would last to the end of the decade, but the label headed for some tough times after that.

The Stax Sound.   Because a good deal of southern soul was recorded in Memphis and Muscle Shoals, southern soul has been associated with "the Stax sound." Even for music that was not recorded at Stax, there may still be some validity to this claim as the musicians involved often attempted to imitate the style and sound of the first few hits by Otis Redding, Wilson Pickett, and Sam and Dave that were recorded at Stax.

Wilson Pickett's "In the Midnight Hour" is representative of the Stax sound—though many of Pickett's later hits were not recorded at Stax, this track was. The track begins with a four-measure introduction featuring horns, followed by two measures of a simple two-chord pattern that forms the basis for the tune. In those measures between the horn intro and the entrance of Pickett's voice, listen to the character of the rhythmic feel: if you count along, you'll notice that the guitar and snare drum play together on beats 2 and 4, and these beats occur so late that they are almost out of time. This is the delayed backbeat rhythm mentioned above, and it permeates this track and many others recorded later. Compared to the Supremes' "Baby Love," "In the Midnight Hour" seems much more unbuttoned and free. There are no backup vocals on the Pickett track (this is typical of the Stax sound), making Pickett's vocal delivery the focus of the song. Pickett's performance makes it seem as if his vocalizing is spontaneous and only loosely planned, leaving the listener to imagine that another performance could well be different. The song is in simple verse form, like the Supremes number, though the instrumental introduction and interlude featuring the horns create a sense of formal variety.

Wilson Pickett (left) working with Atlantic Records producer Jerry Wexler in the Fame Studios in Muscle Shoals, Alabama. Pickett's hit "In the Midnight Hour" displays the "delayed backbeat" feel that Wexler and the Stax band developed, and which became a regular element in the southern soul sound.

Aretha Franklin.   Often called the Queen of Soul, Aretha Franklin was born in Memphis, raised in Detroit, and recorded most of her hits in New York. Of all the artists Wexler had a hand in bringing to Atlantic, Franklin enjoyed the greatest success on both the pop and rhythm and blues charts, even if she did arrive almost last on the southern soul scene.

Franklin is the daughter of the famous Reverend C. L. Franklin, who led the New Bethel Baptist Church in Detroit and was well known around the

Wilson Pickett, "In the Midnight Hour"

Words and music by Wilson Pickett and Steve Cropper, produced by Jerry Wexler.
Rose to #23 on the Billboard Pop charts and #1 on Billboard Rhythm and Blues
charts in the summer of 1965.

FORM: Simple verse, with an instrumental interlude. After an instrumental introduction featuring the horns, the band falls into a repeated figure, often called a "vamp."
In this case, the vamp is made up of two chords played over one measure, and this
measure is repeated. Two 17-bar verses featuring Pickett's lead vocal are followed by
an instrumental interlude made up of the horns playing over new material based on
the intro vamp. Pickett's vocals then return, and he delivers only the first part of a
verse before seeming to improvise over the intro vamp as the song fades out.

TIME SIGNATURE: 4/4, with an accent on the second beat of each measure that is
so late it is almost out of time. This is the famous Stax "delayed backbeat."

INSTRUMENTATION: Electric guitars, bass, drums, horns, lead vocals.

0:00–0:13	**Introduction**, 6 mm.	A 4 mm. harmonized line in horns leads into the 2 mm. vamp.
0:14–0:50	**Verse 1**, 17 mm.	Vocals enter. Note the low sax (baritone sax) that helps propel the song's groove, as well as the way the rhythm guitar and snare drum lock in on beats two and four. "I'm gonna wait . . ."
0:50–1:27	**Verse 2**, 17 mm.	As before, but horns added to the first part of the verse. "I'm gonna wait . . ."
1:27–1:44	**Instrumental Interlude**, 23 mm.	Horns play over new melody loosely based on the introduction.
1:44–2:31	**Verse** (partial), 20 mm.	Pickett seems to start a final verse, as the horns play a new line underneath, but then the vamp continues without changing in the usual place, as Pickett improvises and the song fades out. "I'm gonna wait . . ."

country for his rousing sermons, which were regularly broadcast on the radio. Aretha grew up hearing some of the best gospel singers in the world at close range; she credits Clara Ward's singing of "Peace in the Valley" at a Franklin family funeral with inspiring her to devote herself to a career as a singer. When she turned eighteen and with the blessing of her father, Franklin left Detroit for New York to pursue a singing career. By the early 1960s she was signed to Columbia Records, where she released several records; these were traditional pop songs in a mainstream setting that did not make much of a commercial impact. When the Columbia contract expired in 1966, Wexler moved in, first trying to get Stax to sign Franklin, but eventually signing her directly to Atlantic. In early 1967, in the wake of the fallout with Stax, Wexler brought her to Fame Studios in Muscle Shoals to record her first tracks for Atlantic. Wexler likely hoped that the crew at Fame could work the same magic for Franklin that they had for Wilson Pickett.

The sessions at Fame started well and the first track completed was the hit "I Never Loved a Man (The Way I Love You)" (p37 r9, 1967), which abandoned the supper-club, easy-jazz character of most of Franklin's Columbia work to showcase the gospel roots of her singing. As well as that track came together, the rest of the session fell apart when a dispute broke out between Franklin's husband and somebody else in the studio, perhaps Fame's Rick Hall. Soon thereafter Franklin and Wexler were back in New York working on more tracks with the Muscle Shoals rhythm section, who were flown in without Hall's knowledge. These and later New York sessions—southern soul recorded in the Big Apple—produced a series of hits for Franklin, including a reworking of Otis Redding's "Respect" (p1 r1, 1967), as well as "Baby I Love You" (p4 r1, 1967), "(You Make Me Feel Like) A Natural Woman" (p2 r2, 1967), "Chain of Fools" (p2 r1, 1968), and "Think" (p7 r1, 1968). Redding reportedly said Franklin's performance of "Respect" was so powerful that she more or less owned the tune, even though he wrote it and recorded it first. This record shows the power of Aretha Franklin's soul music from the late 1960s, as she tears through the song, steamrolling her way to the climactic, stop-time coda.

Like many rhythm and blues singers, Aretha Franklin was strongly influenced by gospel. Pictured here is one of Aretha's first-ever recordings, a 1962 live performance at her father's church: New Bethel Baptist Church in Detroit. This album featured sermons from her father, C. L. Franklin, and music from Sammie Bryant, another prominent gospel artist. Aretha never totally abandoned gospel. Her best-selling album was Amazing Grace (1972), which featured "Precious Lord" and "Never Grow Old," two songs also recorded here.

Motown, Atlantic, Stax, and Issues of Blackness.

Some writers have characterized the southern soul of Stax/Atlantic as being truer to black culture than the productions of Motown, which,

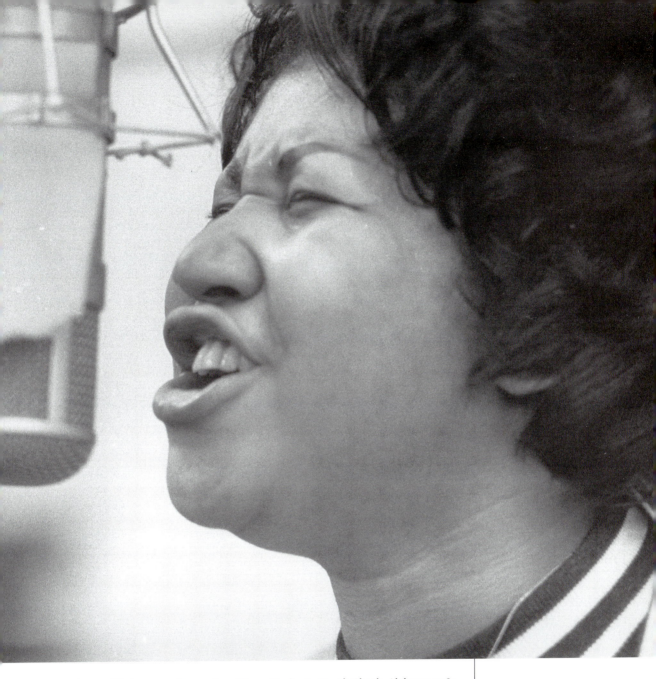

Aretha Franklin in a recording session at Fame Studios in Muscle Shoals, Alabama, 1967. After recording smooth pop songs for Columbia, Franklin left Columbia for Atlantic. There, Jerry Wexler encouraged her to be more expressive, drawing on the passion of gospel. The session pictured here was Franklin's first for Atlantic, and it yielded some of her biggest hits, including "I've Never Loved a Man (The Way I Love You)." While others, like "Respect," were recorded in New York, Franklin and Wexler continued to pursue Franklin's "southern sound" that first surfaced in Muscle Shoals.

Aretha Franklin, "Respect"

Words and music by Otis Redding, produced by Jerry Wexler. Reached #1 on both the Billboard Pop and Rhythm and Blues charts.

FORM: Modified simple verse. Beginning with a 4-bar introduction, this track continues by presenting three very similar 10-bar verses. It then moves into an 8-bar instrumental bridge, which serves to provide a brief contrast before returning to the fourth verse. Perhaps the most notable formal feature of this track is the coda, which begins with what might be Franklin's most memorable passage ("R E S P E C T"). As distinctive as these measures are, they really only help launch the song's ending and are built on the same two-chord vamp that is used for the entire coda and fade-out.

TIME SIGNATURE: 4/4. This is Wexler's attempt to capture the Stax rhythmic feel in Atlantic's New York studios.

INSTRUMENTATION: Electric guitar, organ, piano, bass, drums, tambourine, horns, lead and backup vocals. Note that while Franklin's lead vocals are much looser and unbuttoned than most other female lead singers of the 1960s, the backup vocals are much more restrained and in the girl-group tradition.

0:00–0:09	**Introduction**, 4 mm.	Horns and guitar play in call and response.
0:09–0:30	**Verse 1**, 10 mm.	Vocals enter. Note the backup vocals, which blend girl-group support with a strong gospel element. "What you want . . ."
0:30–0:51	**Verse 2**, 10 mm.	As before. Note that the guitar and snare are not locked in with the same precision as was heard in Wilson Pickett's "In the Midnight Hour," and that the low notes in the piano here take over the role played by the baritone sax in the Pickett song. "I ain't gonna do you wrong . . ."
0:51–1:12	**Verse 3**, 10 mm.	As before, "I'm about to give ya . . ."
1:12–1:28	**Instrumental Bridge**, 8 mm.	Sax solo offers contrasting material in a surprising new key.
1:28–1:50	**Verse 4**, 10 mm.	As before and back in the home key, though harmonic shift back is somewhat awkward. "Your kisses are . . ."
1:50–2:22	**Coda**, 16 mm.	Famous "R E S P E C T" stop-time passage, and then vamp, as Stax-style baritone sax enters just as the song fades out.

despite its tremendous success, is often cast as a kind of sellout to the white market. In terms of musical style, there is ample evidence that much Motown music is more pop-oriented than that of Stax. Still, no company makes records unless it believes the records will sell, so to a certain extent the Stax/Atlantic artists were also directing their music to the marketplace. If we compare the Supremes' "Baby Love" and Wilson Pickett's "In the Midnight Hour," however, the contrast between the two labels is clear—the Supremes track is much more polished in the traditional music-business sense: it focuses on the song and the vocals, and never makes too much of its blackness. If Martha and the Vandellas' "Heat Wave" or "Dancing in the Streets" is brought into the discussion, the differences between the two labels are harder to discern. What further confounds the typical distinctions between Motown and Stax/Atlantic is that it was Motown, not Stax/Atlantic, that was owned and run by black Americans—until the mid 1960s, almost everybody involved with Motown was black and by the end of the decade it was among the country's top black-owned businesses. Stax and Atlantic, on the other hand, both had white owners, and most of their records had white producers. The Stax band—often thought of as "blacker" when compared with the Motown band—was made up of two white performers (Cropper and Dunn) and two who were black (Jones and Jackson) while the Motown one was often (but not always) all black. In addition, in Muscle Shoals almost everyone besides the singers was white. This raises many interesting questions for consideration: What makes music sound black or white? What is it in the music that makes it "sound black"? Can white musicians play black music and do some black artists play music that is somehow "less black"? Does it matter who owns the record company or supervises the sessions in this regard? Is Stax "blacker" than Motown? Effective arguments have been made on both sides of this issue. What do you think?

1968: A Pivotal Year for Black Popular Music.

On April 4, 1968, the Reverend Dr. Martin Luther King Jr. was assassinated on the balcony of his Memphis hotel room. It would be difficult to exaggerate the importance of this event for race relations in America at the end of the 1960s. King had been an important leader in the civil rights movement; he was perhaps the most elegant and probably the most widely known advocate for racial equality in the United States. King's approach to social protest was markedly nonviolent; the reaction to his death, however, led to an escalation of protest violence that had begun months earlier in black neighborhoods in some of the country's major cities (including Detroit).

The death of Dr. King had a palpable impact on black music as well; at Stax, it hit especially hard (the studio was only minutes away from the hotel where Dr. King was killed). But there were other problems as well: in late 1967 Atlantic had been sold to Warner Brothers-Seven Arts, leaving Stax with a six-month option to either continue the distribution agreement with Atlantic or terminate it. Jim Stewart learned that the agreement he had signed with Atlantic some years before was not simply a distribution contract as he had thought; Atlantic attorneys had inserted a clause that gave ownership of the master tapes for all Stax recordings to Atlantic. In addition, Stewart was also reminded that Sam and Dave were Atlantic artists on loan, and if the contract were not renewed they would revert to Atlantic. With the death of his best artist, Otis Redding, in late 1967, Stewart was left with few choices. Disgusted with the Atlantic negotiations, Stewart and his sister eventually opted to sell the label to Gulf & Western, a conglomerate that produced metal bumpers before purchasing other companies, including ones in the entertainment business. Stax did continue under the leadership of Al Bell, and was soon back on the charts with Johnnie Taylor's "Who's Makin' Love (With Your Old Lady While You Were Out Makin' Love)" (p5 r1, 1968). The original community of Stax musicians, writers, and producers began to pull apart, however, and a new era was clearly beginning—an era we will pick up again in Chapter 9.

Over at Motown in April 1968, Holland-Dozier-Holland were gone and Norman Whitfield had become the label's most successful writer/producer. Berry Gordy was set on moving the label to Los Angeles in order to become more involved with movie productions and had turned over much of the day-to-day operation to others. In the wake of Dr. King's death, Motown records began to deal more directly with issues facing black America: the Supremes' "Love Child" (p1 r2, 1968), for instance, confronts the realities of urban life through the lens of an illegitimate child. By the early 1970s, Whitfield and the Temptations, Marvin Gaye, and Stevie Wonder would all focus on issues in black urban life in unmistakable terms.

James Brown: On the Way to Funk

From Doo-wop to Soul. Whatever position you take regarding the blackness of Stax and Motown, there is little room for debate over blackness when it comes to the music of James Brown. In many ways, Brown is perhaps the most important black performer in the 1960s when the history of black pop is considered in its own right.

In light of his tremendous importance and stylistic distinctiveness in the '60s, it is strange to think of James Brown starting his career in the 1950s as a stand-in for Little Richard. Born in South Carolina and raised in southern Georgia, Brown had gained some regional attention in the mid 1950s as a member of the Fabulous Flames. At a Little Richard show just before Richard hit with "Tutti Frutti," Brown and his group delivered an uninvited impromptu performance that impressed Richard's road manager, leading to the Flames being booked across the south by Clint Brantley, Richard's manager. When Richard's "Tutti Frutti" became a hit, Richard left Georgia to capitalize on his success, and James Brown performed as Little Richard for a series of appearances that Brantley had already scheduled. Soon James Brown and the Fabulous Flames enjoyed moderate success with Brown's impassioned delivery of "Please Please Please" (r6, 1956), the first record released on the Cincinnati-based King Records, run by Syd Nathan, which would release all but a handful of Brown's records over the decades to follow. Brown hit again in 1958 with "Try Me," his first number one rhythm and blues hit, which also enjoyed moderate crossover appeal (p48).

Brown's early hits remained within the stylistic range of 1950s doo-wop, as he sang lead vocal supported by the backup vocals of the other Flames. With "Think" (p33 r7, 1960), however, Brown began to develop the soul style for which he would become so well known. The song is driven by the horns and the rhythm section in a tight accompaniment. Brown's aggressive singing and the rhythmic groove created to support it are the clear focal points of the music, and not the lyrics, harmony, or background vocals as in other pop styles of the time.

By the early 1960s, Brown was well known around the R&B circuit for his stage show, which already featured his athletic dancing and the famous closing routine in which he is led off stage exhausted, only to vault back into the spotlight with fresh energy. In hopes of capturing on record the excitement of James Brown and the Fabulous Flames in concert, Brown and manager Ben Bart hit on the idea of releasing a live album that was recorded during a 1962 Apollo Theater performance in New York. As in most other styles in the early 1960s except jazz, folk, and classical, albums were not the focus of record sales in rhythm and blues. Even so, Brown's *Live at the Apollo* went to number two in the pop album charts in the summer and fall of 1963 and showcases not only his energetic performance but also his stylistic range. While "Think" had already anticipated Brown's turn toward a domination by tight rhythmic grooves, "Out of Sight" (p24, 1964) from the fall of 1964 went even further in this direction, introducing the hard-driving soul style that would be continued with "Papa's Got a Brand New Bag, Pt. 1" (p8 r1, 1965), "I Got You (I Feel Good)" (p3 r1, 1965), "It's a Man's Man's Man's World" (p8 r1, 1966), and "Cold Sweat, Pt. 1" (p7 r1, 1967).

Unlike most of the other artists discussed in this chapter, James Brown exerted almost total control over his music from early on. He has written and produced most of his hits; and after the deaths of King Records' Syd Nathan and his manager Ben Bart in 1968, he has made most of his own business decisions as well. Brown is thus something of a special case in 1960s rhythm and blues, being a kind of combination of Wilson Pickett, Norman Whitfield, and Berry Gordy. In his artistic and musical independence, he parallels Brian Wilson, Bob Dylan, and the Beatles, who also won significant control over their music and careers during the 1960s. As a bandleader, Brown picked the best musicians he could find and rehearsed them vigorously, sometimes fining players who made mistakes during performances. Though some of his musicians found this work environment too much to bear, Brown's rigorous approach produced some of the best ensemble playing in popular music in the 1960s.

"Papa's Got a Brand New Bag, Pt. 1" is a good example of his band's instrumental precision. The track opens with a sustained chord, and soon falls into the first verse (the verses employ the 12-bar blues structure). Listen to how the entire ensemble works together rhythmically to create the groove that drives the song. The stops at the end of the verses help distinguish this track from a Stax arrangement and show off the ensemble skills of Brown's band. The form of the song mixes verses with a bridge, which is sung once and then used as the basis for the vamp in the coda. Note the absence of background

Brown in Boston

One could argue that the single most important political issue in the United States throughout the 1960s was neither the war in Vietnam nor the cultural struggle between generations, but the war on institutionalized racism. Black musicians not only reflected and reacted to the civil rights movement in their songs; they exerted a profound influence upon it.

The key role of music in the long struggle of black Americans for freedom and equality extends back hundreds of years to the birth of the Negro spiritual and the infusion of African musical elements into predominantly white music, particularly in the south. As the civil rights movement picked up momentum in the 1950s, black performers like Harry Belafonte, Lena Horne, and Louis Armstrong became important spokespersons, fund-raisers, and drawing cards for it. In the early '60s, several black artists began to incorporate explicit political statements into their music. Sam Cooke's "A Change Is Gonna Come," Nina Simone's "Mississippi Goddamn," and Joe Tex's "The Love You Save" are all popular examples of political music. Curtis Mayfield's vocal group the Impressions scored several hits with subtly challenging yet positive anthems like "People Get Ready" and "Keep On Pushing." More than artist endorsements and political lyrics, however, the conscious adaptation of more and more elements drawn from black musical traditions into mainstream pop music both reflected and affected the growing Black Pride movement. All these trends accelerated in the late 1960s.

James Brown performing in Boston less than twenty-four hours after the assassination of Martin Luther King Jr. Boston's mayor, Kevin White (pictured in center image), agreed to allow the concert to be televised, and many credit White and Brown with keeping the peace in Boston as other cities were engulfed in riots.

But nowhere is the influence of black musicians on American life more graphically demonstrated than in a single concert appearance by James Brown on April 5, 1968—one night after the assassination of Martin Luther King Jr. in Memphis. Brown had just returned from his first trip to Africa—a pivotal event in his life—and was scheduled to play at the Boston Garden. Rioting had begun in cities all across America on April 4, as the news of the assassination spread. But the next night was a Friday and much greater violence was anticipated. Boston Mayor Kevin White asked Brown to broadcast his concert on live television to help maintain order. The show was broadcast on the local public television station, WGBH, and picked up by a number of other stations across the country. Brown began the show with a direct appeal to the viewers: "Let's not do anything to dishonor Dr. King. You kids, especially, I want you to stay home tonight and think about what Dr. King stood for. Don't just react in a way that's going to destroy your community." There were devastating riots in more than a hundred American cities that night, including Washington, D.C. But in Boston and several other cities where the concert was broadcast it was unusually quiet. On April 6, Brown traveled to Washington and gave a speech that was televised locally. The rioting stopped there, too. Only a black musician could restore peace in the aftermath of King's assassination, demonstrating the truth of Brown's own assessment: "The music wasn't a part of the revolution. The music *was* the revolution."

James Brown, live at the Apollo. Brown worked with top-notch musicians and rehearsed them tirelessly. His live shows were equally tiring, with Brown passionately dancing, belting out lyrics, and directing the band. His performances at the Apollo Theater in Harlem, New York City, have become legendary.

James Brown, "Papa's Got a Brand New Bag, Pt. 1"

Words and music by James Brown, produced by James Brown. Rose to #1 on the Billboard Rhythm and Blues charts and #8 on the Billboard Pop charts in the fall of 1965.

FORM: Modified simple verse. The 12-bar verses return without alterations (except for new lyrics), and are based on the 12-bar blues structure. The 8-bar bridge enters after two verses, and this might seem to indicate an AABA form, especially since a verse returns right after the bridge. The bridge, however, is static, vamping on a single chord and not really driving toward the return of the verse as bridges typically do in an AABA form. The structure of this song is perhaps best viewed as a verse-verse-bridge structure, which is then repeated with the bridge serving as the ending as the song fades. The form of this track thus turns out to be closest to a simple verse form, though one might also see it as a hybrid of simple verse and AABA forms.

TIME SIGNATURE: 4/4. Note the precise interplay between the instruments and how they work together to project an intricate rhythmic background over which Brown delivers his lead vocal.

INSTRUMENTATION: Electric guitar, bass, drums, horns, and lead vocal.

0:00–0:26	**Verse 1**, 12 mm.	After opening upbeat chord, vocal enters and verse locks in based on the 12-bar blues, "Old feel sisters . . ."
0:26–0:48	**Verse 2**, 12 mm.	As before. Note the use of the baritone sax, playing the same role here as it does in Pickett's "In the Midnight Hour." Similarly, the rhythm guitar and snare are locked in on beats two and four throughout. "Come down brother . . ."
0:48–1:03	**Bridge**, 8 mm.	Lead vocals over vamp on single chord, with horn backups. "He did the jerk . . ."
1:03–1:26	**Verse 3**, 12 mm.	As before, "Come down sister . . ."
1:26–1:48	**Verse 4**, 12 mm.	As before, "Oh and father . . ."
1:48–2:06	**Coda** (Bridge), 8 mm. +	Based on single-chord vamp from bridge and then fade out, "C'mon, hey hey . . ."

vocals—a feature that not only helps distinguish Brown's approach from that of Motown but also highlights the contrast with his music in the 1950s, which often featured doo-wop backups.

Black Pride and the Birth of Funk.   After the assassination of Dr. King, James Brown and his music were increasingly valued within the black community for his markedly "black" approach, which seemed to many to be uncompromised by the stylistic adjustments made by Motown (and Atlantic) that would create music more marketable to whites. While this perception was not entirely accurate, Brown was counted among the most important figures in black popular music when "Say It Loud, I'm Black and I'm Proud" (p10, r1) climbed the charts in the fall of 1968. Brown's music would soon turn toward funk, making him one of the principal influences on 1970s black pop. In Chapter 9, the story of funk is discussed and our consideration of James Brown's music will continue. In the next chapter, however, we turn back toward the rock scene to explore how rock music developed out of psychedelia, and how the business grew into a multinational financial enterprise in the 1970s. The issues of race addressed in this chapter will return again, especially in regard to the rise of disco, and later in the emergence of rap.

Questions for Review and Discussion

1. What was Berry Gordy's approach in running Motown? How does this relate to previous approaches used by others?
2. Who are the important songwriters and producers at Motown? Who are the important artists at Motown and who produced them in each case?
3. What role did the following figures play at Motown: the Funk Brothers, Maxine Powell, Cholly Atkins?
4. How did the relationship between Atlantic and Stax begin? Who are the important figures on the business end?
5. Who are the important artists at Atlantic/Stax? How were production and songwriting duties handled at Atlantic/Stax?
6. What role did the following play in southern soul music: Booker T. and the MG's, Rick Hall, and Jim Stewart?
7. How did James Brown's career develop from the mid 1950s to the end of the 1960s?
8. Is it possible for one kind of black pop to be "blacker" than another? If so, in which aspect(s) of the music does this occur: image, publicity, performance, or recording? Can you hear this "blackness"?

Further Reading

Rob Bowman, *Soulsville, U.S.A.: The Story of Stax Records* (Schirmer, 1997).

James Brown, with Bruce Tucker, *James Brown, the Godfather of Soul* (Macmillan, 1986).

Gerald Early, *One Nation under a Groove: Motown and American Culture* (Ecco Press, 1995).

Nelson George, *Where Did Our Love Go? The Rise and Fall of the Motown Sound* (St. Martin's Press, 1985).

Berry Gordy, *To Be Loved: The Music, the Magic, and the Memories of Motown* (Warner Books, 1994).

Peter Guralnick, *Sweet Soul Music: Rhythm and Blues and the Southern Dream of Freedom* (HarperCollins, 1986).

Brian Ward, *Just My Soul Responding: Rhythm and Blues, Black Consciousness, and Race Relations* (University of California Press, 1998).

Otis Williams, with Patricia Romanowski, *Temptations* (Fireside, 1989).

chapter 7

Many cite the Beatles' Sgt. Pepper's Lonely Hearts Club Band (1967) as the most influential album ever made. While successful albums were produced before it, it was Sgt. Pepper that made the album into an art form— and the dominant musical medium from then on. The Beatles conceived of this album as one complete artistic production, not just a string of stand-alone songs; later, this would be called a "concept album." Musically, the songs are wide-ranging, drawing on many styles including rhythm and blues, Indian music, and even brass bands, all the while employing groundbreaking recording techniques. Lyrically—and visually, considering its cover—Sgt. Pepper tells the story of a fictional band, though only some of the songs can be linked to that story. Another one of the many innovations here was the Beatles' choice to print all the song lyrics on the album jacket. Sgt. Pepper and the concept album approach influenced many artists working in a wide variety of styles.

Psychedelia

June, July, and August of 1967 are frequently referred to as the Summer of Love: a summer in which Scott McKenzie's "San Francisco (Be Sure to Wear Flowers in Your Hair)" played on radios across the United States and England, eventually hitting number one in the UK and number four in the United States. The song, written by Mamas and Papas leader John Phillips, celebrates the emerging hippie culture and flower power, locating the movement's center in San Francisco. At the same time in London, the Beatles released *Sgt. Pepper's Lonely Hearts Club Band*—perhaps the most influential album from one of rock's most influential bands. The summer of 1967 also saw an American guitarist fronting a British band and emerging as an international musical figure at a large outdoor rock festival in Monterey, California. When Jimi Hendrix set his guitar aflame at the climax of his virtuosic and outrageous performance, it was one important signal among many that rock music was taking a turn down a new path in 1967, a path that was soon dubbed "psychedelia." As in 1955 when rock and roll moved into the pop mainstream, and again in 1964 with the arrival of the Beatles and the start of the British invasion, the Summer of Love does not mark the beginning of psychedelia per se, but rather the breakthrough of psychedelia into mainstream popular culture. Psychedelic music and culture can be traced back to regional underground scenes in both London and San Francisco that have their roots in the 1950s and were well established by the end of 1965.

This chapter traces the rise of psychedelia from its origins in the London and San Francisco underground movements (consisting of bands, clubs, shops, and newspapers primarily known only to people in these geographical regions), through its emergence into mainstream pop culture (where it became available to anyone), to its pervasive influence on rock culture at the end of the '60s. At the beginning of 1966, while only hints of what would soon become psychedelic music can be found on the records of major rock artists, relatively unknown musicians were developing the new style; some of these bands would soon become well known and commercially successful (the Grateful Dead, Pink Floyd, the Jefferson Airplane), while others would never make the jump to the next level (Soft Machine, Tomorrow, the Charlatans). It is thus important to examine the development of psychedelic music on two fronts, exploring the underground scenes in London and San Francisco while also keeping an eye on the acts with major-label recording contracts. When the ideas of the underground make their way into the mainstream—either because the groups themselves become major acts or because major acts adopt psychedelic ideas—psychedelic music begins to exert its influence. But before we trace its history, we need to define it: What is psychedelia and how can music be psychedelic?

Drugs and the Quest for Higher Consciousness

The Doors of Perception: Ken Kesey, Timothy Leary, and LSD. At its root, the psychedelic movement was concerned with exploring new ways people could experience the world. Young adults in the mid 1960s felt that the cultural values of the 1950s were too focused on being "normal," so they began to challenge middle-class values by seeking out alternative approaches to life and culture. Influenced in part by the civil rights movement and an ever-growing resistance to the Vietnam War, young people began to be suspicious of most institutions in American life: government, schools, churches, big business, the military, and the police. Teens in the mid 1950s had been the first to experience a youth culture that could be clearly distinguished from adult culture. The counterculture that emerged in the mid 1960s, however, was much more assertive in its separation from adult culture, making "generation gap" into a household phrase by the end of the decade. As far as the hardliners within the counterculture were concerned, institutions were corrupt and everything young people had been taught was a lie.

Drugs generally—but marijuana and LSD especially—played a central role in providing the basis for the new worldview many young people were seeking. Led by author Ken Kesey and ex-Harvard professor Timothy Leary, two older men who had publicly rejected "the establishment," many young people came to see hallucinogenic drugs as essential to unlocking "the doors of perception" (a reference to Aldous Huxley's essay of the same name, in which the author describes his experience with the hallucinogenic drug mescaline). Leary's advice to "turn on, tune in, drop out" became a slogan of the counterculture, as many college-age youngsters earnestly explored drug use, radical philosophy, and Eastern religion.

LSD (lysergic acid diethylamide) was developed accidentally by Swiss scientist Albert Hoffmann in 1943 while he was working on a cure for migraine headaches; along with mescaline, LSD was tested by the CIA during the 1950s as a truth serum and was known among psychiatrists as a potential treatment for alcoholism. LSD was also used recreationally by a relatively small group of people in some major cities in the United States and the UK. To the young adults who came to the drug in the mid-to-late 1960s, LSD was thought to allow the user to suppress all the false and misleading modes of understanding that had been foisted on him or her—in school specifically and in society generally —and to perceive the world and life itself as it really is. "Dropping acid" supposedly allowed one to see new possibilities, opening the mind to new knowledge and modes of understanding. In short, LSD was viewed as a kind of magic pill that led to a "higher consciousness" that had previously been available only to spiritual mystics and visionaries.

A Journey to the East: The Beatles and the Maharishi.   Until the summer of 1967, most of the actual counterculture activity was restricted to regional scenes in San Francisco and London. As discussed in Chapter 5, the Byrds' "Eight Miles High" hit the U.S. charts in the summer of 1966 and was among the first public signs that drug use was becoming a central part of rock music and youth culture.

The unlikely blend of Eastern spirituality and drug use that "Eight Miles High" evokes had been advocated by Timothy Leary in his 1964 book *The Psychedelic Experience*. Co-written with Ralph Metzner and Richard Alpert (who would change his name to Ram Dass and play an important role in popularizing Eastern religion among the hippies), the book offered a guide to acid use based on the ancient Tibetan Book of the Dead. The association of drugs with eastern philosophy was further reinforced somewhat unintentionally by the Beatles, who became students of transcendental meditation with the Maharishi Mahesh Yogi during the same summer that they released *Sgt. Pepper's Lonely Hearts Club Band*. While the use of drugs is not part of the practice of yoga in most Eastern traditions, they did nonetheless become linked in the eyes of the burgeoning hippie culture via the quest for higher consciousness: as Eastern gurus sought truth through spiritual discipline, so the hippies sought truth through the use of LSD. In the late 1960s, a variety of lifestyle philosophies emerged that blended aspects of Eastern spirituality and drug use, sometimes including avant-garde art, and both radical and utopian politics. Taken together, these sometimes contradictory approaches make up what is generally called the 1960s counterculture—a hippie worldview committed to cultural change with music at the center.

Two Psychedelic Approaches to Music.   Considering the counterculture's focus on achieving higher consciousness, one might well wonder what kind of role music can play. There are two general tendencies to be found in late 1960s music. The first places music in a secondary role to drugs, seeing it as a way of enhancing the drug trip. According to this view, the important thing is the drug experience itself; the music is only a soundtrack to the trip, perhaps provoking response with novel and unfamiliar sounds but not itself providing a trip in the absence of the drugs. We will encounter instances of this tendency in our discussions of both the San Francisco and London underground scenes and groups like the Grateful Dead and Pink Floyd. A second approach is to understand the music itself as the trip. In this case, it is the musician's job to craft music that acts as an aesthetic drug, taking the listener on an aural journey that may be enhanced by the use of drugs but in which the music remains primary. The music of the Doors and the Beatles offer good instances of this approach, discussed in more detail below. In both approaches, the trip and the quest for higher consciousness are essential; the difference is in whether music is primary or secondary to the trip. In either case, musicians became more experimental and ambitious about writing, performing, and recording music. For music to enhance or provide a trip, however, it had to move beyond the two- or three-minute radio format that was standard for AM radio in the mid 1960s. As rock became more psychedelic, it often became more ambitious, and tracks became longer and spacier.

Psychedelic Ambition: The Beach Boys and the Beatles

Two Bands, One Label. As it turns out, the cultural rise of psychedelia coincided well with a musical tendency toward more ambitious approaches to rock songwriting, arranging, and recording. The music of both the Beatles and the Beach Boys became increasingly complicated as the '60s progressed: lyrics addressed more serious topics, a wider range of instrumentation was used, harmonic language became more innovative, standard formal types were often modified or abandoned, and greater time was taken in the studio, recording tracks that were often not reproducible in live performance. Clearly with the Beatles, the band gradually moved away from the model of professional craftsmen (best exemplified by the Brill Building songwriters) and toward a more self-consciously "artistic" stance (akin to that of a classical-music composer or artist). With the Beach Boys, a quest to match and surpass the accomplishments of Phil Spector seemed to drive Brian Wilson to an increasingly experimental approach. The parallel development of the Beatles and the Beach Boys was partly because in the United States both bands were on the same record label, Capitol. This meant that they not only competed for the public's attention but also for the attention of their own record company. Since the Beatles' primary contract was with British EMI, this competition had less of a direct effect on them; but for the Beach Boys—who had already scored a number of hits for Capitol before the Beatles invaded—the rivalry was much more acute (though also friendly). The combined effect of the increased artistic ambitions of both bands with a direct commercial rivalry between them produced a sequence of records that transformed rock from dance music to listening music.

The Beatles' George Harrison (left) and John Lennon (right) with the Beach Boys' Mike Love (center) in New Delhi, India, February 1968. The Beach Boys and the Beatles had a friendly rivalry in the 1960s. Both bands deeply respected each other and were trying constantly to outdo the other's expert songwriting and recording techniques. Members of both bands were also interested in Eastern philosophy, which they studied together in India.

We have already considered the Beatles' music through *Revolver* and the Beach Boys' music through *Pet Sounds* in Chapters 4 and 5, respectively. Here we consider some of the ways these bands influenced and even inspired one another. Brian Wilson has remarked, for instance, that he admired the way the songs on *Rubber Soul* all seemed to hang together as an album; not simply another collection of singles, the album as a whole was greater than the sum of its parts. This inspired Wilson to think of *Pet Sounds* as an album of related songs. Paul McCartney remembers that he played *Pet Sounds* constantly in the period immediately after its release, admiring the production and songwriting. With *Revolver*, and especially "Tomorrow Never Knows," the Beatles pushed the limits of studio experimentation, producing a track that many see as the first to introduce psychedelia into the mainstream.

"Good Vibrations."   Not to be outdone by the ambition of "Tomorrow Never Knows," Wilson and the Beach Boys released "Good Vibrations"—a single that consumed more studio time and budget allocation than any other pop single ever had at the time; Wilson called it his "pocket symphony," and many consider this single his finest achievement. As the Listening Guide shows, "Good Vibrations" begins by using a contrasting verse-chorus approach. But after the second time through the chorus, the track continues with a sequence of three sections that were originally recorded separately and spliced together later, using something like the cut-and-paste function in a word-processing program but employing old-fashioned recording tape, scotch tape, and scissors. Wilson spent a great deal of time experimenting with the order of these sections before arriving at the final version. Years later Capitol released some of the alternate versions and studio rehearsals of "Good Vibrations" and these tapes clearly reveal the centrality of recording studio techniques and a sense of experimentation in the creation of this song. The alternate versions make for interesting comparisons with the official version—some sections are left out and new ones are inserted. The rehearsal tapes reveal how diligently Wilson worked at finding the precise instrumental sounds he employed, providing a rare glimpse of his working method. In the released version, each of the three sections introduces some new musical material. Section 1 employs a tack piano (an upright piano with tacks stuck in the hammers to create a sharper attack), a Jew's harp (a small instrument held against the teeth or lips and plucked with the fingers), and then bass harmonica and sleigh bells in addition to voices, bass, tambourine, and organ. The splice into Section 2 can be heard clearly, as the music immediately gets quieter, starting only with organ and percussion; after the vocals, organ, and bass enter, the passage works its way toward a beautiful harmony on "ah" to end the section (listen carefully for the echo as the vocals die out). The third section then enters as if it might be

---

Rising Rock Ambitions

Beatles, *Rubber Soul* (late 1965)
   Beach Boys, *Pet Sounds* (early to mid 1966)
Beatles, *Revolver* (late summer 1966), "Tomorrow Never Knows"
   Beach Boys, "Good Vibrations" (late 1966)
Beatles, "Penny Lane/Strawberry Fields Forever" (early 1967)
   Beach Boys, *SMiLE* (late 1966/early 1967; not released)
Beatles, *Sgt. Pepper's Lonely Hearts Club Band* (June 1, 1967)
   Beach Boys, *Smiley Smile* (August 1967)

Most of the Beach Boys' creative songwriting and production came from Brian Wilson (pictured here in the studio, 1966). Like his hero Phil Spector, Wilson demanded total control of the musical production and experimented with nontraditional instruments and recording technology. Wilson was constantly pushing himself to outdo the Beatles and their legendary producer, George Martin.

LISTENING GUIDE   GET MUSIC ▶▶   wwnorton.com/rockhistory

The Beach Boys, "Good Vibrations"

Words and music by Brian Wilson and Mike Love, produced by Brian Wilson. Reached #1 on the Billboard charts and in the UK in late 1966.

FORM: The first half of the song uses contrasting verse-chorus form, which breaks off after the second statement of the chorus (1:41). At that point, a series of three sections begin, the last of which uses music from the chorus to help round the song off as it fades out. Taken as a whole, the song does not fit neatly into any conventional pop formal pattern, except in the most general sense that contrasting material often follows the second statement of the chorus.

TIME SIGNATURE: 4/4 time throughout.

INSTRUMENTATION: Organ, guitar, bass, drums, woodwinds, cellos, Theremin (an early electronic instrument played by moving the hands around two antennae that controlled the sound), bass harmonica, Jew's harp, tambourine, sleigh bells, maracas, lead and backing vocals.

0:00–0:25	**Verse 1**, 16 mm. (8 mm. phrase with repeat)	Lead vocals enter immediately, note repeated chords in the organ and orchestral-style drumming and subtle use of woodwinds in second 8 mm. "I love the colorful clothes . . ."

another chorus, only to introduce a new three-part vocal counterpoint passage before resuming the chorus music for the fade-out. While "Good Vibrations" starts out as a contrasting verse-chorus form, the addition of these three sections after the second chorus and the way they introduce new sounds and material represented an important departure for pop music. In the music of the Beach Boys and Brian Wilson, it marked a high point in the band's musical ambition that they would never equal again.

Sgt. Pepper's Lonely Hearts Club Band.   After the release of *Revolver*, the Beatles abandoned touring to devote their energies to recording. By the summer of 1966, the band decided that touring had become too limiting: they couldn't play some of their most recent songs and they felt the audiences were no longer listening anyway. In the wake of the controversy surrounding Lennon's remarks about Christianity, live appearances had also become too dangerous. In the fall of 1966 the Beatles began working on the album that would become *Sgt. Pepper's Lonely Hearts Club Band*. At first the idea was to unite all

0:25–0:50	**Chorus**, 16 mm. (four 4 mm. phrases)	Multipart vocals in counterpoint, note entrance of cellos low in the texture and Theremin melody on the top. "I'm pickin' up . . ."
0:50–1:15	**Verse 2**, 16 mm.	As before. Note that verse is quieter than chorus—this dynamic contrast comes out clearly in this shift back to the verse. "Changed my mind . . ."
1:15–1:41	**Chorus**, 16 mm.	As before, end leads into section 1. "I'm pickin' up . . ."
1:41–2:13	**Section 1**, 20 mm.	New music used, piano, bass harmonica, sleigh bells, Jew's harp enter, "Excitations . . ." Listen for tape splice to section 2.
2:13–2:57	**Section 2**, 24 mm.	More new music, quieter now, starting with organ and ending with vocal "ah." Listen again for tape splice into section 3. "Gotta keep . . ."
2:57–3:35	**Section 3**, 22 mm.	Based on chorus, with new vocal counterpoint. Starts louder, then gets quieter and then louder again before fade-out. "I'm pickin' up . . ."

the songs on the album around a central theme—their memories of growing up in Liverpool. But by early 1967, the group was getting pressure from EMI to at least release a single, as the label professionals knew it was never good for a pop act—even the Beatles—to be off the pop charts for too long. The band decided to release "Penny Lane" and "Strawberry Fields Forever" as a double-A-sided single. The lyrics to "Penny Lane" describe a variety of scenes that McCartney felt captured a cross-section of everyday life in his hometown, while Lennon's lyrics to "Strawberry Fields Forever" are less specific, generally recalling a neighborhood park in which he used to play as a child.

The group's growing musical ambitions can be heard in the piccolo trumpet solo in "Penny Lane," inspired by a performance of a Bach concerto McCartney had heard while they were working on the track. "Strawberry Fields Forever" is the more adventurous track in terms of recording; it uses a wide variety of instruments, including cellos, inside-the-piano playing, reversed-tape sounds, and the Mellotron, an early sampling keyboard that uses taped sounds to create orchestral strings, choral voices, and an ensemble of recorders (simple wooden flutes). This keyboard can be heard at the very beginning using its recorder-ensemble setting. The final version of "Strawberry Fields Forever" is actually a spliced together combination of two versions that had been recorded at different tempos and in different keys; producer George Martin varied the tape speed on the two versions so they could be joined without the listener noticing the splice. "Strawberry Fields Forever" also includes a novel feature: after the song fades at the end, there is a moment of silence and then a brief passage of new music fades back in. This must have surprised disc jockeys the first time they played the song: just as the jock is talking over the end as the song fades, the music marches back in!

The initial idea of creating an album based on the band's childhoods in Liverpool was dropped when the "Penny Lane"/"Strawberry Fields Forever" single was released. According to EMI policy at the time, a single could not also be on an album if both were released within the same calendar year; this was to protect fans from being forced to buy the same record twice. Paul McCartney then hit on the idea of the band's assuming the role of the fictional Sgt. Pepper's Lonely Hearts Club Band. The album would be a recorded performance of various acts, hosted by the made-up band. Thus, the album begins with "Sgt. Pepper's Lonely Hearts Club Band," in which the group introduce themselves and then announce singer "Billy Shears" (played by Ringo) to sing "With a Little Help from My Friends." After the two initial tracks, however, the plan breaks down until the very end, where a reprise of the first track appears just before the last one, "A Day in the Life." Because of the Sgt. Pepper idea, and the way the album packaging participates in the charade (the original album came in a gatefold cover, complete with pictures of the band dressed in uniform), *Sgt. Pepper's Lonely Hearts Club Band* is often cited as rock's first "concept album"— an album that is organized around some central idea or story. John Lennon resisted thinking of *Sgt. Pepper* this way, claiming that his songs could have appeared on any Beatles album; however, Lennon's objections did little to discourage rock fans from lauding and musicians from imitating this aspect of *Sgt. Pepper*, and in the wake of its release concept albums seemed to pop up everywhere.

Sgt. Pepper's Lonely Hearts Club Band is one of the most important albums in the history of rock music. In the weeks after its release, most of the important figures in rock music were listening carefully to the album. There are many aspects of the album that marked a fundamental change in rock music. In addition to the elaborate photographs intimately bound up with the "concept," the complete lyrics for all the songs were printed on the album cover, signaling that the lyrics were central to the experience and perhaps worth reading on their own. Stylistically the album ranges widely, bringing together a variety of styles from British music hall to Indian music to chamber music to rock and roll. The use of techniques borrowed from avant-garde music is central to "Being for the Benefit of Mr. Kite," which uses taped organ sounds randomly assembled to create a kaleidoscopic aural background. The album's most influential track, "A Day in the Life," employs two passages in which the orchestral string players start from a note low on their instrument and then continue to gradually play higher notes until given a cue, when they play one of the notes in an E-major chord that is closest to where they happen to end up. Such chance techniques, called "aleatoric" in classical music, were very much a part of avant-garde music in the 1960s; the Beatles were well aware of the connection—avant-garde composer Karlheinz Stockhausen appears on the cover of the album. The use of such techniques further underscores the seriousness with which the Beatles now approached their music.

Perhaps one of the most important and influential aspects of *Sgt. Pepper* is that it created a new focus on the album as opposed to the single—in fact, *Sgt. Pepper* had no hit single. In the years following *Sgt. Pepper*, single-oriented pop would be directed at a teen audience via AM radio, and album-oriented rock (AOR) would be directed at older teens and college-age listeners on FM. While the Beatles would continue to have hit singles after *Sgt. Pepper*, the new album-as-basic-unit idea served as a model for much late '60 and '70s rock.

Collapse and Retreat: SMiLE *and* Smiley Smile.   While the Beatles were recording "Penny Lane" and "Strawberry Fields Forever," Brian Wilson was at work on perhaps the most famous album not to be released (though the album was re-recorded and released in 2004, almost forty years later!). Working from the idea that laughter and "good vibes" were what made the world a better place, Wilson planned to call his new concept album *SMiLE*. After a planned release date of December 1966 was missed, he continued working through the first months of 1967 before eventually abandoning the project, according to some reports with more than 70 percent of the album finished. The Beach Boys released *Smiley Smile*, which is a significantly different album from what *SMiLE* would have been (and turned out to be). In the years since, many myths about *SMiLE* have arisen; some writers argue that it would have been Wilson's masterpiece; others that his high intake of drugs left him confused and unable to manage the complexity of the music; and still others that he was so frustrated and/or paranoid that he destroyed all the tapes in a fit of rage (and more). As it turns out, most of the music has been saved, and in the years since, scholars have gotten a good idea of how the album might have sounded from studio material released by Capitol in the 1990s, as well as from bootleg recordings that have circulated for years. One track that was released at the time provides a representative sample of the original *SMiLE*; much like "Good Vibrations," "Heroes and Villains" is a product of the recording studio, with separately recorded and highly produced sections later spliced together to create a sequence of musical episodes; and while the released version rose to number twelve in the United States during the summer of 1967 (uk8), several alternate versions exist that are much more experimental—one reportedly runs over ten minutes. Wilson's re-recorded version from recent years stays

---

LISTENING GUIDE　　　GET MUSIC ▶▶ | wwnorton.com/rockhistory

The Beatles, "A Day in the Life"

Words and music by John Lennon and Paul McCartney, produced by George Martin. Included on the album *Sgt. Pepper's Lonely Hearts Club Band*, which hit #1 in the United States and the UK in the summer of 1967.

FORM: Compound ABA form, with both the A and B sections using a simple verse scheme. The A section is an incomplete song by John Lennon, while the B section is an incomplete song by Paul McCartney. The two songs are stitched together by an interlude that leads from the A section to the B section, and by a bridge that returns to the A section. In the interlude, the Beatles employ the strings in an avant-garde manner, creating a strange growing rush of sound that gets repeated at the end of the song.

TIME SIGNATURE: 4/4 in both sections.

INSTRUMENTATION: Acoustic guitar, piano, bass, drums, maracas, strings, brass, alarm clock, lead vocal.

A	0:00–0:12	**Introduction**, 8 mm.	Strummed acoustic guitar, with bass, drums, and percussion joining in second 4 mm.
	0:12–0:44	**Verse 1**, 20 mm.	Vocal (Lennon) enters. Note the echo on the voice. Starts with guitar, piano, and maracas only. "I read the news . . ."
	0:44–1:11	**Verse 2**, 20 mm.	As before. Drums enter, but played in an orchestral manner, with a lot of fills in dialogue with vocal line. "He blew his mind . . ."
	1:11–1:41	**Verse 3**, 19 mm.	As in verse 2, but last measures overlap with beginning of interlude, "I saw a film . . ."

completely within the spirit of the original, and many argue that this is the *SMiLE* album he had in mind all along.

With the considerable status *SMiLE* has achieved in the years since it was abandoned, it seems surprising that it created such controversy within the band when Wilson was working on it. The other Beach Boys spent a good deal of time on the road performing the band's earlier hits. When they encountered Brian's newest music in late 1966, they thought it would never be popular with fans. To a certain extent this was true, as *Pet Sounds* had not sold as well as

1:41–2:16	**Interlude**, 23 mm.	Orchestral sound builds up, creating an enormous crescendo that cuts off abruptly, forming a transition to the second big section. "I love to turn you on . . ."
B 2:16–2:21	**Introduction**, 4 mm.	Repeated chords on acoustic piano help establish a quieter contrasting mood. Note the alarm clock.
2:21–2:36	**B Verse 1**, 9 mm.	Vocal (McCartney) enters. Note how little reverb there is on the vocal. Bass plays a happy walking line on the second half, "Woke up . . ."
2:36–2:49	**B Verse 2**, 9 mm.	As before, "Found my coat."
2:49–3:18	**Bridge**, 20 mm.	10 mm. phrase occurs twice, sung by Lennon and soaked in reverb. Note the ominous orchestral backdrop.
A' 3:18–3:46	**Verse 4**, 19 mm.	As in verse 3 of the A section, with last measures overlapping with beginning of ending section. "I read the news . . ."
3:46–4:57	**Interlude** as ending, 24 mm.	Orchestral crescendo as in the previous occurrence of the interlude, but with a giant chord played on the piano to end at 4:21. This chord is sustained for almost 40 seconds using electronic means to keep the sound audible.

previous albums. Released in place of *SMiLE* in the summer of 1967, *Smiley Smile* (p41 uk9) marked a distinct turn away from the highly produced approach Wilson had been cultivating since he had taken over as the band's producer. On *Smiley Smile* and subsequent albums through the rest of the decade, the Beach Boys made an effort to simplify their sound, though this never resulted in a significant return to the kind of commercial success they had enjoyed earlier. Wilson was still writing for the band and performing on the recordings, but the albums were now listed as "produced by the Beach Boys." Though the Beach Boys played a crucial role in extending the musical possibilities of rock music, the psychedelic hippie culture that followed in the wake of the Summer of Love largely dismissed the band as too "square." Jimi Hendrix, whose own studio experimentation is an extension of Wilson's music, once referred to the Beach Boys as a psychedelic barbershop quartet.

And in the End: The Beatles after Sgt. Pepper.

Lennon may have insisted that *Sgt. Pepper* was not a concept album, but much of what the Beatles did after *Sgt. Pepper* was driven by organizing ideas, often dreamed up by Paul McCartney. *Magical Mystery Tour*, for instance, was built around the idea that the band would get on a bus and travel the English countryside, making a movie as they went. In early 1968, the band traveled to India to study meditation at the ashram of the Maharishi Mahesh Yogi, bringing back dozens of songs, many of which would appear on *The Beatles* (often called the "White Album"). At about the same time, the band was approached about making an animated film that would use them as characters in a surrealist adventure in Pepperland. The result, *Yellow Submarine*, could be described as a kind of psychedelic *A Hard Day's Night*. McCartney then devised a plan to create a film that would document the Beatles writing, rehearsing, and recording an album; the film was to end with a performance of the finished music. The "Get Back" project went badly, producer George Martin walked out, and the camera frequently captured band members arguing. The film and album were scrapped and the Beatles reunited with Martin and moved on to what would be their last studio album, *Abbey Road* (1969). The film and studio tracks from "Get Back" were later salvaged and released as *Let It Be* in 1970; but since Martin had removed himself from the project, *Let It Be* was produced by Phil Spector. More recently, the Beatles re-released these same recordings as *Let It Be Naked*, which erased much of Spector's production to return the music to a more elemental and raw sound.

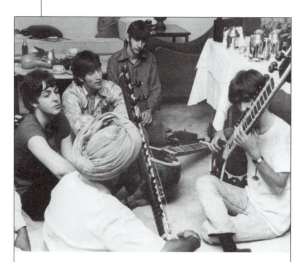

In the late 1960s, the Beatles became increasing interested in eastern philosophy and religion, studying transcendental meditation with the Maharishi Mahesh Yogi. Here, in summer 1966, months before Sgt. Pepper, *George Harrison (right) gets a lesson in the Indian sitar, as (from left) Paul McCartney, John Lennon, and Ringo Starr look on.*

In the summer of 1967, the Beatles suffered the loss of their manager, Brian Epstein. The band eventually decided to take over the business end of their careers themselves, renting offices and forming Apple Records (the Beach Boys had formed Brother Records at about the same time). Apple was launched with much fanfare: the Beatles would not only run their own careers but would also promote the work of deserving artists who might otherwise be turned away by mainstream commercial backers. It was based on a generous idea, but Apple was soon losing money and professionals had to be called in to stem the losses and reorganize the group's finances. By late 1969 all four Beatles were ready to call it quits, and in April 1970, the Beatles officially broke up. In the years that followed, each of the Beatles would score successful albums and singles as solo artists.

Despite some failed projects and the Apple fiasco, the Beatles' success never lagged during the 1967–70 period: every album and single they released placed high in the charts, several at number one in both the United States and the UK. In many ways, late Beatles music would prove to be more influential for future rock musicians than their earlier music. In terms of the development of psychedelic music, the friendly competition between the Beach Boys and the Beatles during 1966–67 had an important consequence. The ways these bands applied themselves to developing the stylistic, timbral, and compositional range of rock music was a model for other groups. *Pet Sounds*, "Good Vibrations," "Strawberry Fields Forever," and *Sgt. Pepper* demonstrated that rock could stand on its own as music and thus be taken seriously: rock music was no longer simply dance music about teen romance. Because these bands were so successful, Capitol and EMI gave them a certain freedom to experiment; when these experiments produced hit singles and albums, other groups were given greater license as well. By mid 1967 this meant that bands well known in the underground psychedelic scenes around San Francisco and London were now poised to break into national and international prominence.

The San Francisco Scene and Haight-Ashbury

Between the summers of 1966 and 1967, the Beatles and the Beach Boys were dominating national rock with increasingly ambitious music, but a local psychedelic scene had been developing since mid 1965 in San Francisco. One of the first important signs that something new was burgeoning in the city was the Human Be-In, held in San Francisco's Golden Gate Park in January 1967. Posters advertising the event called it a "gathering of the tribes," and it brought together clusters of hippies from northern California (between ten and twenty thousand, perhaps more) for a day of poetry, spirituality, and music provided by local bands the Grateful Dead and the Jefferson Airplane, among others. The Be-In drew media attention to San Francisco's growing hippie culture and within a few months the event was imitated in New York and Los Angeles. A local San Francisco bus-tour company began offering a "Hippie Hop Tour." In many ways the San Francisco psychedelic scene grew out of the area's Beat movement of the late '50s and early '60s—a bohemian scene that celebrated the poetry of Allen

Ginsberg and the prose of Jack Kerouac and that gathered in the North Beach City Lights Bookstore of Lawrence Ferlinghetti. Ginsberg and fellow beats Michael McClure and Gary Snider mentored the emerging hippie movement, even helping to organize the Human Be-In. Despite the many parallels between the beats and the hippies, however, there were also significant differences, the most crucial being music: the jazz of be-bop musicians Charlie Parker and Dizzy Gillespie was the choice of most beats; hippies favored the music of the Rolling Stones, Bob Dylan, and the Beatles.

The Red Dog, the Family Dog, Kesey's Acid Tests.   San Francisco, and the old Victorian neighborhood of Haight-Ashbury especially, soon became the center of the American psychedelic scene, although the first stirrings of psychedelia actually took place in Virginia City, New Mexico, at a restored western-style bar called the Red Dog Saloon. In June 1965, a group of San Francisco musicians called the Charlatans became the house band at the Red Dog, and for the next several weeks evenings of free-form music-making and acid tripping increasingly drew young people out to Virginia City for the first round of psychedelic happenings that would serve as the model for later ones in the Bay Area. By the fall of 1965, a group of friends calling themselves the Family Dog began organizing psychedelic dances at local San Francisco ballrooms. The first was held in October at the Longshoremen's Hall under the title "A Tribute to Dr. Strange" and featured the Charlatans along with the newly formed Jefferson Airplane and the Great Society. The second dance, "A Tribute to Sparkle Plenty," was held several days later with the Charlatans and the Lovin' Spoonful (a New York band) playing.

At about the same time novelist Ken Kesey was organizing something he called the "acid test." Since 1964 Kesey and a band of vigorously bohemian friends who called themselves the Merry Pranksters had been traveling the country in a brightly painted schoolbus emblazoned with the destination FURTHUR. Like Timothy Leary, Kesey celebrated the liberating effects of LSD and wanted to share the drug as broadly as he could. But unlike Leary, Kesey was not seeking spiritual wisdom through methods of quiet contemplation and revelation; instead Kesey and the Pranksters wanted to provide an environment rich in unpredictable stimulation to those who paid their dollar to enter the acid tests and experience LSD. In addition to a dose of the drug, participants were treated to light and slide shows, bizarre sound effects, and rock music, all in hopes of intensifying the effects of the acid. Kesey first offered his acid tests to the public in November 1965 in Santa Cruz, but by January 1966, 2,400 people

A poster advertising a Ken Kesey "Acid Test." Unlike others of the period who sought higher consciousness through quiet contemplation, Kesey strove to provide an environment rich in unpredictable stimulation. In addition to a dose of LSD, participants were treated to light and sound effects, and rock music—all in hopes of intensifying the effects of the drug.

attended an acid test at San Francisco's Fillmore Auditorium. The house band for Kesey's acid tests was a group called the Warlocks, who soon changed their name to the Grateful Dead.

It Takes a Village to Raise a Ruckus: Concerts, News, the Psychedelic Shop, FM Radio. The multiple-bill dances combined with the unpredictable and multi-media aspects of Kesey's acid tests became the model for psychedelic events in San Francisco for the next few years. Soon psychedelic evenings of LSD and rock music were a regular feature in the Bay Area; Bill Graham began organizing shows at the Fillmore while Chet Helms promoted shows at the Avalon Ballroom. Ron and Jay Thelin opened their Psychedelic Shop in the Haight-Ashbury district to meet the countercultural needs of the hippies, as local bands rented large Victorian houses in the neighborhood that also served as rehearsal spaces. (The Grateful Dead lived at 710 Ashbury.) By September 1966, the *San Francisco Oracle* became the first hippie newspaper and a precursor to *Rolling Stone Magazine*, which published its first issue in November 1967. Thus, while many outside the hippie subculture may have learned about it only in early 1967 with news of the Human Be-In (and many more in the summer of 1967), by the fall of 1966 the hippie underground in San Francisco was firmly established.

One place where psychedelic music was absent, however, was on the radio. Pop music radio was still entirely on the AM dial and oriented toward short hit singles, and clearly the new, lengthier psychedelic rock would not fit that format. The FM dial had been available for some years and mostly featured public-service programming—university lectures, classical music concerts, and foreign-language shows. Many radios in the mid 1960s did not even have an FM dial. Living in San Francisco, dropping acid, and disgruntled with the AM radio business in which he had worked for years, Tom Donahue (discussed in Chapter 8) developed a new, free-form approach to radio programming that featured longer tracks placed back-to-back with more freedom given to the disc jockey and less in-your-face between-song chatter. Donahue's wife Rachel reports that he phoned a number of FM stations in the local phone book until he found one where telephone service had been disconnected; figuring that any radio station that could not pay its phone

A San Francisco Timeline

June 1965: Charlatans begin at Red Dog Saloon

October 1965: Family Dog's "A Tribute to Dr. Strange," Longshoremen's Hall, Charlatans, Great Society, Jefferson Airplane

October 1965: Family Dog's "A Tribute to Sparkle Plenty," Charlatans, Lovin' Spoonful

November 1965: Kesey's first public acid test, Warlocks (Grateful Dead)

December 1965: acid test draws 400 in San Jose after Rolling Stones concert

January 1966: acid test at the Fillmore Auditorium draws 2,400, Grateful Dead

January 1966: 3-evening Trips Festival, Longshoremen's Hall, Grateful Dead, Big Brother

Early to mid 1966: Psychedelic Shop opens

September 1966: first issue of *Oracle*

January 1967: Human Be-In draws 20,000, Quicksilver, Jefferson Airplane, Big Brother

April 1967: KMPX-FM goes on the air

November 1967: first issue of *Rolling Stone*

bill might be receptive to new ideas, Donahue eventually came to terms with KMPX-FM. Starting with an evening slot in April 1967, Donahue and a growing staff soon took over the full day's programming, mostly playing records from their own collections. While Donahue may not have been the first to launch a free-form FM radio show—a New York station had briefly run one in 1966 and another disc jockey had even tried one at KMPX just a month before Donahue went on the air—Donahue was the first person to make the format work. Within months he was also successfully running a station in Los Angeles, while FM rock stations were popping up across the country in the wake of the breakthrough of psychedelia in the summer of 1967.

The Grateful Dead.   Music was at the center of San Francisco psychedelia, and the group at the center of psychedelic music in the Bay Area was the Grateful Dead. The roots of this band go back to the folk movement of the early 1960s. Guitarist Jerry Garcia started out as a folk, bluegrass, and jug-band musician, playing traditional music on guitar and banjo. Like many young American musicians of his generation, he was introduced to American electric blues by the Rolling Stones. By spring 1965, Garcia was playing covers of the Rolling Stones and Chess blues numbers with the Warlocks. Based in the Bay Area, the Warlocks also included Ron "Pigpen" McKernan (organ), Bob Weir (guitar), Bill Kreutzmann (drums), and eventually Phil Lesh (bass). As the house band for the Kesey acid tests, the band soon changed its name to the Grateful Dead and began to develop a highly improvisational approach in which single songs could last longer than most albums. While the group's free-form style worked well in the context of the acid tests and the subsequent performances at the Fillmore and Avalon, it posed such significant difficulties when the group was signed by MGM to record an album in 1966 that the band and the label parted ways without a record being released. The band then signed with Warner Brothers and in March 1967 it released a debut album, *The Grateful Dead*, containing short tunes that give no real indication of the improvisatory nature of the band's live shows.

The group's second album, *Anthem of the Sun* (1968), did not solve the problem of how to record a portrayal of their live act, but it does provide an important instance of the band's improvisational bent. Made up of segments drawn from live and studio recordings, the album consists of two sides that were each assembled via multiple tapes in real time: just as the Beatles had mixed tape loops in real time on "Tomorrow Never Knows," Garcia and Lesh "mixed" each side of the album on the fly with a considerable amount of studio improvising subject to the element of chance. According to Garcia, the album was mixed with the goal of intensifying the acid experience. Lesh, who had been a composition student before he joined the band and was familiar with the tape and electronic avant-garde music, has remarked how impressed the band was to hear "Tomorrow Never Knows." The parallels between Lennon's lyrics drawn from Leary's *The Psychedelic Experience* (which counsels one during an acid trip) and the psychedelic aesthetic of *Anthem of the Sun*, combined with the similarities concerned in the manipulation of taped sounds, make the Grateful Dead album a clear extension of the Beatles track. The band had still not captured its live show on record, however, though their 1970 album *Live/Dead* would go a good way toward achieving that; *Live/Dead* contained new material (with the exception of "St. Stephen," which had appeared on 1969's *Aoxomoxoa*) and was recorded before a group of friends live in the recording studio. It contains a twenty-five-minute version of "Dark Star," a song written with poet Robert Hunter (a friend of Garcia's from his army days) that is one of the songs most often associated with the band. This track is representative of the band's extended improvised instrumental solos, which frequently occur over simple chord progressions and feature the use of modal scales (as opposed to the more common major and minor scales), as might be found in much modal jazz of about the same period, though perhaps with less technical display. Released later in 1970, *Workingman's Dead* and *American Beauty* return to shorter, more country- and folk-oriented tracks, and taken with *Live/Dead*, form a trio of albums that launched the Grateful Dead as one of the most successful live American bands in the 1970s and '80s.

The Jefferson Airplane and the Grateful Dead were mainstays of the San Francisco psychedelic scene. As evidenced by this concert poster, psychedelia was supported by a unique, "trippy" look in rock art. The Fillmore Auditorium, where the concert advertised on this poster took place, was the performance "home" of psychedelia in San Francisco—many bands played there throughout the '60s and '70s.

The Jefferson Airplane.　　Formed by singer Marty Balin and guitarist Paul Kantner in mid 1965 about the same time the Grateful Dead were going electric, the Jefferson Airplane actually established themselves slightly earlier on the San Francisco scene than the Dead. The group had been formed to play in a club Balin owned called the Matrix; when the band played the club opening in August 1965, a positive review from *San Francisco Chronicle* critic Ralph Gleason (who was to mentor young editor Jann Wenner in the early years of *Rolling Stone*) led to a recording deal with RCA. Along with original members Jorma Kaukonen (guitar) and Signe Anderson (vocals), bassist Jack Cassady and drummer Spencer Dryden eventually made up the band that recorded *Jefferson Airplane Takes Off*. Recorded in late 1965, it was not released until late 1966 and rose only as high as number 128 on the U.S. album charts. By October 1966, however, Anderson had been replaced by Grace Slick, who had been a member of another San Francisco group, the Great Society. Slick brought two songs with her to the Airplane, both of which became hit singles: "Somebody to Love" (p5, 1967) and "White Rabbit" (p8, 1967). The band's second album, *Surrealistic Pillow* (1967), rose to number three on the American album charts. This lineup subsequently recorded a series of successful and often innovative albums, including *After Bathing at Baxter's* (p17, 1967), *Crown of Creation* (p6, 1968), the live *Bless Its Pointed Little Head* (p17 uk38, 1969), and the politically inspired *Volunteers* (p13 uk34, 1969), all of which became staples of late 1960s progressive FM radio. The group's early influences were primarily American folk and blues, but elements of modal jazz and Indian music can be found throughout their music, especially in the sometimes extended instrumental solos.

The single "White Rabbit" shows how the Jefferson Airplane were able to blend musical ambition with the AM single format. The song is in AABA form, with an introduction. The first two verses are followed by a bridge and then an expanded verse, which also includes the dramatic ending. The lyrics of the song refer to Lewis Carroll's *Alice in Wonderland* stories, although, as Slick has pointed out, the clear reference in lines like "feed your head" is to the use of psychedelic drugs. Slick's surreal images resonate with those of many other psychedelic songwriters, especially John Lennon, whose "Lucy in the Sky with Diamonds" was also inspired in part by *Alice in Wonderland*. The Jefferson Airplane modeled the music in "White Rabbit" on the Spanish bolero, heard especially in Kaukonen's Spanish-sounding guitar lines in the introduction. Slick recalls listening to the Miles Davis and Gil Evans orchestral jazz album *Sketches of Spain* for inspiration, but the overall dynamic shape of the piece closely resembles a well-known orchestral work by the French composer Maurice Ravel entitled *Bolero* (1927–28). Often used by music educators to illustrate the wide variety of tone colors available to the master orchestrator, Ravel's *Bolero* employs a single Spanish-tinged melody that is scored at each repetition to exploit the full range of orchestral colors. More important to our discussion of "White Rabbit," however, *Bolero* is constructed as a single long crescendo—it continually and gradually builds toward its violent musical climax. This is precisely what "White Rabbit" does (see the Listening Guide below), though on a more compressed time scale (the Ravel piece lasts almost fifteen minutes). With "White Rabbit," as with the Grateful Dead's *Anthem of the Sun* and the Beatles' "Tomorrow Never Knows," we again find a song dealing with the acid experience and employing ambitious techniques borrowed from classical music, though in the case of "White Rabbit" the classical music involved is not avant-garde music, but rather early twentieth-century orchestral music.

Big Brother and the Holding Company, Janis Joplin.   Like the Grateful Dead and the Jefferson Airplane, Big Brother and the Holding Company experimented with classical and avant-garde music. At one point the band regularly performed a version of Edvard Grieg's "Hall of the Mountain King" from *Peer Gynt* and contemplated a piece called "Bacon," which would last as long as it took to fry a plate of bacon on stage. The band enjoyed its greatest acclaim and success, however, backing up singer Janis Joplin on electric blues numbers. Joplin had left her hometown of Port Arthur, Texas, in the early 1960s to sing in clubs in Austin. By mid-decade she had made her way to San Francisco, where she sang for a brief period before giving up music to return to Port

Arthur. When Big Brother and the Holding Company formed, concert promoter Chet Helms convinced her to return to San Francisco to join the band. The band's self-titled first album was released in fall 1967 and rose as high as number sixty on the U.S. charts. The group's second album, *Cheap Thrills*, was an enormous commercial success, hitting number one on the U.S. album charts in the fall of 1968 while the single "Piece of My Heart" rose to number twelve. Joplin left Big Brother to embark on a solo career, and by fall 1969 her debut album, *I Got Dem Ol' Kozmic Blues Again Mama!*, went to number five on the U.S. charts, while the single "Kozmic Blues" rose to number forty-one. Throughout her adult life Joplin struggled with drug and alcohol abuse and on

---

LISTENING GUIDE

GET MUSIC ▶▶ wwnorton.com/rockhistory

The Jefferson Airplane, "White Rabbit"

Words and music by Grace Slick, produced by Rick Jarrard. Reached #8 on the Billboard Pop charts in the summer of 1967. Also released on the album *Surrealistic Pillow* (#3 U.S., spring 1967).

FORM: AABA form, with the last verse expanded to create a musical climax. The entire piece builds gradually, beginning quietly and ending loudly.

TIME SIGNATURE: 4/4, with the drums suggesting a Spanish flavor in imitation of a bolero rhythm.

INSTRUMENTATION: Electric guitars, bass, drums, lead vocals.

0:00–0:28	**Introduction**, 12 mm.	Bass guitar and snare drum suggest "bolero" rhythm, as the guitar enters with winding lines that evoke Spanish music.
0:28–0:55	**A-Verse**, 12 mm.	Vocals enter quietly, with only bass, guitar and snare drum accompaniment. "One pill makes you . . ."
0:55–1:23	**A-Verse**, 12 mm.	Just a little louder and more forceful, "And if you go . . ."
1:23–1:42	**B-Bridge**, 8 mm.	Second guitar now enters, drums go into a more traditional rock beat, and the music gains intensity, getting markedly louder. "When men on . . ."
1:42–2:27	**A-Verse** (expanded), 21 mm.	Vocal now much more forceful, as rhythm in the accompaniment gets much more insistent, driving toward the climax at the end. "Go ask Alice . . ."

Janis Joplin (left) singing with her group Big Brother and the Holding Company at a 1967 concert in San Francisco. As evidenced by her aggressive, passionate blues style, Joplin drew inspiration from singers like Bessie Smith and Ma Rainey. Their hard lives proved a model for Joplin, who died of a drug over-dose in 1970, just months before her album Pearl *was released and quickly climbed the charts to num-ber one.*

October 4, 1970, she was found in a hotel room dead from an overdose. Her posthumously released album *Pearl* was number one in early 1971, while her version of Kris Kristofferson's "Me and Bobby McGee" hit the top of the U.S. singles charts. Both Joplin's powerful blues style and hard-living image were reminiscent of the earlier blues singers like Ma Rainey, Bessie Smith, and Big Mama Thornton that Joplin so admired. Her singing style has almost nothing to do with psychedelia, though she was a central figure in the Haight-Ashbury scene leading up to the summer of 1967. The musicians in Big Brother were more in step with the psychedelic aesthetic, and while acknowledging the importance of blues in their music, also stressed how they were striving to find something new—a style they called "blues in Technicolor."

Country Joe and the Fish. Led by the Washington, D.C.–born singer-guitarist Joe McDonald and New York–born Barry "The Fish" Melton, Country Joe and the Fish were not part of the Haight-Ashbury scene initially but were active in radical politics in nearby Berkeley, California. While the politics of the Berkeley radicals and the counterculture of the San Francisco hippies are typically thought of as different aspects of the same local scene, the two communities often had difficulty agreeing on issues of cultural and political change. To many of the radicals, the hippies seemed spacey and generally detached from the political issues that most concerned them; to many hippies, the radicals seemed too intense and hung up on political action. Country Joe and the Fish were something of a bridge between the two communities. In 1966, for instance, the band issued an extended-play (EP) recording that was included in an issue of *Rag Baby*, a radical magazine that circulated in the San Francisco/Berkeley area. The three songs from that EP, "Bass Strings," "(Thing Called) Love," and "Section 43" were later included on the band's markedly psychedelic debut album, *Electric Music for the Mind and Body* (p39, 1967). While this album clearly displays the band's origins in acoustic blues and folk, it is most noteworthy for its many moments influenced by the band's use of LSD; the atmospheric and experimental "Section 43" is the best example of this. According to band accounts, the entire record was designed, like the Grateful Dead's *Anthem of the Sun* (but earlier), to enhance the listener's acid trip. The group's next album, *I-Feel-Like-I'm-Fixin'-to-Die* (p67, 1968), included the title song, originally recorded in 1965 and an outspoken denouncement of the Vietnam War, and the "Fish Cheer," which the band made famous by inserting another four-letter word in place of "Fish" at live performances, most notably at Woodstock in the summer of 1969. While *Together* (p23, 1968) brought the group's greatest commercial success, it already marked the musical decline of the band.

Quicksilver Messenger Service.   Among the first San Francisco bands on the scene, Quicksilver Messenger Service began performing in the Bay Area in late 1965. With the Grateful Dead, Jefferson Airplane, Big Brother, and the Charlatans, they were one of the top bands in the city's psychedelic underground. But unlike most of these other bands, Quicksilver did not release an album until mid 1968, when *Quicksilver Messenger Service* rose as high as number sixty-three on the U.S. charts. Within a style of music that often preferred long instrumental jams to shorter and tighter song-based numbers, Quicksilver made their mark as a live band, featuring guitarists Gary Duncan and John Cipollina in extended improvised solos. The band's second album, *Happy Trails*, included tracks recorded live at the Fillmore in San Francisco and the Fillmore East in New York, and rose to number twenty-seven in the United States in mid 1969. British pianist Nicky Hopkins joined when Duncan left the band early in 1969, and his playing can be heard on *Shady Grove*, which hit number twenty-five on the U.S. charts after its release in late 1969. Like the Charlatans, however, Quicksilver's stature within the San Francisco underground never translated to national success, as it did for the Jefferson Airplane, Janis Joplin, and (somewhat later) the Grateful Dead.

Other Important San Francisco Bands: Moby Grape, the Steve Miller Band.
One San Francisco group that missed the Summer of Love in the Haight was Moby Grape. The band was formed in the fall of 1966 by former Jefferson Airplane manager Matthew Katz and included the Airplane's original drummer, Skip Spence (now back to playing guitar). Working with producer David Rubinson, Moby Grape signed with Columbia and released their first album, *Moby Grape*, in June 1967. Encouraged by Rubinson's confidence in the album, the label released five singles simultaneously—an action that was perceived by many as a publicity stunt. Of these five singles, only "Omaha" (p84, 1967) charted, though the album rose to number twenty-four in the United States. Because of the June release and the promotion associated with it, Moby Grape

spent most of the Summer of Love on the road. The band's next album, *Wow*, did even better than the first, reaching number twenty on the U.S. charts in the summer of 1968, though this success was short-lived and its follow-up, *Moby Grape '69*, never charted.

Moby Grape blended a blues-rock guitar-driven sound (there were three guitarists) with rich vocal harmonies derived from folk rock. "Omaha," for instance, is a hard-rocking number with some psychedelic touches (backward-tape and other studio effects), while "8:05" (one of the other singles released simultaneously) is a quieter folk-influenced tune sung in close vocal harmonies.

Another musician who missed San Francisco's Summer of Love was guitarist Boz Scaggs. Scaggs arrived in the Bay Area in the fall of 1967 to join the Steve Miller Band—a group led by blues guitarist Miller and well known in the Haight since late 1966. Owing to a scarcity of recording studios well suited to rock music, most San Francisco bands recorded somewhere else, often in Los Angeles. The Steve Miller Band, however, recorded its first album in London. Co-produced by the band and British producer Glyn Johns (who had engineered recordings for many British bands, including the Rolling Stones), *Children of the Future* received much FM airplay when it was released in early 1968 but only charted at number 134 in the United States. The band's second album, *Sailor*, did better, reaching number twenty-four on the U.S. charts in late 1968. Miller and Scaggs would each go on to much greater success on both sides of the Atlantic in the 1970s.

The London Scene

The Rise of the British Underground. The arrival of the Steve Miller Band at London's Olympic Studios to record their first album in January 1968 was not the first contact between the psychedelic scenes in San Francisco and London. Two and a half years earlier, at about the same time the Grateful Dead were turning to electric blues and the Jefferson Airplane were rehearsing for their debut performance, beat poet Allen Ginsberg was in London helping bookstore owner Barry Miles organize a poetry reading that eventually featured several American and European beats, including Lawrence Ferlinghetti and Gregory Corso. Convinced that Miles' Better Books was far too small a shop to contain the crowd they were hoping to draw, the organizers rented the Royal Albert Hall. In June 1965, "Poets of the World/Poets of Our Time" drew over 5,000 people—many under the influence of pot or acid—and inaugurated the London psychedelic underground. The following September, Michael Hollingshead (who had introduced Timothy Leary to LSD), opened the World Psychedelic Center in London, which would soon become the English center for psychedelic music and culture.

Drugs were not entirely new to rock culture in the UK. The Beatles had been introduced to marijuana in late 1964 (reportedly by Bob Dylan) while in the United States, and John Lennon and George Harrison had already experienced LSD in the spring of 1965 when it was secretly slipped into their coffee after dinner at the home of an acquaintance. But as in San Francisco, a community of young people in London was beginning to form around drugs, Eastern philosophy, radical politics, and experimental music. By the end of January 1966, a series of weekly events called the Spontaneous Underground were initiated that combined performance art, poetry, music, and avant-garde weirdness. Held in the Marquee Club on Sundays, these events were akin to Kesey's acid tests, though on a smaller scale. In February, a bookstore and gallery called the Indica was launched by Barry Miles, John Dunbar (the husband of Marianne Faithfull), and Peter Asher (of Peter and Gordon and brother of Paul McCartney's girlfriend, Jane). The Indica, similarly to the Psychedelic Shop, specialized in counterculture items, and it was here that John Lennon came across Leary's *The Psychedelic Experience* for the first time. Unlike the San Francisco scene, the London underground boasted a kind of countercultural night school at which students could study topics such as housing problems, race relations, mental health, and law, among many others. Called the London Free School, it began meetings in March 1966.

Despite the many parallels, the San Francisco and London scenes were quite different. Members of the early London psychedelic underground had only a few descriptions of the San Francisco scene as a guide. In the late 1960s, when air travel was far less commonplace than it is today, there were few people in London who had actually experienced the San Francisco underground, and since the San Francisco scene remained underground until mid 1967, published reports were very scarce. From Ginsberg and a few others, psychedelic Londoners knew the main points of San Francisco psychedelia but were forced to work out the specific applications according to their own imaginations. The result was a London scene that was at once very similar to but also very distinct from the one in California.

Underground Clubs in Swinging London. In April 1966, just as the London psychedelic scene was gaining momentum and was still unknown to most anyone outside of it, *Time* magazine ran a cover story on "Swinging London," focusing on what the editors in New York perceived as a refreshing urban lifestyle filled with glamorous nightspots attended by hip stars adorned in daring and colorful fashions (this is the image of '60s London that is the target of so much of the humor in the Austin Powers movies). The summer of 1966 saw young tourists flocking to London to catch some of the excitement, but the underground psychedelic scene developed mostly way from the view of these tourists. By October, the *International Times* began publication, providing the burgeoning scene with a newspaper devoted to its concerns, and the UFO Club was established. Unlike the Fillmore or the Avalon in San Francisco, the UFO was not so much a place as an organization. On the weekends, UFO evenings would take place in a bar that on other nights of the week was an Irish pub. When using that bar later became a problem, the UFO simply relocated. While other clubs also featured psychedelic music (even some of the same bands, such as Pink Floyd, Soft Machine, Tomorrow, and the Crazy World of Arthur Brown), the UFO was the home of the psychedelic underground in London. The Saville Theater (owned by Brian Epstein) provided a larger venue for Sunday night shows as well. In late April 1967 an evening of psychedelia brought 10,000 London hippies together. Called "The 14-Hour Technicolor Dream," the all-night event was held at the Alexandra Palace, a Victorian palace overlooking London. Avant-garde happenings (one supervised by Yoko Ono), a light show, and a long roster of bands were meant to intensify the chemically enhanced experiences of those in attendance. A month later Pink Floyd sponsored a similar event, "Games for May," which was held in Queen Elizabeth Hall, and in July, a "Love-In" back at Alexandra Palace featured Floyd, Tomorrow, the Crazy World of Arthur Brown, and the Animals. By August, when the Middle Earth Club was established for evenings similar to those hosted by the UFO, little about psychedelia was underground anymore: in the wake of *Sgt. Pepper's Lonely Hearts Club Band*, it seemed that psychedelia was everywhere.

Musical Notes from the Underground: Pink Floyd, Soft Machine, Tomorrow.

There were generally two types of bands on the London scene during the 1966–69 period: those who enjoyed commercial success in the United States and UK (the Beatles, the Stones, Cream, Jimi Hendrix, Donovan), and those whose success was limited to the London underground. The first band to make its name on the London underground scene formed in 1965 and took its name from American bluesmen Pink Anderson and Floyd Council. Initially calling themselves the Pink Floyd Sound, then the Pink Floyd, and eventually simply Pink Floyd, the band became regulars at Spontaneous Underground events, and later at the UFO Club.

The band took its name from the blues, but much of its approach was more indebted to avant-garde art music; the group's extended improvisations would often dispense with chord patterns and/or scales and wander into exploratory noise-making, produced by playing their instruments in unconventional ways or feeding their electric guitars and keyboards through tape-echo devices. While leader and guitarist Syd Barrett, bassist Roger Waters, organist Richard Wright, and drummer Nick Mason could play "Interstellar Overdrive" for half an hour, they also had a pair of hit singles in mid 1967, written by Barrett. "Arnold Layne," a song about a transvestite who steals women's clothing off other people's clotheslines at night—a recording that somehow avoided being banned by the BBC—reached number twenty in the UK charts; the follow-up, "See Emily Play," hit number six. The band refused to play these

> ### A London Timeline
>
> June 1965: "Poets of the World/Poets of Our Time," Albert Hall
> September 1965: Michael Hollingshead opens World Psychedelic Center
> January 30, 1966: Spontaneous Underground weekly events begin (Marquee Club)
> February 1966: Indica Bookshop and Gallery opens
> March 1966: London Free School is launched
> April 1966: *Time* cover story on Swinging London
> October 1966: *International Times* begins publication
> December 1966: UFO evenings begin
> April 1967: "The 14-Hour Technicolor Dream," Alexander Palace
> May 1967: "Games for May," Pink Floyd, Queen Elizabeth Hall
> July 1967: "Love-In," Pink Floyd, Tomorrow, the Animals, Arthur Brown, Alexander Palace
> August 1967: Middle Earth evenings begin

songs live, however, preferring to perform their extended improvisations instead. Pink Floyd's first album, *Piper at the Gates of Dawn* (uk6, 1967), was recorded in the same Abbey Road facility and during the same period as the Beatles' *Sgt. Pepper*; Paul McCartney is reported to have visited at least one of the sessions. Barrett soon began to show signs of mental illness, and during an American tour in 1968, he became unable to perform reliably. Guitarist and Barrett friend David Gilmour was brought in, at first to cover for Barrett's lapses but eventually to replace him entirely. In light of the tremendous success the band enjoyed worldwide in the 1970s (to be discussed in Chapter 8), it is surprising that their success before *The Dark Side of the Moon* (1973) was limited to the UK. The group scored a string of hit albums in Britain, including *A Saucerful of Secrets* (uk9, 1968), *More* (uk9, 1969), *Ummagumma* (uk5 p74, 1969), and *Atom Heart Mother* (uk1 p55, 1970), but they could never break the Top 40 album charts in the States. Their concert performances in London during 1966–68, often accompanied by elaborate light shows and played for audiences tripping on acid, made them one of the most important bands in the London psychedelic underground.

Like San Francisco, London had a strong psychedelic scene that remained underground until mid 1967. The UFO Club—less an actual place than an organization—hosted many important bands of the era. This 1967 poster advertises a Pink Floyd concert (they were regulars at the UFO) and reveals a clear artistic connection with the rock posters of the Fillmore in San Francisco.

Soft Machine also performed regularly for the UFO Club and other psychedelic events in London. They blended a passion for experimental weirdness with a penchant for the free jazz of Ornette Coleman and John Coltrane. Formed in Canterbury in 1966, the band included Mike Ratledge on keyboards, Kevin Ayers on bass, Robert Wyatt on drums, and—at least for the first album—Daevid Allen on guitar. Unlike Pink Floyd, the group never had a hit single and had only modest success with their albums. The first one, *The Soft Machine*, was released in late 1968 in the States only, where it did not chart (the band was touring this country at the time, opening for Jimi Hendrix). *Soft Machine Volume 2* (1969) was released in the UK but did not chart, though *Third* (uk18, 1970) and *Fourth* (uk32, 1971) each did somewhat better commercially. In 1966–68, the band alternated short song-like sections (often with Wyatt singing) with avant-garde improvisations. After this, the band tended toward jazz fusion and became pioneers of the British jazz fusion called Canterbury progressive rock.

Tomorrow became regulars at UFO events and around the London scene slightly later than Pink Floyd and Soft Machine. Featuring guitarist Steve Howe (who would later play in the 1970s progressive rock band, Yes) and vocalist Keith West, along with bassist John "Junior" Wood and John Adler ("Twink"), the band released a pair of singles that were popular around London but failed to chart. One of these, "My White Bicycle," exhibits many of the psychedelic features found in a wide range of other records: backward tape sounds, exotic Eastern-sounding scalar melodies, and simple pop lyrics bordering on naïve. By the time the band's first album, *Tomorrow*, was released in early 1968, the psychedelic parade had mostly passed by. Along with the Crazy World of Arthur Brown (featuring a young Carl Palmer, future drummer for Emerson, Lake & Palmer), Tomorrow was highly regarded on the London scene.

The Public Face of British Psychedelia: The Major Acts.   As important as Pink Floyd, Soft Machine, Tomorrow, and Arthur Brown were to the burgeoning London psychedelic underground in 1966–67, other British-based bands and artists enjoyed a much higher profile within the UK and sometimes abroad as well, especially after June 1967. First among these was certainly the Beatles; the Rolling Stones also continued to score hit singles and albums throughout the second half of the 1960s. New bands such as Cream, the Jimi Hendrix Experience, and Traffic emerged in the months leading up to the Summer of Love, each building on the Stones' passion for electric blues, while folk-singer Donovan Leitch turned to flower power and provided a lighter take on British psychedelia.

The Rolling Stones: Psychedelic Rhythm and Blues?   By late 1966, Brian Jones's contribution to the Rolling Stones' music had diminished considerably, and the Jagger-Richards songwriting partnership began to dominate the band's music. The band's seventh album, *Aftermath*, was the first to contain all Jagger-Richards songs, securing the pair's role as group leaders. Despite their now well-established position as one of rock music's leading bands, however, the Stones remained junior colleagues of the Beatles, and this can be seen clearly in the second half of 1967, as the band prepared *Their Satanic Majesties Request* in response to *Sgt. Pepper*. Jagger had been present at sessions for *Sgt. Pepper* and appeared with the Beatles on their worldwide broadcast of "All You Need Is Love" in July 1967; he had also accompanied them when they traveled to Wales to study with the Maharishi later in the summer. The summer and fall of 1967 had been difficult months for Jones, Jagger, and Richards; each was convicted on drug possession charges and for some time faced the possibility of serving prison sentences. The single "We Love You" was the band's way of thanking fans for their support during the trials; it hit number eight (uk) in the fall of 1967 and provided a somewhat darker echo of the Beatles' "All You Need Is Love." Released in December 1967, *Their Satanic Majesties Request* (p2 uk3) sported a cover employing a holographic image of the band dressed in wizard outfits—if the Beatles were a happy-go-lucky brass band, the Stones would pose as menacing magi of the occult. The single "She's a Rainbow" (p25) provides a representative instance of the *Sgt. Pepper* influence on the Stones: the tune employs orchestral instruments and a classical-sounding piano figure that recurs frequently, each time breaking the steady beat of the music.

Their Satanic Majesties Request remains a source of disagreement among rock writers; some consider the album to be the Rolling Stones' low point— a project that fails by attempting to imitate the Beatles too closely; others find the album an interesting and perhaps necessary step in the band's development. Most writers do agree that the Rolling Stones seemed to come into their own as a band when they stopped worrying about what the Beatles were doing and turned back to their rhythm and blues roots. The hard-driving rhythm of "Jumpin' Jack Flash" (p3 uk1, 1968) gives the first indication of this new stylistic orientation, and the band's next album, *Beggar's Banquet* (p5 uk3, 1968), confirms it. As discussed in Chapter 4, the Stones' manager Andrew Loog Oldham had marketed the band as bad boys beginning in 1964. By the end of 1967, Oldham was no longer managing the group, but this did not keep the Stones from amplifying the outlaw image that had been crystallized by the scandal over "(I Can't Get No) Satisfaction." In the wake of their much-publicized drug busts and trials, and at a time when the utopian peace and love of 1967 was beginning to share space within the counterculture with the riots and antiwar protests of 1968, the Stones' "Street Fighting Man" was banned from the radio because authorities were concerned it might fuel further violence. When Jagger adopted the role of Lucifer to sing "Sympathy for the Devil" in 1968, it was clear the band's involvement with flower power was over.

Cream: British Blues on Acid with Pop on the Side.

Perhaps the first rock band ever to be billed as a "supergroup" was formed in July 1966 when Eric Clapton (formerly of the Yardbirds), bassist Jack Bruce, and drummer Ginger Baker formed Cream. Individually they had played in British blues bands with Alexis Korner, John Mayall, and Graham Bond, and the initial idea was that the trio would focus on traditional blues—the band eventually covered several traditional blues numbers, including Robert Johnson's "Crossroads" and Muddy Waters's "Rollin' and Tumblin'." Clapton had helped develop the instrumental "rave-up" sections that had been a feature of the Yardbirds' live shows, and these long sections featuring extensive soloing became an important element in Cream's blues adaptations as well. The live version of Willie Dixon's "Spoonful" found on *Wheels of Fire* is typical. It includes a lengthy instrumental rave-up and runs to almost seventeen minutes. While the focus of the music was often on Clapton's guitar playing, Bruce and Baker were also accomplished players who would solo from time to time as well; Baker's drum solo on "Toad," for example, became a model for many other rock drummers. Clapton was widely celebrated in England as the best rock guitar player in the world (at least until Jimi Hendrix also became a favorite) and helped make the use of distortion and the wah-wah pedal common among guitarists. Although the blues were a central element in Cream's music, the band also had a knack for pop singles, as confirmed by "I Feel Free" (uk11, 1966) and "Strange Brew" (uk17, 1967) in the first year of their career.

Cream's first three albums helped establish the idea that rock musicians could begin to rival classical or jazz musicians in terms of instrumental ability and prowess. Whereas the focus of the Beatles' or the Beach Boys' music was in expanding the limits of rock songwriting and recording techniques, Cream relied more on virtuosic playing. Initially, the band's success was greater in the UK where the band members were already well known. The band's first album, *Fresh Cream*, hit number six on the UK charts in late 1966/early 1967, though it only barely squeaked in the U.S. Top 40. However, in the wake of the Summer of Love and the new passion for trippy music that came with it, *Disraeli Gears* hit number four in the U.S. charts (uk5) in the fall of 1967, and *Wheels of Fire* was number one (uk3) a year later. In many ways, Cream's penchant for instrumental soloing parallels that of the San Francisco bands, many of whom were initially inspired by the Rolling Stones' and Yardbirds' adaptations of American electric blues. But while the San Francisco guitarists remained less well known than the bands they played in, Clapton and then Hendrix became famous as individuals, ushering in the idea of the "guitar hero." For all the excitement generated by Cream, it was all over by November 1968, when the band performed a farewell concert in London's Royal Albert Hall and broke up. All three members went on to have solo careers, though Clapton's was the most successful, spanning the 1970s, '80s, and '90s with successful singles and albums.

Cream—(from left) Jack Bruce (bass), Ginger Baker (drums), and Eric Clapton (guitar)—performing live at the Fillmore Auditorium in San Francisco, 1967. Strongly influenced by the blues, Cream showcased the virtuosic instrumental solos of Eric Clapton (formerly of the Yardbirds) and the powerful drumming of Baker.

Cream's Blues Adaptations.   One of Cream's best-known tracks is "Sunshine of Your Love," written by Clapton, Bruce, and lyricist Pete Brown. The song is built around a central guitar figure (sometimes called a "riff" or "lick") that is repeated in the guitar and bass throughout much of the song. (The technique of building a blues number around a central lick is a familiar one within American electric blues; Bo Diddley's "I'm a Man" is a representative example.) In "Sunshine of Your Love," this central riff is combined with the 12-bar blues structure to create the verses that repeat throughout the tune according to the simple verse formal design. The 12-bar pattern is doubled to twenty-four measures, though the proportions remain the same—the first 4-bar phrase is now eight bars, while the second and third are expanded in the same manner. The third phrase departs somewhat from the standard blues version, but is clearly derived from that pattern. By modifying elements within the 12-bar blues structural framework, Cream creates an original blues-rock song that builds on and expands traditional blues techniques and patterns.

The Jimi Hendrix Experience: Psychedelic Blues Meets the Avant-garde.
Along with Clapton, Seattle-born Jimi Hendrix is one of the most influential guitarists in the history of rock music. Hendrix spent the first half of the 1960s

Cream, "Sunshine of Your Love"

Words and music by Eric Clapton, Jack Bruce, and Pete Brown, produced by Felix Pappalardi. Reached #5 on the Billboard Pop charts in early 1968, and #25 on the UK singles charts in fall of the same year. Also released on the album *Disraeli Gears* (uk5, p4, late 1967).

FORM: Simple verse, with each verse employing the same 24-bar pattern, created by doubling each measure in the standard 12-bar blues structure so that each single measure becomes two measures. The song draws on the "lick blues" tradition of building a tune around a repeating riff or lick. Note the interesting expansion of the 24-bar pattern that occurs in the last verse.

TIME SIGNATURE: 4/4.

INSTRUMENTATION: Electric guitar, bass, drums, and lead vocal.

0:00–0:16	**Introduction**, 8 mm.	2 mm. lick stated four times in guitar and bass. Note that the drum part employs no cymbals.
0:16–1:06	**Verse 1**, 24 mm.	Vocal enters, as lick continues. Clapton and Bruce trade off singing vocal phrases. "It's gettin' near dawn . . ."
1:06–2:00	**Verse 2**, 26 mm.	A 2 mm. link precedes a repetition of the 24-mm. verse. Vocal trade-off continues and the verse is performed as before. "I'm with you my love . . ."
2:00–2:50	**Instr. Verse**, 24 mm.	Clapton blues-based guitar solo. After laying off the cymbals in the previous verses, Baker employs them heavily now.
2:50–4:08	**Verse 3**, 32 mm. and fade-out	This last verse is much more forceful, owing to the now copious use of cymbals carried over from the solo. The verse proceeds as before until the "I've been waiting so long," where the 24 mm. structure is expanded by repeating that line to create a dramatic ending before the fade-out. "I'm with you my love . . ."

(with the exception of a short term of service in the U.S. Army) playing in various bands, including stints with Little Richard and the Isley Brothers. By 1964 he had moved to New York, where he began working with soul singer Curtis Knight before forming his own band, Jimmy James and the Blue Flames in 1966. In July of that year, Animals bassist Chas Chandler saw Hendrix's act at the Café Wha? in Greenwich Village and soon offered to manage the guitarist. Chandler brought Hendrix to London in September, where he formed the Jimi Hendrix Experience with Hendrix, drummer Mitch Mitchell, and bassist Noel Redding. By early 1967, the Experience's rendition of "Hey Joe" was number six on the UK charts, followed by "Purple Haze" (uk3) in May. The band's first album, *Are You Experienced?* (uk2 p5, 1967), was a tremendous success in the UK during the second half of 1967; it rose to the number two spot and was only kept from number one by *Sgt. Pepper*. Despite being an American, Hendrix actually arose out of the London psychedelic scene. His success in the United States did not begin until after his appearance at the Monterey festival in the summer of 1967—the first album was not released in the United States until August, and while it did well, "Purple Haze" reached only number sixty-five and "Foxey Lady" stalled at number sixty-seven on the American singles charts. In the wake of *Sgt. Pepper*, album success is a much more accurate measure than rank on the singles charts, and by early 1968 *Axis: Bold as Love* was at number three in the United States (uk5), followed by *Electric Ladyland* (uk6 p1, 1968) and the compilation *Smash Hits* (uk4, 1968; p6, 1969). Hendrix released albums after the breakup of the band in the summer of 1969, just weeks before his legendary Woodstock performance, but his work with the Experience is his most influential. On September 18, 1970, Jimi Hendrix died of a drug overdose.

"Purple Haze" and "Foxey Lady" from the first album are good examples of Hendrix's distinctive blend of blues and pop. Both tracks employ chord progressions and melodic materials derived from electric blues to form effective pop "hooks": the line, "S'cuse me while I kiss the sky," is followed by a catchy response in the guitar in "Purple Haze," just as the line "foxey lady!" is answered in a parallel manner by the guitar in that song.

A good example of Hendrix's more experimental music can be found on *Axis: Bold as Love*: "If 6 Was 9" runs to over five minutes, with three minutes being instrumental playing featuring novel guitar sound effects and some counterculture narration. "1983 (A Merman I Should Turn to Be)" from *Electric Ladyland* clocks in at just under fourteen minutes and is perhaps Hendrix's most ambitious experimental track. After a few minutes of the song proper (which is filled with backward tape effects), the band launches into a series of loose atmospheric instrumental sections that allow Hendrix, Mitchell, and Redding each ample opportunity to shine (Chris Wood from Traffic also contributes on flute) before ending with a reprise of the song. A short electronic piece, "Moon, Turn the Tides . . . gently, gently away" follows immediately and adds a clear avant-garde final touch to "1983." Hendrix's experimentation in the recording studio (he often worked very closely with engineer Eddie Kramer) clearly extends the work done by others, especially the Beatles and the Beach

Boys (Hendrix's aversion to surf music notwithstanding). His virtuosity as a guitarist served as a model for many important rock musicians who followed, and his sonic innovations employing feedback and the vibrato bar on the electric guitar were much imitated. His flamboyant and often sexually suggestive or physically destructive performances—setting the guitar on fire or otherwise destroying it—became the stuff of rock legend.

Traffic, Van Morrison. In April 1967, the Spencer Davis Group was enjoying great success; in the previous six months the band had two hit singles break the Top 10 in both the United States and the UK. In that time, however, rumors had also circulated that eighteen-year-old Stevie Winwood would leave the group. The tremendous success of the Spencer Davis Group brought with it musical limitations that Winwood was eager to abandon in favor of exploring more "musicianly" concerns. Winwood quit Davis's band and formed Traffic with drummer Jim Capaldi, guitarist Dave Mason, and flutist/saxophonist Chris Wood. The band's first single, "Paper Sun" (uk5 p94), was released in May and captured well the whimsical character of emerging British flower power with its opening measures of sitar and upbeat vocal melody. The band's next single,

---

🎧 **LISTENING GUIDE**   GET MUSIC ▶▶ | wwnorton.com/rockhistory

The Jimi Hendrix Experience, "Purple Haze"

Words and music by Jimi Hendrix, produced by Chas Chandler. Reached #3 on the UK charts in 1967. Contained on the album *Are You Experienced?*, which rose to #2 in the UK and #5 in the United States.

FORM: Simple verse, with contrasting instrumental bridge. The introduction plays an important role in the track, and it returns after the instrumental bridge, serving to re-launch the tune. The practice of using an instrumental bridge, as well as of returning to the introduction to set up the last verse, are both features that will become commonplace in later rock music.

TIME SIGNATURE: 4/4.

INSTRUMENTATION: Electric guitars, bass, drums, lead vocal, and extra spoken voices.

0:00–0:32	**Introduction**, 14 mm.	The first 2 mm. introduce the famous dissonant riff in the guitar and bass, followed by 8 mm. of blues-based melodic phrases on the guitar. The introduction concludes by setting up the chord progression that will follow in the verse.

"Hole in My Shoe" did even better, going to number two in the UK. By the end of 1967, the band had released its first album, *Mr. Fantasy*, which rose to number eight in the UK. With their second album, *Traffic* (uk9 p17, 1968), the group finally scored success in the United States, which increased with the release of *Last Exit* (p19, 1969). While the Spencer Davis Group had been rooted securely in rhythm and blues, Traffic experimented with a broad range of styles; tracks from the first album blend psychedelic pop and blues ("Heaven Is in Your Mind") with latin rhythms ("Dealer"), classical instrumentation ("No Face, No Name, No Number"), and jazz soloing ("Coloured Rain"). The group disbanded in early 1969 and Winwood went on to play with Clapton and Baker in Blind Faith before reforming Traffic with Wood and Capaldi in early 1970 (Traffic's music from the '70s is discussed in the next chapter).

Irish singer-songwriter Van Morrison first hit the charts as a member of the band Them, whose "Baby Please Don't Go" (uk10, 1964) and "Here Comes the Night" (uk2 p24 1965) enjoyed success mid-decade. The band's recording of "Gloria"—the B side of "Baby Please Don't Go"—became a garage-band classic and was covered most famously by Patti Smith (1976). By 1967, Morrison had set out on a solo career, and this move was given a substantial boost by the

0:32–0:52	**Verse 1**, 9 mm.	Vocal enters. Note call and response between the vocal ("S'cuse me") and the lead guitar at the end of the verse. "Purple haze all in my brain . . ."
0:52–1:12	**Verse 2**, 12 mm.	The first 9 mm. are as before, but then a 3-mm. transition ("Help me") leads into the guitar solo. "Purple haze all around . . ."
1:12–1:35	**Instrumental Bridge**, 8 mm.	Guitar solo. While blues based, this solo also invokes sitar-like lines. Note speaking voices in the background.
1:35–1:53	**Return of Introduction**, 8 mm.	A repetition of the melody from the intro.
1:53–2:12	**Verse 3**, 9 mm.	As before, "Purple Haze all in my eyes . . ."
2:12–2:49	**Coda**, 17 mm. and fade	Music is drawn from the instrumental bridge.

Jimi Hendrix is cited by many as the most innovative and explosive rock guitarist ever. Hendrix's music displays a strong blues influence mixed with psychedelic elements and catchy lyrics and melodies. Hendrix was famous for getting many sounds from the guitar, including his signature fuzz and feedback, but using them in creative ways. His stage shows were exciting, improvisational, and often destructive.

commercial success of "Brown Eyed Girl" (p10), a song that has been a staple of American FM radio ever since. As catchy as his hit songs can be, Morrison also has a more experimental side, and this showed itself clearly on the 1968 album *Astral Weeks*. Recorded in New York in less than two days, the album's raw looseness was influential to many later singer-songwriters, though the album was more a critical than a commercial success. The tracks on *Astral Weeks* bring together a wide variety of styles, including acoustic folk music, jazz, classical, and rhythm and blues, and many of the tracks were recorded with top-notch studio players improvising as Morrison strums and sings. This highly improvised dimension of the music has a certain aleatoric (chance) quality that was popular in both jazz and avant-garde performances of the 1960s, but the connections to the experimental aspects of performances by Pink Floyd or the aleatoric studio practices found on the Grateful Dead's *Anthem of the Sun* are also interesting. The music is loose and improvisatory, but it is not often dissonant or angular—impressionistic, jazzy, and filled with a sense of poetic mysticism. Morrison went on to be an important singer-songwriter in the 1970s, and we will consider his music further in Chapter 8.

Donovan and Psychedelic Folk. Born Donovan Philips Leitch, Donovan first attracted international attention as a traditional folksinger/guitarist/songwriter with his 1965 hit single "Catch the Wind" (uk4 p23). Much like the music of Bob Dylan from approximately the same period, Donovan's early folk music was strongly influenced by Woody Guthrie. As folk rock developed in mid 1965, Donovan adapted his music to the new style by using electric guitars, keyboards, bass, and drums in his arrangements, sometimes provided by future Led Zeppelin musicians Jimmy Page and John Paul Jones. Donovan enjoyed a series of hit singles in the UK and United States, including "Sunshine Superman" (uk2 p1, 1966) and "Mellow Yellow" (uk8, 1967; p2, 1966). When psychedelia and flower power emerged from regional underground scenes into mainstream culture in the United States and UK in 1967, Donovan's gentle melodic sense, eclectic stylistic range, and often mystical lyrics made him a leading figure for hippie pacifism, as his success continued with more hit singles including "Wear Your Hair like Heaven" (p23,1967) and "Hurdy Gurdy Man" (uk4 p5, 1968), the second of which features the playing not only of Page and Jones but also future Led Zeppelin drummer John Bonham. With "Atlantis" (uk23, 1968; p7, 1969), Donovan reached the edge of counterculture utopianism, reciting the tale of

---

Six Albums That Changed Rock Guitar Forever

When Chas Chandler asked Hendrix to go with him to London, Hendrix asked Chandler if he could introduce him to Clapton. Clapton was immediately impressed with Hendrix's playing, and a friendly rivalry began. The Jimi Hendrix Experience and Cream brought out an alternating sequence of albums that progressively raised the bar on rock-guitar virtuosity.

Band: Album	Release date UK/US
Cream: *Fresh Cream*	Dec 1966 /Jan 1967
Hendrix: *Are You Experienced?*	May 1967/Aug 1967
Cream: *Disraeli Gears*	Nov 1967
Hendrix: *Axis: Bold as Love*	Dec 1967/Feb 1968
Cream: *Wheels of Fire*	Aug 1968/Jul 1968
Hendrix: *Electric Ladyland*	Nov 1968/Oct 1968

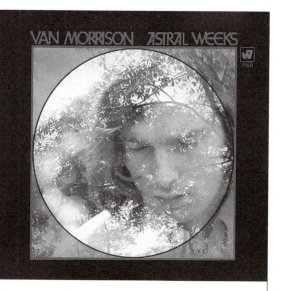

Though he may be better known for his more catchy pop songs, Van Morrison's psychedelic Astral Weeks *(1968) might be his most influential album. Recorded in less than two days, this highly improvizational album brings together many styles, including acoustic folk music, jazz, classical, and rhythm and blues.*

the lost city in a manner suggesting its lost wisdom might help rebuild Western culture, followed by a long sing-along section similar to the one that concludes the Beatles' "Hey Jude." Donovan remained active in the 1970s, releasing albums such as the commercially successful *Cosmic Wheels* (uk15 p25, 1973) and providing music for films including Franco Zeffirelli's *Brother Sun, Sister Moon* (1973).

Los Angeles and Elsewhere

The Byrds, the Buffalo Springfield. San Francisco and London were homes to the most important psychedelic subcultures, but other American cities also participated in the growth of the psychedelic movement. Along with the Mamas and the Papas and the Beach Boys, the Byrds were among the most successful bands to come out of Los Angeles in the mid 1960s. After the controversy over "Eight Miles High" in the summer of 1966, the group released the album *Fifth Dimension* (p24 uk27, 1966), which not only contained "Eight Miles High" but also another song that would prove to be the first sign of a new direction the band would soon follow: "Mr. Spaceman" (p36, 1966), the band's first attempt to mix rock with country music. While this was more the exception than the rule for the band in 1966, by 1968 they had released the album *Sweetheart of the Rodeo*, often cited as a pivotal album in the development of country rock. By the end of 1967 David Crosby had left the Byrds to join Hollies vocalist Graham Nash and guitarist Stephen Stills. Stills had enjoyed moderate success with the Buffalo Springfield, whose single "For What It's Worth" (the chorus of which, "Stop children. What's that sound?" inspires this textbook's title) had hit number seven in the U.S. charts in early 1967. Crosby, Stills, and Nash (sometimes joined by ex-Buffalo Springfield guitarist Neil Young) became one of the first supergroups of the 1970s; their music will be considered in Chapter 8. As these established artists were heading off in new musical directions other musicians were emerging from the Los Angeles scene.

Love and Arthur Lee, the Great Unknowns. Formed in Los Angeles in 1965 by singer/guitarist Arthur Lee, Love played an important role in the L.A. psychedelic scene, though the group never achieved the level of national success in the United States enjoyed by groups like the Byrds or the Doors. Love was actually signed to Elektra before the Doors and recommended the band to the record label. Love's first single, "My Little Red Book" (1966), was a rock cover version of a Bacharach-David song and it reached number fifty-two on the U.S. charts, though "7 and 7 Is" made number thirty-three later the same year. Much of the group's early music shows strong Byrds and Rolling Stones influences, and "Can't Explain" from the band's first album, *Love* (p57, 1966), is a good example. In the wake of the Beatles' *Sgt. Pepper's Lonely Hearts Club Band*, Love released their third and most celebrated album, *Forever Changes* (1967), which featured ambitious tracks, at times employing orchestral accompaniment and psychedelic recording studio effects. *Forever Changes* was more of a musical and critical success than a commercial one, partly owing to Lee's reluctance to tour outside southern California. The album earned the respect of many other rock

musicians in the late '60s, especially in England, where it hit number twenty-four in the UK album charts, making Love a rare instance of a local success in the United States scoring much greater success in the UK. In 1969, Lee and a new lineup released *Four Sail*, but neither this nor subsequent releases would enjoy the influence or acclaim of *Forever Changes*, though *Out Here* did reach number twenty-nine in the UK album charts in 1970.

The Doors and Jim Morrison, Turning to the Dark Side. The Doors was formed in Los Angeles in 1965 by singer/lyricist Jim Morrison and keyboardist Ray Manzarek, taking their name from eighteenth-century British poet William Blake (via Aldous Huxley's book *The Doors of Perception*). The Doors first attracted attention in the United States with their 1967 hit single "Light My Fire" (p1 uk49, 1967). Together with Robbie Krieger and John Densmore, the foursome produced an often-moody brand of late 1960s blues-based psychedelia with a tendency to linger over the darker aspects of emotional life, perhaps best exemplified by "The End," a dramatic and shocking piece in which Morrison recites and then shouts his Oedipal desires. If most psychedelia in 1967 seemed to focus on the positive side of drug use—the path to higher consciousness and liberation—Morrison seemed determined to explore avenues opened up by the "bad trip," beginning with the first track on the first album, "Break on Through." His lyrics are filled with grotesque and unsettling images of alienation and repression, and his on-stage antics took the bad-boy, nonconformist, overtly sexual image, fostered first by

The Doors' Jim Morrison (front) and keyboardist Ray Manzarek (behind), in a 1968 concert at the Hollywood Bowl. Unlike many in the psychedelic scene, Morrison chose to explore the darker side of life, exemplified by his songs "The End" and "Break on Through," the latter of which examines a "bad [acid] trip."

Elvis Presley and then by Mick Jagger, to a new level. With the band's third album, *Waiting for the Sun* (p1 uk16, 1968), Morrison introduced an alter ego, the Lizard King. The idea of a rock singer assuming an onstage persona would influence many singers, including Alice Cooper, David Bowie, Peter Gabriel, and Madonna. While the group's music became increasingly refined over the course of the six studio albums from *The Doors* (p1, 1967) to *L.A. Woman* (p9 uk26, 1971), and the style remained relatively stable as the band produced several hit singles, including "Hello, I Love You" (p1 uk15, 1968), "Touch Me" (p3, 1969), and "Love Her Madly" (p11, 1971). Morrison died under mysterious circumstances in 1971.

Iron Butterfly: Heavy Duty Rock and Roll. As dark as the Doors could get, nobody got any heavier in the late 1960s than Iron Butterfly. The band formed in San Diego in 1966 but bounded onto the scene on the strength of their second album, *In-A-Gadda-Da-Vida*, which hit number four in the United States during the summer of 1968. The title track of this album is seventeen minutes long and filled with extended organ, guitar, bass, and drum solos that would serve as the model for almost every rock band that did a live show over the next few years (it reappeared in pop culture over twenty years later in an episode of *The Simpsons* in which Bart smuggles the tune into church as the hymn, "In the Garden of Eden"). An edited version of "In-A-Gadda-Da-Vida" even hit number thirty on the U.S. singles charts in 1968, and the follow-up album, *Ball*, rose to number three in the first half of 1969. The heavy, menacing opening lick from the tune, as well as the references to classical organ music (perhaps overdone to become somewhat melodramatic in the manner of a bad horror movie), provided some of the first tendencies that would soon develop into the early heavy metal music of Black Sabbath, Deep Purple, and even Led Zeppelin (see chapter 8).

Vanilla Fudge and Psychedelic-symphonic Cover Versions. Back in New York, Vanilla Fudge had formed in 1965 as the Pigeons, changing their name in late 1966 when they signed to Atlantic records. The band's first album, *Vanilla Fudge* (p6 uk31), did moderately well on both sides of the Atlantic in the fall of 1967. The first single, "You Keep Me Hangin' On," had been released a few months earlier, and while it stalled at number sixty-seven in the United States, it hit number eighteen in the UK. The group's trademark was taking simple pop songs and turning them into elaborate and often lengthy cover versions. "You Keep Me Hangin' On" is a representative example: the band takes a two-minute song by the Supremes and Holland-Dozier-Holland and turns it into a psychedelic movement of over five minutes' length, complete with dramatic dynamic shifts and sitar lines. The group's second album, *The Beat Goes On* (p17), takes a motive from the Sonny and Cher song to unify—somewhat unsuccessfully, it must be admitted—a series of tracks that move chronologically from the style of Mozart forward to the Beatles. The musical ambition exemplified by these psychedelic-symphonic cover versions ensured that Vanilla Fudge would serve as an early influence for many of the progressive rock bands that would emerge in the early 1970s.

Upstate Americana: Dylan and the Band.   While the Byrds had turned to country music by 1968, Bob Dylan was making a similar turn in his own music about the same time. Sidelined by a motorcycle crash in 1966, Dylan retreated to Woodstock, New York, where he began to record with a group of mostly Canadian musicians known formerly as the Hawks, but now playing under the name the Band. Drummer Levon Helm (the lone American), guitarist Robbie Robertson, bassist Rick Danko, pianist Richard Manuel, and organist Garth Hudson had played the Ontario bar circuit behind rockabilly singer Ronnie Hawkins in the early 1960s, and without Helm, had backed Dylan on his world tour in 1965–66. The extensive sessions with Dylan were later released in 1975 as *The Basement Tapes* (p7 uk8), but the albums released in 1968, the Band's *Music from Big Pink* (p30) and Dylan's *John Wesley Harding* (p2 uk1), are both important records for the emergence of country rock. It might seem strange that a band mostly made up of Canadians could play such a central role in redefining the "American-ness" of American rock, but the members of the Band were experienced students of rural American musical styles. If it took a bunch of British bands to introduce many Americans to their own electric blues, it took a clutch of Canadians to help introduce them to musical Americana. The musical directions that Dylan and the Band were exploring in Woodstock, New York, might remain shrouded in mystery, but by the summer of 1969 the whole country was focusing on Woodstock for an entirely different musical reason.

A Woodstock Nation: Festivals, Audiences, and Radio

Do You Know the Way to Monterey?   Large, open-air music festivals became an important element of rock culture for the first time in the late 1960s. In the spring of 1967, John Phillips of the Mamas and the Papas and record-company executive Lou Adler organized the Monterey International Pop Festival, modeling it on the already established Monterey Jazz Festival. Monterey Pop was the first important international rock festival and it brought together bands from San Francisco, Los Angeles, and London to perform on June 16–18 at the Monterey County Fairgrounds in California. The Jefferson Airplane, the Grateful Dead, Big Brother and the Holding Company, the Byrds, the Mamas and the Papas, the Animals, the Who, and many others played for free, receiving only travel expenses. Jimi Hendrix's appearance introduced him to important musicians and businessmen in the United States and was crucial to his subsequent success. The Mamas and the Papas performed for the last time live in their original lineup, and the Beach Boys' decision not to play was widely thought to have hurt their reputation within the burgeoning counterculture. Even though attendance figures for any single outdoor event often vary widely, most responsible accounts seem to agree that between 55,000 and 90,000 people attended the Monterey festival. In many ways, Monterey was simply an expansion and development of the hippie concert events that had been occurring with increasing regularity in San Francisco since 1965. But while the San Francisco events featured mostly local and regional acts, the Monterey

International Pop Festival placed a broader range of acts on the same bill and provided a model for the open-air rock festival that would be followed over the next two years or so across the country, as major concert events were staged in Newport (1968 and 1969), Miami (1968), Toronto (1969), Atlanta (1969), and Denver (1969), among other locales. Monterey Pop was filmed by D. A. Pennebaker, and the release of the *Monterey Pop* film in December 1968 (as well as a not-very-representative album) further added to the importance of the festival.

Good Trip, Bad Trip: Woodstock and Altamont. If Monterey marked the beginning of the era of large outdoor rock festivals, Woodstock was the culmination of the era. Held on a large patch of farmland in Bethel, New York, on August 15–17, 1969, the Woodstock Music and Art Festival drew at least 400,000 hippies; the roadways in upstate New York were so unexpectedly crowded that many had to be closed to avoid large-scale regional gridlock. Tickets had been offered for sale in advance, but most fans turned up at the event without tickets expecting to get in for free. The meager security forces were overwhelmed—all in the spirit of hippie fellowship—and many people ended up crashing the event without paying. In addition, heavy rain stopped the show and created pools of mud. Despite these potentially devastating financial and logistical setbacks, the event was tremendously successful, making the festival's slogan, "Three Days of Peace and Music," into an ideal that represented the power and influence of the hippie counterculture. Many of the important American and British bands performed (the Grateful Dead, Jimi Hendrix, the Jefferson Airplane, Janis Joplin, the Who), and there were important performances by Santana; Crosby, Stills, and Nash; Joe Cocker; and Sly and the Family Stone. The 1970 release of Michael Wadleigh's documentary film, *Woodstock*, and a multi-disc live album helped make the event a financial success and, like the Monterey film and album, added to the event's significance.

The sixties went out on a sour note, however, as a festival at the Altamont Speedway in Livermore, California, held December 6, 1969, ended in violence and tragedy. The original plan for the event was that the Grateful Dead would sneak the Rolling Stones into San Francisco's Golden Gate Park for a free surprise show for the hippie faithful; the Stones saw the show as a way of thanking loyal fans. The Stones announced the concert at a press conference some days before, however, and the original plans were quickly canceled when San Francisco city officials got word of the event. Finally a venue was located out of town at an old racetrack. Two decisions seem to have led to the disaster that followed: first, the Stones employed a motorcycle gang, the Hells Angels, to provide security; and second, the Stones waited until nightfall to begin their portion of the show, leaving an open spot in the day's program that left concert-goers with nothing much to do. The Stones were waiting for darkness because they had planned a light show and were filming a movie, later released as *Gimme Shelter* in 1970. The Hells Angels were without some of their senior members, and a few got out of control, beating fans if they got too close to the stage (the Jefferson Airplane's Marty Balin was knocked out cold at one point). When Meridith Hunter, an eighteen-year-old black fan, pulled a gun at the front of the stage, he was beaten to death—all captured on film and in front of the band's eyes as they tried to perform. Many writers have since pointed out that given the sometimes haphazard organization that went into these events, it was only a matter of time before something tragic occurred, and something similar could have happened at many other events. But Hunter's murder did occur at Altamont, and this has caused many to view Altamont as the event that marked the end of the hippie era.

Festivals in the UK and Europe. As Monterey had expanded on Family Dog events and outdoor gatherings like the Human Be-In, so too did the Festival of Flower Children in the Woburn Abbey (late August 1967) expand the 14-Hour Technicolor Dream for British hippies. This three-day outdoor festival included performances by Jimi Hendrix, Tomorrow, the Jeff Beck Group, and the Small Faces, among others. (The Duchess of Bedford attended, mistakenly believing it would be a flower show.) Rock acts also appeared on the bill of the National Jazz and Blues Festival, an annual event that had begun in 1961. In August 1967 the festival was held in Windsor and included Cream, Tomorrow, the Nice, Donovan, and the Crazy World of Arthur Brown. Other festivals followed in France, Italy, and Switzerland, while the most important later British festivals include one in London's Hyde Park (July 1969), organized by the Rolling Stones to honor the recently deceased Brian Jones, and the Isle of Wight Festival (August 1970). The Isle of Wight festivals actually began in 1968, when about 10,000 enjoyed a one-day bill that included the Crazy World of Arthur Brown and the Jefferson Airplane. The 1969 festival was a far more ambitious enterprise, expanded to two days and including Bob Dylan and the band on a roster that also featured the Who, the Moody Blues, and the Nice, among many others, and drawing about 150,000 attendees. Conservative estimates place the attendance at the enormous 1970 Isle of Wight Festival at 500,000, and this festival remains among the largest ever to take place in Great Britain. The program included a mix of established artists and emerging acts that would make their name in the years that immediately followed. The Doors, Donovan, and Jimi Hendrix (his last public performance), for instance, were joined by Emerson, Lake & Palmer, Jethro Tull, and Chicago.

The Fracturing of the American Radio Audience: AM vs FM. Psychedelic music was never meant to appeal to young teens or preteens; like folk had been earlier in the decade, it was a music targeted at college-age listeners. With the development of free-form FM radio in 1967 and its spread to radio markets across the country, an important distinction between singles-oriented AM pop and album-oriented FM rock began to develop: younger listeners tended toward the AM dial while their older siblings listened to FM. By the end of the decade, the free-form format began to show signs of becoming somewhat more organized, and by the mid 1970s the increasing constraints of the album-oriented rock (AOR) format would spark great debate within the rock community. In the last few years of the '60s, though, it was possible to tune in an AM station and hear the Monkees, the Fifth Dimension, the Association, and many other hit-oriented artists, while the FM dial might play longer album tracks by groups that did not

Woodstock

The Woodstock Music and Art Festival was more than just the largest and most important of the open-air music festivals of the late 1960s. Woodstock was a defining cultural moment, a confluence of powerful social movements that were changing mainstream attitudes about music, politics, race, the war in Vietnam, religion, socially acceptable behavior, the use of drugs, and the role of youth in American culture.

The festival was organized by Michael Lang, Joel Rosen-man, and Artie Kornfeld, and financed by John Roberts. It was held in Bethel, New York, about forty miles away from Woodstock, the famous idyllic artists' colony where Bob Dylan had retired in 1967. By using the name "Woodstock" and putting the Band on the bill, the festival organizers subtly encouraged the mistaken idea that Dylan would perform. With the festival's proximity to New York City, a lineup of major stars (including the Who, Jimi Hendrix, and Janis Joplin), and some aggressive promotion, Woodstock mushroomed in size, drawing a peak crowd of between 300,000 and 600,000 people.

In 1969 the counterculture was frequently demonized by the mainstream. As a result the unprecedented gathering of hundreds of thousands of "hippies" in a single rain-soaked field, with insufficient food, medical care, traffic plans, and organization, alarmed both the government and the media. Yet despite the problems, Woodstock was

Virtually no one anticipated the huge crowd that would descend on Bethel, New York, for the Woodstock Music and Art Festival (1969). Over 400,000 people attended, sharing peace, love, drugs, and music, and getting soaked by rain. The Who, Sly and the Family Stone, Richie Havens (right), Santana (below), and Jimi Hendrix provided just some of the standout musical performances.

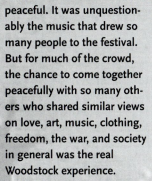

peaceful. It was unquestionably the music that drew so many people to the festival. But for much of the crowd, the chance to come together peacefully with so many others who shared similar views on love, art, music, clothing, freedom, the war, and society in general was the real Woodstock experience.

Not all of the music was a success: some of the shows were poorly timed, plagued by technical problems, interrupted by rain, or simply ordinary. But most of the artists rose to the challenge of playing before such a large and unpredictable crowd. There were breakout performances by new or lesser-known acts like Santana, Joe Cocker, Richie Havens, and Crosby, Stills, Nash, and Young, and incendiary shows by Sly and the Family Stone, the Who, and Jimi Hendrix. Sly and the Family Stone powerfully demonstrated the crossover appeal of funk to a largely white rock audience. The Who played their new, innovative rock opera *Tommy* and gained further notoriety when Pete Townshend assaulted radical activist Abbie Hoffman with his guitar after Hoffman interrupted their show. Just as at Monterey, however, a brilliant performance by the Who was upstaged by Jimi Hendrix. The highlight of Hendrix's set was his instrumental rendition of "The Star-Spangled Banner." Hendrix used his guitar to mimic the sounds of bombs, explosions, screams, and gunfire, and quoted "Taps" as a memorial to the victims of war. This single song, played by a former paratrooper, was perhaps the most eloquent antiwar statement of the entire era and by itself demonstrated how far rock music had come in terms of ambition, creativity, and virtuosity. Yet as a testament to the chaos of Woodstock this defining moment came on Monday morning, after all but about 30,000 stragglers had left.

have hit singles. There was some crossover: the Doors' "Light My Fire" charted as a pop single, for instance, but in an edited version that removed much of the instrumental soloing from the center section.

This separation by age group within the rock market foreshadows the even greater fragmentation of that market in the 1970s, even among FM rock stations. As we will see in Chapter 8, rock music in the 1970s takes the psychedelic era as a point of departure but splits into many distinguishable styles—it takes musical features that coexisted within psychedelia and separates them out for further development. It is to this expansion and fragmentation of psychedelia in the 1970–75 period that we turn next.

Questions for Review and Discussion

1. Describe what is meant by "counterculture" and "psychedelia." What are some of the important elements of the hippie worldview? How can music be psychedelic?
2. How did the relationship of the Beatles and the Beach Boys contribute to the development of ambitious music in the second half of the decade?
3. What are the origins of the Haight-Ashbury hippie scene in San Francisco and how did it develop? Who are some the most important bands and/or artists of this scene?
4. Did any bands from Los Angeles or New York play an important role in the development of rock music in the late 1960s? If so, name them and briefly summarize their activities.
5. What are the origins of the London psychedelic scene? Are there important parallels and differences with the scene in San Francisco? Which groups were important to the underground scene in London?
6. How did Jimi Hendrix and Eric Clapton contribute to the idea of instrumental virtuosity in rock music?
7. What role did radio play in the development of psychedelic music in the United States?
8. Name some of the most important hippie music festivals in the United States and the UK. How are these extensions of earlier concert events?

Further Reading

Ray Coleman, *Clapton! An Authorized Biography* (Warner Books, 1986).

Jim DeRogatis, *Kaleidoscope Eyes: Psychedelic Rock from the '60s to the '90s* (Citadel Press, 1996).

James Henke and Parke Puterbaugh, eds., *I Want to Take You Higher: The Psychedelic Era 1965–1969.* (Chronicle Books, 1997).

Jerry Hopkins and Daniel Sugerman, *No One Gets Out of Here Alive* (Warner Books, 1980).

Timothy Leary, Ralph Metzner, and Richard Alpert, *The Psychedelic Experience: A Manual Based on the Tibetan Book of the Dead* [1964] (Citadel Press, 1995).

Ray Manzarek, *Light My Fire: My Life with the Doors* (Century, 1998).

John McDermott with Eddie Kramer, *Hendrix: Setting the Record Straight* (Warner Books, 1992).

Gene Sculatti and Davin Seay, *San Francisco Nights: The Psychedelic Music Trip, 1965–68* (St. Martin's Press, 1985).

Joel Selvin, *Summer of Love: The Inside Story of LSD, Rock and Roll, Free Love, and High Times in the Wild West* (Cooper Square Press, 1999).

Grace Slick with Andrea Cagan, *Somebody to Love? A Rock-and-Roll Memoir* (Warner Books, 1998).

Derek Taylor, *It Was Twenty Years Ago Today* (Simon and Schuster, 1987).

Chris Welch with Steve Winwood, *Steve Winwood: Roll with It* (Perigee, 1990).

Tom Wolfe, *The Electric Kool-Aid Acid Test* (Farrar, Straus & Giroux, 1968).

The Nineteen Seventies

1970s

By the early 1970s, the counter-culture of the late 1960s had become mainstream. While a few years earlier, peace signs, long hair, tie dye, incense, and hippie values were found only on college campuses, hippie fashions and lifestyles were now popular in middle-class suburbs and shopping malls across the country. This commodification of counterculture might have been a signal that some of the problems that had divided America in the '60s were "solved" in the '70s. However, people continued to question these "solutions" and expose new problems that kept the country in a state of turmoil throughout the decade.

In the first years of the 1970s, Richard Nixon reached an agreement with the North Vietnamese, effectively ending the Vietnam War. The war had been the one of the most divisive issues of the 1960s. Though its real horrors were over, the scars from Vietnam ran deep. Many called it the first war America lost and questioned government's attention to "the people" in matters of policy. This skepticism exploded in 1974, when a Republican break-in to the Democratic offices at the Watergate office building in Washington, D.C., was covered up by members of the Nixon White House. This scandal forced Nixon to be the first president to resign.

Though Jimmy Carter, promising America a brighter future, was elected in 1976, his presidency was plagued with problems. In the last few years of the decade, the American economy was stagnant and inflation was high, a situation so pronounced that economists coined a new term to describe it: "stagflation." Part of the problem was a fuel shortage, leading to occasional long lines at gas stations and a general sense of an "energy crisis." Nuclear power seemed to offer a viable alternative, but an accident at a nuclear power plant at Three Mile Island in Harrisburg, Pennsylvania, in 1979 raised public fears about the safety of such facilities. Finally, a political revolution in Iran ultimately led to the taking of American hostages—a situation that gave more than a hint of political problems to come in the Middle East.

As mentioned above, the hippie values of the 1960s became mainstream in the 1970s. Feminism of the 1960s

became known as "women's liberation"—or simply "women's lib"—in popular culture. Gloria Steinem established *Ms.* magazine in 1972, providing a high-profile media forum for feminist issues. In a long-running series of advertisements beginning in 1969, Virginia Slims promoted a cigarette made especially for women with the slogan, "You've come a long way, baby." Women's lib also found its way into sports and mainstream music. Tennis pro Bobby Riggs challenged Billie Jean King to a match in 1973, claiming that a man could easily beat a woman (he lost), and Helen Reddy won

a Grammy for the feminist anthem, "I Am Woman."

Advocates for gay rights also began to be more visible in pop culture. After the 1969 "Stonewall Riot" erupted in reaction to a police raid of a New York City gay club, the movement organized and worked to change state laws prohibiting homosexual activity. An important step forward occurred when the American Psychological Association removed homosexuality from its list of diseases in 1973.

Television began to reflect these social and cultural changes. *All in the Family* debuted in 1971 and addressed

Tennis star and vocal advocate for women's rights Billie Jean King after defeating Bobby Riggs in the "Battle of the Sexes," 1973. The "Women's Lib" movement of the 1970s had its first sports star in King, which showed that the movement had become part of the mainstream.

All in the Family *was one of television's most popular shows in the 1970s. Archie Bunker (Carroll O'Connor) constantly battled cultural changes of the time. Here he spars with his liberal son-in-law Michael (Rob Reiner) and his women's lib–inspired daughter Gloria (Sally Struthers), as his wife Edith (Jean Stapleton) looks on.*

many of the burning issues of the time. Set in the home of a working-class New York City family, the show's central character was Archie Bunker, a middle-aged, poorly educated bigot. Archie frequently, and humorously, locked horns with those around him, including his liberal, college-educated son-in-law Michael (whom he called "Meathead"), his women's lib–inspired daughter Gloria, and even his bighearted but somewhat dimwitted wife Edith.

Archie sometimes tangled with neighbor George Jefferson on issues of race. Jefferson was Archie's black counterpart—just as bigoted but markedly more successful in his career. In 1975, *The Jeffersons* became the first *All in the Family* spin-off, followed by *Maude*, whose central character was a strong-willed woman who had also traded barbs with Archie.

The show that best captured the growing sense that women could make careers for them-

selves without the support of a husband was *The Mary Tyler Moore Show*. From its first episode in 1970, the show consistently dealt with issues that women typically faced in the workplace, though these were handled most often in a light-hearted manner. By mid-decade, *Chico and the Man* was raising the country's awareness of Hispanic life, making television programming more diverse than it had ever been.

The 1970s also saw the rise of rock-music television, a step forward from 1960s teen-oriented shows such as *American Bandstand*. Brill Building mogul Don Kirshner produced a new series in 1972, *In Concert* (later called *Rock Concert*), that featured live performances by leading rock bands and artists. *The Midnight Special* debuted the next year, featuring famous radio disc jockey Wolfman Jack. R&B found a television home on Don Cornelius's *Soul Train*, which broke through in 1971 and continues to this day. By the late 1970s, *Saturday Night Live* would become the premiere live showcase for rock groups, with many making their first marks in America there.

On the radio waves, FM radio grew into big business, and the album-oriented rock (AOR) format dominated, often with two or three stations in each city fighting for listeners (and advertising revenue). As FM developed, AM radio was increasingly the home of pre-teen pop, oldies, and what was left of traditional network-style programming. As the decade progressed, however, FM rock radio became more and more tightly formatted, allowing the disc jockeys less control over what got played and thus reducing their influence on the music and culture.

Outer space remained a fascination for American moviegoers, though it now had a definite hippie tinge. When George Lucas's *Star Wars* appeared in 1977, record crowds flocked to see Luke Skywalker fight totalitarianism in a galaxy far, far away. At the climactic moment of the movie, when Skywalker must destroy the evil Death Star, he hears the voice of his guru, Obi Wan Kenobi, telling him to "use the force." Skywalker turns off his high-tech equipment, plugs into the cosmic oneness, and fires the shot that saves his people.

Throughout the 1970s, blacks struggled with whites, men struggled with women, and gays struggled with straights. However, these groups were standing closer to each other than ever before. If the '60s was about the problems of segregation (or division), the '70s was about the problems of diversity. As we will see, this diversity was reflected in the music of the time. Folk and progressive rock, disco and punk, rhythm and blues, and funk all fought for—and received—attention. Every social group, it seemed, had a band. And every band had an audience.

chapter 8

The cover of Led Zeppelin's untitled fourth album, often called Zoso. This album contains one of Led Zeppelin's most recognizable songs, "Stairway to Heaven." This song, the album, and the group that produced them represent one answer to the early 1970s central musical and stylistic question: How would musicians after psychedelia incorporate, extend, or reject "the hippie aesthetic" (the focus on musicians' virtuosic playing usually involving guitars, complex experimental arrangements, and lyrics focused on "deep" topics like spiritual enlightenment)? As exemplified by Zoso and "Stairway to Heaven," Led Zeppelin chose to combine the "hippie aesthetic" with elements of electric and acoustic blues, as well as folk music.

The Growing Rock Monster

The late 1960s provided fertile music-stylistic ground for rock musicians in the 1970s. Most of the styles we will explore in this chapter grow out of some aspect of '60s rock, though elements that coexisted within psychedelia in the '60s get increasingly separated and developed as distinct styles in the '70s. The first half of the 1970s is characterized by bands still experimenting musically and testing the limits of the rock style. The second half of the decade, however, is somewhat more controversial. As the stylistic range of rock music was expanding over the course of the decade, the business of rock music was also growing and transforming from a business owned and run mostly by entertainment companies into a business owned and run by multinational corporations with little previous involvement in music. For some writers, the stylistic and corporate expansions are linked, such that one way of telling the story of rock in the 1970s is to cast it as a story of rock music in decline (similar to one view of the early 1960s, as described in Chapter 3). According to this interpretation, most of what's best about music in the late 1960s gets progressively corrupted by big money and even bigger egos, all motivated by the corporate bottom line, resulting in the much-despised corporate rock of the late 1970s, which is dismissed as a formulaic exploitation of rock designed only to make money—music that has sold its rock and roll soul. One problem with this take on rock history is that the music of many of the bands these writers tend to hate—Led Zeppelin, Deep Purple, and Jethro Tull from earlier in the decade, for instance, and Bad Company, Boston, Kansas, and Foreigner from later—has become the core of the "classic rock" radio format as it developed throughout the 1990s. For many young listeners, the rock music of the 1970s that we will consider in this chapter and the next is not seen as a decline from anything, and in fact, its connection to 1960s rock is often forgotten or only dimly acknowledged.

As we consider rock in the 1970s then, we are faced with at least two interpretations of this music: one sees much classic rock as a corruption, and thus tends to celebrate the underground punk scene during the first half of the decade and the emergence of punk and new wave in the second half; another view understands classic rock almost entirely in terms of the way it has been recast by FM radio and cable television in the period since about 1990. Both perspectives have their problems: in the first case, the connection to the 1960s is acknowledged but misunderstood, and in the second, the music that has come to represent the 1970s via classic rock radio often leaves important music out, mostly because some tracks are too long to be accommodated within current radio formats. This chapter will explore rock music in the first half of the 1970s with an eye toward the ways this music develops out of the psychedelic music we studied in Chapter 7. Chapter 9 examines black pop, disco, and reggae during the same period. In this chapter we will track each 1970s style out of its '60s roots and follow its development during the decade. Chapter 10 focuses on the second half of the decade, charting the growth of the business side of rock and examining the development of punk and new wave music during the 1970s. After studying this chapter and the next two, you can decide for yourself whether either of the interpretive positions briefly outlined above should be rehabilitated, incorporated into another view, or abandoned entirely.

The Hippie Aesthetic

Psychedelic Legacies.   One of the most important changes brought about in the 1966–69 period by artists such as the Beach Boys, the Beatles, and Bob Dylan was to change the focus of rock music from the single to the album, and from dancing music to listening music. While hit singles did not go away—in fact, as we've already seen, some psychedelic groups had hit singles—there was a growing sense that singles were a distinctly different part of the business, or maybe even a different business altogether. The focus of bands in the years after *Sgt. Pepper's Lonely Hearts Club Band* was increasingly fixed on creating albums that provided a musically provocative listening experience; in short, an album was a "trip."

As discussed in Chapter 7, musicians expanded rock's stylistic range by incorporating elements drawn from classical music, electronic music, and jazz. Musicians also came to depend increasingly on the recording studio as a creative tool, producing records that would have been difficult to reproduce live in many cases (at least back then). By the early 1970s, this focus on musical and technological craft, combined with a distinctly artistic approach to music-making (even among those groups who cultivated a no-nonsense, hard-rocking image), led to an aesthetic approach to rock that will be called the "hippie aesthetic." The basic idea behind the hippie aesthetic is that the rock musician is an artist who has a responsibility to produce sophisticated music using whatever means are at his or her disposal. The music should stand up to repeated listening and the lyrics should deal with important issues or themes. Musical prowess is especially valued: fans at this time began voting in annual polls sponsored by music magazines selecting performers in categories like Best Guitarist, Best Keyboardist, Best Drummer, Best Bassist, and Best Vocalist, in addition to typical categories like Best Album and Best New Act. Polls like this had been common for years in jazz publications (*Down Beat* especially), in which musical virtuosity and improvisatory fluency were often highly valued. Now rock musicians and their fans began taking themselves and their music just as seriously.

The hippie aesthetic is central to understanding what connects a wide variety of 1970s rock styles; as strange as it may sometimes seem, artists as diverse as Yes, the Eagles, the Allman Brothers Band, Steely Dan, and even Alice Cooper share elements of a common aesthetic approach. The hippie aesthetic also helps us realize that '70s rock is a clear development of psychedelia, making the period from about 1966 to 1979 seem much more unified than typically assumed. When we consider music in the 1980s in later chapters, we will also see how aspects of the hippie aesthetic surface even in the work of artists who seem to be soundly rejecting it. For now, however, we will begin by considering how '60s roots and the hippie aesthetic influence the music of the British blues rockers.

Blues-Based British Rock

Roots in the Rolling Stones, the Yardbirds, and Cream. Blues-based rock music coming out of Britain in the 1970s represents an important extension of earlier blues-influenced rock. The blues, especially the Chicago electric blues of musicians like Muddy Waters and Howlin' Wolf, played a large part in our discussion of rock music in the 1960s. The Rolling Stones were especially crucial in bringing this American music style back to America, or perhaps more specifically, introducing it to white American teenagers. In the wake of the Stones came the Yardbirds, which at various points featured guitarists Eric Clapton, Jeff Beck, and Jimmy Page. Many British bands like Deep Purple, Led Zeppelin, and Black Sabbath built on the stylistic foundation established by the Stones, the Yardbirds, and Cream. In fact, by the early 1970s, the Stones themselves were still enjoying tremendous commercial success employing a sound that returned them to their blues roots after a brief adventure in psychedelia. Chart-topping albums such as *Sticky Fingers* (p1 uk1, 1971), *Exile on Main Street* (p1 uk1, 1972), and *Goat's Head Soup* (p1 uk1, 1973) brought the Stones out of the Beatles' shadow, making them one of the most important groups to continue its '60s success into the 1970s (and beyond). Yardbirds alumni also remained active: Clapton continued as a solo artist after his stint with Cream and then Derek and the Dominoes, emerging with a hit single, "I Shot the Sheriff" (p1 uk9, 1974), while Jeff Beck led a succession of bands that tended toward a jazz-fusion approach (discussed below). Clapton and Jimi Hendrix had set the standard for guitar virtuosity and showmanship, mixing blues roots with psychedelic sounds and heavy rock volume, and Jimmy Page would play an important role in continuing that aspect of rock music. Drafted into the group toward the end of its career, Page was the only one left in the band by 1969. In order to fulfill a series of Yardbirds performing obligations, Page called on bassist John Paul Jones, a seasoned session musician, and two newcomers: vocalist Robert Plant and drummer John Bonham. After working for a short time under the name the New Yardbirds, the band changed their name to Led Zeppelin.

Led Zeppelin: Blues, Folk, and Psychedelia Take the Next Step. With a string of eight number one albums in the UK and six number ones in the United States, Led Zeppelin was among the most successful new British groups in the 1970s. Led by Jimmy Page, who co-wrote most of the group's music (often with Robert Plant providing the lyrics) and managed by Peter Grant, Led Zeppelin were so devoted to the idea of the album that they resisted releasing any tracks as singles. When Page first approached Robert Plant about forming a band, he described it as a blend of traditional electric blues, acoustic folk, and a fair amount of experimentation. It has thus frustrated Page and Plant somewhat over the years that listeners and critics seem to focus on the heavier elements in the group's music, forgetting how much of their total output is acoustically based. This blend is clear even on the first two albums, *Led Zeppelin* (p10 uk6, 1969) and *Led Zeppelin II* (p1 uk1, 1970) which, though they are usually thought of as '70s rock, were recorded in 1969. On the first record, "Babe I'm Gonna Leave You" is a nice reflection of the band's acoustic tendencies, while "Good Times, Bad Times" shows off the band's harder edge. The more psychedelic side is showcased in "Dazed and Confused," a staple of the band's live shows that featured Page playing his guitar with a violin bow. A blend of the harder elements with the psychedelic ones can also be found in "Whole Lotta Love," discussed on p. 312.

Perhaps the best blend of acoustic, blues, and psychedelic elements in Led Zeppelin's music can be found in what is arguably their best-known track, "Stairway to Heaven," from their fourth, untitled album (p2 uk1, 1972). The song features an acoustic guitar opening, backed at first only by recorders and then as accompaniment to Plant's vocals. As the arrangement builds, electric twelve-string guitar, bass, and drums are added; in the final section the track moves into heavy rock, featuring a blues-influenced electric guitar solo from

Led Zeppelin's Robert Plant (vocals) and Jimmy Page (guitar) in performance. Led Zeppelin's music combined complex arrangements with guitar mastery. Page's playing displayed strong blues and folk roots. Though the band was known for their harder, electrified music, they often used acoustic instruments and produced quieter, simpler songs.

Page and Plant's distinctive high wailing vocals. The vocals to "Stairway to Heaven" deal with the question of spiritual enlightenment, a perennial concern among hippies of the late 1960s, and a recurrent theme in 1970s rock. Led Zeppelin would return to themes of spirituality and the wisdom of the ancients and/or the East, perhaps most famously in "Kashmir," from *Physical Graffiti* (p1 uk1, 1975).

Led Zeppelin lyrics often focus on sexual topics as well; Plant's swaggering on "Whole Lotta Love" or "Black Dog" takes the playful hokem blues lyrics of songs like "Shake, Rattle, and Roll" beyond metaphor to direct references to sexuality. Page produced all of the band's albums and he was especially masterful at layering electric guitars—adding one after another, each playing distinct parts. "The Song Remains the Same" from *Houses of the Holy* (p1 uk1, 1973) is a particularly good example of this technique.

Deep Purple: Blues, Classical, and Psychedelia. Like Led Zeppelin, Deep Purple had its origins in late 1960s rock. Formed in London in 1968, the group had a number four U.S. hit single that year with a version of Joe South's "Hush." From its inception, the band mixed its blues-based rock with classical music, bringing out one of the first albums to combine a rock band with a symphony orchestra, *Concerto for Group and Orchestra* (uk26, 1970). After three relatively unsuccessful albums ("Hush" notwithstanding), founding members Jon Lord (keyboards), Ritchie Blackmore (guitar), and Ian Paice (drums) replaced original singer Rod Evans and bassist Nick Simper with singer Ian Gillan and bassist Roger Glover; this second lineup became the classic Deep Purple that stormed the rock charts in the first half of the 1970s. *Deep Purple in Rock* went to number four in the UK in 1970, followed by *Fireball* (p32 uk1, 1971) and *Machine Head* (p7 uk1, 1971), an album perhaps best known for containing "Smoke on the Water" and "Highway Star," two songs that have been staples of rock radio stations ever since ("Smoke on the Water" is discussed in detail in Interlude 2).

"Highway Star" is often cited as one of the songs that most influenced the development of heavy metal in the late 1970s and early 1980s, but in the context of the hippie legacy, it is a good example of how Deep Purple attempted to blend rock music with classical. The song features two long instrumental sections—one each for guitar and keyboard solos. Both solos make use of harmonic and melodic practices more often associated with the European baroque music of Bach and Vivaldi than with the blues of Muddy Waters or Elmore James. While the earlier *Concerto for Group and Orchestra* had merely juxtaposed the band with a classical orchestra, here classical music is integrated much more effectively, though no orchestra is used. A third track from *Machine Head*, "Lazy," provides a nice instance of the ways the band blended aspects of psychedelic trippiness into their blues-rock style. The track begins with a moody Jon Lord organ solo, which seems to blend church music, blues, and a bit of phantom-of-the-opera style organ playing together in a way reminiscent of Iron Butterfly's "In-A-Gadda-Da-Vida." Both Lord and Blackmore turn in strong blues solos during the course of the rest of the track, and Gillian delivers some of the falsetto screams that became the model for much rock singing of the late

Deep Purple in concert, 1972. Deep Purple was innovative in mixing its blues-based rock with classical music. Like Led Zeppelin, Deep Purple focused much of their music on instrumental solos, often displaying strong blues and classical influences. Roger Glover (bass), Ian Gillan (vocals), and Ian Paice (drums) are shown here; not pictured are Jon Lord (keyboards) and Ritchie Blackmore (guitar).

'70s and '80s (Gillan's vocal style also became well known through his performance as Jesus on the 1970 Tim Rice/Andrew Lloyd Webber concept album, *Jesus Christ Superstar*). The classic lineup folded by 1974 and singer David Coverdale and bassist Glenn Hughes joined the band for several albums, most notably *Burn* (p9 uk3, 1974). Except for a handful of cover versions, Deep Purple wrote its own material and also produced its own records, though Glover had an important hand in production when he was in the band. By the end of the decade, Deep Purple members had formed other bands, including Rainbow (Blackmore), Whitesnake (Coverdale), and Gillan.

Black Sabbath: British Rock Meets Boris Karloff and the Gothic Beginnings of Metal.   Though their roots are sometimes forgotten, Black Sabbath began as a blues band like Deep Purple and Led Zeppelin in the late 1960s. But early on, singer Ozzy Osbourne, guitarist Tony Iommi, bassist Geezer Butler, and drummer Bill Ward got the idea that they needed a trademark approach if they were to have any hope of getting noticed, and they opted for renaming the band, until that time known as "Earth," after the Boris Karloff horror movie *Black Sabbath*. The first track on their first album, *Black Sabbath* (p23 uk8, 1970), begins with the tolling of distant church bells, followed by a sinister riff using the interval of the tritone, a dissonant and unstable musical interval well known among classical-music aficionados as the devil's interval (as in Igor Stravinsky's *L'histoire du soldat*, for instance). The band's next album, *Paranoid* (p12 uk1, 1970), contains "Iron Man," which begins with the low-pitched tolling of guitars to accompany Ozzy's distorted voice intoning "I am Iron Man." Despite these gothic touches, the music remains based in blues riffs and structures, though often with guitar, bass, and voice playing variants of the same riff simultaneously ("Iron Man" is a good example of this practice). These two early albums, along with *Master of Reality* (p8 uk5, 1971) and *Black Sabbath, Vol. 4* (p13 uk8, 1972), were great commercial successes and laid the foundation for the use of darker images that would become central to much heavy metal only a few years later. By the end of the decade, the original lineup had parted ways and Ozzy went on to a solo career as one of the most prominent practitioners of 1980s heavy metal.

Go Your Own Way: The Faces, Humble Pie.   Much as the demise of the Yardbirds produced Led Zeppelin, the reorganization of the Small Faces at the end of the 1960s also had consequences for 1970s British blues rock. In this case, however, two new bands emerged. As the Small Faces, singer/guitarist Steve Marriott, bassist Ronnie Lane, and drummer Kenney Jones had released six albums in the UK, and a few of these did well on the charts. *Ogden's Nut Gone Flake*, a concept album released in the wake of *Sgt. Pepper* in the summer of 1968, went to number one in Britain. The band's only significant success in the United States was the single "Itchicoo Park," which hit number sixteen in late 1967 (uk3). In 1969, Marriott left the band to return to his blues roots, forming Humble Pie, and Lane and Jones likewise turned to blues rock, bringing in singer Rod Stewart and guitarist Ron Wood, both recent members of the Jeff Beck Group (in which Wood had played bass). Calling themselves simply the Faces, the new band's third album, *A Nod's as Good as a Wink . . . to a Blind Horse* (p6 uk2, 1971), established them on both sides of the Atlantic, as "Stay with Me" (p17 uk6, 1971) also became a hit. The Faces followed with *Ooh La La* (p21 uk1, 1973), which contained the hit "Cindy Incidentally" (p48 uk2, 1973).

At the same time the Faces were establishing themselves as a band, Stewart was recording solo with even greater success. His number one album *Every Picture Tells a Story* (p1 uk1, 1971) and hit single "Maggie May" (p1 uk1, 1971) made him one of the most recognized voices in rock music; his trademark husky voice was hard to miss. Stewart went on to release a string of successful albums and singles, including *Never a Dull Moment* (p2 uk1, 1972), which contained "You Wear It Well" (p13 uk1, 1972); *Sing It Again Rod* (p1 uk1, 1973); and *Atlantic Crossing* (p9 uk1, 1975). By 1974 the Faces had disbanded, as Wood went on to join the Rolling Stones and Stewart continued his solo career before turning to disco.

In 1978, Kenney Jones joined the Who to replace Keith Moon, who had died of a drug overdose. In forming Humble Pie, Marriott pulled together guitarist Peter Frampton, bassist Greg Ridley, and drummer Jerry Shirley. The new band scored a British hit with "Natural Born Bugie" (uk4, 1969), but it was their third album that established them as an international act. *Performance—Rockin' the Fillmore* (p21 uk32, 1971) contained such hard-rockin' blues-rock numbers as "I Don't Need No Doctor," as well as a cover version of Ray Charles's "Hallelujah (I Love Her So)." Frampton then left the band for a solo career (more about that in Chapter 9) and was replaced by Dave Clemson. The band enjoyed more commercial success with *Smokin'* (p6 uk28, 1972), which featured "30 Days in the Hole," and *Eat It* (p13 uk34, 1973). Just as the Faces' music was easily identified by Stewart's gruff tenor voice, Marriott's bluesy high tenor was a trademark of the Humble Pie sound.

Hippie Blues Rock. As we have seen already in our discussion of Cream's "Sunshine of Your Love" in Chapter 7, adapting blues practices to rock can often result in tracks that can no longer be thought of as blues in the traditional sense. Led Zeppelin's 1969 track "Whole Lotta Love" provides another chance to see this transformation at work and gives a sense of how British blues rock in the early 1970s combined the blues with other elements. While originally credited to Jimmy Page and Robert Plant, the song is actually an adaptation of a Willie Dixon blues number called "You Need Love." (After some legal wrangling over the years, the song is now credited to Dixon and all four members of Led Zeppelin.) While the blues is clearly a central component in "Whole Lotta Love," elements of psychedelia can be found in the song, as well as features that anticipate the rock that followed in the 1970s. The song begins as a simple verse-chorus form, presenting two verse-chorus pairs based on the same music after the brief guitar-riff introduction. A long central section then follows— longer, in fact, than all the music that preceded it. The spacey sounds, stereo effects, and Plant's moaning lend a distinctively psychedelic flavor to this section (which lasts approximately thirty-nine measures), while Page's aggressive guitar solo that follows in the next six measures continues the psychedelic blues-rock virtuosity earlier associated with Eric Clapton and Jimi Hendrix. The song then returns to the verse-chorus pair, presented a third time with only slight alterations. The track ends with a coda, which begins with a free-form Plant vocal phrase (a kind of vocal "cadenza" in which the music stops and Plant provides a solo flourish), followed by a return to the tune's guitar riff and fade-out.

The overall formal structure of "Whole Lotta Love" follows a pattern that became common among rock bands in the 1970s. After two verse-chorus pairs,

LISTENING GUIDE

GET MUSIC ▶▶ wwnorton.com/rockhistory

Led Zeppelin, "Whole Lotta Love"

Words and music by Jimmy Page, Robert Plant, John Paul Jones, John Bonham, and Willie Dixon, produced by Jimmy Page. Released as a single and rose to #4 on the Billboard Pop charts in late 1969. Also released on the album *Led Zeppelin II*, which reached #1 on the Billboard album charts and #1 in the UK in late 1969.

FORM: Compound AABA. The A sections follow simple verse-chorus form, with verse and chorus based on the same musical material. An extended central section forms the B section, leading to a return of the A section and a coda, which begins with a vocal "cadenza" in free time before the riff kicks back in and the song fades out.

TIME SIGNATURE: 4/4.

INSTRUMENTATION: Electric guitars, bass, drums, lead and backup vocals.

	0:00–0:11	**Introduction,** 4 mm.	Begins with guitar alone, playing 2-bar blues-derived riff. Bass joins for the second time through this riff.
A	0:11–0:35	**Verse 1,** 9 mm.	Lead vocal enters, riff continues in guitar and bass. "You need coolin' . . ."

some kind of contrasting section occurs; this section can merely be a guitar, sax, or keyboard solo over the verse material, or it can be a new section. A return to either the verse-chorus pair or only the verse usually concludes this pattern. If the verse-chorus pairs are thought of as A sections and the contrasting section is considered the B section, a large-scale AABA pattern emerges. When an AABA section is made up of verse-chorus components, the term "compound AABA" will be used (reserving "AABA" for the song forms discussed earlier). Considering the blues roots of the tune, the trippy, psychedelic character of the central section, the aggressive guitar virtuosity, and the use of compound AABA form, "Whole Lotta Love" provides a bridge from the 1960s into the 1970s, at once looking forward and backward in the development of rock.

American Blues Rock and Southern Rock

The Allman Brothers Band and Southern Rock. The influence of 1960s British blues rock was not restricted to English bands. Many aspiring young rockers were drawn to electric blues in the '60s, and by the early 1970s that blues influence

	0:35–0:47	**Chorus**, 4 mm.	Drums enter, as backup vocals provide vocal hook. Note sliding guitar effect in call-and-response to vocal. "Got a whole lotta love . . ."
A	0:47–1:10	**Verse 2**, 9 mm.	As before, except that drums now continue from previous section. "You been learnin'. . ."
	1:10–1:21	**Chorus**, 4 mm.	As before, but the fourth bar of the chorus serves as the first bar of the central section that follows.
B	1:21–3:22	**Central Section**, 45 mm.	39 bars of spacey psychedelia. Drums keep a light beat, as guitar sounds and vocal wails move from side to side, amid avant-garde sound effects. An aggressive 6-bar guitar break concludes this section.
A	3:22–3:50	**Verse 3**, 11 mm.	As in verse 2, but extended by 2 bars at the end. "You've been coolin' . . ."
	3:50–4:00	**Chorus**, 4 mm.	As before. "Got a whole lotta love . . ."
	4:00–5:30	**Coda**, 24 mm.	Vocal "cadenza" in free time begins this final section, and then the song's riff returns as Plant improvises vocally and the song fades out.

could be clearly heard in a style that would be called southern rock. During the late 1960s, Nashville-born guitarist Duane Allman became a favorite studio guitarist for Rick Hall at his Fame Studios in Muscle Shoals, adding his blues-drenched playing to the mix in numerous sessions for Hall and Atlantic's Jerry Wexler, including Wilson Pickett's version of the Beatles' "Hey Jude." Through his playing at Muscle Shoals, Allman came to the attention of Phil Walden, who had managed several southern rhythm and blues singers during the 1960s, including Otis Redding. By the end of the decade, Walden was managing Allman and the young guitarist was pulling together former bandmates and other fellow southern musicians to form what would become the Allman Brothers Band. By 1969, Allman had enlisted bassist Berry Oakley, guitarist Dickey Betts, and drummers Jai Johnny Johnson ("Jaimoe") and Butch Trucks; brother Gregg Allman was the last to join, and his blues-influenced vocals and organ playing rounded out the most important band in 1970s southern rock.

Duane Allman of the Allman Brothers, performing at the Fillmore East, New York, 1971. Allman was a gifted studio musician, playing on many important recordings for Jerry Wexler and others in Muscle Shoals, Alabama. The Allman Brothers Band, formed in 1969, were famous for a rhythm and blues–influenced southern rock style and long improvised solos. Live at the Fillmore East *(1971) displays both of these elements.*

The use of the term "southern rock" in the early 1970s is perhaps misleading; it was more the result of writers in the north and on the west coast describing bands from the south than it was a label embraced by the southern musicians themselves. In many ways, the "southern rock" label allowed music-business people to categorize this music for marketing purposes, playing on the almost stereotypical images of the south fostered by the media in the north—images featuring hard-drinking men and women driving pickup trucks with Confederate flags and gun racks in the rear window, for instance.

The Allman Brothers Band indeed drew their influences from the blues and rhythm and blues that they heard growing up in the south, but blending this heritage with rock was also influenced by the British blues rockers of the 1960s, and playing live shows that featured extended improvised solos—something for which the band have become legendary over the years—was part of the San Francisco psychedelic legacy. Like the British blues rockers Led Zeppelin and Deep Purple, the Allman Brothers Band developed and extended ways of blending blues and rock that had begun in the 1960s, and their embrace of both their musical and cultural

heritage would serve as a model for many other southern bands, though some
would come up with their own distinctive blends as well.

The Allman Brothers were important from both a music and a business
standpoint. Phil Walden, who established Capricorn Recording Studios in
Macon, Georgia, eventually signed the band to his Capricorn label, making
Capricorn and Macon central for those groups who followed in the wake of the
Allmans' commercial success during the 1970s. After a modest degree of commercial success on their first two studio albums, the band released a double live
album, *Live at the Fillmore East*, which rose to number thirteen in the United
States during the summer of 1971. The album contains the band's signature
song from their first studio album, the Gregg Allman–penned "Whipping
Post," which is perhaps the best single example of the band's strong blues influences and penchant for extended soloing, and makes for an informative comparison with Led Zeppelin's approach to blues.

Despite the death of Duane Allman in a 1971 motorcycle accident, the
band's next album, *Eat a Peach*, hit number four on the U.S. album charts in
early 1972. Slightly more than a year after Allman's death, Berry Oakley was
also killed in a similar accident. Now depending much more on Betts, the group
also added Lamar Williams on bass and Chuck Leavell on piano. The album
Brothers and Sisters hit number one in the United States (uk42) in the fall of
1973, also yielding a hit single with "Ramblin' Man" (p2); this Dickey Betts track
brings the band's country influences to the fore.
The band enjoyed further success with *Win, Lose,
or Draw* (p5, 1975) before beginning a series of
breakups and reformations that have continued
ever since. Much of the band's music during the
first few years was produced by veteran Atlantic
engineer and producer Tom Dowd, who had
worked on many of the Stax and Muscle Shoals
records released by Atlantic, in addition to much
else that had been released by the label since the
late 1950s.

Lynyrd Skynyrd built on the southern
rock sound set down by the Allman
Brothers but produced catchier, more
radio friendly songs. Skynyrd was very
proud of their southern heritage, evidenced by their hit "Sweet Home
Alabama" and the Confederate flag they
often used on stage (pictured here).

Lynyrd Skynyrd. Among other rock groups
from the south, perhaps the greatest beneficiaries of the Allmans' success were a collection of
slightly younger rockers who named their band
after a high school teacher with whom they had
tangled as students (but changing the name
from Leonard Skinner to Lynyrd Skynyrd); the
band was originally courted by Walden and
Capricorn. Figuring that they might get more
attention from a label that did not already have
a southern rock band, however, Skynyrd signed
with Al Kooper's label, Sounds of the South, based in Atlanta, and released a
series of successful albums, beginning with *Pronouced Leh-nerd Skin-nerd*
(p27, 1973) and peaking with *Street Survivors* (p5 uk13, 1977). Kooper was a

veteran in the recording studio, having played organ on most of the Dylan sessions from 1965 to 1966. Under Kooper's production, Skynyrd's tracks tended to be somewhat more radio-friendly than those of the Allmans, with plenty of guitar and Ronnie Van Zant providing clear lyrical and melodic hooks setting stories of everyday life in the south, such as those found on "Sweet Home Alabama" (p8, 1974), "Saturday Night Special" (p27, 1975), and "What's Your Name?" (p13, 1977). Ever since its release on the live album, *One More from the Road* (p9 uk17, 1976), "Free Bird" has been a staple on rock radio playlists. A tragic plane crash in late 1977 killed Ronnie Van Zant and two other band members—Steve and Cassie Gaines—only days after the release of *Street*

🎧 **LISTENING GUIDE**   **GET MUSIC** ▶▶   wwnorton.com/rockhistory

The Allman Brothers Band, "Whipping Post"

Words and music by Gregg Allman, produced by Adrian Barber. Contained on *The Allman Brothers Band*, which was released in 1969.

FORM: Contrasting verse-chorus. Each verse consists of two 4-bar phrases over the same repeating 2-bar chord progression, followed by a 2-bar buildup to the chorus. Each chorus consists of three 1-bar phrases, followed by a stop-time phrase, and then a bar of instrumental response that echoes the vocal. Note the instrumental interlude that follows the second instrumental verse. It creates a passage that dramatically builds up to the final statement of the chorus, and does so in an almost symphonic manner, using an ascending scale and then stop-time lead-guitar blasts. Note also how the final chord at the end shows some of the band's jazz influences.

TIME SIGNATURE: 12/8, with sections in 11/8 as indicated. In this case, 11/8 can be counted as 1 & uh, 2 & uh, 3 & uh, 4 &, as if it were 12/8 with the last element lopped off. It is also possible to count this song in 6/8, in which case all measure numbers below can simply be doubled and the 11/8 sections would be counted as a measure of 6/8 followed by a measure of 5/8.

INSTRUMENTATION: Two electric guitars, bass, organ, two drummers, and lead vocals.

0:00–0:26	**Introduction**, 8 mm. (in 11/8 time)	This section begins in the bass, adding drums, guitars, and finally organ one by one along the way to provide a gradual buildup that leads to the first verse.
0:26–1:04	**Verse 1**, 10 mm. (in 12/8)	Lead vocal enters, singing two 4-bar phrases, and then a 2-bar phrase that leads to the chorus. "I've been run down . . ."

Survivors, and while this event raised the band's profile and prompted radio stations to begin playing much of the band's older music, the remaining members found it difficult to go on, though the band did eventually regroup some years later.

More Sounds of the South.   Unlike Lynyrd Skynyrd, the Marshall Tucker Band had no reservations about signing with Capricorn. Working with Walden's label, the band placed six albums in the Top 40, including *The Marshall Tucker Band* (p29, 1973) and *Searchin' for a Rainbow* (p15, 1975), before placing two more (with Warner Brothers) on the charts by the end of the decade. Formed in 1971

Time	Section	Description
1:04–1:38	**Chorus**, 9 mm.	Music gets louder and more dramatic, as 1-bar vocal phrase is repeated to lead to stop-time climax. Guitars then echo vocal phrase, and then lead into a 4-bar transition in 11/8 based on the introduction. ". . . Tied to the whipping post . . ."
1:38–2:07	**Instrumental Verse**, 8 mm.	Guitar solo over the first eight bars of the verse.
2:07–2:45	**Verse 2**, 10 mm.	As in verse 1. "My friends tell me . . ."
2:45–3:19	**Chorus**, 9 mm.	As before, once again leading to a guitar solo. ". . . Tied to the whipping post . . ."
3:19–3:49	**Instrumental Verse**, 8 mm.	A second guitar solo, structured just like the first one.
3:49–4:31	**Interlude**, 10 mm.	This instrumental buildup consists of four bars of an ascending scale that leads to four bars of dramatic stop-time. The music then stops, as Allman introduces the 2-bar buildup to the chorus found in the previous verses ("Sometimes I feel"), and this drives headlong into the final statement of the chorus.
4:31–5:18	**Chorus**, 5 mm.	As before, but with more energy and a tremendous sense of arrival. The final echo of the vocal presented previously by the guitars is here replaced with a gentle and mysterious jazz-influenced ending. ". . . Tied to the whipping post . . ."

by brothers Tommy (bass) and Toy Caldwell (guitar)—there is no Marshall Tucker in the group—the band opened for the Allman Brothers early in their careers before establishing themselves as headliners. The band's most successful single was "Heard It in a Love Song" (p14, 1977), which shows more of country influence than blues.

In contrast to the Marshall Tucker Band and Lynyrd Skynyrd, the Charlie Daniels Band is actually named after a member of the band, in this case a guitarist/singer/fiddle player who was a bit older than most of the other southern rock musicians. Daniels had been playing professionally since the late 1950s and had done stints as a studio musician in Nashville during the 1960s, playing on a wide variety of records, including the Dylan sessions in the late '60s. Forming his own band in the early 1970s, Daniels had five Top 40 albums in the years between 1975 and 1982, including *Million Mile Reflections* (p5, 1979) and *Full Moon* (p11, 1980), and enjoyed a number three hit single in the States in 1979, "The Devil Went Down to Georgia," which became his trademark song. Daniels's style is sometimes thought of as more country than rock, though he moved in southern rock circles in the 1970s and as an older musician, and was looked to as a mentor by some members of the other southern rock bands.

In light of the personal and business struggles that beset the Allman Brothers Band and the tragic events surrounding Lynyrd Skynyrd in 1977, it seemed as if southern rock might be over late in the decade, the success of the Marshall Tucker Band and Charlie Daniels notwithstanding. But just as it seemed that the lights were going out in Georgia, a new band called .38 Special updated and carried southern rock into the 1980s with a series of successful records, including *Wild-Eyed Southern Boys* (p18, 1981) and *Strength in Numbers* (p17, 1986). Other bands that are often labeled as southern rock include Wet Willie, the Outlaws, Grinderswitch, and Blackfoot, all of whom had at least some degree of commercial success.

Texas and South of the Border: Santana and ZZ Top.   As we have seen, southern rock refers to bands from the southeast that emerged in the wake of the Allman Brothers' success. But the use of the word "south" in southern rock does not seem to extend west of the Mississippi or south of the border. Nevertheless, the influence of electric blues can be heard clearly in the music of Texas-based ZZ Top and the south-of-the-border-tinged sounds of Santana.

Led by Mexican-born guitarist Carlos Santana and featuring the organ playing and singing of Greg Rolie (who would later form Journey), Santana emerged not from Mexico but from the San Francisco psychedelic scene in 1969, the band's success fueled in part by their performance at Woodstock. *Santana* (p4 uk26, 1969) featured the band's trademark blend of jazz- and blues-influenced improvisation set to the accompaniment of latin rhythms and percussion. "Evil Ways" (p9, 1970), the band's first hit, provides a representative example of the Santana style from the first half of the 1970s. They built on the success of their first album by releasing *Abraxas* (p1 uk7, 1970), which contained "Black Magic Woman" (p4, 1970) and "Oye Como Va" (p13, 1971); *Santana III* (p1 uk6, 1971); and *Caravanserai* (p8 uk6, 1972). If Duane Allman

Led by virtuoso guitarist Carlos Santana (pictured here), Santana took influences from psychedelia (their performance at Woodstock is legendary) and combined them with Latin rhythms and percussion. This unique sound didn't keep the spotlight from shining on Carlos Santana, whose guitar improvisations put him in the same league as Allman, Hendrix, Clapton, Page, and other guitar greats.

was the south's answer to Eric Clapton, Carlos Santana's smooth soulful playing was the Latino response to the electric blues explosion of the 1960s.

Texas-based ZZ Top became a staple of rock radio by the end of the 1970s and enjoyed continued success into the 1980s. In the early 1970s, however, Texas blues was not yet the force it would later become, and guitarist Billy Gibbons, bassist Dusty Hill, and drummer Frank Beard struggled for recognition. While *First Album* (1971) did not chart, *Tres Hombres* fared much better, hitting number eight in the U.S. charts in 1973, while *Fandango!* (p10 uk60, 1975) showed the first signs of international appeal, containing the track "Tush" (p20, 1975), an up-tempo 12-bar blues tune that was likely the first number by ZZ Top many rock listeners heard. While Santana's music is often referred to as "latin rock," and ZZ Top is considered Texas blues, neither is typically thought of as southern rock (much less country rock). Stylistically, however, the music of both bands is similar to that of the southern rock bands, with Santana perhaps most closely paralleling the Allman Brothers in the emphasis on improvisation, while the tighter arrangements in ZZ Top's music are similar to those found in Lynyrd Skynyrd's music. The important central element in all this music is a significant stylistic debt to the electric blues.

What Were Once Vices: Steppenwolf, Three Dog Night, Grand Funk Railroad, Edgar Winter, the Doobie Brothers.   The musical effects of the blues in American rock were not restricted to the south, and many other groups were influenced by the blues as well as rhythm and blues, including Steppenwolf, Grand Funk Railroad, Edgar Winter, and the Doobie Brothers. German-born singer/guitarist John Kay spent time in many of the important musical hot spots of the 1960s. He had visited the folk scene in New York, experienced San Francisco psychedelia, and hung around Los Angeles in the months before Love and the Doors burst on the scene. Together with organist Goldy McJohn and drummer Jerry Edmunton—two musicians he had worked with in Canada— Kay formed Steppenwolf (named after the Hermann Hesse novel) in Los Angeles (the band used a series of guitarists and bassists as well). The band's first album, *Steppenwolf* (p6, 1968) contained the hit single "Born to Be Wild" (p2, 1968), and "Magic Carpet Ride" (p3, 1968) was released on the next album, *Steppenwolf the Second* (p3, 1969). Either single can be taken as representative of Steppenwolf's approach to blues rock: Kay's gruff vocals are supported by driving guitars and drums, with McJohn's distorted organ often coming to the front of the texture. The band continued into the 1970s but disbanded after a special concert played on Valentine's Day in 1972. Three Dog Night were also based in Los Angeles, and early on they were produced by Brian Wilson. The group's blue-eyed soul focused on the song and the vocals, with an AM-friendly approach that made them a kind of late 1960s Righteous Brothers (except that there were three lead singers). The band had a series of hit records, many written by songwriters who would later establish themselves as performers. Successful singles included Harry Nilsson's "One" (p5, 1969), Laura Nyro's "Eli's Coming" (p10, 1969), and Randy Newman's "Mama Told Me (Not to Come)" (p1, 1970). Often overlooked by rock writers, Three Dog Night enjoyed enormous success until their breakup in the mid 1970s.

Hailing from Flint, Michigan, Grand Funk Railroad also had roots in 1960s pop; as members of Terry Knight and the Pack, guitarist/vocalist Mark Farner and drummer/vocalist Don Brewer had a minor hit in 1967 with "I (Who Have Nothing)" (p46). Soon Farner and Brewer brought in bassist Mel Schacher to form Grand Funk Railroad, and Knight managed the new band. The group enjoyed success almost immediately, as *On Time* hit number twenty-seven on the U.S. charts in 1969, and the band went on to place their next nine albums in the Billboard Top 10. Among these, *We're an American Band* (p2, 1973) was the most successful, as the single of the same name went to number one in 1973. The band followed with *Shinin' On* (p5, 1974), which contained a version of Little Eva's 1962 hit "The Loco-Motion" (p1, 1974), as well as the single "Shinin' On" (p11, 1974). The band scored on the singles charts again with the old rhythm and blues number, "Some Kind of Wonderful" (p3, 1975), but that was to be their last taste of strong commercial success. Grand Funk's music is deeply rooted in 1960s soul, and Mark Farner's singing shows these influences at almost every point. Though often ignored by critics, the band's sustained success during the early 1970s made them one of the most popular acts in rock music of the time, though the group did not enjoy similar success in the UK.

Beginning with his band White Trash, keyboardist/saxophonist/vocalist Edgar Winter was an important influence in American blues rock. After the success of the White Trash live album *Roadwork* (p23, 1971), Winter teamed with bassist Dan Hartman, drummer Chuck Ruff, and guitarist Ronnie Montrose to form the Edgar Winter Group. The band's *They Only Come Out at Night* (p3, 1972) contained the instrumental monster hit "Frankenstein" (p1 uk18, 1973), as well as "Free Ride" (p14, 1973). The band followed this success with *Shock Treatment* (p13, 1974), adding guitarist Rick Derringer (who had played in the McCoys as well as White Trash) when Montrose left to form his own band.

Based in San Francisco, the Doobie Brothers hit the album and singles charts at about the same time with a similar blues-rock sound. *Toulouse Street* (p21, 1972) contained the hit "Listen to the Music" (p11, 1972), while *The Captain and Me* (p7, 1973) contained "Long Train Runnin'" (p8, 1973) and "China Grove" (p15, 1973). The band did even better with *What Were Once Vices Are Now Habits* (p4 uk19, 1974), which not only placed on the UK charts but also included the number one single "Black Water." Accompanied by bassist Tiran Porter, drummers Dave Shogren and Michael Hossack, and fellow guitarist Pat Simmons, Tom Johnston's blue-eyed soul singing is much like that of Winter or Farner, and like Steppenwolf, all three bands had a knack for a good pop hook, producing rock that fit nicely into evolving FM radio formats (radio formats and how they changed over the 1970s will be considered in Chapter 9, as will the late 1970s success of the Doobie Brothers after Johnston left the band). The stylistic approaches of Winter, the Doobies, and Grand Funk are very similar, growing out of the combination of heavy rock guitars and drums with vocals strongly influenced by black pop of the 1960s.

Aerosmith, J. Geils Band. In the wake of the success of Edgar Winter, Grand Funk, and the Doobie Brothers, in addition to the success of the British blues-rock bands, two American groups continued the American blues-rock style into the mid and late 1970s. Though their first album, *Aerosmith* (1973), did not chart and the track "Dream On" rose only as high as number fifty-nine in the U.S. charts, Aerosmith's early music would get more attention with subsequent success. The band's second album, *Get Your Wings* (p74, 1974), despite such energetic tracks as "Same Old Song and Dance" and a version of the blues classic "Train Kept a Rollin'," did not chart well. With the success of *Toys in the Attic* (p11, 1975) and the single "Sweet Emotion" (p36, 1975), however, the music from the earlier records saturated American FM radio during 1975 and after. The success of *Rocks* (p3, 1976) and the re-release of "Walk This Way" (p10, 1976) give some idea of how much more popular Aerosmith's music had become. Led by lead singer Steven Tyler and guitarist Joe Perry, Aerosmith were often compared to the Rolling Stones. Tyler was very similar in appearance and stage performance to Mick Jagger, and Perry's stoic tough-guy demeanor paralleled that of Richards.

Another American blues-based rock band, led by guitarist J. Geils and featuring lead vocalist Peter Wolf and harmonica player Magic Dick, became FM radio regulars about a year before Aerosmith. Neither the band's self-titled debut, *The J. Geils Band* (1971), nor their sophomore effort, *The Morning After* (1972), charted, though the track "Looking for a Love" (p33, 1972) did moderately well on the singles chart. Like early Aerosmith albums, *Full House* (p54, 1972) did not chart particularly well initially, though the earlier records were revived with the subsequent success of *Bloodshot* (p10, 1973), which contained the track "Give It to Me" (p30, 1973), and *Nightmares . . . and Other Tales from the Vinyl Jungle* (p26, 1974), which contained "Must of Got Lost" (p12, 1974). Both Aerosmith and the J. Geils Band went on to continued success in the late 1970s and '80s, and the role played by Aerosmith's "Walk This Way" in helping rap cross over to the rock audience in the mid 1980s will be considered in Chapter 11.

Taken together, the American blues rockers from the Allman Brothers to the Doobie Brothers balance their Led Zeppelin– and Deep Purple–led British counterparts, and it is easy to see how both sets of bands could share fans and concert bills. Stylistically, these groups extended the blues rock of the 1960s into the 1970s and forged a mainstream rock style of the first half of the decade that enjoyed tremendous commercial success. Most of these groups subscribed to the hippie aesthetic that developed in the psychedelic era: some bands blended in classical, folk, or country elements; others focused on virtuosic soloing influenced by blues and jazz; and some engaged serious issues in their lyrics. Other bands in the 1970s extended the ideas of psychedelia in very different ways, and for the British progressive rockers, the blues tradition was far less central than the traditions and practices of classical music.

Progressive Rock: Big Ideas and High Ambition

Philosophical Lyrics and Concept Albums. As we saw in Chapter 7, *Sgt. Pepper's Lonely Hearts Club Band* was understood to be a concept album—even though John Lennon insisted his songs had nothing to do with the Sgt. Pepper idea.

And in the wake of *Sgt. Pepper*, many bands on both sides of the Atlantic began releasing concept albums. The idea of turning an album into a self-contained artistic statement was already a few years old by the 1970s, but only after the British progressive rock bands grabbed the idea did it really develop into something of an obsession within rock music. The progressive rock bands also took their cue from *Sgt. Pepper* in lavishing attention on the album covers—indeed, the bizarre covers Hipgnosis did for Pink Floyd and the fantasy landscapes created for Yes by Roger Dean are an integral part of experiencing the music (an impact somewhat lost now due to CD covers' smaller size). These groups also felt an obligation to avoid lyrics dealing with romance or sexual prowess, opting instead to address big philosophical issues such as religion and spirituality, politics and power, the forward march of technology, and existential angst. Some fans devoted to the idea that rock should be a direct form of emotional expression might have been repelled by such ambitious topics (some critics would dismiss progressive rock as pretentious) in the context of the hippie aesthetic, but these elaborately packaged concept albums that were focused on the fate of mankind were clearly an extension of the idea that music should provide a trip. Progressive rockers may have taken themselves and their music very seriously, but the style was a logical development of the increasingly loftier ambitions that rock had adopted over the course of the 1960s.

Designed by the art house Hipgnosis, the cover of Pink Floyd's album Wish You Were Here (1975) is representative of the progressive rock's interest in album art (the U.S. release is pictured here). Like Sgt. Pepper before them, these covers were designed to be part of the listening experience, and many fit with themes in the lyrics that often address big philosophical issues like religion and spirituality, politics, and technology.

The Use of Classical Music with Rock. A primary element of British progressive rock in the 1970s was the clear and self-conscious use of classical music—and in some cases even an attempt to "raise" rock music to the level of classical music. The Beatles were the most obvious source of this practice, though as we saw in Chapter 7, many other psychedelic groups employed elements drawn from classical music. Among the earliest attempts to blend classical music into a concept album is the Moody Blues' *Days of Future Past* (p3 uk27, 1967). The Moody Blues had already scored a hit single with "Go Now" (p10 uk1, 1965) when their label, Decca, asked them to record a rock version of Dvořák's *New World* Symphony as a stereo demonstration record to help them sell stereo units manufactured by the company. Instead the group came up with a song suite, and a professional arranger was brought in to compose the orchestral interludes between tracks, eventually creating the album *Days of Future Past*. The Moody Blues went on to place a string of albums on the charts, including *A Question of*

The Growth of FM Rock Radio

FM is a type of radio broadcast developed in 1933 by Edwin Howard Armstrong. It uses the same radio waves as AM but in a different way: information is transmitted by varying the frequency of the carrier wave, instead of the amplitude of the wave. FM broadcasts have less static and a shorter range than AM, so they are a purely local but higher-quality broadcast.

The development of FM was bitterly contested by the radio industry, despite its obvious virtues. Because broadcasting corporations like RCA had millions of dollars invested in AM radio equipment, programming, and marketing, they had no desire to invest in an expensive new medium just so they could compete with them-

selves. But the tide for FM turned in the 1950s with improvements in home audio equipment, the development of stereo recording and the LP, and the Federal Communication Commission's 1967 order that dual-license owners had to provide original FM programming for at least 50 percent of the broadcast day. Beginning that year, stations moved quickly to differentiate themselves from AM. "Free-form"

or "Progressive" radio was the format that worked best.

Free-form radio was probably first developed at New York's WOR-FM, but Tom Donahue became the most influential proponent of the format when he adopted it at KMPX-FM in San Francisco in the spring of 1967. Thanks to Donahue's success in the Bay Area and subsequently in Los Angeles, the format spread nationwide by 1968. It also was the main format

Tom Donahue, pictured here, was one of rock's most important disc jockeys. At KMPX-FM in San Francisco, Donahue adopted the "free-form" radio format, helping to promote more conceptual, progressive rock music.

for student-run college stations. (Although never widely popular, college radio was a key element in the rise of alternative rock in the 1980s, when commercial stations resisted playing it.)

On progressive radio, DJs programmed their own sets with little or no attention to playlists. They chose songs as they saw fit for musical or other reasons—even for political purposes. As a result, the taste and personality of the particular DJ became the major commercial asset of FM radio. The DJ evolved into a combination music critic, musicologist, counterculture revolutionary, and entertainer. This was primarily demonstrated through the two major innovations of progressive radio: "The rap" and the "segue."

"The rap" refers to the style and content of a DJ's voice. Because of FM's higher fidelity, progressive DJs usually spoke in a more intimate, less affected style. Free-form DJs educated their listeners by rapping (speaking) about musical, political, or social issues. They also used their familiar personalities as a way to bring listeners closer to musicians through broadcast interviews. Free-form DJs

developed a method of stringing songs together by means of a musical, thematic, or historical connection between songs, a device known as a "segue." For instance, two songs might be put together simply because the end of one led well into the beginning of another. Or an entire set might be made out of songs about rain (e.g., Dylan's "It's a Hard Rain [Gonna Fall]," followed by Creedence Clearwater Revival's "Who'll Stop the Rain?" and the Doors' "Riders on the Storm"). After the Beatles' invention of the concept album, progressive DJs sometimes played entire uninterrupted album sides as a single set. By combining their programming choices and their rap, free-form DJs both entertained and enlightened.

Progressive radio was mainly album-based, rather than single-based like Top 40 radio. DJs chose the best songs available, whether they were released as singles or not, and usually the best version of a given song was found on the album. As a

result, progressive radio came to be called "Album-Oriented Radio," or AOR. The mutual influence of radio on rock music and rock music on radio eventually freed both from the two- to four-minute restriction of song length.

Because stylistic variety was not as important as in other fonrmats, AOR DJs led listeners into deeper knowledge of specific styles, musicians, and even songs. At the same time, AOR fragmented FM into an array of stations associated with specific musical styles. Rock stations would play little or no dance music, dance-music stations would play little or no rock, and jazz stations would play little of either. Just as the social fragmentation caused by "urban renewal" programs in the 1970s led to renewed racial segregation in housing, the stylistic fragmentation of AOR led to renewed segregation in music.

Balance (p3 uk1, 1970), *Every Good Boy Deserves Favor* (p2 uk1, 1971), and *Seventh Sojourn* (p1 uk5, 1972). Procol Harum also blended classical music with rock, and their best-known track, "A Whiter Shade of Pale" (p5 uk1, 1967), combines the feel of Percy Sledge's "When a Man Loves a Woman" with a harmonic progression drawn from a cantata by J. S. Bach. Procol Harum also scored a series of moderately successful albums well into the 1970s, including *A Salty Dog* (p32 uk27, 1969), *Procol Harum in Concert* (p5 uk48, 1972), and *Grand Hotel* (p21, 1973).

The Who: Townshend's Big Projects.

Though they are not often thought of as a progressive rock band, the Who were tremendously influential in the development of rock ambition at the end of the 1960s. Made up of guitarist Pete Townshend, vocalist Roger Daltrey, bassist John Entwistle, and drummer Keith Moon, the band were managed by Kit Lambert, whose father, Constant Lambert, was a well-known classical-music composer in Britain. The younger Lambert was well acquainted with the structure of classical music, and he began encouraging Townshend to borrow classical-music ideas for the music the guitarist was writing for the Who. Townshend's first tries were two relatively short pieces, "A Quick One While He's Away" (from *A Quick One* [uk4, 1966]) and "Rael" (from *The Who Sell Out* [uk13, 1968]). These laid the groundwork for Townshend's much larger work, *Tommy* (p4 uk2, 1969). *Tommy* tells the story of a deaf, dumb, and blind boy who gains spiritual enlightenment through playing pinball. When Tommy is cured of his handicaps, he is cast as a guru, possessing the great wisdom of the ages. The story is a parable about the superficiality of much hippie spirituality. When Tommy tells his followers that to gain spiritual insight they will need to renounce smoking pot and drinking, mute their senses, and play pinball, the crowd soundly rejects him. Townshend's message seems to be that most talk of spiritual seeking expects the process to be quick and easy; when it is found to require effort and sacrifice, most of these seekers are no longer interested. Ironically, many of the hippies who were the target of this album never understood its message. Musically, Townshend employs a variety of material that is brought back at important

The Who continued their success throughout the 1970s, with their music growing increasingly complex and conceptual. Guitarist and songwriter Pete Townshend used elements of classical music and opera to create concept albums like Tommy (1969), Who's Next (1971), and Quadrophenia (1973). Here Townshend leaps through the air during a performance of Tommy at the Metropolitan Opera House in New York, June 9, 1970.

moments of the album, just as occurs in much opera. The Who followed up with two more concept albums, *Who's Next* (p4 uk1,1971) and *Quadrophenia* (p2 uk2, 1973). The first of these was actually not the project Townshend began with; this project was called *Lifehouse* and the hope was to merge the band and its listeners through a series of concert experiences that would somehow be captured on record. When this didn't work out, the band took much of the music and made *Who's Next* out of it. With *Quadrophenia*, Townshend returns to his mod past, crafting a story about a young mod seeking meaning in his life. The Who had continued success throughout the remainder of the 1970s, though they moved away from big projects. Over the years since, Townshend has returned to a number of the projects he had left incomplete during the first half of the 1970s.

In the Beginning: King Crimson, Emerson, Lake & Palmer.

As influential as the Beatles, the Moody Blues, Procol Harum, and the Who were on 1970s progressive rock, the album that set the template for the style was King Crimson's *In the Court of the Crimson King* (p28 uk5, 1969). Led by guitarist Robert Fripp and including Greg Lake on bass and vocals, Michael Giles on drums, and Ian McDonald on keyboards and woodwinds, King Crimson blended the harder, more dissonant aspects of twentieth-century music and the softer and more consonant elements of nineteenth-century classical music into a rock context, with a modern jazz influence added in as well. The album opens with "21st Century Schizoid Man," a track that features Lake belting out the vocals in the aggressive manner similar to much of John Lennon's singing with the Beatles in the late 1960s, and a virtuosic middle section filled with odd rhythmic syncopations and angular melodic riffs. The group endured a number of personnel changes, though the lineup that settled in for several albums in the early 1970s, featuring Fripp with drummer Bill Bruford, bassist/vocalist John Wetton, and violinist David Cross, produced some of the band's finest music, including *Larks' Tongues in Aspic* (p61 uk20, 1973) and *Red* (p66 uk45, 1974).

While King Crimson were influential, they enjoyed far less commercial success than the bands centered on multi-keyboardist Keith Emerson. As early as 1967, Emerson was well known on the London scene as a member of the Nice, a band that enjoyed two hit albums in Britain, *The Nice* (uk3, 1969) and *Five Bridges Suite* (uk2, 1970). During his time with the Nice, Emerson built a reputation for virtuosic playing, as well as for destroying (or seeming to destroy) keyboards during shows—clearly an idea he got from Hendrix (the Nice toured with the Jimi Hendrix Experience in the late '60s). Emerson also became known for his clever adaptations of classical-music favorites for rock band. While touring the United States on the same bill with King Crimson during late 1969, Emerson and Lake decided to form their own band together, drawing in Carl Palmer, who had played drums with Arthur Brown. Together Emerson, Lake & Palmer ("ELP") picked up where the Nice had left off and the new band's self-titled debut album rose to number 4 in the UK (p18) in 1970. For their second album as ELP, the band considered releasing a double album made up of one record of original material and a second containing a live performance of their version of Mussorgsky's piano suite, *Pictures at an*

Exhibition. The dual-release plan was scrapped and the albums were released separately as *Tarkus* (p9 uk1, 1971) and *Pictures at an Exhibition* (p10 uk3, 1971). These two records capture well the two key characteristics of ELP's approach to progressive rock. The original music on *Tarkus* features long tracks that alternate lyrical songs with Emerson's versatile keyboard playing on organ, piano, and synthesizer. *Pictures* provides a representative instance of how the band could rework classical music, dropping some parts and adding newly composed ones, to produce a new work in its own right. The band followed up with *Trilogy* (p5 uk2, 1972) and *Brain Salad Surgery* (p11 uk2, 1973) and continued to be one of the most successful bands of the 1970s.

Hippie Spirituality: Jethro Tull, Yes.

Tommy had touched on the role of spirituality in hippie culture, setting the stage for subsequent bands to engage such issues. Jethro Tull and Yes both focused their most ambitious work on religious institutions and traditions. Unlike most of the other progressive rock bands, Jethro Tull began as a blues band. On early albums such as *Stand Up* (p20 uk1, 1969), group leader Ian Anderson plays more harmonica than his trademark flute (in addition to singing lead vocals). By the beginning of the 1970s, however, Anderson became increasingly focused on issues of religion and spirituality, and like Townshend, was highly suspicious of religious and political institutions. The first album to express these kinds of ideas is *Aqualung* (p7 uk4, 1971), which is part a condemnation of society's treatment of the poor and part a bitter indictment of the Church of England. The band's next album, *Thick as a Brick* (p1 uk5, 1972), is an attack on bourgeois values (including religion), setting a poem by "Little Milton" (a fictitious character created by the band), while *A Passion Play* (p1 uk13, 1973) takes on the topic of life after death and reincarnation. While *Aqualung* is divided into separate tracks, both of the other albums are divided only by the obligatory break required to turn the record over and are thus essentially single tracks of about forty minutes' length. The band's personnel shifted over the decade, though the lineup consisting of Anderson, Martin Barre (guitar), John Evans (keyboards), Barrie Barlow (drums), and Jeffrey Hammond played on most of the more conceptual albums.

Keyboardist for Yes, Rick Wakeman, in concert. Yes's music was known for the strong playing of Wakeman (notice the many stacked keyboards here), guitarist Steve Howe, drummer Bill Bruford, and bassist Chris Squire. The band's progressive themes centered around issues of spirituality, especially those picked up from Eastern religion. These were placed in music that used complex formal structures, often taken from classical music.

Led by vocalist Jon Anderson (no relation to Ian), Yes's music was also concerned with issues of spirituality inspired by the hippie mélange of Eastern religious ideas. Though the group had released three albums previously, *Fragile* (p4 uk7,

1971) marks the first album by the band's definitive lineup, consisting of Anderson with guitarist Steve Howe, bassist Chris Squire, drummer Bill Bruford, and flamboyant multi-keyboardist Rick Wakeman. All of the progressive rock bands depended on the instrumental prowess of their members, but Yes were perhaps the most accomplished all around, with Howe, Squire, Wakeman, and Bruford consistently winning awards for their playing in music-magazine polls on both sides of the Atlantic. While spiritual themes can be found on *Fragile*, with *Close to the Edge* (p3 uk4, 1972) they are much more obvious. Based in part on Hermann Hesse's novel *Siddhartha*, the eighteen-minute title track is inspired by the quest for spiritual wisdom with very little of the caustic critique found in Jethro Tull. (If any band from the 1970s perfectly captures the naïve and hopeful innocence of psychedelia, Yes is that group.) The band's follow-up, *Tales from Topographic Oceans* (p6 uk1, 1973), is inspired by Eastern scripture (drawn from a footnote in Paramahansa Yogananda's *Autobiography of a Yogi*, a favorite hippie book of the time) and consists of four tracks on two albums. After the release of *Tales*, Wakeman left to pursue a solo career and the band drafted Swiss keyboardist Patrick Moraz for *Relayer* (p5 uk4, 1974), the epic track of which ("The Gates of Delirium") is inspired by Tolstoy's *War and Peace*. The band's heady blend of instrumental virtuosity and spiritual subject matter proved to be a fan-winning combination; together with ELP and Jethro Tull, Yes was among the top bands in rock music during the first half of the 1970s in terms of commercial success.

Symphonic Expansion.   Most progressive rock bands were eager to integrate classical-music influences into their music to create longer, more intricate arrangements, but the elements in these more symphonically styled rock tracks are drawn from common pop-music forms. Yes's "Roundabout" provides a representative illustration of how a long track—it runs to almost nine minutes—can be constructed out of shorter, more familiar components. The piece uses the same compound AABA form that we saw in Led Zeppelin's "Whole Lotta Love." With "Roundabout," however, the A sections are made up of verse-bridge combinations, rather than verse-chorus as in the Led Zeppelin track. After a classical guitar introduction played in a rhythmically free manner—musicians call this "rubato"—the track launches into the first A section, made up of two verses and a bridge. Next follows the second A section, made up of a single verse and a bridge. The central B section is made up of a large, fifty-two–bar middle section, followed by a return to material drawn from the introduction and bridge during the quiet section at 4:57–5:50. The B section ends with alternating organ and guitar solos, all played over material drawn from the bridge. After a return to a verse-chorus pair for the last A section, the track concludes with a coda, ending with a distinctive passage on the guitar drawn from the end of the introduction.

"Roundabout" is a complex piece of music, filled with many interesting musical features that show classical-music influences. Notice, for instance, how a melodic line drawn from the opening guitar introduction returns during the transition to the second A and B sections. The idea of reusing melodic material in new ways is a central feature of much classical music, and many more such connections can be found in "Roundabout." The piece also incorporates a number of interesting rhythmic features. Notice how the bridge sections cannot be counted according to a simple four-beat pattern. If you begin counting at 1:45, you will need to count 1234 1234 1234 12, and then 1234 1234 1234 12, etc. In the

---

LISTENING GUIDE GET MUSIC ▶▶| wwnorton.com/rockhistory

Yes, "Roundabout"

Words and music by Jon Anderson and Steve Howe, produced by Yes and Eddie Offord. Reached #13 on the Billboard Pop charts in early 1972. Contained on the album *Fragile*, which reached #7 in the UK and #4 on the Billboard Album charts.

FORM: Compound AABA form. The A sections consist of verse and bridge sections, but no chorus. The B section falls into three parts: new verses based on a repeating riff, a return of the introduction and bridge section, and a series of solos in the organ and guitar. Note how the return of the introduction (marked by asterisks) re-starts the song—a practice we noted in Hendrix's "Purple Haze" and a formal strategy that became common in the 1970s, especially in longer and more complicated songs.

TIME SIGNATURE: Mostly in 4/4, with measures of 2/4 and 3/4 occurring along the way.

INSTRUMENTATION: Acoustic and electric guitars, bass, organ, piano, synthesizer, mellotron, drums, percussion, lead and backup vocals.

*	0:00–0:44	**Introduction**	Rubato, acoustic guitar free rhythm, punctuated by tape effect created by playing tape-recorded grand-piano bass notes backward.
A	0:44–1:18	**Verse 1**, 20 mm.	Entire band plays 8 bars to prepare for the entrance of the lead vocals, which then present a 2-bar verse. "I'll be the roundabout . . ."
	1:18–1:45	**Verse 2**, 16 mm.	4 bars now prepare the return of the vocals, which present the 12-bar verse as before, but with backup vocals added and leading to the bridge. "The music dance . . ."
	1:45–2:15	**Bridge**, 18 mm.	Starts with guitar, high hat, and vocal only, then organ and finally bass enter. "In and around the lake . . ."
A	2:15–2:49	**Verse 3**, 20 mm.	8 bars prepare vocal return, then the 12 mm. verse as before with slight changes in instrumentation. Note the use of synthesizer here,

coda beginning at 7:53, you must count 1234 1234 and then 1234 123 1234 123, and so on. This kind of rhythmic patterning (called "changing meter") is standard in much twentieth-century classical music and some jazz, but is not often a feature in 1950s and '60s rock (the Beatles' "All You Need Is Love" is a notable

			as well as the new fast melodic figure that occurs just before the singing returns. "I will remember . . ."
	2:49–3:25	**Bridge**, 21 mm.	As before, but without staggered entrance in bass and drums and new backup vocal part. Fast melodic figure returns to create transition to middle section. "In and around the lake . . ."
B	3:25–4:57	**Middle Section**, 50 mm.	Twelve times through a 4-bar phrase based on a riff in the bass and guitar. Choral vocals present melody, with some instrumental interludes along the way. The end of the section re-introduces the verse melody to transition back to the introduction. "Along the drifting cloud . . ."
*	4:57–5:50	**Reprise of Introduction and bridge**	Rubato during intro and then 9 bars that reinterpret the music from the bridge. "In and around the lake . . ."
	5:50–7:05	**Instrumental solos**, 45 mm.	The organ and guitar alternate solos based on music drawn from the bridge. An ascending scale passage creates a transition to the return of the verse.
A	7:05–7:26	**Verse 4**, 12 mm.	The verse returns varied somewhat, but using the lyrics from verse 1. "I'll be the roundabout . . ."
	7:26–7:53	**Bridge**, 17 mm.	This is the fullest presentation of the bridge so far, leading directly into the coda. "In and around the lake . . ."
	7:53–8:30	**Coda**, 20 mm.	Layered harmony vocals over a strummed acoustic guitar, as the song ends with a guitar phrase drawn from the end of the introduction.

exception—try it using three- and four-beat counting). We also saw a similar use of changing meter in the Allman Brothers' "Whipping Post."

With its formal patterning drawn from simpler pop forms and its manipulation of melodic and rhythmic material drawn from classical music, "Roundabout" provides a good illustration of how progressive rock depends on both pop and classical traditions. While formal patterns within progressive rock vary considerably, the pattern found in "Roundabout" recurs regularly (though with some variation) in Yes's music from the 1970s. The Listening Guide also shows that the track falls into two big parts, marked by the classical guitar introduction and its return at 4:57 (shown by asterisks). This division does not line up with the AABA one, revealing a formal structure that is operating at two levels at least, another feature of classical music.

Bizarre Tales and Progressive-rock Theater: Genesis and Pink Floyd.

By the middle of the 1980s, Genesis, Phil Collins, Peter Gabriel, and Mike + the Mechanics would constitute a small empire in rock music, selling millions of records and dominating the charts and FM airwaves. But in the first half of the 1970s, Gabriel was singing with Genesis, as Collins sang backup and played drums, with Michael Rutherford on bass, Steve Hackett on guitar, and Tony Banks on keyboards. The band members were focused on lengthy, carefully worked out arrangements, as Gabriel spun bizarre tales, most of which delivered stinging, if sometimes obscure, criticisms of British life and values. While the band members sat on-stage, absorbed in their playing, Gabriel began acting these stories out, using costumes and props to develop a new kind of rock theater, extending the rock-opera ambitions of *Tommy*. An early instance of this new approach to rock stagemanship is live performances of "The Musical Box" from *Nursery Cryme* (1971), in which Gabriel donned a mask to help him act out the role of a reincarnated spirit that has aged seventy or more years but built up decades of unsatisfied sexual longing. On *Foxtrot* (uk12, 1972), the feature track is the twenty-minute "Supper's Ready"; playing the role of the returning Messiah at the end of the performance of this number, Gabriel was lifted from the stage via wires to increase the effect of divine presence. In *The Lamb Lies Down on Broadway* (p41 uk10, 1974), much as in Jethro Tull's *A Passion Play*, we follow the main character, Rael (remember the Who piece mentioned above), as he makes his way in the land after death and before rebirth. Gabriel's costumes for performances of *The Lamb* became so elaborate that he sometimes found it difficult to hold the microphone close enough to his mouth to sing.

Gabriel's penchant for the bizarre is paralleled by Roger Waters's fascination with madness that can be found on many Pink Floyd albums from the 1970s. After their success on the London psychedelic scene late in the 1960s, Pink Floyd—featuring Waters on bass and vocals, Rick Wright on keyboards, Nick Mason on drums, and guitarist David Gilmour replacing Syd Barrett—scored a series of successful albums in the UK, including *Ummagumma* (uk5, 1969), *Atom Heart Mother* (uk1, 1970), and *Meddle* (uk3, 1971). True to the psychedelic ethos, these albums were markedly experimental, depending more on interesting electronic timbres than on instrumental virtuosity. *The Dark Side of the Moon* (pi uk2, 1973) firmly established the band in the United States: the album was enormously successful and many of its tracks have been staples of FM rock radio since its release. Barrett had been forced to leave the group in the late 1960s by the onset of mental illness and Waters seemed obsessed with this, as well as with the death of his own father during World War II. Most Pink Floyd lyrics can be traced to these two themes: *Wish You Were Here* (pi uk1, 1975), for instance, directly deals with Barrett's madness, especially in the track "Shine On You Crazy Diamond." While Genesis made Peter Gabriel the focus of the live show, Pink Floyd chose to extend the idea of the psychedelic light to include a variety of elaborate stage effects, such as a crashing airplane and a flying pig. The tour for the band's two-record concept album *The Wall* (pi uk3, 1979) featured a stage show that was so complex hardly a second of it was left to chance.

Providing impressive lighting and prop effects during performances was a part of almost all progressive rock shows, though, as we have seen, some bands took this idea farther than others. The notion that rock musicians can be virtuoso performers is a characteristic not only derived from Hendrix and Clapton, but also a stylistic component that links progressive rock with jazz rock in the 1970s. Concept albums and rock operas developed first in the late 1960s, as did the notion of addressing important and serious-minded issues. In all these ways, progressive rock in the 1970s extends and refines tendencies found in psychedelic music, while also having roots that extend as far back as the playlets of Leiber and Stoller. In many ways, progressive rock is the style of music in the 1970s that remains most faithful to the hippie aesthetic. Because of this, it was the prime target against which punk rebelled later in the decade (more about that in Chapter 10). For now we'll turn our attention back to the United States: while the British progressive rock bands were blending classical-music ideas with rock, American musicians were mixing rock with jazz to develop a new kind of music-stylistic fusion.

Jazz-Rock Fusion and Jazz-Influenced Rock

Jazz and the Studio Musician. As rock musicians became increasingly ambitious about their music, they also became increasingly concerned with achieving technical mastery on their instruments. In the late 1960s, Clapton and Hendrix challenged the boundaries of rock in the extended improvisations that were a central component of their live shows. As we have just learned, progressive rock musicians in the 1970s looked chiefly to classical music as a model for technical virtuosity. But jazz also provided a model that many other musicians embraced. For decades, jazz had been revered for the musical prowess of its players, with artists such as Charlie Parker, Dizzy Gillespie, John Coltrane, and Art Tatum setting very high standards for music-technical and aesthetic achievement. Jazz is essentially a soloist's music, and the focus placed on solos in jazz encourages players to develop their improvisatory skills to the highest degree possible. As solos assumed a more central role in rock music, it was natural that many players would look to jazz as a source for new ideas. Jazz players had been involved in popular music for years; in addition to playing clubs by night, many jazz

Miles Davis (pictured here) was the most influential artist of the jazz-rock style. Though Davis was a key player in jazz from the late '40s through the '60s, in the late '60s and early '70s his influences included Jimi Hendrix, James Brown, and Sly and the Family Stone. Davis's album Bitches Brew (1970) influenced many in jazz-rock fusion and included many artists who would go on to form important fusion groups, including Chick Corea (pictured in the background on keyboards) of Return to Forever, John McLaughlin of the Mahavishnu Orchestra, and Joseph Zawinul and Wayne Shorter of Weather Report.

musicians also made a living playing pop recording sessions by day. The Funk Brothers who played the Motown sessions, for instance, were all gifted and experienced jazz players, as were Los Angeles studio musicians like guitarist Barney Kessel, who played on everything from Phil Spector records to those by the Monkees. In the 1970s, the "studio musician" came to stand for the idea of a player who was fluent in all styles, could read music well, and could be counted on to play expertly in any musical situation. Jazz-schooled players such as drummer Steve Gadd, bassist Tony Levin, or guitarists Lee Ritenour and Larry Carlton played on many records and their high level of professionalism served as a model for many aspiring rock musicians.

Jazz-Rock Fusion: Miles and Beyond. As some rock musicians were beginning to look to jazz, some jazz musicians were also looking into where rock was headed at the end of the 1960s. Trumpeter Miles Davis, who had played with many of the jazz greats since the 1940s and was already one of the most important figures in the style, began noticing that the extended jams of Cream and Hendrix were not all that different from what a lot of jazz players were doing. What impressed Davis most, however, was that rock audiences would sit and listen to this kind of music. Jazz audiences were much smaller than those that assembled for even a moderately well attended rock show, and Davis decided that he would love to play for festival-sized crowds. Davis pulled together a cast of jazz musicians that he thought might be able to fuse rock with jazz, including guitarist John McLaughlin, keyboardists Joseph Zawinul, Chick Corea, and Herbie Hancock, and saxophonist Wayne Shorter. The resultant double album, *Bitches Brew*, rose to number thirty-five on the U.S. album charts in the summer of 1970, and introduced rock audiences to jazz-rock fusion.

In the years following the success of *Bitches Brew*, and in the wake of the rising appreciation for technical virtuosity triggered by the progressive rock bands, members of Davis's band formed their own groups and enjoyed a similar level of commercial success. John McLaughlin formed the Mahavishnu Orchestra, bringing rock, jazz, and Eastern mysticism together in the debut album *Inner Mounting Flame* (1972) and subsequently enjoyed chart success with *Birds of Fire* (p15 uk20, 1973). Herbie Hancock hit with *Headhunters* (p13) in 1974, while Chick Corea's band, Return to Forever, appeared on the album charts several times, with *Romantic Warrior* (p35, 1976) owing the clearest debt to progressive rock. Shorter and Zawinul formed Weather Report and scored later in the decade with *Heavy Weather* (p30 uk43, 1977). Violinist Jean-Luc Ponty left McLaughlin's band to pursue a solo career and did well; his *Enigmatic Ocean* (p35, 1977) is a representative example of jazz-rock fusion in the second half of the 1970s. Former Yardbird Jeff Beck also turned to jazz; his *Blow by Blow* of 1975 climbed to number four on the American charts. In Britain, Soft Machine emerged from the 1960s to establish an English branch of fusion, releasing several albums during the 1970s. Brand X (including Genesis drummer and now front man Phil Collins) enjoyed moderate success in the UK; *Moroccan Roll* (uk37, 1977) provides a good instance of their approach, which parallels rather closely that of Return to Forever and Jean-Luc Ponty from about the same time. Not since the days of the big bands had so much instrumental music enjoyed such commercial success. Taken together the fusion bands were only moderately successful in pop terms, but compared with usual jazz sales and audiences they were enormously successful.

Frank Zappa: Satire and Complexity. Few artists in the history of rock have flourished for decades on the fringes of the popular-music business, but among those Frank Zappa is easily the foremost example. Beginning with the Mothers of Invention's *Freak Out!* (1966), for thirty years Zappa's music blended compositional sophistication, musical virtuosity, and satire that at times pressed the bounds of good taste. Zappa's penchant for often cynical satire can be seen in the 1968 album sending up *Sgt. Pepper* called *We're Only in It for the Money* (p30 uk32). Zappa, with the support of a long line of band members, would chalk up eight more Top 40 albums in the United States; his most successful album in

Featuring Walter Becker (bass/guitar, second from left) and Donald Fagen (vocals/piano, right), Steely Dan used jazz elements and virtuoso studio musicians to create a winning jazz-rock sound. Every one of their seven albums in the 1970s charted in the Billboard Top 40. Though they did perform concerts, Steely Dan focused their attention on the studio, where they wrote carefully organized arrangements, punctuating them with improvised solo sections.

the UK was *Hot Rats* (uk9), while in the States, *Apostrophe* (p10, 1974) made the strongest showing. "I'm the Slime" from *Overnite Sensation* (p32, 1973) provides a representative example of Zappa's blend of jazz-fusion style playing with his cartoonish vocals and satirical lyrics that offer a bitter critique of television. Though Zappa clearly took his music-making seriously, he was vigilant in deflating any effort to interpret his music in terms of the usual categories, insisting that he didn't care whether it was "commercial," "artistic," or "relevant." Zappa also composed a number of pieces for small and large ensembles (or adapted pieces written for rock band) that are best classified as twentieth-century classical music, despite titles such as "Mo and Herb's Vacation."

Low Sparks and Pretzel Logic: *Traffic* and *Steely Dan*.

Perhaps the jazz-rock band with the clearest ties to the psychedelic era is Traffic, a British band that flourished in the 1970s in a style dominated by American acts. After their breakup following their success in the late 1960s, Steve Winwood (keyboards/vocals), Jim Capaldi (drums), and Chris Wood (flute and sax) teamed up again to release *John Barleycorn Must Die* (p11 uk5, 1970). Soon Capaldi left and with drummer Jim Gordon, bassist Rick Grech, and percussionist Reebop Kwaku-Baah, the band released their signature album of the 1970s, *The Low Spark of High-Heeled Boys* (p7, 1971). The title track to that album provides a good example of how Traffic blended Winwood's bluesy vocals with Wood's Coltrane-inspired sax soloing. After more personnel changes, the band went on to release more successful albums, including *Shoot Out at the Fantasy Factory* (p6, 1973) and *When the Eagle Flies* (p9 uk31, 1974). Winwood left the band in 1975 to embark on what would prove to be a successful solo career.

Back in the States, Steely Dan emerged in 1972 with the debut album *Can't Buy a Thrill* (p17, 1972), which contained two hits, "Do It Again" (p6, 1972) and "Reelin' in the Years" (p11, 1972), both sung by David Palmer. Led by keyboardist/vocalist Donald Fagen and bassist/guitarist Walter Becker, the band initially contained a lineup of talented musicians, including guitarist Jeff "Skunk" Baxter. But after the first album Palmer was gone, Fagen took over lead vocals, and soon Becker and Fagen began using the best studio musicians in New York and Los Angeles to provide the instrumental tracks and virtuosic solos. Perhaps the best album showing this arrangement at work is *Aja* (p3 uk5, 1977), which included three hit singles: "Peg" (p11, 1977), "Deacon Blues" (p19, 1978), and "Josie" (p26, 1978). Steely Dan arrangements, like those of Zappa and other jazz rockers, were often completely written out before recording began. Solos, however, were left open and became showcases for the pros the duo hired to play on particular tracks. "Peg" provides a good example of this, as the horns and rhythm section play mostly worked-out parts while Lee Ritenour's guitar solo was improvised live in the studio. As both a band and as a duo using studio players, Steely Dan placed all seven of their albums from the 1970s in the American Top 40, in addition to scoring ten Top 40 singles.

Horn Bands: *Blood, Sweat, & Tears*, *Chicago*.

The jazz rock of Miles Davis, Frank Zappa, Traffic, and Steely Dan often relies on horns to provide a jazz element, but two bands are most often thought of as jazz-rock "horn bands":

Blood, Sweat, & Tears, and Chicago. After playing sessions with Bob Dylan but before producing Lynyrd Skynryd, keyboardist Al Kooper formed Blood, Sweat, & Tears, releasing *Child Is Father to the Man*, which hit number forty in the UK in 1968. Kooper soon left the band and teamed with guitarists Michael Bloomfield and Stephen Stills to record *Super Session* (p12, 1968). With Kooper's departure from Blood, Sweat, & Tears, singer David Clayton-Thomas joined and the group enjoyed enormous success with its next album, *Blood, Sweat, & Tears* (p1 uk15, 1969), which contained three hit singles—"You've Made Me So Very Happy" (p2 uk35, 1969), "Spinning Wheel" (p2, 1969), and "And When I Die" (p2, 1969)—in addition to winning a Grammy Award. The follow-up *Blood, Sweat, & Tears 3* (p1 uk14, 1970) contained Goffin and King's "Hi-De-Ho" (p14, 1970) and Clayton-Thomas's own "Lucretia MacEvil" (p29, 1970). Blood, Sweat, & Tears' use of a small horn section was certainly nothing new in the history of rhythm and blues or pop: Stax and Motown arrangements often used horns to "sweeten" the accompaniment. Blood, Sweat, & Tears made the horns more central to the arrangements, however, even providing instrumental showcases for both solo and ensemble playing that are influenced by the big-band tradition in jazz. An example of this can be found on the group's arrangement of the Rolling Stones' "Sympathy for the Devil," which Blood, Sweat, & Tears title "Sympathy for the Devil/Symphony for the Devil." Similar to the Vanilla Fudge symphonic-psychedelic cover version discussed in Chapter 7, Blood, Sweat, & Tears create an almost eight-minute epic out of the Stones tune, including long instrumental passages that employ both jazz and avant-garde classical-musical practices.

Another band to place increased focus on their horn section was Chicago. Beginning with their debut album, *Chicago Transit Authority* (p17 uk9, 1969), the band released thirteen Top 40 albums in the United States during the 1970s (five in the UK) and five of these went to number one. The band also scored twenty-two Top 40 singles (three in the UK) with its blend of melodic pop vocals and sophisticated horn-dominated accompaniments. "If You Leave Me Now" rose to number one in both the U.S. and UK charts in 1976; it features the Paul McCartney-esque singing of bassist Peter Cetera and is a good example of the band's softer side. The track "Does Anybody Really Know What Time It Is?" (p7, 1970) from the first album features singing of keyboardist Robert Lamm and shows how the band blended Beatles-influenced pop with horn arrangements influenced by jazz. The track begins with an instrumental introduction focusing at first on rhythmic ensemble playing and then breaking into a brief trumpet solo from Lee Loughnane. The horns then retreat to the accompaniment as Lamm delivers verses and chorus, supported by Beatle-esque backup vocals. A final flourish at the end is provided by a jazzy trombone lick courtesy of James Pankow.

As popular as jazz rock was during the 1970s, it was also the source of enormous controversy within the jazz community, especially later in the decade. Some jazz musicians and fans welcomed the blending of rock and jazz elements, but many jazz traditionalists hated it, labeling it a sell-out to the pop-music industry. Rock purists rejected the music because it seemed too concerned with instrumental virtuosity and lacked the visceral punch that they felt rock should always deliver. In a parallel manner, the same rock purists rejected progressive rock as too complex and full of itself, while most classical-music listeners found it too pop-oriented to be taken seriously. Jazz rock and progressive rock found themselves in a similar kind of in-between situation with some listeners—"neither fish nor fowl" stylistically speaking. The psyche-delic approach was to blend styles freely and delight in the new combinations; and since the first half of the 1970s was dominated by the hippie aesthetic, most rock listeners and critics embraced jazz rock and progressive rock as an extension of hippie musical values. But as the decade neared its end, jazz rock would join progressive rock as one of the targets of punk rebellion.

Glam Rock and Rock Theater: Shocking Characters

Dressing Up and Acting Out. In our discussion of Genesis, we touched on Peter Gabriel's use of costumes, makeup, and props in performance and linked this to Pink Floyd's growing fascination with providing a highly visual stage show. As the 1970s arrived, big rock shows were mostly staged in arenas and stadiums rather than theaters and ballrooms, as they had been in the late 1960s, and this led to a growth in production standards across the rock-music industry; increasingly, audiences expected a show with professional stage lights and some kind of special effects. Thus, Genesis and Pink Floyd are two bands that stand out in the context of many bands that offered elaborate extra-musical excitement. Amid this new attention to the more theatrical elements of rock performance, it was perhaps inevitable that certain artists would come to spe-cialize in acting out the role of a fictional character onstage. The two most important figures in this regard during the 1970s are Alice Cooper and David Bowie. Cooper and Bowie each adopted a distinct on-stage persona that audi-ences understood (mostly) was a character they were portraying. The roots of this practice in rock go back to the Beatles and the Doors. The "concept" of the *Sgt. Pepper* album was that the Beatles were portraying the Lonely Hearts Club Band. On Doors albums and in performance, Jim Morrison had adopted the role of the Lizard King. With the growth of the theatrical side of the rock-concert business in the 1970s, it became possible to put on and tour a sophisti-cated show with elaborate props and effects—a kind of rock theater with increasingly higher production values.

Alice Cooper: Welcome to My Nightmare. It is perhaps a measure of how far hippie androgyny had developed by the early 1970s that a band of hard-drinking, tough-looking rock and rollers could have a front man whose name was Alice. But on stage, Vincent Furnier became Alice Cooper and led his audi-ences into the darkest parts of the imagination, often ending the show in some gruesome way: on different tours, Cooper was hanged, executed in an electric chair, and beheaded by a guillotine. Cooper's obsession with such ghoulish top-ics was influenced by his admiration for Jim Morrison, who befriended the young Cooper in the late 1960s. After two commercially unsuccessful records produced by Frank Zappa and released on Zappa's label, Cooper and his band released *Love It to Death* (p35, 1971), which contained the single "I'm Eighteen" (p21, 1971), an almost gothic study in teenage depression and anger. Bob Ezrin (who would later produce *The Wall*) produced this album and continued to work with the group. The band, made up of guitarists Glen Buxton and Michael Bruce, drummer Neal Smith, and bassist Dennis Dunaway, remained intact, and Cooper enjoyed rising success with the release of *Killer* (p21 uk27, 1971), which featured the semi-autobiographical "Be My Lover" (p47, 1972); *School's Out* (p2 uk4,1972); which contained the single "School's Out" (p7 uk1, 1972), and *Billion Dollar Babies*, which hit number one on both sides of the Atlantic in 1973. With Cooper and Bruce doing most of the writing and Ezrin producing, the band's often dramatic music had just enough self-satire in it to keep things from getting too heavy. "Be My Lover" provides a clear instance of this, as Cooper and the band go into the kind of bump-and-grind ending more often found in strip clubs than on rock stages, prefaced by Cooper's spoken "oh," done in a manner made famous by movie sex goddess Mae West. By the middle of the decade the original Alice Cooper Band had split up, as Cooper went solo, enjoying more success with *Welcome to My Nightmare* (p5 uk19, 1975). By this time, however, Cooper had traded in the shock value found in his earlier music for a cartoonish and campy approach far removed from the music of the Doors.

Kiss and Make Up.   While Cooper's music over the first half of the 1970s started in Morrisonesque psychodrama and ended in horror-movie campiness, Kiss's music began from a cartoonish approach to rock theater. Rather than only the lead singer donning makeup and costumes, all four member of Kiss—bassist Gene Simmons, drummer Peter Criss, and guitarists Paul Stanley and Ace Frehley—cast themselves as distinct characters onstage, with elaborate face makeup that for years kept their countenances secret. From the beginning, the idea of the band was to provide a bombastic live show, using lights, flames, and explosions to create a high-energy rock spectacle. The first few albums—*Kiss* (p87, 1974), *Hotter Than Hell* (p100, 1974), and *Dressed to Kill* (p32, 1975)—did not do particularly well. The band then released a live version of "Rock and Roll All Nite," which went to number twelve in the United States (1975) and prepared the way for the success of *Destroyer* (p1 uk22, 1976). The live album *Alive* (p9 uk49, 1976) contained songs from the band's earlier albums, which now began to sell and get increased playing time on

Alice Cooper (kneeling, center) acts out a ghoulish drama on stage. Cooper was strongly influenced by Jim Morrison's darker outlook on life, one that Cooper combined with Peter Gabriel and Pink Floyd's sense of theater and musical heaviness (note the double bass drums behind Cooper).

rock radio. By the end of the decade, Kiss had masterfully exploited the marketing opportunities provided by their success, starring in their own feature film and even selling action figures. Stylistically, the band was essentially a blues-

David Bowie performing as his alter ego, Ziggy Stardust. Like Alice Cooper and Peter Gabriel, Bowie pushed the boundaries of sexual and gender identity, though in a campier, fashion-conscious way. Ziggy Stardust emerged on the album The Rise and Fall of Ziggy Stardust and the Spiders from Mars (1972), and Bowie continued to reinvent the character throughout the decade.

rock band; "Rock and Roll All Nite" is a good example of the band's approach, which blends verses not unlike those of Bad Company or Foghat with an anthemic sing-along chorus that works well as the song's hook.

Ziggy Played Guitar: David Bowie.   Of all the British glam stars that stormed the UK charts in the first half of the 1970s, only David Bowie was able to make a significant impact in the United States. His first important success in the UK came with the single "Space Oddity" (uk5, 1969; p15, 1973), a song inspired by the Stanley Kubrick film adaptation of Arthur C. Clarke's *2001: A Space Odyssey*. By the early 1970s, Bowie had formed the Spiders from Mars, a band with shifting personnel that featured Mick Ronson on guitar. He also created the character of Ziggy Stardust for the album *The Rise and Fall of Ziggy Stardust and the Spiders from Mars* (p75 uk5, 1972), which contained "Suffragette City" (uk10, 1972). The release of *Aladdin Sane* (p17 uk1, 1973) and *Pin-Ups* (p23 uk1, 1973) reinforced Bowie's stature in the UK, while helping him gain ground in the United States (though *Diamond Dogs* [uk1, 1974] was a bit of a setback). The album that made Bowie's reputation in America was *David Live* (p8 uk2, 1974), which featured a generous selection of songs from the earlier Bowie albums that had topped the charts in the UK. The success of *Young Americans* (p9 uk2, 1975), which contained the single "Fame" (p1 uk17, 1975), and *Station to Station* (p3 uk5, 1976) solidified Bowie's star status in America. In light of our discussion of Alice Cooper, it is important to recognize both the similarities and differences between Bowie and Cooper. Each adopted a stage persona that was based in fantasy and both pushed the boundaries of sexual and gender identities. While Cooper enjoyed his greatest commercial success in the UK when glam was at its peak, his roots do not lie in the world of urbane fashion consciousness that Bowie's do. Also, it soon became Bowie's practice to change characters with every album, while Cooper stuck with his Alice character all along. Despite the differences, Cooper and Bowie, with the addition of Peter Gabriel, were in many ways sharing a common aesthetic goal that had its roots in psychedelia: making the music a trip—even if the trip ended up being weird, campy, or ghoulish.

The Singer-Songwriters

The Importance of Being Earnest.   The singer-songwriter style of the 1970s arose in part from the folksingers of the 1960s—Dylan especially—as well as the music of the Beatles in the last year or so of their career. When Dylan delivered a song from behind his acoustic guitar, or Paul McCartney while at the piano, it was understood that each was sincerely expressing the results of his own personal reflection. The singer-songwriters thus stood as the direct antithesis to Bowie and Cooper: they were not playing characters but rather revealing their true selves. Much of this, it is important to understand, is only an ideal; no matter how authentic a performance is, it is almost always mediated by issues of show-business concern for projecting the proper image. No matter how much the real person and stage performer are or are not similar, it is still crucial that audiences believe that these are one and the same. Sometimes a singer-songwriter in the 1970s would be accompanied only by an acoustic piano or acoustic guitar, but if other instruments were used, it was important that they not draw attention to themselves. The aural impression of sincerity and intimacy created by most singer-songwriter records is achieved by placing the singer front and center, with the accompaniment clearly in a secondary and supporting role. Dylan's career in the 1970s was as a singer-songwriter, as was John Lennon's, who enjoyed several hit singles and albums in the first half of the decade, perhaps most notably *Imagine* (p1 uk1, 1971), the title single of which went to number three in United States. In the case of both these artists, the focus is always the singer and the song.

1960s Connections: James Taylor, Carole King, Paul Simon. One of the important new singer-songwriters to emerge out of the late 1960s was Chapel Hill–born James Taylor. Taylor was among the first acts signed to the Beatles' new record label, Apple, in 1968. His debut on Apple, *James Taylor* (1968), did not chart, though it contained "Carolina in My Mind," a song that would

LISTENING GUIDE

GET MUSIC ▶▶| wwnorton.com/rockhistory

Carole King, "You've Got a Friend"

Words and music by Carole King, produced by Lou Adler. Contained on *Tapestry*, which hit number one on the Billboard Album charts in 1970.

FORM: Compound AABA form. The A section is based on contrasting verse-chorus form, and consists of a 16-bar verse and a 14-bar chorus. The 10-bar bridge section is followed by a partial return of the A section, consisting of only the chorus. The song ends with a quiet coda.

TIME SIGNATURE: 4/4.

INSTRUMENTATION: Acoustic piano, acoustic bass, acoustic guitar, congas, string quartet, lead and backup vocals.

	0:00–0:12	**Introduction**, 4 mm.	Solo acoustic piano sets the intimate tone of the song.
A	0:12–0:58	**Verse 1**, 16 mm.	Vocal enters, as piano continues but with the support of the acoustic bass. "When you're down . . ."
	0:58–1:49	**Chorus**, 18 mm.	Congas and harmony vocal are added. James Taylor's acoustic guitar playing can just barely be heard in the background. The

become much better known a few years later. Taylor soon moved to a new label, and his "Fire and Rain" hit number three on the U.S. charts in 1970, while *Sweet Baby James* (p3 uk7, 1970) established Taylor on both sides of the Atlantic. He enjoyed continued success in the first half of the decade with albums like *Mud Slide Slim* (p2 uk4, 1971) and *One Man Dog* (p4 uk27, 1972). Taylor's single "You've Got a Friend" (p1 uk4, 1971) was written by a familiar name in American popular music, Carole King. By the end of the 1960s, King had decided to step out from behind the scenes, becoming one of the most important and influential female artists of the 1970s. She scored a string of successful albums, beginning with *Tapestry* (p1 uk4, 1970), which contained the hit "It's Too Late" (p1 uk6, 1971) as well as her own version of "You've Got a Friend" and a reinterpretation of her "Will You Still Love Me Tomorrow?" Follow-ups included *Music* (p1 uk18, 1972) and *Rhymes and Reasons* (p2 uk40, 1972).

Another familiar name among the singer-songwriters was Paul Simon. In the wake of his tremendous run of hit records with Art Garfunkel, Simon decided to strike out on his own, updating his 1960s approach and releasing *Paul Simon* (p4 uk1, 1972), which contained "Mother and Child Reunion" (p4

			chorus consists of 14 bars, to which 4 bars are added drawn directly from the additional introduction. "You just call . . ."
A	1:49–2:34	**Verse 2**, 16 mm.	As before, but now with acoustic guitar continuing and string quartet added. "If the sky . . ."
	2:34–3:13	**Chorus**, 14 mm.	All instruments continue, as harmony vocal and congas return. "You just call . . ."
B	3:13–3:42	**Bridge**, 10 mm.	Same instrumentation as verse 2, "Now ain't it good . . ."
A′	3:42–4:21	**Chorus**, 14 mm.	As in the first chorus, as string quartet drops out until the very end. Note how the guitar gets busy toward the end as well. "You just call . . ."
	4:21–5:05	**Coda**, 15 mm.	Repeat of vamp drawn from first 2 bars of the introduction, with King improvising vocal lines on top. "You've got a friend . . ."

In Concert at the Forum-April 15th · 8:30 PM

Carole King   **Barbra Streisand**   **James Taylor**

McGovern
3/4
Use the Power 18 Register and Vote

Quincy Jones and his Orchestra

Ushers: Warren Beatty · Jack Nicholson · Julie Christie · Sally Kellerman · James Earl Jones · Jacqueline Bisset
Michelle Gilliam · Mike Nichols · Shirley MacLaine · Goldie Hawn · Gene Hackman · Elliott Gould
Marlo Thomas · Burt Lancaster · Jon Voight · Raquel Welch · Michael Sarrazin · Britt Ekland and more

In the 1970s, singer-songwriters continued their popularity and their focus on social issues. This poster advertises a concert to benefit the liberal Democrat George McGovern's 1972 campaign for president. Carole King (a longtime behind-the-scenes songwriter—see Chapter 3) started a solo career, and with her album Tapestry *became one of the most influential women songwriters of the decade.*

uk5, 1972)—a song using Jamaican musicians in the years before reggae became well known. In a series of albums and singles including *There Goes Rhymin' Simon* (p2 uk4, 1973), "Kodachrome" (p2, 1973), *Still Crazy After All These Years* (p1 uk6, 1975), and "50 Ways to Leave Your Lover" (p1 uk23, 1975), Simon increasingly incorporated jazz elements in his music, often employing studio musicians to play on his tracks. A clear example of Simon's blend of jazz into the singer-songwriter style is his "Still Crazy After All These Years." The lyrics reflect on meeting an old lover by chance and reassessing the course his life has taken. The backup playing is subdued but sophisticated during the verses, while the middle section features a soaring and melodic jazz-tinged saxophone solo.

American Poets Society.   Carly Simon (no relation to Paul) came to the attention of most rock listeners first with her singles "That's the Way I Always Heard It Should Be" (p10, 1971) and "Anticipation" (p13, 1971). Her album *No Secrets* (p1 uk3, 1973) stands as the peak of her popular appeal, and contains the single "You're So Vain" (p1 uk3, 1972), which features the backup vocals of Mick Jagger and was rumored to refer to Simon's brief romantic relationship with the Rolling Stones singer. Other important American singer-songwriters include Harry Chapin, whose "Taxi" (p24, 1972) and "Cat's in the Cradle" (p1, 1974) both reflect on life's twists and turns, and Don McLean, whose "American Pie" (p1 uk2, 1972) attempts to summarize the previous two decades of rock and roll history, while "Vincent" (p12 uk1, 1972) offers a portrait of the painter Vincent Van Gogh. Jim Croce was at the height of his popularity when he was killed in an airplane crash. His "Bad, Bad Leroy Brown" (p1, 1973) was at the top of the U.S. charts at the time, and the release a few months later of his "Time in a Bottle" (p1, 1974), a reflection on the unwelcome approach of death and recorded months before the crash, gave the song an eerie poignancy.

British Singer-Songwriters: Van Morrison, Cat Stevens, Elton John. The singer-songwriter style was not restricted to Americans; Van Morrison, Cat Stevens, and Elton John all enjoyed considerable success during the early and mid 1970s. Van Morrison continued his 1960s success into the new decade, bringing his blend of jazz and rhythm and blues influences to albums like *Moondance* (p29, 1970) and *Tupelo Honey* (p21, 1971). Cat Stevens first stormed the U.S. charts with his single "Peace Train" (p7, 1971). A string of albums made him a regular on the album charts on both sides of the Atlantic, including *Teaser and the Firecat* (p2 uk3, 1971), *Catch Bull at Four* (p1 uk2, 1972), and *Buddha and the Chocolate Box* (p2 uk3, 1974). Perhaps the most successful of all the singer-songwriters discussed here is Elton John. After four Top 40 albums in the United States and the UK, Elton established himself with the single "Your Song" (p8 uk7, 1971) and a series of hugely successful albums: *Honky Chateau* (p1 uk2, 1972), *Don't Shoot Me I'm Only the Piano Player* (p1 uk1, 1973), *Goodbye Yellow Brick Road* (p1 uk1, 1973), and *Caribou* (p1 uk1, 1974). John wrote most of his songs with lyricist Bernie Taupin, and as a songwriting team their success rivals that of Lennon-McCartney or Jagger-Richards. Taupin's images are clever and compelling, and John's melodic-harmonic sense draws on a wide range of influences. Except for the fact that John performs the tunes, the John-Taupin partnership is strongly reminiscent of the Tin Pan Alley and Brill Building songwriting teams of previous decades. There is thus an especially clear parallel between John and Carole King and a clear link to the American pop song tradition, perhaps less than to folk songwriting. John began employing a backup band in the early 1970s (most often drummer Nigel Olsson, bassist Dee Murray, and guitarist Davey Johnstone) and this idea of the singer-songwriter now placed at the front of a rock band became the model for many singer-songwriters in the second half of the decade. Even though this arrangement went back to Dylan's turn to electric music, John's band prepared the way for the next batch of harder-rocking singer-songwriters, including Billy Joel, Bob Seger, and Bruce Springsteen (all to be discussed in Chapter 10).

Elton John, pictured here in a 1975 concert, was the most successful singer-songwriter of the early 1970s. John blended folk and rhythm and blues influences (he performed on the black dance show Soul Train) *with some of David Bowie's glam-rock sensibility. John's worldwide popularity continues to this day.*

Canadian Voices: Joni Mitchell, Neil Young, Gordon Lightfoot. Like that of Paul Simon, Joni Mitchell's music in the 1960s was very much indebted to folk music, and like Simon, she also began experimenting with the use of jazz in the 1970s. Mitchell first climbed the pop charts as a songwriter when Judy Collins recorded "Both Sides Now" (p8 uk14, 1968). Her music developed quickly, as she made a practice of using very talented and sometimes well-known musicians to back her up. Her biggest commercial success was *Court and Spark* (p2 uk14, 1974), which contained the single "Help Me" (p7) and featured the playing of Tom Scott's LA Express. A year later she explored new, sometimes avant-garde stylistic territory with *The Hissing of Summer Lawns* (p4 uk14, 1975), and later in the decade she explored esoteric jazz with *Mingus* (p17 uk24, 1979). Sometimes misunderstood by critics, Mitchell is probably the most musically eclectic and experimental singer-songwriter of the decade.

Also with roots in the 1960s, Neil Young enjoyed success as a member of Buffalo Springfield, and then in his on-again, off-again relationship with Crosby, Stills, and Nash. As a solo artist, Young placed a string of albums high on the charts. The decade began with *After the Gold Rush* (p8 uk7, 1970), containing "Southern Man." While that track never charted, it received enough airplay that Lynyrd Skynyrd felt they had to answer it in the lyrics to "Sweet Home Alabama" (the entire second verse responds to Young's sharp criticism of racism in the south, concluding that a southern man doesn't need him around anyhow). Young enjoyed his greatest commercial and critical success with *Harvest* (p1 uk1, 1972), which contained the hit "Heart of Gold" (p1 uk10). Performing in a style in which voices are often pretty and controlled, Young's singing voice is frequently thin, somewhat out of tune, and seemingly unsure. But as with Dylan's voice, these qualities can be deeply expressive and evocative.

Gordon Lightfoot's music is more traditional than that of Mitchell or Young. Several of his quiet and thoughtful songs, delivered in his polished baritone voice, became staples of FM and AM radio during the decade, including "If You Could Read My Mind" (p5 uk30, 1971), "Sundown" (p1 uk33, 1974), and "The Wreck of the Edmund Fitzgerald" (p2 uk40, 1976), which chronicled the 1975 sinking of a freighter in Lake Superior.

With her music ranging from folk to avant-garde rock to jazz, Joni Mitchell (pictured here in a 1974 concert) is probably the most musically eclectic and experimental singer-songwriter of the decade. She combined her own strong songwriting skills with very talented backup bands—a combination that resulted in many winning albums.

Country Rock

The Gift to be Simple. In many ways, the country rock style that emerged in the early 1970s was the result of the late 1960s reaction against the growing excesses of psychedelic rock. The attraction of country music for many rockers is similar to that exerted by blues or folk: somehow, in its apparent simplicity, country music seems more honest and authentic than most music on the pop charts. As we saw in Chapter 1, this occurs partly because country music has traded for decades in the perception that it is down-home music, and this goes back to the first days of the *Grand Ole Opry*. Among the first rockers to head out to Nashville to record were the Byrds. By 1968, most of the original Byrds had left the band and Roger McGuinn brought guitarist Gram Parsons on board. Parsons knew the country style well, and this shows in the band's influential *Sweetheart of the Rodeo* (1968). Bob Dylan also headed to Nashville to record *Nashville Skyline* (p3 uk1, 1969), which contains a duet version of "Girl from the North Country" sung with Johnny Cash. Now out of the Byrds, David Crosby teamed up with the Buffalo Springfield's Stephen Stills and the Hollies' Graham Nash to record *Crosby Stills and Nash* (p6 uk25, 1969). The next album included Neil Young (who had been in Buffalo Springfield with Stills); *Deja Vu* (p1 uk5, 1970) was followed by the live album, *Four Way Street* (p1 uk5, 1971). Crosby, Stills, and Nash (with or without Young) blended the folk rock of the Byrds with touches of jazz, country, and blues. "Suite: Judy Blue Eyes" (p21, 1969) provides a good example of the band's blend of acoustic and electric instruments, close vocal harmony, and catchy pop songwriting. While working with Dylan in upstate New York, the Band had also managed to record *Music from Big Pink* (p30, 1968). Led by drummer Levon Helm and guitarist Robbie Robertson, this group of mostly Canadian musicians had a deep love for the music of the American south, including country music. A series of successful albums, including *The Band* (p9 uk25, 1970), *Cahoots* (p21 uk41, 1971) and *Rock of Ages* (p6, 1972), established them among American listeners. The band's first hit, "Up on Cripple Creek" (p25, 1970) had as its B side "The Night They Drove Old Dixie Down," the song that came to be most associated with the group. "Dixie" tells the story of the fall of the south during the Civil War and draws on both folk and country styles.

Another 1960s musician who turned to country rock at the end of decade was Rick Nelson, who with the Stone Canyon Band revisited the charts with "She Belongs to Me" (p33, 1970), a cover version of a Dylan song. His later hit "Garden Party" (p6, 1972) told the story of playing a rock and roll revival show at Madison Square Garden with the Stone Canyon Band and the rejection he experienced there. Ex-Monkees guitarist Michael Nesmith got into the act as well; featuring the playing of steel guitarist Red Rhodes, the First National Band scored with "Joanne" (p21, 1970).

Poor Boys Make Good: Creedence Clearwater Revival. Most listeners in the late 1960s were surprised to learn that the band made up of brothers John and Tom Fogerty on guitars, Stu Cook on bass, and Doug Clifford on drums were from the San Francisco Bay area. Their music sounded country, John Fogerty's singing sounded black, and San Francisco was the home of psychedelia. Recording for the small Fantasy label, however, Creedence Clearwater Revival (CCR) placed a long string of singles on the charts, beginning with "Suzie Q" (p11, 1968), and extended their success to Britain with "Proud Mary" (p2 uk8, 1969) and "Bad Moon Rising" (p2 uk1, 1969). John Fogerty wrote most of the band's music, delivering songs that pushed *Green River* (p1 uk20, 1969), *Willy and the Poor Boys* (p3 uk10, 1970), and *Cosmo's Factory* (p1 uk1, 1970) to significant commercial success. The hippie component was not entirely missing in CCR's music. *Willy and the Poor Boys* showed the influence of *Sgt. Pepper*, as the members of CCR became the jug band pictured on the cover and named in the title. From the first track, "Down on the Corner," to "Poor Boy Shuffle" and "Fortunate Son," the tracks seem to be generated from the central "concept" of the album.

The Avocado Mafia. While the idea of blending rock with country music occurred to musicians in many parts of the United States—Los Angeles, Woodstock, and San Francisco—southern California became the home of country rock by the early 1970s, and the Eagles were the leading band in the style. Guitarist Glenn Frey and drummer Don Henley got to know one another while playing in the touring band for singer Linda Ronstadt. Ronstadt had earlier sung for the Stone Poneys, a folk-rock band that had a hit with "Different Drum" (p13, 1967), a song written by then-Monkee Michael Nesmith. After the recording of Ronstadt's *Silk Purse* (1970), Frey and Henley were hired as backup players. Soon bassist Randy Meisner joined the band, and for one gig at least, guitarist Bernie Leadon joined the Ronstadt show. The foursome quickly decided to strike out on their own, leaving Ronstadt and recording their debut album—ironically in London and not sunny southern California—under the production of Glyn Johns. *Eagles* (p22, 1972) was followed by *Desperado* (p41, 1973), a country-rock concept album about the Old West. Guitarist Don Felder joined the band after the second album, and *On the Border* (p17 uk28, 1974) and *One of These Nights* (p1 uk8, 1975) followed. Beginning with "Take It Easy" (p12, 1972), the band placed eight singles in the American Top 40 by 1975, including "Best of My Love" (p1, 1974) and "One of These Nights" (p1, 1975). In many ways the Eagles brought several 1960s elements together. Like the Beach Boys, the Beatles, and the Byrds, the Eagles were a superb singing group with the primary focus on the song, two very strong lead voices (Frey and Henley), and skillful harmony singing. They wrote their own music, played on their own albums, and kept close control of production decisions. By mid-decade, Leadon was replaced by ex-James Gang guitarist Joe Walsh, and the band headed away from its country rock sound to become even bigger stars; we discuss the next stage of the band's career in Chapter 9.

The Eagles' "Take It Easy." The Eagles bring together many elements of previous rock styles; their first hit "Take It Easy" is as a good example. The first seventeen seconds of the tune already tell the listener a lot about where the band is coming from musically. Opening with big, brilliant electric guitar chords

The Eagles, "Take It Easy"

Words and music by Jackson Browne and Glenn Frey, produced by Glyn Johns. Reached #12 on the Billboard Pop charts in the summer of 1972. Contained on the album *The Eagles*, which reached #22 on the Billboard Album charts.

FORM: Simple verse form. The verse structure is complicated, involving three distinct phrases, each 8 bars in length. The middle phrase sounds like it might be a chorus, and the last phrase has a refrain. The song cycles through the verse four times, with the third time through (instrumental verse) consisting of only twice through the verse.

TIME SIGNATURE: 4/4.

INSTRUMENTATION: Acoustic and electric guitars, bass, banjo, drums, lead and backup vocals.

0:00–0:17	**Introduction**, 10 mm.	8 bars of big-sounding guitars, then 2 bars with entire band that set the country-flavored mood of the song.
0:17–0:58	**Verse 1**, 24 mm., (8 + 8 + 8)	Lead vocal enters, joined by rich vocal harmonies in the second 8-bar phrase. "Well I'm runnin' . . ."
0:58–1:44	**Verse 2**, 26 mm.	2-bar country guitar riff from introduction is followed by the 24-bar verse, performed mostly as in verse 1, with the addition of a second backup vocal part in the first and third 8-bar phrase. "Well I'm standin' . . ."
1:44–2:13	**Instr. Verse**, 16 mm.	Guitar solo based on first two phrases of the verse. Note the addition of banjo to the accompaniment.
2:13–2:55	**Verse 3**, 24 mm.	As before, but with the addition of even more backup vocals. The banjo continues percolating in the background. "Well I'm runnin' . . ."
2:55–3:31	**Coda**, 19 mm.	10 bars of vamp with choral vocals on top and the banjo moving to the front of the mix, then a new 9-bar melody based on the verse that ends with a surprise chord.

reminiscent of the Byrds and folk rock generally, another electric guitar soon enters with a lick that is meant to imitate the sound of the steel guitar, found in so much country music. As the song continues and the lead vocal enters, it sounds as if Glenn Frey is singing with a western accent; when the backup vocals enter, they show a marked Beatles/Beach Boys influence (notice how the harmonies are set high in the male voice register). With the second verse, a high harmony is added to make the verse a duet, much in the style of the Everly Brothers or Lennon and McCartney. The guitar continues the steel guitar references during the solo, as banjo is added in the accompaniment to reinforce the country connection. In the third verse, a new vocal part is added above the lead vocal to create interest and keep the arrangement fresh. In the coda the banjo comes more to the front of the mix, and the band again showcases their harmony vocals. The song is in simple verse form—there is no clear chorus or bridge—but the verse structure is more complicated than is usually found in a simple verse form. In this case, it consists of three eight-bar sections to total twenty-four bars. Notice that only the first two eight-bar sections are used in the instrumental verse.

The Eagles, live at Wembley Stadium, London, July 1975: (left to right) Timothy B. Schmidt (bass), Glenn Frey (electric guitar), Don Henley (drums), Joe Walsh (banjo), and Don Felder (acoustic guitar). The Eagles were the leaders in the California country-rock scene. They placed eight singles in the U.S. Top 40 by 1975. Like the Beach Boys, the Beatles, and the Byrds, the Eagles employed strong, harmonically rich singing and retained nearly total control over their music production.

This chapter has followed the development of several rock styles of the first half of the 1970s, tracing their roots in the music of the psychedelic era. Surveying the music of the first half of the 1970s, you can see how aspects of psychedelia that existed side by side in the late 1960s became separated out to form new styles. Country rock focused on the integration of country music into rock, for instance, while progressive rock refined the use of classical music, and jazz rock refined the use of jazz. What had been one eclectic stylistic hodge-podge was refined into distinct styles that then developed in some cases away from one another. The close connections that are found in rock music between 1966 and 1976—this unfolding of the stylistic possibilities of the late 1960s in the music of the early 1970s—might cause one to wonder whether a stylistic division is actually valid or useful. In some ways such a division is helpful, but in many more ways it is probably better to view the music discussed in Chapters 7 and 8 as more unified than divided. What unifies the music is the hippie aesthetic, and until about 1975 there was nothing to deter significantly the idea that rock music would simply continue to progress and develop as many thought it had been doing. But three things happened mid-decade: (1) multinational corporations got involved in the music business, (2) the punk movement began to form, and

(3) disco began to make a play for putting dancing back at the center of popular music. The struggle caused by the rise of disco will be explored in Chapter 9. The disputes that arose over the first two of these events will be the topic of Chapter 10.

Questions for Review and Discussion

1. Name the most important British blues-rock bands of the early 1970s and discuss how each has roots in 1960s blues rock.
2. What American bands were influenced by blues rock?
3. Discuss the similarities and differences between southern rock and country rock. How does each style develop out of the 1960s, and which bands are the most central to each style?
4. Compare and contrast progressive rock and jazz rock. Which bands are the most important to the style and what are the features that distinguish each?
5. What was glam rock and how can its influence be seen in 1970s rock?
6. Discuss the development of a new kind of rock theater in the 1970s. What are the important acts and how does this approach grow out of psychedelia?
7. Who are the important singer-songwriters in the early 1970s? Describe the important features of the style.
8. What is the hippie aesthetic? How can this idea be used to unify rock music in the 1967–75 period? How can this idea be used to find similarities among the styles prevalent in the early 1970s? Cite bands, artists, songs, and any other elements you think are important to this discussion.

Further Reading

Hank Bordowitz, *Bad Moon Rising: The Unofficial History of Creedence Clearwater Revival* (Schirmer, 1998).

Marley Brandt, *Southern Rockers: The Roots and Legacy of Southern Rock* (Billboard Books, 1999).

Henry Edwards and Tony Zanetta, *Stardust: The David Bowie Story* (McGraw-Hill, 1986).

John Einarson, *Desperados: The Roots of Country Rock* (Cooper Square Press, 2001).

Susan Fast, *In the Houses of the Holy: Led Zeppelin and the Power of Rock Music* (Oxford University Press, 2001).

Edward Macan, *Rockin' the Classics: English Progressive Rock and the Counterculture* (Oxford, 1997).

Dave Marsh, *Before I Get Old: The Story of the Who* (St. Martin's, 1983).

Stuart Nicholson, *Jazz Rock: A History* (Schirmer, 1998).

Philip Norman, *Sir Elton: The Definitive Biography* (Carroll & Graf, 2001).

Nicholas Schaffner, *A Saucerful of Secrets: The Pink Floyd Odyssey* (Delta, 1991).

Marc Shapiro, *The Long Run: The Story of the Eagles* (Omnibus, 1995).

Paul Stump, *The Music's All That Matters: A History of Progressive Rock* (Quartet Books, 1997).

Brian Sweet, *Steely Dan: Reelin' in the Years* (Omnibus, 1994).

Dave Zimmer, *Crosby, Stills, and Nash: The Authorized Biography* (Da Capo, 2000).

Interlude 3

In the Studio: The Role of Recording Techniques in Rock Music

Records, tapes, and CDs are central to the history of rock music, and since the mid 1990s, digital downloading and file sharing have also become significant factors in how music gets from the artists to listeners. Live performance is also important, and some groups—such as the Grateful Dead, the Allman Brothers Band, and more recently Phish and Widespread Panic—have been more oriented toward performances that change from night to night than with authoritative versions of tunes that are produced in a recording studio. But even when fans exchange tapes of various live shows, what is changing hands is still a recording of some kind. Because of the importance of recordings in rock music, some scholars argue that the rock repertoire is not simply a collection of songs, but that it is a collection of *specific recordings* of songs. There is, for instance, only one recording of *Sgt. Pepper's Lonely Hearts Club Band* that we value, and it's the one made by the Beatles in 1967. Who would prefer a copy of this album done by a group of sound-alikes? Further, different recordings have what might be thought of as "sonic signatures"—features that mark them in terms of where and when they were recorded, as well as by whom. Elvis's early recordings with Sam Phillips at Sun have a distinctive recorded sound that is, in a sense, separable from the songs themselves or the actual performances of them. For scholars with this view, rock is largely a recorded art, and thus, when we talk about rock songs, we are almost always also talking about rock *records*, even if we don't realize it.

This interlude will help you enter this important realm of recorded sound. It will provide an introductory glimpse into the recording process, describing the techniques and equipment used by engineers and producers in the recording studio and outlining some of their key concerns. We will then consider two contrasting tracks in detail, directing our attention to features of the music that will help us hear aspects of musical style imbedded in the way the recording itself has been made.

Ambience

Is It Live or Is It Memorex? There are two principal ways of thinking about what a recording represents. The first is to think of the recording as an "audio snapshot"; in this case, the recording is meant to reproduce a live performance as faithfully as can be done on tape (or digitally). As much as possible, the listener should be unaware that a recording process is involved: all of the sounds seem natural and almost indiscernible from an actual performance. This approach to recording is frequently used in classical, jazz, and folk music. The second way of approaching recording is to exploit the possibilities offered by the studio—an approach that produces sounds that would be impossible to re-create in the same way in a live setting. The records of Les Paul and Mary Ford are a good early example of this second approach: by progressively building up tracks of Paul's guitar and Ford's voice, Paul was able to create a recorded sound that was very much a consequence of the recording technology that produced it. The recording studio allows instruments to be combined in ways that would not easily work in a natural acoustic setting; one of the most common of these is putting an acoustic guitar together with drums and distorted electric guitar, as heard on a myriad of tracks, including Boston's "More Than a Feeling" discussed in Chapter 9. The fact that live performance technology since the early 1970s has made it increasingly possible to combine acoustic instruments with louder electric ones is in large part a result of sounds that occurred first in the studio. Since the days of Elvis Presley's Sun recordings, rock music has depended more on this second approach to recording—exploiting the possibilities of the studio—than it has on the audio snapshot approach. Other styles, such as classical and jazz, remain devoted to the first approach.

Reverb and Echo. Whether we are aware of it or not, every space we enter has specific acoustic properties. Whenever a sound is made, it is the result of a series of vibrations moving through the air; some of these vibrations reach our ears directly from the source while others bounce around the room and reflect back to us. Hard surfaces reflect sound; more porous ones (like carpeting, curtains, or furniture) absorb sound. Architects who design concert halls are keenly aware of this, and they devote considerable energy to determining the balance of harder and softer surfaces in a hall and how these surfaces will be angled. The idea, of course, is to create a space that makes the performances in the hall sound as acoustically rich as possible. If there's too much reflection, the sound can be too bright or boomy; if there's not enough, the music can sound dry and lifeless. When recording according to the audio snapshot approach, it is crucial to find a space with "good acoustics"—that is, with the right kind of reflected sound for the ensemble or soloist involved. Major record companies have in the past maintained their own studios, some bigger and some smaller, that have been acoustically engineered for the best natural sound. For them, the task is not only to capture the way the musicians sound but also to commit to tape how those musicians sound in that specific room. In rock music, stories abound of vocals that were recorded in bathrooms, or guitar parts that were recorded in hallways or stairwells in order to take advantage of the natural acoustics of those spaces. It is also possible to create a room sound—often referred to as "ambience"—via electronic means, and this effect is called "reverb." Most commercially available electronic reverb units offer settings that reproduce the sound of small rooms, medium-size rooms, large rooms, auditoriums of various sizes, and churches, as well as a number of "unnatural" spaces. When an engineer knows that she will use reverb, she records the sound as "dry" as possible, meaning an acoustic space is used that reflects little sound (these spaces often use special sound-absorbing material). This dry sound is then fed through the reverb device to produce the desired sound. Reverb is used to some extent on almost all rock recordings, meaning that the "spaces" captured on tape are often not real spaces at all. In addition, different kinds of reverb can be used on different instruments or voices, producing sounds that are the result of multiple "spaces," none of which could naturally coexist in a world with only three dimensions.

Reverb must be distinguished from echo. In the natural world, an echo occurs when sound bounces back to our ears to create two sonic images of the same event—we hear the original and then its reflection. This sound can be produced electronically as well, though some recording studios have built their own trademark "echo chambers" (the chamber at Gold Star Studios in Los Angeles—now destroyed—has almost mythical standing within the recording world). Echo tends not to be of much concern to those who employ the audio snapshot approach; mostly they try to avoid it. In rock, echo is used extensively and often on voices. Together with reverb, echo can make the singing voice sound much richer and even mask certain imperfections in tone or intonation. The beginning of the Supremes' "Where Did Our Love Go?" is a good example of studio reverb. The clapping (actually two-by-fours being slapped together) is drenched in a rich reverb that makes it sound like the clapping is occurring in a large gymnasium or some other big, reflective space. The most famous echo can be found on Elvis Presley's Sun recordings. For many years after Elvis's success, studio engineers all around the world tried to reproduce the distinctive echo found on songs such as "That's All Right (Mama)," in which the quick echo (often called "slap-back echo") gives Presley's voice a quality that he could never have produced live. Reverb and echo provide what might be thought of as the ambient dimension of the music, and the use of these effects can make instruments sound closer or farther from the listener, depending on how much reverb or echo is employed—the more reverb or echo, the farther away the sound seems to be.

EQ, Stereo, and Mixing

River Deep, Mountain High: EQ. If we think in terms of three dimensions, ambience (along with volume level) accounts for the "depth" of a recording. Things sound nearer or farther away based on how loud they are and how much reverb or echo is present. The "height" of a recording is its frequency range. In traditional terms, musicians think of frequency range in terms of the available pitch range of various instruments; thus, a flute or violin is relatively high in the frequency range compared to a double bass, trombone, or tuba. A piano or organ has a wide range, extending from the lowest to the highest note possible by other instruments. The most common classical ensembles, from orchestra to string quartet, encompass a broad frequency range by virtue of the instruments included, and composers who write for these groups attend constantly to the balance of sounding pitches in the low, middle, and high ranges. Rock also brings together combinations of instruments that fill out the frequency range; bass covers the low end, while guitars, keyboards, and voices fill out the middle and upper ranges. The actual note played by an instrument is called its "fundamental"; but along with this note, every instrument also subtly produces other, higher notes that are heard not as harmony notes, but rather as the tone, or "timbre" (pronounced to rhyme with "amber") of the instrument. You have probably noticed that if you adjust the treble and bass settings on your stereo you can greatly affect the sound—more treble and the sound is brighter, less treble and it sounds muffled. These tone settings adjust the volume of the frequencies in the sounds you hear and affect not only the fundamentals but also the higher notes that are generated in each case (called "upper partials" or "harmonics"). In the process of recording instruments, an engineer has a significant amount of control over the timbre of each recorded sound; for each microphone in use he has four or more controls that work like the treble and bass on your stereo. In addition to being concerned that the frequency range for any given track is balanced with regard to the fundamental notes being produced by the instruments and voices involved, the engineer can also balance the sound by adjusting the timbre of each. This area of concern is usually referred to as "EQ," which is short for equalization. A good recording is "EQ-ed" to produce a balanced distribution of frequencies. EQ can also help to bring out certain instruments, as well as to keep instruments in a similar range from covering each other up, resulting in a crisper, clearer, and more defined sound.

Every Breadth You Take: Stereo Placement.   The third dimension of recorded sound, the "width" of the music, is stereo placement. When we hear sounds in the natural world, we can locate the position of a sound source because the sound enters each of our ears in a different way. Our mind calculates where a sound is coming from on the basis of the "stereo" effect. In music that is recorded in stereo, the engineer can control whether a sound comes out of the right or left speaker, or some combination of the two. In order to hear this clearly, sit exactly between your stereo speakers. Put on a stereo recording and close your eyes: you will notice that there is a kind of "sonic landscape" in the space between the two speakers. Some sounds seem to come from the center, while others seem to come from the right or left, or mid-right or mid-left. It is, of course, impossible for the sounds that seem to be coming from the center to really be coming from there; after all, you are sitting between the speakers and there is no center speaker physically present. Stereo sound is thus an aural illusion or image that we construct as a result of how we hear. Engineers use this phenomenon to separate sounds from one another to allow us to hear more detail in the recording. For instance, if a rhythm guitar and organ are playing almost the same thing in the same frequency range, the listener may not be able to distinguish them from one another—one will cover up or "mask" the other. If you adjust one to sound like it is coming from the right ("pan right") and the other from the left, each will be much more distinct. In a stereo

recording, then, the instruments and voices are arranged across the stereo field and the result is that the recording sounds clearer and more complex sonically.

The three dimensions of the recorded sound—ambience/volume, EQ, and stereo placement—are controlled from a mixing board. A mixing board is used in two ways: first, to record the sound to tape (or more recently to the hard disk of a digital recorder) and second, to play the tape back. In classical music, the engineer's job is to capture the sound in the natural ambient space as faithfully as possible; a playback will not color the sound much more (though it may, and sometimes adjustments are made at this second stage). In rock, sounds are often committed to tape dry (except when special room effects are desired) and stored for playback. Early recording tape could store three tracks of music (meaning that the three tracks could be played back simultaneously), but as the '60s and '70s progressed, tapes could contain eight, sixteen, twenty-four, thirty-two, forty-eight, and even more tracks. With the advance of digital technology in recent years, the number of tracks available is so large that track space is no longer a technical limitation. Once all the tracks are stored on tape, the engineer is then ready to "mix down," meaning that she will adjust the ambience, EQ, stereo placement, and relative volume of the tracks to produce the final version of the song. (Notice that "track" is used in recording to specifically designate a recorded part, while the word "track" is also used more generally among fans and writers as synonymous with "song" or "tune," as in "Let's hear the second track on that CD.") Mixing is a complicated and creative process, and engineers and producers who do this are highly skilled professionals, often known for their distinctive "sound." Since the mid 1960s, bands have frequently spent more time mixing an album than they spent recording the individual tracks.

Mono and Stereo

For its first decade or so, most rock music was recorded and released in monophonic sound, meaning that there was assumed to be only one speaker for playback and thus no possibility of stereo imaging. Almost all of the Beatles' records, for instance, were released principally in mono, with later stereo versions being prepared mostly (and sometimes hastily) for hi-fi enthusiasts, often without the band participating in the stereo mixes. By the late 1960s, however, stereo was the preferred format for albums and FM radio, and by the mid 1970s complex stereo mixes had become the norm even for music that nurtured an image of simplicity and directness. The development of more and more tracks, the greater use of the stereo field, and increasingly ambitious musical projects progressed hand-in-hand throughout the late '60s and '70s, as listeners

A sound engineer adjusting a mixing board, 1971. This board is from the Rolling Stones' mobile recording unit, used to record Deep Purple's multi-platinum album Machine Head.

Steely Dan, "Josie"

Words and music by Walter Becker and Donald Fagen, produced by Gary Katz. Reached #26 on the Billboard Pop charts in 1978. Contained on the album *Aja*, which reached #3 in the United States and #5 in the UK in late 1977.

FORM: Compound AABA form, with A sections employing a verse-chorus pair.

TIME SIGNATURE: 4/4.

	0:00–0:32	**Introduction**, 16 mm.	8 mm. guitar figure then 8 mm. vamp.
A	0:32–1:03	**Verse 1**, 16 mm.	"We're gonna break out . . ."
	1:03–1:28	**Chorus**, 12 mm.	8 mm. chorus then 4 mm. link to verse 2.
A	1:28–1:59	**Verse 2**, 16 mm.	As before, "Jo would you love . . ."
	1:59–2:15	**Chorus**, 8 mm.	No link this time, "When Josie . . ."
B	2:15–2:31	**Bridge**, 8 mm.	Instrumental.
A	2:31–3:03	**Instr. Verse**, 16 mm.	Guitar solo.
	3:03–3:19	**Chorus**, 8 mm.	As second chorus, "When Josie . . ."
	3:19–4:24	**Coda**, 32 mm.	8 mm. as intro, then 24 mm. vamp and fade.

INSTRUMENTATION

Rhythm section	Singing	Solos	Sweetening
Electric piano	Solo w/ some	Electric guitar	Horns
2 rhythm guitars	harmony on		Synth strings
"Funky" guitar	verse and chorus		Percussion
Drum set			
Bass			

MIX

Left		Center		Right
Cymbal	Solo guitar	Lead vocal	Backup vocals	High-hat
Rhythm guitar	Backup vocals	Electric piano	Horns	Cymbal
Tom-tom	Horns	Percussion		"Funky" guitar
Synth strings		Snare drum		Rhythm guitar
		Bass		Tom-tom
		Bass drum		

purchased more and more sophisticated stereo equipment to get the full effect of the music. Among the most successful of the producers to work in mono was Phil Spector, and some of the most sophisticated recorded sounds in stereo came from Steely Dan. Spector and Steely Dan will thus make for a good comparison as representatives of mono and stereo, respectively. But since most of the rock music we listen to is in stereo, we'll begin our detailed listening there.

Steely Dan's "Josie" is structured according to the compound AABA form found so often in 1970s music. After an angular introduction featuring the electric guitar, there are several measures of vamp before the first verse begins. There are then two verse-chorus pairs making up the large-scale A sections, followed by an instrumental bridge making up the B section. The return to the verse-chorus pair in this case features a guitar solo over the verse material, with the vocals returning for the chorus. A return to the introduction and vamp close the song, as it fades out. In terms of the instrumentation, the track uses a fairly standard rhythm section of rhythm guitars, electric piano, bass, and drums. The vocals are mostly solo, with some harmony added during both the verse and chorus sections. Horns, percussion, and synthesizer strings are added to sweeten the mix. The stereo aspect of the record can be heard most readily in the drums: note that while the snare and bass drums are in the center, the high-hat is panned right, while tom-toms and cymbals are panned both right and left. As is usual for most rock, the lead vocals and bass are in the center. Three electric guitars are involved in the rhythm section: two of these are panned right and left and play an almost identical part with piano, which is panned center. There is a third guitar, which plays a funky single-note part, panned right. When the synthesizer strings enter in the second chorus, they are panned left. Note that the horns and backup vocals are both panned mid-right and mid-left to keep them distinct in the mix. Listen for the reverb and echo that have been added to the lead vocals and the heavy reverb on the synthesizer strings and solo guitar; by contrast, the bass, bass drum, and high-hat are very dry. Thus, in addition to the separation that occurs through stereo placement, ambience is also used to help keep the parts distinct. The distribution of instruments and equalization across the full frequency range makes the recording sound full, with plenty of low end balanced by bright highs.

As discussed in Chapter 3, Phil Spector is known for his Wall of Sound approach to production, and his recordings from the early 1960s sound very different from Steely Dan's "Josie." While the ambience, stereo placement, and EQ in the Steely Dan track were all employed to make each part aurally distinguishable in the mix, Spector's Wall of Sound technique strives to achieve the exact opposite effect. Spector worked to blend the backup instruments together in such a way that they melt into one another aurally. This was done by recording most of the backup music with all the musicians together in the same studio. With drums, piano, guitar, and bass (plus whatever else Spector had playing) all together in a small space, the sound from the guitar ended up in the piano microphone and the drums bled through the guitar mic, and so on. The result produces a different imaging from sounds in the Steely Dan tune. Since the track is in mono, there is no breadth through stereo placement. Instead, there is a foreground space for the lead vocal and a background space for everything else (though the backup vocals are farther forward in the background space than the instrumental parts). Notice in "Da Doo Ron Ron" that the lead vocal is enhanced by double tracking; the singer, Darlene Love, likely recorded the vocal and then recorded it again along with herself, giving the lead voice an added richness. There seems to be reverb on everything in this recording, even the drums, producing some cavernous tom-tom fills. Since Spector

LISTENING GUIDE

GET MUSIC ▶▶▌ wwnorton.com/rockhistory

The Crystals, "Da Doo Ron Ron"

Words and music by Phil Spector, Jeff Barry, and Ellie Greenwich, produced by Phil Spector. Reached #3 on the Billboard Pop charts in 1963 (UK5).

FORM: Simple verse, with an instrumental verse that is a shortened version of the sung ones.

TIME SIGNATURE: 12/8 (shuffle in four).

0:00–0:06	**Introduction**, 4 mm.	
0:06–0:35	**Verse 1**, 18 mm.	16 mm. verse plus 2 mm. link, "I met her . . ."
0:35–1:04	**Verse 2**, 18 mm.	Same as above, "I knew what she . . ."
1:04–1:17	**Instr Verse**, 8 mm.	Sax solo using first 8 mm. of verse.
1:17–1:46	**Verse 3**, 18 mm.	As verses 1 and 2, "Well, I picked her up . . ."
1:46–2:11	**Coda**, 16 mm.	Repetition of first 4 mm. of verse and fade.

INSTRUMENTATION

Rhythm section	Singing	Solos	Sweetening
Piano	Solo, with	Saxophone	Horns
Guitar?	Echoes and		Percussion
Drums	Harmony		Hand claps
Bass			

MIX

Foreground	Background
Solo vocal, sax solo	Backup vocals
	Horns
	Rhythm section
	Percussion
	Hand claps

was working with only a few tracks available, most of the EQ-ing was likely done during the recording stage as opposed to being done at playback. The instruments sometimes blend together so completely in a Spector recording that it can be difficult to discern exactly what instruments are present; can you detect a guitar in the rhythm section of "Da Doo Ron Ron," for instance?

This brief consideration of recording technique barely scratches the surface of the complexities of recorded rock music. Most listeners never realize that the sounds they are hearing are so heavily mediated by electronic means. They may even believe—however tacitly—that most records are "audio snapshots," representing performances that occurred in real time just as a live performance would. In order to hear the subtle features of recordings, it is useful to listen to the same song many times, maybe once or twice each for stereo placement, instrumentation, ambience/volume, and frequency distribution. Once you have heard deeply into a single recording, you may be surprised at what you begin hearing in records you have known for years.

Further Reading

Mark Cunningham, *Good Vibrations: A History of Record Production* (Sanctuary, 1996).

Howard Massey, *Behind the Glass: Top Record Producers Tell How They Craft the Hits* (Backbeat Books, 2000).

Albin Zak III, *The Poetics of Rock: Cutting Tracks, Making Records* (University of California Press, 2001).

chapter 9

Released in 1971, Marvin Gaye's What's Going On *signaled an important change in direction for Motown. Departing from the traditional Motown formula, which featured singles over albums, Gaye drew on the concept album idea laid down by the Beatles to create* What's Going On. *On this album, Gaye's songs are not self-contained but linked together, flowing seamlessly from one to the next, creating the feeling of a larger, complete artistic work. Diverging from traditional (though not all) Motown material, Gaye focused his lyrics on important social issues like the Vietnam War ("What's Going On" and "What's Happening Brother"), the environment ("Mercy Mercy Me [The Ecology]"), and urban blight ("Inner City Blues [Make Me Wanna Holler]"). While certainly popular and influential in its own time,* What's Going On *is often cited by industry professionals as one of the most important albums ever made, evidenced by its number six ranking on* Rolling Stone *magazine's list of the "500 Greatest Albums of All Time" (November 2003).*

Black Pop and the Rise of Disco

When rock and roll emerged in the mid 1950s, it was controversial for a number of reasons. One of the ways rock and roll challenged mainstream white middle-class values was in its blending of rhythm and blues and country and western into pop. For many in America, the increased emphasis on musical elements clearly drawn from black music elicited the strongest reaction. Early rock and roll, it is often claimed, acted as a force for breaking down racial and cultural barriers in the 1950s. In the context of rock's early history, it is ironic that by the end of the 1970s fans of mainstream rock were almost entirely white, as were most of the musicians and others involved with making, performing, and selling rock. This chapter will survey black popular music in the 1970s, which in many ways is a separate stylistic world from that of the rock discussed in the previous two chapters. While the music of some black artists was known to rock listeners, much of it was not, as black and white listeners often had record collections with only a few albums in common. Black pop in the 1970s deserves a much fuller treatment than can be provided here—one that sets this music primarily in the context of the black pop traditions from which it emerges. We will consider 1970s black pop mostly in terms of how it relates to the history of rock music that we have been studying up to this point, as well as explore how white misunderstandings of black pop in the '70s led to the dramatic reactions against disco. Like mainstream rock of the 1970s, black pop in the '70s developed out of '60s music—styles developed by Motown and Stax artists and production teams, James Brown, and a new artist who emerged out of the San Francisco hippie scene in the late 1960s. We will begin this chapter by charting the path of black pop out of the '60s and into the '70s.

Black Pop Roots in the 1960s

Sly and the Family Stone: Sly Crosses Over. It is difficult to exaggerate the influence that Sly and the Family Stone had on the course of black pop at the end of the 1960s; Sly's music was important to many black musicians, and his blend of funk with aspects of psychedelia defined black pop for white listeners in the early 1970s as well. Beginning with "Dance to the Music," which went to number eight on the pop charts (r9, 1968), Sly and the Family Stone topped the charts with a series of crossover hit singles, including number one hits on both pop and rhythm and blues charts: "Everyday People" (1969), "Thank You (Falettinme Be Mice Elf Agin)" (1970), and "Family Affair" (1971). Sly Stone (Sylvester Stewart) was born in Texas but moved to the San Francisco area as a child. During the mid 1960s he was a disc jockey and record producer, working with many artists, including the Beau Brummels and the Great Society (the band Grace Slick left to join Jefferson Airplane). In 1967, Sly and the Family Stone began playing in the Bay Area and circulating in the San Francisco psychedelic music scene. With bassist Larry Graham, drummer Gregg Errico, and guitarist Freddie Stone laying down a rhythmic backdrop strongly influenced by James Brown's bands, and the catchy vocals and solid keyboard playing of Sly and his sister Rose Stone Banks (topped off by the trumpet and sax playing of Cynthia Robinson and Jerry Martini), the band stood out not only for its distinctive blend of white and black musical styles, but also because it was one of the few racially and sexually integrated bands of the era. The early tracks are

---

LISTENING GUIDE

GET MUSIC ▶▶ wwnorton.com/rockhistory

Sly and the Family Stone, "Thank You (Falettinme Be Mice Elf Agin)"

Words and music by Sylvester Stewart, produced by Sly Stone. Hit #1 on both Billboard Pop and Rhythm and Blues charts in 1970.

FORM: Simple verse-chorus. The entire song is based on the groove laid down in the introduction. Twice in the song the bass drops out to create an instrumental interlude after each chorus, allowing the bass to reenter sounding fresh. After the third verse-chorus pair, a contrasting verse occurs, providing further contrast.

TIME SIGNATURE: 4/4.

INSTRUMENTATION: Electric guitars, bass, drums, horns, and vocals.

0:00–0:18	**Introduction**, 8 mm.	Groove established first with guitar, bass, and high-hat only, with drums and horns entering for second 4 bars.
0:18–0:54	**Verse 1**, 16 mm.	Unison vocals, music continues as in introduction. "Lookin' at the devil . . ."
0:54–1:12	**Chorus**, 8 mm.	Harmony added to vocal part. "Thank you . . ."

optimistic and dance-oriented, and "Thank You (Falettinme Be Mice Elf Agin)" is representative of this approach. The entire song is built over a repeating riff in the bass, which established the song's rhythmic feel or "groove." It is the catchiness of this groove that is central to the song's effectiveness, and this can be said for much of Sly's music.

With the 1971 album *There's a Riot Goin' On* (p1 r1), the band's music began to adopt a more militant stance, at times focusing on controversial racial and political issues of the day. The next album, *Fresh* (p7 r1, 1973), which contains the hit single "If You Want Me to Stay" (p12 r3), would prove to be the last major commercial success for the group, but by that time the overwhelming crossover appeal of the band was already much imitated among black artists. From the beginning of Sly's commercial success, CBS subsidiary Epic Records had marketed the band as if they were a rock act, emphasizing both singles and albums. One result was that the band got significant airplay on white rock radio; but another result was that other black pop acts, in imitation of Sly, began devoting more attention to albums, a shift in focus that had already occurred in rock with the Beatles' *Sgt. Pepper's Lonely Hearts Club Band* in 1967.

1:12–1:21	**Interlude**, 4 mm.	Bass drops out and leaves guitar and drums only.
1:21–1:57	**Verse 2**, 16 mm.	As before, but with horns fading in and out to create a train-whistle effect. "Stiff all in the collar . . ."
1:57–2:15	**Chorus**, 8 mm.	As before, with horn line added. "Thank you . . ."
2:15–2:24	**Interlude**, 4 mm.	As before.
2:24–3:01	**Verse 3**, 16 mm.	As in verse 2, with slightly busier accompaniment filling in the spaces between vocal phrases. "Dance to the music . . ."
3:01–3:19	**Chorus**, 8 mm.	As before, with horns. "Thank you . . ."
3:19–3:37	**Contrasting Verse**, 8 mm.	A new verse is presented over the same music. Note the marked trebly tone of the vocals, which adds timbral contrast. "Flamin' eyes . . ."
3:37–3:55	**Chorus**, 8 mm.	As before, with horns. "Thank you . . ."
3:55–4:13	**Chorus**, 8 mm.	As before, with horns.
4:13–4:32	**Chorus**, 8 mm.	As before and fade-out.

Sylvester Stewart, lead singer and guitarist of Sly and the Family Stone, in concert in 1974. With his racially mixed group, Stewart combined James Brown–like bass patterns with aspects of psychedelia. As a result, Sly and the Family Stone appealed to both black and white audiences. While influencing many black artists, the group also put on an incendiary performance at Woodstock (in front of a largely white audience) and got significant airplay on white rock radio.

In Sly's Wake: Ohio Players, Kool and the Gang. After Sly and the Family Stone topped the pop charts, the way was clear for other funk-oriented acts to follow suit. The emergence of George Clinton and Parliament-Funkadelic in the mid 1970s is perhaps the clearest consequence of Sly's success, and this will be discussed in greater depth below. Other bands, however, enjoyed greater notoriety and success before Clinton and his P-Funk crew did, and the success of these bands helped define black pop in the 1970s. Hailing from Dayton, for instance, the Ohio Players began as Robert Ward and the Untouchables back in 1959. Over the course of the next decade, the band—the Ohio Untouchables and then the Ohio Players—released a series of singles without much commercial success. In 1973, the band stormed the charts with a novelty number called "Funky Worm," which hit number one on the rhythm and blues charts and rose as high as number fifteen on the pop charts. The band followed up with a string of number one rhythm and blues albums, all of which placed high on the pop charts as well, including *Skin Tight* (1974), *Fire* (1975), *Honey* (1975), and *Contradiction* (1976).

Another Sly-influenced band was Kool and the Gang, who started out as the Jazziacs and developed their musical skills in Jersey City, New Jersey, among such jazz luminaries as Thelonious Monk, Pharoah Sanders, and McCoy Tyner. By the late 1960s, however, the group had turned to a more commercial sound and enjoyed modest success on the rhythm and blues charts, with singles including "Let the Music Take Your Mind" (r19, 1970) and "Funky Man" (r16, 1970). The band emerged as an important crossover act in 1973 with the album *Wild and Peaceful*, which developed the pop funk of Sly Stone and hit number six on the rhythm and blues charts (p33), while spawning three crossover hit singles, "Funky Stuff" (r5 p29), "Jungle Boogie" (r2 p4), and "Hollywood Swinging" (r1 p6). Both the Ohio Players and Kool and the Gang built on Sly's blending of funky rhythms with catchy vocal hooks, and while the Ohio Players' popularity peaked in 1975 with "Love Rollercoaster" (r1 p1), Kool and the Gang would enjoy even greater success later in the decade after disco became popular, hitting with "Ladies' Night" (r1 p8, 1979) and "Celebration" (r1 p1, 1980), two songs that have since become popular staples of the party-band repertory.

6), and *Journey Through the Secret Life of Plants* (p4 r4, 1979). "Living for th[e] [Cit]y" (p8 r1), from *Innervisions*, is a representative example of these traits in [W]onder's music. The track tells the tale of a poor black country youth whose [fa]mily scrimps and saves to send him to the city to seek his fortune. He is [du]ped into carrying drugs for a pusher and summarily convicted and jailed. In [t]he last verse, Wonder's gravelly voice testifies to the suffering undergone by [t]his young man and his family. The full version of the track (there is a shorter [r]adio edit) provides a spoken vignette over Wonder's synthesizer accompani[ment] telling of the youth's arrival, duping, arrest, and conviction. The portrayal of the urban tragedy seems to indict society at large rather than pit black society against the white power structure; the song's tone is nonconfrontational. Easy to see is the general thematic kinship with "Papa Was a Rolling Stone," *What's Goin' On*, or even Sly's *There's a Riot Goin' On*. In its extended length (over seven minutes) and harmonic and melodic sophistication, "Living for the City"

LISTENING GUIDE

GET MUSIC ▶▶ wwnorton.com/rockhistory

The Temptations, "Papa Was a Rolling Stone"

Words and music by Norman Whitfield and Barrett Strong, produced by Norman Whitfield. Hit #1 on the Billboard Pop charts in 1972, and #5 on the rhythm and blues charts.

FORM: Simple verse-chorus. Like Sly Stone's "Thank You (Falettinme Be Mice Elf Agin)," the entire song is built over the same repeating bass line. Perhaps the most striking feature of this track is its drama and scope, running to almost seven minutes, employing orchestral strings, harp, and jazz trumpet to establish a menacing atmosphere.

TIME SIGNATURE: 4/4.

INSTRUMENTATION: Electric guitars (one with wah-wah), electric piano, bass, drums, hand claps, trumpet, orchestral strings, harp.

0:00–1:57	**Introduction**, 60 mm.	Lengthy and atmospheric introduction, beginning with bass and high-hat, but then adding orchestral strings, wah-wah guitar, jazzy trumpet improvisation, hand claps, and even harp.
1:57–2:28	**Verse 1**, 16 mm.	Lead vocal enters, counterpointed by bluesy guitar lines and wah-wah guitar. "It was the third . . ."

The Rock Connection: Tower of Power and War. Before he emerged as a performer, Sly Stone had been a well-known figure in the San Francisco psychedelic scene of the late 1960s, and this connection to the big-money world of rock music opened doors for many other black artists and bands. Like Sly, the Oakland-based band Tower of Power were also part of the Bay Area hippie scene, counting among their first important supporters Fillmore concert promoter Bill Graham and record producer David Rubinson (mentioned in the discussion of Moby Grape in Chapter 7). A band comprising white, Latino, and black musicians, Tower of Power became especially celebrated for their hard-driving funk grooves as well as the high caliber of their horn section, which often guested on the recordings of other artists (Elton John, the Rolling Stones, Rod Stewart). Recording for Warner Brothers, the band had a series of moderately successful albums during the first half of the 1970s, including *Bump City* (r16, 1972), *Tower of Power* (r11 p 15, 1973), and *Back to Oakland* (r13 p26, 1974), almost always finding more success on the rhythm and blues charts than they did on the rock charts.

Kool and the Gang during one of their trademark elaborate stage shows. The group started as a funk band strongly influenced by Sly and the Family Stone. As the '70s wore on, however, their sound became smoother and they became major players in disco, scoring hits with "Ladies' Night" and "Celebration."

Another notable rock connection in 1970s black pop comes via Eric Burdon, who had become famous in the mid 1960s as lead singer for the Animals. The members of War had moved in the Los Angeles rhythm and blues circuit throughout the 1960s. As the Nightriders, they had been hired to back up Deacon Jones, a famous football player who was making a failed attempt to build a new career in music. While backing Jones, the band was spotted by Burdon, Danish harmonica player Lee Oskar, and producer Jerry Goldstein. With Burdon and Oskar, War recorded *Eric Burdon Declares War*, which hit number eighteen on the pop album charts (r47) in 1970 and contained the number three pop single "Spill the Wine." Burdon soon left the group, though this did nothing to weaken their musical powers. War's *All Day Music* (r6 p16, 1971) began a string of highly successful albums and singles for the group, who often tended to blend latin styles with their rhythm and blues roots. *The World Is a Ghetto* (r1 p1, 1973) was the band's most commercially successful album overall, containing the crossover hit singles "The World Is a Ghetto" (r3 p7) and "Cisco Kid" (r5 p2), both of which provide representative examples of the group's style.

Later in the '70s: Earth, Wind, and Fire, the Commodores. The second half of the 1970s saw the continued popularity of bands that built on Sly's breakthrough success. Maurice White had been a studio drummer at Chess Records during the mid 1960s and had played behind Curtis Mayfield on Impressions records. In 1969, he moved to Los Angeles and formed Earth, Wind, and Fire. Soon lead singer Philip Bailey joined the band, and though the rest of the personnel shifted during the 1970s, Earth, Wind, and Fire scored a series of crossover hits with catchy pop hooks and sophisticated and sometimes intricate horn arrangements. "Shining Star" (r1 p1, 1975) provides a representative example of the band's approach. The tune begins with a hard-driving funk groove in the style of Sly and the Family Stone, setting up vocals that alternate sophisticated vocal harmonies with gritty solo singing, all complemented by rhythmic horn shots and held down by a catchy chorus.

The Commodores were also among the most commercially successful black pop bands of the late 1970s. The group started in 1968 as a party band in Tuskegee, Alabama, but soon came under the influence of Sly and the Family Stone. In 1971, the band was hired by Motown to open for Jackson 5 concerts. The Commodores' earliest roots in funk can be heard clearly in tracks such as "Brick House" (r4 p5, 1977), but it was the band's approach to ballads, written by singer Lionel Ritchie, that yielded the greatest commercial success. Ritchie's "Easy" (r1 p4, 1977) and "Three Times a Lady" (r1 p1, 1978) both offer representative examples of the Commodores' smooth, pop-ballad style, featuring Ritchie's polished lead vocals and refined and tasteful horn arrangements.

Motown Marches On: Norman Whitfield, the Temptations, Marvin Gaye.

Motown was quick to absorb the changes in black pop that characterized the late 1960s. According to the Temptations' Otis Williams, "Cloud Nine" (p6 r2, 1968) was recorded under the influence of Sly's "Dance to the Music." The group had recently suffered the departure of lead singer David Ruffin, who was replaced by Dennis Edwards in the summer of 1968. Now sharing the songwriting duties with Motown veteran Barrett Strong, Whitfield's production style steered a more aggressive and groove-oriented course. This new stylistic turn would prove even more successful with "I Can't Get Next to You," which hit the number one slot on both the pop and rhythm and blues charts in the summer

Anchored by Maurice White's compositions and led by Philip Bailey's soaring voice, Earth, Wind, and Fire, like Kool and the Gang, took Sly and the Family Stone–like funk and often combined it with the smoother sounds and complicated production of disco.

of 1969. The string of funk-oriented hits c (p7 r2, 1970) and "Ball of Confusion" (p3 r2 the gentle lyricism of "Just My Imagination topped both the pop and R&B charts in the s Temptations turned toward addressing more Rolling Stone" (p1 r5, 1972), a dramatic and ati problems within black urban life, features a ha Paul Riser, and ranks as Whitfield's finest achiev "Thank You," "Papa Was a Rolling Stone" is built line, now extending to almost seven minutes.

As much as the ambition of "Papa Was a Rolli by the recent seriousness of Sly and the Family Sto was also inspired by fellow Motown producer Marvi few Motown artists to win writing and production co the 1971 album *What's Going On* (p6 r1), Gaye produc albums in black pop, reflecting yet another link with r remaining faithful to his Motown roots. Containing th "What's Goin' On" (p2 r1), "Mercy Mercy Me (The Ecolo City Blues (Make Me Wanna Holler)" (p9 r1), Gaye's alb lems of urban life as Sly was soon to do, but with none o posture of some of Sly's music. Gaye's music, unlike that did not draw much on Sly's funk orientation. Gaye's music to the album, however, and in doing so Gaye borrowed the approach from the white rockers. Gaye's *What's Going On* is discussed in Chapter 7; it would also be possible to think of ' Stone" as a trip as well, but maybe just a shorter one.

Stevie Wonder Comes of Age.

While Sly brought funk and dan pop mainstream, and Marvin Gaye and Norman Whitfield brou of musical ambition to Motown, it was Stevie Wonder who put a ments of late 1960s and early 1970s black pop together into the s In the 1970s Wonder was given complete artistic control over his i proceeded to produce a series of albums that, if not always concept tainly take the sum of the tracks to be at least as important as any si This album-oriented mentality was most immediately influenced by *Going On*, but is more generally a sign of late '60s rock influence on music-making—in many ways Wonder's approach extends the black p approach to the hippie aesthetic initiated by Gaye. Unlike any other M artist of the time, Wonder often wrote, produced, and played many of th ments on his albums. And while he was able to place several singles hig the pop and rhythm and blues charts during the '70s, Wonder also paral the British progressive rockers in his emphasis on complex arrangement: search for new sounds and timbres (including extensive use of the synthe and lyrics devoted to serious topics.

Beginning with *Talking Book* (p3 r1, 1972), Wonder's albums explored a ety of musical styles and ambitious approaches, as can be heard on *Innervisio* (p4 r1, 1973), *Fulfillingness' First Finale* (p1 r1, 1974), *Songs in the Key of Life* (p1 shows a connection to the progressive rock of Yes, Genesis, or Jethro Tull. The relationship of Wonder's music to white rock in the '70s was not missed by rock listeners: Wonder received more rock-radio airplay than any other black musician except perhaps Jimi Hendrix, and if white rock fans had only one album by a black artist from the '70s, it was probably one of Stevie's.

The Last Train for the Coast: Diana Ross, Marvin Gaye, the Jackson 5, Rare Earth. By the early 1970s, Motown was mostly run from Los Angeles, as Berry Gordy had left Detroit to pursue a broader range of possibilities for his company in southern California. And while many consider the 1960s to be the "golden age" of Motown, Gordy's label continued to record an impressive roster of successful artists in addition to the Temptations and Stevie Wonder. Diana Ross, now a solo act, continued her hit making, though no longer at quite the level she had achieved with the Supremes. In the wake of his success with *What's Goin' On*,

2:28–3:00	**Chorus**, 16 mm.	Choral vocals share melody with lead vocal. Note the double-time hand claps that begin with the second 8-bar phrase. "Papa was a rolling stone . . ."
3:00–3:31	**Interlude**, 16 mm.	Jazzy trumpet and wah-wah guitar return, along with orchestral strings.
3:31–4:03	**Verse 2**, 16 mm.	Melody now traded between singers, "Hey mama . . ."
4:03–4:35	**Chorus**, 16 mm.	As before, but hand claps begin immediately, doubled by the wah-wah guitar. "Papa was a rolling stone . . ."
4:35–4:59	**Interlude**, 12 mm.	Trumpet returns, now with pronounced echo effect and supported by electric piano, bass, and drums, and wah-wah guitar.
4:59–5:30	**Verse 3**, 16 mm.	This verse mostly features the high tenor voice of Eddie Kendriks. "Hey mama . . ."
5:30–6:02	**Chorus**, 16 mm.	As before, but without hand claps. "Papa was a rolling stone . . ."
6:02–6:18	**Chorus**, 8 mm.	Hand claps kick in with this partial repeat of the chorus.
6:18–6:52	**Coda**, 16 mm.	Strings enter as vocals fade and double-time hand claps continue, then track fades out.

Stevie Wonder, one of Motown's most successful artists, in performance. In the 1960s Wonder was a staple of Motown's lineup of pop stars. In the 1970s, Wonder broke with Motown tradition and took total control of his music—writing, producing, and playing all instruments. Wonder combined the driving, danceable funk of Sly and the Family Stone with Sly and Marvin Gaye's social consciousness to create several albums of lasting influence: The Music of My Mind (1972), Talking Book (1972), and Songs in the Key of Life (1974), among others.

Stevie Wonder, "Living for the City"

Words and music by Stevie Wonder, produced by Stevie Wonder. Rose to #1 on the rhythm and blues charts and #8 on the pop charts in 1973.

FORM: Modified compound AABA. The A sections are made up of two verses and one instrumental bridge each. The verse contains the "Livin' just enough for the city" refrain, while the instrumental bridges make clear references to classical music through their use of more complicated harmony, melody, and rhythm. The B section is not really a musical section, but rather a mini-drama that has some musical accompaniment. The compound AABA form is modified in the use of a third A section before the B section (though this A section is itself a modified version). The repetitions of the bridge section at the end of the track help create a strong sense of ending and are not exceptional in such larger forms. The closest comparison in terms of form among the pieces we have studied would be to "Roundabout" by Yes.

TIME SIGNATURE: 4/4 in the 12-bar verses, with a 9-bar section made up of six bars of 3/4, one of 2/4, and then two of 4/4 used in the instrumental bridges.

INSTRUMENTATION: The rhythm section is made up of synthesizer bass, electric piano, hand claps, and drums. Wonder's lead vocal is featured with sparing use of backup vocals, and multiple synthesizers are employed to lend a symphonic quality to the track. All instruments on this track are played by Stevie Wonder.

	0:00–0:11	**Introduction**, 4 mm.	Electric piano and synthesizer bass establish the song's basic chord progression.
A	0:11–0:40	**Verse 1**, 12 mm.	Lead vocals added, along with bass drum. "A boy is born . . ."
	0:40–1:09	**Verse 2**, 12 mm.	Drumbeat kicks in. "His father works . . ."
	1:09–1:26	**Bridge**, 9 mm.	Synthesizers enter, playing a classical-sounding passage with lead vocal on the syllable "la." Time signature changes to 3/4, with the final bar in 2/4 before returning to 4/4.
A	1:26–1:56	**Verse 3**, 12 mm.	As before, though the vocal may now be a little more urgent. "His sister's black . . ."
	1:56–2:30	**Verse 4**, 14 mm.	As before, with new synthesizer line added. Two extra bars are added to end of verse. "Her brother's smart . . ."
	2:30–2:47	**Bridge**, 9 mm.	As before.

continued

A'	2:47–3:56	**Vamp**, 28 mm.	A vamp drawn from the verse is played as Wonder provides vocal improvisations supported by gospel-flavored backup vocals and hand claps. Synthesizer lines weave in and out, and synthesizer bass gets busier.
	3:56–4:13	**Bridge**, 9 mm.	As before, and then vamp and fade create transition.
B	4:13–5:19	**Central Drama**	"Bus for New York City . . ." with spoken dialogue portraying story of deception, arrest, trial, and prison. The music continues to play underneath, and then breaks down to synthesizer incidental music (with some drumming), and then verse music fades back in.
A	5:19–5:47	**Verse 5**, 12 mm.	Lead vocals become bitter and gruff, backup vocals added, as synthesizer lines continue to weave in and out. "His hair is long . . ."
	5:47–6:21	**Verse 6**, 14 mm.	Lead vocals are still gruff, as second vocal part is added and synthesizers now play in harmony. Two bars added to end of verse as music seems to break down briefly. "I hope you hear . . ."
	6:21–6:38	**Bridge**, 9 mm.	As before, but now with more elaborate counterpoint in the synthesizer part.
	6:00–6:54	**Bridge**, 9 mm.	Repeat of previous 9 bars.
	6:54–7:24	**Bridge**, 16 mm.	As before, but here extended to create majestic ending. Note that this section is all in 3/4, with no time signature change at the end as in previous statements.

Marvin Gaye continued to be a fixture of black pop with middle-of-the-road hits such as "Let's Get It On" (p1 r1, 1973) and (with Diana Ross) "Got to Give It Up, Pt. 1" (p1 r1, 1977). Motown broke into the teen market with a group of brothers from Gary, Indiana. The Jackson 5, featuring the high prepubescent vocals of young Michael, scored a string of top bubblegum hits, starting with "I Want You Back" (1969) and continuing with "ABC" (1970), "The Love You Save" (1970), and "I'll Be There" (1970)—all of which hit number one on both the pop and rhythm and blues singles charts. The Jackson 5 as a group, and Michael as a solo artist, placed over a dozen more hits on the charts before leaving Motown for Epic in the mid '70s. In the second half of the decade, the

Jacksons (as they were now called, since Gordy owned the Jackson 5 name), continued to enjoy success, as Michael began a solo career that made him one of the most successful artists in the history of popular music.

Perhaps the most interesting indication of Gordy's desire to branch out into all possible music markets was has signing of Rare Earth, a white rock band from Detroit. Released under the Rare Earth subsidiary label, the band hit with "Get Ready" (p4 r20) in 1970 as well as with the album *Get Ready* (p12), the second side of which features a twenty-one-minute version of the title track. Ironically, while Gordy was abandoning his Detroit operation for a broader portfolio of interests, a pair of producers in Philadelphia were making plans to form a label that would use Motown as a model and reshape black pop in the process.

The Jackson 5 in a 1972 television performance. While Marvin Gaye and Stevie Wonder were demanding control over their music, the Jackson 5 were in the traditional Motown mold: Berry Gordy controlled most aspects of their sound, style, and look. The Jackson 5's tight arrangements and short, catchy songs, combined with Michael Jackson's powerful voice and charismatic performances, made the brothers teen idols and enormously successful worldwide.

The Philadelphia Sound: Gamble and Huff.   In the late 1950s, Leiber and Stoller developed the idea of the independent record producer. Before they came along, record producers had always been employees of the record company that was releasing the record, but after Leiber and Stoller established this new model, many—perhaps most importantly Phil Spector—followed their lead. At Atlantic, the practice was often to give producers had the new autonomy and freedom that Leiber and Stoller had opened up, while these producers were also working for the label; Jerry Wexler is perhaps the best example of this practice (though Atlantic also bought the distribution rights of regional hits from smaller labels, who effectively acted as independent producers in that situation). Motown (and on a more modest scale, Stax) followed Atlantic's lead in having a roster of producers, all of whom worked for the label exclusively, while Spector started his own label devoted specifically to his releases. In Philadelphia in the second half of the 1960s, Kenny Gamble and Leon Huff began as independents, writing songs and producing records for the rhythm and blues market. They released some of these records themselves, such as the Intruders' "(We'll Be) United" (r14, 1966), which appeared on the Gamble label. Other records were released through major labels, including hits by Archie Bell ("I Can't Stop Dancin'" from 1968) and Wilson Pickett ("Don't Let the Green Grass Fool You" from 1971), both of which appeared on Atlantic. In the early 1970s—as Sly was enjoying his greatest success and Whitfield's Temptations records were getting increasingly funky—CBS provided the money for the rising songwriting and production team of Gamble and Huff to begin their own label, Philadelphia International, which would be devoted specifically to their records but distributed through the well-established CBS network.

Creators of the "Philadelphia sound,"
producers Kenny Gamble and Leon Huff.
As Motown moved toward funk in the
1970s, Gamble and Huff used smoother
sounds and more complicated arrangements to score hits for Billy Paul ("Me
and Mrs. Jones") and the O'Jays ("Back
Stabbers"), and their backing band performed the theme song for the groundbreaking black dance and music show
Soul Train.

The Gamble and Huff approach, often called the "Philadelphia sound," typically blends lyric vocals and a driving rhythm section with elegant string arrangements provided by Thom Bell and Bobby Martin. In 1972, Philadelphia International began a series of hit releases with the easygoing ballad from Billy Paul, "Me and Mrs. Jones," which hit the number one slot on both pop and rhythm and blues charts in the fall of that year. Gamble and Huff's most consistently successful acts were Harold Melvyn and the Blue Notes (featuring Teddy Pendergrass), whose string of hits were often limited to the rhythm and blues charts, and the O'Jays, whose singles regularly crossed over to the pop charts. The O'Jays' "Back Stabbers" (r1 p3, 1972) is a representative example of the Philadelphia sound. After a dramatic solo piano opening, a latin-flavored groove begins, which is then overlaid with strings and brass. As the O'Jays enter singing the hook-oriented chorus, it is easy to hear the Motown influence of the Temptations or the Four Tops. The happy, up-tempo groove is also central to "Love Train," which made number one on both the pop and rhythm and blues charts in 1973, and may be one of the most widely known of the Gamble and Huff records, at least among white listeners. A big part of the success of Gamble and Huff productions was their house band, Mother Father Sister Brother (MFSB). This group had a hit of their own when they provided the theme music to *Soul Train*, a television show devoted to black pop hosted by Don Cornelius and directed specifically at a black audience. This song, "TSOP (The Sound of Philadelphia)," hit number one on both pop and rhythm and blues charts in 1974. Because *Soul Train* featured dancing, much as *American Bandstand* always had, many white rock listeners would generalize—wrongly, as we shall see—that "TSOP" was what all black pop in the '70s sounded like, and this would feed into the controversy over disco some years later.

Thom Bell, the Spinners, Stylistics. In addition to his work with Gamble and Huff, Thom Bell produced artists on a freelance basis. The Spinners had a history in Detroit going back to the late 1950s and had been signed to Motown during the '60s. Though they scored a handful of hits for Motown—"It's a Shame" (r4 p14, 1970) did the best—in 1972 they left the label and were picked up by Atlantic. With Bell now producing them, the group stormed the pop and rhythm and blues charts with a string of top records, including "I'll Be Around" (r1 p3, 1972), "Could It Be I'm Falling in Love" (r1 p4, 1972), "They Just Can't

Directed by
GORDON PARKS

Music Composed by
'Hot Buttered Soul Man'
Isaac Hayes

Shaft, directed by Gordon Parks, proved to Hollywood that movies directed at an African American audience could sell. The movie featured the strong, virile, and stylish police officer John Shaft (Richard Roundtree), who fights off the (mostly white) bad guys, all to the sound of Isaac Hayes's Oscar-winning soundtrack. The success of Shaft paved the way for other so-called blaxploitation films—all with funky original soundtracks—including Superfly (soundtrack by Curtis Mayfield) and Coffy (soundtrack by Roy Ayers).

Stop It (The Games People Play)" (r1 p5, 1975), and "Rubberband Man" (r1 p2, 1976). Bell had similar results with the Stylistics, who were a Philadelphia group signed to Avco Records. Along with lyricist Linda Creed, Bell wrote many of the Stylistics' hits in addition to producing them, including "Betcha by Golly, Wow" (r2 p3, 1972) and "You Make Me Feel Brand New" (r5 p2, 1974). With both groups Bell continued to work in the polished Philadelphia style, emphasizing upbeat themes and elegant string arrangements.

"Blaxploitation": Isaac Hayes and Curtis Mayfield.   One of the factors influencing black musicians to explore issues in their music regarding problems in the urban black community was a new genre of film that appeared at the beginning of the 1970s—a genre often called "blaxploitation." A 1971 independent film entitled *Sweet Sweetback's Baad Asssss Song* painted a more realistic picture of urban black life than had been done before and was made entirely outside the usual Hollywood establishment. The film's unexpected success tipped the major studios off to the realization that there was money to be made in movies that cast strong, aggressive main characters in tough urban situations. In 1971, *Shaft* became the first important movie in this new genre, and Isaac Hayes's music for the film earned him an Oscar. Hayes had been part of the team at Stax during the 1960s, writing and producing a series of hits with David Porter for Sam and Dave. After the sale of the label (as discussed in Chapter 6), the opportunity arose for Hayes to record as a solo artist. His first album, *Hot*

Soul Train

Since its debut in 1970, the syndicated dance-party show *Soul Train* has played a similar role to *American Bandstand*, as an independently produced and nationally distributed show that provides America with a weekly dose of dance music. But while *Bandstand* was more broadly pop-oriented and a force for integration, *Soul Train* has always explicitly been a celebration of black styles of music and dance.

Soul Train was created in 1969 by Don Cornelius, a Chicago-based disc jockey and sports anchor. Cornelius thought a dance-party show aimed at the black, urban market would be a hit, so he produced a pilot episode himself and found the show's first sponsors. His first show was broadcast on August 17, 1970, on the independent Chicago TV station WCIU, and was a rapid success. With an important black-owned company, Johnson Products, as a primary sponsor, Cornelius moved his production to Los Angeles and syndicated the show nationally. *Soul Train* quickly spread in exposure and popularity until it was broadcast nation-

wide. It is still broadcast today to more than 80 percent of American households.

Soul Train has survived by continually adapting to changing tastes. But it has always mixed established styles with both newer and more traditional ones. Most of the performers on the first nationally syndicated season, 1971–72, were established stars with current hits on the rhythm and blues charts, such as the Staples Singers, Al Green, and Bill Withers. But it featured rhythm and blues, soul, and blues veterans like Little Richard, Jackie

Soul Train was the brainchild of the show's host, Don Cornelius (right) a disc jockey and sports anchor from Chicago. While the show started in 1969, its first nationally syndicated season was 1971–72, with Edwin Starr (below) as one of the featured performers. While the performers were not always black, Soul Train emerged as an important celebration and vehicle for black culture in the 1970s.

Wilson, and B. B. King alongside cutting-edge performers like the Ohio Players and the Bar-Kays. The 2005 season included some hip-hop acts, such as Shawna F with Ludacris, but mostly featured more conservative neo-soul artists like Brian McKnight, Usher, and Alicia Keys, and even some '90s-style boy bands such as Boyz II Men. The occasional videos feature more popular artists like R. Kelly or Beyoncé Knowles.

Soul Train's dance-party format is similar to *American Bandstand*. Cornelius was the weekly host until 1993, when he was followed by a series of guest hosts and eventually by other regular ones. The bulk of the show features young men and women dancing to current hits, interspersed with two to three live performers, and occasional comedy monologues, celebrity cameos, dance contests, and music videos. The performers are drawn from black styles but are not necessarily black—an important distinction. *Soul Train* has often featured dance hits by white artists, such as Hall & Oates, Sheena Easton, Elton John, Culture Club, and Don Henley. Because of this, *Soul Train* serves as a celebration and vehicle for black culture, rather than for black artists exclusively. Much of the focus

of the show is on the individual dancers. Some of them, like Pebbles, Jody Watley, and Rosie Perez, have gone on to fame as musicians or movie stars.

Soul Train played an important role in the popularity of Philly soul and disco. Artists produced by Gamble and Huff or Thom Bell were regularly featured throughout the show's early years. And disco's characteristic "four-on-the-floor" drumbeat developed out of the style of Earl Young, the drummer for Philadelphia International house band MFSB, which was heard every week on the *Soul Train* theme song, "TSOP (The Sound of Philadelphia)." Cornelius

didn't shy away from the overtly sexual material that was so important to disco. On April 10, 1976, for instance, *Soul Train* featured two key early disco songs with notoriously sexual lyrics, Johnny Taylor's "Disco Lady" (r1 p1, 1976) and Donna Summer's "I Love to Love You Baby" (r3 p2, 1976). Although *Soul Train* has not played a significant role in the rise of new styles since disco, it remains an important, independently produced, national outlet for black dance and music styles, providing access to airwaves otherwise dominated by mainstream acts.

Buttered Soul (r1 p8, 1969), became the first in a series of seven number one rhythm and blues albums. Hayes crossed over to the pop charts in a big way with "The Theme from *Shaft*" (r2 p1, 1971), while the soundtrack album, *Shaft*, hit number one on both the pop and R&B charts. "The Theme from *Shaft*" may be the first track to firmly associate the rhythmic sound of the wah-wah guitar with black pop; though white and black musicians had used it before in other contexts, its prominent place in this track made it a kind of stylistic flag for black pop in the 1970s. Hayes's ultra-cool vocal delivery—part spoken and part sung—also served as a model for many black artists who followed him.

Like Hayes, Curtis Mayfield also had deep roots in 1960s rhythm and blues. Throughout the decade he had been a member of the Chicago-based vocal group, the Impressions, who had scored a long series of rhythm and blues hits, with some that crossed over, such as "It's All Right" (r1 p4, 1963) and "We're a Winner" (r1 p14, 1968). Inspired by Hayes's success with *Shaft*, Mayfield enthusiastically accepted the challenge of writing music for the 1972 film *Superfly*. Mayfield's high tenor voice soars above the rhythmic wah-wah guitar and elegant strings on "Freddie's Dead" (r2 p4, 1972), showing the influence of Hayes and Sly as well as the smooth production of Philadelphia and Motown. Mayfield followed with "Superfly" (r5 p8, 1972), a track from the movie that reveals his funk influences. To white audiences of the early 1970s, Curtis Mayfield was perhaps the most widely known voice for the problems of black urban life; he performed frequently on prime-time network television shows and became something of a cultural ambassador to the white community.

Curtis Mayfield in a 1971 performance. Though Mayfield started his career as a songwriter and singer for the doo-wop group the Impressions, he struck out on his own and forged a strong solo career. Much of Mayfield's music tackled social issues with an optimistic outlook, praising black culture while not harshly condemning whites. His soundtrack to the 1972 "blaxploitation" film Superfly *(directed, like* Shaft, *by Gordon Parks) contained some of Mayfield's biggest hits, including "Pusherman" and "Freddie's Dead."*

James Brown, George Clinton and Parliament/Funkadelic

Soul Brother Number 1. Sly Stone became a model for other black bands and artists by effectively negotiating the crossover into the white rock market, much as Motown and Stax had done in the 1960s. But there was also a strong funk component to Sly's music, and the harder-edged aspects of funk tended not to cross over into the rock world as effectively. In fact, in the first half of the 1970s, funk was closely associated with black culture in the minds of both black and white listeners, mostly because the style had been so successfully developed by James Brown. As discussed at the end of Chapter 6, James Brown's career began in the 1950s and by the mid 1960s, his groove-oriented soul made him one of the most important figures in black pop, also enjoying some crossover success with white audiences. Brown's success on both of these fronts continued into the first half of the 1970s, as hits such as "Get Up (I Feel like Being a) Sex Machine (Part 1)" (p15 r2, 1970), "Super Bad" (p13 r1, 1970), and "Hot Pants" (p15 r1, 1971) kept him on both the pop and rhythm and blues charts until mid-decade. In the period after the 1968 assassination of Martin Luther King Jr., Brown became an important voice within the black community, encouraging black pride—"Say It Loud, I'm Black and I'm Proud" (p10 r1, 1968)—and often coming out strongly against drug abuse. His songs "King Heroin" (p40 r6, 1972) and "Public Enemy #1" both contain strong anti-drug messages and are delivered more in the manner of a sermon than a song, and with far less groove-driven energy than some of Brown's other records from the same period. Many of his '70s tracks put more emphasis on the rhythmic interlocking of guitar, bass, and drums than his '60s records had, though horns still play an important role in these later tracks. Brown's music influenced and served as a model for many of the acts discussed already in this chapter; Sly Stone, Stevie Wonder, and Norman Whitfield all drew on Brown's characteristic emphasis on the rhythmic groove and tight ensemble playing as well as his flamboyant approach to live performance. Despite Brown's influence on a wide range of black pop bands and artists, it was an ambitious musician and songwriter from Detroit, George Clinton, who is most closely associated with the extensive development of funk in the 1970s.

The Mothership Connections: George Clinton and Company.   James Brown was perhaps the first to prove that a black performer could surround himself with first-rate musicians and create and sustain a lucrative business. While Brown had others to help him do this, he had a tremendous amount of control over his career and music. Berry Gordy had shown that a black man could own and operate his own record company, building Motown from a modest rhythm and blues label into one of the most important record companies in the country. George Clinton brought together aspects of Brown's and Gordy's accomplishments to establish one of the most successful music-business operations in the second half of the 1970s. Originally from New Jersey, Clinton moved to Detroit with his group, the Parliaments, during the first Motown boom of the 1960s. Clinton sang, wrote, and produced songs for the Parliaments, who likely aspired to be the next Temptations or Four Tops and had a number three rhythm and blues hit with "(I Wanna) Testify" (p20) in 1967. Because of a dispute over the name of the group, Clinton began recording under the name Funkadelic to avoid legal complications. When the legal wrangling ended, Clinton's group began using the name Parliament—eventually recording with different labels as Parliament (Casablanca) and Funkadelic (Westbound, and then Warners). From the beginning, Parliament was considered the more

George Clinton in concert, 1978. Clinton was strongly influenced by James Brown's high musical standards. In fact, Clinton's bassist, Bootsy Collins, and saxophonist, Maceo Parker, were both from Brown's band. Clinton, however, drew influence for his stage shows from bands like Kiss and Genesis. Often Clinton's shows had an otherworldly, comic-book feel, with a spaceship—"the mothership"—landing on stage, ready to take the band away.

commercial act, while Funkadelic was considered more avowedly experimental. The first few Funkadelic albums from the 1970–73 period blend psychedelic rock with soul, showing such diverse influences as Jimi Hendrix, Sly Stone, Miles Davis, and James Brown. The group also developed a reputation for dressing outrageously during performances, as well as for wild on-stage antics.

By 1974, Clinton had convinced Neil Bogart of Casablanca Records to sign Parliament, and the band released *Up for the Down Stroke* (r17, 1974), an album that would be the first in a series of successful releases for Clinton and crew under the Parliament moniker. The band's important breakthrough record was *Mothership Connection* (p13 r4, 1976), which contained the hit "Tear the Roof Off the Sucker (Give Up the Funk)" (p15 r5). For the tour to support this album, Clinton developed an elaborate stage show that featured a spaceship descending onto the stage, from which he would emerge as the character he called Dr. Funkenstein. Casablanca was to fund this elaborate show, but considering that Bogart also had Kiss on his label, it is perhaps no surprise that he supported the idea. *Mothership Connection* brought a kind of comic-book quality to Parliament shows and albums, and Clinton liked to emphasize this aspect of the music. He was borrowing and adapting considerably from white acts such as Alice Cooper and Genesis, but much like other black artists in the 1970s, Clinton felt free to adopt, adapt, and further develop ideas that were then current in white rock. Subsequent albums such as *The Clones of Dr. Funkenstein* (p20 r3, 1976) and *Funkentelechy vs. the Placebo Syndrome* (p13 r2, 1977) continued to develop the concept-album idea, though with a healthy dose of irony and humor.

During the string of successful Parliament albums in the second half of the 1970s, Funkadelic were also releasing albums that enjoyed considerable success on the rhythm and blues charts. *One Nation Under a Groove*, for instance, went to number one on the rhythm and blues charts in 1978 (p16) and *Uncle Jam Wants You* hit number two in 1979 (p18). Clinton was leading the songwriting and producing on these records; he was using a stable of musicians including many who had previously played in James Brown's bands, such as sax player Maceo Parker and bassist Bootsy Collins. Because of his success with Parliament and Funkadelic in the period after 1975, Clinton was able to negotiate deals for other artists within his "Parliafunkadelicment Thang" collective, and albums were released by Bootsy's Rubber Band (led by bassist Collins), the Horny Horns (the horn section), the Brides of Dr. Funkenstein (female backup singers), and Parlet (more female backup singers), among others. By building on the examples set by Brown and Gordy, George Clinton became one of the most influential figures in black pop during the second half of the 1970s, and has remained the prime exponent of funk in the years since.

Average White Band, the Band That Did Get Airplay on White Rock Radio.
Despite the popularity of Parliament and Funkadelic among black listeners, and despite the respectable positions on the pop charts earned by some of the albums these bands released, white rock listeners heard very little Parliament or Funkadelic on the radio. Ironically, the funk band that many rock listeners would have known best was a group from Scotland called the Average White Band. The band's first American album, *Average White Band*, hit number one in the fall of 1974, propelling the single "Pick Up the Pieces" to number one on the singles chart. *Cut the Cake* (p4, 1975) and *Soul Searching* (p8, 1976) also did well and received significant airplay on rock radio. The first two albums also hit number one on the rhythm and blues charts, while the third rose to number two. It is some measure of how far apart white and black audiences had grown that many white listeners who enjoyed the Average White Band had very little awareness of funk's development in the first half of the 1970s. This lack of understanding of funk—and of black pop generally—would contribute significantly to the furor that developed in the rock community over the rise of disco.

Reggae Comes Ashore

New Orleans and New York. Reggae cannot be considered an African American pop style, but its rise in the 1970s has its roots in the history of much American rock and rhythm and blues that preceded it as well as aftershocks in pop styles that follow, especially punk and rap. Jamaican music has played at

LISTENING GUIDE

GET
MUSIC ▶▶ wwnorton.com/rockhistory

Parliament,
"Tear the Roof Off the Sucker (Give Up the Funk)"

Words and music by George Clinton, Bootsy Collins, and Jerome Brailey, produced by George Clinton. Rose to #5 on the rhythm and blues charts and #15 on the pop charts.

FORM: Modified contrasting verse-chorus. This track employs two choruses rather than a verse and chorus, and these two choruses use music that is different enough for it to be considered contrasting. The form is built up generally through an alternation of these two choruses. The first time through, chorus 2 is expanded, creating an 8-bar interlude. The second time through this interlude itself is expanded by four measures. The third time through presents the most extensive expansion: chorus 1 is repeated once and then chorus 2 occurs seven times. The track ends with a fourth time through chorus 1 and chorus 2, returning them to the texture and length found at the beginning of the tune.

TIME SIGNATURE: 4/4. Note especially how bass and electric guitar weave often complicated rhythmic patterns against the more straightforward patterns in the drums.

INSTRUMENTATION: Drums, bass, and guitar form rhythmic background throughout. Horns employed for emphasis and embellishment, and vocals throughout are sung in a choral, sing-along style. Note the use of synthetic orchestral strings, a keyboard sound more often associated with mainstream rock during the mid 1970s, but also later in the 1970s with disco.

0:00–0:19	**Introduction**, 8 mm.	Low male voice intones "Tear the roof off the mutha . . ." to the accompaniment of the drums, and then to the rest of the band.
0:19–0:37	**Chorus 1**, 8 mm.	Choral, sing-along vocals; note syncopated bass line and sustained keyboard chords. "You've got a real type of thang . . ."

least a peripheral role in mainstream popular music since the 1940s and '50s. In Chapter 3, we mentioned the late 1950s craze for calypso music and the popularity of songs such as "Jamaican Farewell," and the fact that the Kingston Trio took its name from that Jamaican town. While Americans were enjoying Jamaican music in the late 1950s, however, Jamaicans were listening to American pop, and especially rhythm and blues. For years, Jamaican radio stations had been quite conservative, based on the British model of the BBC. But

0:37–0:56	**Chorus 2**, 8 mm.	Choral vocals continue, but notice change in bass line and keyboard part, and sparer texture in the rhythm section. "We want the funk . . ."
0:56–1:14	**Interlude**, 8 mm.	This section employs the music from chorus 2. "La la la . . ."
1:14–1:33	**Chorus 1**, 8 mm.	As before, but now with bass voice at the front of the mix. "You've got a real type of thang . . ."
1:33–1:51	**Chorus 2**, 8 mm.	As before. "We want the funk . . ."
1:51–2:09	**Interlude**, 8 mm.	As before. "La la la . . ."
2:09–2:19	**Interlude extension**, 4 mm.	New vocal added over same music, as sustained keyboard chord returns. "We gotta turn this mutha out . . ."
2:19–2:54	**Chorus 1**, 16 mm.	Length is doubled by repetition of 8-bar section, "You've got a real type of thang . . ."
2:54–3:30	**Chorus 2**, 16 mm.	Length is also doubled here, as the texture builds up by adding layers, "We want the funk . . ."
3:30–5:00	**Chorus 2**, 40 mm.	Extension here comprises five times through the 8-bar pattern, beginning by returning to a simpler texture and then building up again, adding the material from the interlude extension. "We want the funk . . ."
5:00–5:18	**Interlude**, 8 mm.	"La la la . . ." Note that chorus 1 melody enters early.
5:18–5:35	**Chorus 1**, 8 mm.	As at the beginning, "You've got a real type of thang . . ."
5:35–5:44	**Chorus 2**, 8 mm.	As at the beginning, with fade-out. "We want the funk . . ."

when portable radios become more affordable—and thus accessible—Jamaicans could tune in to American radio stations, especially those broadcasting from New Orleans. As a consequence, many Jamaicans developed a strong taste for artists such as Fats Domino and the rolling feel of much New Orleans–based rhythm and blues. Although tuning in to listen to this music on the radio was easy, obtaining it in the form of records was another thing altogether. The scarcity of American rhythm and blues records on the island led to the appearance of the "sound system man"—an entrepreneur who assembled a powerful sound system on the back of a truck and drove it from town to town, stopping to play records for whoever gathered to hear the music. Competition soon arose among these mobile music promoters, leading some to scratch the labels off their most recently acquired records (often purchased on special trips to New Orleans or Miami) so that competitors would not know who the artist was. It also led sound system men to begin featuring disc jockeys who would talk over records, often inventing rhyming verses to display their cleverness and verbal dexterity. In the 1970s Kool Herc, a Jamaican living in New York's Bronx began to demonstrate how this kind of "toasting" was done, and before too long New York had mobile sound systems with DJs and MCs who were developing a style of music that would be called rap.

LISTENING GUIDE   GET MUSIC ▶▶ wwnorton.com/rockhistory

Bob Marley and the Wailers, "Get Up, Stand Up"

Words and music by Bob Marley and Peter Tosh, produced by Chris Blackwell and the Wailers. Contained on *Burnin'*, which was released in 1973.

FORM: Contrasting verse-chorus, with verse and chorus based on different but similar bass lines. Choruses and verses alternate regularly with no interludes in between. Like "Papa Was a Rolling Stone" and "Thank You (Falettinme Be Mice Elf Agin)," this track is driven by the bass part and drumbeat, even if it does not use the same bass line all the way through.

TIME SIGNATURE: 4/4.

INSTRUMENTATION: Electric guitar, clavinet (an electric keyboard similar to a harpsichord in design, but sounding more like an electric guitar), electric piano, bass, drums, percussion, lead and backup vocals.

| 0:00–0:04 | **Introduction**, 4 mm. | After drum lead-in, clavinet, guitar, bass, and drums enter, setting up entrance of the voices. |
| 0:08–0:32 | **Chorus**, 16 mm. | Unison, sing-along vocal melody, "Get up, stand up. . ." |

In the early 1960s, however, New Orleans rhythm and blues began to fade, so Jamaican musicians began to provide their own version referred to as "ska." As the 1960s progressed, ska was replaced by a newer style called "rock steady," and reggae developed out of this second style. Writers often claim that the lilting reggae rhythms are derived from rhythmic feels established by earlier Jamaican musicians who thought they were playing a rhythm and blues beat, but got it wrong. This "wrongly played" feel was catchy, and it developed an identity of its own within Jamaican music. Whatever the case, most of the musicians who led the reggae movement in the 1970s had backgrounds in Jamaican pop that stretched back into the early 1960s. Of these, the most important was Bob Marley. With Peter Tosh and Bunny Livingston, Marley had been a member of a vocal trio in the 1960s called the Wailers. The Wailers were signed by Jamaican producer Lee "Scratch" Perry, who recorded the trio using his backing band, the Upsetters; the group's records did well enough locally. Perry also convinced the Wailers that they needed to play instruments themselves to be successful.

At about the same time, Chris Blackwell established Island Records in the UK and began releasing records for the British market that had been recorded in Jamaica. The market for such records was stronger in England than it was in

0:32–0:57	**Verse 1**, 16 mm.	Lead vocal takes over; note the change in the line played by the bass and guitar. "Preacher man . . ."
0:57–1:21	**Chorus**, 16 mm.	Choral vocals return. Note the percussion in the background. "Get up, stand up . . ."
1:21–1:46	**Verse 2**, 16 mm.	Lead vocal takes over again. Note wah-wah guitar lines in background. "Most people think . . ."
1:46–2:11	**Chorus**, 16 mm.	Choral vocals return, but now Marley improvises over the melody. "Get up, stand up . . ."
2:11–2:35	**Verse 3**, 16 mm.	New lead singer, Peter Tosh, changes the melody somewhat. "We're sick and tired . . ."
2:35–3:00	**Chorus**, 16 mm.	Choral vocals return, and both Marley and Tosh improvise over the melody. "Get up, stand up . . ."
3:00–3:13	**Chorus**, 8 mm.	As before, as song fades out.

Bob Marley, the world's most famous reggae musician, in a 1976 concert. Here, Marley performs in front of the image of Haile Selassie, the leader of the Rastafarian religion, which preached salvation for African people all over the world. Often catchy and danceable, Marley's lyrics focused on political and social freedom, making Marley an icon for social justice movements around the world.

America, largely because there was a substantial subculture of Jamaicans living in the UK who were eager to hear music from home. The homesick Jamaicans enjoyed the music, but so did British kids, and this new availability of reggae in the UK during the early 1970s influenced many of the English musicians who would later end up in punk and new-wave bands. Blackwell signed the Wailers to Island and advanced them the money they needed to record an album. In the spring of 1973, *Catch a Fire* was released, followed by *Burnin'* at the end of the year. "Get Up, Stand Up" appeared on the second of these records, a representative example of Bob Marley's approach to reggae. Like much funk-influenced rhythm and blues of the early 1970s, the track is built on a groove, laid down by the bass and drums, that remains steady throughout the tune and provides a clear example of the reggae rhythmic feel, with its emphasis on the upbeats. While the verse and chorus are built on different bass lines, they aren't much different, and the contrast is provided by the use of group vocals on the chorus and solo vocals during the verses. Like much folk or singer-songwriter music, the focus in reggae is on the message of the lyrics, and the lyrics here advocate political freedom.

As popular as Marley and the Wailers were among fans of reggae, their music remained mostly off the pop radar screen. Two events helped bring a broader audience to reggae. The first was the independent film *The Harder They Come*, which chronicled the rise and fall of a fictional pop singer in Jamaica. Released in the United States in 1973, the movie became a popular cult attraction. A soundtrack album was released by Island and featured tracks by Jimmy Cliff (who had starred in the movie) and other Jamaican artists, including Toots and the Maytals. The second event that raised reggae's profile was the success of Eric Clapton's cover of Marley's "I Shot the Sheriff," which had originally appeared on *Burnin'*; Clapton's version topped the U.S. charts during the summer of 1974 (uk9). Soon fans of Clapton's record were seeking out Marley's music. About this time, both Tosh and Livingston left the Wailers to pursue solo careers, but Marley's career was the one that really took off. By the end of the decade, Bob Marley was highly revered not only as a musician but also as a cultural hero and fighter for political and social justice. His albums sold well, especially in the UK, and he played to sold-out audiences around the world. Late in the 1970s, Marley developed cancer and in 1981 he passed away at the age of thirty-six. In the years since his death, both Tosh and Livingston (as Bunny Wailer) have continued their solo careers, and Marley's son Ziggy has enjoyed success with his band, the Melody Makers.

Though not a style of black pop in the strict sense, reggae can be seen as a parallel consequence of 1950s and '60s black pop. When 1950s rock and roll and electric blues went out of style in the United States, it continued to develop in the UK, returning to the States—with a distinctive accent—via the Beatles and the Rolling Stones. New Orleans rhythm and blues and 1960s soul had a similar effect in Jamaica, returning to the mainland transformed into reggae. Reggae is similar in many ways to 1970s black pop, and this is due in large part to the common influence of earlier styles of black popular music.

The Rise of Disco

I Should Be Dancin'; a New Dance Craze.   By the mid 1970s, rock had become music that was meant primarily for listening. People could dance along with much rock music, and many did, but dancing was not the most important element in '70s rock, which continued to be created mostly under the influence of the hippie aesthetic discussed in Chapter 8. In most clubs and bars, live bands were much preferred to disc jockeys, who were thought to be a budget alternative to live music. Within black pop, dancing was still a central element, so for those interested in dancing to records, black pop provided plenty of beat-driven material. Disco emerged on the national stage in a powerful way in 1977, but already early in the 1970s dancers were visiting small clubs that specialized in spinning records of dance music all night. According to many accounts, this practice first began to grow significantly within the New York gay community. Even though gays generally found more acceptance in the early 1970s than they had in the 1950s or '60s, many rock bands still would not go near a gay club. The gay community was forced to develop an alternative to live rock, so it relied heavily on disc jockeys playing danceable music. All of this occurred far off the radar screen of most fans of popular music; until it hit the mainstream in 1977, disco was mostly an underground style that occasionally popped up into greater visibility. Among the first hits to arise from the disco subculture were George McCrae's "Rock Your Baby" (r1 p1, 1974) and Van McCoy's "The Hustle" (r1 p1, 1975). These songs blended a direct dance beat with a catchy pop hook that is repeated frequently. Barry White's Love Unlimited Orchestra also scored with "Love's Theme" (r10 p1, 1974), which added lush strings to the disco mix. A series of early hits came from Florida's KC and the Sunshine Band, the most widely known of which is probably "That's the Way I Like It" (r1 p1, 1975). While all of these songs would have been known to rock listeners, they were viewed more as novelty tunes than as serious threats to the rock world order.

Disco emerged from local dance clubs onto the national scene in 1977 with the release of *Saturday Night Fever*, a film starring John Travolta, who at the time was best known for his role in the television comedy *Welcome Back, Kotter*. A gifted dancer, Travolta became the model for the macho disco dancer, establishing a markedly heterosexual context for disco. The soundtrack to *Saturday Night Fever* featured a number of tracks by the Bee Gees that soon became disco staples: "Stayin' Alive" (r4 p1, 1978) and "Night Fever" (r8 p1, 1978) both topped the pop charts and fueled a craze for disco music that began to worry rock fans who now saw rock radio stations beginning to change to a disco format. Amid the excitement of Travolta, *Saturday Night Fever*, and the Bee Gees, many hippies cut their hair, put on sleek polyester shirts, and headed out to the disco. Suddenly many major artists were turning out disco-flavored tracks: rockers Rod Stewart ("Do You Think I'm Sexy?"), the Rolling Stones ("Miss You"), and even Kiss ("I Was Made for Loving You") jumped on the disco bandwagon. Disco versions of well-known songs began popping up, including a disco version of the first movement of Beethoven's Fifth Symphony! Extended disco mixes, which had previously circulated only among disc jockeys who needed longer tracks to keep the dancers on the floor, now began selling over the counter in significant numbers. The disco craze was on.

The Return of the Producers.   By the mid 1970s, the rock industry had given over much of the production authority to the musicians themselves; bands used producers, but they often retained a significant amount of say in how the record sounded. Disco returned the authority to the producers, and these records were made according to the Brill Building or Motown models—in many cases, it

Saturday Night Fever *(1977) featured the story of Tony Manero (John Travolta), a young man from Brooklyn caught between his friends— who are content with their lives—and the dream of something more. Much of the film centers on Tony's disco dancing. The film and the wildly popular soundtrack (featuring the Bee Gees' "Stayin' Alive") epitomized disco culture and music, and set off a craze for both.*

didn't really matter who was singing since the focus was not on the artist, but instead on the song and its beat. One of the first disco acts to emerge with a strongly identifiable image was the Village People. Assembled by producer Jacques Morali as a kind of "gay Monkees," the group specialized in songs that took a playful slant on life in the gay underground. It is therefore somewhat amazing that most listeners missed this aspect of the Village People entirely. The group's 1978 hit "YMCA" (r16 p2) is devoted to the YMCA as a place where young gay men can meet, and even today, this song is regularly played at sporting events, as the entire family— mom, dad, the kids, and grandma—all get up and dance to the chorus without the slightest idea what they are singing about. By contrast, it would be tough not to know what Donna Summer was singing about on "I Love to Love You Baby" (r3 p2, 1976). Produced by Munich-based Giorgio Moroder and Pete Bellotte, Summer moans and groans her way through a seventeen-minute extended mix that tended to underscore the sensual aspects of disco dancing. Summer's records, along with those of Silver Convention and Kraftwerk, represent the Euro-

Donna Summer, shown here in concert in 1979, was one of disco's biggest stars. Her hits "I Love to Love You Baby," "Hot Stuff," and "Bad Girls" are disco classics. Summer's music reveals disco's strong funk roots, now with a beat and groove made for dancing courtesy of Euro-disco.

disco style—a style in which the beat is often provided electronically to guarantee metronomic precision. After disco broke into the mainstream, Summer became one of its biggest stars, hitting the top of the charts with "Hot Stuff" (r3 p1, 1979) and "Bad Girls" (r1 p1, 1979), both contained on the album *Bad Girls*, which is in many ways a disco concept album. Michael Jackson also took advantage of the disco craze in 1979, releasing the album *Off the Wall*, which contained the hit "Don't Stop 'Til You Get Enough" (r1 p1). *Off the Wall* began Jackson's collaboration with producer Quincy Jones—a partnership that would enjoy overwhelming success in the 1980s.

Disco and the Hippies

Disco Sucks?   The rise of disco in the days and months after the release of *Saturday Night Fever* caused a violent reaction within parts of the rock-music community. Perhaps the clearest instance of this can be seen in the anti-disco rally held by Chicago rock DJ Steve Dahl in 1979 before a White Sox baseball game. Dahl arranged to have a large crate of disco records placed in the outfield, and these records were then ceremoniously blown up. The resulting rioting was so extreme that the scheduled baseball game had to be called off. Shock-jock antics aside, this hatred of disco was widespread among rock fans, whose slogan became "disco sucks." In retrospect, one wonders what could have caused these rock fans to hate disco with such a passion. A few explanations have been offered. One, for instance, holds that rockers were reacting against the origins of disco in the gay community. There may be some truth in this, but remember that—at the time, at least—most rock fans had no idea that disco originated in gay night spots; for them, disco originated in the very heterosexual context of John Travolta and *Saturday Night Fever*. In any case, rock fans tolerated a fair amount of androgyny without a similar reaction, and by the end of

---

LISTENING GUIDE

GET MUSIC ▶▶| wwnorton.com/rockhistory

Donna Summer, "Bad Girls"

Words and music by Donna Summer, Eddie Hokenson, Bruce Soldano, and Joe Esposito, produced by Giorgio Moroder and Pete Bellotte. Rose to #1 on both the pop and rhythm and blues charts in 1979.

FORM: Modified contrasting verse chorus, but with the chorus preceding the verse. Each statement of the chorus is preceded by an instrumental interlude featuring a melody in the horns. The verses that follow the chorus are split into two 8-bar subsections. Note that again we see the re-starting of a song through a return to the introduction, much as shown in the analysis of "Purple Haze" and "Roundabout."

TIME SIGNATURE: 4/4; note the strong disco beat provided by emphasizing the regular groove and mixing the bass drum, high-hat, and snare forward throughout.

INSTRUMENTATION: The rhythm section is made up of drums, bass, guitar, and piano, with horns used in the traditional rhythm and blues manner. Summer's lead vocal is supported by female backups, and miscellaneous percussion is used throughout (the whistles are the most noticeable of these).

0:00–0:32	**Introduction,** 16 mm.	Texture builds up gradually, with eight bars of groove played by guitars and drums only. The next eight bars add horns, whistles, and "toot, toot."
0:32:0:40	**Interlude,** 4 mm.	Melody presented in the horns.
0:40–0:56	**Chorus,** 8 mm.	Lead vocal with rhythm section only. "Bad girls . . ."
0:56–1:11	**Verse,** pt 1, 8 mm.	Girl-group style backup vocals are added at the ends of phrases, "See them out on the street . . ."
1:11–1:28	**Verse,** pt. 2, 8 mm.	Horn hits are added in, "You ask yourself . . ."

the decade many rock musicians happily admitted their homo- and bisexual orientations. Another explanation is that disco was largely music that facilitated meeting members of the opposite sex at bars for quick, one-night stands, and as such, rockers were offended by this blatant promiscuity. Sexual practices may have been somewhat different within disco culture, but it is difficult to square such puritanical attitudes with rock and roll—Foreigner's "Hot Blooded" is not exactly an anthem for sexual moderation, and swaggering braggadocio is hardly foreign to rock culture.

1:28–1:36	**Interlude**, 4 mm.	Uses horn line from last 4 mm. of introduction.
1:36–1:52	**Chorus**, 8 mm.	This time backup vocals echo Summer, "Bad girls . . ."
1:52–2:08	**Verse**, pt 1, 8 mm.	As before. "Friday night and the strip is hot . . ."
2:08–2:24	**Verse**, pt. 2, 8 mm.	As before. "Now don't you ask yourself . . ."
2:24–2:32	**Interlude**, 4 mm.	As before.
2:32–2:48	**Chorus**, 8 mm.	Changed to include taunt from backup vocals. Note also new guitar line in the background. "Bad girl, such a naughty bad girl . . ."
2:48–3:04	**Verse**, pt 1, 8 mm.	As before, but guitar continues. "You and me, we're both the same . . ."
3:04–3:19	**Verse**, pt. 2, 8 mm.	Guitar solo emerges from the background to take the melody previously handled by the lead vocals.
3:19–3:59	**Reprise of Introduction,** 20 mm.	Varied and expanded to encompass four 8-bar sections based on introduction material and Summer speaking and singing ("Hey mister . . .") over groove.
3:59–4:14	**Interlude**, 8 mm.	Expanded to eight bars and emerges directly out of reprised introduction, as "Hey mister . . ." in vocals returns.
4:14–4:54	**Chorus and ending,** 20 mm.	8-bar chorus is followed by 8-bar return to interlude material that immediately preceded it, though the horn melody continues throughout this section. The backup vocals add a 4-bar ending.

Two other explanations of rock fans' reactions to disco are more plausible. The first holds that part of the negative reaction among almost entirely white rock fans to disco music was a result of racial misunderstanding. To many of these white rock fans, disco was associated with black pop, and as such, it was not welcome within rock culture. In associating disco with black pop, these fans were at least partially correct. Their error, however, was in failing to see that disco did not stand for *all* black pop. Nobody was more sensitive to this misconception than many of the black pop acts, who resented being lumped in with disco; George Clinton has been particularly outspoken about the mistake of seeing funk as a part of the disco movement, which he held in as much musical contempt as the white rockers did. Because the worlds of white rock music and black pop had grown so far apart during the 1970s, most white rock fans no longer had much idea of what was happening in black pop; all they knew about was the music that crossed over. Even though black pop singles were crossing over onto the pop charts, these records were not getting much airplay on album-oriented rock stations across the country. It has to be counted as a low mark in the history of rock music, however, when music associated with black culture is unwelcome in rock, even if that rejection is the result of a music-stylistic misunderstanding. In 1955 rock and roll was born out of the blending of black and white pop styles, but by 1978, some rock fans (and maybe only a minority of these) had no time for black music.

Another explanation perhaps reaches deeper to the heart of why disco was viewed as such a threat within the rock community. In many ways, disco stood in direct confrontation to the hippie aesthetic that had been developing in rock music since the mid 1960s. Disco music was not about listening to music but rather about dancing to it. It was not concerned with important spiritual or social issues; it was about fun. And perhaps most important to the musicians involved, disco was not about the specific artists but about the beat in general—and this beat was often provided by a machine. It took the production authority away from the artist and turned it back over to the producer. In fact, disco threatened to take back everything that rock had won since the Beatles' *Sgt. Pepper's Lonely Hearts Club Band* had made rock a more serious-minded, "listening" music. Strangely enough, disco and punk were united in their rejection of the hippie aesthetic, and rock fans, whether they could articulate it precisely or not, at least sensed that their approach to music was under attack from these new styles. True, racism probably played a role in the reaction of some rock fans to disco, but more often, rock fans rejected the very anti-hippie aesthetic of disco. A further consequence of white rockers' misunderstanding of black pop was the assumption that black musicians generally rejected the hippie aesthetic, and this was not the case at all. As we have seen in this chapter, many black pop musicians took their music very seriously, engaged serious issues, experimented with ambitious approaches, and produced music that stands up well to repeated listenings. As things turned out, neither disco nor punk displaced rock. Both did have a marked effect on rock, however, and in the next chapter we will chart punk's assault on what it called "corporate rock," and more importantly, on the hippie aesthetic.

1. Discuss the importance of Sly and the Family Stone for black pop in the late 1960s. How was Sly's music related to rock culture?
2. How did Motown's music change toward the end of the 1960s and into the 1970s?
3. Discuss the "Philadelphia sound" and the ways in which it built upon previous music-business practices.
4. What is meant by the term "blaxploitation" and how does this figure into the history of black pop in the 1970s?
5. Discuss the music of George Clinton during the 1970s. How did Clinton build on the accomplishments of previous figures in the history of black pop, both musically and businesswise?
6. How does reggae relate to black pop in the 1970s? What are its sources and who are its best-known practitioners?
7. Consider the rise of disco and discuss why it might have been rejected by some rock listeners.

Further Reading

Lloyd Bradley, *This Is Reggae Music: The Story of Jamaica's Music* (Grove Press, 2000).

Nelson George, *The Death of Rhythm and Blues* (E. P. Dutton, 1989).

John Jackson, *A House on Fire: The Rise and Fall of Philadelphia Soul* (Oxford University Press, 2004).

Arthur Kempton, *Boogaloo: The Quintessence of American Popular Music* (Pantheon Books, 2003).

Dave Thompson, *Funk* (BackBeat Books, 2001).

Rickey Vincent, *Funk: The Music, the Rhythm, and the Power of the One* (St. Martin's Griffin, 1996).

Timothy White, *Catch a Fire: The Life of Bob Marley* (Henry Holt, 1998).

chapter 10

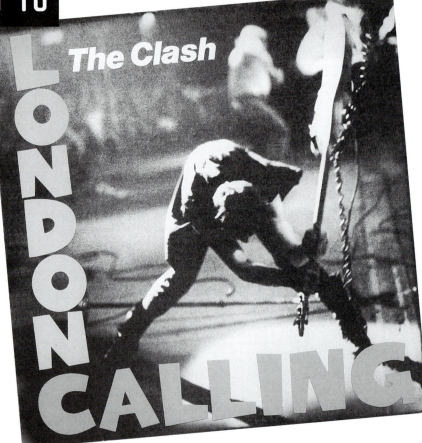

As evidenced on the cover of the Clash's London Calling (1980), punk was about rebellion: politically, socially, and musically. Government and traditional moral values were the focus of punk's political and social attacks, while disco and overproduced concert rock were the focus of punk's musical attacks. London Calling was a highly influential punk album, and the Clash's first success in the United States. The band drew on the musical style of the Sex Pistols, but took punk in a different, more political direction. Punk first started in the New York underground, and later it developed and gathered steam in London. With the success of the Sex Pistols, the Clash, the Buzzcocks, and others, punk soon broke into the UK and U.S. mainstream. The movement culminated in new wave, which many saw as a smoothed-out, more radio-friendly version of punk.

Mainstream Rock, Punk, and New Wave

If rock music in the first half of the 1970s can be traced back to 1967, one might well wonder how far forward into the decade these styles extend. In many ways, the spirit of late '60s psychedelic music continues well into the '70s, at least to the end of the decade. By the mid 1970s, this hippie rock—invested as it frequently was in the hippie aesthetic discussed in Chapter 8—had become the status quo. Also by mid-decade, a move was afoot on the fringes of the rock world to overthrow the rock establishment, and punk and new wave became two musical movements that would challenge mainstream rock's commercial domination. Rock music had increasingly become a bigger business than it had ever been, and the increased opportunity to make money seemed to crowd not only the business side of music, but also, some would argue, the musical end as well. Rock musicians, some claimed, were growing fat on the ever-increasing amounts of money to be made, and as a result some were designing their music for greatest popular appeal rather than as a sincerely rendered musical expression.

This chapter will explore how mainstream rock in the late 1970s constitutes a continuation of earlier '70s rock styles. While the first half of the decade was mostly a time of emerging new styles that developed aspects of psychedelic music, the second half can be seen as a consolidation of earlier styles. We will also investigate how the punk movement developed in underground scenes in New York and London, largely off the mainstream rock radar screen, eventually emerging into the mainstream as new wave. Punk and new wave positioned themselves against mainstream rock, rejecting the highly produced and sophisticated sounds of the hippie bands in favor of a return to the simplicity they believed had been central to pre-hippie rock. Before we can understand what the punks were rebelling against in their attempt to reclaim the power and directness of rock from the clutches of hippiedom, however, we first need to explore how the rock music business grew so much over the course of the 1970s, becoming bigger than many had imagined it could ever be.

Building the Business: Frampton Comes Alive

FM Radio Goes from Late '6os Free Form to AOR.   Radio was one front that saw tremendous growth in the 1970s. One important development in rock radio during the 1960s was the development of FM rock radio (as described in Chapter 7). By the early 1970s, FM stations across the country were broadcasting rock music and focusing not on hit singles, as had been the case on AM radio, but rather on album cuts, following the model established by Tom Donahue in San Francisco (a format that developed into "album-oriented rock," or AOR). It became clear that young people were tuning in to these stations and that a lot of money could be made selling advertising on them. Since listeners tune in for free, commercial radio stations must look to advertising to provide the profits needed to stay in business. Advertising rates are based in large part on how many people can be expected to listen to a station, and radio stations do extensive research to determine who listens to their station, how old these listeners are, how much money they make, and how long they are likely to stay tuned in before they switch to another station. All of this information figures heavily into how much stations can charge their advertisers, and since the kind of music played on the station has a direct influence on who listens, advertising concerns can often affect what music gets played. At the beginning of the 1970s, most FM rock stations were still relatively free form, leaving the music choices to the disc jockeys. By the end of the decade, however, most of these stations were heavily formatted, with program directors or consultants calling the shots and the disc jockeys choosing far less of the music played. By the late 1970s, rambling jam tracks and rock symphonies were no longer considered "radio friendly"; they were too long, and either did not leave enough time for commercials or prompted listeners to change the station. Musicians and record companies understood that there was an ideal length for a radio track (about four to five minutes), and bands that did not conform would simply not get their music played. When rock became increasingly profitable in the middle of the decade, a number of major corporations invested in the music business, buying record labels and radio stations. Because the corporations seemed interested only in the financial bottom line, and the restrictions on what was played arose mostly to maximize advertising profits, many suspected that the music that was played had been designed specifically for radio play. The perception was that this music had sold out to corporate concerns and it was labeled "corporate rock" by its detractors.

Show Me the Way: The Advent of the "Big Album."   The corporations that prompted such concern among mainstream rock's critics were not restricted to the radio business; the record business experienced a transformation during the 1970s as well. The growth of the rock-music business in general was fueled by the steady growth of hippie culture; the psychedelic rock culture celebrated at

Fleetwood Mac's Stevie Nicks sings at a concert in San Francisco. Building on the success of other "big albums" like Frampton Comes Alive!, *Fleetwood Mac's* Rumours *stayed on the Billboard charts for thirty-one weeks in 1977, helping to make the band one of the 1970s' most popular groups.*

Fleetwood Mac would never duplicate the success of *Rumours*, though they continued to release successful albums into the 1980s, including *Tusk* (p4 uk1, 1979), *Mirage* (p1 uk5, 1982), and *Tango in the Night* (p7 uk1, 1987). One effect of the quest for the mega-hit album within the recording industry was to encourage a conservative attitude. In looking for the next Frampton, Eagles, or Fleetwood Mac, record companies were less willing to take a chance on a band that might be interesting but was likely to sell only 350,000 records—a figure that had been acceptable only a few years before. Every new band was an entry in the big-album lottery, so record-company folks asked themselves, Why waste a chance on a group that can't win? When critics lament the late '70s, it is often because they feel that record companies killed the music when they became obsessed with the big album—music became just another way to make money, and it didn't matter how the music sounded or what it stood for so long as the financial benefits could be realized.

Mainstream Rock, 1975–1980

It's Still Rock and Roll to Me. In Chapter 8 we saw how the wide range of rock styles found in the first half of the 1970s emerged out of the primordial rock soup of psychedelia. Rock in the early 1970s was teeming with competing stylistic approaches that are relatively easy to distinguish from one another. By mid-decade, however, these styles began to blend, reducing the usefulness of the old stylistic labels. Instead, rock moved back in the direction of a more unified style in which elements of earlier styles can be easily detected in many cases but combinations of features are less predictable. This "evening out" of the earlier '70s styles is sometimes attributed to the conservative attitude that increasingly became a part of the record-company decision-making processes, a charge leveled by those who complain of the banality of "corporate rock." So while we saw early '70s rock in Chapter 8 as a stylistic expansion, mainstream rock in the second half of the decade will be viewed in this chapter as a stylistic consolidation. It is thus important to understand how mainstream rock in the late '70s continues and *extends* earlier styles while also pulling together elements that had previously been used to *distinguish among* styles.

same year with "Albatross." By 1971 Green and Spenser were gone and keyboardist/vocalist Christine McVie had joined, and by 1975, guitarist/vocalist Lindsay Buckingham and singer Stevie Nicks came on board. The quintet released *Fleetwood Mac*, which rose to number one in the United States in 1975 and contained "Rhiannon" (p11) and "Say You Love Me" (p11 uk40). It was *Rumours*, however, that raised the stakes; the album spent thirty-one weeks at number one on the Billboard charts in 1977 and contained the hit tracks "Don't Stop" (p3 uk32), "Dreams" (p1 uk24), and "You Make Loving Fun" (p9 uk45). No album had ever sold so many copies or dominated pop music in this way. There is no reliable formula for success like this, but the songs were catchy and dealt with relationships in a band that contained plenty of romantic intrigues, and these elements probably figure into the album's phenomenal appeal.

		from the introduction, again featuring voice-box lead guitar. "I want you . . ."
1:30–2:07	**Verse 2**, 20 mm.	As before, "Well I can see no reason . . ."
2:07–2:29	**Chorus**, 12 mm.	As before, but now the 4-bar phrase is sung three times and then goes right into the guitar solo. "I want you . . ."
2:29–2:58	**Instrumental Verse**, 16 mm.	Twice through the 8-bar phrases, featuring a solo on the voice-box lead guitar.
2:58–3:20	**Verse 3**, 12 mm.	Only once through the 8-bar phrase, then to the 4-bar phrase leading to the chorus. The sung verse is shortened here because we have just heard an instrumental verse and a full sung verse following that might become too repetitive. "I wonder if . . ."
3:20–3:49	**Chorus**, 16 mm.	As before, but four times through the 4-bar phrase. "I want you . . ."
3:49–3:56	**False Ending**, 4 mm.	Song sounds as if it will end, but comes charging back.
3:56–4:18	**Chorus**, 12 mm.	As before, but three times through the 4-bar phrase. "I want you . . ."
4:18–4:32	**Coda**, 5 mm.	Once through the 4-bar progression from the introduction, plus one last bar on the final chord, provide the real ending for the tune.

sweepstakes was the Eagles' *Hotel California*, which hit number one in the United States (uk2) in early 1977 and included three hit tracks: "New Kid in Town" (p1, uk20), "Hotel California" (p1 uk8), and "Life in the Fast Lane" (p11). On this album, guitarist Joe Walsh replaced Bernie Leadon, as the band seemed to abandon their easygoing country rock approach for a harder-rocking, more mainstream style. The Eagles followed with *The Long Run* (p1, uk4), which was among the top albums of 1979. However, as well as Frampton and the Eagles did, Fleetwood Mac soon took the big album phenomenon even further.

Fleetwood Mac had started out as a British blues band in the late 1960s, led by guitarist Peter Green and including guitarist Jeremy Spenser, drummer Mick Fleetwood, and bassist John McVie. The band enjoyed some success in England with *Peter Green's Fleetwood Mac* (uk10, 1968) and a number one single the

---

LISTENING GUIDE　　　　　　　GET MUSIC ▶▶　wwnorton.com/rockhistory

Peter Frampton, "Show Me the Way" (Live)

Words and music by Peter Frampton, produced by Peter Frampton. As a single, the song hit #6 on the Billboard Pop charts in 1976, but the song was also contained on the album *Frampton Comes Alive!*, which topped the charts.

FORM: Contrasting verse-chorus. The verses consist of an 8-bar phrase, its repetition, and a 4-bar phrase that leads to the chorus, and the chorus is based on a contrasting 4-bar phrase that can occur two to four times. Note the false ending at 3:49, probably provided to fool the audience into thinking the song was ending so as to charge back into the chorus by surprise. Since this version is taken from a live recording, timings may differ among CD re-issues.

TIME SIGNATURE: 4/4.

INSTRUMENTATION: Acoustic guitar, electric guitar, bass, drums, lead and backup vocals.

0:05–0:33	**Introduction**, 16 mm.	Strummed acoustic guitar opens the song as band comes in after first four bars, first in stop time and then in regular time. Note the use of the voice box on the lead guitar, which makes the guitar seem to speak.
0:33–1:09	**Verse 1**, 20 mm.	Lead vocal enters with two 8-bar phrases, followed by 4 bars that drive toward the chorus. "I wonder how . . ."
1:09–1:30	**Chorus**, 12 mm.	Backup vocals enter to sing two 4-bar phrases, followed by a 4-bar transition drawn

Woodstock in the summer of 1969 became the hippie rock culture that flourished on every college and suburban high school campus across the country in the first few years of the 1970s. For the most part, the people in charge of record labels and radio stations in the early '70s were the same ones who had run these concerns before. By the middle of the decade, however, it became clear that far more money was to be made in rock music than anybody had ever imagined, and a significant factor in this realization was the emergence of the "big album." Generally, before 1975 most bands and their record labels would be happy if an album sold 300,000 to 500,000 copies. But early in 1976, Peter Frampton's live album *Frampton Comes Alive!* exceeded all expectations by selling millions rather than thousands of copies. Frampton had been a member of Humble Pie but left that group to go solo after the *Rockin' the Fillmore* album. His first two solo albums did respectably, and his third and fourth releases, *Something's Happening* (p25, 1974) and *Frampton* (p32, 1975) did better. Not much of his previous success prepared Frampton for the enormous commercial domination of *Frampton Comes Alive!*, which hit number one on the U.S. album charts (uk6) and contained the hit tracks "Show Me the Way" (p6 uk10), "Baby, I Love Your Way" (p12 uk43), and "Do You Feel Like We Do" (p10 uk39). Frampton followed with *I'm in You* (p2 uk41, 1977), the title track of which hit number two in the United States (uk41), but he was unable to duplicate this success on subsequent records.

The substantial financial returns of Frampton's success helped transform the record business into an attractive possibility for investment, and before long, large multinational corporations with no previous experience in music—Philips Petroleum, for instance—were buying up record labels in hopes of cashing in on the "big album." The concert circuit had been changing as well, as venues became larger and national and international tours became the norm for bands signed to major labels. Theaters and ballrooms were no longer big enough for major acts; shows moved into stadiums and sports arenas and new attendance records were regularly set and then broken. With this growth in record and concert revenues, the musicians themselves began enjoying the fruits of increased profits within the music business, leading to the use of private jets, long stays in expensive recording studios, and the ingestion, in many cases, of significant quantities of expensive—and illegal—drugs.

Peter Frampton live at New York City's Madison Square Garden, 1977. Frampton was the poster boy for the "big album" and "corporate rock." His album Frampton Comes Alive! *set a benchmark by selling over 13 million copies, while Frampton consistently played to huge, sell-out crowds.*

Life's Been Good to Me So Far: More Big Albums.
Among the several albums that followed *Frampton Comes Alive!* in the big money

The Rock Connection: Tower of Power and War. Before he emerged as a performer, Sly Stone had been a well-known figure in the San Francisco psychedelic scene of the late 1960s, and this connection to the big-money world of rock music opened doors for many other black artists and bands. Like Sly, the Oakland-based band Tower of Power were also part of the Bay Area hippie scene, counting among their first important supporters Fillmore concert promoter Bill Graham and record producer David Rubinson (mentioned in the discussion of Moby Grape in Chapter 7). A band comprising white, Latino, and

black musicians, Tower of Power became especially celebrated for their hard-driving funk grooves as well as the high caliber of their horn section, which often guested on the recordings of other artists (Elton John, the Rolling Stones, Rod Stewart). Recording for Warner Brothers, the band had a series of moderately successful albums during the first half of the 1970s, including *Bump City* (r16, 1972), *Tower of Power* (r11 p 15, 1973), and *Back to Oakland* (r13 p26, 1974), almost always finding more success on the rhythm and blues charts than they did on the rock charts.

Kool and the Gang during one of their trademark elaborate stage shows. The group started as a funk band strongly influenced by Sly and the Family Stone. As the '70s wore on, however, their sound became smoother and they became major players in disco, scoring hits with "Ladies' Night" and "Celebration."

Another notable rock connection in 1970s black pop comes via Eric Burdon, who had become famous in the mid 1960s as lead singer for the Animals. The members of War had moved in the Los Angeles rhythm and blues circuit throughout the 1960s. As the Nightriders, they had been hired to back up Deacon Jones, a famous football player who was making a failed attempt to build a new career in music. While backing Jones, the band was spotted by Burdon, Danish harmonica player Lee Oskar, and producer Jerry Goldstein. With Burdon and Oskar, War recorded *Eric Burdon Declares War*, which hit number eighteen on the pop album charts (r47) in 1970 and contained the number three pop single "Spill the Wine." Burdon soon left the group, though this did nothing to weaken their musical powers. War's *All Day Music* (r6 p16, 1971) began a string of highly successful albums and singles for the group, who often tended to blend latin styles with their rhythm and blues roots. *The World Is a Ghetto* (r1 p1, 1973) was the band's most commercially successful album overall, containing the crossover hit singles "The World Is a Ghetto" (r3 p7) and "Cisco Kid" (r5 p2), both of which provide representative examples of the group's style.

Later in the '70s: Earth, Wind, and Fire, the Commodores. The second half of the 1970s saw the continued popularity of bands that built on Sly's breakthrough success. Maurice White had been a studio drummer at Chess Records during the mid 1960s and had played behind Curtis Mayfield on Impressions records. In 1969, he moved to Los Angeles and formed Earth, Wind, and Fire. Soon lead singer Philip Bailey joined the band, and though the rest of the personnel shifted during the 1970s, Earth, Wind, and Fire scored a series of crossover hits with catchy pop hooks and sophisticated and sometimes intricate horn arrangements. "Shining Star" (r1 p1, 1975) provides a representative example of the band's approach. The tune begins with a hard-driving funk groove in the style of Sly and the Family Stone, setting up vocals that alternate sophisticated vocal harmonies with gritty solo singing, all complemented by rhythmic horn shots and held down by a catchy chorus.

The Commodores were also among the most commercially successful black pop bands of the late 1970s. The group started in 1968 as a party band in Tuskegee, Alabama, but soon came under the influence of Sly and the Family Stone. In 1971, the band was hired by Motown to open for Jackson 5 concerts. The Commodores' earliest roots in funk can be heard clearly in tracks such as "Brick House" (r4 p5, 1977), but it was the band's approach to ballads, written by singer Lionel Ritchie, that yielded the greatest commercial success. Ritchie's "Easy" (r1 p4, 1977) and "Three Times a Lady" (r1 p1, 1978) both offer representative examples of the Commodores' smooth, pop-ballad style, featuring Ritchie's polished lead vocals and refined and tasteful horn arrangements.

Motown Marches On: Norman Whitfield, the Temptations, Marvin Gaye.
Motown was quick to absorb the changes in black pop that characterized the late 1960s. According to the Temptations' Otis Williams, "Cloud Nine" (p6 r2, 1968) was recorded under the influence of Sly's "Dance to the Music." The group had recently suffered the departure of lead singer David Ruffin, who was replaced by Dennis Edwards in the summer of 1968. Now sharing the songwriting duties with Motown veteran Barrett Strong, Whitfield's production style steered a more aggressive and groove-oriented course. This new stylistic turn would prove even more successful with "I Can't Get Next to You," which hit the number one slot on both the pop and rhythm and blues charts in the summer

Anchored by Maurice White's compositions and led by Philip Bailey's soaring voice, Earth, Wind, and Fire, like Kool and the Gang, took Sly and the Family Stone–like funk and often combined it with the smoother sounds and complicated production of disco.

of 1969. The string of funk-oriented hits continued with "Psychedelic Shack" (p7 r2, 1970) and "Ball of Confusion" (p3 r2, 1970) before being interrupted by the gentle lyricism of "Just My Imagination (Running Away with Me)," which topped both the pop and R&B charts in the spring of 1971. Whitfield and the Temptations turned toward addressing more serious issues with "Papa Was a Rolling Stone" (p1 r5, 1972), a dramatic and atmospheric track that focuses on problems within black urban life, features a haunting string arrangement by Paul Riser, and ranks as Whitfield's finest achievement as a producer. Like Sly's "Thank You," "Papa Was a Rolling Stone" is built over a single repeated bass line, now extending to almost seven minutes.

As much as the ambition of "Papa Was a Rolling Stone" may seem inspired by the recent seriousness of Sly and the Family Stone, it is likely that Whitfield was also inspired by fellow Motown producer Marvin Gaye. Gaye was one of the few Motown artists to win writing and production control of his music. With the 1971 album *What's Going On* (p6 r1), Gaye produced one of the first concept albums in black pop, reflecting yet another link with rock-music practice while remaining faithful to his Motown roots. Containing the crossover hit singles "What's Goin' On" (p2 r1), "Mercy Mercy Me (The Ecology)" (p4 r1), and "Inner City Blues (Make Me Wanna Holler)" (p9 r1), Gaye's album confronts the problems of urban life as Sly was soon to do, but with none of the confrontational posture of some of Sly's music. Gaye's music, unlike that of the Temptations, did not draw much on Sly's funk orientation. Gaye's music did draw attention to the album, however, and in doing so Gaye borrowed the concept-album approach from the white rockers. Gaye's *What's Going On* is a musical trip as discussed in Chapter 7; it would also be possible to think of "Papa Was a Rolling Stone" as a trip as well, but maybe just a shorter one.

Stevie Wonder Comes of Age. While Sly brought funk and dance grooves to the pop mainstream, and Marvin Gaye and Norman Whitfield brought a new sense of musical ambition to Motown, it was Stevie Wonder who put all these elements of late 1960s and early 1970s black pop together into the same package. In the 1970s Wonder was given complete artistic control over his records and proceeded to produce a series of albums that, if not always concept albums, certainly take the sum of the tracks to be at least as important as any single song. This album-oriented mentality was most immediately influenced by *What's Going On*, but is more generally a sign of late '60s rock influence on Wonder's music-making—in many ways Wonder's approach extends the black pop approach to the hippie aesthetic initiated by Gaye. Unlike any other Motown artist of the time, Wonder often wrote, produced, and played many of the instruments on his albums. And while he was able to place several singles high on the pop and rhythm and blues charts during the '70s, Wonder also paralleled the British progressive rockers in his emphasis on complex arrangements, search for new sounds and timbres (including extensive use of the synthesizer), and lyrics devoted to serious topics.

Beginning with *Talking Book* (p3 r1, 1972), Wonder's albums explored a variety of musical styles and ambitious approaches, as can be heard on *Innervisions* (p4 r1, 1973), *Fulfillingness' First Finale* (p1 r1, 1974), *Songs in the Key of Life* (p1 r1,

1976), and *Journey Through the Secret Life of Plants* (p4 r4, 1979). "Living for the City" (p8 r1), from *Innervisions*, is a representative example of these traits in Wonder's music. The track tells the tale of a poor black country youth whose family scrimps and saves to send him to the city to seek his fortune. He is duped into carrying drugs for a pusher and summarily convicted and jailed. In the last verse, Wonder's gravelly voice testifies to the suffering undergone by this young man and his family. The full version of the track (there is a shorter radio edit) provides a spoken vignette over Wonder's synthesizer accompaniment telling of the youth's arrival, duping, arrest, and conviction. The portrayal of the urban tragedy seems to indict society at large rather than pit black society against the white power structure; the song's tone is nonconfrontational. Easy to see is the general thematic kinship with "Papa Was a Rolling Stone," *What's Goin' On*, or even Sly's *There's a Riot Goin' On*. In its extended length (over seven minutes) and harmonic and melodic sophistication, "Living for the City"

LISTENING GUIDE   GET MUSIC ▶▶   wwnorton.com/rockhistory

The Temptations, "Papa Was a Rolling Stone"

Words and music by Norman Whitfield and Barrett Strong, produced by Norman Whitfield. Hit #1 on the Billboard Pop charts in 1972, and #5 on the rhythm and blues charts.

FORM: Simple verse-chorus. Like Sly Stone's "Thank You (Falettinme Be Mice Elf Agin)," the entire song is built over the same repeating bass line. Perhaps the most striking feature of this track is its drama and scope, running to almost seven minutes, employing orchestral strings, harp, and jazz trumpet to establish a menacing atmosphere.

TIME SIGNATURE: 4/4.

INSTRUMENTATION: Electric guitars (one with wah-wah), electric piano, bass, drums, hand claps, trumpet, orchestral strings, harp.

0:00–1:57	**Introduction**, 60 mm.	Lengthy and atmospheric introduction, beginning with bass and high-hat, but then adding orchestral strings, wah-wah guitar, jazzy trumpet improvisation, hand claps, and even harp.
1:57–2:28	**Verse 1**, 16 mm.	Lead vocal enters, counterpointed by bluesy guitar lines and wah-wah guitar. "It was the third . . ."

One reason
that mainstream rock in the late '70s extended earlier styles is that the bands
and musicians in the earlier and later periods were in some cases the same
ones. A number of bands and artists built on the success they had first achieved
in the '60s, continuing to top the charts and saturate FM radio and creating a
situation that was new to rock music at the time: the idea that rock musicians
could sustain active careers after the age of thirty (or, in some cases, forty). The
Rolling Stones brought in ex-Faces guitarist Ron Wood to replace Mick Taylor,
releasing *Black and Blue* (p1 uk2, 1976) containing "Fool to Cry" (p10 uk6),
Some Girls (p1 uk2, 1978) containing "Miss You" (p1 uk3), and *Emotional Rescue*
(p1 uk1, 1980), containing "Emotional Rescue" (p3 uk9). The band continued to
tour, playing to packed stadiums around the world.

Only a few years after the breakup of the Beatles, Paul McCartney formed
Wings with his wife Linda, guitarist Denny Laine, and drummer Denny Seiwell.
Considering the popularity of the front man, it was perhaps no surprise when
the new band's first album, *Red Rose Speedway*, hit number one on the U.S.
charts (uk5) in 1973, and the ballad "My Love" topped the American singles
charts (uk9). Wings' most successful album, commercially and aesthetically, is
Band on the Run (p1 uk1, 1974), in which McCartney successfully updates his
style with the Beatles to create an album of well-crafted tracks, including "Jet"
and "Band on the Run" (p1 uk3). McCartney and Wings continued to enjoy success with the albums and singles that followed, including *Venus and Mars* (p1
uk1, 1975), "Listen to What the Man Said" (p1 uk6), *Wings at the Speed of Sound*
(p1 uk2, 1976), "Silly Love Songs" (p1 uk2), *London Town* (p2 uk4, 1978), and
"With a Little Luck" (p1 uk5).

As mentioned in Chapter 8, Pink Floyd built on the earlier success of *The
Dark Side of the Moon* with *Wish You Were Here* (p1 uk1, 1975), *Animals* (p3
uk2, 1977), and *The Wall* (p1 uk3, 1979). *The Wall* is perhaps the most extreme
and thorough manifestation of the concept-album idea—an album and a stage
show timed down to the second. Grace Slick and Paul Kantner updated the
Jefferson Airplane, changing the name to Jefferson Starship and releasing
Dragonfly (p11, 1975). Singer Marty Balin rejoined the band, as the group's
next album *Red Octopus* rose to the top of the U.S. album charts in 1975. The
single "Miracles" (p3) features Slick and Balin in a powerful vocal duet. The
band followed with *Spitfire* (p3 uk30, 1976), *Earth* (p5, 1978), and *Freedom at
Zero Point* (p10 uk22, 1980). The group's success continued in the 1980s even
after Kantner left the band, when the name was shortened to "Starship."
Fellow members of the late 1960s San Francisco scene, the Steve Miller Band,
enjoyed more success in the 1970s than they ever had in the '60s. Beginning
with *The Joker* (p2, 1973), which contained the number one U.S. single "The
Joker," Miller and company were regular entries on the American album and
singles charts. *Fly Like an Eagle* (p3 uk11, 1976) is perhaps the band's best-
known album, containing the tracks "Fly Like an Eagle" (p2), "Rock 'n' Me"
(p1 uk11), and "Take the Money and Run" (p11), though *Book of Dreams* (p2
uk12, 1977), containing "Jet Airliner" (p8), is also representative of the band's
late '70s style.

Gaining Ground: Aerosmith, Bad Company, Kiss, the Doobie Brothers. In addition to the bands with roots in the 1960s, some of the groups discussed in Chapter 8 continued to build on their success during the first half of the 1970s in the remainder of the decade. In the wake of their 1975 album *Toys in the Attic* (p11), Aerosmith followed with *Rocks* (p3, 1976), *Draw the Line* (p11, 1978), and *Night in the Ruts* (p14, 1979), establishing the band among the decade's top acts. Likewise, Bad Company scored with a series of albums in the mid and late '70s, including *Run with the Pack* (p5 uk4, 1976), *Burnin' Sky* (p15 uk17, 1977), and *Desolation Angels* (p3 uk10, 1979). In many ways, Kiss reached its commercial peak during this same period with *Alive!* (p9, 1976), *Rock and Roll Over* (p11, 1977), *Love Gun* (p4, 1977), and *Dynasty* (p9, 1979). Faced with the departure of Tom Johnston due to illness, the Doobie Brothers brought pianist/singer Michael McDonald on board and adopted a stylistic approach that laid more emphasis on jazz influences. The resultant records *Takin' It to the Streets* (p8, 1976) and *Livin' on the Fault Line* (p10 uk23, 1977) reestablished the band, but *Minute by Minute* (p1, 1979) pushed the group to new levels of commercial success. The album contained three hit tracks, "Minute by Minute" (p1 uk31), "What a Fool Believes" (p14), and "Dependin' on You" (p25), all of which quickly became staples of FM radio. The group followed with *One Step Closer* (p3, 1980) to finish out the decade.

Though successful in the first half of the decade with a harder, straight-ahead rock style, later in the 1970s the Doobie Brothers turned to a more laid back, jazz-influenced rock, with the help of lead singer and songwriter Michael McDonald and ex–Steely Dan guitarist Skunk Baxter (left).

Rethinking Previous Approaches: Boston, Foreigner, Journey. Following the careers of bands with roots in the 1960s and early 1970s helps us realize that while new bands and styles emerged during the second half of the decade, older styles also survived and prospered. Whatever your opinion on the idea of corporate rock, a number of bands that emerged in the second half of the decade seemed to adopt features of earlier music, shaping them to fit the new, more restricted radio formats. The band Boston, for instance, blended blues rock with aspects of progressive rock to produce music that sold well and received generous radio play. Their first album, *Boston*, was released in early 1977 and quickly climbed to number three on the album charts (p11); the track "More Than a Feeling" (discussed below) is representative of the group's approach. Boston's next album, *Don't Look Back* (p1 uk9, 1978) seemed to assure the band's continued success, but a dispute with their record label kept the third album from being released until 1986, when *Third Stage* went to number one (uk37).

If any late '70s band had a formula for chart and radio success, it was probably Foreigner. Formed by guitarist Mick Jones and featuring the lead vocals of newcomer Lou Gramm, the band's debut *Foreigner* (p4, 1977) and the tracks

"Feels Like the First Time" (p4, 1977; uk39, 1978) and "Cold as Ice" (p6, 1977) quickly established them, especially with American audiences. The next album, *Double Vision* (p3 uk32, 1978), contained three hit tracks: "Double Vision" (p2), "Hot Blooded" (p3 uk42), and "Blue Morning" (p15 uk45, 1979). Gramm's vocal approach is influenced by Paul Rodgers and rhythm and blues singing generally, while Jones's blues-rock guitar hooks drive the songs forward. The first few albums feature keyboards prominently, clearly influenced by progressive rockers like Yes and Emerson, Lake & Palmer, but pared down to radio-friendly dimensions. Foreigner enjoyed sustained success into the 1980s with *Head Games* (p5, 1979), *Four* (p1 uk5, 1981), and *Agent Provocateur* (p4 uk1, 1984).

Journey was formed by guitarist Neal Schon and organist Greg Rolie, both formerly of Santana, along with bassist Ross Valory (ex–Steve Miller) and drummer Ansley Dunbar (ex-Zappa). The band experienced only moderate success until they added singer Steve Perry for their fourth album. This was a wise move, as *Infinity* rose to number twenty-one in the United States in 1978. Drummer Steve Smith then replaced Dunbar for *Evolution* (p20, 1979), which contained such radio staples as "Lights" (a good example of the band's power ballad style) and "Feelin' That Way" (an example of the band's harder-rocking approach). As the decade closed, Journey's popularity grew, as *Departure* hit number eight in the U.S. charts in 1980 and *Escape* found the top spot in 1981 (uk32). If Boston's image played to the male science-fiction nerd and Foreigner aroused the fantasies of teenage-boy sexual conquests, Journey seemed designed to appeal to the girlfriends of Boston and Foreigner fans. Perry's lyrics often evoked a sense of nonthreatening vulnerability, perhaps most noticeably in the song "Loving, Touching, Squeezing," which would never be mistaken for a Foreigner track.

Boston's Tom Scholz performing in concert, 1978. Boston blended blues rock with aspects of progressive rock, producing music that sold well and received generous radio play. Scholz wrote and co-produced "More Than a Feeling," one of the band's most popular songs.

Old Wine, New Bottles: Cheap Trick, Blue Öyster Cult, Van Halen.

Several bands found their own distinctive and commercially successful blend of new and old features. Combining power-chord guitar with pop hooks, for instance, Cheap Trick hit its stride on its fourth album, *Live at Budokan* (p4 uk29, 1979), which contained the track "I Want You to Want Me" (p7 uk29), for which the band is best known. The group followed with *Dream Police* (p6 uk41, 1979), whose title track rose to number twenty-six on the American charts. Blue Öyster Cult employed a guitar-heavy sound and hit with their fourth album, a live release called *On Your Feet or on Your Knees* (p22, 1975). The band's next album,

Mick Jones (left) and Lou Gramm of Foreigner, in concert. Foreigner took guitar and vocal influences from rhythm and blues and combined them with a progressive rock keyboard style to create a winning combination for radio and record sales. Their hits "Feels Like the First Time" and "Cold as Ice" made Foreigner into megastars in America.

Agents of Fortune (p29 uk26, 1976), contained "(Don't Fear) the Reaper" (p12, 1976; uk16, 1978), which quickly became a radio staple and probably the song most often associated with the group. Emerging from Los Angeles and featuring the virtuosic guitar playing of Eddie Van Halen and the wildman antics of singer David Lee Roth, Van Halen stormed the charts with a style that blended hard-driving rock with blues-based vocals. The band's *Van Halen* (p19 uk34, 1978) contains a cover version of the Kinks' "You Really Got Me" (p36), as well as what is arguably the band's most well-known track, "Runnin' with the Devil." The band quickly became a radio favorite, and the albums *Van Halen II* (p6 uk23, 1979), containing "Dance the Night Away" (p15) and "Beautiful Girls," and *Women and Children First* (p6 uk15, 1980) clearly established the band among the most promising of the new mainstream rockers. In many ways, Van Halen's approach owes much to the earlier British blues rockers, Deep Purple especially, and we will return to them in our discussion of heavy metal in Chapter 12.

Progressive Rock Revamped. For the most part, the progressive rock movement of the first half of the decade had expended its energies by mid-decade: King Crimson had broken up, Peter Gabriel had quit Genesis, and many of the other bands were winding down. Yes were the exception in this regard, as 1977's *Going for the One* went to number one in the U.S. charts, and even hit number one in the UK (this in the year punk began to make its mark in Britain). The next two records also did well: *Tormato* (p10 uk8, 1978) was the last album for singer Jon Anderson and keyboardist Rick Wakeman, as singer Trevor Horn and keyboardist Geoff Downes were brought in for *Drama* (p18 uk2, 1980), which took a somewhat new wave turn. Horn and Downes recorded separately as the Buggles, scoring a number one UK hit (p40) with "Video Killed the Radio Star" (which was later the first video ever played on MTV). Emerson, Lake & Palmer released *Works 1* (p12 uk9, 1977), which would prove to be the band's last significant album. Jethro Tull continued to do well with a series of albums, including *Songs from the Wood* (p8 uk13, 1977), *Heavy Horses* (p19 uk20, 1978), *Stormwatch* (p22 uk27, 1979), and *A* (p30 uk23, 1980), but they largely abandoned the progressive style in favor of a leaner, more song-oriented approach.

In many ways, it fell to two American bands to revamp the progressive rock style for late-1970s radio. Kansas enjoyed only moderate success until its fourth album, *Leftoverture* (p5, 1977), which contained the hit "Carry On Wayward Son" (p11). Powered by the songwriting of keyboardist Kerry Livgren and the singing of Steve Walsh, Kansas pruned away some of the progressive rock extravagance, getting their tracks down to the four-minute range encouraged by radio. The band's most successful album was *Point of Know Return* (p4, 1978), which contained "Dust in the Wind" (p6). Like Kansas, Chicago's Styx recast progressive rock grandeur in a more economical manner. After scoring a hit with "Lady" (p6, 1975), the band had to wait until their seventh album to enjoy significant commercial success. *The Grand Illusion* rose to number six on the U.S. charts in 1977, and contained "Come Sail Away" (p8) and "Fooling Yourself" (p29), two tracks that blend Wakeman-esque keyboards with a simpler pop-rock approach. With *Pieces of Eight* (p6, 1978), the band turned to a harder-rocking style with fewer progressive rock frills, best exemplified by "Blue Collar Man" (p21) and "Renegade" (p16). Styx continued to enjoy hit albums and singles into the 1980s with *Cornerstone* (p2 uk36, 1979), "Babe" (p1, uk6), *Paradise Theater* (p1 uk8, 1981), and *Kilroy Was Here* (p3, 1983).

Revamped Prog from the North: Rush. Perhaps the most enduring of the progressive rock–influenced bands to emerge in the second half of the 1970s is the Canadian power trio Rush. The band first made its mark in 1976 with its fourth album, the concept album *2112*, and followed with a string of records that did better and better on the album charts. In 1980, *Permanent Waves* hit the number four spot in the United States (uk3) when most bands were turning away from ambitious concept albums. Because the band included no keyboards during the first few years and depended on Alex Lifeson's guitar playing for its harmonic color, their sound avoided some of the classical pretension that generated so much criticism of the original prog bands. Bassist Geddy Lee's high-pitched vocals were reminiscent of both Jon Anderson of Yes and Led Zeppelin's Robert Plant, and it was probably the similarity to Plant that kept many rock critics from including Rush in the prog-bashing diatribes. Still, the

Rush's guitarist Alex Lifeson (left) and bassist Geddy Lee perform live in 1978 on dual double-necked guitars. Rush was one of the most enduring of the prog-influenced bands. They produced top-selling albums and performed to sell-out crowds in the late '70s and throughout the '80s and '90s.

band kept the prog flame alive in the rock mainstream, and Neil Peart's virtu-osic drumming and ambitiously poetic lyrics made it clear that there was no return-to-simplicity to be found in Rush's music. The Canadian trio were able to remain commercially successful into the 1980s and 1990s, with top-selling albums and sold-out tours, long after most other prog bands had broken camp.

Alan Parsons, ELO, Queen.   North American acts were not the only ones reworking the progressive-rock style. British recording engineer Alan Parsons had been behind the mixing board for many well-regarded albums, including the Beatles' *Abbey Road* and Pink Floyd's *The Dark Side of the Moon*, before he set out on his own as a musician, leading the Alan Parsons Project. His first foray was a concept album based on the poetry of Edgar Allan Poe entitled *Tales of Mystery and Imagination* (p38, 1976). Parsons stuck with the concept-album approach on the subsequent series of albums, including *I Robot* (p9 uk30, 1977), which contained the track "I Wouldn't Want to Be Like You" (p36), *Pyramid* (p26, 1978), and *Eve* (p13, 1979). Parsons's stylistic approach was more grounded in straight-ahead rock than the contemporaneous music of Yes or Emerson, Lake & Palmer, with strong emphasis on blues-based vocals provided by a series of studio singers. Parsons's success continued into the 1980s with albums such as *The Turn of a Friendly Card* (p13 uk38, 1980), *Eve in the Sky* (p7 uk28, 1982), and *Ammonia Avenue* (p15 uk24, 1984).

Electric Light Orchestra (ELO) was originally formed out of the ashes of the British psychedelic band the Move. Soon it became the vehicle for the singing and songwriting of guitarist Jeff Lynne, whose stylistic indebtedness to *Sgt. Pepper*–era Beatles is unmistakable. ELO took the idea of rock band with cham-ber strings accompaniment, developed by the Beatles on tracks such as "Strawberry Fields Forever" and "I Am the Walrus," and made it their trade-mark. After moderate success in the UK during the first half of the decade, ELO broke through in the United States with their fifth album, the conceptually driven *Eldorado* (p16, 1975), which contained the hit "Can't Get It Out of My Head" (p9, 1975). The band followed with a series of hit albums and singles, including *Face the Music* (p8, 1975), "Evil Woman" (p10 uk10, 1976), *A New World Record* (p5 uk6, 1977), "Telephone Line" (p7 uk8), *Out of the Blue* (p4 uk4, 1977), *Discovery* (p5 uk1, 1979), and "Don't Bring Me Down" (p4 uk3).

Queen also seemed inspired by the campier and stylistically eclectic aspects of some late Beatles music. Featuring the singing of Freddie Mercury and the sometimes symphonically conceived guitar playing of Brian May, the band

Freddie Mercury of Queen, live in concert. Queen combined the "glam" tendencies of David Bowie with the scope of classical-influenced prog rock, exemplified in the ambitious song "Bohemian Rhapsody." Mercury died in 1991, a day after announcing he had AIDS— solidifying his position as an icon in the gay community.

scored its first success in the UK with *Queen II* (uk5, 1974). *Sheer Heart Attack* (p12 uk2, 1975) brought the band's music to the attention of listeners in the states, while *A Night at the Opera* (p4 uk1, 1976), featuring the extravagant "Bohemian Rhapsody" (p9 uk1), established the band as a kind of cross between the glam aspects of David Bowie and the classical ambitions of the progressive rockers. Queen continued their success with *A Day at the Races* (p5 uk1, 1977) and *News of the World* (p4 uk3, 1977), the latter of which contained the anthemic one-two punch "We Will Rock You" and "We Are the Champions." More success followed with the release of *Jazz* (p6 uk2, 1978) and *The Game* (p1 uk1, 1980), which contained "Another One Bites the Dust" (p1 uk7). During the 1980s, the band's success continued, especially in the UK, with albums like *Hot Space* (p22 uk4, 1982), *The Works* (p23 uk2, 1984), *A Kind of Magic* (uk1, 1986), and *The Miracle* (p24 uk1, 1989). While many fans were convinced that Mercury was gay, perhaps prompted by his use of sometimes flamboyant stage costumes, Mercury himself never fully disclosed his sexual orientation to the public. When he died from AIDS in 1991, however, his death served to raise public awareness of a disease that had been devastating the gay community for several years already.

Singers, Songwriters, and Bands: Bob Dylan, Elton John, Paul Simon. By the mid 1970s singer-songwriters were often fronting bands, keeping the intimate bond created by soul-searching lyrics but exploring harder-edged rock styles. In most cases this meant that the bands themselves, though now more prominent, were still not the focus of the act. The dean of American singer-songwriters, Bob Dylan, enjoyed a career resurgence with the hit album *Planet Waves* (p1 uk7, 1974). Dylan had been the first of the folksingers to front a band back in the mid 1960s, and he now followed up on this approach with *Blood on the Tracks* (p1 uk4, 1975), which contained "Tangled Up in Blue" (p31); *Desire* (p1 uk3, 1976), which contained "Hurricane" (p33 uk43); and *Street Legal* (p11 uk2, 1978). Famous for career shifts that confuse and confound his followers and critics, Dylan began espousing a relatively fundamentalist brand of Christianity with *Slow Train Coming* (p3 uk2, 1979), which contained "Gotta Serve Somebody" (p24), and *Saved* (p24 uk3, 1980).

Elton John continued his string of hit albums and singles begun earlier in the decade by placing two singles in a row at the top of the American charts: a cover version of "Lucy in the Sky with Diamonds" (p1 uk10, 1974) and his own "Philadelphia Freedom" (p1 uk12, 1975). *Captain Fantastic and the Brown Dirt Cowboy* (p1 uk2) was one of the top albums of 1975, with "Someone Saved My Life Tonight" (p4 uk22) highlighting Elton's more lyrical side. John followed up with *Rock of the Westies* (p1 uk5, 1975), which contained the hit "Island Girl" (p1 uk14) and a single recorded with singer Kiki Dee called "Don't Go Breaking My Heart" (p1 uk1, 1976). Other successful albums and singles include *Blue Moves* (p3 uk3, 1976), "Sorry Seems to Be the Hardest Word" (p6 uk11, 1976), and *A Single Man* (p15 uk8, 1978).

Paul Simon's music continued to highlight his interest in jazz, rhythm and blues, and gospel. His *Greatest Hits, etc.* (p18 uk6, 1977) blended a best-of package with new tracks, including "Slip Slidin' Away" (p5 uk36), in which jazz and gospel influences are pronounced. Simon then embarked on an album and movie, *One Trick Pony*, bringing on a band of studio pros including bassist Tony Levin, guitarist Eric Gale, pianist Richard Tee, and drummer Steve Gadd. While the movie received mixed reviews, the accompanying album *One Trick Pony* (p12 uk17, 1980) is the most musically complex of Simon's career. The album's single "Late in the Evening" (p6) is not particularly representative of this complexity, but tracks like "Jonah" and "How the Heart Approaches What It Yearns" showcase Simon and his band at their most musically sophisticated.

Billy Joel, Jackson Browne, Bob Seger, Bruce Springsteen.   By mid-decade new artists were building on the idea of the singer-songwriter fronting a band. Among these was Billy Joel, whose second album, *Piano Man* (p27, 1973), contained the track "Piano Man" (p25), which helped launch Joel's career in early 1974. The singer's career stalled a bit with the releases that followed: *Streetlife Serenade* (1974) reached only number thirty-five on the U.S. charts and *Turnstiles* (1976) missed the Top 40 completely. These low rankings made the impact of Joel's next album all the more dynamic: *The Stranger* (p2 uk25, 1977), which contained the tracks "Just the Way You Are" (p3 uk19), "Movin' Out" (p17 uk35), "Only the Good Die Young" (p24), and "She's Always a Woman" (p17), began a string of hit albums and singles that continued into the 1980s. His *52nd Street* hit number one in 1978 (uk10), buoyed by the popularity of "My Life" (p3 uk12) and "Big Shot" (p14, 1979). With the arrival of new wave on the scene at the end of the decade, Joel released an album that also engaged earlier rock and pop styles as many new wave bands were doing. *Glass Houses* (p1 uk9, 1980) contained two hits that referred to other music: "You May Be Right" (p7) seemed to evoke the Rolling Stones while "It's Still Rock and Roll to Me" (p1 uk14) seemed modeled on late 1950s rockabilly.

Pianist, singer, and songwriter Billy Joel performs in an Austin, Texas, concert. Joel drew on the singer-songwriter tradition and produced a string of popular songs and albums from the mid 1970s through the 1990s. Joel's music centers around his strong piano playing and easy-to-follow, catchy lyrics.

Jackson Browne had been part of the early 1970s country rock scene in southern California, and in addition to co-writing the Eagles' "Take It Easy," he scored a hit single with "Doctor My Eyes" (p8) in 1972. While Browne's third album *Late for the Sky* (p14, 1974) did well, he was far more successful after 1975 with a series of albums and singles that included *The Pretender* (p5 uk26, 1976), *Runnin' On Empty* (p3 uk28, 1978), and *Hold Out* (p1, 1980). The tracks "Runnin' On Empty" (p3 uk28, 1978) and "Stay" (p20 uk12, 1978) became staples of FM radio.

Detroit-native Bob Seger had enjoyed brief success in 1968 with the single "Ramblin' Gamblin' Man" (p17), but then struggled, even leaving the music business to return to college for a couple of years. With the album *Beautiful Loser* (1975), Seger began to perfect the style for which he would become known—folksy lyrics about everyday problems set to the often hard-rocking accompaniment of the Silver Bullet Band. The album *Live Bullet* (p34, 1976) got the attention of many rock listeners, and with *Night Moves* (p8, 1977) Seger established himself commercially with the help of the singles "Night Moves" (p4) and "Mainstreet" (p24). He followed with *Stranger in Town* (p4 uk31, 1978), which contained "Still the Same" (p4) and "Old Time Rock & Roll" (p28, 1979), and *Against the Wind* (p1 uk26, 1980). Seger's success continued well into the 1980s.

It is in this context of the mid 1970s singer-songwriter that Bruce Springsteen first emerged. Backed by the E-Street Band, Springsteen established himself as an important new voice in rock music with his third album, *Born to Run* (p3 uk17, 1975). Much like the others discussed here, Springsteen wrote lyrics that were understood to be largely autobiographical and

---

LISTENING GUIDE GET MUSIC ▶▶▶ wwnorton.com/rockhistory

Boston, "More Than a Feeling"

Words and music by Tom Scholz, produced by John Boylan and Tom Scholz. Reached #5 on the Billboard Pop charts in September 1976. Contained on the album *Boston*, which reached #11 on the UK charts and #3 on the Billboard Album charts.

FORM: Compound AABA, with each A section based on contrasting verse-chorus form, while the bridge offers new material employing lead guitars playing in harmony. Note that the verse and chorus lengths are different in each presentation of the A section, giving some indication of the variety employed when these sections reappear.

TIME SIGNATURE: 4/4.

INSTRUMENTATION: Electric and acoustic guitars, bass, drums, hand claps, lead and backup vocals.

	0:00–0:18	**Introduction**, 6 mm.	Acoustic guitar fades in, as electric guitar and bass join in.
A	0:18–0:42	**Verse 1**, 11 mm.	Vocals and drums enter, music remains quiet, ending gets louder and transitions into chorus via lead guitar melody. "I looked out . . ."
	0:42–1:17	**Chorus**, 16 mm.	Louder, with backup vocals and hand claps added to create excitement. Again, ending

frequently confessional. He also embraced rock's past, and the single "Born to Run" (p23) seemed inspired by Phil Spector's Wall of Sound. Springsteen and the E-Street Band enjoyed continued success with *Darkness on the Edge of Town* (p5 uk16, 1978) and *The River*, which was number one in the United States (uk2) in 1980.

Form or Formula? In considering how bands in the late 1970s recast aspects of music from earlier in the decade, it is helpful to focus on formal design. The lengthiest tracks by earlier artists often employed multiple sections organized so that at least a part of the music from early in a track would return in some form later in the tune. In Chapter 8 we looked at Led Zeppelin's "Whole Lotta Love" and Yes's "Roundabout," noting that both employed a compound AABA formal scheme overall, with verses, choruses, or bridges used within the A sections. Boston's "More Than a Feeling" squeezes a level of organizational complexity comparable to the almost nine-minute Yes example into a track about

			provides a transition, this time back to the verse. "It's more than a feeling . . ."
A	1:17–1:51	**Verse 2**, 15 mm.	Quieter again, with 4 bars of interlude before singing returns. Transition to verse gets louder, as before. "So many people . . ."
	1:51–2:30	**Chorus**, 18 mm.	As before, but now a new transition leads to the instrumental bridge. "It's more than a feeling . . ."
B	2:30–2:55	**Instrumental Bridge**, 11 mm.	Melodic guitar solo featured, frequently doubled in harmony. The feel in this section is symphonic, similar to earlier progressive rock.
A	2:55–3:48	**Verse 3**, 24 mm.	Quieter again, with 4 bars of acoustic guitar preparing the introduction of the lead vocal. This time the verse is extended by repeating the end of the last phrase before beginning the transition to the chorus. "When I'm tired . . ."
	3:48–4:41	**Chorus**, 20 mm.	As before, and then fade out. "It's more than a feeling . . ."

half that long. The Boston track uses a compound AABA design, with a verse-chorus pair making up each A section and an instrumental guitar solo—actually two guitars playing in harmony—as the B section. Note that each verse and chorus varies in length, with no two being exactly the same; this creates a more complicated arrangement than simply repeating material would have done. Foreigner's "Feels Like the First Time" offers an interesting twist on the compound AABA design. It begins as if the A sections will consist of verse-chorus pairs like those found in the Boston track; but with the second A section, a bridge is inserted between verse two and the chorus. This bridge would usually occur after the second iteration of the chorus, but in that spot Foreigner places a second bridge, this time with a guitar solo (note that a guitar solo often follows the second verse-chorus pair in much '70s rock). The final A section contains only a chorus, with no return to the verse, and the entire track clocks in at under four minutes—perfect for radio.

While both songs feature the distorted guitar sounds that are a central feature in blues-based rock (both American and British), there are a few progressive rock touches as well. With Foreigner, these are found mostly in the use of

LISTENING GUIDE　　　　GET MUSIC ▶▶　wwnorton.com/rockhistory

Foreigner, "Feels Like the First Time"

Words and music by Mick Jones, produced by John Sinclair and Gary Lyons. Reached #4 in the United States, and #39 in the UK in mid 1977. Contained on the album *Foreigner*, which reached #4 in the United States but did not chart in the UK.

FORM: Modified compound AABA, with A sections based on contrasting verse-chorus form. The second A second includes bridge, based on the chorus, inserted between the verse and the chorus. The last A section is abbreviated, using only the chorus section.

TIME SIGNATURE: 4/4, with bridge 1 in 2/2.

INSTRUMENTATION: Electric guitars, bass, synthesizer, organ, lead and backup vocals.

0:00–0:27	**Introduction**, 12 mm.	Begins with distorted guitar, then stop-time bass and drums enter, with sparkling progressive rock synthesizer above. Full band and drumbeat enter at m. 9.
A 0:28–1:02	**Verse 1**, 16 mm.	Vocals enter, as music builds from quiet to loud, first adding distorted guitars, and then backup vocals, as chords get higher and higher. "I would climb . . ."

the high synthesizer arpeggios in the introduction and choruses, as well as in the synthesizer melody in the first chorus (though the harmonic movement in that section is influenced by classical music). In the Boston example, the harmony guitar parts throughout (and especially in the bridge) are carefully coordinated—"composed" in the classical sense—showing a concern for matching these harmonized guitar melodies with the parts being played by the other instruments. In these ways, both Boston and Foreigner condense qualities of earlier rock, blending them together and fitting them into shorter tracks. On one hand, this can be seen as a culmination of earlier musical practices; on the other, it can be seen as applying a kind of formula.

The Roots of Punk in the United States, 1967–1975

Safety Pins and Leather. To an FM-rock radio listener in the mid 1970s, things would not seem to have changed drastically since the beginning of the decade. Many of the same bands were played regularly, and most of the newer ones that

	1:03–1:21	**Chorus**, 8 mm.	Loud, with choral vocals, with sparkling synthesizer on top. "It feels like . . ."
A	1:21–1:56	**Verse 2**, 16 mm.	As before, but now with rhythmic guitar underneath during the quiet part, and backup vocals entering earlier. "I have waited . . ."
	1:56–2:38	**Bridge 1**, 18 mm.	Change of meter to 2/2, change of key to minor, with classical-music references in the synthesizer part and in the accompanying harmony. "It feels like . . ."
	2:39–2:56	**Chorus**, 8 mm.	As before, but now with improvised lead vocals playing off the choral-vocal statement of the melody. "It feels like . . ."
B	2:56–3:14	**Bridge 2**, 8 mm.	Virtuosic guitar solo, with stop in the bass and drums, and improvised vocal interjections. "Open up the door . . ."
A'	3:14–3:32	**Chorus**, 8 mm.	As in the second statement of the chorus. "It feels like . . ."
	3:32–3:49	**Chorus**, 8 mm.+	Repeat of chorus and then fade out.

emerged did not depart too radically from the established acts. Listeners would have perhaps noticed that the playlists were becoming slightly more restricted, and certain big albums were in heavy rotation, but there was not much else that signaled the changes that were on the horizon for rock music. By the fall of 1977, however, American rock fans would begin hearing about a movement in the UK called "punk," spearheaded in large part by the Sex Pistols, whose outrageous antics, and not the actual music itself, were often the focus of news reports. Punk took hold first in the UK, where groups like the Sex Pistols, the Buzzcocks, and the Clash became popular in the second half of the decade, placing singles and albums high on the British charts. But because of the sometimes aggressive and dangerous images associated with punk, American record labels were quick to tone down the style somewhat, producing a style they dubbed "new wave." In many ways, the mainstream American market barely experienced punk as the British music world had done. Strangely enough, punk actually had its most important roots in an American underground scene that goes back to the mid 1960s and was centered mostly in New York. Punk was thus exported from the United States to the UK, later to return and be reintroduced as new wave.

Punk Roots: The Velvet Underground, the Stooges, the MC5. During the years between 1967 and 1975, when most of the rock world was focused on the music discussed in Chapters 7 and 8, punk was brewing underground. Among the most important early influences on what would later develop into punk and new wave was the early music of the Velvet Underground. The group emerged when Lou Reed, who had studied creative writing in college and then worked as a professional songwriter, and John Cale, who had studied avant-garde composition and was playing with a performance ensemble led by avant-garde composer LaMonte Young, came together in the mid 1960s. Reed's lyrics focused

From left, Lou Reed, John Cale, and Nico of the Velvet Underground in concert. While hippies and "flower power" were dominating rock in the late '60s, the Velvet Underground chose to look at the darker side of life. Many of the creative artists of the punk and glam scenes—David Bowie and Patti Smith, among others—often cite the Velvet Underground as a major influence.

on the darker side of urban life, while Cale was eager to employ avant-garde ideas in a pop context. With Reed on guitar and vocals, Cale on bass and viola, Sterling Morrison on guitar, and Maureen Tucker on drums, the band recorded *The Velvet Underground and Nico* in late 1966. The addition of the singer Nico to the band came at the insistence of Andy Warhol, who produced the album. Warhol had included the Velvets in some of his pop-art happenings, including his Exploding Plastic Inevitable multimedia show that ran in 1966. Warhol was among New York's leading young artists at the time, championing a style that adapted elements from everyday American culture, refocusing them in an artistic context; you may have seen Warhol's multicolor prints of Campbell's Soup cans or Marilyn Monroe. It is easy to see how pop music would fit into Warhol's project, and considering the avant-garde aspirations of Reed and Cale, Warhol was a valuable ally. In the summer of 1967, when much of rock culture was focused on the fantastic images of *Sgt. Pepper*, the Velvets' first album, containing tracks such as "Heroin" and "Venus in Furs," went largely unnoticed. The Velvets split from Warhol soon thereafter and continued performing in New York and Boston through the rest of the decade.

Iggy Pop was one of the young musicians who did notice the Velvet Underground, and by August of 1969 his band, the Stooges, had released their first album. While the Velvets were avant-garde experimenters obsessed with the dark downtown reality, Iggy Pop made his mark as an outrageous performer. Iggy seemed to challenge the audience at every show, in some cases walking on the audience's hands and smearing peanut butter all over his body. The band's raw sound is best captured on its second release, *Fun House* (1970). The Stooges were based in Detroit, and another Detroit band, the MC5, are also important to the later punk scene. The band's *Kick Out the Jams* (p30, 1969) is representative of the raw aggressive sound of the band, especially the title track, which contained profanities (anticipating the vulgarity of later punk). All three bands have an aspect of confrontation: with the Velvets it's an aesthetic confrontation, with the Stooges it's a performance confrontation, and with the MC5 it's a confrontation with the sheer aggressiveness of the music. All of this would prove influential for the New York punk rockers who would soon follow.

The Beginnings of the New York Scene. The Velvet Underground had performed frequently in New York, but by the early 1970s the most important band to connect the late '60s with the mid '70s was the New York Dolls. Fronted by the flamboyant David Johansen, the band incorporated elements of the British glam scene into their performances of gritty, hard-driving rock music. The Dolls used makeup and costumes, though they nevertheless projected an image of toughness, danger, and reckless disdain for convention that would become central to punk music. Their two albums, *The New York Dolls* (1973) and *Too Much Too Soon* (1974), sold poorly and the group never gained national recognition. But during the first half of the decade, others in New York began developing an approach that drew to some extent on the music of the Velvets, the Stooges, the MC5, and the Dolls. In November 1973, poet Patti Smith teamed up with guitarist and rock critic Lenny Kaye. The two had performed together years before, with Smith usually reciting poetry while Kaye accompanied on guitar. Smith had already begun to develop a reputation as a poet, so initially these performances were less musical events than literary ones. But soon the duo added pianist Richard Sohl and by August 1974 had released "Hey Joe," a cover version of the song made famous by Jimi Hendrix. The Patti Smith Group, which eventually included Ivan Krahl on bass and Jay Dee Daugherty on drums, signed a deal with Arista records, the first band from the developing New York punk scene to do so. Late in 1975 the band released *Horses*, which rose to number forty-seven on the American charts. The band's version of "Gloria" provides a representative example of how their numbers would often unfold: Smith begins with a recitation that seems to have nothing to do with the tune itself but eventually builds in intensity and winds its way to an energetic rendering of the chorus. At about the same time Smith and Kaye were beginning to work together, school friends Richard Hell and Tom Verlaine formed Television. The two were interested in literature and had even published a collection of poetry under an assumed name. In early 1974 Hell and Verlaine began searching around New York for someplace their new band could perform. They landed a regular Sunday evening spot at an almost-deserted bar called CBGB (the name is an acronym for Country, BlueGrass, and Blues). In March 1974 they began playing at CBGB, and shortly Television and the Patti Smith Group were sharing the bill and attracting attention. CBGB became the home for the New York punk scene, though soon Max's Kansas City would begin booking punk acts as well.

The Ramones and Blondie.   Among the other bands to play CBGB in its earliest days as punk headquarters were the Ramones. Playing under the stage names of Joey (vocals), Johnny (guitar), Dee Dee (bass), and Tommy (drums) Ramone, the quartet produced a stripped-down, high-energy style of rock that focused on short, simple songs played very fast. The band signed with Sire Records—an important New York label—and released *Ramones* (1976), which contained "Blitzkrieg Bop." Because of the resurgence of interest in the Ramones' music years later, many are surprised to learn that the band never had any significant success in the United States. A series of albums including *Leave Home* (uk45, 1977), *Rocket to Russia* (1977), *Road to Ruin* (uk32, 1978), *It's Alive* (uk27, 1979), and *End of the Century* (uk14 p44, 1980) were mostly flops in America, even during the late 1970s when many of their CBGB colleagues were topping the charts (though the band's music was better received in the UK). In May 1974, the Stillettos—a band influenced by the early '60s girl groups—played CBGB. At that time, the band included singer Debbie Harry and guitarist Chris Stein. Soon, however the band reconfigured itself and became Blondie. By 1976 the group featured Harry, Stein, keyboardist Jimmy Destri, guitarist Frank Infante, drummer Clem Burke, and bassist Nigel Harrison, and this lineup released *Blondie* on the small Private Stock label. The track "X Offender" provides an aural glimpse of the early girl-group influences, with the spoken introduction, happy driving beat, backup vocals, '60s combo organ sounds, and Ventures-like guitar solo. The first Blondie album did not do well, however, and at that point there was little indication that the band would become one of the most commercially successful of the CBGB

Patti Smith in concert at CBGB in New York. Though Smith started her career as a poet, she formed a band, calling it the Patti Smith Group. Smith's group and Television (another punk band) began performing at CBGB in 1974 and the club quickly became the center of the U.S. punk rock scene. Smith's vocal style continued to be strongly influenced by poetry.

bands. But that would occur only after the Sex Pistols brought punk to the attention of the mainstream rock audience in America; for now, punk was an underground scene in the United States, known for the most part only to those who hung around in the clubs and neighborhoods of New York's bohemian community.

The Rise of Punk in the UK, 1974–1977

No Hope: Malcolm McLaren, British Punk, and the Sex Pistols. Unlike the situation in the United States, the rise of punk in the UK can be linked to specific socioeconomic circumstances: Britain in the mid 1970s was suffering a crushing economic recession. For Britain's youth, this meant jobs were hard to find, and those that were available had no significant opportunity for advancement. Whether or not these feelings were justified by the country's economic troubles, many British teens were prone to despair; that despair, in turn, bred anger, and punk became the music of that anger. Malcolm McLaren is a central character in how this socioeconomic frustration found its voice of expression in punk music and culture. In the early 1970s, McLaren ran a clothing store in London. He was interested in early rock and roll, and his shop was initially called Let It Rock, specializing in biker jackets and other '50s clothes. McLaren was also fascinated with the career of Larry Parnes, the manager who had launched several rock singers in the years before the Beatles hit the UK scene (recall from Chapter 4 that an early Beatles gig was backing up a Parnes singer, Johnny Gentle). By 1973 McLaren had re-launched his shop as Too Fast to Live, Too Young to Die and befriended members of the New York Dolls, who had

The Sex Pistols—(from left) Sid Vicious (bass), Paul Cook (drums), Johnny Rotten (vocals), and Steve Jones (guitar)—performing at their debut U.S. concert, January 5, 1978, in Atlanta. The Sex Pistols were key members in the punk scenes in the UK and the United States. Their first single, "Anarchy in the UK," epitomizes their rebellious attitude, musically and socially.

wandered into the shop while in London to perform. McLaren provided matching red leather suits for the band, which they sported during performances in New York in early 1975. McLaren helped manage the band during the first months of 1975, but returned to London when the group dissolved amid bitter disputes among band members. In New York, McLaren had been impressed by the underground punk scene there, and especially with Richard Hell's manic performing style and sense of punk fashion. McLaren opened his shop again, this time calling it Sex and specializing in leather clothing and fetish wear. In the meantime, guitarist Steve Jones and drummer Paul Cook had started a band, playing mostly on equipment that Jones had stolen from bands all around London. Soon Glen Matlock, who worked in Sex part-time, had joined on bass and the band was searching for a singer. John Lydon used to hang around McLaren's shop and auditioned for the lead singer job by singing along to Alice Cooper's "School's Out" on the jukebox. McLaren changed Lydon's name to Johnny Rotten after the band pressured McLaren to manage them. With McLaren now calling the shots, the Sex Pistols began playing gigs in late 1975 and by November 1976 they had signed with EMI, releasing their first single, "Anarchy in the UK" (uk34). In early December the band filled in at the last minute for Queen on a British television show; provoked by the host, they uttered a few forbidden words, causing a scandal and becoming notorious overnight. Embarrassed by their punk behavior, EMI dropped the band but paid off their promised advance money, and McLaren quickly signed them to A&M. A&M then got cold feet and dropped them, again paying off the advance money promised, and McLaren signed the band to Virgin Records. Before their first album was released in late 1977, the Sex Pistols had already collected advances from three record companies, a fleecing of the music-business establishment that only enhanced their reputation as rebellious troublemakers. When *Never Mind the Bollocks, Here's the Sex Pistols* was released, it went straight to the number one slot in the UK. By then the band had also placed three singles in the UK Top 10 since "Anarchy in the UK," including the highly controversial "God Save the Queen," the cover of which featured a picture of the Queen with a safety pin through her face. The scandals surrounding the Sex Pistols lasted just over a year, and by early 1978 the band had broken up (with Sid Vicious replacing Matlock on bass during the final months). In the UK, the Sex Pistols were the catalyst for punk; in every spot the band played, it seemed, new punk bands would start up, inspired by the experience. McLaren, Rotten, and company also made punk a dirty word—in the American music industry at least—and none of those labels wanted to sign new punk bands if this meant they would go through what EMI and A&M had experienced with the Sex Pistols, even though these record companies were interested in the commercial potential of the developing punk scene.

The Clash, the Buzzcocks, the Jam, Siouxsie and the Banshees.   After the Sex Pistols, punk bands seemed to spring up all over England, and their emergence gave British punk a greater stylistic range. Early on in the history of British punk, for instance, a familiar relationship was forged between the Sex Pistols and the Clash. Managed by Bernard Rhodes, the Clash adapted a positioning strategy that had worked over a decade before for the Rolling Stones: if the Sex Pistols were the nihilists of punk, the Clash would be its political protesters. Thus with Joe Strummer (vocals/guitar), Paul Simonen (bass), Mick Jones (guitar), and Tory Chimes (drums), in April 1977 the band released *The Clash* (uk12), which contained the single "White Riot" (uk38). After the demise of the Pistols and with Topper Headon on drums, the Clash did even better in late 1978 with *Give 'em Enough Rope* (uk2). *London Calling* (p27 uk9, 1980) marked the band's entry into the American market, where "Train in Vain (Stand by Me)" (p27) became a radio favorite.

Among the groups to emerge in the excitement caused by the success of the Sex Pistols and the Clash, the Buzzcocks adopted a more pop-influenced approach to punk than the other two bands. Led by Pete Shelley, the group released a series of successful albums and singles, including *Another Music in a Different Kitchen* (uk15, 1978), *Love Bites* (uk13, 1978), and "Ever Fallen in Love (with Someone You Shouldn't've?)" (uk12). The Jam drew their musical influences from mid '60s Kinks and Who singles, and their distinctive look from mods. Comprised of Paul Weller (guitar/vocals), Bruce Foxton (bass), and Rick Buckler (drums), the Jam signed with Polydor and released *In the City* (uk20) in May 1977. The band followed up later that year with *This Is the Modern World* (uk22), the title track of which is representative of the band's blend of hard-driving rhythm with catchy pop hooks. The group's success built through the end of the decade and into the 1980s with the albums *All Mod Cons* (uk6, 1978), *Setting Sons* (uk4, 1979), and *Sound Affects* (uk2, 1980), and the number one UK single "Start!" The Sex Pistols' Sid Vicious had previously played drums in a band fronted by Siouxsie Sioux, who together with bassist Steven Severin would lead Siouxsie and the Banshees. The band signed with Polydor and released "Hong Kong Garden" (uk7) in the fall of 1978, followed by *The Scream* (uk12, 1978), a dark, brooding album that contained a gothic cover of the Beatles' "Helter Skelter." The band enjoyed continued success into the 1980s with *Join Hands* (uk13, 1979), *Kaleidoscope* (uk5, 1980), *Ju Ju* (uk7, 1981), and a cover version of "Dear Prudence" (uk3, 1983). Siouxsie was not the only woman in British punk in the late 1970s; X-Ray Spex, fronted by Poly Styrene, enjoyed brief success with *Germ Free Adolescents* (uk30, 1978), which contained "The Day the World Turned

The Clash's guitarist Mick Jones performs during the band's 1979 tour of America. The Clash took the Sex Pistols' musical rebelliousness but focused it more squarely on politics. Unlike many punk bands that emerged after the Sex Pistols, the Clash was able to break into the American mainstream: their album London Calling *was popular in the United States and even found its way into regular FM radio rotation.*

Dayglo" (uk23); and the Slits, an all-female punk trio that opened for the Clash on their spring 1977 tour and released *Cut* (uk30) in September 1979. The groups discussed here did at least moderately well in the British market, but none enjoyed American success except the Clash, and that was not until 1980. The British punk scene did not make the Atlantic crossing; other British acts did, however, though not as punk acts. They came under the label "new wave."

Punk Poetics—Organization or Anarchy? Punk fashion attacks the status quo and punk lyrics often advocate social or political change, but punk music is often fairly conventional in its structure. This is partly because of punk rock's "return-to-simplicity" aesthetic—the idea of eliminating the complexity and expansiveness that hippie rock had developed. The Sex Pistols' first single, "Anarchy in the UK," provides an interesting example in terms of musical structure. Overall, the song employs a simple verse structure; each verse is sixteen measures in length, with the last eight measures in each verse carrying the same lyrical refrain (a "mini-chorus"). This eight-bar refrain is repeated three times at the end of the track, creating a coda that drives home the song's catchiest line (its "hook"). The exceptions are the two bridges inserted along the way, the first between verses two and three, and the second between verses three and four. Ironically, this insertion of bridges into a typical formal design is similar to the Foreigner example explored earlier in this chapter. It is significant that unlike the bridges found in the Foreigner or Boston examples, this Sex Pistols track features no elaborate guitar solos or synthesizer riffs. In fact, the return-to-simplicity approach is perhaps most obvious in the driving guitar, bass, and drums accompaniment and the self-consciously untrained and amateurish character of Johnny Rotten's singing. The fast tempo and driving, steady eighth notes in the guitar, bass, and drums are also clear features of early punk. The use of simple verse form—inserted bridges notwithstanding—links this music with early rock and rhythm and blues, as well as with much traditional folk music, and contrasts strongly with the examples from Yes, Boston, and Foreigner discussed earlier.

The Rise of New Wave, 1977–1980

The Next Big Thing. As late as fall 1977, rock listeners in America were largely unaware of either British or American punk. CBGB was popular among some in New York, but with the overwhelming success of big albums from Peter Frampton, the Eagles, Stevie Wonder, and Fleetwood Mac; the continued success of Wings, Aerosmith, and others; and the emergence of Boston, Foreigner, and Billy Joel, it is easy to see that punk would have had a tough time getting listeners' attention, especially on FM rock radio with its increasingly restricted playlists. In late 1977 and early 1978, the Sex Pistols did tour the United States, but instead of playing rock clubs in the northeast and on the west coast, the band toured the south—a move designed, it seemed, to invite trouble and provoke yet more headlines (which it did). Late in 1977, Elvis Costello (see p. 430) appeared on *Saturday Night Live* (filling in for the Sex Pistols, who had trouble getting into the country in time), marking perhaps the first time most mainstream rock fans in the United States had been exposed to punk. At about the same time, rock magazines like *Rolling Stone* were beginning to take notice of punk and give it more attention. Punk, however, had already begun to build a reputation for being dangerous and potentially embarrassing within the music business; on the other hand, every record company had its eye out for "the next big thing," and with disco already beginning to challenge rock, why not punk? For much of the music business, new wave was the solution; new wave tamed the more aggressive elements of punk, making it more of an artsy aesthetic statement than a statement of nihilism or protest. Punks seemed angry whereas new wavers were ironic. Punk's answer to frustration was to lash out, perhaps break a window and form a band; new wave's was to reflect on urban alienation, have a cup of coffee, and write a clever lyric. Since many of the CBGB bands had backgrounds in the arts, the turn to new wave worked to their advantage. Blondie and Talking Heads, both regulars at CBGB (see p. 425), became stars, leaving the Ramones behind. Strangely enough, Television seemed as poised as any of the other CBGB bands to achieve broad commercial success, but Hell left the group in 1975 and Verlaine took over the band. Having signed with Elektra,

LISTENING GUIDE　　　　　GET MUSIC ▶▶　wwnorton.com/rockhistory

The Sex Pistols, "Anarchy in the UK"

Words and music by Paul Cook, Steve Johns, Glen Matlock, and Johnny Rotten, produced by Chris Thomas and Bill Price. Reached #38 in the UK in late 1976. Contained on the album *Never Mind the Bollocks, Here's the Sex Pistols*, which went to #1 in the UK in late 1977.

FORM: Modified simple verse, with instrumental bridges inserted. Each verse ends with an 8-bar refrain.

TIME SIGNATURE: 4/4.

INSTRUMENTATION: Electric guitars, bass, drums, lead and backup vocals.

0:00–0:14	**Introduction**, 8 mm.	Music derived from the refrain sets the stage for the entrance of the vocals.
0:14–0:43	**Verse 1 w/refrain**, 16 mm.	Vocals enter, raw and urgent. "I am an antichrist . . ."
0:43–1:11	**Verse 2 w/refrain**, 16 mm.	As before, with no significant changes. "Anarchy for the UK . . ."

the band's debut album, *Marquee Moon* (uk28) flopped in the United States in the first half of 1977. The next album, *Adventure* (uk7), was released in April 1978 and did no better in the States. It was a different story for the Patti Smith Group, who scored on both sides of the Atlantic with *Easter* (p20 uk16, 1978), which contained the hit single "Because the Night" (p13 uk5), and followed with *Wave* (p18 uk41, 1979).

Blondie, the Talking Heads.   Even though Blondie had signed with Chrysalis, in early 1978 it looked as if the band might be in for the same fate as Television —successful in England and unknown at home. Released in February 1978, Blondie's *Plastic Letters* (uk10) did well in the UK, in part on the strength of the hit singles "Denis" (uk2) and "(I'm Always Touched by Your) Presence, Dear" (uk10). But in the fall of that year, the band brought out *Parallel Lines* (p6 uk1, 1978), which contained a single that hit number one on both sides of the Atlantic, "Heart of Glass," as well as two more UK hits, "Hanging on the Telephone" (uk5) and "Sunday Girl" (uk1). Blondie followed with *Eat to the Beat* (p17 uk1, 1979)—which contained "Dreaming" (p2 uk27)—released "Call Me" (p1 uk1, 1980) as a single, and began the new decade with *Autoamerican* (p7 uk3, 1980), "The Tide Is High" (p1 uk1), and "Rapture" (p5 uk1, early 1981). In

Time	Section	Description
1:11–1:31	**Bridge 1**, 11 mm.	Simple guitar solo over new musical material. Note occasional rude vocal sounds throughout.
1:31–1:59	**Verse 3 w/refrain**, 16 mm.	As before, but now with repeated note on the guitar. "How many ways . . ."
1:59–2:14	**Bridge 2**, 8 mm.	New musical material, melodic but driving, as repeated note in guitar becomes sustained note, with feedback throughout the first half of the following verse.
2:14–2:42	**Verse 4 w/refrain**, 16 mm.	As before. "Is this the M.P.L.A. . . ."
2:42–2:57	**Refrain**, 8 mm.	Repeat of refrain to create ending. "I want to be . . ."
2:57–3:11	**Refrain**, 8 mm.	Repeat; note guitar licks in the background throughout the ending.
3:11–3:29	**Refrain**, 8 mm.	Repeat; ends with menacing vocal on the word "destroy" and guitar feedback.

The Talking Heads during their first performance at CBGB as a foursome (left to right: Jerry Harrison, Chris Frantz, David Byrne, and Tina Weymouth), in spring 1977. Like many so-called new wave groups that would follow, the Talking Heads took punk's rebellion in a new, "artsy" direction. If punk turned passion into violence, new wave turned it into intro-spective vocals and more complex music.

a few short years, Blondie had gone from a band many at CBGB thought were the least likely to make any headway in the business to the most successful of the lot.

Made up of students from the Rhode Island School of Design and led by songwriter David Byrne, and featuring Jerry Harrison (guitar), Chris Frantz (drums), and Tina Weymouth, the Talking Heads debuted at CBGB in May 1975 and also seemed to exceed initial commercial expectations. The group gained recognition in New York almost immediately but held off signing with a label, though they were courted by a few. Eventually the band signed with Sire and released *Talking Heads 77* in September 1977. The track "Psycho Killer" provides a representative example of the early Talking Heads approach, with spare instrumental accompaniment and Byrne's spastic vocal delivery. The next album *More Songs about Buildings and Food* (p29 uk21) was released in summer 1978 and enjoyed moderate success, though interest in that album began to heat up considerably when the track "Take Me to the River" (p26) was released as a single in October. The next two releases, *Fear of Music* (p21 uk33, 1979) and *Remain in Light* (p19 uk21, 1980), established the band as one of new wave's leading groups, especially since they were well liked by many music critics, who praised the intellectual and artsy character of Byrne's songs.

New Wave, American-style: the Cars, Tom Petty, Devo, B-52s, the Knack.   As central as New York is to the development of American punk and new wave, many of the most successful of the new wave bands in the late 1970s did not arise out of the CBGB scene. The Boston-based Cars, led by guitarist/vocalist Ric Ocasek and drummer David Robinson, were among the first new wave bands to break onto the FM rock radio playlists. Signed with Elektra, the band's debut release, *The Cars* (p18 uk29, 1978), contained two tracks that got significant airplay on mainstream rock radio stations in the fall of 1978 and into 1979: "My Best Friend's Girl" (p35 uk3, 1978) and "Just What I Needed" (p27, 1978; uk17, 1979).

The band followed with *Candy-O* (p3 uk30, 1979), which contained "Let's Go" (p14), and *Panorama* (p5, 1980), and continued to top the charts well into the 1980s. Also hailing from outside the Big Apple, Florida's Tom Petty and the Heartbreakers adapted the '60s folk-rock style of Dylan and the Byrds, so much so that the Byrds' Roger McGuinn likes to joke that the first time he heard "American Girl" (uk40) from *Tom Petty and the Heartbreakers* (uk24, 1977), he thought it was one of his own songs. As new wave was gaining in popularity in the second half of 1978, Petty and company released *You're Gonna Get It* (p23 uk34), which contained "I Need to Know" (p41). When the band's label, Shelter, was sold, the group ended up recording for MCA, releasing in late 1979 *Damn the Torpedoes* (p2), which rose to number two in the United States on the strength of several tracks, including "Don't Do Me Like That" (p10) and "Refugee" (p15, 1980), which became staples of FM rock radio.

Perhaps the most ironic of all new wave bands were Devo, led by brothers Bob and Mark Mothersbaugh. The band adopted the image of futuristic beings from 1950s science-fiction movies. The Ohio band's first album, *Q: Are We Not Men? A: We Are Devo!* (uk12), containing the band's mechanistic cover of "(I Can't Get No) Satisfaction" (uk41) and their theme song "Jocko Homo," did well in England when released in September 1978. The band did not really enjoy commercial success in the United States until *Freedom of Choice* (p22 uk47, 1980), which contained the single "Whip It" (p14). If any band could challenge Devo for irony, Georgia's B-52s are that band. Led by singer Fred Schneider and featuring singers Kate Pierson and Cindy Wilson done up in '50s-style bee-hive hairdos, the band made its first significant showing in the UK with *The B-52s* (uk22,1979), which contained "Rock Lobster" (uk37), a track that has since become much better known. The band enjoyed broader commercial success with the release of *Wild Planet* (p18, uk18) in 1980.

Devo took new wave to the peak of irony, often employing a high-tech feel in their music and a 1950's space-movie look in their videos and live performances. Their robot-like version of the Rolling Stones "I Can't Get No Satisfaction" and the pseudo-sexual "Whip It" epitomize the detached humor of the band's music and videos.

No new wave band in the late 1970s was more cynical and calculating in the use of musical styles and images drawn from rock's pre-hippie history than the Knack. Based in Los Angeles and led by guitarist Doug Feiger, the band signed with Capitol and did its best to suggest they were the new Beatles. The first album, *Get the Knack* (p1, 1979), was indeed a smash and was supported by a hit single, "My Sharona" (p1 uk6). The front cover of the record featured the band in Beatle-esque attire and the back cover was meant to suggest the Beatles' appearance on the *Ed Sullivan Show*. The band even had Capitol revert to using the same logo on the record labels as it had back in the mid 1960s. All this worked only briefly, and the next album, *But the Little Girls Understand* (p15, 1980), was their last album to climb the charts.

Music on *Saturday Night Live*

We have seen all along how national radio and television shows like the *Kraft Music Hall*, the *Ed Sullivan Show*, and *Soul Train* served as showcases to draw national attention to new and important musical acts—often dramatically reshaping the history of rock and roll in the process. Since 1975 *Saturday Night Live*, a ninety-minute sketch-comedy show broadcast live every Saturday evening on NBC, has consistently filled this role as an important national music venue.

Saturday Night Live debuted in 1975 and quickly became very popular for its irreverent, satirical brand of humor and the performances of a talented company of comedians. Each show features a guest host—typically a film star but occasionally a politician, athlete, or musician—along with a musical guest. Each musical guest performs twice, about half an hour into the show and again just before closing.

Although the show is broadcast live, this has led to far fewer controversies and mishaps than might be expected. After the producers asked him not to sing "Radio, Radio" during his 1977 appearance, Elvis Costello abruptly switched to it halfway through his performance of "Less than Zero," ruining the show's delicate timing. And when Sinead O'Connor performed in 1992, she ceremoniously tore up a picture of Pope John Paul II, sparking outrage among Roman Catholic viewers. The most disastrous performance in *SNL* history was given by Ashlee Simpson in 2004. When her drummer accidentally cued the wrong song, it became obvious to the national audience that she lip-synched her vocals. She abruptly ended the song in disgrace, while dancing an embarrassing "hoedown."

Like the *Ed Sullivan Show*, an appearance on *Saturday Night Live* is an important career landmark. It has been the high-water mark for countless one-hit wonders, from Dexy's Midnight

From the beginning of Saturday Night Live *in the mid 1970s though the present, music has been a key component of the show, and the producers have used it in many different ways. Sometimes they created their own musical groups like the Blues Brothers (left), played by Dan Aykroyd and John Belushi. Often they presented parodies of musicians —like Gilda Radner's impersonation of Patti Smith (center, compare with Smith herself on p. 419). The show also featured many groundbreaking (and often controversial) traditional performances—in 1992 Sinead O'Connor (right) sang Bob Marley's "War," ending the song by destroying a picture of Pope John Paul II.*

Runners to the Crash Test Dummies, and heralded the arrival on the national stage for major stars and even entire musical styles. For example, when Run-DMC became the first hip-hop act to appear, in 1986, their appearance not only announced that Run-DMC were major stars but also served notice that hip-hop was now a national force. Similarly, Nirvana saw their 1992 appearance as proof that the band had arrived as superstars and that grunge was a major style.

SNL performers are typically rock-oriented but also include rhythm and blues, country, and hip-hop. Less mainstream guests occasionally appear for the sake of variety. Among the most unusual performers to appear were the Yale glee club known as the Whiffenpoofs, jazz trumpeter Miles Davis, the South African pop choir Ladysmith Black Mambazo, minimalist composer Philip Glass, and the 96-year-old, Depression-era tunesmith Eubie Blake. *SNL* has been particularly important to the history of punk rock and hip-hop, because of landmark performances by the Talking Heads, the Clash, Nirvana, and Green Day, and by Run-DMC, Public Enemy, and the trio of Snoop Dogg, Dr. Dre, and Eminem.

Musicians and music are also often satirized in comedy sketches. Frequent targets include VH1's *Behind the Music* series, benefit concerts ("Musicians for Free-Range Chickens"), U2 lead singer Bono, and especially Frank Sinatra. Other famous parodies include John Belushi's impressions of Joe Cocker and Ludwig Van Beethoven, Gilda Radner's Patti Smith, and Adam Sandler's imitation of Axl Rose singing nursery rhymes. But by far the most famous use of music on *Saturday Night Live* was John Belushi and Dan Aykroyd as "The Blues Brothers." The Blues Brothers recorded a #1 album in 1979 (*Briefcase Full of Blues*), toured nationally, made a hit film, and revived interest in the music of John Lee Hooker, Booker T. & the MG's, and the blues in general.

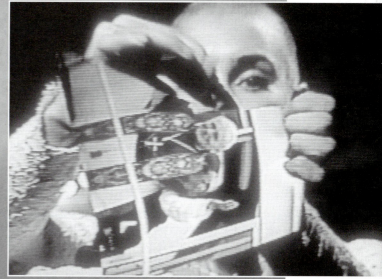

Elvis Costello's legendary performance on Saturday Night Live *(December 17, 1977) was an important moment in his career and helped launch punk and new wave into the mainstream. Costello did not have approval to play "Radio, Radio," but halfway through his performance of "Less Than Zero," he stopped the band and told the audi-ence, "Sorry, ladies and gentleman, there's no reason to do this song here." He then did a rollicking version of "Radio, Radio" with its lyrical attack on the radio industry—just what the producers didn't want. For many, this was a triumphant expression of the punk music attitude.*

British New Wavers in America: Elvis Costello, the Police, Joe Jackson. Besides the Sex Pistols and the Clash, most of the British punk bands that dominated the charts in England never made an impact in the states. Those acts that fit the American new wave profile, however, did enjoy success, and first among these was Elvis Costello. Signed with Stiff in the UK but distributed by Columbia in the United States, Costello's releases were among the first British new wave records to make the U.S. Top 40 in the first half of 1978. While *My Aim Is True* (p32 uk14) contained the ballad "Alison," Costello became much better known for aggressive and clever attacks on the status quo. His second album, *This*

Year's Model (p30 uk4, 1978)—recorded with a backup band called the Attractions—contained "Pump It Up" (uk24), which is a good example of Costello's more raucous side, as is the single "Radio, Radio" (uk29, 1978). Elvis Costello and the Attractions followed with *Armed Forces* (p10 uk2, 1979), completing a trio of albums that would establish Costello as one of rock's most interesting songwriters. The Police also debuted in this new wave context, as their first album *Outlandos d'Amour* (p23) from the first half of 1979 contained both "Roxanne" (p32 uk12) and "Can't Stand Losing You" (p42 uk2). Initially blending a strong reggae influence into their style, the Police became well known for the complex drumming of Stewart Copeland, the literary lyrics of Sting, and the atmospheric guitar of Andy Summers. The series of albums and singles that followed included *Regatta de Blanc* (p25 uk1, 1979), "Message in a Bottle" (uk1), *Zenyatta Mondatta* (p5 uk1, 1980), and "Don't Stand So Close to Me" (p10 uk1). The Police became one of the most important bands of the early 1980s, and will be discussed further in Chapter 11. Another important new wave artist who is sometimes overlooked is Joe Jackson. Jackson's debut effort, *Look Sharp!* (p20 uk40, 1979) contained the tracks "Is She Really Going Out with Him?" (p21 uk13) and "Sunday Papers"—two songs that were played at least as much as any other new wave on the radio at the end of the decade. Jackson followed up with *I'm the Man* (p22 uk12, 1979), but then headed off in new stylistic directions, abandoning new wave by 1980.

Pangs of Rock History?   One aspect of new wave sets it apart from the hippie rock that preceded it: new wave bands had a clear fascination with earlier musical styles and—perhaps more important—with the visual images associated with those styles. Thus, it's *Elvis* Costello who wears horn-rimmed glasses like Buddy Holly and straight leg pants and short hair in an era of bellbottoms and shoulder-length hair. Why this dimension of new wave was important to these musicians and their fans is discussed below, but for now we will focus on the music itself. Spotting the references to rock history in the visual aspect of new wave is easy, but how can we hear stylistic references to earlier rock *in the music itself*? The Cars' "My Best Friend's Girl" offers an example rich in new wave references to past styles. Notice first the hand claps that enter during the introduction, reminiscent of early '60s girl-group recordings ("My Boyfriend's Back") or early Beatles tracks ("I Want to Hold Your Hand"). The rockabilly guitar lick that occurs in the passages linking the choruses to the following verses seem inspired by Carl Perkins, Elvis Presley, or Gene Vincent records from the late '50s. The repeated organ chords that enter with the second verse bring to mind the mid '60s garage-band sound, a good example of which is "96 Tears" by ? & the Mysterians. Ocasek's vocal delivery is full of vocal hiccups that imitate those of Buddy Holly and the naïve innocence of much teen music before the mid '60s. These many references to pre-hippie rock are not particularly well reinforced by the form, which follows a compound AABA design not too different from Boston's "More Than a Feeling," employing verse-chorus pairs for A sections and a guitar solo for the bridge. The Cars material here is far simpler in its harmonic content than the harmonies in the Boston track, and notice that all the sections are repeated without much structural change (the measure counts

The Cars, "My Best Friend's Girl"

Words and music by Ric Ocasek, produced by Roy Thomas Baker. Reached #35 in the United States and #3 in the UK in mid 1978. Contained on the album *The Cars*, which reached #18 in the United States and #29 in the UK.

FORM: Compound AABA, with A sections based on contrasting verse-chorus form. The B section is instrumental, featuring a guitar solo and based on the music from the chorus.

TIME SIGNATURE: 4/4.

INSTRUMENTATION: Electric guitars, bass, synthesizer, organ, drums, hand claps, lead and backup vocals.

	0:00–0:16	**Introduction**, 8 mm.	Clean guitar for 4 bars, and then hand claps enter at 0:09.
A	0:16–0:48	**Verse 1**, 16 mm.	Vocals enter, with full band joining in after 4 bars, along with backup vocals. "You're always dancin' . . ."
	0:49–1:08	**Chorus**, 10 mm.	Choral vocals, as organ enters. Ends with 4 mm. rockabilly guitar that leads to next verse. "She's my best friend's . . ."
A	1:09–1:40	**Verse 2**, 16 mm.	As before, but now with "96 Tears" organ and lightly arpeggiated guitar in first half and rockabilly pattern in second half. "You got your nuclear boots . . ."
	1:40–2:00	**Chorus**, 10 mm.	As before, 4 mm. link leads to instrumental chorus this time. "She's my best friend's . . ."
B	2:00–2:20	**Instrumental Chorus**, 10 mm.	6-bar guitar melodic solo, then 4-bar link leads back to last verse.
A	2:20–2:51	**Verse 3**, 16 mm.	Repeat of verse 1 lyrics with verse 3 accompaniment.
	2:51–3:11	**Chorus**, 10 mm.	As before, 4 mm. link leads to coda.
	3:11–3:43	**Coda**, 10 mm.	New melody based on chorus with chords from verse. Synthesizer strings enter in the background at 3:19, and hand claps at 3:27, as fade-out begins, "My best friend's girlfriend."

for verses and choruses are identical). This Cars example, like much new wave, is less an attempt to duplicate earlier rock styles than an eclectic view of earlier rock taken in through a late 1970s "lens." We can begin to separate these out as the '60s stylistic references are placed within a '70s formal design.

The Rejection of Hippie Values and the Rise of Historical Self-Consciousness

New Wave and the Hippie Aesthetic.   New wave's relationship to past rock-music styles is the key to understanding how it differentiated itself from mainstream rock. Rock music from psychedelia through late 1970s mainstream rock was founded on the hippie aesthetic: the idea that rock music should take the listener on a kind of trip and use all the possibilities of technology—in terms of both equipment and instrumental and compositional skill—to do so. Rock should deal with important issues, not teen love, and should reflect on man's place in the universe. New wave musicians would have none of that: they scaled back the musical complexities and shortened the tunes; they returned to topics of teenage romance; and they no longer paraded their musical prowess for their listeners. Thus the music-stylistic and visual references in new wave were almost always to rock before *Sgt. Pepper*—and this is important because *Sgt. Pepper* marks the beginning of hippie culture. The new wave haircuts, clothes, album art, music, and lyrics all seem to reject hippie culture and music. But in rejecting the hippie present, were new wavers advocating a return to rock's past? The answer is no; instead, new wave musicians were making ironic references to earlier music—they were not embracing past styles but rather using them to offer a critique of the present.

Gary Wright and Gary Numan.   One way to see the contrast between the mainstream rock and new wave approaches in the late 1970s is to compare bands and artists with obvious similarities but also with telling differences. Both Gary Wright and Gary Numan relied heavily on keyboards and synthesizers in their music, for instance. American Gary Wright had been a member of Spooky Tooth (along with Mick Jones in his days before Foreigner), but set out on a solo career. He released *The Dream Weaver* (p7) in late 1975 and his music caught on in 1976 with two hit tracks, "Dream Weaver" (p2) and "Love Is Alive" (p2). Englishman Gary Numan was originally a member of Tubeway Army, whose second album *Replicas* was number one in the UK in the summer of 1979 with the help of the hit single, "Are We 'Friends' Electric?" (uk1). Numan went solo as well, releasing *The Pleasure Principle* (p16 uk1) in September 1979, which contained the hit "Cars" (p9 uk1). Comparing Wright's "Dream Weaver" with Numan's "Cars" reveals that both tracks rely almost exclusively on synthesized sounds. But whereas Wright's warm timbres, saturated with reverb and echo, are similar to the broad textures used by progressive-rock keyboardists such as Rick Wakeman or Keith Emerson, Numan's sounds are much harsher, creating a drier and more focused sound more reminiscent of Germany's Kraftwerk.

Wright's vocals show a blues influence; Numan's are clipped and almost mechanical. Both Wright and Numan employ futuristic images on the album sleeve: Wright's future seems optimistic and utopian while Numan's seems cold and mechanical, dominated by machines. Since Wright's music comes first, it is clear that Numan's approach takes its meaning as much from what it is not as from what it is; despite similarities to "Dream Weaver," Numan's "Cars" makes its mark by rejecting the hippie dreams of fantastic voyages into the bright technological future—Numan rejects the trip, or at least suggests a very different kind of trip.

Heart and Blondie.   Another comparison can be drawn between the music of Heart and Blondie. Led by sisters Anne and Nancy Wilson, Heart's debut album, *Dreamboat Annie* (p7 uk36), rose on the U.S. charts with the help of the tracks "Crazy on You" (p35) and "Magic Man." The band followed with *Little Queen* (p9 uk34, 1977), containing "Barracuda" (p11); *Magazine* (p17, 1978); *Dog & Butterfly* (p17, 1978), containing "Straight On" (p15); and *Bebe Le Strange* (p5, 1980). The group's music has both a harder edge, in which Anne Wilson can belt out her vocals with power and authority, and a softer, more acoustically oriented side, often showcasing Nancy's guitar playing. Anne Wilson adopted the stage persona of the tough, hard-driving woman, perhaps following and extending the image established by Janis Joplin. Her singing is often forceful and technically schooled, filled with bluesy melodic twists and turns similar to those found in the singing of Steve Winwood, Paul Rodgers, or later, Lou Gramm. Debbie Harry (of Blondie) has a vocal approach that is much more limited, far less free rhythmically, and devoid of any blues influence whatsoever. This is immediately evident in comparing Heart's "Straight On" with Blondie's "Heart of Glass." Here again, Harry's style is motivated by a rejection of hippie technical virtuosity; her style is almost amateurish, and this amateur quality is exactly what many new wave musicians were attempting to project. Harry's singing in this regard is similar to that of David Byrne, Ric Ocasek, or Elvis Costello, none of whom would be considered "polished" vocalists in a traditional sense. That was part of new wave's return-to-simplicity charm, and central to its rejection of rock's hippie legacy.

Although new wave defined itself against hippie rock, it was never able to escape it completely. Indeed, by the early 1980s, most new wave was incorporated within the mainstream rock playlists of FM radio, attesting to the influence of new wave but also to the underlying similarities between the styles. By the end of the decade, record-company and radio pressures had reduced the length of most mainstream rock tracks to less than five minutes, and this reduction within hippie rock led to a pulling back of the ambition and scale that had been the norm earlier in the decade. As mainstream rock consolidated, it became less experimental and, in many ways, simpler. New wave was not the only style to challenge mainstream rock and the hippie aesthetic in the second half of the 1970s: as we saw in the last chapter, the disco craze caused many rock fans to throw away their beads and put on their dancing shoes. To many rockers, it was as if the gains made in the 1960s from "The Twist" to *Sgt. Pepper* were being reversed, as some young rockers gave up the sedentary contemplation of rock in favor of the physical abandon of disco. Disco had mostly played itself out by the end of the 1970s, however, and ceased to pose any real threat to mainstream rock. Mainstream rock and new wave had come together sufficiently by the beginning of the 1980s that it seemed as if hippie rock had run its course and that an era had ended. Elements of the hippie aesthetic would re-emerge over the course of the 1980s and '90s—especially in heavy metal and MTV videos—but for the most part, the era of ambitious rock devoted to the idea of music as a trip was over.

Questions for Review and Discussion

1. How did the growth of the rock-music business in the second half of the 1970s affect the development of radio and expectations for album sales and profits?
2. Some bands and artists with roots in the 1960s and the early 1970s continued to enjoy success in the late 1970s. Who were these bands and what are some of their important albums?
3. If the first half of the 1970s can be seen as a time of stylistic expansion and specialization, how can the second half of the decade be characterized?
4. Summarize the roots of punk in the United States. How does this scene compare with the rise of punk in the UK?
5. How does new wave differ from punk? How did new wave bands refer to earlier musical styles and images? How can this be contrasted with mainstream rock during the same period?
6. Can the hippie aesthetic account for the rise of new wave?

Further Reading

Victor Bockris, *Transformer: The Lou Reed Story* (Simon & Schuster, 1994).

Craig Bromberg, *The Wicked Ways of Malcolm McLaren* (Harper & Row, 1989).

Jerome Davis, *Talking Heads* (Vintage, 1986).

Toby Goldstein, *Frozen Fire: The Story of the Cars* (Contemporary Books, 1985).

Debbie Harry, Chris Stein, and Victor Bockris, *Making Tracks: The Rise of Blondie* (Da Capo, 1998).

Brian Hinton, *Let Them All Talk: The Music of Elvis Costello* (Sanctuary, 1999).

Joe Jackson, *A Cure for Gravity: A Musical Pilgrimage* (Da Capo, 2000).

Glen Matlock with Pete Silverton, *I Was a Teenage Sex Pistol* (Omnibus, 1990).

The Nineteen Eighties

1980s

The 1980s began with the defeat of incumbent president Jimmy Carter and the election of Ronald Reagan, a Hollywood actor turned politician. Reagan's presidency marked a new conservative attitude in much of the country and also in popular culture. In his speeches and public remarks, Reagan evoked images of America's idyllic past, and his amiable, "grandfatherly" style helped many to regain confidence in government after Watergate and the Iran hostage crisis.

Reagan's economic policy was driven by "supply-side economics"—lower taxes on wealthy Americans that would, arguably, inspire everyone to work harder (because they'd be keeping more of their income). His foreign policy embraced building up American military forces and weapons systems. Reagan believed that an arms race would cripple the Soviet Union (which he referred to as the "evil empire"), whose economy could not afford to keep pace with American advances. However, in the midst of this Cold War buildup, Mikhail Gorbachev became leader of the Communist Party in 1985, advocating policies of *glasnost*

(openness) and *perestroika* (restructuring of Soviet government along Western lines). Historians differ on who gets credit for it, but in November 1989 (almost a year after Reagan left office), the Berlin Wall—a symbol of the division between the Soviet Union and the Western powers—fell, signaling an end to a cold war that had lasted almost half a century. By 1991, the Soviet Union had broken apart and the United States emerged as the world's leading superpower.

The 1980s also mark the emergence and growth of the AIDS epidemic, with over 150,000 cases diagnosed and

over 90,000 AIDS-related deaths reported in the United States from 1981 to 1989.[1] AIDS was made most publicly visible by movie star Rock Hudson, who died from the disease in 1985. Hudson had been a leading man in romantic comedies for years, and his homosexuality came as a surprise for many of his fans. Despite the sensationalism following the disclosure of Hudson's gay lifestyle, many Americans learned about AIDS for the first time, leading to an increased awareness of the dis-ease and its seriousness. In 1991, Queen frontman Freddie Mercury succumbed to the disease, further raising the music world's awareness of AIDS.

The American economy grew in many ways during the 1980s, but no sector advanced as impressively and publicly as high tech. The space program had provided many spin-off benefits and technologies, and the development of ever smaller, more powerful computers made it possible for home computers to be useful and affordable to most Americans. The earliest Apple computers from the mid 1970s were made from kits. By the early 1980s

AIDS victims and supporters in the March on Washington for Lesbian and Gay Rights, 1987. Over 150,000 cases of AIDS were diagnosed from 1981–89. Many AIDS activists did not think the Reagan administration sufficiently supported their cause.

1 Statistics compiled from AVERT: www.avert.org/usastaty.htm

The Cosby Show *was one of the 1980s' most popular shows. It featured a middle class African American family dealing not with issues of race, but usually with the more mundane problems of their school-age children. Here, Cliff Huxtable (Bill Cosby) and his son Theo (Malcolm Jamal Warner) discuss marijuana found in Theo's school book.*

however, Steve Jobs and Steve Wozniak were marketing a more refined home unit, while Microsoft founders Bill Gates and Paul Allen were offering the MS-DOS operating system for the IBM PC. In 1984, a now-famous commercial during the Super Bowl announced the arrival of the Macintosh computer, and by 1985, the first version of Windows was available for the PC. These years also marked the beginnings of Internet use by the general public; CompuServe offered home e-mail in 1979 and real-time chat in 1980, and the number of users increased throughout the decade, though the real Internet explosion would not occur until the 1990s.

While many benefited from technologies developed by NASA, the space agency also experienced one of its greatest disasters in the mid 1980s. The space shuttle *Challenger* exploded minutes after taking off, killing all the astronauts aboard, including Christa McAuliffe. McAuliffe was a high school teacher who was making the journey in order to bring aspects of the space program into more direct contact with schoolchildren.

Another technology that experienced dramatic growth during the decade was cable television. By mid-decade, many American homes were wired to receive premium movies, news, and sports from channels like

HBO, CNN, and ESPN. Most important for the history of rock music, MTV was launched, creating competition for FM radio, which had been the central way to expose the music to a large body of listeners. And just as it was having to share its audience with MTV, FM was also losing sponsors to a new kind of radio emerging over the AM band: talk radio. Taking advantage of the neglect into which many AM stations had fallen, entrepreneurial broadcasters such as Rush Limbaugh began offering hours of daily political and cultural commentary, sometimes from the left of the political spectrum, but most often from the right. Soon Limbaugh and others built up syndication networks, in a sense reinventing the radio networks of the '30s and '40s, as millions of listeners heard the same programming across the country (though National Public Radio had also been doing the same thing on the FM band for years).

Television reflected America's renewed fascination with money and power. Perhaps no show captured this more vividly than *Dallas*, which debuted in 1978 and focused on a rich Texas oil family led by the shifty J. R. Ewing. Viewers got caught up in the cliffhanger ending to the show's second season, and during the summer of 1980 the phrase "Who shot J. R.?" saturated the media. *Family Ties* also reflected this new conservative trend, featuring a middle-aged liberal couple bantering with their conservative and financially astute son, Alex.

If *Family Ties* underscored the changes taking place in the white middle class, the *Cosby Show* reinforced shifts occurring in the black community. The show's main characters, Cliff and Clare Huxtable, were both professionals (he was a doctor, she was a lawyer), and the comedy turned on family issues arising among them and their several school-age children, and never on issues of race (unlike *The Jeffersons* in the 1970s, for instance). The Huxtables lived in a nice home in a desirable part of town, and their markedly upper-middle-class standing emphasized the rise and visibility of the black middle class during the decade. Middle-class values were in for a completely different treatment, however, when *The Simpsons* debuted in 1989. This animated prime-time comedy irreverently lampooned almost every dimension of American life; playing no political favorites and pulling few punches, it established the model for many animated series in the 1990s.

As the hippies got older, the general cultural middle-class transformation from 1970s idealistic dreamers into well-appointed 1980s Yuppies (young urban professionals) created a cultural crisis for some. Such hand-wringing over identity and authenticity is captured effectively in *The Big Chill*. In this 1983 film, set to the beat of late '60s rock and soul, a group of thirty-something college friends reunite for the funeral of a friend. While there, each takes in the changes that have occurred in their lives over the years. Amid the success that some of these friends have achieved, the viewer senses that they have lost touch with the things that originally inspired and motivated them.

The idea of selling out arises much more obviously and forcefully in Oliver Stone's 1987 film *Wall Street*. Stone set out to capture the ruthless lust for money and power that he believed characterized stock market professionals. Epitomized by the phrase "Greed is good," the film provided a glimpse into the dark side of the Reagan years and illustrated how the conservative '80s were viewed by those with 1960s sensibilities. For a younger generation that came of age in the 1980s, youth-oriented films like *The Breakfast Club* and *St. Elmo's Fire* grappled with the social issues of young adult life and helped to define new cultural attitudes free from the baggage of the 1960s and '70s ideologies for those subsequently dubbed "Generation X."

Likewise, though rock music benefited from the wealth and technology of the times, it still often displayed the critical stance of the 1960s and 1970s. Hyper-marketed pop stars competed with musicians critical of the growing divide between rich and poor, and the continued gaps between black and white, straight and gay, and male and female.

chapter 11

Soon after its release in 1983, Michael Jackson's Thriller *became the best-selling album of all time. It contained several major hits, including "Billie Jean," "Beat It," and "Thriller." Jackson took full advantage of MTV to help promote his talents as both a musician and a performer. His innovative videos became instant MTV classics. Jackson teamed up with director John Landis (who also directed the 1981 film* American Werewolf in London, *among others), to make the video for "Thriller," a short film featuring Jackson as a loveable boyfriend who turns into a gruesome monster. Despite the monster-movie aesthetic, the video provides Jackson ample time to show off his exquisite dancing. With this album and these videos, Jackson was one of the first performers in the MTV era to successfully combine hit music with artistic visuals.*

I Want My MTV

The late 1970s saw a struggle among musical styles for the hearts and ears of America's youth. As rock became increasingly influenced by the idea of the smash album, disco and punk challenged the rock status quo. As it turned out, most rock fans in the 1980s had little to worry about with disco and punk. By early in the decade, punk retreated into an underground scene that continues to this day, replaced in the music-business limelight by new wave, and new wave quickly blended into mainstream rock radio playlists. The craze for disco music ended almost as quickly as it had begun; its big influence was reminding musicians that rock was not only for listening but also for dancing. By the middle of the 1980s, however, big changes were taking place in rock music. Music Television (MTV) began to challenge radio for priority in establishing hit records and artists, as heavy metal and rap began a climb from the underground into the spotlight by the end of the decade. This chapter will focus on the rise of MTV and many of the visually oriented acts that emerged during the 1980s, as well as the continued development of mainstream rock and new wave, which brought with it some new faces mixed with familiar ones. Chapter 12 will focus on the rise of heavy metal and rap, as well as the emergence of alternative rock in the early 1990s.

MTV Is on the Air

The Roots of MTV in Promotional Video.   Since the beginning of rock music, artists have used films as a vehicle for advancing their careers and increasing their popularity. Perhaps the most obvious examples of this are the films made by Elvis and the Beatles during the 1960s. Short films made to promote a single song also date back at least to the 1960s, though these were more a part of the European market than the American one. Given the wide range of television shows on the three major networks in the United States, most artists promoted their newest records by performing (or lip-synching) on *American Bandstand*, *Hullabaloo*, *Shindig*, *Where the Action Is*, and variety shows like the *Ed Sullivan Show*. For the European market, it became practical to make short films that could be shown not only in Europe but also in far-flung corners of the British Commonwealth like Australia and New Zealand—places that were difficult and expensive to visit in person. Among the first important promotional videos to be shown in the United States in place of actual performances were several made by the Beatles. In 1966, the band made videos for "Rain" and "Paperback Writer." Judged by later standards, these seem unimaginative and bland: the band lip-synchs performances in various scenes all shot in the same outdoor garden setting. But because the Beatles were growing weary of touring, these and later videos—most especially those for "Penny Lane" and "Strawberry Fields Forever"—became important tools in promoting new Beatles releases.

In the late 1960s, the idea of a television network devoted to nothing but promotional videos would have seemed absurd. In fact, the idea seemed strange to many broadcasters even in the early 1980s. The history of MTV grows not only out of the history of promotional videos but also out of the way cable television developed in the United States during the 1970s. Initially, cable was seen as necessary in areas where antenna transmission was unsatisfactory. For people who lived in hilly or mountainous areas, for instance, cable television provided a much more reliable way of delivering programming than standard transmission did. Then cable television, like any industry, looked for ways to expand, even in areas where over-the-air transmission was perfectly viable. In order to develop new markets, cable had to offer something the networks and local stations could not, and at first the focus was on recent movies broadcast without commercial interruptions. Because there were no commercials, customers were required to pay for the service, and many in the industry thought viewers would never pay for something they could otherwise get free. Soon, however, cable channels such as Home Box Office (HBO) proved these critics wrong. And when cable providers saw that movies were popular, they looked for more specialty channels to add to their roster. Soon sports, news, and weather were added to the list. MTV was the cable channel that added music to this list.

Rock music was no newcomer to television in the early 1980s; going back to *American Bandstand* in the late 1950s, teenagers had proved that they would happily tune in to listen to new music and watch (often lip-synched) performances. In 1966, the Monkees proved that teens would faithfully watch pop-music shows that were not just variety or dance shows. The question for the people who developed MTV was not whether teens would tune in, but whether they would watch music television around the clock on a specialty channel. In the early days of planning MTV, two models were on the table. The first was to show nothing but promotional videos provided by the record companies at their expense. Critics of this approach pointed out that it would make MTV nothing more than an advertising billboard for the labels. This faction, led by former Monkees guitarist Michael Nesmith, pushed for a more artistic approach. They argued that the videos should be experimental and innovative, not simply commercials. They saw great potential in music videos for expanding the artistic range of pop music by bringing filmmaking and music together in a symbiotic relationship. In the end, Nesmith and company lost the debate, and on August 1, 1981, MTV went on the air with a video of the Buggles' "Video Killed the Radio Star" (provided by the record company, of course).

MTV debuted on August 1, 1981, and its first video was, appropriately, "Video Killed the Radio Star" by the Buggles. The song and the visuals associated with it—exploding radios replaced by televisions—signaled the new direction MTV would take music in the coming decades.

On the Air, but Who's Watching?   MTV faced enormous challenges in its earliest days, the first of which was having enough videos to fill the broadcasting hours. Initially the record companies were not entirely convinced that investing money in music videos would pay off in additional sales, and many of the first music videos were shot on shoestring budgets. One reason for the record companies' reservations was that cable television was not yet widely available in America in the first half of the 1980s. As viewers learned about the benefits of cable, however, more and more communities added the service, and by the end of the decade cable was much more accessible. But in the first couple of years of broadcasting, artists would often have videos playing on MTV and not even know exactly what MTV was (or even have seen it). It turned out that MTV had its biggest audience wherever HBO and other premium cable movie services had enjoyed success—mainly in the midwest. Unlike HBO, MTV did sell advertising, so their programming choices—once they had enough videos to begin to reject some of them—were driven by a target audience. For its first couple of years, MTV's main audience was white teenagers in the midwest; and to appeal to these viewers, MTV played videos by mainstream rock artists who were, with only rare exceptions, white as well. In early 1983, Michael Jackson's "Billie Jean" was climbing the pop charts. By some accounts, MTV refused to play Jackson's video because he is black (or because they believed their white viewers would not want to see it because Jackson is black). Legend in the music business is that Jackson's label, Epic, threatened to pull all their artists off MTV if the video was not aired, though this has been disputed by other accounts. However it happened, Jackson's video played on MTV in March 1983, and in many ways Jackson's enormous success increased the popularity of the network. Before long, record companies considered music videos to be crucial promotional tools for their artists, and MTV began to rival FM radio as the place to make or break hit records.

Can Video Really Kill the Radio Star?   By the mid to late 1980s, MTV was an important aspect of the popular-music business; it was also the source of much controversy. The principal criticism was that it tended to privilege the visual aspects of artists over the musical ones: if the artists looked good in the video, it hardly mattered what the music sounded like. And conversely, no matter how good the music was, if the "look" wasn't right, the music would be unsuccessful. Regardless of whether you agree with these complaints, it is certainly true that MTV provided the perfect platform for artists who used the visual dimension as an important part of their act. For Michael Jackson and Madonna, MTV allowed new ways of projecting their music and the images that went with it, and they and many other artists took full advantage of this.

Music Video's New Elite: Michael Jackson and Madonna.   As discussed in Chapter 9, Michael Jackson's career began at Motown with the Jackson 5. While singing in that group with his older brothers, Jackson also released singles as a solo artist, scoring a series of top hits, including "Rockin' Robin" (p2 r2, 1972) and "Ben" (p1 r5, 1972). When the pop world was swept with the disco craze in the late 1970s, Jackson teamed with veteran producer Quincy Jones to record the album *Off the Wall* (p3 r1, 1979), which contained four Top 10 hits, three of which also placed in the rhythm and blues top five (two at number one). The next two albums did even better: *Thriller* (p1 r1, 1983) contained three number one crossover singles, "Billie Jean," "Beat It," and "The Girl Is Mine"; the last, with Paul McCartney, placed at number two on the pop charts. Two more in the albums cracked the top five. *Bad* (p1 r1, 1987) did as well; it contained four songs that hit the number one slot on both pop and rhythm and blues charts: "Bad," "The Way You Make Me Feel," "I Just Can't Stop Loving You," and "The Man in the Mirror." Throughout this incredible run on the charts, Jackson not only sold tens of millions of records for Epic, but he also won numerous awards, making him arguably the biggest star in popular music during the 1980s and earning him the title King of Pop.

Jackson was an artist who seemed perfect for the newly emerging video age of pop. As a performer, he continued the tradition of slick and sometimes athletic choreography made famous by the Temptations, updated with his silver glove and patented "Moonwalk" dance step. His video performances provided an opportunity to showcase his enormous dancing skill, making his videos a cut above the others of the mid 1980s, many of which still had the performers alternating between lip-synching and jumping around for no apparent reason. Jackson soon became ambitious about music videos, producing an extended video for "Thriller"; it was directed by Hollywood's John Landis and employed state-of-the-art special effects. Jackson's music in the 1980s is almost always driven by a strong beat, showing not only his roots in 1970s black pop but also his experience with disco. "Billie Jean" is representative, beginning with a groove laid down in the bass and drums that serves as the musical foundation for everything that follows. Jackson's vocals project a sense of restrained emotional urgency during the verses, and the chorus provides the more open and catchy melodic hook. Jackson's famous high-voiced "ooo" can be heard scattered throughout the track, which features a Quincy Jones arrangement that builds continuously as the song unfolds.

Although Jackson's records after the mid 1970s no longer appeared on Motown, Jackson continued Berry Gordy's practice of courting white listeners. Two of *Thriller*'s top hits featured white musicians who were well known to mainstream rock fans at the time; the duet with Paul McCartney on "The Girl Is Mine" paired Jackson with the most publicly visible Beatle, and Eddie Van Halen's guitar solo on "Beat It" brought a rising guitar icon into the picture. This was all smart business, but Jackson's crossover practices drew the fire of many critics who accused him of selling out his blackness. This argument goes back to the 1960s, and Jackson's close association with Motown during the first half of the 1970s made him an especially inviting target. Jackson, however, never backed down from his efforts to bridge the gaps he saw between white and black culture, as proved by his video for 1991's "Black or White" (p1 r3).

Like Michael Jackson, Madonna Louise Ciccone depended as much on the visual aspect of her music as the sonic dimension. Unlike the King of Pop, however, the "Material Girl's" appeal was almost exclusively to white audiences. Madonna had worked as a professional dancer in New York, appearing at various points with the Pearl Lange and Alvin Ailey dance troupes. Her first recordings enjoyed success within the New York dance-club scene, and she was signed by Sire records, which had recently been one of the most important labels in New York new wave. Her 1984 debut album *Madonna* (p8) contained two hit singles, "Borderline" (p10) and "Lucky Star" (p4), and the videos for these songs provide an early glimpse of what would soon become one of the most controversial figures in the video age. By early 1985, Madonna's *Like a Virgin* (p1) was climbing the pop album charts, while four singles hit the top five, including "Like a Virgin" (p1) and "Material Girl" (p2). *True Blue* did even better, reaching number one on the pop album charts in 1986 and producing three number one singles—"Live to Tell," "Papa Don't Preach," and "Open Your Heart"—as well as two more that made the top five.

Like Jackson's, Madonna's music is often driven by a dance beat, perhaps under the influence of her dance-club background. "Like a Virgin" provides an interesting comparison with Jackson's "Billie Jean." The tracks start out in a similar manner, though while the repeating bass line in Jackson's song is somewhat menacing, the bass line in Madonna's song is buoyant and celebratory. Madonna also seems to borrow Jackson's high-voiced "ooo's," which can be heard in her chorus as "hey." "Like a Virgin" also betrays a dance-club influence in its layers of synthesizers that create an accompanimental backdrop for Madonna's singing. Later tracks expand Madonna's stylistic range to include

LISTENING GUIDE

GET MUSIC ▶▶ wwnorton.com/rockhistory

Michael Jackson, "Billie Jean"

Words and music by Michael Jackson, produced by Quincy Jones. Rose to #1 on the U.S. pop and rhythm and blues charts, as well as on the UK charts, in 1983. Contained on the album *Thriller*, which also topped all three charts.

FORM: Almost the entire song is built over a repeating bass line (heard in the introduction) and a simple four-chord succession. Both the verse and the chorus use this material, making the form a simple verse-chorus type. This song also features a section called a "pre-chorus." A pre-chorus is a section that is no longer the verse but not yet the chorus and functions primarily as a way of intensifying the arrival of the chorus. In this case, the pre-chorus contrasts with the material used in the verse and chorus, making the form as a whole a simple verse-chorus with contrasting pre-chorus. The arrangement is constructed traditionally, adding new elements along the way, starting with less activity and becoming increasingly busy as the song unfolds.

TIME SIGNATURE: 4/4.

INSTRUMENTATION: Drums, electronic percussion, synthesizers, electric piano, guitar, lead and backup vocals. Notice that all the voices are Jackson's and that he frequently doubles the melody an octave higher than the main voice.

0:00–0:28	**Introduction**, 14 mm.	10 mm. of drums and bass set up the song's groove, and then the synthesizer enters playing a repeating 4-chord pattern.
0:28–0:53	**Verse 1**, 12 mm.	Lead vocal enters; note the heavy reverb on Jackson's voice and the use of vocal octaves at the end, "She was more like a beauty queen . . ."

moodier songs such as "Papa Don't Preach" and sensual songs like "Justify My Love" (the video for which was banned on MTV). Throughout her career, Madonna has played an active role in the creative aspects of her music, earning songwriter and production credits on many of her albums.

Madonna's commercial success has not flagged much in the years since these albums and singles established her as an important figure in pop music, and she remains among the most successful acts in the music business. She has continually challenged aspects of what she perceives to be some of society's most troubling issues and practices. Early on, her "boy toy" image cast her as a sex object, though this was done with great irony—Madonna put on the role of sex object in order to call it into question, and in this way she can be

0:53–1:10	**Verse 2**, 8 mm.	As before, "She told me her name . . ."
1:10–1:26	**Pre-Chorus**, 8 mm.	Contrasting musical material, as arrangement builds through the addition of new synthesizer melody, electric piano, and splash cymbal. "People always told me . . ."
1:26–1:50	**Chorus**, 12 mm.	Harmony vocals enter. Note rhythmic octaves in the guitar, "Billie Jean is not my lover . . ."
1:50–2:15	**Verse 3**, 12 mm.	As before, with added string melody in the synthesizer part and more activity between voice parts, "For forty days . . ."
2:15–2:32	**Verse 4**, 8 mm.	As verse 3, "She told my baby . . ."
2:32–2:48	**Pre-Chorus**, 8 mm.	Builds as before, but now with new string melody, "People always told me . . ."
2:48–3:05	**Chorus**, 8 mm.	As before, but now with new string melody at end of phrase, "Billie Jean . . ."
3:05–3:28	**Chorus**, 12 mm.	Guitar line and synthesizer trumpet line are added.
3:28–3:54	**Interlude**, 12 mm.	Rhythmic guitar line highlighted, with vocals at end.
3:54–4:18	**Chorus**, 12 mm.	As before, but with guitar line mixed forward and more vocal interjections. "Billie Jean . . ."
4:18–4:50	**Coda**, 16 mm.	Various improvised singing along with harmony vocals as song fades out.

Motown 25

On March 25, 1983, Motown Records held a concert in Pasadena, California, to celebrate its twenty-fifth anniversary. The show was broadcast on national television two months later. It was meant as a way to recognize the great history of the record label while simultaneously providing it with some much needed publicity. Motown had fallen on hard times in the 1970s after moving its operations to Los Angeles, investing heavily in film production, and disbanding the Funk Brothers. At the time of the concert the label's only consistent star was Stevie Wonder. Newer acts such as DeBarge had failed to capture large audiences and older stars like Diana Ross and Marvin Gaye had changed labels. In an era of slow record sales and expensive music video production costs, Motown struggled to compete.

Adding insult to injury, the last artist groomed by Berry Gordy during Motown's Detroit years, Michael Jackson, was now the biggest star in the world—for another record label. His 1982 album *Thriller* was well on its way to becoming the most popular record in history and Jackson had single-handedly racially integrated MTV with the wildly popular, high-

production videos for "Billie Jean," "Beat It," and "Thriller." Yet despite several years of conflict between Motown and the Jackson family (except for brother Jermaine, who had remained with Motown), the Jackson 5 decided to put on a reunion performance—provided that Michael would get the spotlight at the end of the show. Desperate for the network audience a Jackson appearance would bring, Motown agreed, and Jackson delivered one of the most memorable performances in television history. Wearing a sequined tuxedo, glittering socks, and his trademark single glove, Jackson sang and danced with a dazzling combination of grace, style, and flash. The climax of his set was "Billie Jean," during which Jackson unveiled a spectacular, smoothly deceptive new dance move: the "Moonwalk." All across America, teenagers spent the next few weeks perfecting their own moonwalks. Jackson's rise to an Elvis-like level of superstardom was complete.

It is powerfully ironic that the Motown Twenty-Fifth Anniversary Special is legendary for the performance of

a non-Motown artist, Michael Jackson, when so many artists who had made much bigger contributions to Motown Records itself also performed. But it was the presence of James Jamerson that provided a tragic footnote and a vivid demonstration of the cruelty of the music industry. As a virtuoso bassist and the central member of the Funk Brothers, Jamerson was arguably the single most important musician in the history of Motown Records. He was the unquestioned leader of the band that had performed on every hit record in the company's first fifteen years. Yet not only was Jamerson not invited to perform at the anniversary show; he even had to buy a ticket just to get in the door. Jamerson died shortly after the concert and remained unrecognized by the public for his role at Motown until the release of the 2002 documentary *Standing in the Shadows of Motown*.

Though his album Thriller was a hit for Epic at the time, Michael Jackson agreed to perform on Motown 25—a tribute to the Jackson 5's longtime label. Jackson's performance became legendary; it was here he first performed the "Moonwalk." With this performance Jackson brought down the house and further solidified his status as the world's most popular entertainer.

Madonna, "Like a Virgin"

Words and music by Billy Steinberg and Tom Kelly, produced by Nile Rodgers. Hit #1 on the Billboard Pop charts and #9 on the rhythm and blues charts in 1985; contained on the album *Like a Virgin*, which went to #1 (r10).

FORM: Compound AABA. The A sections are based primarily on simple verse-chorus form, except that the chorus is built on the first part of each verse only. The second part of each verse differs from the first part in that its last 6 bars break off the pattern set by the first part, creating a section that functions similarly to the pre-chorus in "Billie Jean." The bridge presents contrasting material drawn from the last 6 bars of the second part of the verse, but developed and changed. The return of the final A section brings back only the second part of the verse, but the repeats of the chorus help balance the end of the song.

TIME SIGNATURE: 4/4.

INSTRUMENTATION: Layers of synthesizers, drums, guitar, lead vocals.

	0:00–0:08	**Introduction**, 4 mm.	Synthesizer bass and drums begin, with synthesizer chords added in last 2 bars.
A	0:08–0:24	**Verse 1** (first part), 8 mm.	Vocals enter, as drumbeat locks in. "I made it through . . ."
	0:24–0:44	**Verse 1** (second part), 10 mm.	Note how the first four bars repeat the first part of the verse, but then add new material that propels the song toward the chorus. "I was beat . . ."
	0:44–1:00	**Chorus**, 8 mm.	Added synthesizer lines and rhythmic guitar. "Like a virgin . . ."
A	1:00–1:16	**Verse 2** (first part), 8 mm.	As before, with added synthesizer interjections. Note how this verse emerges directly out of the chorus. "Gonna give you . . ."
	1:16–1:36	**Verse 2** (second part), 10 mm.	As before, "You're so fine . . ."
	1:36–1:52	**Chorus**, 8 mm.	As before, but note Michael Jackson-esque high-voiced "hey." "Like a virgin . . ."
B	1:52–2:08	**Bridge**, 8 mm.	Material derived and developed from second part of verse, with vocals on "Whoa."

A	2:08–2:29	**Verse 3** (second part), 10 mm.	As verse 2, "You're so fine . . ."
	2:29–2:45	**Chorus**, 8 mm.	As before, with extra background parts added. "Like a virgin . . ."
	2:45–3:01	**Chorus**, 8 mm.	Repeat, but with a sensual vocal variation at the end.
	3:01–3:09	**Chorus**, 4 mm.	Repeat, with vocal improvisation as song fades out.

The many faces of Madonna. Madonna was an expert in reinventing herself, keeping her music and image exciting and relevant to fans every time. These images from her performances and videos represent just some of the images Madonna promoted (counterclockwise, from below): The innocent sensuality of "Virgin," her first concert tour (1985); the approachable glamour of Marilyn Monroe in the "Material Girl" video (1985); and the dominant, gender-bending sexuality of her "Blond Ambition" tour (1988), which featured the hits "Vogue" and "Express Yourself."

linked to previous figures such as Jim Morrison, Alice Cooper, David Bowie, and Kiss, all of whom adopted personae. Throughout her career she has explored the boundaries of sexual conduct, racial issues, women's roles, and spirituality. Detractors have accused her of seeking publicity by titillating and shocking audiences, while her supporters have praised her methods of bringing up important social issues for debate. Whatever position you take on Madonna's place in popular culture, video images clearly play a central role in her music. Her music videos are rich in symbolism and striking juxtapositions—a factor that has caused many academics to offer extended interpretations of their deeper meanings.

Dirty Minded? Prince and Janet Jackson.   Michael Jackson is often credited with opening up MTV for black artists and Madonna for testing the boundaries of sexuality in music; the Minneapolis-based singer-songwriter-producer Prince deserves credit on both these fronts as well. His video for "1999" aired on MTV before Jackson's storied "Billie Jean" video, and Prince's practice of using blatant sexual images, both in his songs and in live performance, goes back to the late 1970s, when the Material Girl was still in college. Born Prince Rogers Nelson, Prince was one of the most prolific artists of the 1980s, writing and producing a long string of hit records under his own name—often playing all the instruments on his records—and writing and producing other artists, such as the Time, Vanity 6, and Sheila E. Prince's musical roots are in the black pop and funk of the 1970s, and in many ways his careful control of both his music and the music of satellite projects is modeled on the practice of George Clinton, while his one-man-band approach to recording is reminiscent of Stevie Wonder. Prince's first four albums did well in the rhythm and blues market, with both *Prince* (1979) and *Controversy* (1981) reaching number three and containing hit singles. During this early period Prince developed his image as a sexually charged and somewhat androgynous figure, and songs such as "Head" and "Jack U Off" provided ample opportunity for him to project this image in live performance.

While he had enjoyed modest crossover success before the late 1982 release of *1999* (4r, 9p), this album made Prince a star in the pop world, fueled by the singles "1999" (4r 12p) and "Little Red Corvette" (15r 6p) and his exposure on MTV. The title track finds Prince employing a synthesizer-heavy backdrop, driven hard by a strong beat in the drums. His technique of using different voices for each line in the verse goes back at least to Clyde McPhatter and the Drifters, but here the most immediate influences are probably Sly and the Family Stone or the Temptations. At the very end of "1999" you can hear the strong funk influences that support Prince's music. In 1984, Prince released the semi-autobiographical feature film *Purple Rain*, which was greeted with critical acclaim and accompanied by a soundtrack album that quickly hit the top spot on both pop and rhythm and blues charts, while the singles "When Doves Cry" and "Let's Go Crazy" did the same on both singles charts. More hit albums and singles followed over the next few years, including *Around the World in a Day* (4r 1p, 1985), *Batman* (5r 1p, 1989), and *Diamonds and Pearls* (1r 3p, 1991), each of which sold over two million copies. Prince's blending of the funk

Like Marvin Gaye and Stevie Wonder before
him, Prince had total control over his music
(and like Wonder often played all the instruments). Unlike the other two, however,
Prince demanded this arrangement from the
beginning of his career. Prince combined
Michael Jackson's crossover appeal with
Madonna's blatant sexual imagery, and with
this mixture scored hits throughout the '80s
and '90s. Prince's heavy use of synthesizers
and his placement of the bass guitar on the
beat influenced many other musicians and
dominated the sound of 1980s pop.

grooves and outrageousness of George Clinton and Parliament with a strong pop sensibility made him one of the most influential artists of the decade generally, and among black artists he is rivaled only by Michael Jackson.

As Prince was developing his musical style in the late 1970s, Michael Jackson's younger sister Janet was a regular on the television sitcom *Good Times*. During the early 1980s Janet was releasing albums and singles on the side while continuing to act in television shows such as *Diff'rent Strokes* and *Fame*. In 1986, however, she teamed with the producer-songwriting team of Jimmy Jam and Terry Lewis, two musicians who had been in the Prince-produced band, the Time. Under their direction, Janet's 1986 album *Control* shot to the top of the pop and rhythm and blues charts and contained six top five singles. Janet projected a new image of confidence and independence, in sharp contrast to her previous image as a teen actress, and the hard-driving beats behind this new music showed the influence of hip hop and funk. The Jackson/Jam/Lewis team followed with *Rhythm Nation 1814* (1989), which again topped both charts and surpassed *Control* by producing seven top five hit singles—the first album ever to have so many hits. While *Rhythm Nation 1814*

LISTENING GUIDE

GET MUSIC ▶▶ wwnorton.com/rockhistory

Prince, "1999"

Words and music by Prince, produced by Prince. Contained on the album *1999*, which went to #26 on the Billboard Pop charts in 1983.

FORM: This track is a contrasting verse-chorus form with an extended coda. Notice how extra measures are added to the end of each chorus: first 4 measures, then 8 measures, and then the final extended coda. It is also interesting that the repeating chord progression in the synthesizer part is based on the Mamas and the Papas' hit single "Monday, Monday."

TIME SIGNATURE: 4/4.

INSTRUMENTATION: Electric guitar, bass, drums, synthesizer, synthesized percussion, and lead, all provided by Prince, plus female backup vocals.

0:00–0:50	**Introduction**, 16 mm.	Begins with electronically modified voice, as drumbeat enters, and then synthesizer.
0:50–1:22	**Verse 1**, 16 mm.	Vocal enters; notice exchange of voices, perhaps influenced by Sly or the Temptations. "I was dreaming when I wrote this . . ."
1:22–1:39	**Chorus**, 8 mm.	Harmony vocals, no extension added yet, "Two thousand zero zero . . ."

took on a more serious, socially conscious tone than its predecessor, the original plan had been for it to project a sexier and more seductive image for the singer. It would be the next release, *janet* (1993), that would launch the new, more adult-oriented image, underscored by an infamous *Rolling Stone* cover photo featuring a topless Jackson, her breasts covered by the hands of an unseen friend that emerge from behind her back. Of the six hit singles on *janet*, the chart-topping "That's the Way Loves Goes"—which uses music taken directly from the recording of James Brown's "Papa Don't Take No Mess" (a process called "sampling")—serves as a representative example of the Jackson/Jam/Lewis approach. Jackson went on to be one of the most successful artists of the 1990s. Throughout her career, video has played a central role in Janet Jackson's musical presentation; as with her famous brother, dancing is as important as singing in Janet's videos (Paula Abdul directed Janet's dance moves). Some critics have claimed that the musical dimension in these videos takes a backseat to the visual one, making Janet's sexier videos—like those of Madonna—more focused on titillation than on musical edification.

1:39–2:12	**Verse 2**, 16 mm.	As before but with new synthesizer and guitar lines, "I was dreaming when I wrote this . . ."
2:12–2:37	**Chorus**, 12 mm.	As before, but now extended by 4 mm., "Two thousand zero zero . . ."
2:37–3:10	**Verse 3**, 16 mm.	Now sung in harmony, with small variations in the accompaniment. "If you didn't come to party . . ."
3:10–3:25	**Chorus**, 8 mm.	As the first time, "Two thousand zero zero . . ."
3:25–3:58	**Chorus**, 16 mm.	As the second time, but now extended by 8 mm., with plenty of vocal improvisation.
3:58–4:13	**Chorus**, 8 mm.	One more time through the coda, before heading into the extended ending.
4:13–6:14	**Coda**, 60 mm.	Extension of chorus now becomes a lengthy coda. Note that the last 16 mm. are quieter, with a sudden stop in the last measure. The funk influence comes out especially in these last measures.

Often teaming with producers Jimmy Jam and Terry Lewis, Janet Jackson placed many Top 10 hits in the '80s and '90s. Jackson often portrayed the image of a strong, powerful African American woman, as on her albums Control *(1986) and* Rhythm Nation 1814 *(1989). Like her brother Michael and Madonna before her, Jackson placed a heavy emphasis on dancing, often employing top choreographers to help plan her videos and concert performances.*

Let's Get Physical: Olivia Newton-John.

Among the highest-profile women in pop music during the early 1980s was the Australian-born singer Olivia Newton-John. In many ways, her image and career changes in the years before MTV paved the way for Madonna and Janet Jackson. Newton-John first appeared on the pop radar in the 1970s with a series of country-flavored hits, including "Let Me Be There" (p6, 1973) and "If You Love Me Let Me Know" (p5, 1974), and easy-listening pop songs such as "I Honestly Love You" (p1, 1974) and "Have You Never Been Mellow?" (p1, 1975). Newton-John's profile was raised considerably when she starred in the film *Grease* in 1978, playing the role of the "good girl" opposite John Travolta in the musical set in the same idyllic 1950s as *American Graffiti* and the television show *Happy Days.* The film produced more hits for Newton-John, including the chart-topping "You're the One That I Want." At the end of *Grease*, Newton-John's character develops from a demure, polite high school student into a rock and roll bombshell, and this turn to the sexier side largely parallels the singer's image of the 1980s. *Totally Hot* (p7, 1979) helped establish this new direction, powered by "A Little More Love" (p3). Another movie, *Xanadu* (1980), was less successful at the box office but nevertheless contained the number one single "Magic." By the end of 1981, Newton-John had released *Physical* (p6), which held "Make a Move on Me" (p5) and the dance-beat driven, synthesizer-powered "Physical" (p1)—among her most widely known hits.

Brit Pop Hits MTV: Duran Duran, Culture Club.

During its first few years on the air, MTV suffered from a shortage of usable videos. A twenty-four hour rotation requires hundreds of videos, and MTV had not quite convinced the American record companies that videos paid off on the investment of resources, but after their exposure in the first video to be played on MTV the Buggles found their records were selling in markets in America they had never even played, much less marketed to. A new crop of British pop acts knew how to use video and MTV to advance their careers, however. Bands and artists such as Bow Wow Wow, Adam and the Ants, A Flock of Seagulls,

Howard Jones, Thomas Dolby, and ABC, who might otherwise never have cracked the American market, profited handsomely from the exposure their music received on MTV. Among the most successful of these groups were Duran Duran, whose synthesizer- and guitar-heavy new wave sound was driven by infectious dance beats, and whose visual dimension was marked by a concern for style and rebellious elegance. The band first made its mark in the United States with *Rio* (p6 uk2, 1983), containing "Hungry like the Wolf" (p3 uk5), and the video for this song, which went into MTV rotation. The success of this album spurred interest in the band's 1981 first album, *Duran Duran* (p10, 1983), which had risen to number three in the UK when it was originally released. Appearing in late 1983, *Seven and the Ragged Tiger* (p8 uk1) continued Duran Duran's run on the international charts, spawning three Top 10 hits, including "The Reflex" (p1 uk1).

Culture Club also exploited the visual side of their act. The band was fronted by singer George "Boy George" O'Dowd, who dressed in women's clothes and sported long dreadlocks. One of the band's first appearances on British television prompted one critic to write, "It's a bird, it's a bloke, it's Boy George." *Kissing to Be Clever* (p14 uk5, 1983) included three Top 10 hits, including the easygoing "Do You Really Want to Hurt Me" (p2 uk1), which was played heavily on both MTV and radio. The next album, *Colour by Numbers* (p2 uk1, 1983), brought three more Top 10 hits, including the ubiquitous "Karma Chameleon" (p1 uk1). Culture Club's music was unabashedly pop-oriented in the Brill Building sense: catchy tunes and hooks established a generally happy tone, while Boy George's fluid and laid-back singing style seemed influenced by black pop singers of the 1960s and '70s.

Thinking Person's MTV: Eurythmics, Tears for Fears. Eurythmics took advantage of the synthesizer-pop sound that had emerged in the UK at the end of the 1970s and combined it with an innovative approach to music video. Combining the soul-influenced vocals of Annie Lennox, the synthesizer wizardry of David Stewart, and a penchant for intellectual experimentation, the band released *Sweet Dreams (Are Made of This)* (p15 uk3, 1983), the title song of which hit number one in the United States (uk2) and was supported by an avant-garde–influenced video that featured a cow attending a corporate board meeting, as well as a board meeting being held in a pasture. During a period in which many videos were relatively inane, the sophisticated "Sweet Dreams" video became must-see MTV and the Eurythmics capitalized on this to great advantage. Following with *Touch* (p7 uk1, 1984) and *Be Yourself Tonight* (p9 uk3, 1985), the band was able to remain successful in America, though subsequent albums, such as *We Too Are One* (uk1, 1989), while very popular in England, did not make significant inroads on the American market.

Influenced by the primal scream therapy of Arthur Janov, keyboardist Roland Orzabal and bassist Curt Smith called their UK-based band Tears for Fears. Basing their stylistic approach in British synthesizer-pop, the duo released its debut album, *The Hurting* (uk1), in 1983. The first album barely created a ripple in the United States, but the second one, *Songs from the Big Chair* (p1 uk2, 1985), was an international sensation, fueled by two number one American hits, "Everybody Wants to Rule the World" (uk2) and "Shout" (uk4), and bolstered by heavy rotation on MTV. In many ways, the ambition of *Songs from the Big Chair* is reminiscent of the progressive rock albums from the early to mid 1970s: the lyrics deal with serious topics, the music is sometimes complicated, and tunes run into one another to create long tracks. Perhaps owing to their seriousness of purpose, the duo was not able to produce a timely follow-up, and while *The Seeds of Love* (p8 uk1, 1989) enjoyed success, it was the last big record for the band.

The Hippie Aesthetic Returns Transformed.   As mentioned above, MTV and the video age are often thought to challenge some of rock's deeply held values: the centrality of video images seems to take attention away from the music itself, raising suspicions that the music could never stand on its own without the visual images to prop it up. Viewed from a broader historical perspective, however, the ambitious scope of some music videos—and especially those of Michael Jackson, Madonna, and the Eurythmics—clearly reinterpret and redirect at least one aspect of the hippie aesthetic. Concept albums in the 1970s pushed at the boundaries of rock music by exploring a variety of musical styles while pursuing serious-minded themes. As the 1980s progressed, music videos followed a similar path, though now the focus was no longer on exploring a variety of musical styles as much as it was on exploring the ways in which music and images can work together to create a compelling synthesis. In each case, there was a strong element of artistic ambition: in the '70s this ambition was focused on the album—its packaging, its music, and its message. This kind of focus often shifted to the video in the 1980s, revealing an important aesthetic connection between these two decades that is often missed by critics who focus more on the differences between '70s and '80s music than on the underlying continuities.

Featuring bassist and lead singer Sting, guitarist Andy Summers, and drummer Stewart Copeland, the Police were one of the 1980s' most popular rock bands. They combined the hard driving guitar sound of punk, reggae's rhythmic complexity, and serious-minded lyrics to create eight Top 10 hits in the early '80s.

The Wave Continues

Keepers of the Wave: The Police, U2.   While a new crop of bands took advantage of the visual dimension made available by MTV, mainstream rock and new wave continued to develop into the 1980s, mostly with more emphasis on the aural than on the visual. One of the most successful bands to come out of the new wave movement at the end of the 1970s was the Police. Formed in England by Brits Andy Summers (guitar) and Sting (bass and vocals), and American drummer

Stewart Copeland, the band's first hit single, "Roxanne" (p32, 1979), showed a strong reggae influence. Though their first album, *Outlandos d'Amour* (p23, 1979), picked up on the return-to-simplicity approach of punk, the group clearly were interested in creating sophisticated musical arrangements along with self-consciously poetic and at times intellectual lyrics. The title of the band's fifth album, *Synchronicity* (p1 uk1, 1983), for instance, is drawn from the psychological writings of Carl Jung. The band's music dominated the rock-music business in the first half of the 1980s; eight singles placed in the American Top 20 during that time, and even though only one of these ever went to number one ("Every Breath You Take" in 1983), the band's music was a staple of FM rock radio. While Police's initial success was in the U.S. market, they ultimately did even better in the UK, with four of their five studio albums going to number one, and five singles hitting the top spot as well. "Don't Stand So Close to Me" provides a representative example of the Police's musical approach. The music is relatively spare but skillfully executed, creating a mysterious atmosphere to go with Sting's lyrics, which tell of a teacher's unhealthy romantic attraction to his young student. Andy Summers's guitar playing is more focused on creating washes of sound than with soloing, as Copeland's drumming lays down an often complex rhythmic grid beneath the other instruments. There is a sense of agitation in this song that reflects the uneasiness of the teacher who, according to the lyrics, ends up being publicly accused.

Bono, the lead singer for U2, performs at the Live Aid concert at Wembley Stadium in London. Like the Police, U2 produced hard-driving rock hits that often tackled serious social issues. At Live Aid, the concerts held in London and Philadelphia—featuring U2 and many other artists—raised over $70 million for famine relief in Ethiopia.

As the Police's active career was coming to a close in the mid 1980s, the career of Ireland's U2 was just getting started. The band's first five albums made good showings; *War* (p12 uk1, 1983) and *The Unforgettable Fire* (p12 uk1, 1984) did somewhat better than the others. With 1987's *The Joshua Tree* (p1 uk1, 1987), however, U2 began a string of enormously successful albums that continues to the present day. U2 built on the sophisticated approach of the Police: both bands wrote simple songs but arranged them in innovative ways. Lead singer Bono's lyrics often strive for a poetic quality, while lead guitarist The Edge layers sound behind Bono's voice to create a rich backing texture. The band often composed their songs by jamming for hours in the studio, then leaving for the day as producers such as Brian Eno and Daniel Lanois

460

WHAT'S THAT SOUND?

LISTENING GUIDE

GET
MUSIC ▶▶

wwnorton.com/rockhistory

The Police, "Don't Stand So Close to Me"

Words and music by Sting, produced by the Police and Nigel Gray. Rose to #1 on the UK charts and #10 in the United States in 1981; contained on the album *Zenyatta Mondatta*, which also hit #1 in the UK and #5 in the United States.

FORM: The use of differing material makes this track an example of contrasting verse-chorus form. Notice how each verse builds up a bit more, adding new parts with each occurrence—an arranging approach we have seen often. The timbre-rich instrumental verse thus arrives as a natural extension of this process. The lyrics describe a teacher who is attracted to an underage student. The agitation in the music, and perhaps the central instrumental verse, attempt to capture this sense of uneasiness.

TIME SIGNATURE: 4/4.

INSTRUMENTATION: Drums, bass, guitars, synthesizer, lead and backing vocals.

0:00–0–37	**Introduction**	Free-form synthesizer and guitar sounds establish a mysterious texture to open the track, and then drums usher in 4-bar reggae-inspired vamp as groove locks in.
0:37–1:04	**Verse 1**, 16 mm.	Lead vocal enters, accompanied by a quiet repeating guitar line, two-part harmony on second half of verse, "Young teacher . . ."
1:04–1:19	**Chorus**, 9 mm.	Harmony vocals, as music gets fuller and louder, "Don't stand so close . . ."
1:19–1:46	**Verse 2**, 16 mm.	As before, but sung higher and with added guitar parts. Harmony vocals on second half of verse are also sung higher, creating a sense that the song is getting more intense "Her friends are so jealous . . ."
1:46–2:02	**Chorus**, 9 mm.	As before, "Don't stand so close . . ."
2:02–2:29	**Verse 3**, 16 mm.	As in verse 2, "Loose talk in the classroom . . ."
2:29–2:48	**Chorus**, 11 mm.	As before, "Don't stand so close . . ."
2:48–3:15	**Instrumental Verse**, 16 mm.	Synthesizer sweeps added. Are these sounds meant to capture the emotional confusion of the main character in the song?

3:15–3:29	**Chorus**, 8 mm.	as before, but with counter line added in vocals. "Don't stand so close . . ."
3:29–3:42	**Chorus**, 8 mm.	repeated with counter line.
3:42–3:56	**Chorus**, 8 mm.	repeated again as song fades out.

LISTENING GUIDE   GET MUSIC ▶▶   wwnorton.com/rockhistory

U2, "Pride (In the Name of Love)"

Words and music by U2, produced by Brian Eno and Daniel Lanois. Single rose to #3 in the UK and #33 in the United States; contained on the album *The Unforgettable Fire*, which went to #1 in the UK and #13 in the United States in 1984.

FORM: In this compound AABA form, the A sections employ simple verse-chorus structure that is based on the same chord pattern, while B section presents a new melody in the guitar, supported by a new chord progression, as well as a return to the introduction.

TIME SIGNATURE: 4/4.

INSTRUMENTATION: Electric guitars, bass, drums, lead and backing vocals. Notice the use of the repeated-note guitar sound throughout, and how avoiding that repeated-note sound in verses 2 and 3 adds excitement to its return.

	0:00–0:28	**Introduction**, 12 mm.	Rhythmic guitar with echo featured with drums, before bass enters and song begins the repeated progression that will form the basis of the verse and chorus.
A	0:28–0:46	**Verse 1**, 8 mm.	Vocal enters over music established in the introduction, sung in the middle register. "One man come in the name of love . . ."
	0:46–1:04	**Chorus**, 8 mm.	Vocal continues over same music, but now sung higher and with more urgency. "In the name of love . . ."
A	1:04–1:23	**Verse 2**, mm.	As before, but note that rhythmic guitar gives way to broad arpeggios to create a sense of contrast. "One man come on a barbed-wire fence . . ."
	1:21–1:41	**Chorus**, mm.	As before, as rhythmic guitar returns, "In the name of love . . ."

continued

B	1:41–1:58	**Bridge** (instrumental), 8 mm.	Contrasting music featuring a repeated guitar melody consisting of a three-note figure repeated as an echo, but in tempo.
	1:58–2:26	**Re-Intro**, 12 mm.	Same material as intro, last 4 mm. hummed. The technique of re-starting a song by returning to the introduction can be traced back to "Purple Haze" and can be seen in much 1970s music.
A	2:26–2:44	**Verse 3**, 8 mm.	As in verse 2, with broad guitar arpeggios. "Early morning, April 4 . . ."
	2:44–3:02	**Chorus**, 8 mm.	As before, as rhythmic guitar returns. "In the name of love . . ."
	3:02–3:21	**Chorus**, 8 mm.	As before, but backup vocals add counter melody.
	3:21–3:47	**Coda**, 8 mm. + fade-out	Same material as verse, chorus, and intro, as Bono improvises on the song's melody.

picked through the material for the best bits, which were then reassembled into tracks for the band's approval the next day. "Pride (In the Name of Love)" illustrates some of the musical features of U2's music from the middle of the decade. The Edge plays repeated-note figures on the guitar, soaked in echo, that provide one of the band's most recognizable sonic signatures. During the verses, Bono croaks out accounts of people who have given their lives in the name of love, including Dr. Martin Luther King Jr., while his wailing on the chorus underscores the passion of the cause for which their lives were given. U2 has remained an important band throughout the 1990s and to the present day, with a string of successful albums and sold-out tours, while Bono has become an outspoken advocate for humanitarian issues.

The Sun Never Sets on New Wave: Split Enz, Crowded House, Men at Work, XTC, Squeeze. New wave also emerged from Australia, as Split Enz broke on the international scene with *True Colors* (uk43 p40, 1980), which contained the infectious single "I Got You" (uk12 p53). Led by brothers Tim and Neil Finn, the group had formed in the 1970s as an often experimental, post-psychedelic band. By the end of the '70s, the group's sound had become securely pop based, and their penchant for Beatle-esque tunes helped them catch the new wave that was breaking in the United States. Neil Finn later formed Crowded House, whose first album reached number twelve on the U.S. charts in 1986 on the strength of the single "Don't Dream It's Over" (uk27 p2, 1987). Also hailing from the land down under were Men at Work, whose Police-like sound is best heard on *Business as Usual* (uk1 p1 1982), which contained the two hits "Who Can It Be Now" (uk45 p1) and "Down Under" (uk1 p1). The Beatles also exerted a strong influence on new wavers back in England. Led by the songwriting of guitarist Andy Partridge and bassist Colin Moulding, XTC made their mark with *Black Sea* (uk16 p41, 1980), which contained the catchy and clever "Generals and Majors." Like XTC, Squeeze invited Beatles comparisons, and songwriters Chris Difford and Glenn Tilbrook were compared to Lennon and McCartney in the British music press during the first few years of the 1980s. The band enjoyed British chart success with singles such as "Cool for Cats" (uk2, 1979) and albums like *East Side Story* (uk19 p44, 1981), which includes perhaps the most un-Squeeze-like tune the band ever recorded, "Tempted." While "Tempted" features the soulful lead vocal of Paul Carrack, most Squeeze tracks have a markedly British-invasion influenced style, with emphasis on clever lyrics and concise forms. Neither XTC nor Squeeze enjoyed significant success in the United States, though they were both celebrated and well-respected by British critics.

College Rock Underground: R.E.M. and the Smiths. The return-to-simplicity credo of the late 1970s was the working principle for a scene that would develop on U.S. college campuses in the second half of the 1980s. In many ways, college rock got its start in Athens, Georgia, home of the University of Georgia and a local band called R.E.M. Led by guitarist Peter Buck and vocalist Michael Stipe, R.E.M. emerged from Athens to have a string of successful albums in the second half of the 1980s that would propel them well into the

1990s. The band's fifth album, *Document*, rose to the number ten position on the U.S. charts in 1987 (uk28), while the single "The One I Love" hit number nine on the American charts. R.E.M. had much more chart success in the States than in England, but with 1991's *Out of Time*, the band finally reached the number one spot on both sides of the Atlantic, fueled in part by the success of the singles "Losing My Religion" (p4 uk19) and "Shiny Happy People" (p10 uk6). Like the Police and U2, R.E.M. drew its inspiration from late 1970s new wave, but where these British bands were influenced by the return-to-simplicity aspect of new wave, R.E.M. seemed to be strongly influenced as well by new wave's sense of irony and alienation. Despite their commercial success, R.E.M. became heroes of the burgeoning college rock scene in the second half of the 1980s—a scene that celebrated its lack of affiliation with major labels and corporations, and in which music was circulated through recordings released by small independent labels (or sometimes by the bands themselves), airplay on college radio stations, and live performances at clubs that formed a circuit of the country's

Led by guitarist Peter Buck and vocalist Michael Stipe, R.E.M. was one of the leaders of "college rock." This music had a return-to-simplicity feel—it had none of the slick production techniques or elaborate stage shows of mainstream pop—and these bands prided themselves on placing their music with independent or homegrown labels.

most important college towns. In the UK at about the same time, the Smiths became the darlings of the British underground. Combining the songwriting talents of guitarist Johnny Marr and vocalist Morrissey, the band first tasted success outside the underground scene in 1984 with *The Smiths* (uk2, 1984), containing the single "What Difference Does It Make?" (uk12). While the band's chart success never crossed the Atlantic, their music nonetheless helped fuel the college rock scene in the States. Back home in England, the Smiths topped the charts with *Meat Is Murder* (uk1, 1985) and *The Queen Is Dead* (uk2, 1986).

Girls Just Wanna Have Fun: The Go-Go's, Cyndi Lauper, and the Bangles.

The late 1970s had ushered in a new era for women in rock music; Blondie and the B-52s, for instance, ironically employed images drawn from the girl groups of the early 1960s, both musically and visually. Pat Benatar and Olivia Newton-John had nurtured more aggressive and sensual female images. There had been a handful of all-female rock and punk bands in the '70s as well, so perhaps it was no surprise when the Go-Go's became the first successful all-female new wave band. Fronted by singer Belinda Carlisle, the band's *Beauty and the Beat* hit the top of the U.S. charts in 1981, powered in part by the catchy single "We Got the Beat" (p2). The Go-Go's worked pre-hippie '60s images to the hilt: the band name is derived from "go-go girls," while the *Beauty and the Beat* cover featured a shot of the ladies clad in bath towels, seemingly in the middle of a slumber party. The band's success was fleeting, though Carlisle returned to the charts regularly as a solo artist. Her second album, *Heaven on Earth* (p13 uk4, 1987), contained three hits including "Heaven Is a Place on Earth," which topped both the American and British charts.

Cyndi Lauper, seen here in a 1986 concert, capitalized on woman-focused new wave groups like the Go-Go's and produced the girl-power rock anthem "Girls Just Want to Have Fun." Lauper projected an image of a strong and fiercely independent woman, and this was supported by her powerful voice, woman-focused lyrics, and creative dress and video production.

Capitalizing on the girl-specific images of the Go-Go's, Cyndi Lauper emerged into the mainstream spotlight with the hit album *She's So Unusual* (p4 uk16, 1984), which included a hit that might be considered an anthem for girl power in rock, "Girls Just Want to Have Fun" (p2 uk2). The album also included hits that showed other aspects of Lauper's musical personality; "Time after Time" (p1 uk3) is a haunting ballad, while "She Bop" (p3 uk46) is a thinly veiled engagement with the topic of female masturbation. In the wake of Lauper's and Madonna's success mid-decade, the Bangles emerged from California with *Different Light* (p2 uk3, 1986), an album propelled up the charts by a song provided by Prince, "Manic Monday" (p2 uk2), and a tongue-in-cheek, B-52s-esque track, "Walk like an Egyptian" (p1 uk3). The Bangles blended the jingle-jangle of '60s folk rock with smooth vocal harmonies and further reinforced the idea—building on evidence provided by Heart, Fleetwood Mac, the Pretenders, the Talking Heads, and the Go-Go's—that women can not only sing in rock bands, but they can also play instruments.

The New Traditionalists: No Irony, Just a Healthy Love for Earlier Styles.

During the first years of new wave in the late 1970s, the fact that a band or artist made use of features associated with pre-hippie rock was enough to include them under the "new simplicity" banner. The rejection of hippie values—even if only on the surface in some cases—was such an overriding characteristic that it tended to eclipse important differences within the first cluster of new wave bands. But as the 1980s began and hippie rock started to recede into history, it became increasingly clear that there were actually two distinct approaches to appropriating earlier rock music styles and features. The first was to employ these sounds and images in an ironic manner, not so much to endorse earlier rock as to reject the corporate rock of the 1970s—Devo are probably the clearest example of this tendency. A second approach was to employ such sounds and images in earnest—that is, bands used elements of earlier rock music because they sincerely thought the music sounded better this way. This collection of bands and artists were not exploiting earlier music to create a kind of art-school pastiche but rather were traditionalists concerned with returning rock to what they considered to be its core aesthetic values. These musicians are referred to here as the "new traditionalists."

I Won't Back Down: Tom Petty, with and without the Heartbreakers.

Perhaps the best example of an artist who was originally taken to be a new waver, only to be reinterpreted as a new traditionalist, is Tom Petty. Ironically, Petty never really did anything to change his style throughout the 1970s and '80s. In the early 1970s—and thus at a time when it was out of fashion—Petty's music had a strong '60s element. In many ways, he didn't come to new wave as much as new wave came to him. As the 1980s began, Petty and the Heartbreakers built on their successful practice of blending rootsy jingle-jangle guitar sounds with catchy melodies and thoughtful lyrics. *Hard Promises* (p5 uk32, 1981) contained the radio favorite "The Waiting" (p19), while *Southern Accents* (p7 uk23, 1985) featured "Don't Come Around Here No More" (p13). Petty's music had tended to enjoy more success in the United States than in England, though his first solo album, *Full Moon Fever* (p3 uk8, 1989), finally cracked the UK Top 10, while producing the hits "Free Fallin'" (p7) and "I Won't Back Down" (p12) in the States. Petty's position as keeper of the rock and roll flame was further solidified with the formation in 1988 of the Traveling Wilburys, led by ex-Beatle George Harrison and including Petty, Bob Dylan, Roy Orbison, and Electric Light Orchestra frontman Jeff Lynne. This all-star, roots-of-rock-and-roll band released *Traveling Wilburys Volume 1* (p3 uk16, 1988), containing the single "Handle with

Care" (p45 uk21); it featured all the members singing phrases of the lead vocal and quickly became an FM rock radio staple. Displaying a Beatle-esque sense of humor—itself a throwback to those carefree mop-top days—the band named their second album *Traveling Wilburys Volume 3* (p11 uk14, 1990).

New Jersey Nostalgia: Bruce Springsteen and the E-Street Band. Unlike Tom Petty, Bruce Springsteen was never lumped in with the new wavers in the 1970s; since his songs relied so much on the lyrics and his impassioned vocal delivery, Springsteen was better thought of as a colorful, Jersey-based singer-songwriter. The larger-than-life sound of his third album with the E-Street Band, *Born to Run* (p3 uk17, 1975), showed more than a hint of Phil Spector's influence and marked Springsteen as an important force in rock music. Springsteen's greatest success would come in the 1980s, however, beginning with his fifth album, *The River* (p1 uk2, 1980), with the hit "Hungry Heart" (p5), and continuing with the more introspective *Nebraska* (p3 uk3, 1982). Springsteen's landmark release is 1984's *Born in the U.S.A.*, which topped the charts in both the United States and Britain and produced six Top 10 American hits, including "Glory Days" (p5 uk17) and "Born in the U.S.A." The album *Live 1977–1985* (p1 uk4, 1986) introduced Springsteen's many new fans to his older material and sparked renewed sales and radio play for his '70s music. Springsteen followed up with *Tunnel of Love* (p1 uk1, 1987) and the simultaneous release of two albums in 1992: *Human Touch* (p2 uk1) and *Lucky Town* (p3 uk2).

Springsteen's image relies on the idea that he is the voice of an average working-class guy, and his lyrics reflect on common emotional and social problems. "Born in the U.S.A.," for instance, paints a vivid picture of the decay of American values in the industrial heartland, all seen from the perspective of someone who is powerless to effect change. (In a strange turn of events, "Born in the U.S.A." was mistakenly appropriated by the Reagan administration as a paean to traditional values and American pride.) The song's form seems simple: it employs the same eight-bar progression and two-bar melody, both of which are unrelentingly repeated. But formally, the song threatens to lose its way in the middle, as verses break off incomplete. The constant repeat of the music, combined with the formal wandering of the song's midsection, creates a sense that the Vietnam veteran in the lyrics is not sure which way to turn. Throughout much of his career, Springsteen has projected an image reminiscent of a late 1950s or early 1960s white rock and roll singer, though the thoughtfulness of his lyrics hark back to Dylan of the 1960s. His musical material is mostly simple, rootsy, and sometimes influenced by Stax soul.

Bruce Springsteen belts out "Born in the U.S.A." in Washington, D.C., the first stop on his 1986 concert tour. This song, though used by Ronald Reagan, was deeply critical of American values. Springsteen's music is marked by a big, seemingly traditional rock and roll sound combined with poetic, socially conscious lyrics reminiscent of Bob Dylan's.

Americana on Both Sides of the Pond: John Mellencamp, Dire Straits.
Emerging in 1979 with the radio hit "I Need a Lover" under the name John Cougar, John Mellencamp made his commercial and critical mark with his third album, *American Fool* (1982), which topped the U.S. charts and contained the hits "Hurts So Good" (p2) and "Jack and Diane" (p1). Mellencamp followed up with *Scarecrow* (p2, 1985), which featured "Small Town" (p6), a song similar in spirit to Springsteen's "Born in the U.S.A." Throughout his career, the Indiana-born Mellencamp has embraced an image of a small-town Midwesterner—plain-spoken, nothin' fancy, and interested in social justice and emotional self-understanding. This homespun image—projected both lyrically and musically—makes Mellencamp a central figure in an Americana strain of new

LISTENING GUIDE

GET MUSIC ▶▶ wwnorton.com/rockhistory

Bruce Springsteen, "Born in the U.S.A."

Words and music by Bruce Springsteen, produced by Bruce Springsteen, Jon Landau, Chuck Plotkin, and Steve Van Zandt. Rose to #9 in 1984; contained on the album *Born in the U.S.A.*, which topped the album charts in the United States and the UK.

FORM: A 2-bar melodic figure permeates this track, which is further built on almost identical repeating 8-measure sections for both verse and chorus sections, making this a simple verse-chorus form. After breaking the verse-chorus pattern after verse 3 and seeming to wander formally, notice how verses 4 and 5 also break off lyrically. The overall effect is to drive to verse 6 and toward the final statements of the chorus. Springsteen wants to parallel the sense of abandonment portrayed in the lyrics by allowing the music, formally, to wander somewhat. At certain points the song seems unsure of where it wants to go, but is nevertheless pushed forward by the nagging 2-bar melody.

TIME SIGNATURE: 4/4.

INSTRUMENTATION: Drums, guitar, bass, piano, synthesizers, lead vocal.

0:00–0:16	**Introduction**, 8mm.	Snare drum, piano, and synthesizer playing repeated 2 mm. melody.
0:16–0:33	**Verse 1**, 8 mm.	Vocal enters over this stark music of the intro, "Born down in a dead man's town . . ."
0:33–0:49	**Chorus**, 8 mm.	Lead vocal doubles the 2 mm. melody that has been repeating since the beginning of the song. "Born in the U.S.A. . . ."

traditionalism. Perhaps because of his pronounced celebration of middle-American culture, Mellencamp's stateside success has never effectively translated to the UK. The English band Dire Straits, on the other hand, have had the reverse experience. Led by singer-songwriter-guitarist Mark Knopfler, the band emerged during the first excitement of new wave in late 1978 with *Dire Straits* (p2 uk5), which had the single "Sultans of Swing" (p4), a song that celebrates the virtues of anonymous jazz virtuosos and features Knopfler's accomplished guitar playing, rendered without the usual amplifier distortion so characteristic of '70s mainstream rock. In the years after, however, Dire Straits had markedly better luck in the UK than in America; *Love over Gold* (p19, 1982), for instance, topped the UK charts, powered in part by the single "Private Investigations"

0:49–1:05	**Verse 2**, 8 mm.	Guitars and bass enter and drums break into a beat, as the song gets louder and more intense. "Got in a little hometown jam . . ."
1:05–1:21	**Chorus**, 8 mm.	As before, but with new parts added in verse 2 continued. "Born in the U.S.A. . . ."
1:21–1:36	**Verse 3**, 8 mm.	As in verse 2, "Come back home to the refinery . . ."
1:36–1:52	**Interlude**, 8 mm.	Music continues without vocal melody, Springsteen improvises quietly in the background.
1:52–2:07	**Verse 4**, 8 mm.	Partial verse, as last phrase is broken off, "I had a brother . . ."
2:07–2:23	**Verse 5**, 8 mm.	Partial verse, verse is broken off even sooner, "He had a woman . . ."
2:23–2:39	**Verse 6**, 8 mm.	Music goes back to spare texture of verse 1. "Down in the shadow . . ."
2:39–2:55	**Chorus**, 8 mm.	Spare, as in chorus 1. "Born in the U.S.A. . . ."
2:55–3:10	**Chorus**, 8 mm.	Music gets fuller again, as in chorus 2. "Born in the U.S.A. . . ."
3:10–4:28	**Coda**, 40 mm.	Vocal melody drops out, as Springsteen improvises and screams in the background. The music goes through the 8-bar pattern 5 times, with a dropout in the 4th one.

(uk2). The band's re-emergence as international chart-toppers came with *Brothers in Arms* (p1 uk1, 1985), containing the hit "Money for Nothing" (p1 uk4), which included Sting on background vocals and was supported by an innovative music video that went into strong rotation on MTV, despite its critiques of that station. Like the other new traditionalists, Dire Straits employed a no-nonsense approach in their music, with a strong respect for older styles and a simpler, more transparent approach to production.

Rockabillies in Exile: The Stray Cats. Led by virtuoso guitarist and lead vocalist Brian Setzer, the Stray Cats celebrated rock and roll's rockabilly past by blending pop sensibility with instrumental prowess. Unappreciated on Long Island in the late 1970s, the band moved to London just when a rockabilly revival was taking hold, due largely to the efforts of Dave Edmunds and his band Rockpile. Performing with drummer Slim Jim Phantom and bassist Lee Rocker, Setzer powered through a series of British hits, including "Runaway Boys" (uk9, 1980) and "Rock This Town" (uk9, 1981), without making much of a mark on the American market. After signing with EMI America and on the strength of their MTV videos, the Stray Cats saw "Rock This Town" climb to number nine in the United States, "Stray Cat Strut" ascend to number three, and their first American album, *Built for Speed*, hit number two. While the band's appropriation of 1950s music and fashion seemed a bit cartoonish at first, Setzer's dedication to rockabilly has proved to be very much in earnest, and he is currently esteemed as the world's foremost rockabilly guitarist. In the 1990s, he formed the Brian Setzer Orchestra and rode the fashion for swing that was fueled by the success of bands such as the Squirrel Nut Zippers and the Cherry Poppin' Daddies. His *Dirty Boogie* (1998) put him back on the charts, as the album rose to the number nine spot in the states and earned him two Grammy awards.

Blue-eyed Soul, '80s Style: Hall and Oates, George Michael, and Michael Bolton. Another strain of traditionalism can be found among white artists who were strongly influenced by 1960s black pop styles. Daryl Hall and John Oates can probably claim the most direct connections to late '60s and early '70s rhythm and blues, since Hall grew up in Philadelphia and had worked with Leon Huff, Kenny Gamble, and Thom Bell. Hall and Oates's soul-drenched singing fueled their first American hits, "Sara Smile" (p4, 1976) and "Rich Girl" (p1, 1977), but the pair really came into their own with the release of *Private Eyes*, which rose to number five on the U.S. charts in 1981 (uk8), and contained two number one hits, "Private Eyes" and "I Can't Go for That." Hall and Oates followed with *Big Bam Boom* (p5 uk28, 1984), which had another number one hit with "Out of Touch" and established the duo as the most important American blue-eyed soul act of the first half of the 1980s. The British duo Wham! (George Michael and Andrew Ridgeley) was similar stylistically to Hall and Oates and emerged during the height of Hall and Oates's popularity. Michael produced the albums and wrote much of the material, as Wham! scored first in the UK with *Fantastic* (uk1, 1983). The next year, the duo reached number one on both sides of the Atlantic with the aptly titled *Make It Big*, which had three U.S. number one

George Michael and Andrew Ridgeley of Wham! in concert, 1984. Michael's singing had roots in 1960s rhythm and blues, and helped to produce hits for Wham! ("Wake Me Up before You Go-Go" [1984]) and as a solo artist ("Faith" [1987]). Like Madonna, Boy George, and Prince, Wham! often projected images of androgyny, and in doing so became icons in the gay community.

hits—"Wake Me Up before You Go-Go" (uk1), "Careless Whisper" (uk1), and "Everything She Wants"—plus a fourth single that rose to number three: "Freedom" (uk1). Despite the success of Wham!, Michael decided to go solo, releasing the chart-topping *Faith* (p1 uk1, 1987), fueled by four number one hits and two more top five hits in the United States, with three of these scoring in the British Top 10 as well. Michael's music, both with Wham! and solo, is deeply indebted to the soulful singing of 1960s black pop, continuing a tradition established by earlier British singers such as Joe Cocker and Stevie Winwood. In the wake of George Michael's international success, American Michael Bolton emerged with two moderately successful singles, "That's What Love Is All About" (p19, 1987) and a cover version of Otis Redding's classic "(Sittin' on) the Dock of the Bay" (p11, 1988). Bolton escorted blue-eyed soul into the 1990s with his *Soul Provider* (p3 uk4, 1990), which ascended the charts on both sides of the Atlantic powered by three Top 10 American hits, including "How Am I Supposed to Live without You" (p1 uk3). Bolton soon became one of the most successful singers of the first half of the 1990s, further reinforcing his strong debts to 1960s soul by covering Percy Sledge's "When a Man Loves a Woman" (p1, 1991).

The Revenge of the Prog Nerds and Mainstream Rock

The Dinosaurs Adapt.   When punk and new wave of the second half of the 1970s challenged the rock music of earlier in the decade, no group of artists felt more under attack than the progressive rock bands. Progressive bands such as Yes and Genesis had built their careers on long, complicated album tracks—just the kind of thing the return-to-simplicity advocates despised. As a consequence, progressive rock in the late 1970s was simplified by bands like Kansas and Styx, and by the end of the decade the original British prog bands were considered dinosaurs. But if the progressive rock style had died out, the musicians themselves remained active and in many cases enjoyed far more commercial success in the 1980s than they ever had in the '70s. By streamlining their sound and making it more accessible and radio friendly, members of Yes, Genesis, and Emerson, Lake & Palmer remained in the mainstream rock limelight with chart-topping albums and sold-out tours. While many had predicted the extinction of these prog-rock dinosaurs, the musicians instead adapted to changes in the pop climate and reinvigorated their careers.

From Genesis to Corporation.   During the first half of the 1970s, Genesis enjoyed moderate success but were never as popular as other prog bands such as Yes or Jethro Tull. When Peter Gabriel left the band mid-decade, drummer Phil Collins took over the lead vocal duties, and initial predictions were that the group would probably lose some of its popularity. The first two albums after Gabriel's departure held their own with the previous releases, though they did better in Britain than in the United States. With the album . . . *And Then There Were Three* (p14 uk1, 1978), the band's music began to turn more toward pop, and the single "Follow You Follow Me" (p23 uk7) was a moderate hit. The next series of albums solidified Genesis's shift to a poppier style, as *Duke* (p11 uk1, 1980), *Abacab* (p7 uk1, 1981), and *Invisible Touch* (p3 uk1, 1986) went to the top of the charts, with the single "Invisible Touch" hitting the number one spot in the United States (uk15). At the same time, individual members of Genesis enjoyed further success outside of the band. As a solo artist, Phil Collins released *Face Value* (p7 uk1) in 1981, which contained the single "In the Air Tonight" (p19 uk2)—a track that got significant radio play at the time. Collins followed up in 1985 with *No Jacket Required*, which topped the charts in both the United States and the UK, producing the two hits "One More Night" (p1 uk4) and "Sussudio" (p1 uk12), and again in 1989 with . . . *But Seriously* (p1 uk1), which contained "Another Day in Paradise" (p1 uk2). Collins's solo music eschewed the clever and/or philosophical lyrics, sophisticated harmonies, and extended forms of earlier Genesis music in favor of direct lyrics, simple harmonies, and tight, radio-friendly arrangements. Genesis bassist Michael Rutherford led Mike + the Mechanics, whose first album did moderately well (p26, 1985) and produced two Top 10 hits, "Silent Running" and "All I Need Is a Miracle" (p6, 1986). The next release, *The Living Years* (p13 uk2, 1988), did better, and contained the hit single "The Living Years" (p1 uk2).

Former Genesis frontman Peter Gabriel released four solo albums in the years following his departure from the band, all of which were named *Peter Gabriel*, though the fourth also went under the title *Security* in the United States. These albums all did better in the UK than in America, though Gabriel received substantial radio airplay in the States. The third of these early albums did the best, hitting number one in Britain, and number twenty-two in America. Gabriel's breakthrough album came in 1986 with *So* (p2 uk1), featuring the hits "Sledgehammer" (p1 uk4) and "Big Time" (p8 uk13), both of which were the subject of innovative videos that received lots of MTV airplay. "Sledgehammer" offers an opportunity to see the roots of rock and roll in what may be considered an unlikely place. The lyrics to this track are Gabriel's tribute to the hokem blues discussed in Chapter 1 with Big Joe Turner's "Shake, Rattle, and Roll" (1954), as the lyrics playfully allude to sexuality, giving the title of the song a double meaning. The two-part form seems to hark back to southern soul, where the end of the song becomes a kind of loose jam of a groove, as occurs in Aretha Franklin's "Respect." Gabriel's follow-up to *So*, *Us* (p2 uk2, 1992), established him as one of the most influential songwriters of the 1990s.

MTV seemed to fit Peter Gabriel perfectly; with Genesis he constantly experimented with elaborate visuals in their concerts. With his classic video "Sledgehammer" (1986), Gabriel used many types of animation and creative camera techniques to create a dreamlike mood that paralleled the metaphors in the song's suggestive lyrics.

Going for the One: Yes and Asia. By the end of the 1970s, singer Jon Anderson and keyboardist Rick Wakeman had left Yes, replaced by Trevor Horn and Geoff Downes, who existed separately as the synthesizer-pop band the Buggles (it was their "Video Killed the Radio Star" that inaugurated MTV). The band released *Drama* (p18 uk2, 1980), which would prove to be the last gasp of '70s prog, and then Downes, Horn, and guitarist Steve Howe left the group. Yes recruited Trevor Rabin, a South African singer-songwriter-guitarist who had had regional success with Rabbitt in the mid 1970s and had since released a couple of solo albums. With Anderson back in the band and with Horn now producing, Yes released *90125* (p5 uk16, 1983), an album full of Rabin rockers, one of which, "Owner of a Lonely Heart," gave the band its first-ever number one single in the United States (uk28). Howe and Downes had also been busy after leaving Yes, forming Asia with drummer Carl Palmer and King Crimson bassist/lead vocalist John Wetton. The band's first album, *Asia* (uk11), topped the charts in the United States in 1982, spawning the hit singles "Heat of the Moment" (p4) and "Don't Cry" (p10). The next album, *Alpha* (p6 uk5, 1983), continued the band's success, though Howe left to form G.T.R. with former Genesis guitarist Steve Hackett. That band's only album, *G.T.R.* (p11, 1986), produced an American hit single, "When the Heart Rules the Mind" (p14) in the same year that keyboardist Keith Emerson and bassist/lead vocalist Greg Lake regrouped, this time with veteran drummer Cozy Powell aboard, to release *Emerson, Lake & Powell* (p23, 1986).

I Will Survive: 1960s and '70s Rock Bands Continue to Thrive. If the progressive rock musicians maintained a central role in rock long after they were predicted to be finished, they were not alone. Many bands and artists from the 1960s and

'70s remained active during the '80s. Foreigner, for instance, continued to dominate mainstream rock with albums such as *4* (p1 uk5, 1981) and *Agent Provocateur* (p4 uk1, 1984), the latter of which had the hit "I Want to Know What Love Is" (p1 uk1). Styx continued their success from the late 1970s with *Kilroy Was Here* (p3, 1983), producing "Mr Roboto" (p3), while Boston contributed *Third Stage* (p1, 1986), with the hit "Amanda" (p1). David Bowie's *Let's Dance* (p4 uk1, 1983) saw him returning to the rhythm and blues orientation of earlier records while enjoying a number one hit on both sides of the Atlantic. Billy Joel's *An Innocent Man* (p4 uk2, 1983) featured some of his strongest material to date, including "Tell Her About It" (p1 uk4) and "Uptown Girl" (p3 uk1), as did *Storm Front* (p1 uk5, 1989), which contained "We Didn't Start the Fire" (p1 uk7). Sixties rockers the Rolling Stones seemed not to be slowed much by age, as *Tattoo You* (p1 uk2, 1981) produced the classic "Start Me Up" (p2 uk7), and subsequent albums like *Undercover* (p4 uk3), *Dirty Work* (p4 uk4, 1986), and

---

LISTENING GUIDE GET MUSIC ▶▶ wwnorton.com/rockhistory

Peter Gabriel, "Sledgehammer"

Words and music by Peter Gabriel, produced by Daniel Lanois and Peter Gabriel. Rose to #1 in the United States (uk4) in 1986; contained on the album *So*, which reached #2 in the States (uk1).

FORM: This track falls into two large sections, consisting of a contrasting verse-chorus form in the first half followed by a simple verse form in the second. The influence of southern soul is obvious throughout the track, and this two-part form may be modeled on tracks like Aretha Franklin's "Respect," which have a high-energy ending filled with vocal improvising. The lyrics mark the song as a tribute to hokem blues songs such as Big Joe Turner's "Shake, Rattle, and Roll."

TIME SIGNATURE: 4/4.

INSTRUMENTATION: Drums, bass, guitar, piano, synthesizers, brass, percussion, lead and backup vocals.

A	0:00–0:30	**Introduction**, 12 mm.	Rhythm and blues horns play a repeated melodic line, propelled by a driving beat.
	0:30–1:00	**Verse 1**, 12 mm.	Vocals enter, as the lyrical allusions remain fairly innocent. Organ comes in. "You could have a steam train . . ."
	1:00–1:20	**Verse 2**, 8 mm.	As before, the allusions get a little sexier. "You could have a big dipper . . ."

Steel Wheels (p3 uk2, 1989) topped charts worldwide. Ex-Beatle Paul McCartney didn't do so badly in the 1980s, either, hitting the number one slot in both England and America with 1982's *Tug of War*. In many ways, the 1980s made it clear that rock artists need no longer think of their careers as only a few years in the sun; rock careers could in fact span decades, and acts could successfully continue even after the style with which they were originally associated had passed from popular favor.

Old School Newcomers: AC/DC, Huey Lewis and the News. While older, more established bands continued to thrive, and a host of new styles arrived on the scene, it was still possible for new acts to enjoy success playing music that seemed more suited to an earlier time. The music of AC/DC is strongly influenced by the British blues rock of bands like Led Zeppelin and Deep Purple, but this Australian group did not make its first important mark on the U.S.

	1:20–1:40	**Chorus**, 8 mm.	Backup vocals are added, "I want to be your sledgehammer . . ."
	1:40–1:51	**Interlude**, 4 mm.	Accompanimental groove continues.
	1:51–2:11	**Verse 3**, 8 mm.	Horn line added, as lyrics push a little farther. "Show me 'round your fruit cage . . ."
	2:11–2:31	**Chorus**, 8 mm.	As before, "I want to be . . ."
	2:31–2:51	**Chorus**, 8 mm.	As before, "I'm gonna be . . ."
	2:51–3:01	**Interlude**, 4 mm.	Creates transition to second section.
B	3:01–3:21	**Verse**, 8 mm.	Spacey synthesizer melody, based on new musical material.
	3:21–3:41	**Verse**, 8 mm.	Vocal enters, note the gospel-style call and response backup vocals, "I kicked the habit . . ."
	3:41–4:00	**Verse**, 8 mm.	Vocal harmony added to lead vocal, "Show for me . . ."
	4:00–4:21	**Verse**, 8 mm.	Lead vocal improvisation begins, as arrangement builds, "Show for me . . ."
	4:21–4:40	**Verse**, 8 mm.	Vocal improving continues, influenced by southern soul, as song seems to fade out. "Show for me . . ."
	4:40–4:49	**Interlude**, 4 mm.	Drumbeat continues alone until snuffed out electronically.

charts (and on American radio) until the 1970s were almost over. AC/DC had formed in 1973—during the salad days of British blues rock—and established themselves at home during the decade. With the release of *Highway to Hell* (p17) in 1979, however, the band's music broke in the United States, powered by the powerful lead guitar playing of Angus Young and the raspy vocals of Bon Scott. Scott did not live to enjoy the band's stateside success, however, and he was replaced by Brian Johnson. The band did not skip a beat on the charts, as *Back in Black* (p4, 1980) and *Dirty Deeds Done Dirt Cheap* (p3, 1981) further established AC/DC's position as old-school rockers and influenced the heavy metal bands that were beginning to assemble in southern California.

Huey Lewis and the News made a trademark of being somewhat out of step with the times, perhaps best exemplified by their 1986 hit "Hip to Be Square" (p3). Veterans of the San Francisco rock scene of the 1970s, the band formed in 1980 and scored their first chart success in 1982 with "Do You Believe in Love" (p7). The albums *Sports* (1983) and *Fore!* (1986) topped the album charts and the song "The Power of Love" was number one in 1985 when it appeared in *Back to the Future*, a film starring Michael J. Fox that celebrates the idyllic 1950s and early rock and roll. Huey Lewis and the News videos were in regular rotation on MTV and their songs became fixtures of FM rock radio during the decade. The easy-rockin', sunny, and wholesome feel of much of their music stood in stark contrast to some of the edgier music of the decade and made them favorites for listeners who perhaps yearned for the good old days when pop music was more often fun than scandalous.

By the late 1980s, new wave and mainstream rock acts would have to make way for a steady stream of heavy metal and rap artists, who not only began to dominate the charts but also developed a strong presence on MTV. In the next chapter we will explore how heavy metal and rap rose from their respective underground scenes during the 1980s to emerge as important styles in the popular music world by the end of the decade.

Questions for Review and Discussion

1. What were the models for MTV when the channel was in the planning stages? Which won out initially? Could you argue that both eventually became a part of music video?
2. How did Michael Jackson and Madonna make use of the visual dimension in their pop music?
3. What role does sexuality play in 1980s music and videos?
4. How did new wave continue into the 1980s and how is it distinguished from the music of the "new traditionalists"?
5. Discuss the role of women in 1980s pop. Compare and contrast this with the role of women in 1970s rock.
6. How did 1970s progressive-rock musicians return in the 1980s?
7. In what ways did 1980s rock reject the hippie aesthetic? In what ways did it adapt it to new purposes?

Bill Flanagan, *U2 at the End of the World* (Delacorte Press, 1995).

Alex Hahn, *Possessed: The Rise and Fall of Prince* (Billboard Books, 2003).

Dave Marsh, *Born to Run: The Bruce Springsteen Story, Volume 1* (Thunder's Mouth Press, 1996)

Dave Marsh, *Glory Days: Springsteen in the 1980s* (Thunder's Mouth Press, 1996).

Tom McGrath, *MTV: The Making of a Revolution* (Running Press, 1996).

chapter 12

Though it was not their first album, Run-DMC's Raising Hell (1986) was the first rap album to make a major impact on white audiences. This crossover appeal was driven by Run-DMC's sound, which featured strong lyrics mixed with samples from rock music. Their version of Aerosmith's "Walk This Way" exemplified this blend, and the video "duel" between Run-DMC and Aerosmith's Steven Tyler and Joe Perry brought the mix to MTV. The strong sales of Raising Hell—released on the Def Jam label owned by Rick Rubin and Russell Simmons—to whites and blacks and the consistent airplay of "Walk This Way" on MTV proved to industry professionals that they could make money selling rap, which in turn caused the genre to explode into the mainstream.

Heavy Metal, Rap, and the Rise of Alternative Rock

During the first half of the 1980s, while new wavers, new traditionalists, revamped progsters, and mainstream rockers were sharing the FM radio waves and MTV was transforming the visual aspects of rock music, two underground scenes were developing that would emerge into the pop-music spotlight later in the decade. As with most new styles, both rap and heavy metal had their roots in previous music, and this chapter will trace the ways each drew upon these earlier musical styles and practices throughout the decade. In the case of both, MTV played a crucial role first in exposing the music to a broader audience, and second in marking the success rap and metal artists began to enjoy as these styles began to assume increasingly central positions in popular music in the second half of the decade. As the 1980s drew to a close, a new underground rock scene was developing in Seattle that also was rooted in earlier styles, especially punk. In the early 1990s, the success of Nirvana ushered grunge into the mainstream and fueled a movement that came to be called alternative rock. All three styles discussed in this chapter developed in the underground, emerging later to enjoy tremendous commercial success. In some sense, each positioned itself as the voice of some disenfranchised segment of the culture. Interestingly, each style was able to keep that sense of identity—and often to play on it—even in the midst of overwhelming popularity.

Heavy! Duty! Heavy Metal in the 1980s

Heavy Metal Thunder.   Nobody seems to be sure exactly how heavy metal got its name. The phrase "heavy metal thunder" is in the lyrics of Steppenwolf's "Born to Be Wild," and Beat writer William Burroughs had also used the phrase before the style ever developed. If the origins of the label are unclear, the origins of the style are much easier to identify. Heavy metal rock music developed out of the harder, more aggressive aspects of late 1960s and early 1970s rock music. Iron Butterfly's "In-A-Gadda-Da-Vida" could be seen as an early precursor, though most writers prefer to cite Black Sabbath as the originators of the style. The heavy and gothic character of Sabbath's early music—driving riffs, dark themes, extended guitar solos—is an important source for later metal bands, as is the heavier side of Led Zeppelin's music. The ways Deep Purple blended some of these same musical features with aspects of classical music would also serve as a model, as would the extravagant showmanship of Alice Cooper and Kiss. Until the early 1980s, all the stylistic features that would prove inspirational to metal musicians existed in music that was not set apart from other rock under the category of "heavy metal." Metal bands drew out these elements and refined them later, and there are other aspects of the music of Led Zeppelin, Alice Cooper, and Deep Purple that heavy metal musicians did not typically adapt. Heavy metal as a separate stylistic category does not emerge in a significant way until the early 1980s when several bands, developing as part of close-knit musical communities and movements mostly in England and Los Angeles, begin to break out of their underground venues with the help of successful albums and constant touring.

Blue-Collar Man: Image and Class.   Heavy metal musicians and fans were often referred to as "headbangers," in part owing to fans' tendency to bang their heads in the air while listening to the music. But the term also captured a sense that many in the music world shared (however unfairly) that heavy metal music was primitive and its adherents were simple-minded and generally unsophisticated. Heavy metal was also thought of as the music of blue-collar whites, so part of the image the music developed was tied up with class prejudices that can be found in American culture even today. The more lovable aspects of '80s metal culture—honesty, loyalty, unselfish devotion to partying—are portrayed by actors Mike Myers and Dana Carvey in the *Wayne's World* movies (1992 and 1993), while the negative aspects of the metal stereotype—ignorance, vulgarity, laziness—come through loud and clear in the *Beavis and Butthead* cartoon series. In terms of the general showbiz glitziness that characterized the successful MTV acts during the early to mid 1980s, it is easy to see how heavy metal bands used their ragged image to oppose the status quo. Even when metal bands were glitzy, it was almost always more the tawdry, strip-club kind of glitz than the mainstream pop music-business kind. In any case, metal fans saw this rejection of the commercial status quo as a mark of authenticity and embraced it with enthusiasm, making metal a gesture of cultural defiance.

The New Wave of British Heavy Metal.   During the late 1970s in the UK, punk and new wave were the most visible reactions against the mainstream rock that the major labels had been releasing. But instead of the return-to-simplicity solution offered by punk and new wave, other musicians opted for what might be termed a "return to heavy rock and roll." By 1977, Ozzy Osbourne had quit Black Sabbath to pursue a solo career. Black Sabbath continued with Ronnie James Dio on lead vocals (though he was followed by a series of lead singers through the 1980s), and Ozzy recruited virtuoso guitarist Randy Rhoads and released a pair of successful solo albums, *Blizzard of Ozz* (uk7 p2, 1980) and *Diary of a Madman* (uk14 p16, 1981), that helped keep the spirit of heavy rock and roll alive. While Ozzy and Sabbath were high-profile acts, playing for stadium crowds and enjoying the benefits of many past successes, other English bands were also developing their music under the pop-industry radar. Judas Priest had formed in Birmingham in 1970, but it wasn't until 1979 that their album *Hell Bent for Leather* (uk32, 1979) earned them a broader audience in England. The follow-up, *British Steel* (uk4 p34, 1980), helped them break through in the United States on the strength of tracks like "Breaking the Law" and "Living after Midnight." Iron Maiden formed in England in 1976, and like Judas Priest, first hit in their home country with *Iron Maiden* (uk4, 1980), and then in America with *The Number of the Beast* (uk1 p33, 1982). Def Leppard made their mark in 1981 with *High 'n' Dry* (uk26 p38), following with *Pyromania* (uk18 p2, 1983), containing the track "Photograph," the video for which became an early staple of MTV. After emerging into rock's mainstream in the early 1980s, these British bands, often referred to collectively as the "new wave of British heavy metal," continued to record and tour successfully throughout the decade. Their music is primarily guitar-driven, following the early 1970s Black Sabbath/Deep Purple model, often featuring pyrotechnical soloing and unrelentingly propelled by heavy drumbeats. It is in most cases an attempt to get back to an earlier style. In terms of the forward development of heavy metal, however, most of the action was not in England but in Los Angeles.

Early Los Angeles (LA) Bands and the American Heavy Metal Underground.

During the 1970s, Los Angeles had increasingly become the place to "make it" in the music business. As a result, musicians from all over the country migrated to southern California seeking rock stardom and fame. Sometimes it seemed that every guitar player in America had moved to Los Angeles in the late 1970s. Heavy metal is a style dominated by the electric guitar—most metal bands did not include keyboard players and often featured dual guitarists. So it makes a certain amount of sense that a heavy metal underground would have developed and sustained itself in Los Angeles. The hopes and dreams of metal aspirants were fed by the success at the end of the 1970s of Van Halen, who had worked their way up through the LA scene and enjoyed a series of successful albums. By 1984, however, the relationship between virtuoso guitarist Eddie Van Halen and flamboyant lead singer David Lee Roth had gone

Nikki Sixx (left) and Vince Neil of Mötley Crüe in performance, 1986. Mötley Crüe's music epitomized the hard guitar-driven sound that came out of Los Angeles in the mid 1980s. Like much music in this style, Mötley Crüe's lyrics were simple and easy to follow, making audience participation a major part of their live performances.

sour. Roth's last album with the band was *1984* (p2 uk15, 1984), and Sammy Hagar joined the band for *5150* (p1 uk16, 1986). Roth released *Eat 'em and Smile* (p4 uk28) that same year, employing a backup band featuring guitarist Steve Vai. As the Van Halen personnel saga was playing out, other bands from Los Angeles were beginning to emerge. Quiet Riot was among the first, as their *Metal Health* reached the top spot on the U.S. charts in 1983. The album contained a cover version "Cum On and Feel the Noize," a hit for British heavy rock band Slade a decade earlier. Although the band did not like the tune and thought they turned in a poor performance, the track went to number five on the singles charts and became a staple of FM radio.

LISTENING GUIDE   GET MUSIC ▶▶ wwnorton.com/rockhistory

Mötley Crüe, "Shout at the Devil"

Words and music by Nikki Sixx, produced by Tom Werman. Contained on the album *Shout at the Devil*, which went to #17 in 1983.

FORM: Like much 1970s rock, this song is in compound AABA form. The A sections are made up of a verse-chorus pair, while the middle B section features a guitar solo and employs a melodic figure drawn from the introduction. The intro itself begins with 8 measures of guitar, bass, and drums, followed by a statement of the chorus, leading to 4 measures of lead guitar melody. This melody returns not only during the bridge, but also during the coda. In the last A section, the chorus occurs three times, once with only vocals and drums. This repetition places strong emphasis on the anthemic chorus, which is the song's hook. It's easy to imagine a crowd singing along to this chorus during live shows. Notice that the arrangement does not really build much, with verses and choruses throughout the song done in mostly the same way each time.

TIME SIGNATURE: 4/4 throughout, with the beat at the beginning being clearly articulated by the high-hat, snare, and bass drum. The tempo is moderate, not nearly as fast as those found among speed metal bands.

INSTRUMENTATION: Heavily distorted electric guitar, bass, and drums make up the rhythm section. Vince Neil's high lead vocals border on screaming at some points and are generally aggressive throughout. The background vocals enter on the chorus. Notice that the guitar is doubled and panned hard right and left, while drums, bass, and lead guitar are panned to the center. The backup vocals are panned left and right, while the lead vocal remains in the center most of the time.

0:00–0:41	**Introduction**, 16 mm.	Powerful figure played by guitar, bass, and drums in the first 8 bars, then 8 mm. that return as the song's chorus.

Mötley Crüe, featuring singer Vince Neil and drummer Tommy Lee, hit big first with *Shout at the Devil* (p17, 1983) and later in the decade with *Girls Girls Girls* (p2 uk14, 1987) and *Dr. Feelgood* (p1 uk4, 1989), both of which contained hit singles. Also coming out of LA were Ratt, whose *Out of the Cellar* (p7, 1984) had the hit single "Round and Round" (p12), though Ratt would not repeat this level of success. Based out of New York, Twisted Sister also enjoyed their first success at about the same time the LA bands were emerging. Led by singer Dee Snider, Twisted Sister's *Stay Hungry* hit number fifteen in the U.S. charts in 1984 (uk34) and contained the hit "We're Not Gonna Take It" (p21).

A	0:41–1:01	**Verse 1**, 8 mm.	Lead vocals enter. Note the high, almost screaming quality of Neil's voice, reminiscent of Led Zeppelin's Robert Plant. Note also the stops between vocal phrases. "He's a wolf screaming lonely . . ."
	1:01–1:11	**Chorus**, 4 mm.	Catchy backup vocals added. This is the material that appeared in the introduction. "Shout! Shout! . . ."
A	1:11–1:31	**Verse 2**, 8 mm.	As before. "He'll be the love in your eyes . . ."
	1:31–1:41	**Chorus**, 4 mm.	As before. "Shout!"
B	1:41–1:57	**Instrumental Bridge**, 6 mm.	Lead guitar solo over material based on the chorus.
A	1:57–2:17	**Verse 1**, 8 mm.	Repeat of first verse, done as before, "He's a wolf . . ."
	2:17–2:27	**Chorus**, 4 mm.	As before, "Shout!"
	2:27–2:37	**Chorus**, 4 mm.	Lead and backup vocals with drums only. This is the place where the crowd sings along in a live setting. "Shout!"
	2:37–2:47	**Chorus**, 4 mm.,	Guitar and bass return. "Shout!"
	2:47–3:12	**Coda and fade**, 8 mm.+	Backup vocals continue, but music changes feel and lead guitar enters after 4 mm. with melody from introduction.

Mötley Crüe's "Shout at the Devil" is a good example of the kind of guitar-driven, pop-oriented metal that came out of Los Angeles in the mid 1980s. Vince Neil's singing is high, almost screaming, showing the influence of Led Zeppelin's Robert Plant, while the drumming is loud and assertive. The unison, sing-along vocals on the chorus give the song an anthem-like quality, and the band drops out late in the track, allowing the listener to focus on the vocal hook (in live performance, this is the spot where the audience sings along and claps their hands). This track has less virtuosic guitar playing than many others, but even at that, the guitar is the focus of the instrumental bridge section.

The Rise of the Metal Mega-Stars and Hair Bands.

Even though the British and LA metal bands had enjoyed significant commercial success in the first half of the decade, heavy metal had yet to produce a band of megastar status. In spite of the strong metal scene in California, the first metal superstars were a band from New Jersey, Bon Jovi. Led by singer Jon Bon Jovi, the group's *Slippery When Wet* topped the U.S. album charts in 1986 (uk6), containing a handful of hit singles, including the two number ones "You Give Love a Bad Name" (uk14)

Guns n' Roses' lead singer Axl Rose performing in concert. Though Guns n' Roses was one of the most popular heavy metal groups in the 1980s ("Welcome to the Jungle" [1987] was a number one hit), Rose and the band fought constantly—with each other and sometimes with fans—thus cutting their career short.

and "Livin' on a Prayer" (p1 uk4). The band's 1988 follow-up, *New Jersey*, did even better, topping the album charts on both sides of the Atlantic as well as containing a clutch of hit singles, including "Bad Medicine" (p1 uk17) and "I'll Be There for You" (p1 uk18). By late in the decade, many metal fans were claiming that Bon Jovi had become too pop-oriented to be considered heavy metal; for Bon Jovi's part, the band began moving toward a more mainstream style—a move that helped them survive the demise of metal in the '90s. Guns n' Roses were the next big winners in the heavy metal sweepstakes. Singer Axl Rose and lead guitarist Slash (Saul Hudson) fronted the quintet, releasing *Appetite for Destruction* (p1 uk5) in 1987. Though the album stalled at first, by the fall of 1988 the singles "Welcome to the Jungle" (p1 uk24) and "Sweet Child o' Mine" (p7 uk24) caught fire on the charts, making Guns n' Roses one of the most successful rock acts of the year. Relationships within the band tended to be stormy even during the best of times, however, and though the group simultaneously released two enormously successful albums in 1991, *Use Your Illusion I* (p2 uk2) and *Use Your Illusion II* (p1 uk1), they had split up within a few years.

By the end of the decade, many heavy metal bands were referred to as "hair bands." In the 1970s, Alice Cooper, Kiss, David Bowie, Genesis, and others had employed makeup and costumes as a way of enhancing their visual images. For the English glam movement, in fact, make-up played a central role. Following these models, Mötley Crüe wore makeup, outrageous clothes, and heavily teased and sprayed hair, as did many of the other metal bands. Poison, however, took this approach so far that some fans initially mistook them for women. As unsettling as this was within the often macho-man world of metal, Poison began to attract a lot of female fans. Often, metal audiences in the 1980s would be almost entirely male, but when Poison played, the ladies showed up. Their 1986 album *Look What the Cat Dragged In* hit number three in the United States, and *Open Up and Say . . . Ahh!* (p2 uk18, 1988) did even better. The latter album contained the hit single "Every Rose Has Its Thorn" (p1 uk13), a representative of a type of song that developed during the second half of the 1980s called the "power ballad." In a power ballad, the singer—in this case Bret Michaels—is given a chance to display his sensitive side, as the song often begins with a quiet expressive section, before the heavy guitars and drums enter to pump up the arrangement. Pretty-boy hair bands were sometimes accused of targeting female teens, and often band members were featured in teen magazines. Other late 1980s hair bands of note are Warrant, who scored with *Dirty Rotten Filthy Stinking Rich* (p10, 1988) and *Cherry Pie* (p7, 1990); Winger, who hit with *Winger* (p21, 1988) and *In the Heart of the Young* (p15, 1990); and Skid Row (featuring singer Sebastian Bach), who enjoyed success on both sides of the pond with *Skid Row* (p6 uk30, 1989) and *Slave to the Grind* (p1 uk5, 1991).

Metal Ambition.   There was clearly a significant amount of dandyism in the world of heavy metal, especially toward the end of the 1980s, but metal also had its more serious-minded, musically earnest, and ambitious practitioners. Perhaps no metal band fits this description better than Metallica; the band began in Los Angeles but moved to the San Francisco area, where they felt that metal fans had a deeper appreciation of their approach to the style. Like other metalheads, Metallica were influenced by Black Sabbath, Led Zeppelin, and Deep Purple. But the band was also influenced by the new wave of British heavy metal, and especially by Motörhead. Formed by Lemmy Kilmister in the mid 1970s after the bassist had done a stint with Hawkwind, the band brought together the guitar-dominated sound of British blues rock, the hectic tempos of punk, and a love for biker leather and culture. Though influential, Motörhead never enjoyed marked commercial success in the United States, though albums such as *Motörhead* (uk43, 1977), *Ace of Spades* (uk4, 1980), and *Iron Fist* (uk6, 1982) did well enough in England.

Metallica's music is often referred to as speed metal, marking the fast tempos and blazing guitar passages that occur on some of their records. Many metal musicians like those in Metallica, Megadeth, Anthrax, and Slayer, came to view speed metal as being too narrow (and some considered it too technically demanding) and developed thrash metal, which allowed for a broader range of musical textures and tempos. Metallica's music indeed displays a wide variety of textures, and this can be found on their early records, such as *Master of Puppets* (p29 uk41, 1986). The band's breakthrough album is . . . *And Justice for All* (4uk 6us 1988), and it contains the track "One," a representative example of the

486

WHAT'S THAT SOUND?

LISTENING GUIDE

GET
MUSIC ▶▶

wwnorton.com/rockhistory

Metallica, "One"

Words and music by James Hetfield and Lars Ulrich, produced by Metallica with Flemming Rasmussen. Single rose to #35 in the United States (uk13) in 1989. Contained in the album . . . *And Justice for All.*

FORM: In the largest sense, this track is in two-part form, and these sections are marked "A" and "B" below. After a lengthy introduction, the A section is in contrasting verse-chorus form, with the addition of the instrumental interlude that appears three times and acts as an instrumental refrain. The fourth time this interlude occurs, it is developed and expanded musically. The second section begins as a simple verse form, but then breaks off into a through-composed instrumental composition.

TIME SIGNATURE: This track begins in 4/4, but the last 9 bars of the introduction shift to 3/4, and the A section stays in 3/4, though extra bars of 2/4 are added throughout, often at the ends of phrases. The chorus is the exception in the first section, as it mixes 4/4 and 2/4. The B section is entirely in 4/4.

INSTRUMENTATION: Two guitars, bass, drums, and lead vocal.

A	0:00–0:20	**Taped war sounds**	Machine gun fire, helicopter sounds establish the mood.
	0:20–1:31	**Introduction**, 25 mm.	Three 8-bar phrases (the last extended by a measure) then a 9-bar anticipation of the verse using quiet, clean guitar sounds.
	1:31–1:46	**Instrumental interlude**, 8 mm.	This music returns as refrain several times, music remains quiet and this passage is sunny and might be mistaken for '70s prog-rock.
	1:46–2:13	**Verse 1**, 16 mm.	Lead vocal enters, as mood turns back to quiet and mysterious. "I can't remember anything . . ."
	2:13–2:20	**Chorus**, 4 mm.	Backup vocals enter, music contrasts strongly with verse, turning much heavier and more aggressive, using distorted guitar sounds, "Hold my breath . . ."
	2:20–2:34	**Instrumental interlude**, 8 mm.	Sunny, quiet music from the first interlude returns.
	2:34–3:02	**Verse 2**, 16 mm.	Mysterious, as before. "Back in the womb . . ."

	3:02–3:09	**Chorus**, 4 mm.	Heavy and aggressive, as before. "Hold my breath . . ."
	3:09–3:37	**Instrumental interlude**, 16 mm.	Twice through the returning quiet and sunny interlude music.
	3:37–3:54	**Chorus**, 10 mm.	The heavier and more aggressive 4-bar chorus is repeated once and then extended by 2 bars. "Now the world . . ."
	3:54–4:38	**Instrumental interlude (developed)**, 27 mm.	Mostly in 3/4, and in 4-bar phrases and based on the earlier interlude but now much heavier, though still melodic. Toward the end (4:20), a machine-gun rhythm begins in the drums, preparing the way for the next section, while also recalling the taped sounds that began the track.
B	4:38–4:55	**Instrumental transition**, 8 mm.	"Machine-gun" rhythm now played by entire band. This is the most aggressive and angular music so far in the track, and it sets up the mood for the second half of the song.
	4:55–5:13	**Verse 1**, 8 mm.	Lead vocal enters, as the mostly pastoral mood of the first half of the song is shattered by angry aggression. "Darkness imprisoning me . . ."
	5:13–5:22	**Verse 2**, 4 mm.	As before, "Landmine has taken my sight . . ."
	5:22–7:25	**Instrumental Finale**, 57 mm.	Mostly in 4/4, this long section can be broken into sections of 12, 13, 14, and 19 measures. Note the tight playing between band members, as well as virtuosic guitar soloing.

Metallica in concert, 1987. Though their guitar-driven style might seem to connect them with '80s "hair bands," Metallica, led by guitarist and singer James Hetfield (center), brought a more musically complex style to heavy metal. Pictured with Hetfield are bass guitarist Jason Newsted (left) and guitarist Kirk Hammett (right).

band's music. Cast in a large-scale two-part form, "One" begins quietly, but gains intensity and speed in the second section of the track. The follow-up, *Metallica* (p1 uk1, 1991), marked the group's arrival as one of the most important bands in heavy metal and includes "Enter Sandman," perhaps the most popular track in all of metal.

Another important thrash metal band is Megadeth, led by former Metallica guitarist and singer Dave Mustaine; representative records are *Peace Sells . . . but Who's Buying?* (1986), *Countdown to Extinction* (p2 uk5, 1992), and *Youthanasia* (p4 uk6, 1994). New York's Anthrax, whose 1987 offering *Among the Living* (p62 uk18, 1987) is probably their best, and LA's Slayer, whose *Reign in Blood* (p94 uk47, 1986) is representative, are also important.

The Role of Virtuosity and the Hippie Aesthetic. Although not all metal bands embraced instrumental virtuosity, many did. Indeed, blistering guitar solos are one of the features most often associated with heavy metal, even by its harshest critics (who often label such solos "empty" or "self-indulgent" technical displays). Most metal guitarists would trace their musical pedigree back to Deep Purple's Ritchie Blackmore; his solo on "Highway Star" as a prime example of proto-metal virtuosity. Eddie Van Halen, whose two-hand tapping techniques can be heard on his solo "Eruption" from the first album, and Randy Rhoads, whose "Mr. Crowley" solo with Ozzy's band is representative, are also links in the metal guitar tradition. Perhaps the clearest instance of a self-consciously virtuosic approach to metal guitar playing within the frame of the traditional classical-music definition is Swedish guitarist Yngwie Malmsteen. Malmsteen moved to California in 1982, where he played the LA clubs with Steeler and then Alcatrazz before forming Rising Force. This band released its debut album in 1984, and the track "Dark Star" provides a showcase for Malmsteen's formidable technique. In many ways, heavy metal—or at least the more technically oriented strain of it—clearly continues the propagation of the hippie aesthetic, and as such, constitutes a direct continuation of late 1960s and 1970s musical sensibilities into the 1980s and 1990s. In its elevation of classical-music models, extended forms, virtuosic solos, and even concept albums devoted to serious-minded issues, heavy metal can be seen as perhaps the most "traditional" style of rock music in the 1980s—an aspect of the music that may seem strange for a style that features plenty of leather, chains, hairspray, and makeup.

The Emergence of Rap

Rap Music and Hip-Hop Culture.   As with heavy metal, it is not difficult to determine the cultural and class association of rap. Most writers agree that rap has its origins in New York's urban black communities, where rap was one element within hip-hop culture generally. Two other important elements of hip-hop, graffiti and break dancing, actually came to the attention of mainstream culture years before rap music began to emerge from its underground regional origins. New York graffiti artists in the mid to late 1970s would splash their names across the city's subway cars—often in vibrant colors—and these cars would then broadcast the names as they circulated the city on their regular scheduled rounds. At about the same time, break dancing—which involves performing athletic spins and other movements on a piece of cardboard or hard plastic placed on the ground—was developed. The first break dancers were mostly black teens, but the practice was soon taken up by Hispanic youths, and the exciting displays of both brought the activity to the attention of the general

Break dancing, which developed in the late 1970s was, along with graffiti art, a major part of hip-hop culture. As seen here, break dancers choreographed elaborate routines that showed off the acrobatic nature of the style. Like rival rap groups, break dance teams challenged each other to put on the best routine—and put down the competition at the same time.

public. The origins of rap are thus best understood within this mix of urban art, dancing, and music. The first hip-hop DJs played records at neighborhood parties, often in one of the city's many parks. Adapting a practice from Jamaican DJs, hip-hop DJs would often carry their own sound systems and employ MCs to comment on the music and encourage the partygoers. One of the most popular of the early hip-hop DJs was Kool Herc, who would often pull up to a city park in his truck, plug his powerful sound system into a city power box, and begin spinning records loud enough for everyone in the neighborhood to hear. Herc was perhaps the first to use an MC (Coke La Rock), and such MCs would soon develop into rappers, blending the original role of the MC with the clever patter of black radio disc jockeys.

Early hip-hop DJs such as Kool Herc and Grandmaster Flash can claim credit for innovations in mixing that would affect most rap that followed. Radio stations had for years employed at least two turntables, one for the record being played and a second for the record that would follow, and most dance clubs employed the same arrangement. Using a pair of turntables, DJs or technicians could transition from one record to the next seamlessly, employing a mixing board to fade the volume of one record while increasing the volume of the next. Kool Herc and Grandmaster Flash employed portable turntables and mixers based on this radio/dance-club set-up, but in addition to transitioning from song to song, they also used their equipment to develop techniques in "break spinning." The DJs took the catchiest instrumental breaks or passages (often drawn from latin-music recordings) and used two copies of the same record to prolong these sections by playing the passages over and over between the two turntables—just as the passage ended on one, it would be replayed on the other. This was done to incite the dancers to greater excitement, but it also created new music (in a sense) out of recorded "samples"—an idea that would form the aesthetic basis for the rap that followed. Grandmaster Flash also popularized "scratching," a technique in which the record is rotated in the reverse direction and then forward, quickly and repeatedly, to create a distinctive rhythm. In addition to the technological expansions of Kool Herc and Grandmaster Flash, another early DJ, Afrika Bambaataa, expanded the range of source recordings employed within hip-hop. Known in the community as the "master of the record," Bambaataa incorporated obscure or unlikely tracks such as the Mohawks' "Champ" and Kraftwerk's *Trans-Europe Express* into his mixes. Bambaataa also founded Zulu Nation in 1974, an organization devoted to building a sense of fraternity and to de-emphasizing the role of fighting and crime in the urban neighborhoods of New York.

Seen here with his group the Furious Five, Grandmaster Flash (center) was one of the most important DJs in early rap. Flash popularized "scratching" and was instrumental in bringing socially conscious lyrics ("The Message" [1982]) to what was often seen as simply "party music."

From the Park to the Radio: The First Rap Records. During the early years of
hip-hop, there were no hip-hop records—mixing and MCing was strictly a live
affair, something you had to be there to experience. However, in 1979 Sugar
Hill Records, based in Englewood, New Jersey, and run by Joe and Sylvia
Robinson, released "Rapper's Delight." Credited to the Sugar Hill Gang, the
record went to number four on the rhythm and blues charts that year, even hitting number thirty-six on the pop charts. Before this unexpected success with
Sugar Hill, the Robinsons had run an indie label called All Platinum until the
mid 1970s, and Sylvia had enjoyed hit records as half of Mickey and Sylvia
("Love Is Strange," 1957) and as a solo performer ("Pillow Talk," 1973). As the
story goes, Sylvia heard guests at a Harlem party chanting rhymes over the
instrumental passages in disco records. Thinking this might be catchy enough
to sell some records, she rounded up several
young men and they "rapped" over a rhythm
track drawn from Chic's "Good Times" to produce "Rapper's Delight." The success of this single demonstrated that the live hip-hop
experience could indeed be transferred to vinyl,
though in this transition the rapping became the
focus, with the mixing serving now as the musical backdrop. This also tended to make the rapper the star of the act, relegating the DJ—who up
until then had run the show in a live setting—to
the role of supporting player. Soon after the success of "Rapper's Delight," Kurtis Blow scored
with a hit for Mercury Records; "The Breaks
(Part 1)" went to number four on the rhythm and
blues charts in 1980. Sugar Hill, however, developed into the most important rap label in the
early 1980s, signing an impressive roster of rappers and DJs, and releasing a series of what are
now considered classic old-school rap tracks,
including Grandmaster Flash and the Furious
Five's "The Message" (r4 p62, 1982).

***Russell Simmons, Rick Rubin: Crossing Over to
White Audiences.*** Inspired by the success of
Sugar Hill, two college students at New York
University, Russell Simmons and Rick Rubin,
decided to begin their own rap label. In the mid
to late 1980s, Def Jam Records released records
by the decade's leading rappers (LL Cool J, the
Beastie Boys, Public Enemy), while Simmons's
management, Rush Entertainment, handled
some of rap's top acts (Run-DMC, Kurtis Blow,
DJ Jazzy Jeff and the Fresh Prince). Some writers
have compared Def Jam to Motown in the 1960s,

*Run-DMC—(from left) MC Darryl
McDaniels ("DMC"), DJ Jason Mizell
("Jam Master Jay"), and MC Joseph
Simmons ("Run"). Run-DMC combined
traditional rap lyrics with rock breaks
and samples. They were one of the most
important innovators in rap, influencing
every rap and hip-hop artist who followed them.*

as Simmons and Rubin presided over the most impressive stable of talent on any indie devoted to rap during the decade. As the Motown businessmen had realized earlier, Simmons and Rubin saw that the real money was to be made in crossover, and the two set about bringing rap to white teens. Among their first successes was LL Cool J, whose career was jump-started in 1985 by an appearance in the movie *Krush Groove*, and a hit rhythm and blues single, "I Can't Live without My Radio" (r15). The album *Radio* rose to number six on the rhythm and blues charts in 1986, hitting a respectable number forty-six on the pop charts as well. LL Cool J crossed over to the pop singles charts in 1987 with "I Need Love" (r1 p14), a track that is perhaps the first rap ballad, while the album *Bigger and Deffer* hit number one on the rhythm and blues album charts (p3).

About the same time LL Cool J was enjoying this success, another Def Jam act was crossing over in an even more direct way. Run-DMC consisted of two rappers, Joseph Simmons ("Run," Russell's younger brother) and Darryl

---

LISTENING GUIDE

GET MUSIC ▶▶▌ wwnorton.com/rockhistory

Run-DMC, "Rock Box"

Words and music by Larry Smith, Joseph Simmons, and Darryl McDaniels, produced by Russell Simmons and Larry Smith. Single rose to #22 on the rhythm and blues charts in 1984; contained on the album *Run-DMC*, which hit #14 on the rhythm and blues charts.

FORM: This track features 2-measure vocal phrases played over a repeating 1-measure riff in the accompaniment. In the first verse sections, eight of these 2-bar vocal phrases occur, while in the second verse section twenty such phrases are heard. The last verse section is shorter than either of the previous two, containing only four 2-bar phrases. Interludes one and two create contrast by focusing the listener's attention on the background music. The coda features segments of relatively free verse, delivered over the same accompaniment found throughout the track. There is no chorus present in this track, making the form a version of the simple verse design.

TIME SIGNATURE: The meter is 4/4 throughout.

INSTRUMENTATION: The background music contains multiple electric guitars, bass, drums, and electronic percussion over which the two rappers deliver their verses. The style of the accompaniment is mainstream rock, with emphasis on distorted electric guitars and a big drum sound.

0:00–0:33	**Introduction**, 13 1/2 mm., 1 1/2 mm. pick up, then 12 mm.	Using sampled beat and multiple distorted, hard-rock guitar melodies.

McDaniels ("DMC"), and DJ Jason Mizell ("Jam Master Jay"). The group enjoyed some crossover success initially with the single "Rock Box" (r22, 1984), mainly because the video for the song was played on MTV. Run-DMC rapped over breaks from rock records, and the rock influence can be heard clearly throughout "Rock Box." Another break Run-DMC used was the opening drum beat from Aerosmith's "Walk This Way." Rick Rubin, a big fan of harder-edged rock and heavy metal who would later go on to produce Slayer and Danzig, invited Steven Tyler and Joe Perry to re-record tracks for the tune rather than sampling them from the record, and the new Run-DMC version thus featured both the rappers and the rockers. By using Aerosmith and their music, Rubin and Run-DMC brought rap to many white rockers who probably would have ignored it otherwise, and "Walk This Way" (r8 p4, 1986) became an important record for bringing rap into the pop mainstream. The band's first album, *Run-DMC* (r14 p53, 1984), is often cited as among the most influential

0:33–1:11	**Verse 1**, 16 mm.	Rapping begins, using eight 2-bar vocal phrases over the repeating guitar riff and beat from the introduction. "For all you sucker MCs . . ."
1:11–1:30	**Interlude 1**, 8 mm.	No vocal, focus on guitars and drums, as repeating guitar riff goes into stop time and multiple guitar melodies cascade.
1:30–3:01	**Verse 2**, 40 mm.	Twenty 2-bar phrases, the first two over only the drumbeat, then the repeated guitar riff returns. The last phrase employs scratching but no rapping. "Because the rhymes I say . . ."
3:01–3:16	**Interlude 2**, 4 mm.	No vocal, with emphasis on drumbeat as music breaks down.
3:16–3:35	**Verse 3**, 8 mm.	Four 2-bar phrases, guitar riff occurs in stop time. "We got all the lines . . ."
3:35–5:27	**Coda and fade**, 44 mm. +	Repeated guitar riff returns and is interrupted with stop time, then continues, as lead guitar solos and rappers improvise, creating a long, atmospheric ending section. "Jay, Jay, Jay . . ."

in early rap music, but *Raising Hell* (r1 p6, 1986) was the album that made the band stars. Taking a page from the Sam Phillips playbook, Def Jam then produced a band of white rappers, the Beastie Boys, whose "(You Gotta) Fight for Your Right (to Party)" hit number seven on the pop charts in 1987 (it did not score on the rhythm and blues charts), while their album *Licensed to Ill* became the first rap record to hit number one on the pop album charts (r2). The Beastie Boys were among the first bands to take advantage of the new digital sampling technology—instead of working with records and turntables, passages could now be recorded digitally and looped with far more precision than turntables would allow. By the end of the 1980s digital sampling was a widespread practice among rappers—so much so that lawsuits began to fly over whether bands are required to pay for the rights to the samples (it turned out that they are).

As seen in this picture, Public Enemy, led by rappers Chuck D (seated center) and Flavor Flav (seated right), brought militancy to rap. Public Enemy often railed against the racism in the police department, in Hollywood with "Burn, Hollywood, Burn" (1990—foreshadowing the LA riots of 1992), and even ambulance response time to black neighborhoods, in "9-1-1 is a Joke" (1990).

Although Def Jam was a dominant force during the second half of the 1980s, other labels and artists also enjoyed success. Ice-T is among the most important of these. Tracy Morrow was born in New Jersey but moved to Los Angeles as a child, where he became one of the most important representatives of west coast rap in the late 1980s and early 1990s. His "I'm Your Pusher" (r13, 1988) returns to themes of urban life and its problems that had been explored by black musicians twenty years earlier, though often in a more graphic and angry manner, earning such music the label "gangsta rap." Consistent with its influences from the 1970s, the track employs samples drawn from Curtis Mayfield's "Pusherman." While the 1988 album *Power* (r6 p35) did well commercially, Ice-T would enjoy much greater crossover success in the 1990s with *O.G. Original Gangster* (r9 p15, 1991) and *Home Invasion* (r9 p14, 1993).

Challenging the Status Quo. Among the rap artists who began to engage in social and political criticism, Boogie Down Productions (BDP), led by KRS-One (Kris Parker), is often cited as the most significant. The band's first album, *Criminal Minded* (r73, 1987), influenced many rappers who followed in its sometimes uncompromising and harsh depictions of urban life. BDP reached the peak of its crossover success with *Ghetto Music: The Blueprint of Hip-Hop* (r7 p36, 1989) and *Edutainment* (r9 p32, 1990). Building on the rhythmic style of Run-DMC and the social and political approach of BDP, Public Enemy first stormed the rhythm and blues charts in 1988 with *It Takes a Nation of Millions to Hold Us Back* (r1 p42), containing the single "Don't Believe the Hype" (r18). The band's single "Fight the Power" (r20, 1989) was featured in Spike Lee's film *Do the Right Thing*, as the next album, *Fear of a Black Planet* (r3 p10, 1990), crossed over onto the pop charts. Led by Chuck D and Flavor Flav, Public Enemy became one of the most influential groups in rap, enjoying their greatest crossover success with *Apocalypse 91—The Enemy Strikes Back* (r1 p4, 1991). With the success of Public Enemy, Los Angeles' N.W.A. (Niggaz with Attitude) brought an even angrier approach to rap, creating much controversy in the process. The band's 1989 album, *Straight Outta Compton* (r9 p37), contained a track entitled "Fuck Tha Police," which earned the band's record company, Ruthless, a warning letter from the FBI. The band's penchant for depicting dangerous urban life appealed strongly to white kids in America's shopping malls, however, and *EFIL4ZAGGIN* hit number one on the pop album charts in 1991 (r2), much to the consternation of many parents and community leaders.

Fear of a Black Planet? The Flap over Rap.   It is something of an understatement to say that rap has been controversial; almost since the days of "Rapper's Delight," critics have argued that rap is not really "music" since many rappers don't play instruments or sing. Maybe it's a kind of poetry, these critics will often allow, but it's not music. Others are more offended by the words and images employed in some rap: critics claim that rap can be misogynistic, homophobic, vulgar, and violent. To a certain extent, rap again trips the wires of race and class distinctions among some white listeners—a phenomenon that goes back at least to 1955 and never quite goes away during the decades that follow. The video for Run-DMC's "Walk This Way" captures the racial tension between rock and roll and rap perhaps more accurately than anybody involved in making it intended. During the first half of the video, neither Run-DMC nor Aerosmith seems to have much patience for one another, and as Tyler breaks down a wall that physically separates the two groups in the video, it is hardly a happy moment of reconciliation. As much as issues of race and class may account for some of the tension over rap, they also account for some of its attraction. Many young white rap fans in the late 1980s and early '90s were clearly fascinated by the worlds of urban violence and struggle that played a role in much of the harder-edged rap—worlds that were very different from the affluent and mostly white suburban environment in which they lived (though perhaps not as different in reality as is often imagined). Against claims that rap is not really music, it is worth noting that rap musicians often take preexisting music and refashion it into something new, and this reworking of commonly available materials has been an accepted aesthetic approach at least since World War II in the visual and musical arts. Many listeners might object to the music of contemporary composers such as John Cage or Karlheinz Stockhausen, but few would go so far as to say that they are not musicians. Refashioning preexistent materials—even if this comes from records—can be just as "musical" as working with new material; it just depends on how it is done.

In many ways, rap and heavy metal might seem to be opposed to one another during the second half of the 1980s, but actually they developed along parallel paths. Interestingly, both styles developed devoted followings on MTV. Headbangers' Ball premiered in 1987, playing metal videos exclusively, while Yo! MTV Raps debuted in August 1988 and quickly became one of the most popular shows on the network. Both styles maintained a kind of "outsider" status, depending in large part on class differences—and in the case of rap, race issues must be figured into the equation. Both styles became emblematic of the lower end of the class spectrum and used this class distinction as part of their appeal, often drawing in middle- and upper-class fans as well. While rap continued to develop throughout the 1990s, enjoying continued success (as well as inciting new criticism), heavy metal began to lose favor as a new guitar-heavy sound began to emerge, at first from Seattle, and then from around the country as well as from England.

LISTENING GUIDE GET MUSIC ▶▶▌ wwnorton.com/rockhistory

Public Enemy, "Don't Believe the Hype"

Words and music by Carlton Ridenhour, Hank Shocklee, Eric Sadler, and Charles Drayton, produced by Hank Shocklee and Carl Ryder. Single rose to #18 on the rhythm and blues charts in 1988; contained on the album *It Takes a Nation of Millions to Hold Us Back*, which rose to #1 on the rhythm and blues charts (p42).

FORM: After a 4-measure introduction, this track falls into simple verse-chorus form. The verses are made up of 4-bar vocal phrases; the first verse uses four such phrases, the second uses five, and the third employs ten. The first chorus is also a 4-measure phrase, as is the third. The second and fourth choruses employ an 8-bar structure in which a 4-bar phrase is followed by a contrasting 2-bar phrase and then by a return to the first phrase. Note how the rhyme schemes and rhythms change often and sometimes cross over from one phrase to the next.

TIME SIGNATURE: 4/4.

INSTRUMENTATION: The accompaniment consists of a funk groove played by guitar, bass, and drums that is likely sampled and looped to create a constant and repetitive backdrop. An electronic whistle sound also recurs regularly.

0:00–0:10	**Introduction**, 4 mm.	Electronically sampled and altered sounds over looped groove.
0:10–0:49	**Verse**, 16 mm.	Rapping enters in four 4-bar phrases, as looped groove continues underneath. "Bang, caught you lookin' . . ."

Into the 1990s: Alternative Rock

America's Punk?   In Chapter 10 we focused on the rise of punk in the second half of the 1970s and on the differences between the British and American punk scenes. In many ways, British punk was more motivated by socioeconomic frustration and despair during those years than American punk was; because of the depressed economy, young people in the UK had much more to rebel against than did their American brothers and sisters, who mostly had little to complain about economically. This has led some rock writers and artists to argue that America never really experienced "punk" in the sense that the Brits did, and that punk did not really arrive in the United States until the emergence of Nirvana and the Seattle bands in the early 1990s. This argument is certainly thought provoking, but it would likely be rejected by the

0:49–0:58	**Chorus**, 4 mm.	Recited two 2-bar phrases with nonverbal vocal interjections, "Don't believe the hype . . ."
0:58–1:47	**Verse**, 20 mm.	Rapping now presents five 4-bar phrases, with loop continuing with occasional stop time. "Yes was the start . . ."
1:47–2:07	**Chorus**, 8 mm.	First two 2-bar phrases as before, then one contrasting phrase, followed by a return to first 2-bar phrase.
2:07–3:44	**Verse**, 40 mm.	Rapping now presents ten 4-bar phrases, with loop continuing uninterrupted. Note the exchange of rapped phrases. "Don't believe the hype, it's a sequel . . ."
3:44–4:04	**Chorus**, 8 mm.	The first 4 mm. are without vocals, followed by two 2-bar vocal phrases.
4:04–5:00	**Verse**, 23 mm.	Rapping uses five 4-bar phrases then one 3-bar phrase, "I got flavor . . ."
5:00–5:19	**Chorus**, 8 mm.	As before, two 2-bar phrases, one contrasting phrase, then return to first 2-bar phrase.

The Parents Music Resource Center Hearings

In the 1980s, the members of the baby boom generation came of age and assumed roles of responsibility as parents and workers. When this happened, many of them began to rethink the rebellious excesses of their youth and turned in a strikingly conservative direction. As a direct result, conservative Republicans led by Ronald Reagan gained political control in Washington for the entire decade. But there is no single clearer example of the conservative counterrevolution of the 1980s than the Parents Music Resource Center (PMRC) hearings held by the U.S. Senate in 1985.

Tipper Gore, the wife of Tennessee Democratic senator Al Gore (later the vice president), was disturbed one day to find her eleven-year-old daughter listening to Prince's "Darling Nikki," an explicitly sexual song on an album (*Purple Rain*) that Mrs. Gore had purchased for her.

Believing that a rating system or warning label would have alerted her that the album contained potentially offensive material, Mrs. Gore formed the PMRC with her friend Susan Baker, the wife of Republican treasury secretary James Baker, and a number of other powerful Washington, D.C., parents. The PMRC initially sought to educate parents about the "alarming" content of much popular music. Later, however, they used their considerable political and media clout to advocate the "voluntary" use of warning labels by the record industry.

The effectiveness of such warning labels has long been debated. Since much of the appeal of popular music is based in rebellion against authority figures, it is always possible that alerting parents to objectionable content will only enhance that appeal. And while advisory stickers can be effective on store-bought CDs, they don't affect live performances, copies, bootlegs, or counterfeits. And in any case, the PMRC offered no solution for the countless songs dealing with adult topics like sex or drug use that were already widely available—from Big Joe Turner's "Shake, Rattle, and Roll" to the Knack's "My Sharona," and from Nina Simone's "Lilac Wine" to Lou Reed's "Heroin." It would also have been very difficult to write legislation that forced the industry to use labels because the Supreme Court had ruled that music was free speech, protected by the Constitution. But the appeal of this movement seems to have been that it gave concerned parents at least some sense that they could limit their children's exposure to adult content, so the PMRC took their campaign to a new arena: the Senate.

Al Gore was a member of the Senate Commerce,

Founders of the Parents Music Resource Center (PMRC), Tipper Gore (left) and Susan Baker testifying before the U.S. Senate, May 6, 1985. The PMRC was able to get record companies to agree to put warning labels on their "explicit" products, but this seemed to help, not hinder, sales.

Luther Campbell of 2 Live Crew in concert. In the wake of the PMRC hearings, 2 Live Crew's lyrics came under close scrutiny. As this concert shows, 2 Live Crew did use blatant sexual images, but the Supreme Court ruled that they were not illegal and couldn't be censored. As you can see from the T-shirt on one of their members (bottom right corner), 2 Live Crew was vehemently opposed to any form of censorship.

Technology, and Transportation Committee, which held hearings in September 1995 investigating the "pornographic content" of popular music. Testimony was given by members of the PMRC, representatives of the record industry, a University of Texas at San Antonio professor who discussed subliminal and hidden messages in heavy metal, and a child psychiatrist who pointed out associations between metal lyrics and various antisocial behaviors. The musicians were represented by a curious trio: mild-mannered folk-pop star John Denver, whose song "Rocky Mountain High" was sometimes mistakenly interpreted as referring to drug use; avant-garde counterculture hero Frank Zappa, who had been battling censorship for years; and glam/metal singer Dee Snider of Twisted Sister, whose lyrics had also been frequently misinterpreted. All three were critical of the PMRC's proposals. Although the committee advocated no legislation, the public attention surrounding the hearings created pressure for a labeling system. In a clever political maneuver, the record industry conceded to labeling in exchange for a tax on blank audiocassette sales in order to offset revenue lost to audio duplication (setting a precedent for the Digital Millennium Copyright Act of 1998).

As Frank Zappa warned, the system of labeling CDs with advisory stickers has never been effective. Not only did it not prevent the spread of music with explicit lyrics, but it actually enhanced it. In the era of gangsta rap that followed shortly after the hearings, an advisory label became a de facto certificate of authenticity. Musicians even competed for media attention by using progressively *more* offensive lyrics. This process reached a climax in 1992 with a trial to determine whether the 2 Live Crew album *As Nasty as They Wanna Be* was legally obscene. A Florida court found that the record was obscene, but that decision was overturned on appeal. After the U.S. Supreme Court upheld the appellate court's decision, both sides seemed to back down from the issue, although the record industry's use of warning labels continues today.

many young Americans who participated in local punk scenes around the country in the late 1970s as well as in the underground punk scenes that flourished throughout the 1980s, after punk had receded from the music-business spotlight. There were many guitar-oriented, self-consciously "post-punk" bands throughout the 1980s, and the best known and most widely respected of these minimalistic underground rockers were probably Minnesota's Hüsker Dü and New York's Sonic Youth (see Chapter 13). However much some might object to it, the "America's punk" interpretation of Nirvana and company at least brings out a clear historical connection, even if some ultimately reject its conclusions. The new style of rock music that began to win strong adherents in the early 1990s—called alternative rock—embraced punk's return-to-simplicity aesthetic and its directness of expression. As 1970s punks had reacted against the big labels and what they believed was the over-produced rock of Jethro Tull, Pink Floyd, and Led Zeppelin, the 1990s alternative rockers were reacting against the visually oriented MTV artists and the flashy (and often virtuosic) heavy metal bands. Alt rockers dressed very casually (no spandex or teased hair), many projected themselves as amateur instrumentalists (no long guitar solos), and often rejected the idea of recording for a major label, opting instead to work with smaller indie labels. This do-it-yourself aesthetic was one way of rejecting the crass commercialism of popular music, as well as most of the trappings of fame. Alt rockers and their fans became rock's new bohemians—self-consciously scruffy and full of attitude.

Seattle's Grunge Scene: Nirvana, Hole.   When Nirvana's second album *Nevermind* (p1 uk7) was released in late 1991, it not only rose to the top of the pop charts on both sides of the Atlantic—partly with the help of the single "Smells like Teen Spirit" (p6 uk7)—but also launched a movement that would soon be called alternative rock, a stylistic explosion that would resonate for over a decade. Though they played their first shows in Olympia, Washington, Nirvana is perhaps the most significant of the "grunge" bands that came out of Seattle in the first half of the 1990s. Led by singer/songwriter/guitarist Kurt Cobain, the band quickly became stars, despite Cobain's dedication to the idea that Nirvana's music rejected the entire rock star apparatus in show business. The two albums that followed the debut release further solidified the band's status as one of the hottest new acts in rock; *In Utero* (1993) and *Unplugged in New York* (1994) both hit the number one slots in the United States and the UK. Although Cobain and Nirvana projected an image of amateurism—fans were supposed to think that the group were not concerned about their technical capabilities as musicians (in strong distinction to the heavy metal bands)—Cobain was in fact a gifted songwriter and a tasteful guitarist. But as the punks and new wave bands had done in the late 1970s, the alternative movement bands (led however reluctantly by Nirvana) embraced a return-to-simplicity/return-to-authenticity aesthetic. Nirvana's career, however, was cut tragically short by Cobain's suicide in April 1994 and it would be left to others to carry the alternative torch.

Nirvana's lead singer Kurt Cobain performing in England, 1992. Nirvana combined simple but intense guitar work with poetic, sometimes disturbing, longing lyrics to create a new sound: "grunge." This sound seemed to appeal especially to young, white suburbanites who felt alienated from mainstream American values. Cobain's suicide in 1994 helped turn him into an icon of "alternative" music and culture.

In 1992, Cobain married Courtney Love, whose band Hole developed a reputation for being one of the most aggressive on the new alternative rock scene, due in large part to Love's combative persona. Formed in Los Angeles in 1989 and relocated to Seattle by 1990, the band's first release, *Pretty on the Inside* (1991), drew favorable reviews. Their 1994 release, *Live Through This*, did well in the UK, hitting number 13 (uk56) and garnering critical praise on both sides of the Atlantic, though tragically for Love, most of this success came just after Cobain's suicide. Hole went on to enjoy greater chart success in the following years, with *Celebrity Skin* (1998) reaching number nine in the United States.

LISTENING GUIDE   GET MUSIC ▶▶▌ wwnorton.com/rockhistory

Nirvana, "Smells like Teen Spirit"

Words and music by Kurt Cobain, Krist Novaselic, Dave Grohl, produced by Butch Vig. Single rose to #7 in the United States (#6 in the UK) in early 1992; contained on the album *Nevermind*, which rose to #1 in the United States (#7 in the UK).

FORM: This song is in simple verse-chorus form with a few interesting twists. The 16-bar introduction is made up of two 2-bar phrases played solo on the guitar, then four 2-measure phrases played loudly by the entire band, followed by the same phrase played twice more but quietly and arranged differently. This last "quiet" 2-bar phrase returns again as a lead-in to the second verse and abbreviated to 2 bars to lead into the third verse. Each verse and chorus is built on the same 2-bar phrase heard in the introduction. The 16-bar verses cycle through the phrase eight times; the first 8 bars in each case employ new lyrics while the second 8 bars repeat the "Hello/how low" lyric. The 16-bar choruses contain the 2-bar phrase six times each, with a contrasting 4 bars added to the end in each case. After the second verse-chorus pair, the verse is played instrumentally, as the guitar plays the vocal melody. The song ends with a chorus containing ten statements of the basic 2-bar phrase.

TIME SIGNATURE: 4/4 throughout.

INSTRUMENTATION: Two guitars, bass, and drums accompany Cobain's solo vocal. Notice the contrast between the clean sounding guitar at the beginning of each sung verse and the heavily distorted guitars heard in the choruses.

0:00–0:33	**Introduction**, 16 mm.	Solo guitar plays 2-bar phrase twice through relatively quietly, then the entire band comes in playing the same music for 8 bars, followed by a return to a quiet, but differently arranged version of the same music.

Pearl Jam. In Nirvana's wake, a host of alternative rock bands began to enjoy a level of commercial success in the 1990s that had eluded post-punk bands like Sonic Youth (see Chapter 13) in the 1980s. Also coming out of Seattle were Pearl Jam, led by singer Eddie Vedder, whose albums *Ten* (p2 uk18, 1992), *VS* (p1 uk2, 1993), and *Vitology* (p1 uk6, 1994) established them as a top act by mid-decade. Pearl Jam's music was in many ways closer to the heavy metal that had immediately preceded it, and this similarity made it easy to program on the mainstream rock radio stations of the mid 1990s. The group was central to the alternative rock scene of the decade, but they were also important to the anti-

0:33–1:06	**Verse 1**, 16 mm.	Lead vocal enters to the accompaniment of the "quiet" music in the first 8 bars, and to the "loud" music in the second 8 bars. "Load up on guns and bring your friends . . ."
1:06–1:47	**Chorus**, 20 mm., 12 mm.	Played and sung at its most aggressive, plus 4 bars of contrasting music, then a 4 mm. lead-in to the next verse using the "quiet" music, "With the lights out it's less dangerous . . ."
1:47–2:20	**Verse 2**, 16 mm.	As in verse 1, "I'm worse at what I do best . . ."
2:20–2:53	**Chorus**, 16 mm.	As before, but without the "quiet" music lead-in to the next verse. "With the lights out it's less dangerous . . ."
2:53–3:34	**Instrumental Verse**, 20 mm.	16 mm. guitar solo plays the melody almost exactly as it is sung in the verses, then the 4 mm. "quiet" music again serves to lead into the verse, though this time it is a little different, allowing space for the lead guitar to die out.
3:34–4:05	**Verse 3**, 16 mm.	As in verses 1 and 2, "And I forget just why I taste . . ."
4:05–4:58	**Chorus**, 21 mm.	As before, but now extended to include ten times through the 2-bar phrase, plus a last chord added to create an ending. Cobain's vocals become the most frenzied toward the end.

commercial aesthetic of the alt-rock lifestyle. The band battled with Ticketmaster, a national service that handles ticket sales for many large rock concerts, because Pearl Jam believed the agency was forcing individual tickets to sell for more than $20, thus making it difficult for some fans to attend the band's shows. Although Pearl Jam eventually lost a long legal battle with Ticketmaster, their willingness to fight the big-establishment, big-business company—and to lose the revenue they would have earned through concert appearances during this time—made them heroes within the alt movement, which generally scorned the trappings of commercial success. By the end of the decade, *Yield* (1998) hit number two on the U.S. charts, and the band scored a surprise single with "Last Kiss" (p2, 1999), a cover of the 1964 splatter platter hit single by J. Wilson and the Cavaliers that Pearl Jam had recorded especially for their fan club.

Other Seattle Bands: Soundgarden, Alice in Chains, Foo Fighters.

Led by the vocals of Chris Cornell and the guitar playing of Kim Thayil, Soundgarden also emerged from Seattle. Formed in the late 1980s and widely expected by many in Seattle to be the band that would first break onto the national scene, the band's blend of heavy metal, '70s blues rock, and '60s psychedelia had to wait until after Nirvana broke to enjoy national commercial success with *Superunknown* (p1 uk4, 1994). Alice in Chains was formed by singer Layne Staley in the late 1980s and was initially signed by Columbia Records as a metal band. Staley's penchant for dark lyrics dealing with drug addiction and death are similar to those of speed metal bands like Metallica or Megadeth, and the group's 1991 debut album, *Facelift*, was initially directed to metal fans. In the wake of Nirvana, Alice in Chains were promoted as a Seattle band, which helped the sales of *Facelift* and pushed the next album, *Dirt*, to number six in the United States. In 1994, the acoustically oriented *Jar of Flies* became the first extended play ever to top the Billboard album charts, while 1995's *Alice in Chains* debuted at number one in the States. In the wake of Nirvana's demise, drummer Dave Grohl formed Foo Fighters, which developed around a collection of solo recordings he had made. Released first on inexpensively produced cassettes, the collection of tracks became the band's first album, *Foo Fighters* (1995), which reached number twenty-three on the U.S. charts and did even better in the UK (uk3). The

Pearl Jam's Eddie Vedder sings at the Lollapalooza music festival, 1992. Pearl Jam was central to the alternative rock scene and their battle with concert ticket handler Ticketmaster was important to the anti-commercial aesthetic of the alt-rock lifestyle.

success of several subsequent releases has made the band among the most successful of those that emerged out of Seattle scene in the '90s.

California Bands. Although Seattle is often thought of as the home of the new alternative movement, a number of bands farther down the west coast were developing along parallel lines. San Francisco's Green Day, led by singer/songwriter/guitarist Billy Joe Armstrong, formed in 1989 and had already released one full-length album before Nirvana broke into national attention. The band enjoyed its first significant commercial success in 1994, however, with *Dookie* (p2), following in 1995 with *Insomniac* (p2). The band's music is often hard driving and aggressive, making their stylistic debt to '70s punk and '60s pop clear, but their softer side can be heard in the ballad "Good Riddance (Time of Your Life)," which became known to millions of Americans when it was played during the final episode of the enormously successful television show *Seinfeld*. The wildly eclectic Faith No More was formed in San Francisco in 1982 by bassist Billy Gould, keyboardist Roddy Bottum, and drummer Mike Bordin; guitarist Jim Martin joined soon thereafter. After releasing a couple of albums, the band added Mike Patton on vocals in 1988; Patton also sang in the even-more-eclectic San Francisco–based band, Mr. Bungle. With Patton on board, Faith No More released *The Real Thing* (p11, 1990), which produced the number nine single "Epic." *Angel Dust* (p10) followed in 1992 and further established the band's reputation. In many ways, Faith No More's musical approach may be more akin to the comic irreverence of Frank Zappa than to the angry rebelliousness of the Sex Pistols. The Red Hot Chili Peppers also do not fit neatly into the alternative template. Formed in 1983 in Hollywood, the group seemed just as influenced by '70s funk as by '70s punk, and this is especially evident in the playing of the band's bassist, Flea. Their second album, *Freaky Styley* (1985), was produced by George Clinton, while 1989's *Mother's Milk* contained a cover version of Stevie Wonder's "Higher Ground." The band enjoyed its first commercial success with the Rick Rubin–produced *BloodSugarSexMagik*, which rose to number three in 1991. Following with hit albums such as *One Hot Minute* (p4, 1994) and *Californication* (p3, 1999), the Red Hot Chili Peppers also developed a reputation for innovative videos, many of which became staples on MTV. Formed in 1987 even farther south in San Diego, Stone Temple Pilots drew heavily on the style of Seattle bands like Alice in Chains and Pearl Jam, while at the same time drawing in elements of '70s guitar-oriented mainstream rock. The band was dismissed by some critics for being too derivative, but Stone Temple Pilots' first three albums—*Core* (1992), *Purple* (1994), and *Tiny Music* (1996)—all cracked the top five on the U.S. charts.

Revisiting the 1960s and 1970s. In many ways, the alternative scene of the 1990s was fueled by a reinterpretation of 1960s and 1970s rock styles. Led by singer/songwriter/guitarist Billy Corgan, for instance, Chicago's the Smashing Pumpkins became one of the most successful acts of the 1990s by reworking aspects of progressive rock, psychedelia, and early heavy metal. After a couple of relatively successful album releases, *Mellon Collie and the Infinite Sadness* (4uk 1us) topped the charts in 1995. Similarly, England produced Oasis, a band heavily influenced by the Beatles—so much so that some critics have never been able to see past this aspect of the group's sound. Oasis reached the top of the British charts in 1994 with *Definitely Maybe*, and scored a transcontinental hit the next year with *(What's the Story) Morning Glory*. Within the UK, where the success of Oasis was more overwhelming than it was in the States, Blur also rose to the top of the charts with *Parklife* (1uk, 1994), as did Suede with *Suede* (uk1, 1993). Drawing heavily on the more atmospheric music of Pink Floyd, Radiohead scored first in the UK with *The Bends* (uk6, 1995), later hitting the number one slot in the United States with *Kid A* (2000) and becoming one of the most critically celebrated bands at the turn of the new century.

Some interesting questions follow the rise of alternative music in the 1990s. Why, for instance, did alternative rock have such broad appeal? Was it because it rejected the glamor of the many MTV acts that seemed to be more concerned with their looks and dance steps than they were with their music? Or was it because heavy metal had pushed the instrumental aspect of rock so far toward virtuosity and complexity that some kind of correction was needed to keep rock from getting too self-involved and full of itself? Could it just be that the rock public constantly requires something new? If so, why was alternative seen as new when the punk and new wave acts had embraced the return-to-simplicity approach only a little more than a decade before? Because many of the alternative artists discussed in this chapter are still active, gaining a sense of historical perspective and understanding is difficult. In the next chapter we will survey many more artists whose music became popular in the 1990s, and at this point in our study of the history of rock, a historical perspective becomes increasingly difficult to establish—perhaps because the era we are beginning to consider is not yet history in the traditional sense!

Questions for Review and Discussion

1. Discuss the roots of 1980s heavy metal in earlier rock music. Who are the strongest influences on '80s metal bands?
2. Consider metal's development in the 1980s from an underground scene to a style in the rock mainstream. Who were the British forerunners and why was the Los Angeles scene so important? Which bands or artists helped to push metal into the music-business limelight?
3. Discuss the roots of rap in earlier music and culture. How did rap music develop out of hip-hop culture?
4. What were the important record labels in rap's history, and what role did they play in raising the profile of rap?
5. What role did MTV play in fueling the growing popularity of heavy metal and rap?
6. Compare and contrast the stereotypical images of heavy metal and rap musicians and fans. How accurately do such images portray these communities?
7. How did alternative rock emerge in the early 1990s? Who are the most important bands or artists?

8. In what ways did alternative music engage the return-to-simplicity aesthetic? How does alternative music refer to earlier music, and how does this parallel other moments in rock's history?

Further Reading

Ian Christie, *Sound of the Beast: The Complete Headbanging History of Heavy Metal* (Harper, 2003).

Nelson George, *Hip-hop America* (Penguin, 1998).

David Konow, *Bang Your Head: The Rise and Fall of Heavy Metal* (Three Rivers Press, 2002).

Russell Simmons, with Nelson George, *Life and Def: Sex, Drugs, Money, and God* (Crown, 2001).

The Vibe History of Hip-hop, edited by Alan Light (Three Rivers Press, 1999).

Robert Walser, *Running with the Devil: Power, Gender, and Madness in Heavy Metal Music* (Wesleyan University Press, 1993).

Deena Weinstein, *Heavy Metal: A Cultural Sociology* (Lexington Books, 1991).

The Nineteen Nineties and Beyond

1990s and Beyond

The fall of the Berlin Wall in 1989 marked the end of the Cold War and left the United States as the world's only true superpower. Clear military superiority had its responsibilities. In the decades that followed the Cold War, several important armed conflicts arose, and the world often looked to the United States to take the lead in both war and peacemaking efforts. In 1991 Iraq invaded oil-rich Kuwait, and American troops intervened, pushing Iraq's army back across the Kuwait border. This first Gulf War was seen as major victory for President George Bush, but as he and his son George W. Bush would find out, this was not the last conflict the United States would have in the Middle East.

Though the Cold War was over and America was riding high after victory in the Gulf, Bush's efforts at reelection were disappointed by Bill Clinton (and a recession economy) in 1992. The election of the youthful Clinton and his running mate Al Gore seemed to bring a fresh, new spirit to government. Though Clinton had many policy setbacks (losing a battle to reform America's health care system, most notably), the econ-omy boomed during his presidency, and he was easily reelected in 1996. Clinton's presidency, however, was marred by one of the most public scandals since Watergate. Clinton was accused of, and finally admitted to, having a sexual affair with a White House intern and lying to Congress about it under oath. Though Congress impeached him, Clinton (the self-proclaimed "comeback kid") stayed in office, and his approval ratings grew as the economy continued to surge.

The economy was driven by the explosion of the high-tech industry. Computer sales soared as more people used the Internet to communicate, shop, date, and do research. In the late 1990s businesses rushed to tap into the awesome power they believed the Internet held. "Dot coms" seemed to come and go with each passing day, some making tens of millions of dollars as their stock prices sky-rocketed. Wall Street professionals seemed to care less about a company's profits than about how well it appeared to take advantage of new technologies. High-tech innovators like Bill Gates (co-founder of Microsoft)

and Steve Case (co-founder of America Online) achieved rock star status, and many investing novices became serious day traders, seeking the quick bucks the market yielded every day. Finally, when cooler heads began to outnumber irrational ones, the market dropped nearly as quickly as it had risen.

One of the most contentious segments of the Internet economy was in the music industry. In 1999, twenty-year-old Shawn Fanning created Napster, a file-sharing service that allowed users to exchange music, free of charge, over the Internet. Napster made music available to all, but cut record labels and artists out of the process. The Record Industry Association of America (RIAA), which represents five major record labels and a host of smaller labels, didn't like seeing Napster cut their profits, and they sued. Napster was forced to shut down (though it was eventually reborn as a legal downloadable music company). As Napster proved, many Internet users felt that anything on the Web should be free—including artistic material. The music industry continues to struggle with issues of ownership to this day.

Though the American military dominated and the economy boomed in the 1990s, all was not well at home. In 1992, four white police officers in Los Angeles stopped a speeding Rodney King and beat him senseless before arresting him. This was surely not the first instance of white police officers' brutality toward an African American but it was the first to be caught on videotape and broadcast around the country. The public outcry to punish the officers became public rage when they were acquitted on

Shawn Fanning (with guitar) and Sean Parker founded Napster.com, the first important Web site to make downloading of music files possible. Napster became so popular in the late 1990s that the major record companies believed the site was hurting sales of new CDs. Lawsuits were brought against Napster, as teens and college students across the country debated the ethics of file sharing. Napster was eventually converted to a law-abiding music-downloading service, but the genie was out of the bottle, and the practice of illegal file sharing remains widespread.

After the acquittal of the four police officers who beat Rodney King, several parts of Los Angeles exploded in riots. For many, the King case confirmed the racism of white America, especially the police. This building's graffiti recalls N.W.A.'s (Niggaz with Attitude) song "Fuck tha Police." In light of the King beating and the ensuing destruction (in 1992), the song, recorded in 1988, seemed prophetic.

nearly all charges. To many, this confirmed the racism of white America and of the Los Angeles Police Department. When the verdict was issued, riots ensued, and several neighborhoods in Los Angeles were destroyed.

Suburbia also saw its share of tragedy. In 1999 two students at Columbine High School in Colorado brought guns to school and opened fire, killing thirteen of their classmates and teachers before killing them- selves. Though no one will ever know the true intentions of the perpetrators, many speculated that the boys saw themselves as social outcasts who were often harassed by the more "popular" students. Some parents blamed "grunge" and heavy metal music, gothic clothing, video games, and violent television and movies. What was clear to

everyone, however, was that young people, for whatever rea- son, were angry at the establish- ment to the point of violence, and that guns in schools were a serious and widespread prob- lem. All of this—and much of the decade's news events—was captured by twenty-four-hour cable news channels, led by CNN. The worlds of violence, entertainment, and cable news came together most noisily in the high-profile trial of football- star-turned-actor O. J. Simpson. Simpson was accused (and eventually acquitted) of the mur- der of his ex-wife and her friend. The country followed every moment of the proceedings on television: from the car chase, through the trial, to the verdict.

Movies in the 1990s tapped into America's high-tech and (perceived) violent culture. One

of the most popular movies of the decade was Quentin Tarantino's *Pulp Fiction* (1994), which featured John Travolta and Samuel L. Jackson as thugs who would rather kill than see their boss's valuables stolen. Another innovative film was *The Blair Witch Project* (1999), which was marketed as actual footage recovered from three student filmmakers who disappeared into the Maryland woods. The seemingly amateur camera work and true story made *Blair Witch* one of the scariest films of the decade. To promote the myth surrounding the movie, *Blair Witch* used the Internet to form an underground community, spurring the movie's popularity and making Web sites standard movie advertising tools. Main- stream films also combined fic- tion and reality. *Jurassic Park*

(1993), *Forrest Gump* (1994), and *Titanic* (1997) topped the decade's list of box-office smashes, each exploiting the quickly developing digital technology to produce stunning special effects.

Television also blurred the line between fiction and reality in the 1990s. In 1992 MTV launched *The Real World*, which took young people from diverse backgrounds and made them live together, with cameras following their every move. As MTV expected, the cast fought over many issues, from roommate dating to racism. CBS's hit "reality" show, *Survivor* (2000), placed strangers on a tropical island where they fought, backstabbed, and negotiated while competing for a $1 million prize. Though viewers of *The Real World*, *Survivor*, and their imitators felt like voyeurs in these strangers' lives, others felt that "reality" TV was as contrived as any soap opera.

Though the millennium came and went without the technological breakdowns many predicted, America was soon shocked out of its comfort zone. On the morning of September 11, 2001, two planes struck the World Trade Center in New York, one struck the Pentagon in Washington, D.C., and another went down in a field in Pennsylvania; in all, over 3,000 people were killed. It quickly came to light that these planes had been hijacked by members of the Al-Qaeda terrorist network, headed by Osama bin Laden. In response, President George W. Bush sent American troops to Afghanistan, which he considered a terrorist breeding ground, and eventually to Iraq, where he believed President Saddam Hussein was hiding weapons of mass destruction.

After the events of September 11, many Americans no longer felt the total confidence that comes with being the world's economic and military superpower. Power, they now knew, had its price and the future seemed more uncertain than ever. Would America continue to try to rid the world of those it saw as dangerous, or would the country reach out, attempting to bring order to the chaos and unpredictability of the contemporary world?

Dylan Klebold (right) and Eric Harris with their weapons in the Columbine High School cafeteria, April 20, 1999. Klebold and Harris killed twelve students and one teacher before killing themselves. The Columbine shooting brought public attention to the violence that many believed had infiltrated American youth culture.

511

Though some say that popular music in the 1990s and beyond was dominated by overly commercial boy bands and teen idols, record sales indicate otherwise. Alanis Morissette's album Jagged Little Pill (1995) was the number three best-selling album of the 1990s (Shania Twain and Whitney Houston held the top two spots). Decidedly not writing commercial pop, Morissette drew on the personal, intimate musical legacy of female singer-songwriters like Carole King and Joni Mitchell, placing the music in a 1990s context (as did Ani DiFranco, Tori Amos, Liz Phair, and others). Morissette's music is rough and in-your-face, and proved to the world (again, like Aretha Franklin, Janis Joplin, and many others) that a strong woman could be successful commercially.

Conclusion

We have now reached a point in our survey when it becomes increasingly difficult to gain a reliable historical perspective on the development of rock music. Historians usually need at least twenty years to pass before an era settles into the culture enough for them to determine what the really important elements are—or at least to begin the critical and scholarly debate on this topic. In this chapter, then, we will survey a variety of styles that made their mark in the 1990s, but we will keep our eye on how these styles fit with some of the themes we have been following throughout the book. Rather than provide a comprehensive survey of the decade, this chapter will consider relatively recent rock music through the lens provided by the history of the style itself. The focus will be the ways the events and performers in the 1990s extend, repeat, of react against musical styles or other elements that are part of rock's past. And one of the first things that characterizes the rock music (and its business) in the 1990s is its relationship to its own past; many things seem to come back, sometimes in a very clear way—dance music, teen idols, singer-songwriters, roots rock, rhythm and blues—while others extend and blend recent styles and practices—rap, metal, and indie rock. Technology and the commercial maneuvering of record companies, cable television, and radio stations figure into the picture as well. In fact, one of the most obvious ways rock's history played a role in the 1990s was through a reconstruction of that past via the idea of "classic rock," and so we'll begin our survey there.

The Rise of Classic Rock

The Age of the CD Re-Issue: Selling the Same Music Again.   Most college-age students today who are fans of rock music from the 1960s and 1970s were born years after this music was first popular. In many ways, this is the music of their parents'—or even their grandparents'—generation. Considering the role that rock music has often played in establishing a generation's sense of identity, an important exception in the history of the style is that teens in the second half of the 1990s began listening in large numbers to decades-old rock music, in some cases even preferring this music to newer and more current rock. Many of these fans of what has come to be called "classic rock" were first exposed to this music through their parents (or their parents' record collections), but many also encountered classic rock on the radio, on cable television, and in CD stores. In fact, by the end of the 1990s, more music from the 1960s and '70s was available for rock fans than there had been back when this music first made its mark. How did this happen?

One factor in the return of older rock was the change in format from records to compact discs that began in the 1980s. The compact disc was first introduced to the world by Sony and Philips back in 1980, though research and development of CDs had been under way for over ten years by then. By the mid 1980s, record companies were able to offer a small number of albums in this new format and by 1990, CDs had become commonplace, with almost one-third of all American households using them in one form or another. From a music lover's point of view, the CD constituted a major advance. Compact discs are much more portable than records, and unlike tapes, you can go directly to the song you want to hear without having to fuss with the rewind or fast-forward buttons. And while each use of a record or tape wears it down a little bit, CDs are supposed to last forever, with no appreciable degradation in audio fidelity no matter how many times you play them. Add this to the claims by some top audio experts that the digital sound of CDs is far superior to the analog sound of records or tapes—a claim that was hotly debated at the time—and CDs seemed to be the perfect format. Compact discs caught on with consumers: by the end of the 1980s, CDs had begun to dig into the music-store shelf space formerly occupied by records, and by the middle of the '90s, CDs had taken over and new vinyl records became hard to find.

For the record companies in the second half of the 1980s, the changeover to compact discs was just the financial shot in the arm the sagging business needed. Although production of CDs was limited by a small number of available pressing plants in the first few years, once new plants were online the companies could manufacture CDs in large enough volume to make them cheap to produce. The price of CDs, however, stayed higher than it had been with vinyl even when production costs came down, and these extra profits went right into record-company coffers. And since the CD had a reputation for superior audio quality, these companies learned very quickly that middle-class baby boomers—now entering middle age and with plenty of disposable income—would buy the same rock music they had grown up with all over again. Older rock albums had long ago covered their initial costs of production, so re-releasing them produced easy money for the big companies. The age of the CD re-issue thus went into full swing, often with advertised features such as "digital remastering" and "bonus tracks" added to tempt the aging rockers and further sweeten the deal. Companies began to put together multi-CD boxed sets for the most serious-minded and dedicated fans, often with extensive and detailed liner notes, previously unreleased tracks or mixes, and endorsements from the original artists themselves.

Radio Killed the Video Star: The Classic-Rock Radio Format. About the same time record companies were beginning the compact disc switchover, Detroit radio consultant Fred Jacobs began trying to convince the FM radio world that baby boomers would tune in to stations playing nothing but the biggest rock hits from 1966–78. Since the rapid-growth years of the mid 1970s, radio stations had relied increasingly on outside consultants to program their playlists. Lee Abrams, for instance, is widely credited (or blamed) for developing the stricter album-oriented-rock format that characterized rock radio in the late '70s. Like most consultants, Abrams sold his format to stations all across the country as a pre-packaged product—a tried-and-tested recipe for radio ratings success. Jacobs was trying to do the same thing when he came up with his classic-rock format, but he couldn't get anyone to try it. In 1985, however, the first classic-rock station went on the air in Lansing, Michigan, and soon began to dominate its market. As word spread of this early success, the format began to catch on around the country. By 1990, classic rock had become one of the most successful formats in radio and went on to lead the business throughout the rest of the decade, sometimes with multiple stations in a single market competing against one another. Classic-rock radio succeeded commercially primarily because it was able to draw in the segment of twenty-five- to thirty-year-old males demographic, and deliver to advertisers a group of listeners who had the money to purchase their goods and services; as this group aged in the 1990s, they stuck with classic rock. Programmers tried to tweak the format along the way, adding songs from the era that were less well known ("deep tracks") or recently released tracks ("fresh tracks") by the original '60s and '70s bands. But these innovations seemed to reduce rather than increase the ratings numbers, and stations returned to the more conservative list of tried-and-true classic hits (though often still bragging about having a large library of tracks). The format was popular with record companies initially, since it seemed to support their re-release of older rock. When classic rock continued to dominate in most markets and the playlists showed little change, however, the record labels began to see classic rock as squeezing out their new artists and releases. Classic rock, it seemed, was a tough playlist to crack.

Behind the Music: The Rise of VH-1 and Rockumentary.   For the first few years of its existence, MTV was the only cable channel specializing in music videos. The MTV audience was young, however, and in 1985 VH-1 debuted, targeting the older demographic—baby boomers who would soon be buying the CD re-issues and tuning in to classic-rock radio. VH-1 did not succeed as quickly as CDs and classic-rock radio did with the boomers, however, and the cable channel struggled for over a decade until hitting on the idea of *Pop-Up Video* in 1996. These videos with little onscreen factoids about the music and bands—sometimes very clever and humorous—drew many viewers who might not have had the patience for music videos otherwise (some even found the factoids more fun and entertaining than the music). VH-1 then developed two new quasi-historical series in 1997, *Behind the Music* and *Legends*. Both of these series focused on famous rock musicians and their careers, following a predictable rags-to-riches template (with disaster sprinkled in along the way) and placing far more emphasis on the sensational aspects of their subjects' personal lives than on their musical or stylistic development. Despite this, VH-1 gave

The 1990s showed the incredible musical and commercial staying power of rock's classic groups. The Rock and Roll Hall of Fame, though established in 1986, opened a stunning new museum in Cleveland in 1995 (pictured here). The success and popularity of the Rock Hall—in addition to sold out concerts by the Rolling Stones, the Eagles, and the Who among many others—shows that the music continues to find new listeners.

viewers the sense that they were learning about rock's history, and in this way it provided a video angle to complement CD re-issues and classic-rock radio. Less than two years before VH-1 developed *Behind the Music* and *Legends*, the *Beatles Anthology* video documentary aired for the first time on ABC; it created enormous excitement because it featured two new tracks that Paul, George, and Ringo had recorded from unfinished John Lennon sessions. "Free as a Bird" went to number six on the American charts in late 1995 (uk2), and "Real Love" hit the number eleven spot early in the new year (uk4). At the same time—the fall of 1995—the ten-episode Time-Life series *A History of Rock and Roll*, debuted, as did the ten-episode PBS series, *The History of Rock 'n' Roll*. Produced by Quincy Jones, the PBS series was sponsored in part by the Rock and Roll Hall of Fame and Museum, which had opened in Cleveland, Ohio, that September. By the end of the 1990s, rock's history was playing an important role in rock culture: there was big money in old music.

You're Never Too Old to Rock and Roll. While the classic-rock stations celebrated rock's past, many of the bands and artists they featured continued to enjoy great success in the '90s. Powered by the release of their multi-episode rockumentary, the Beatles once again hit the top slots on the album charts; *Anthology 1* (p1 uk2, 1995), *Anthology 2* (p2 uk1, 1996), and *Anthology 3* (p1 uk4, 1996), each a two-disc collection of rare tracks and alternate takes, returned the fab four to the charts again. Paul McCartney followed with a solo album of new material, *Flaming Pie*, which went to number two in 1997 (uk2). The Beatles' British-invasion compatriots, the Rolling Stones, also had big albums in the 1990s with *Voodoo Lounge* (p2 uk1, 1994) and *Bridges to Babylon* (p3 uk6, 1997), and ex-Yardbird and Cream guitarist Eric Clapton released one of the decade's biggest selling albums, *Unplugged* (p1 uk2, 1992), drawn from his performance on the MTV show of the same name. The album featured the tender ballad "Tears in Heaven" (p2 uk5), written for his young son, who had been killed in a freak accident. Among 1970s rockers to storm the charts, the reunited Eagles hit the top spot in 1994 with *Hell Freezes Over* (uk28), Peter Gabriel steamed back with *Us* (p2 uk2, 1992), and Santana hit later in the decade with *Supernatural* (p1 uk1, 1999), featuring the hit single "Smooth" (p1), sung by Rob Thomas of Matchbox 20. Stars from the 1980s also scored big, with Sting's *Ten Summoner's Tales* (p2 uk2, 1993) and *Mercury Falling* (p5 uk4, 1996), Tom Petty's Rick Rubin–produced *Wildflowers* (p8 uk36, 1994), and Bruce Springsteen's *Greatest Hits* (pi uk1, 1995)—all extending these artists' career success into the new decade. Perhaps most impressively, U2 hit the top spot on both sides of the Atlantic with *Zooropa* (1993) and *Pop* (1997), establishing themselves among rock's most enduring acts. The success of these older groups reinforced the idea that rock had an important past and that it was a musical tradition that now had senior figures to act as standard-bearers. Many other bands and artists that had been famous in the '60s and '70s, for instance, regrouped and toured the big outdoor theaters during the summer months. While the classic-rock stations would play only the hits in most cases, live shows provided vintage bands an opportunity to play their old album tracks and even throw in few numbers from a recent album. Bands such as Chicago, Yes, Foreigner, Styx, Peter Frampton, Kansas, and others never returned to the charts with the same force as in earlier years, but they were once again capable of filling large venues, especially if they shared the bill with another vintage act or two. Like jazz, blues, or country, it was now possible to grow old in rock and roll—as an artist or as a fan.

New Traditionalism Continues

Roots Rockers and Generation X. Baby boomers were not the only ones affected by the return of vintage rock to the airwaves, CD stores, and live-music venues. A younger generation was also embracing rock traditionalism, and even if some of the old rockers were still on scene, a new breed of younger roots rockers began to emerge. As discussed in Chapter 11 and Chapter 12, the late 1980s were dominated by slick videogenic MTV acts, rappers, and hair metal bands. The alternative rockers led by Nirvana reacted against what they took to be the puffed-up professionalism of the music business by embracing a return-to-simplicity approach reminiscent of late 1970s punk. Nirvana, Pearl Jam, and Smashing Pumpkins all embraced the sound of the '60s

Eric Clapton (shown here in a 1993 concert) proved that artists from rock's past could forge successful careers decades later. His album Unplugged *(1992), with the somber hit "Tears in Heaven," was one of the 1990s' biggest. Clapton's success in the decade was matched by other rock classics, like Santana and Paul McCartney.*

garage bands, but their music was harsher—the guitars more drenched in heavy distortion, the drums played more aggressively, the lyrics at times more ironic or alienated. The new roots rockers who began to emerge about the same time as the alternative bands were in many ways more faithful to the tradition than the alternative rockers. The guitar sounds were cleaner, sometimes emphasizing folk-rock influences by using strummed acoustic guitar and the jingle-jangle of the electric twelve string. The songs were driven by a strong pop sensibility that mostly lacked the anger or rebellion of alt rock, replacing punk attitude with a catchy vocal hook.

Sheryl Crow, Hootie and the Blowfish.   Sheryl Crow's music wears its traditional stylistic influences proudly; her vocal style owes much to Roger McGuinn and Tom Petty, often set to a 1970s-type country-rock accompaniment with a touch of 1960s jingle-jangle. Based out of Los Angeles, Crow worked as a professional backing vocalist in the 1980s, appearing on a string of records and touring with Michael Jackson and Don Henley. Her 1993 album *Tuesday Night Music Club* (p3) contained the hits "All I Wanna Do" (p2 uk5) and "Strong Enough" (p5 uk33), and eventually ranked among the best sellers of the decade. Her subsequent releases included *Sheryl Crow* (p6 uk5, 1996), which contains the infectious "If It Makes You Happy" (p10 uk9), and *The Globe Sessions* (p5 uk2, 1998). Based out of the university town of Columbia, South Carolina, Hootie and the Blowfish projected a good-time, roots-rock style that featured Darius Rucker's soulful vocals (with occasional gospel influences) accompanied by happy, strummed acoustic guitar along with drums, bass, and '70s-oriented electric guitar. The band's breakthrough album, *Cracked Rear View* (p1 uk12, 1994), contained the hits "Hold My Hand" (p10), "Let Her Cry" (p9), and "Only Wanna Be With You" (p6) and made the band's music a staple of mainstream rock radio in the mid 1990s. The group followed up with *Fairweather Johnson* (p1 uk9, 1996) and *Musical Chairs* (p4 uk15, 1998).

Sheryl Crow performing live at a Lilith Fair concert in Pasadena, California, July 1999. Crow's Tuesday Night Music Club *(1993) was one of the best-selling albums of the decade. The Lilith Fair festival concerts, organized by Sarah McLachlan among others, was dedicated to showcasing female musicians—mainly from the folk and rock traditions, but eventually expanding to include other styles.*

Counting Crows, the Wallflowers.   Coming out of the San Francisco area and led by songwriter and lead vocalist Adam Duritz, Counting Crows emerged about the same time as Hootie and Sheryl Crow were making their first marks. The 1993 album *August & Everything After* established the band, going to number four (uk16) and containing the hit singles "Mr. Jones" (p2 uk28) and "Round Here" (p7), the first of which makes a couple of direct references to Bob Dylan in the lyrics. *Recovering the Satellites* topped the charts in 1996 (uk4) and also contained two hit singles, "Angels of Silences" (p3) and "A Long December" (p5). The band's music-stylistic debts to earlier artists can be heard especially in Duritz's vocal style, which sounds at times like Van Morrison and at other times like Bob Seger or Tom Petty. The band's arrangements also employ vintage piano and organ sounds, and '70s-style guitar distortion. Similarly, the Los Angeles–based Wallflowers use '70s-style guitar and keyboard sounds, adding some George Harrison–type slide lead guitar from time to time. The band's music seems particularly influenced by Tom Petty and Bob Dylan, the second of these being completely understandable considering the lead-singer and songwriter is Jakob Dylan, son of the iconic songwriter. The band splashed on the rock scene with *Bringing Down the Horse* (p4, 1996), which had the hits "One Headlight" (p1), "6th Avenue Heartache" (p10), and "The Difference" (p3). Despite the press's desire to focus on Jakob's family ties, the younger Dylan avoided exploiting his dad's fame as much as he could. Still, the band's traditional rock sound would likely have led to comparisons even if there had been no blood relation.

The Return of Jamming: Phish, Widespread Panic, Blues Traveler, Spin Doctors, the Dave Matthews Band.

By the end of the 1990s, the "jam band scene" had become an important underground culture across the country, with a network of clubs (often in college towns), a collection of indie record labels, and a considerable number of dedicated fans supporting the music. The jam band phenomenon arose out of the same return to rock roots that inspired Sheryl Crow and Counting Crows, but in this case the bands revived the idea that live performances were the central focus of the music, and that highly developed playing skill—especially in improvisation—was an important element. While jam bands do albums, you really had to see them live (or hear a live recording) to fully understand how a track could spread out through improvisation or head off in any number of directions stylistically.

The '70s heroes of the '90s jam bands were primarily the Grateful Dead and the Allman Brothers Band, both legendary for their sprawling live shows. Formed in Vermont, Phish were most often thought of as the new Grateful Dead, and though they recorded many studio albums, their 1995 live album *A Live One* (p18) gives the best idea of how the band sounded at shows. Based out of Athens, Georgia, Widespread Panic were considered the new Allman Brothers, and their music is more blues-oriented than Phish's, which seemed more infused with a jug-band sensibility at times. Both bands draw from jazz, country, rhythm and blues, and even classical in their musical excursions. *'Til the Medicine Takes* (p68, 1999) is a representative example of Widespread Panic's studio work. Hailing from the New York area, both Blues Traveler and the Spin Doctors made their reputations on their live shows, though Spin Doctors became one of the few jam-oriented groups to enjoy a hit album when

John Popper (left) lead singer, guitarist, and harmonica player for Blues Traveler. Blues Traveler, like Widespread Panic and Phish, was labeled a "jam band." Like the Allman Brothers and Grateful Dead before them, these bands feature long, improvised solos, often making their live performances the best of these groups' productions.

Pocketful of Kryptonite hit number three in 1991 (uk2). Emerging from Virginia and building their reputation through incessant touring, the Dave Matthews Band merged the happy acoustic guitar strumming of Hootie and the Blowfish with the instrumental prowess of Phish and Widespread Panic to come up with a chart-topping approach to roots rock. The band hit first with *Under the Table and Dreaming* (p11 1994) and *Crash* (p2, 1996), but *Before These Crowded Streets* (p1,

---

LISTENING GUIDE

GET MUSIC ▶▶ wwnorton.com/rockhistory

Sheryl Crow, "All I Wanna Do"

Words and music by Wyn Cooper, Sheryl Crow, Bill Bottrell, David Baerwald, and Kevin Gilbert, produced by Bill Bottrell. Single rose to #2 in the United States (#5 in the UK) in 1994; from the album *Tuesday Night Music Club*, which rose to #3 in the United States.

FORM: Simple verse-chorus, with pre-chorus. The verse and chorus are built on the same 3-chord, 4-bar chord progression, though the chorus diverges from that progression in the last 2 bars each time. The verses lead into a pre-chorus section, which drives the song forward to the chorus. This pre-chorus material is first heard as the introduction to the song. After the first time through the chorus, an instrumental interlude leads to the second verse; after the second chorus, that interlude—which is based on the song's 3-chord progression—is stretched to 8 bars, as a low guitar line that was first introduced during the verse sections comes to the fore, creating a section that might be considered an instrumental verse, especially since that section leads right into the pre-chorus and forward to the final chorus. The last chorus repeats the final four bars—a "tag"—before heading into the ending, which is a 13-bar section that could be heard as an instrumental version of the chorus (note the ending) with an extra bar added for the last chord.

TIME SIGNATURE: 4/4 throughout. Note how the percussion and hand claps work with the drums to create a variety of rhythmic feels that help distinguish the song's different sections.

INSTRUMENTATION: Electric guitar, slide guitar, acoustic guitar, electric piano, synthesizer strings, bass, drums, percussion, hand claps, lead and backing vocals.

0:00–0:14	**Introduction**, 6 mm.	This music becomes the pre-chorus later in the song, as Crow speaks over rhythmic and jazzy guitar, synthesizer strings, and hand claps. "This ain't no disco . . ."
0:14–0:54	**Verse 1**, 20 mm.	Full band kicks in, as slide guitar weaves in and out of the solo vocal, as a low guitar

1998) revealed in a studio recording the band's sense of stylistic adventure, which was already well known to those who had seen them live.

Matchbox 20, Third Eye Blind. By the second half of the 1990s, the poppier aspects of guitar-driven roots rock were beginning to merge with the harder driving and edgier sounds of alt rock, which had begun to become more

		melody enters toward the middle. "All I wanna do . . ."
0:54–1:06	**Pre-Chorus**, 6 mm.	Synthesizer strings return with intro music, now without jazzy guitar but with full band. "They drive their shiny . . ."
1:06–1:38	**Chorus**, 16 mm.	Harmony vocal and acoustic guitar enter, as slide guitar comes back for 12-bar chorus, which is followed by a 4-bar instrumental interlude. "All I wanna do . . ."
1:38–2:02	**Verse 2**, 12 mm.	As in verse 1, though shorter this time. Note Crow's conversational delivery of the lyrics, which don't rhyme and enhance the sense of a story told in free prose. "I like a good . . ."
2:02–2:14	**Pre-Chorus**, 6 mm.	Synthesizer strings return as before, "And a happy couple . . ."
2:14–2:54	**Chorus**, 12 + 8 mm.	Harmony vocal and acoustic guitar enter as before, but this time the instrumental interlude stretches to 8 bars, focusing on a guitar melody first introduced in the verses but that now functions almost as an instrumental verse. "All I wanna . . ."
2:54–3:10	**Pre-Chorus**, 8 mm.	As before, but a little more rhythmically active. "Otherwise the bar is ours . . ."
3:10–3:58	**Chorus**, 20 + 4 mm.	Harmony vocal and acoustic guitar return, as before, but this time the chorus is stretched to 20 bars and is followed by a 4-bar tag. "All I wanna do . . ."
3:58–4:32	**Coda**, 13 mm.	This ending is a 12-bar chorus, played instrumentally, with some of the instruments dropping out in the last couple of measures.

mainstream as the decade wore on. Florida's Matchbox 20 found a blend that combined the elemental energy of punk with a Beatle-esque sensibility, creating a model for much of the modern guitar pop that followed in the late '90s. The band's debut album, *You or Someone Like You*, was released in 1996 and rose to only number five on the charts (uk50), but sold steadily for years after its release, making it one of the best-selling albums of the 1990s. Several of its tracks became staples of rock-radio playlists, including "3 A.M.," "Push," "Back 2 Good" (p24), and "Real World" (p38). Led by singer Rob Thomas (who sang on Santana's 1999 hit "Smooth"), the band followed up with *Mad Season* (p3 uk31, 2000). San Francisco–based Third Eye Blind enjoyed success with a similar sound in 1997 with the singles "How It's Going to Be" (p9) and "Semi-Charmed Life" (p4 uk33) from the album, *Third Eye Blind* (p25). By the end of the decade, this strain of guitar-driven pop existed comfortably with the punkier music of Green Day and the Beatles-influenced material of Oasis (discussed in Chapter 12).

Rhythm and Blues and Black Pop

The Return of Classic Motown: Boyz II Men. While old rockers kept the vintage sounds of earlier decades alive and a new cast of young rockers returned to these traditional approaches, a fresh sense of traditionalism was also assuming a more central place in rhythm and blues. The most commercially successful of the many rhythm and blues artists and groups to return to earlier styles was the Philadelphia-based vocal quartet, Boyz II Men. The band signed to Motown at the beginning of the decade and reinvigorated a label that had struggled during the 1980s. Like the Drifters or the Temptations before them, Boyz II Men's music featured highly crafted and nuanced harmony-vocal arrangements, putting the focus on the rich blending of their voices, as well as on solo passages by the band's members. The band depended on others for songwriting, accompaniment, and production, returning to the Brill Building model that was standard in the early 1960s. The group's more immediate influences included New Edition and New Kids on the Block, two Boston-based vocal groups developed by songwriter-producer Maurice Starr. Both of Starr's groups enjoyed considerable chart success in the late 1980s, especially among teenage girls, and New Edition's Michael Bivens was instrumental in getting the Philadelphia band signed to Motown. The debut Boyz II Men album, *Cooleyhighharmony* (p3 r1, 1991), contained three crossover hit singles, "Uhh Ahh" (p16 r1), "It's So Hard to Say Goodbye to Yesterday" (p2 r1), and "Motownphilly" (p3 r4). The group topped both charts for the first time with "End of the Road" (1992), a song recorded especially for the movie *Boomerang* (starring Eddie Murphy) and the first to match the vocal quartet with the songwriter and producer Kenneth "Babyface" Edmunds. Boyz II Men followed up in 1994 with their second album, *II*, which hit the number one spot on both charts with the help of the hit singles "I'll Make Love to You" (written and produced by Babyface; p1 r1), "Water Runs Dry" (p2 r4), and "On Bended Knee" (p1 r2). Boys II Men's tremendous success with a traditional vocal-harmony approach made them a

Boyz II Men in concert, 1995. Like the Temptations or the Drifters before them, Boyz II Men featured highly choreographed stage shows and a polished, richly harmonized vocal style. Their album Cooleyhighharmony (1991) was a crossover hit and helped revitalize Motown Records, which had struggled in the 1980s.

model—along with the New Edition and New Kids on the Block—for many groups to follow in the second half of the decade, especially the Backstreet Boys and *NSYNC.

Babyface, L.A. Reid, and LaFace.   Among the most influential musicians and businessmen in 1990s rhythm and blues was Kenneth Edmunds. Edmunds had played in funk bands in the late 1970s and early '80s, including a stint with Bootsy Collins's band (Bootsy reportedly came up with the nickname "Babyface"). Edmunds then partnered with Antonio "L.A." Reid in the 1980s, first to form a new funk band called the Deele, and also to write songs for other artists, much as Leiber and Stoller had decades earlier. Babyface enjoyed considerable success not only as a songwriter and producer but also as a performing artist in his own right, especially in the rhythm and blues market. His hit 1989 album *Tender Lover* (p14 r1), for instance, contained the hits "It's No Crime" (p7 r1), "Tender Lover" (p14 r1), "Whip Appeal" (p6 r2), and "My Kinda Girl" (p30 r3). With Reid, Babyface formed the label LaFace, and like other songwriting-production teams before them, they wrote and produced hits for other artists. Singer Toni Braxton is only one of LaFace's success stories. After Braxton signed with the label, she charted in a duet with Babyface, "Give You My Heart" (p29 r2, 1992), while her solo performance of "Love Shoulda Brought You Home" (p33 r2, 1992) appeared on the soundtrack album for *Boomerang*. Her self-titled 1993 album went to number one on both the pop and rhythm and blues charts, and contained six hit singles, including "You Mean the World to Me" (p7 r3), while 1996's *Secrets* (p2 r1) featured the number one crossover hit "You're Making Me High." LaFace also enjoyed success with several other groups, including TLC. While Babyface and Reid did not write and produce all the songs on LaFace releases, their tunes often turned out to be the hit singles. In addition to his solo success and his hits with LaFace, Babyface also worked with some of the decade's highest-profile artists, including Eric Clapton, Celine Dion, Whitney Houston, and Mariah Carey.

LISTENING GUIDE

GET MUSIC ▶▶ wwnorton.com/rockhistory

Boyz II Men, "End of the Road"

Words and music by L.A. Reid, Babyface, and Daryl Simmons, produced by Babyface. Single rose to #1 on both the U.S. pop and rhythm and blues charts in 1992; from the soundtrack album to the 1992 film *Boomerang*.

FORM: Simple verse-chorus, with pre-chorus. The verse and chorus sections are based on the same 8-bar chord progression, as is the introduction. The pre-chorus section introduces contrasting material and drives toward the chorus each time. As in Sheryl Crow's "All I Want to Do" and Michael Jackson's "Billie Jean" (Chapter 11), the pre-chorus acts as a bridge section that links the verse with the chorus. Because these songs do not have choruses built on contrasting material, the pre-chorus offers the only strong structural contrast, not only driving toward the chorus but also helping to make the return of the same material seem fresh. Each verse features a solo voice, which shifts to a different singer in the pre-chorus, while harmony vocals characterize the chorus sections. The song begins with a voice speaking over the background music, and the voiceover returns in the third verse. This last verse is the most complicated vocally, featuring 8 bars spoken, with a solo voice entering in the next 8 bars as the speaking continues and choral vocals, speaking, and solo vocals present in the pre-chorus. The song ends with four times through the chorus, the last two eventually breaking down to nothing but vocals and hand claps.

TIME SIGNATURE: 6/8 throughout. Note the strong accent on beat 4 during the chorus sections, which arrive just a little late and have the effect of creating a strong groove that helps distinguish the chorus from the verse sections.

INSTRUMENTATION: Electric guitar, electric piano, bass, drums, synthesizer strings, French horn, hand claps, solo and backup vocals.

0:00–0:20	**Introduction**, 8 mm.	The song's 8-bar chord progression is introduced here, with voice-over. "Girl, you know . . ."
0:20–0:59	**Verse 1**, 16 mm.	Twice through the 8-bar progression, with solo lead vocal featured throughout. Note the Motown-style guitar melody in the background. "We belong together . . ."

Crossover Divas: Whitney Houston and Mariah Carey. Going back to Bing Crosby and Frank Sinatra, the song stylist has played an important role in American popular music. With the Beatles and Dylan, rock music began its celebration of the singer as songwriter, and this model has dominated most rock

0:59–1:18	**Pre-Chorus**, 8 mm.	Contrasting material with new voice singing solo vocal, as French horn enters. "When I can't sleep . . ."
1:18–1:56	**Chorus**, 16 mm.	Twice through the 8-bar progression, with a new melody sung by harmony vocals with hand claps emphasizing beat 4 of each measure. "Although we've come . . ."
1:56–2:36	**Verse 2**, 16 mm.	As before, note the virtuosic vocal technique, with many melodic twists and turns (melismas). Horn sound enters on second 8 bars this time. "Girl, I know you really . . ."
2:36–2:55	**Pre-Chorus**, 8 mm.	New lead vocal enters, now fuller than before and supported by synth strings along with horn sound. "Will you love me . . ."
2:55–3:34	**Chorus**, 16 mm.	As before, but now with lead vocal improvising over the backup vocals, adding a sense of urgency and intensity. "Although we've come . . ."
3:34–4:12	**Verse 3**, 16 mm.	First 8 bars are spoken, as the second 8 bars add a solo vocal part behind the voiceover. "Girl, I'm there for you . . ."
4:12–4:31	**Pre-Chorus**, 8 mm.	Voiceover continues, now with new back-up harmony vocals, then the urgent solo vocal reenters. "Lonely . . ."
4:31–5:48	**Chorus**, 32 mm.	Four times through the 8-bar progression, with the first two times through the 8-bar progression as before in the second chorus, but with the accompanying instruments dropping out toward the end of the third time and the fourth time performed with only vocals and hand claps. "Although we've come . . ."

styles in the time since. But rhythm and blues did not entirely abandon the idea of the singer who performs songs written by professional songwriters, as the Motown and Philadelphia International approaches of the 1970s demonstrate. Emerging in the mid 1980s, Whitney Houston became one of the most important song stylists in popular music, employing a traditional approach and following in the footsteps of female singers like Diana Ross and Aretha Franklin. Houston starred in several successful feature films in addition to enjoying a string of top crossover singles, including "Saving All My Love for You" (p1 r1, 1985), "Didn't We Almost Have It All" (p1 r2, 1987), "All the Man That I Need" (p1 r1, 1990), the Dolly Parton–penned "I Will Always Love You" (p1 r1, 1992), and "Exhale (Shoop Shoop)" (p1 r1, 1995), written and produced by Babyface and featured in the film *Waiting to Exhale*. Babyface had also written Houston's hit "I'm Your Baby Tonight" (p1 r1, 1990). In addition to the overwhelming success of her singles, which have saturated adult contemporary FM radio ever since, Houston's albums also topped the charts, with four hitting the number one slot, including the soundtrack to *The Bodyguard* (1992), which is the second best selling album of the decade at almost twenty million copies.

Whitney Houston, seen here in concert in 1992, was one of the most successful singers of the 1990s. Working with top-notch professional songwriters like Kenneth "Babyface" Edmunds, she produced many hit singles and best-selling albums. Her soundtrack to the movie The Bodyguard (1992), featuring her version of Dolly Parton's "I Will Always Love You," was the second best selling album of the decade, with over 20 million copies sold.

If anybody could give Whitney Houston a run for her money in the 1990s, it was Mariah Carey. Carey's first number one single, "Vision of Love" (1990), was followed by a series of hits, including "Love Takes Time" (p1 r1, 1990), "Emotions" (p1 r1, 1991), "Hero" (p1 r5, 1993), "Fantasy" (p1 r1, 1995), "One Sweet Day" with Boyz II Men (p1 r2, 1995), and "Always Be My Baby" (p1 r1, 1996). Carey's albums were also among the best selling of the decade, with *Mariah Carey* hitting the top of the pop charts (r3), and *Music Box* (1993) and *Daydream* (1995) topping both the pop and rhythm and blues charts. Both Houston and Carey employ singing styles that showcase their technical dexterity, with sometimes complicated vocal ornamentation and a broad expressive range. By the end of the 1990s, this style had become the standard approach to adult ballads, much imitated by professionals and amateurs, and not always with complete success, as the later *American Idol* television series would prove. While Whitney and Mariah dominated adult-oriented, middle-of-the-road pop in the first half of the 1990s, their music also had an important impact on rhythm and blues. Together with Babyface, Boyz II Men, and Toni Braxton (and many others), Houston and Carey helped establish a clear return to traditional rhythm and blues during the 1990s that paralleled a similar turning back to vintage styles in rock music.

Teen Idols

If You Build It, They Will Come: Backstreet Boys, *NSYNC. From Fabian to the Monkees to David Cassidy, the history of pop music can claim a series of teen idols—performers whose images and music are carefully crafted to appeal to teenage and preteenage girls. The second half of the 1990s experienced a resurgence of acts designed specifically for this audience, though this time the musical style employed was more indebted to the traditionalist rhythm and blues of Boyz II Men, Babyface, and Mariah Carey than to the bubbly but stiff bubblegum pop of previous decades. The two most important "boy bands" of these years were the Backstreet Boys and *NSYNC: both all-male vocal groups modeled on Boys II Men and both managed by millionaire Lou Pearlman. Based in Orlando, Pearlman had initially made his fortune not in the music business but by chartering private planes to celebrities. When New Kids on the Block chartered a plane from Pearlman's company, he tagged along to see what all the fuss was about. Pearlman was impressed at the way the New Kids were able to market their music and image to pubescent girls, and after consulting with some experts (including Motown's Smokey Robinson), Pearlman decided to mold his own pop group to market to these kids. He started with the Backstreet Boys—five men who all had previous experience singing professionally and had formed before coming into contact with Pearlman. The group had its first successes in Europe in 1995–96, with several singles becoming hits without making much impact in the United States. In 1997, Pearlman and his people began to invest heavily in promoting the band in the United States, releasing *Backstreet Boys* (p4, 1997), mostly a collection of tracks that had already been successful overseas. The album was a success, and the singles "Quit Playing Games (with my Heart)" (p2) and "Everybody (Backstreet's Back)" (p4) made the Backstreet Boys teenage heartthrobs. The band's next two albums, *Millennium* (p1, 1999) and *Black & Blue* (p1, 2000), did even better, though by then the group had officially split with Pearlman and his organization.

One factor causing the split between the Backstreet Boys and Pearlman was Pearlman's attention to a new group he was developing—one that would compete directly with the Boys as teen idols. Among the members of *NSYNC were JC Chasez and Justin Timberlake, two young men who were already familiar to the teen crowd from being regular members of the Disney Channel's *The New Mickey Mouse Club*. The new group's first album, **NSYNC* (p2, 1998), did well, producing the hit single "God Must Have Spent a Little More Time on You" (p8), but the band did not really come close to challenging the Backstreet Boys. The second album, *No Strings Attached* (p1, 2000), however, was *NSYNC's blockbuster, generating the hits "Bye Bye Bye" (p4), "It's Gonna Be Me" (p1), and "This I Promise You" (p5), placing them side-by-side with the Backstreet

Since the late 1990s, American television has been dominated by a format known as "reality television." Most reality shows either depict ordinary people in extraordinary situations (examples include MTV's *The Real World*, *Survivor*, *Fear Factor*, and *Who Wants to Marry a Millionaire?*) or depict famous people in ordinary situations (*The Osbournes*, *The Surreal Life*, and *The Simple Life*). The emphasis in both types of shows is on the "reality" of the behavior of the participants. In other words, these programs promise viewers a window into unusual but real-life circumstances. One of the most successful reality shows mixes elements of both types, in a search for future pop singing stars among ordinary people: *American Idol*.

American Idol premiered in the summer of 2002 on the Fox Network. As with many reality shows, it was based on a program that had already succeeded in another country—in this case, the British show *Pop Idol*. But

both programs were merely revivals in a new style of a very old popular tradition: the talent show. In fact, from 1983 to 1995, one of the most popular television shows in syndication was *Star Search*, which was based on a similar premise. But unlike conventional talent shows, each season of *American Idol* is progressive and it focuses exclusively on pop singing.

American Idol begins each season with a nationwide series of auditions of thousands of potential contestants. The first weeks of the broadcast season focus on the worst of the chaff separated during this process. In 2004, William Hung even achieved brief stardom for his comically bad singing in an *American Idol* audition. Eventually, the contestants are narrowed to a group of twenty-four to thirty-two semi-finalists by a panel of three judges: Simon Cowell, Paula Abdul, and Randy Jackson, sometimes supplemented by a fourth celebrity judge. From the semi-finals forward, the judges serve

only as advisors, critics, or commentators, and selection of the twelve finalists is done by the viewers. During the final twelve weeks of each season, one contestant is eliminated per week until only a single winner remains. The winner receives a major label recording contract as a prize, although several other finalists have earned contracts on merit as well. The winner of the first season, Kelly Clarkson, has already made two multi-platinum albums and been nominated for a Grammy award. The winner and runner-up of the second season, Ruben Studdard and Clay Aiken, have also recorded popular albums.

The great popularity of *American Idol* and its contestants, some of whom have gained more attention than all but the biggest established pop stars, is the subject of much speculation. It is undoubtedly related to the popularity of reality television in general and the long-lasting appeal of talent contests. Both are rooted in the

Kelly Clarkson (center), winner of the first American Idol *competition, sings "A Moment like This" to close the show's first season. Runner-up Justin Guarini is behind her, and the show's other contestants look on. Though first accepted by professional judges, Clarkson was the top choice of the millions of judges that mattered most: the viewing audience.*

idea that within ordinary people like ourselves lies extraordinary, untapped potential. But as a reality show, *American Idol* enhances the appeal of the talent contest by showing the full range of the contestants' experiences. Scenes of failure and mediocrity accompany every triumph, adding both tragedy and comedy to the mix. At the same time, the producers of *American Idol* have cleverly revived the formulaic approach to developing pop stars, which worked so well in the late 1950s: a singer is chosen for skill and appeal in order to deliver songs created by professional songwriters, arrangers, studio musicians, and producers. As ever, this approach ensures that the bulk of the profit is retained by the record company (and in this case, the television show). By combining this commercial approach with the talent show format, the producers have given their audience a rooting, competitive interest in the star-making apparatus. After watching Kelly Clarkson or Ruben Studdard emerge from a pack of competitors week by week, it becomes much easier to listen to their music—no matter how formulaic.

Boys in the boy-band sweepstakes. Both bands' music worked from the stylistic model established earlier in the decade by Boyz II Men. Many of the songs and much of the production was provided by Swedish songwriter and producer Max Martin, who sometimes teamed up with his mentor, Denniz Pop, and later with songwriter and singer Rami. Martin was responsible for many of the hits enjoyed by both bands, as well many for Britney Spears and others during the decade; and like Babyface, he worked with a range of artists and groups, including Celine Dion, Bryan Adams, and Bon Jovi.

Girl Power: The Spice Girls.   About the same time the Backstreet Boys were enjoying success in Europe, an all-girl vocal quintet was also topping the charts in the UK. The five original Spice Girls were each experienced in show business when they answered the same 1993 ad placed by a manager forming a singing group. The manager selected the girls, but they rejected him, heading off to organize the act themselves and to be managed by Simon Fuller, who had managed Annie Lennox. By the fall of 1996 their debut album, *Spice*, and the single "Say You'll Be There" were both at the top of the UK charts, making the band stars in Britain. Each Spice Girl had a special name (Ginger Spice, Baby Spice, Scary Spice, Posh Spice, and Sporty Spice) and the group quickly began exploiting their newfound fame by endorsing products of all kinds. Their catchy music, fun-loving image, and distinctive good looks made them not only successful pop stars but also high-profile celebrities. In early 1997, they worked on succeeding in the United States, at roughly the same time Lou Pearlman was pushing the Backstreet Boys. The American release of *Spice* (1997) went to number one, powered by the hit singles "2 Become 1" (p4), "Say You'll Be There," and the catchy "Wannabe" (p1), featuring the rapped line "I tell you what I want." The group's next album, *Spiceworld* (p3, 1997) was released in conjunction with their feature film of the same name. At the height of their success, the group separated from their manager and Ginger Spice quit. The group carried on for a while longer but had split up by late 2000. Like the Backstreet Boys and *NSYNC, the Spice Girls' music owed much to rhythm and blues, which was combined in the up-tempo numbers with the beat of European dance music. The group projected an image of "girl power," by which they meant that they were in charge of what they were doing and were not powerless pawns being pushed around by the music business. They shared writing credits on many of their tracks—including the hits—though they often teamed with professional songwriters such as Matt Rowe and Richard Stannard. In their projection of independence, the Spice Girls credited Madonna as an important influence.

Teen Divas: Britney Spears and Christina Aguilera.   By 1998, the tremendously lucrative market opened up by the Backstreet Boys and the Spice Girls turned into a new teenybopper bubblegum market, and we have already seen how Pearlman was ready to make the most of this with *NSYNC. Late in 1998 a new figure entered this scene: Britney Spears would soon become the most important artist in this burgeoning preteen movement. Like JC Chasez and Justin Timberlake, Spears had also appeared on *The New Mickey Mouse Club* (as had fellow teen diva Christina Aguilera), so she was an experienced performer by the time she

Britney Spears performing live at the 2000 MTV Video Music Awards ceremony. In many ways a classic teen idol, Spears (and her contemporary, Christina Aguilera) also tapped into a large preteen audience. Many overlook Spears's considerable skill as a singer in light of her flair for dramatic performances, huge global successes, and Madonna-like style reinventions.

emerged as a solo artist. In fall 1998, Britney released her debut album, . . . *Baby One More Time*, produced by Max Martin. The Martin-penned single ". . . Baby One More Time" hit the number-one spot on the pop charts, and Spears's video for the song featured her dancing suggestively in a skimpy schoolgirl outfit. A second hit, "You Drive Me Crazy" (p10), further established Britney as the next big thing, and her second album, *Oops . . . I Did It Again* (p1, 2000), confirmed it.

LISTENING GUIDE

GET MUSIC ▶▶ wwnorton.com/rockhistory

Britney Spears, ". . . Baby One More Time"

Words and music by Max Martin, produced by Max Martin and Rami. Single rose to #1 in the United States in 1998; from the album . . . *Baby One More Time*, which rose to #1 in the United States.

FORM: Contrasting verse-chorus. The first two verses are built on a repeating 4-bar progression, played three times through to create a 12-bar section. The first 4 bars of the chorus are built on the same pattern, but the second 4 bars break off and introduce new material. The first two verses and the choruses that follow are almost identical except for the lyrics, and the second chorus is followed by an instrumental 4-bar interlude that is repeated from the introduction. The formal interest in the song arises in the third verse, which introduces fresh material, and the chorus that immediately follows it, which works from this new, varied structure to rework the chorus lyrics. This varied verse-chorus pair is then followed by a return to the chorus as it was presented earlier, and that form of the chorus occurs twice before the song ends on a strong downbeat. The varied verse and chorus introduce contrast into the song to make the return of the chorus fresh, and function much as a bridge or guitar solo might in another song, though here remaining well within the constraints of a contrasting verse-chorus design.

TIME SIGNATURE: 4/4 throughout, with a strong dance-tempo feel and clearly articulated beat.

INSTRUMENTATION: Wah-wah guitar, bass, synthesizers, piano, drums, percussion, lead and backup vocals.

0:00–0:12	**Introduction**, 4 mm.	A simple riff over a drumbeat that establishes the rhythmic feel. Spears interjects "Oh baby baby" twice.
0:12–0:43	**Verse 1**, 16 mm.	The first 8 bars remain quiet and focus on solo lead vocal, while the last 4 measures add backup vocals and build toward chorus. "Oh baby baby . . ."

Like the Spice Girls, Spears credited Madonna with influencing her control over her image, which early on blended sexual aggressiveness with playful innocence. One of the keys to Britney's success was that while her songs attracted the girls, her dance-heavy performances—both live and on video—drew in the boys.

In 1999, fellow ex-Mouseketeer Christina Aguilera debuted with a more uncompromisingly sexy image, and *Christina Aguilera* topped the pop charts,

0:43–1:03	**Chorus**, 8 mm.	Harmony vocals enter along with synthesizer, much bigger sounding to create emphasis on this section. Note clever transition to next verse. "My loneliness . . ."
1:03–1:34	**Verse 2**, 12 mm.	Mostly as before, with backup vocals now added to entire section, and more emphasis on wah-wah guitar in the accompaniment. "Oh baby . . ."
1:34–1:55	**Chorus**, 8 mm.	Big, as before, but almost identical. "My loneliness . . ."
1:55–2:06	**Interlude**, 4 mm.	As in introduction, with lead vocal improvising in dialogue with guitar.
2:06–2:26	**Verse variation**, 8 mm.	The first four bars repeat the verse as before, but the next four bars introduce new music not heard previously in the song. Note the use of a quiet, quasi-classical texture, with emphasis on acoustic piano and soft orchestral strings and a build to next section. "Oh baby . . ."
2:26–2:47	**Chorus variation**, 8 mm.	Begins as if it could be a regular chorus, but then picks up the chords from the second 4 bars of the varied verse. "I must confess . . ."
2:47–3:07	**Chorus**, 8 mm.	As heard after verses 1 and 2. "My loneliness . . ."
3:07–3:29	**Chorus**, 9 mm.	Repeat with added lead vocal part drawn from chorus variation over backup vocals. Note how the ending employs the final crash to reinforce the catchy refrain "Hit me baby one more time."

containing the hits "Genie in a Bottle" (p1) and "What a Girl Wants" (p1). The next year, Aguilera released *Mi Reflejo*, sung in Spanish and intended to capitalize on the boom in latin pop, led by Ricky Martin's ubiquitous hit single "Livin' La Vida Loca" (p1, 1999) and Santana's "Smooth." The album topped the latin charts, while also hitting number twenty-seven on the pop charts. Both Spears and Aguilera are skilled and versatile vocalists—a feature that is easy to miss in the hype over the sensual images they project—and their approaches to singing owe much to the melismatic stylings of Mariah Carey and Whitney Houston, which is more obvious in the ballads than in the faster dance numbers.

Female Singer-Songwriters

Both Sides Now: Another Take on Girl Power. In the discussion of the singer-songwriters of the 1970s (Chapter 8) we traced the development of the style back to those artists in the 1960s, Bob Dylan especially, who wrote their own songs and delivered them with relatively simple accompaniment—often acoustic guitar and piano—with a focus on the vocals and the importance of the lyrics. The singer-songwriter style grew throughout the 1970s to include a great many artists, sometimes using simple acoustic accompaniment and at other times, as in the case of Paul Simon, Bob Seger, or Joni Mitchell, fronting bands and using more elaborate and sophisticated accompaniment. One constant with singer-songwriters, however, is that the listener has to believe the artist is singing about his or her own experiences, or reflecting his or her own thoughts and feelings. A crucial sense of authenticity is based on this projection of sincerity, and sometimes even vulnerability. In the 1980s, singer-songwriters were still present, and many continued to be active while new ones emerged during the 1990s; Dylan, for instance, returned with *Time Out of Mind* (p10 uk10, 1997), as did Billy Joel with *River of Dreams* (p1 uk3, 1993). But perhaps the most significant development for the style in the 1990s was the emergence of a new generation of female singer-songwriters—artists whose lyrics dealt with issues that are important to women generally, and with specifically feminist issues as well. Influenced by well-known singer-songwriters like Carole King, Joni Mitchell, and Carly Simon, as well as lesser known but critically celebrated artists such as Kate Bush, Tracy Chapman, and others, the music of this new generation of younger women ranged from quiet and contemplative to angry and aggressive.

Tori Amos, the Indigo Girls, Liz Phair, Ani DiFranco. Among the first of this new group of singer-songwriters to emerge in the 1990s was Tori Amos. Growing up in Baltimore, Amos had been a piano prodigy who studied at the prestigious Peabody Conservatory. When Amos decided that a career as a concert pianist was not in her future, she nevertheless continued to pursue music, influenced by the songs of Lennon and McCartney and playing piano in gay bars as a teenager. Amos eventually made her way to Los Angeles, and after a brief stint fronting a rock band, recorded her singer-songwriter debut, *Little Earthquakes* (p54 uk14, 1991). Amos's classical training is audible in her use of harmony and melody as well as in her masterful piano playing; the first track on *Little Earthquakes*, "Crucify," provides a good example of her early style. The song which is perhaps most striking on the album, however, is an unaccompanied vocal track called "Me and a Gun," an intimate and gripping portrayal of a rape experience. After an extended play recording consisting of cover versions of songs by Nirvana, Led Zeppelin, and others, Amos released *Under the Pink* (p12 uk1) in 1994, and *Boys for Pele* (p2 uk2) in 1996. The success of these albums established her as one of the most talented and innovative songwriters of her generation.

The Atlanta-based Indigo Girls also enjoyed chart success with their 1994 album *Swamp Ophelia* (p9 uk66, 1994), which showcased the often contrasting songwriting styles of Amy Ray and Emily Saliers. The duo's music is built around Ray and Saliers's duet singing and acoustic guitar accompaniment, with Ray evincing more rock influence, while Saliers projects a gentler, folk-influenced style. The duo's lyrics often addressed feminist issues in addition to environmental issues and other social causes. Another highly respected artist from the early 1990s is Chicago-based Liz Phair, whose album *Exile in Guyville* (1993) is a response to the Rolling Stones' *Exile on Main Street*. Despite critical acclaim heaped on the 1998 album *whitechocolatespaceegg* (p35), Phair's music had trouble crossing over into the pop mainstream as that of Amos and the Indigo Girls did, and she has remained something of an underground sensation. Ani DiFranco's music did cross over into the pop mainstream, though only modestly, since the New York–based DiFranco resisted major label offers and released her music on her own indie label, Righteous Babe. Her 1995 album, *Not a Pretty Girl*, garnered critical acclaim and mainstream media attention, while *Little Plastic Castle* (1998) rose as high as number twenty-two on the pop charts. Phair also recorded for an indie label (Matador), and the music of DiFranco and Phair can thus also be considered in light of the 1990s indie underground, discussed later in this chapter.

Tori Amos in a live performance at George Washington University, 1994. Amos and many female singer-songwriters of the period (Ani DiFranco and Sarah McLachlan, among others) were the antithesis of the mass-marketed pop diva. Amos, a classically trained pianist, wrote, produced, and sang songs about highly personal, intimate moments. Though the music was produced on the small scale, Amos proved that such music could sell in large numbers: she had several successful albums through the 1990s and beyond.

Canadian Contrasts: Sarah McLachlan, Alanis Morissette.

Hailing from Nova Scotia, Sarah McLachlan enjoyed moderate chart success in 1993 with *Fumbling toward Ecstasy* (p50, 1993). Two years later, her single "I Will Remember You" (1995), written and recorded for the movie

Alanis Morissette, pictured here in a 1996 concert, is known for her aggressive vocal style. Her Jagged Little Pill *(1995) was one of the 1990s' best-selling albums. Like Tori Amos, Ani DiFranco, and others, Morissette's highly personal music was indebted to Joni Mitchell, Carole King, and Janis Joplin, but updated for a 1990s audience.*

The Brothers McMullen, went to number fourteen. It was with her 1997 release, *Surfacing* (p2), that McLachlan broke through into the pop mainstream, partly on the strength of the singles "Building a Mystery" (p13), "Adia" (p3 uk18), and "Angel" (p4). McLachlan's music, produced by Pierre Marchand, is often gentle, and even quite delicate, sometimes using conventional rock instrumentation of guitars, bass, and drums, but other times employing a more electronic backdrop of synthesizers and electronic percussion. She was an important organizer of a music festival called the Lilith Fair which was devoted to music by women, and toured North America; and while initially seeming partial to white, acoustic songwriters, the festival soon included a wide range of artists and styles, including Liz Phair, the Indigo Girls, Sheryl Crow, Tracy Chapman, and Queen Latifah. Canadian Alanis Morissette's first album would not likely be accused of being too gentle or delicate. Her enormously successful *Jagged Little Pill* (p1 uk1, 1995) contained the hits "Ironic" (p4 uk11) and "You Learn" (p6). The album also includes "You Oughta Know," a track that captures the sense of angry frustration and outrage experienced after a romantic breakup. Morissette followed in 1998 with *Supposed Former Infatuation Junkie* (p1 uk3), making her one of the most successful of the female singer-songwriters of the second half of the decade.

Projecting Feminine Identities: Teen Idols and Singer-Songwriters.

Despite the radically different approaches to image, the teen idols and the female singer-songwriters appealed to the same general audience: teenage girls. The singer-songwriters were also able to appeal to older, college-age women, since their songs often dealt with the experiences and concerns of adult women (this was especially true of those who recorded for indie labels). It may be that both styles appealed to teens, but perhaps not the same teens; or maybe they both appealed to the same teens but at different times in their development. Whatever the case, critics of the Spice Girls, Britney Spears, and Christina Aguilera might charge them with making themselves into sexual objects, reinforcing unhealthy images of young women that are the source of a wide range of sociocultural problems. Defenders might point out that these women retained significant control in their careers and provided a positive feminine image focused on women taking charge of their lives and careers. It is easy to see that there is a big difference between Tori Amos singing "Me and a Gun" and Britney Spears singing ". . . Baby One More Time"; but no matter what conclusion you draw from this disparity, by the end of the 1990s, women and their music were playing a central role in popular music, and both the singer-songwriters and the teen idols were back.

Electronic Dance Music

Dance, Dance, Dance. In the early 1960s, America's youth embraced a craze for dance music, typified by dances like the twist, the mashed potato, and the swim; many adults soon joined in the fun, prompting Dick Clark to cite "The Twist" as the moment in rock's history when parents could admit that they liked rock and roll too. Again in the late 1970s, a dance movement re-emerged with the rise of disco, as many put away their tie-dye shirts, jeans, and beads in favor of sleek polyester outfits and gold chains. In a certain sense, dancing has always played a role in rock music; even during the halcyon days of the hippie aesthetic, listeners often danced to the music. The hippies rejected disco not so much because it advocated dancing but because it placed dancing above listening, and in so doing took the focus off the artists and put it on the dancers themselves. By the early 1980s, disco had receded from the pop mainstream, as dancing moved from clubs to cable-television screens to take a central role in music videos. But in many places in the United States, dance music did not disappear; like other styles we have discussed so far, dance music went underground after its time in the pop limelight, and regional dance scenes developed in major cities like New York, Chicago, and Detroit. Throughout the 1980s, dance music developed mostly off the pop-music radar screen, as devoted dancers populated specialized clubs and DJs crafted sets designed to keep the dance floor full. By the late 1980s, America's underground dance music had made its way to England, where a dance craze began to build, placing hit singles on the UK charts by the early 1990s. The UK scene then spread back across the Atlantic to New York, San Francisco, and Los Angeles, forming the basis for the rise of electronic dance music throughout the decade. By the late 1990s, many observers of pop-music trends were predicting that electronic dance music—often referred to broadly as "techno"—would be the next big thing, replacing rock as the music of America's youth.

New York, Larry Levan, and the Paradise Garage. The story of the rise of 1990s electronic dance music begins just as disco was fading from the scene. When it became clear to record companies that disco was on its way out, the flow of new disco records dried up to almost nothing. At dance clubs like New York's Paradise Garage (which had opened in 1977, just before *Saturday Night Fever* appeared), DJs still had crowds who wanted to dance. It was thus up to the DJs to find ways of keeping the music coming without playing the same old records over and over again. Many began to use European disco records, especially disco from Italy. Despite these European imports, good dance records were still in short supply, and DJs were forced to become inventive; they thus developed a number of techniques to create new music—or at least music that wasn't exactly like it originally was on the record. One technique required the DJ to have two copies of the same record and to prolong the length of the song by switching from one copy to the other, repeating the same passage seamlessly. Another was to calculate the tempos of various records, mixing from one record to the next without the dancers feeling any marked change in the beat. Many DJs developed eclectic record collections, using a broad range of music to create distinctive and striking contrasts within their sets. As techniques and practices like this developed, DJs became central to the dance-music experience; and as they became more important, they became increasingly skilled, competing with one another for priority within the regional culture.

At the Paradise Garage in New York's SoHo district, Larry Levan established himself as one of the city's top dance DJs while disco was still popular.

LISTENING GUIDE

GET MUSIC ▶▶ wwnorton.com/rockhistory

Alanis Morissette, "You Oughta Know"

Words and music by Alanis Morissette and Glen Ballard, produced by Glen Ballard. From the album *Jagged Little Pill*, which rose to #1 in the United States and the UK in 1995.

FORM: Contrasting verse-chorus. Each 20-bar verse is made up of six times through the same 4-bar chord pattern, though the last 8 measures each time are much louder and more aggressive, and repeat the same lyrics in verses 1 and 2. The chorus is made up of two times through a contrasting 4-bar pattern, with the second 4 bars extended by 1 measure to create a 9-bar section. The song presents this verse-chorus pair three times, with an extra time through the chorus added at the end. Contrast is provided by the third verse, which features no lyrics during the first 12 bars, but only Morissette's expressive moaning and shouting, indicative of the emotional suffering that is the basis of the lyrics. The focus of the song is on the anger and resentment felt by the protagonist after a romantic breakup, and each verse-chorus pair begins quiet and brooding and builds to a stormy chorus.

TIME SIGNATURE: 4/4 throughout.

INSTRUMENTATION: Electric guitars, bass, organ, drums, and lead vocals.

0:00–0:55	**Verse 1**, 20 mm.	Begins quietly with vocals and snare drum only, with guitar, bass and drums entering and building toward the chorus with the addition of distorted guitar. "I want you to know . . ."

Employing a spectacular sound system and often controlling the lighting as well, Levan would combine a wide range of music to create his sets, sometimes blending records together and at other times moving abruptly from one to another. Levan controlled the dance experience at the Garage, and it was a strong sense of the dramatic that made him a star on the New York scene. As disco faded, Levan began developing his own approach to reworking and combining records, sometimes using electronic reverb or echo to create special effects, at other times employing an electronic drum machine to underscore the beat. Levan's almost total control of the dancing environment made it clear that the records were not the central element in the club—the DJ was. The New York approach to dance music is often called "garage," and the New York City Peech Boys' "Don't Make Me Wait" (1982) provides a representative example of the style.

0:55–1:16	**Chorus**, 9 mm.	This hard-driving section is almost shouted, and is the loudest and most aggressive section of the song. Note the wah-wah guitar. "And I'm here . . ."
1:16–2:10	**Verse 2**, 20 mm.	As before, building from quiet and distressed to angry and sarcastic, but this time with more activity in the electric guitar and bass. "You seem very well . . ."
2:10–2:31	**Chorus**, 9 mm.	As before, heavy and almost manic, with the organ mixed a bit louder in the mix. "And I'm here . . ."
2:31–3:26	**Verse 3**, 20 mm.	The first bars are instrumental, featuring spacey guitar sounds and melodic moaning in the vocals that become sobs, with singing returning in the last 8 bars but with new lyrics.
3:26–3:46	**Chorus**, 9 mm.	As before, driving and insistent. "Well I'm here . . ."
3:46–4:07	**Chorus**, 9 mm.	High guitar added to further intensify the obsessive quality of the music. Ends with vocal alone, as it began. "Well I'm here . . ."

One of the most important DJs in post-disco dance music, Larry Levan, pictured here in 1990 performing at Mars, an important club in the New York City house music scene. With his innovative use of multiple records, lighting, and sound effects, Levan controlled all aspects of the dance club experience. He proved that in this new genre it was not the records that were important; it was the DJ.

Chicago and Detroit.   When the owners of a new Chicago dance club called the Warehouse were searching for a star DJ, they first tried to get Larry Levan. When Levan wouldn't leave New York, they hired Frankie Knuckles, who had worked with Levan, and Knuckles began his DJ career in Chicago in 1977. Knuckles brought the techniques and practices of the New York scene with him, but by the early 1980s he and other Chicago DJs were developing a style that would soon be called "house," after the Chicago club. Remixes became increasingly complex, as passages from various records were spliced together and sometimes new parts were added on top, often using inexpensive synthesizers and drum machines—all this in an attempt to provide a full night's worth of fresh-sounding dance music. New tracks were created using drum machines, synthesizers, loops taken from records, and various sound effects, all designed for the effect they would have on the dance floor; and despite the generally low quality of such recordings, club DJs began working them into sets and Chicago radio stations even began playing them. The first recorded example of house music is probably Jesse Saunders's "On and On" (1983). In Detroit, a group of aspiring DJs, often called the Belleville Three, began blending their love for the European synthesizer music of Kraftwerk with their passion for Parliament-Funkadelic. Juan Atkins, Derrick May, and Kevin Saunderson began producing a refined, futuristic, and sonically sophisticated version of dance music that many originally called "Detroit house," though the style is more generally referred to as "techno." The Detroit approach tends not to employ traditional instruments such as bass, drums, and guitar as can be found in the Chicago and New York dance music, but rather emphasizes the drum machine, synthesizers, and sequencers. A representative example is Juan Atkins's "No UFOs" (1985), released under the name Motel 500. While the New York and Chicago scenes were urban and populated mostly by gay black men, the Detroit scene was black but heterosexual, and more suburban middle-class than urban, at least initially. Nevertheless, there was frequent contact between the DJs and producers in the these cities, and they knew one another's music.

Rise of UK Rave Scene and Its Return to the United States.   By the late 1980s, house and techno—still unknown in the states outside their subcultures—had made their way to London, where dance clubs began to play the records, and this imported American underground music began to catch on. By the summer of 1988, all-night rave parties began to get so large they would sometimes be held outdoors, often at a secret location to avoid police intervention. The drug Ecstasy became an important part of the experience for many dancers, leading some to refer to 1988 as the "second summer of love" because of the blend of trippy music, altered consciousness, and communal and/or tribal sensibilities. Soon British musicians were producing their own version of electronic dance music, and by the early 1990s, dance records were becoming hits on the UK pop charts. In 1990, for instance, Orbital scored with "The Chime" (uk17), and the American musician Moby hit with "Go" (uk10, 1991)—a track that samples a theme from the *Twin Peaks* television show. Other hits included the Prodigy's "Everybody in the Place" (uk2, 1992), Shut Up and Dance's "Raving I'm Raving" (uk2, 1992), and SL2's "On a Ragga Tip" (uk2, 1992). In the early 1990s, dance made its way back to the United States, as British rave culture was transplanted to the New York/New Jersey area, San Francisco, and Los Angeles. In each case, these newly founded rave scenes were driven by DJs who had experienced British rave, and each local scene had its own distinctive musical and cultural profile.

Breakthrough of EDM into the U.S. Pop Mainstream.

Despite the commercial success of dance music in London early in the decade, electronic dance music in the mid 1990s continued to be mostly unknown in American mainstream popular music. In the second half of the decade, however, dance music began to catch on around the country, as more and more local scenes sprang up and major labels began to invest in the style. The mainstream success of electronic dance music in America that began to build during this time was driven primarily by albums sales, not by singles as had been the case in the UK earlier in the decade. MTV also played an important role, airing dance videos that were often innovative and spacey, perhaps owing to the centrality of drug use in dance culture—or at least to a widespread perception that drug use was central. Fatboy Slim's hit 1998 album was, after all, entitled *Better Living through Chemistry*. Important hit electronic dance albums were released by the Chemical Brothers, whose *Dig Your Own Hole* (p14 uk1, 1997) made an early

The DJ and songwriter Moby proved that techno music was viable commercially. He produced several hit albums and his music often found its way into television ads and movie soundtracks. In this picture, Moby handles the turntables during a private party at the New York City club, SPA, July 16, 2001.

mark, and the Prodigy's *The Fat of the Land* (1997), which topped both the U.S. and UK charts. Moby became an important figure during these years, as every track of his 1999 album *Play* (p38 uk1, 1999) was licensed for either commercials or movie soundtracks.

Listening to Dance Music and the "Live" Problem. The most central aspect of electronic dance music is that it is meant to be danced to. This characteristic provided some problems for the mainstream marketing of the music in the late 1990s, since the pop business is set up to sell performances of bands or artists, or recordings that can be understood (and listened to) as performances. While DJ remixes had been available from the earliest days, many DJs still wondered how it would be possible to fit what they did into the conventional pop-music template. Most club DJs prided themselves on their ability to structure an effective set that ran over an hour in length (perhaps much longer), and to respond to the mood and reactions of the dancers: how could this translate into albums or live shows? In many ways, the DJ is more the star in electronic dance music than the producers who record the music, many of whom remain mysterious and release their music under various names. Despite these problems, the music industry still sold electronic dance albums that many of the new fans listened to, and producers—who were often only one or two people—put together ensembles that functioned like rock bands in order to do live shows and tours. Since the 1990s electronic dance music has its historical roots in disco, it is surprising that it shares some of the problems encountered by the hippie-influenced jam bands like Phish and Widespread Panic. In both styles, it's important that fans be at the show or club in order to fully experience the music, which may change from night to night as the artists respond to the crowd and to their own creativity. Both styles are also frequently associated with drug use that many claim enhances the experience of the music. So while jam-band rock and electronic dance music both refer back to starkly contrasting styles of an earlier era, it's interesting to see how many similarities they share.

Rap Rolls On

Gangsta Rap and a Proliferation of Styles. All the styles we have been discussing in this chapter relate in some important way to earlier music of the '50s, '60s, or '70s; and while these returns to rock's past are central to appreciating these styles, they do not fully account for any of them. Each style also builds on musical forms and practices that were present in some form in the 1980s. In the case of rap, by contrast, its development out of its tremendous commercial success of the last years of the 1980s is much more significant than references it makes to earlier styles from the '60s and '70s, which are most often discernible in the sung passages and the samples that often saturate the musical texture. In the 1990s, rap grew into one of popular music's dominant styles, both in the United States and the UK. This growth was so dramatic during the decade that many historians and critics believe the style deserves to be considered as the focal point of its own history, and not as one facet of the history of rock music. In this chapter, we will focus on the continuation of the story of gangsta rap—or "reality rap"—and how it grows out of the music we discussed in the last chapter. With its growth and commercial success, rap fractured into many substyles, much as rock did during the first half of the 1970s.

The rise of rap's popularity brought many more artists and record companies into the mix, and as in any highly populated market, each artist elbowed for his or her own distinctive voice as audiences grew and grew. Some rap was about conflict, some was about peace; some artists talked about partying, others were serious and philosophical; rap could urge you to get your head together or to indulge in the intoxicated fog of drugs. Rap could be musically aggressive or laid back, continuous or full of quick edits and disruptions. In short, rap developed a broad stylistic range.

West Coast: Death Row, Dre, Snoop, Tupac.   Within gangsta rap early in the 1990s, a rivalry developed between southern California and New York, and this feud became the source of much controversy in the music press and eventually ended in tragedy. The west coast faction was led by Death Row Records, owned and controlled by aspiring impresario Suge Knight. Knight signed N.W.A. member Dr. Dre, whose 1993 album, *The Chronic* (p3 r1, 1993), included the rapper Snoop Doggy Dogg, and the track "Nuthin' but a 'G' Thang" (p2 r1) provides a famous example of the album's approach. The track employs two samples: "Uphill (Peace of Mind)," a 1976 track by Kid Dynamite and "I Wanna Do Something Freaky to You" (1979) by Leon

Haywood, both drawn from late '70s soul music. Both Snoop and Dre rap, and rather than being cast in a sing-song and predictable rhyme pattern, the lines weave in and out against the accompanying groove, often employing sophisticated rhythms and phrase groupings. Like Dre, Snoop also signed with Death Row and soon became one of rap's most successful artists with *Doggystyle* (p1 r1 uk38, 1993) and *The Doggfather* (p1 r1 uk15, 1996). While Snoop's music was gangsta, he projected a relaxed, ultra hip image that eventually made him one of the style's most popular celebrities. Things turned out differently for Tupac Shakur, whose albums *Me against the World* (p1 r1, 1995) and *All Eyez on Me* (p1 r1 uk33, 1996) topped the charts like Snoop's records. But Tupac become directly involved in a feud with the New York label Bad Boy, and he was killed in Las Vegas in September 1996 in a drive-by shooting; the exact circumstances of the murder remain unclear. By the end of the decade, both Dr. Dre and Snoop had separated themselves from Death Row. Other rap artists and groups issued from the west coast during the decade, including the pot-promoting band Cypress Hill, whose latin-flavored hip-hop *Black Sunday* (p1 r1 uk13, 1993) sampled Black Sabbath, among others.

One of the most successful recording teams in hip-hop history, Snoop Doggy Dogg (left) and Dr. Dre. Dre was a key player in west coast rap, where he came up with Eazy-E and Ice Cube in the group N.W.A. (Niggaz with Attitude). Snoop and Dre teamed up to create **The Chronic** *(1992), which became the model for west coast gangsta rap. This album includes many George Clinton/Parliament-inspired tracks, like "Let Me Ride," and the gangsta rap anthem, "Nuthin' but a 'G' Thang."*

East Coast: P. Diddy, Notorious B.I.G.   The east coast faction of gangsta rap was led by producer, businessman, and future rap artist Sean Combs, who went by the name Puff Daddy (later changed to P. Diddy). Combs had been in A&R for Uptown Records, working with artists such as Father MC on *Father's Day* (r23, 1990) and Mary J. Blige on *What's the 411?* (p6 r1, 1992). Fired from Uptown, Combs formed his own record label, Bad Boy, and the Notorious

---

LISTENING GUIDE   GET MUSIC ▶▶   wwnorton.com/rockhistory

Dr. Dre, featuring Snoop Doggy Dogg, "Nuthin' but a 'G' Thang"

Words and music by Cordozar Broadus, Andre Young, Leon Haywood, Frederick Knight, produced by Dr. Dre. Single rose to #2 in the U.S. pop charts (#1 on the rhythm and blues charts) in 1993; contained on the album *The Chronic*, which rose to #3 on the U.S. pop charts (#1 on the rhythm and blues charts).

FORM: Simple verse bar form. The verses in almost every case are built on 4-bar phrases, producing either 12- or 16-bar sections. The only exception is verse 1, which is 10 measures in length. Verses 1 and 2 are followed by a 4-bar refrain, as are verses 3, 4 and 5, and this forms a relatively regular and symmetrical formal pattern. Once the groove is set up in the accompaniment, the focus is on the rapping, which is done by both Snoop Doggy Dogg and Dr. Dre. While the rhymes are clever, the ways in which the delivery of these lines flows alternately with and against the rhythmic grouping in the accompaniment is where Snoop and Dre really display their skills. Notice how lines do not always begin or end where you might expect them to— sometimes beginning late or ending early, other times seeming to blur over the underlying 4-bar pattern. To keep the accompaniment interesting, synthesizer lines come and go throughout the track.

TIME SIGNATURE: 4/4 throughout.

INSTRUMENTATION: Electric guitars, bass, synthesizers, drums, percussion, vocals, and samples drawn from Leon Haywood's "I Wanna Do Something Freaky to You" and Kid Dynamite's "Uphill (Peace of Mind)."

0:00–0:11	**Introduction**, 4 mm.	This instrumental section established the laid-back groove. Note the female sighs that saturate this track and the signature synthesizer melody.
0:11–0:36	**Verse 1**, 10 mm.	Snoop begins the rapping, with a brief contribution from Dre. This verse consists of a 4-bar phrase, then a 2-bar phrase, followed

B.I.G. (Christopher Wallace) was among the first to score a top crossover success for Bad Boy; B.I.G.'s *Ready to Die* reached number fifteen on the pop charts in 1995 (13) and *Life after Death* topped the pop and rhythm and blues charts in 1997, even hitting number twenty-three in the UK. In March 1997—about six months after the murder of Tupac—B.I.G. was killed in Los Angeles while he was there to make a video; the murder was never solved. In the wake

		by another 4-bar phrase. "One, two, three . . ."
0:36–1:07	**Verse 2**, 12 mm.	Snoop takes a verse solo. "Back to the lecture at hand . . ."
1:07–1:18	**Refrain**, 4 mm.	This refrain, rapped by Snoop and Dre together, signals the end of this portion of the track, setting up the next verse and introducing Dre. The synthesizer melody from the intro returns. "It's like this . . ."
1:18–1:48	**Verse 3**, 12 mm.	Dre now takes a verse solo. "Well I'm peepin' . . ."
1:48–1:58	**Refrain**, 4 mm.	The refrain again signals the end of this section. Return of synthesizer melody from intro and refrain as before. "It's like this . . ."
1:58–2:07	**Interlude**, 4 mm.	This instrumental section parallels the introduction, as synthesizer melody continues amid vocal samples and scratching.
2:07–2:38	**Verse 4**, 12 mm.	Snoop returns for another solo verse, calling on Dre at the end. "Fallin' back on that . . ."
2:38–3:19	**Verse 5**, 16 mm.	Dre again takes a solo verse. "Here's where it takes place . . ."
3:19–3:29	**Refrain**, 4 mm.	This time the refrain signals the end of the track, as the signature synthesizer melody returns as before. "Like this . . ."
3:29–3:56	**Coda**, 8 mm. and fade.	As in the introduction, this section is instrumental and fades out during the third time through the 4-bar pattern. Signature synthesizer melody continues, as vocal samples and scratching from interlude return.

of B.I.G.'s murder, Puff Daddy recorded the concept album *No Way Out* (p1 r1 uk10, 1997), which in many ways refers back to the philosophical prog-rock albums of the mid 1970s—if not in its musical style, then in its earnest quest for meaning. The single "I'll Be Missing You" (p1 r1 uk1) samples the Police's "Every Breath You Take" and in addition to being an international hit, it became a bittersweet reminder of the consequences of the gangsta feud. P. Diddy followed with *Forever* (p2 r1 uk9, 1999), and other Bad Boy acts enjoyed considerable chart success as well, including Faith Evans, Total, and 112. Whatever the truth about the murders of Tupac and B.I.G., the way they happened reinforced the image of gangsta rap as dangerous music by dangerous men. The fact that some within gangsta rap actually stood trial on felony charges—including Tupac, Snoop, and Knight—further fueled that fire. Acquittals notwithstanding, gangsta rap was widely viewed by parents and authorities during the 1990s as a negative influence on the young fans who embraced it, and as we have seen many times in the history of rock, this only made it more interesting to young fans.

The Great DJ Spin-off: Wu Tang Clan.   As rap in the 1990s mostly continued and developed its styles and practices directly from the 1980s, there is one way in which hip-hop was strongly influenced by earlier music—or at least previous music-business practices. As we have seen, the east and west coast were led by Combs and Knight, respectively—two men who owned companies and controlled several artists. As rap grew in popularity and profitability, many figures in addition to Knight and Combs aspired to become hip-hop impresarios and modeled themselves on George Clinton, who had also managed many musical projects simultaneously during the 1970s. One interesting twist on such commercial aspirations was the New York–based Wu Tang Clan, which consisted of a kind of co-op of nine DJs. The idea of Wu Tang Clan was to produce a smash album that would allow each of the nine DJs to spin off his own solo career. The first album, *Enter the Wu Tang (36 Chambers)*, was released in 1993 and went to number eight on the rhythm and blues charts (p41); the next release, *Wu Tang Forever* (1997), topped the pop and rhythm and blues charts in the United States, also reaching number one in the UK. The nine DJs were RZA, Genius/GZA, Ol' Dirty Bastard, Method Man, Raekwon the Chef, Ghostface Killah, U-God, Inspectah Deck, and Masta Killah (though many also worked under other pseudonyms). The collected spin-off projects produced ten top ten albums in the United States (almost as many in the UK), with several more charting in the Top 40. Similar to Genesis and its members' solo projects during the 1980s (or Beatles solo records during the '70s), Wu Tang Clan became a small company unto itself, placing one record after another on the charts.

Naughty and Nice: Will Smith and Eminem.   As rap's audience expanded late in the 1980s, it also developed a reputation for being dangerous—a reputation that was solidified and expanded by the bi-coastal feud. Playing on the same kind of juxtaposition that had been central to Pat Boone and Elvis Presley in the mid 1950s, the Beatles and the Stones in the mid 1960s, and even the Beatles and the Monkees during psychedelia, Will Smith positioned himself as a family friendly rapper, and crossed over to enormous success during the 1990s. Hailing from Philadelphia, Smith began his career under the name Fresh Prince, rapping with DJ Jazzy Jeff. The duo's 1988 release, *He's the DJ, I'm the Rapper*, crossed over to the pop charts, hitting number four (r5) and containing the hits "Nightmare on My Street" (p15 r9) and "Parents Just Don't Understand" (p12 r10). The 1991 album *Homebase* (p12 r5) produced the hit single "Summertime" (p4 r1), and by then Smith was featured in his own television situation comedy, *The Fresh Prince of Bel Air*. By the mid 1990s, he was starring in a string of successful feature films including *Independence Day* (1996) and *Men in Black* (1997), for which he provided the title musical track. Smith released his first album under his own name in 1997 with *Big Willie Style* (p8 r9), which contained the hit "Gettin' Jiggy wit' It" (p1 r6), a good example of

Smith's upbeat approach to the style. In 1999, Smith followed up with *Willennium* (p5 r8 1999), which included "Wild Wild West" (p1 r3), the title song to his movie of that summer. Despite critics' tendency to disparage Smith as a rapper, he nevertheless won Grammy Awards in 1997 and 1998 for best rap solo performance.

Emerging at the end of the decade, Eminem was in many ways the anti–Will Smith. Born Marshall Mathers (M&M), Eminem grew up as a poor white kid in an urban Detroit neighborhood. After establishing a reputation locally, Eminem won a 1997 freestyle rap competition in Los Angeles and as a result, a copy of his demo tape was heard by Dr. Dre. While Dre was surprised that Eminem was white, he was soon won over by the rapper's wit and talent and produced his breakthrough album, *The Slim Shady LP* (p2 r1 uk12, 1999). While Eminem had sometimes rapped on positive themes on his first album, *Infinite* (1997), for this album he adopted the persona of Slim Shady, a character who could express his deepest emotional pain and hostility. The lead single from the album, "My Name Is" (p36), provides a good example of Eminem's aggressive approach, and the rapper was soon provoking widespread controversy for the violent content of his lyrics, making him rap music's preeminent bad boy. With *The Marshall Mathers LP* (p1 r1 uk1, 2000), Eminem turned his atten-

Dr. Dre discovered Eminem (Marshall Mathers, pictured here at a live concert) in 1997 and soon helped him produce his first album. Eminem had a distinctive vocal style and his lyrics focused not on "gangsta life" or politics, but on his personal experiences growing up as a poor white kid in Detroit. Eminem's mother and his wife Kim were only two of many targets of his aggressive and often violent rhymes.

tion to the problems of his own life, with his portrayal of his wife in "Kim" creating a storm of public and private controversy, and his mother filing a suit against him for defamation of character. The negative reaction to Eminem's music only seemed to make him more successful, and part of this is because many fellow artists—and unlikely ones such as Elton John—strongly defended

Eminem's talent and intelligence. Whatever your view of Eminem, it is difficult to see how anyone could push gangsta rap any further in terms of controversy than he has done.

Metal Extensions and Indie Rock

Rap and Rock: Rage Against the Machine. As rap was expanding into many substyles during the early 1990s, it was also gaining a firmer foothold in the world of white rock. Going back to the years following Run-DMC's crossover cover of Aerosmith's "Walk This Way," rock musicians had taken an interest in employing aspects of rap in their music. Rap and heavy metal rose to mainstream popularity at about the same time, and cross-pollination between the two had played an important role in the second half of the 1980s, though mostly from the rap side. However, eclectic bands like Faith No More began to explore ways of employing rapped passages in a heavy-rock context. Taking their cue from Faith No More and the Red Hot Chili Peppers, the Los Angeles–based band Rage Against the Machine blended hard-driving rock with mostly rapped vocals to establish a stylistic model many after them would follow. The band's first album, *Rage Against the Machine* (p45 uk17, 1992), evinced the group's dedication to political causes while musically drawing much from the Chili Peppers' blend of funk grooves and heavy metal riffs. Zack de la Rocha's vocals share the spotlight with Tom Morello's innovative guitar playing, which blends metal, blues rock, and jazz, while at times using his electric guitar to imitate the sound of DJ scratching. *Evil Empire* (p1 uk4, 1996) followed and established the band as an important force in the rap-rock style, while *The Battle of Los Angeles* (p1 uk23, 1999) served to confirm this. By the end of the decade, de la Rocha had left the grouped and the remaining members reorganized as Audioslave, with Soundgarden's Chris Cornell on lead vocals.

Rage Against the Machine, pictured here in concert, were one of the first groups to successfully combine a rap vocal style with rock. Zack de la Rocha's (left) often political vocals share the spotlight with Tom Morello's (right) innovative guitar playing, which often imitated the sound of DJ scratching.

Getting Heavy: Korn, Limp Bizkit, System of a Down, Kid Rock. Hailing from Bakersfield, California, Korn brought the sound of the seven-string guitar into rap-rock. The electric seven-string had been used by a handful of jazz guitarists over the years to make a wider range of notes available on the instrument. In most configurations, the seventh string was added below the bottom string of a conventional guitar, not only making more bass notes possible but also providing for a greater range within the grip of the guitarist's left hand. Heavy metal virtuoso Steve Vai had introduced the instrument into rock, but Korn guitarists James "Munky" Shaffer and Brian "Head" Welch practically made it into a brand name, using the low strings for heavy, angular, distortion-soaked riffs. The band's first album, *Korn* (1994), introduces the group's trademark sound, while *Life Is Peachy* (p3 uk32, 1996) and *Follow the Leader* (p1 uk5, 1998) established their reputation. As with Rage Against the Machine, Korn's lyrics are most often rapped, but also sometimes screamed, and together with the pronounced influence of heavy metal, create a more menacing stylistic blend. Florida's Limp Bizkit picked up Korn's use of the seven-string guitar, added more screaming in the vocal dimension, and produced *Three Dollar Bill Y'all* (p22, 1997), which included a cover of George Michael's "Faith," and *Significant Other* (p1 uk26, 1999). Led by charismatic vocalist Fred Durst and guitarist Wes Borland, the band received considerable air time on MTV late in the decade. System of a Down (Los Angeles) brought together many of the features of previous bands: with *System of a Down* (1998) and *Toxicity* (p1 uk13, 2001), the group continued the political and social commitment of Rage Against the Machine, blended in the heavy, gothic tones of Korn and Limp Bizkit. Their producer was Rick Rubin, who had produced the Run-DMC records that first brought rock and rap together. Also extending the rap-rock of earlier bands, Detroit's Kid Rock employed a wide range of styles in his late '90s music. *Devil without a Cause* (p4, 1998) uses fewer heavy metal guitar tones and more sounds drawn from traditional blues rock; his grooves are more rock-oriented, with vocals both rapped and sung (at times in a very conventional manner), and showing a stronger flair for a pop hook and a broad range of stylistic references, including country rock. Kid Rock's lyrics are rarely gothic or politically ambitious; they are much more playful and at times ironic and comic.

The Menacing Sounds of Industry: Nine Inch Nails, Marilyn Manson. While bands like Rage Against the Machine and Korn were extending 1980s heavy metal by blending in rap elements, other musicians were exploring a style often called "industrial." The roots of industrial can be traced to British bands of the mid 1970s such as Throbbing Gristle and Cabaret Voltaire, as well as to Skinny Puppy, a Canadian band from the mid to late 1980s. Nine Inch Nails is often considered the premiere 1990s group in the style, and the band's 1994 album *The Downward Spiral* (p2 uk9, 1994) brought industrial to a mainstream rock audience for the first time. In the recording studio, Nine Inch Nails is San Francisco–based composer Trent Reznor, who writes the music and performs all the parts himself, as Stevie Wonder and Prince did on many of their albums. The term "industrial" arises because much of the music contains rhythmic grooves that sound like they might have been produced by large factory machines, though they are almost always the result of looping and synthesizer programming. Nine Inch Nails' music is moody, with frequent shifts in atmosphere, and the lyrics are often concerned with the darker side of the human psyche, not unlike those of Jim Morrison or Alice Cooper. *The Downward Spiral*, for instance, was recorded in the house where Charles Manson and his followers committed the famous (and hideous) murders of actress Sharon Tate and her friends. A similar fascination with the grotesque can be found in the music

Like Alice Cooper and Ozzy Osbourne before him, Marilyn Manson used grotesque, satanic, and often vulgar lyrics and visuals in his music. Manson's outrageousness, which he seemed to flaunt at Middle America as often as possible (this picture is from a performance at the American Music Awards, 2001), appealed to a large audience of teens who longed to rebel against suburbia and the perceived commercialism of music.

of Marilyn Manson; much like Alice Cooper, Marilyn Manson is the name of the band and the lead singer (who is male). Each member of the group adopted a stage name that consisted of a glamorous female celebrity combined with a famous serial killer (the keyboardist, for instance, is Madonna Wayne Gacy). Emerging from Florida, the band made its first commercial mark with its Trent Reznor–produced third album, *Antichrist Superstar* (p3, 1996), following with the even more successful *Mechanical Animals* (p1 uk8) in 1998. Like other shock-rockers before him, Manson did all he could to outrage the more conservative segment of middle America: he dressed outrageously (as a kind of ghoulish transvestite) and included vulgar and satanic content on the albums, practically begging to be banned on the radio. And mirroring the appeal of earlier outrageous bands to previous generations of youngsters, the band's attraction was largely that it misbehaved so proudly and unabashedly, not unlike the gangsta rappers discussed above.

Indie Rock Continues: Yo La Tengo, Pavement, Guided by Voices.   In Chapters 11 and 12 we touched on the indie-rock underground, which began to develop during the 1980s and consisted of a circuit of clubs and bars (often in college towns), college radio stations, independent record labels, and a magazine that chronicled all this called *College Music Journal* (*CMJ*). Perhaps the most prominent feature of indie rock is its do-it-yourself aesthetic: the idea that a band doesn't need the machinery of a major record label to make good music. Such involvement, it is believed, only corrupts; bands must simply take care of all of their business themselves, with minimal intervention by outside forces. The heroes of this movement in the 1980s were R.E.M. (who actually had a major label deal but still celebrated the indie aesthetic), Hüsker Dü, and especially Sonic Youth. Led by guitarist Thurston Moore, the band's *Daydream Nation* (uk99, 1988) is considered a watershed album, with the song "Teen Age Riot" considered particularly iconic. While Sonic Youth did record for a major label, they were respected for having maintained creative control of their material. Most indie bands, however, recorded for small, regional labels, so their records circulated only within the indie-music scene, not getting much mainstream attention or selling in large numbers compared to major label acts. Nirvana and Soundgarden first released their music with the Seattle-based indie label Sub Pop before the Seattle sound emerged onto the national scene. Among the most important indie bands in the 1990s were Yo La Tengo (Hoboken, New Jersey), whose 1993 album *Painful* is representative, and Pavement (Stockton, California), whose *Slanted and Enchanted* (uk72, 1992) is widely considered to be an indie-rock classic. Many indie bands embraced a lo-fi approach, recording on inexpensive equipment (or producing sounds that seem to have been recorded on cheap gear). Ohio's Guided by Voices embraced lo-fi, while also incorporating 1960s pop influences like the Who or the Beatles, as can be heard on *Bee Thousand* (1994).

Despite the small scale on which most of the bands enjoyed success, music critics often warmly praised indie bands and the indie scene generally. For such critics, indie music offered a purer and more direct style of rock music—a style uncorrupted by concerns about marketing and audience demographics.

Georgia Hubley (drums) and Ira Kaplan (guitar) are the core members of Yo La Tengo, one of the most successful indie rock bands of the 1990s. Indie rock centered around a DIY (do-it-yourself) method of production: many bands had their own labels or used small ones (Matador produced many important indie groups, including Yo La Tengo), and the music was supposed to sound simple, nonchalant, and easy-to-create.

Independent record labels played an important role in the scene, and the New York–based Matador dominated the market during the 1990s (Yo La Tengo, Pavement, and Guided by Voices were all Matador artists). Other important labels were Merge in Chapel Hill, North Carolina, a label run by two members of the band Superchunk, and Sub Pop in Seattle, who released records by Boston-based Sebadoh in addition to early tracks by Nirvana and Soundgarden. Over in Olympia, Washington, K Records had the band Beat Happening, while Kill Rock Stars Records released material by Sleater-Kinney. These small labels often worked to develop a distinctive stylistic sound. Since many bands were unknown to indie-rock fans outside the group's native region, knowing something about the label meant that if fans liked one band on a particular label, they might also like another band on the same label. College radio stations also played indie rock, and *CMJ* tracked which stations were playing which records and reported it, much as *Billboard* did for mainstream pop styles. Indie rock was small and it was off the beaten path culturally speaking; for those who loved it, that was part of its charm.

Indie Music in the Mainstream: Beck. Considering the aversion to major labels within the indie world, fans were especially wary of indie bands or artists who signed with big record companies. Among the acts to successfully manage this transition was Beck Hansen, a Los Angeles–based singer-songwriter whose first single, "Loser" (1993), appeared on the indie label Bongload to much acclaim within the southern California indie scene. Beck then signed with a major label (Geffen) and the single was re-released, going to number ten in the United States (uk15, 1994). Perhaps concerned with his credibility as an indie artist, Beck negotiated a deal with Geffen that was exceptional in allowing him to release music on other labels while also releasing material for the major. As a consequence of this deal, two albums subsequently appeared on indie labels, *Stereopathic Soul Manure* (1994) on Flipside and *One Foot in the Grave* (1995) on K Records, while Geffen released *Mellow Gold* (p13 uk41, 1994) and *Odelay* (p16 uk18, 1996) during the same period. Beck's music blends the lo-fi approach of bands like Guided by Voices with hip-hop, country rock, '70s soul, and even classical music, with a keen sense for pop hooks to produce a dizzying succession of styles and stylistic references, often within the same song. Beck seems to enjoy a broad range of earlier styles and often reproduces them faithfully; his music is also full of samples and rapid shifts created by editing, like much rap and dance music from earlier in the decade. Beck continued to enjoy success on the charts and with critics during the second half of the decade with his *Mutations* (p13 uk24, 1998) and *Midnite Vultures* (p34 uk 19, 1999) and into the new century with *Sea Change* and *Guero*.

Conclusion

A New Generation and a Fracturing of the Audience. This chapter has focused on both stylistic continuations out of the 1980s and stylistic returns to the '50s, '60s, and '70s. It is currently too early to know what these continuations mean for the future of rock music. The return of elements from an earlier era of the style would suggest that rock has hit some kind of endpoint in its development, now looking back at its history and establishing a tradition, much as jazz, blues, or classical music have. But the new, younger fans who have been drawn to vintage rock—and the new bands who have created fresh music inspired by it—seem to work against the idea that rock is in its last years. Even though the music business in the 1990s thought it was selling the same music again to

Singer, songwriter, producer Beck, in concert, 1997. For years Beck has successfully straddled the indie-major label divide, scoring hit albums with both. Beck's music blends the do-it-yourself feel of indie rock with elements of hip-hop, country rock, '70s soul, and even classical music. In a musical world where nearly all styles are available streaming over the Internet, Beck always seems to be looking for new ones to embrace.

people who already had it, they also sold it to a generation for which it was new. Unexpectedly, this generation did not see this '60s and '70s music as mom and dad's music; they received it as their own and may well continue to embrace it for many years to come. The important rise of rap in the 1990s suggests that at some point in the future the history of rock may well become a footnote to the development of hip-hop—as a style that ran parallel with rap for a while but was eventually overshadowed by it. In the late 1990s, many critics predicted that the future of popular music was with rap and electronic dance music, but by the middle of the next decade, that had not happened and rock remains strong. As well as rock may be doing in the first decade of the twenty-first century, it nevertheless shares space with a variety of other styles and is no longer the dominant style in popular music that it once was. In fact, the top-selling album of the 1990s was Shania Twain's rock-drenched country release, *Come On Over* (1997), with the soundtrack to *The Bodyguard* coming in second. For much of the 1990s, many critics predicted that country music would be the winner in the next-big-thing sweepstakes. Garth Brooks, for instance, enjoyed tremendous success, placing three albums among the top ten best-selling albums of the decade. The easygoing song stylings of Celine Dion were also popular, with *Falling into You* (1996) selling over thirteen million copies, putting her in the company of Whitney Houston and Mariah Carey as one of pop's top divas.

Technology and the Audience for Popular Music in the Digital Age. The development of digital technology has had broad and far-reaching effects for popular music. Digital recording, for instance, has made it possible for almost any artist or band to record an album inexpensively, and the rise of the Internet makes it easy to sell your CD through a Web page or make MP3s (digital music files) available for download. This new technology allows bands to take over the roles in manufacturing and distribution formerly controlled by record labels. The newfound control has its disadvantages as well; as many bands have discovered, it's one thing to make your music available and another to get fans to visit your site to check it out. With so many bands in cyberspace—each with their own CD and Web site—how do you get people to visit your site? For fans, on the other hand, the Internet provides a vast hunting ground for new music, and many take pride in discovering bands and artists that no one they know has ever heard of. Satellite radio has made hundreds of style-specific channels available, though it's still unclear whether this will encourage listeners to explore new styles or simply reinforce their already established tastes. Personal iPod players allow listeners to configure their own playlists and build their own distinctive collections. Will these technological advances prompt significant stylistic developments as radio and television technology did in the 1950s or as cable television did in the 1980s? Only time will tell.

Questions for Review and Discussion

1. How did rock music of the 1960s and '70s return in the 1990s? What demographic and music-business factors affected this? In what ways did an increased awareness of rock's history arise?

2. Who are some of the most prominent new artists and bands in the 1990s who were strongly influenced by bands from the '60s and '70s? How do these groups differ from alternative rockers from the first half of the 1990s?

3. Outline the return of traditional elements to rhythm and blues in the 1990s. How does this music both continue out of the 1980s and return to the 1960s and '70s?

4. Describe the rise of teen idols in the mid to late 1990s. Who were the important artists and groups, and how were their images designed to appeal to their target audience?

5. What are the important elements in the singer-songwriter approach and how did this style affect the 1990s in a significant way?

6. What are roots of the electronic dance music that became popular late in the decade? How far back can you trace it?

7. In what ways did rap in the 1990s develop out of 1980s rap? How did image and reality merge in the case of gangsta rap?

8. How were elements of heavy metal and indie rock continued in the 1990s? Who were the most important artists and groups?

Further Reading

Bill Brewster and Frank Broughton, *Last Night a DJ Saved My Life: The History of the Disk Jockey* (Grove Press, 2000).

Nelson George, *Hip Hop America* (Penguin, 1998).

Bruce Haring, *Off the Charts: Ruthless Days and Reckless Nights Inside the Music Industry* (Birch Lane Press, 1996).

Jeff Kitts, Brad Tolinski, and Harold Steinblatt, eds., *Alternative Rock: They Launched a Revolution—and Won!* (Hal Leonard Corporation, 1999).

Lucy O'Brien, *She Bop II: The Definitive History of Women in Rock, Pop, and Soul* (Continuum, 2002).

Dick Porter, *Rapcore: The Nu-Metal Fusion* (Plexus, 2003).

Simon Reynolds, *Generation Ecstasy: Into the World of Techno and Rave Culture* (Little, Brown, 1998).

The Vibe History of Hip Hop, edited by Alan Light (Three Rivers Press, 1999).

Credits

Every effort has been made to contact the copyright holders of the material used in **What's That Sound, An Introduction to Rock and Its History**. Please contact us with any updated information.

Text
p. 16: "White Christmas" from the Motion
Picture Irving Berlin's HOLIDAY INN
Words and Music by Irving Berlin
© Copyright 1940, 1942 by Irving
Berlin
Copyright Renewed
International Copyright Secured All
Rights Reserved
p. 52: "Shake Rattle and Roll" By: Charles
Calhoun
© Copyright 1954 (Renewed) Unichappell
Music Inc. (BMI) and Mijac Music
(BMI)
All Rights Administered by Unichappell
Music Inc.
All Rights Reserved. Used by Permission.
Warner Bros. Publications U.S. Inc.,
Miami, FL. 33014

Photos
Intro: p. 2: John Tefteller,
Bluesimages.com; p. 3: John Springer
Collection/Corbis; p. 4: (right)
Bettmann/Corbis; p. 4: (top left)
Douglas Kent Hall/Zuma/Corbis; (bot-
tom left) Ted Williams/Corbis; p. 9:
Michael Ochs Archives; p. 15: (left)
Library of Congress; (right)
Bettmann/Corbis.
Chapter 1: p. 16: © Copyright 1940, 1942
by Irving Berlin; p. 19:
Bettmann/Corbis; p. 20:
Bettmann/Corbis; p. 21:
Reuters/Corbis; p. 22: Courtesy Greg
Van Beek; p. 25: *The Wizard Of Oz*.
1939. Dir. Victor Fleming, Metro-
Goldwyn-Mayer (MGM); p. 28:
Bettmann/Corbis; p. 29:
Bettmann/Corbis; p. 30: Michael Ochs
Archives; p. 36: BMI/Michael Ochs
Archives; p. 37: Bettmann/Corbis; p. 38:
Underwood & Underwood/Corbis; p.
39: Michael Ochs Archives; p. 43:
Corbis; p. 44: Deltahaze
Corporation/Redferns; p. 47:
BMI/Michael Ochs Archives; p. 55:

Bettmann/Corbis; p. 56:
Bettmann/Corbis.
Chapter 2: p. 58: John Tefteller,
Bluesimages.com; p. 62: (top) *The Wild
One*. 1953. Dir. Laszlo Benedek, Stanley
Kramer Productions, Distributor
Columbia Pictures; (middle) *Rebel
Without A Cause*. 1955. Dir. Nicholas
Ray, Warner Brothers; (bottom)
Blackboard Jungle. 1955. Dir. Richard
Brooks, Metro-Goldwyn-Mayer (MGM);
p. 64: Michael Ochs Archives; p. 68:
Bettmann/Corbis; p. 70: Michael Ochs
Archives; p. 73: Michael Ochs Archives;
p. 74: Bettmann/Corbis; p. 76: Michael
Ochs Archives; p. 81: Hulton
Archive/Getty Images; p. 83: Time Life
Pictures/Getty Images; p. 87:
Bettmann/Corbis; p. 88: BBC/Redferns;
p. 91: Bettmann/Corbis.
Chapter 3: p. 104: John Tefteller,
Bluesimages.com; p. 108: Corbis; p. 111:
Bettmann/Corbis; p. 112:
Bettmann/Corbis; p. 113:
Bettmann/Corbis; p. 114: Michael Ochs
Archives; p. 118: Bettmann/Corbis; p.
120: Michael Ochs Archives; p. 121:
Michael Ochs Archives; p. 125: Michael
Ochs Archives; p. 126: Ray
Avery/Michael Ochs Archives; p. 129:
Michael Ochs Archives; p. 131:
Bettmann/Corbis; p. 133: David
Redferns/Redferns; p. 137: Michael
Ochs Archives; p. 145: Capitol/EMI; p.
149: Bettmann/Corbis; p. 150:
Bettmann/Corbis.
Chapter 4: p. 152: Capitol/EMI; p. 155:
Hulton-Deutsch Collection/Corbis; p.
158: Hulton-Deutsch Collection/Corbis;
p. 163: Bettmann/Corbis; p. 170: (top)
David Redferns/Redferns; (bottom)
David Redferns/Redferns; p. 171:
Gunter Zint/Redferns; p. 174:
Bettmann/Corbis; p. 177: Jeremy
Fletcher/Redferns; p. 178:
Wolfgangsvault.com; p. 180: Jorgen
Angel/Redferns; p. 181: Bob
Baker/Redferns.

Chapter 5: p. 186: John Tefteller, Blues
Images.com; p. 189: Michael Ochs
Archives; p. 190: Michael Ochs
Archives; p. 194: Michael Ochs
Archives; p. 196: Henry Diltz/Corbis; p.
197: Michael Ochs Archives; p. 199:
Capitol/EMI; p. 203: Bettmann/Corbis;
p. 205: Henry Diltz/Corbis; p. 207:
Michael Ochs Archives; p. 209: Michael
Ochs Archives; p. 210: Michael Ochs
Archives; p. 212: Henry Diltz/Corbis; p.
217: Henry Diltz/Corbis; p. 218: Fin
Costello/Redferns; p. 219: Roger
Ressmeyer/Corbis.
Chapter 6: p. 224: John Tefteller,
Bluesimages.com; p. 228: Michael Ochs
Archives; p. 229: Michael Ochs
Archives; p. 234: Henry Diltz/Corbis; p.
238: Michael Ochs Archives; p. 240:
Michael Ochs Archives; p. 242:
Universal Music Group; p. 243: Michael
Ochs Archives; p. 248: James Brown
Live In Boston 1968. (from TV)
www.thevideobeat.com; p. 248: James
Brown Live In Boston 1968. (from TV)
www.thevideobeat.com; p. 249: James
Brown Live In Boston 1968. (from TV)
www.thevideobeat.com; p. 250:
Courtesy of Chuck Stewart.
Chapter 7: p. 254: Capitol/EMI; p. 258:
Bettmann/Corbis; p. 260: Michael
Ochs Archives; p. 266:
Bettmann/Corbis; p. 268: Courtesy of
Norman Hartweg & Zane Kesey; p. 272:
Wolfgangsvault.com; p. 275: Ted
Streshinsky/Corbis; p. 280: Courtesy of
Nigel Weymouth & Michael English; p.
283: Ted Streshinsky/Corbis; p. 288:
David Redferns/Redferns; p. 290:
Warner Brothers; p. 291: Henry
Diltz/Corbis; p. 296: Time Life
Pictures/Getty Images; p. 297: Henry
Diltz/Corbis ; p. 301: Bettmann/Corbis;
p. 302: Bettmann/Corbis.
Chapter 8: p. 304: Atlantic/Warner
Brothers; p. 308: Jay
Dickerman/Corbis; p. 310: Fin
Costello/Redferns; p. 314: Jeff

Albertson/Corbis; **p. 315**: Michael Ochs Archives; **p. 319**: Courtesy of Richard Upper; **p. 323**: Capitol/EMI; **p. 324**: Michael Ochs Archives; **p. 326**: Bettmann/Corbis; **p. 328**: Fin Costello/Redferns; **p. 334**: David Redferns/Redferns; **p. 335**: Michael Ochs Archives; **p. 339**: Lynn Goldsmith/Corbis; **p. 340**: Lynn Goldsmith/Corbis; **p. 344**: David J. & Janice L. Frent Collection/Corbis; **p. 345**: Bettmann/Corbis; **p. 346**: Henry Diltz/Corbis; **p. 350**: Henry Diltz/Corbis; **p. 356**: Shepard Sherbell/Corbis SABA.

Chapter 9: p. 362: Motown/Universal; **p. 366**: Dave Ellis/Redferns; **p. 367**: Glenn A. Baker/Redferns; **p. 368**: Charlyn Zlotnick/Redferns; **p. 372**: RB/Redferns; **p. 375**: David Redferns/Redferns; **p. 376**: GEMS/Redferns; **p. 377**: (top left) *Shaft*. 1971. Dir. Gordon Parks, Metro-Goldwyn-Mayer (MGM) & Shaft Productions Ltd.; (top right) *Shaft*. 1971. Dir. Gordon Parks, Metro-Goldwyn-Mayer (MGM) & Shaft Productions Ltd.; **p. 377**: (bottom right) *Shaft*. 1971. Dir. Gordon Parks, Metro-Goldwyn-Mayer (MGM) & Shaft Productions Ltd.; **p. 378**: Everett Collection; **p. 379**: Everett Collection; **p. 380**: Harry Goodwin/Redferns; **p. 382**: Richard E Aaron/Redferns; **p. 388**: Andrew Putler/Redferns; **p. 390**: *Saturday Night Fever*. 1977. Dir. John Badham Paramount Pictures & Robert Stigwood

Organization (RSO); **p. 391**: Richard E Aaron/Redferns.

Chapter 10: p. 396: Sony; **p. 399**: Bettmann/Corbis; **p. 402**: Roger Ressmeyer/Corbis; **p. 404**: Roger Ressmeyer/Corbis; **p. 405**: Corbis; **p. 406**: Ebet Roberts; **p. 407**: Fin Costello/Redferns; **p. 409**: Denis O'regan/Corbis; **p. 411**: Wally McNamee/Corbis; **p. 416**: Mick Gold/Redferns; **p. 419**: Corbis; **p. 420**: Bettmann/Corbis; **p. 422**: Roger Ressmeyer/Corbis; **p. 426**: (c)GODLIS; **p. 427**: Lynn Goldsmith/Corbis; **p. 428**: The Blues Brothers, *Soul Man*. 1978. (Saturday Night Live Performance) NBC Studio; **p. 429**: (right) Yvonne Hemsey/Getty Images; (left) Lynn Goldsmith/Corbis; **p. 430**: Elvis Costello, *Less Than Zero/Radio Radio*. 1977. (Saturday Night Live Performance) NBC Studio; **p. 437**: Bettmann/Corbis; **p. 438**: Jacques M. Chenet/Corbis.

Chapter 11: p. 440: Sony/Epic; **p. 443**: The Buggles, *Video Killed The Radio Star*.1980. (from music video) Distributed by Universal Music Group; **p. 449** Everett Collection; **p. 451**: (top right) Matthew Mendelsohn/Corbis; (bottom right) Photofest; (left) Roger Ressmeyer/Corbis; **p. 453**: Richard E Aaron/Redferns; **p. 456**: Ian Dickson/Redferns; **p. 458**: Lynn Goldsmith/Corbis; **p. 459**: Jacques Langevin/Corbis Sygma; **p. 463**: Richard E Aaron/Redferns; **p. 464**: Ebet

Roberts; **p. 467**: Bettmann/Corbis; **p. 471**: Ian Dickson/Redferns; **p. 473**: Peter Gabriel, *Sledgehammer*. 1986. (from music video) Distributed by Stephen R. Johnson Production Company.

Chapter 12: p. 478: Sony/Arista/Bertlesmann; **p. 481**: Corbis; **p. 484**: Corbis; **p. 488**: SIN/Corbis; **p. 489**: Bettmann/Corbis; **p. 490**: Michael Ochs Archives; **p. 491**: Ebet Roberts; **p. 494**: Corbis; **p. 498**: Wally McNamee/Corbis; **p. 499**: Ebet Roberts; **p. 501**: SIN/Corbis; **p. 504**: Henry Diltz/Corbis; **p. 509**: Gail Albert Halaban/Corbis; **p. 510**: Peter Turnley/Corbis; **p. 511**: Reuters/Corbis.

Chapter 13: p. 512: Maverick/Warner Brothers; **p. 516**: Brownie Harris/Corbis; **p. 517**: Mick Huton/Redferns; **p. 518**: Reuters/Corbis; **p. 519**: Tim Mosenfelder/Corbis; **p. 523**: John Atashina/Corbis; **p. 526**: George Chin/Redferns; **p. 529**: Reuters/Corbis; **p. 531**: Reuters/Corbis; **p. 535**: Matthew Mendelsohn/Corbis; **p. 536**: Mick Huton/Redferns; **p. 540**: Tina Paul@fifibear.com; **p. 541**: Gerardo Somoza; **p. 543**: Mark Peterson/Corbis; **p. 547**: Salifu Idress/Redferns; **p. 548**: Grant Davis/Redferns; **p. 550**: Reuters/Corbis; **p. 552**: Carey Brandon/Redferns **p. 553**: Jon Super/Redferns.

Index

Note: Pages numbers in *italics* refer to illustrations and captions.